CASES AND MATERIALS

INTERNATIONAL LAW AND THE USE OF FORCE

by

MARY ELLEN O'CONNELL
William B. Saxbe Designated Professor of Law
The Ohio State University
Moritz College of Law

FOUNDATION PRESS
NEW YORK, NEW YORK
2005

THOMSON
WEST

© 2005 By FOUNDATION PRESS

     395 Hudson Street
     New York, NY 10014
     Phone Toll Free 1–877–888–1330
     Fax (212) 367–6799
     fdpress.com
Printed in the United States of America

ISBN 1–58778–781–4

 *TEXT IS PRINTED ON 10% POST CONSUMER RECYCLED PAPER*

This book is dedicated to my husband,

Peter Bauer,

*long a soldier who served his country
with pride, courage, and profound
respect for the rule of law.*

*

INTRODUCTION

Throughout history and throughout the world, humanity has constantly striven to control war, particularly through law. We can never know whether these efforts have reduced the incidence of war or mitigated its horrors. We do know that although war persists, so do attempts to control it through law. These efforts are ongoing and today the law relevant to war is actually growing at an unprecedented rate with no decline in sight. In the broader category of international law, perhaps the only fields growing at a faster pace are general human rights law and economic law. As a result, we now have an impressively large and dynamic body of law that regulates both when parties may resort to war and how they must conduct it. The aim of this book is to introduce students to both of these categories—the *jus ad bellum* and the *jus in bello* and to where these categories intersect.

The fact that law on war is growing does not mean, however, that it is accepted in all quarters as useful or even as binding. Even among those who do accept it as binding and useful, controversies abound. Some of these controversies stem from the nature of war, its role in society, and the persistent view that a state of war is the antithesis of legal order. Cicero is credited with saying, *silent enim leges inter armes*—law is silent in war. The very existence of this book is testimony against that view, but it remains an important perspective that we will discuss in more detail in Chapter Three. In fact, the number of controversies and new developments make the study of law on the use of force one of the most challenging, but also compelling, topics in the entire law curriculum. It raises issues from the most profound—can we ever rid the world of war—to the most practical—when and where may a soldier be tried for violating the law of war?

Our study will focus on the public international law aspects of this subject. The book moves beyond classic war to consider all uses of force governed by international law, thus the title *International Law and the Use of Force*. Chapter One is a discussion of what we mean by the use of force and how that term differs from "war," "armed conflict," and related concepts in international law. Chapter Two presents two cases studies of war—the 1990–1991 Persian Gulf War and the 2003 Iraq War. These case studies are built from legal documents and newspaper articles. They are included to provide the facts of actual conflicts to support later discussions, but they also indicate the role law played in two actual conflicts. Chapter Three follows with an in depth consideration of the problem of law and war, focusing on some of the better-known comments on the possibility of law of war.

Chapter Three also introduces the major categories of law on the use of force—the *jus ad bellum*, governing the decision to resort to war and the *jus in bello*, governing the conduct of hostilities. The Chapters in Section II trace the historic development of both categories of law. Section III then considers the contemporary law. The final section, Section IV, looks to the future by providing several proposals for major departures from the current law.

This is a unique collection of cases and materials for law students that combines both the *jus ad bellum* and *jus in bello*. It presents important treaties, cases, principles of customary international law, and general principles, as well as materials on the organizations relevant to regulating force. It is not a book on national security law. Several good student texts already exist on that subject, which generally examine national constitutions and the law regulating force within the domestic legal system. Nor does this book include much on the topic of arms control. We will consider at least briefly the topic of what weapons are lawful to use in battle, but not the large network of treaties and other arrangements to control weapons in peacetime. Finally, this does not purport to be an "operational law" handbook or manual for use by those in the field. Rather, it presents the law at the level of more general principles from which rules guiding conduct in fighting are derived.

While this is a rare book combining law in war and resort to war, it grew from another book written in 1993 with Thomas Ehrlich, *International Law and the Use of Force* (Little, Brown 1993). That book collected cases and materials on resort to war. This book carries on in the tradition of the earlier book with some significant changes. In addition to law on resort to war, this book includes cases and materials on the law in war. For example, in addition to the United Nations Charter rules that were the focus of the other book, this one also introduces the Hague and Geneva Conventions as central to the regulation of war. A major theme of this book is that these two bodies of international law on the use of force have important interconnections and that one understands each category better by understanding the other. This book also provides chapters on the historic development of international law on war with the aim of providing context for today's law.

Further, this book approaches international law from a classical perspective: it relies on positive international law, modified in some important respects by normative or natural law principles. The earlier book focused more on the role of law in foreign policy decision-making. Here you will find the focus on the substantive rules and institutions that emerge from positive acts—treaties, customary international law, and general principles.

With the plethora of treaties and actions by states, international organizations, and courts, we cannot hope to do justice to all the important aspects of the current international law on the use of force. We do hope to provide the basic principles of this law, equipping students with the ability to research and teach themselves the answers to the questions they will confront. We have sought to include a range of materials to demonstrate the array of evidence available on international law. To help students think about this law from a practical perspective, the book has a problem to accompany each chapter. These problems are drawn from actual incidents. They are the kind of problems that daily confront foreign office lawyers, military lawyers, defense lawyers, prosecutors, and plaintiffs' lawyers. International law on the use of force has always been a central theoretical concern of international lawyers. It is now part of the daily practice of lawyers the world over. We hope that our approach both contributes to the continuing development and improvement of international law on the use of force, and that it helps prepare students for their careers in the law.

The book is designed for those who already have a basic knowledge of international law. For those who have not had a basic course—which we highly recommend—reading a good introduction to international law will be essential. David Bederman's *International Law Frameworks* (Foundation 2001) is one of the best available.

MARY ELLEN O'CONNELL

December 2004

*

ACKNOWLEDGMENTS

I wish to especially thank Dr. Andreas Paulus for his careful, thoughtful and erudite comments on the draft of this book. Professor Detlev Vagts, Ms. Brigitte Oederlin, LTC Daria Wollschlaeger, and Professor Gregory Fox made helpful and encouraging comments, and Ms. Amy Beaudreault performed key tasks in preparing the draft for publication. I would also like to thank my student research assistants, Caoilte Joy, Benjamin Hill, Gretchen Drenski, and Barry Naum, as well as members of the seminars on international law and the use of force since 1990.

I also gratefully acknowledge permission extended by the following authors, publishers, and organizations to reprint excerpts from the books, periodicals, and other documents indicated in parentheses and cited in the text: AGENCE FRANCE-PRESS INTERNATIONAL NEWS (excerpt from Copyright 2004 by AGENCE FRANCE-PRESSE (US). Reproduced with permission of AGENCE FRANCE-PRESSE (US) in the format Other Book via Copyright Clearance Center); The American Society of International Law (excerpts from American Journal of International Law and The American Society of International Law Proceedings); The Associated Press (© Reuters 2004. All Rights Reserved); The Chicago Journal of International Law (excerpt from Dörmann & Naresca, The International Committee of the Red Cross and Its Contribution to the Development of International Humanitarian Law in Specialized Instruments, 5 CHI. J. INT'L L. 217, 225–228 (2004)); Council on Foreign Relations, Inc. (excerpt from Copyright 2002–2004 by the Council on Foreign Relations, Inc. All Rights Reserved); David & Charles (excerpt from Key Treaties for the Great Powers, 1814–1916 (1972), by kind permission of the publishers); FT Pharmaceuticals (excerpt from Border and Territorial Disputes, 2nd Revised Edition, Alan J. Day, ed. 1987); H. F. & G. Witherby (excerpt from Claud Mullins, The Leipzig Trials pp. 67–87 (1921)); Frits Kalshoven (excerpt from Constraints on the Waging of War, 1987); The Houston Chronicle (Copyright 2003 Houston Chronicle Publishing Co. Reprinted with permission. All rights reserved); The John Hopkins University Press (excerpt from John Norton Moore, ed. Law and Civil War in the Modern World. pp. 217–228, 229–233, 235–252. © 1974 The John Hopkins University Press. Reprinted with permission of The Johns Hopkins University Press); Melbourne University Law Review (excerpt); The New York Times (Copyright © 1990, 1991, 2003 by The New York Times Company); Oxford University Press (excerpts from Ian Brownlie, International Law and the Use of Force by States and British Yearbook of International Law, vol. 51. By permission of Oxford University Press);

Princeton University Press (excerpt from Paret, Peter; On War. © Princeton University Press, 2004 renewed PUP. Reprinted by permission of Princeton University Press); Rowman & Littlefield Publishers, Inc. (excerpt from The United States and the International Criminal Court, National Security and International Law); Saskatchewan Law Review (excerpt from Forrest Martin, Using International Human Rights Law for Establishing a Unified Use of Force Rule in the Law of Armed Conflict); The University of Chicago Press (excerpt from Quincy Wright, A Study of War (1964)); The Washington Post (© 2003. The Washington Post. Reprinted with permission); Weidenfeld: Nicholson (excerpt from Geoffrey Best, Humanity in Warfare, pp. 10–15 (1980)); Westview Press (excerpt from Stephen C. Schlesinger, Act of Creation: The Founding of the United Nations); The Yale Journal of International Law (excerpt); The Yale University Press (excerpts from Michael Howard, The Laws of War and Geoffrey Parker, Early Modern Europe, in The Laws of War (1994)).

SUMMARY OF CONTENTS

PART IV. The Future Development of International Law on the Use of Force

*

TABLE OF CONTENTS

*

TABLE OF CASES

Principal cases are in bold type. Non-principal cases are in roman type. References are to Pages.

INTERNATIONAL LAW
AND THE
USE OF FORCE

*

PART I

THE STUDY OF INTERNATIONAL LAW ON THE USE OF FORCE

CHAPTER ONE

WHAT DO WE MEAN BY THE USE OF FORCE?

The two case studies of war in Iraq in Chapter Two provide examples of the core subject of this book: two readily identifiable opponents engaging in cross-border, significant armed hostilities. The international law on the use of force has grown up around those kinds of conflicts, and they will be an important part of our study. The subject of this book, however, is broader than classic war. Our subject is the use of force. The Second World War, the Vietnam War, the various Iraq wars, and other wars will feature in the pages that follow, but so will conflicts that are more difficult to categorize, such as conflicts with terrorists, fishing disputes in which shots are fired, and insurgencies to oust an occupying power. It is the use of force that is restricted in the United Nations Charter, not just the use of war. The contemporary law governing the use of force is based on the United Nations Charter, adopted in 1945 at the close of the Second World War.[1] The Charter begins in the Preamble with the statement that the organization was formed to "save succeeding generations from the scourge of war." But the Charter then goes on to prohibit the use of force by states except in self-defense or with the United Nations Security Council's authorization. We will, therefore, look generally at the use of force prohibited by the UN Charter. Given time and space restraints, we will focus primarily on the significant uses of force, those that rise to the level of armed conflict.

This Chapter discusses these various categories: classic war, armed conflict, and other uses of force. While no precise definitions can be provided, broad distinctions can be made. Understanding the broad distinctions and the trends that are affecting them is key to understanding the international law on the use of force in general.

While we cannot provide neat definitions today, it was once possible to find such definitions in this area of international law. Those earlier definitions still influence the law and we will begin by reviewing them. In the 19th century, the era of legal formalism, it was enough for a sovereign to declare war for a war to exist under international law. Two states could

---

1. For general works on the international law governing the use of force, *see* CHRISTINE GRAY, INTERNATIONAL LAW AND THE USE OF FORCE (2d ed., 2004); Thomas Franck, Recourse to Force, Action Against Threats and Armed Attacks (2002); Yoram Dinstein, War, Aggression, and Self–Defense (3d ed., 2001); HILAIRE MCCOUBREY & NIGEL WHITE, INTERNATIONAL LAW AND ARMED CONFLICT (1992); THE CURRENT LEGAL REGULATION OF THE USE OF FORCE (Antonio Cassese ed., 1986); IAN BROWNLIE, INTERNATIONAL LAW AND THE USE OF FORCE BY STATES (1963).

be at war without ever firing a shot. We have since moved away from such unreality. Today it is the fact of fighting that is all-important. This move to greater reality, however, has cost us the clarity afforded by formalism. Yes, the key is actual fighting, but how much fighting and by whom? We know that the most minimal cross-border transgression is not an armed conflict. Yet, we also know that armed conflicts are more than just major cross-border invasions. Important rights and duties turn on the threshold issue. For example, in an international armed conflict, members of the armed forces of an adverse party may be held if captured in detention until the end of hostilities without any criminal charge for fighting. This is a significant departure from the law that prevails in the absence of armed conflict.

Despite the importance of knowing what armed conflict is, current events and legal theories continually challenge the development of even a broad understanding, let alone any neat definition. Concepts of war and what law should apply in war are being pulled in opposing directions. Some now argue that a very low threshold of violence should be considered an armed conflict triggering the law that applies in armed conflict—as opposed to the law applicable in peace. For low-threshold proponents, the law of armed conflict applies even in locations where no armed conflict exists, but where, for example, members of terrorist organizations may be found because these individuals may be planning attacks that could launch an armed conflict. At the opposite extreme, a few scholars argue that in the age of human rights there is no distinct law applying in armed conflicts versus peacetime. They want all violence to be governed by the law of peace without any dualistic categorization. This book is obviously based on the existence of a distinction. The position here is that law is different in armed conflict than in peace and so understanding what an armed conflict is in international law is essential to knowing when the law governing armed conflict applies. Admittedly, the formal division of the law between war and peace is artificial and that fact creates anomalies. This artificiality and the problems it introduces should be born in mind as you read further in the materials below. In the final chapter, Chapter Twelve, we return to some of these basic concepts and discuss the future trends that may impact them.

Here we introduce the phrase "use of force," distinguishing it from "armed conflict" and "war." We also introduce more briefly related terms such as "civil war," "internal armed conflict," "international armed conflict," "incidents," "hostilities," "reprisals" and "countermeasures." We begin by returning to the age of formalism.

A. THE CLASSIC MEANING OF WAR

In the 1906 edition of Lassa Oppenheim's influential treatise on international law, he defined war with precision. It is

> a contention between two or more States through their armed forces, for the purpose of overpowering each other and imposing such conditions of peace as the victor pleases.[2]

2. II LASSA OPPENHEIM, INTERNATIONAL LAW 56 (1906).

This was the definition of war *de facto*, but until the adoption of the United Nations Charter, a *de jure* war could exist as soon as a state declared it, regardless of whether any force was actually used.

Ian Brownlie, International Law and the Use of Force by States

26–28 (1963)*

The practice of states since the early nineteenth century had developed a doctrine which might be considered so absurd as not to merit discussion if it were not for the circumstances that governments have frequently used the doctrine and that it has been resorted to even in more recent times. State practice has emphasized that war is not a legal concept linked with objective phenomena such as large-scale hostilities between the armed forces of organized state entities but a legal status the existence of which depends on the intention of one or more of the states concerned. Thus hostilities resulting in considerable loss of life and destruction of property may not result in a state of war, the term commonly applied to this legal status, if the parties contending do not regard a 'state of war' as existing. This technical concept is also referred to variously in the sources as 'war', '*de jure* war', 'war in the legal sense', and 'war in the sense of international law'. As a legal status it depended on subjective determination by governments of the legal significance of their own actions. This type of determination by individual governments is, of course, a concomitant of the present state of international organization: what is peculiar to the present instance is the fact that, as the nineteenth-century practice shows, the determination did not depend on any objective criteria. In the period between 1798 and 1920 military occupations, invasions, bombardments, blockades, and lesser forms of conflict took place in the absence of any state of war, at least in the opinion of the governments concerned. War became such a subjective concept in state practice that to attempt a definition was to play with words.

In the view of most of the governments there were substantial reasons of policy for avoiding a state of war while at the same time using the desired amount of coercion. In the era of constitutional government the executive was usually bound to observe time-consuming and politically embarrassing procedures before recourse to 'war'. The process involved preparation of public opinion and the rallying of sufficient support in the legislative assembly. Recourse to 'war' incurred a certain odium; 'war' was a term which had acquired a deep psychological and emotional significance. 'War' implied a full-scale combat which offended pacific sentiment

* Footnotes omitted.

and was wasteful of lives and a nation's resources. Furthermore, if a government admitted the existence of a state of war third states could, without embarrassment, demand observance of neutral rights and were themselves under various legal duties. The "state of war" involved a termination of commercial intercourse between the contending states and the invalidation or suspension of treaties. In the more modern period, the appearance of restrictions on the right to resort to war in the League Covenant and other instruments was to provide a further reason for avoiding 'war'. The extreme subjectivity of what may be called the state of war doctrine was tolerable in the period before the League when war was still viewed to some extent as a private duel and not a matter automatically of concern to the community of states. As a rule only powerful states would assert their rights as neutrals in a case in which the parties to a conflict did not themselves admit a state of war. Limited forms of coercion and also large-scale hostilities could take place without the victim of an attack asserting that 'war' existed since the attacker was often a major Power and the victim a relatively weak state anxious not to aggravate the situation.

States often considered that it was desirable to avoid the disruption and embarrassment of full-scale hostilities and war in the legal sense by recourse either to some restricted use of force with a limited object or to extensive operations without any admission of the existence of a "state of war". The constant use in the nineteenth century of various restricted forms of coercion gave rise to a body of legal doctrine on reprisals, pacific blockade, and intervention to protect nationals and their property in foreign states. * * * It is sufficient for the present to notice that, in theory at least, states had to pay for the luxury of avoiding the consequences of a state of war by submitting to some measure of legal regulation of the lesser means of coercion as a reprisal, pacific blockade, or justified intervention. Reprisals and the justified forms of intervention were bounded by the requirement of proportionality to the danger threatened and the restricted object of the use of force.

A famous arbitral award of 1928 described a reprisal by Germany against Portugal, revealing just how serious a use of force reprisals could be. The award also explains some of the precise legal rules that applied to reprisals, rules that would not have applied if Germany had just declared war on Portugal.

Naulilaa

GREEN HACKWORTH, 6 DIGEST OF INTERNATIONAL LAW 154–55 (1943).

On October 19, 1914 a German official and two German officers from German Southwest Africa were killed at the Portuguese post of Naulilaa in Angola under the following circumstances. A party of Germans had crossed, into Angola to discuss with the Portuguese authorities the importation of food supplies into German Southwest Africa. Due to difficulties in interpreting misunderstandings arose between the parties. In the course of the discussion a Portuguese officer seized the bridle of a German official's horse and the official struck him. At that time a German officer drew his pistol. The Portuguese officer ordered his men to fire and the official and two officers were killed. Portuguese authorities subsequently interned the German interpreter and a German soldier. The authorities of German Southwest Africa did not communicate with the Portuguese authorities, but in alleged reprisal for the incident German troops attacked and destroyed certain forts and posts in Angola. These events took place prior to the entry of Portugal into the World War. After the war, the Portuguese Government claimed damages on account of the incident. Alois de Meuron, a Swiss lawyer, was designated on August 15, 1920 as arbitrator to determine in conformance with paragraph 4 of the annex to articles 297–298 of the Treaty of Versailles the amount of the Portuguese claims. On February 9, 1928, two other arbitrators, both Swiss nationals, Robert Guex and Robert Fazy, were added to the tribunal. In an award rendered July 31, 1928 the arbitrators stated that the death of the German official and of the two German officers was not the consequence of an act contrary to the law of nations on the part of the Portuguese authorities. They declared that the *sine qua non* of the right to exercise reprisals is a motive furnished by a preliminary act contrary to the law of nations and that, even had such an act on the part of the Portuguese authorities been established, the German argument that the reprisals were justified would have been rejected because reprisals are only permissible when they have been preceded by an unsatisfied demand. The use of force, they stated, is only justified by necessity. They also stated that, even if it were admitted that the law of nations does not demand that reprisals be in approximate proportion to the offense, it would, nevertheless, certainly be necessary to consider as excessive and illegal reprisals out of all proportion to the act motivating them. They found that there was obvious disproportion between the incident at Naulilaa and the reprisals which followed, and defined reprisals as follows:

> Reprisals are an act of self-help (Selbsthilfehandlung) on the part of the injured state, an act corresponding *after an unsatisfied demand* to an act contrary to the law of nations on the part of the offending State. They have the effect of momentarily suspending, in the relations between the two States, the observance of such or such a role of the law of nations. They are limited by the experiences of humanity and the rules of good faith applicable in relations between State and State.

They would be illegal if a preliminary act contrary to the law
of nations had not furnished a reason for them. . . .

B.   The End of "War," The Continuing Use of Force

1.   The U.N. Charter and the End of "War"

Perhaps not surprisingly, the term "war" fell out of use as a legal term
of art with the adoption of the United Nations Charter in 1945. The
Charter's Article 2(4) prohibits all uses of force, war and lesser actions,
except in self-defense or as mandated by the Security Council. Article 2(4)
of the Charter requires that

> All Members shall refrain in their international relations from the
> threat or use of force against the territorial integrity or political
> independence of any state, or in any other manner inconsistent
> with the Purposes of the United Nations.

This provision was intended to outlaw war and other uses of force.
Following the adoption of the Charter, "war" ministries became "defense"
ministries. States engaging in armed conflict today rarely declare war. They
tend to declare they are acting in self-defense or on behalf of another state
acting in self-defense. The United States has not formally declared war
since the Second World War. The four Geneva Conventions adopted in 1949
for the protection of war victims are triggered by the existence of actual
armed conflict regardless of war declarations. According to Article 2,
common to all four Conventions, the Conventions apply in

> all cases of declared war or of any other armed conflict which may
> arise between two or more of the High Contracting Parties, even if
> the state of war is not recognized by one of them.

What mattered after 1945 was actual fighting, not the 19th century
formalities that might mean a war was occurring legally even if no one ever
fired a shot. We still use the term "war" to refer to any serious armed
conflict. Yugoslavia, Liberia, Sudan and Sri Lanka experienced civil wars
(often called today internal armed conflicts) in the 1990s. We also had the
Gulf War and the Ethiopia–Eritrea War, two international armed conflicts,
in the 1990s. But indicative of the fact "war" is no longer the significant
legal term it once was, the United States fought a war on poverty and a war
on drugs. Declarations of war lost their importance, too, but with the loss
of this formal legal device, the law became more uncertain. The Geneva
Conventions are triggered by "armed conflict;" the Charter's Article 2(4)
actual prohibits "the use of force." What is meant by these terms? Are they
distinguishable? Should they be for the purposes of international law?

2.   The Meaning of Armed Conflict

The Security Council established a tribunal to hear allegations of war
crimes, crimes against humanity, and genocide arising out of the conflicts
in the former Yugoslavia that began in 1991. The first person tried was
Duško Tadić, a Bosnian Serb accused of crimes against Bosnian Muslims.

Tadić challenged the jurisdiction of the tribunal in part by arguing no "armed conflict" had occurred that could give rise to allegations of war crimes.

Prosecutor v. Tadić

Decision on the Defense Motion for Interlocutory Appeal on Jurisdiction.
No. IT–94–1, paras. 66–70 (Oct. 2, 1995).

A.   Preliminary Issue: The Existence of an Armed Conflict

66.   Appellant now asserts the new position that there did not exist a legally cognizable armed conflict—either internal or international—at the time and place that the alleged offences were committed. Appellant's argument is based on a concept of armed conflict covering only the precise time and place of actual hostilities. Appellant claims that the conflict in the Prijedor region (where the alleged crimes are said to have taken place) was limited to a political assumption of power by the Bosnian Serbs and did not involve armed combat (though movements of tanks are admitted). This argument presents a preliminary issue to which we turn first.

67.   International humanitarian law governs the conduct of both internal and international armed conflicts. Appellant correctly points out that for there to be a violation of this body of law, there must be an armed conflict. The definition of "armed conflict" varies depending on whether the hostilities are international or internal ... but, contrary to Appellant's contention, the temporal and geographical scope of both internal and international armed conflicts extends beyond the exact time and place of hostilities.
* * *

70.   On the basis of the foregoing, we find that an armed conflict exists whenever there is a resort to armed force between States or protracted armed violence between governmental authorities and organized armed groups or between such groups within a State. International humanitarian law applies from the initiation of such armed conflicts and extends beyond the cessation of hostilities until a general conclusion of peace is reached; or, in the case of internal conflicts, a peaceful settlement is achieved. Until that moment, international humanitarian law continues to apply in the whole territory of the warring States or, in the case of internal conflicts, the whole territory under the control of a party, whether or not actual combat takes place there.

Applying the foregoing concept of armed conflicts to this case, we hold that the alleged crimes were committed in the context of an armed conflict. Fighting among the various entities within the former Yugoslavia began in 1991, continued through the summer of 1992 when the alleged crimes are said to have been committed, and persists to this day. Notwithstanding various temporary cease-fire agreements, no general conclusion of peace has brought military operations in the region to a close. These hostilities exceed the intensity requirements applicable to both international and internal armed conflicts. There has been protracted, large-scale violence between the armed forces of different States and between governmental forces and organized insurgent groups.

As already quoted above, Common Article 2 of the four Geneva Conventions provides that the Conventions "shall apply to all cases of declared war or of any other armed conflict which may arise between two or more of the High Contracting Parties, even if the state of war is not recognized by one of them." The Commentary to the conventions defines "armed conflict" as used in Article 2 as "any differences arising between two states and leading to the intervention of members of the armed forces."[3] In the Tadić decision above, the Court uses the qualifier "protracted" for conflicts other than those between two states, but also refers to an "intensity" standard for both internal and international armed conflicts. (Para. 70.) Greenwood also takes the position that even between sovereign states, "many isolated incidents, such as border clashes and naval incidents, are not treated as armed conflicts. It may well be, therefore, that only when fighting reaches a level of intensity which exceeds that of such isolated clashes will it be treated as an armed conflict to which the rules of international humanitarian law apply."[4] The Geneva Conventions do incorporate a standard of intensity with respect to their application in civil wars. For international humanitarian law to apply, such conflicts must amount to "more than situations of internal disturbances and tensions such as riots and isolated and sporadic acts of violence."[5] (See discussion of use of force short of armed conflict, below.)

The fighting in an armed conflict is also termed "hostilities" and important humanitarian protections in armed conflict turn on the fact of on-going hostilities. Note how the Tribunal in Tadić found that some rules of international humanitarian law apply away from actual hostilities or the theater of combat and some rules continue even after hostilities are over. This finding indicates that other rules, such as the right to attack enemy military objectives would apply only within a theater of combat and ends with the end of hostilities. Because an armed conflict is necessarily characterized by on-going hostilities, when hostilities end, so does the armed conflict. This point will be discussed in greater detail in Chapter Eleven.

3. III Commentary to the 1949 Geneva Convention Relative to the Treatment of Prisoners of War 23 (Jean Pictet ed., 1960).

4. Christopher Greenwood, *Scope of Application of Humanitarian Law, in* The Handbook of Humanitarian Law in Armed Conflict 42 (Dieter Fleck ed., 1995).

5. Protocol Additional to the Geneva Conventions of 12 August 1949, and Relating to the Protections of Victims of Non–International Armed Conflicts (Protocol II) of 8 June 1977, art. 1(2)1125 U.N.T.S. 609 (1979).

US Supreme Court Justice Sandra Day O'Connor discusses hostilities as a necessary aspect of armed conflict and provides factors as to what constitutes hostilities in the armed conflict that began in Afghanistan on October 7, 2001, with the invasion by the United States and United Kingdom of that country.

Hamdi v. Rumsfeld

542 U.S. ___, 124 S.Ct. 2633 (2004).

It is a clearly established principle of the law of war that detention may last no longer than active hostilities. See Article 118 of the Geneva Convention (III) Relative to the Treatment of Prisoners of War, Aug. 12, 1949, [1955] 6 U. S. T. 3316, 3406, T. I. A. S. No. 3364 ("Prisoners of war shall be released and repatriated without delay after the cessation of active hostilities"). See also Article 20 of the Hague Convention (II) on Laws and Customs of War on Land, July 29, 1899, 32 Stat. 1817 (as soon as possible after "conclusion of peace"); Hague Convention (IV), * * *, Oct. 18, 1907, 36 Stat. 2301 ("conclusion of peace" (Art. 20)); Geneva Convention, * * *, July 27, 1929, 47 Stat. 2055 (repatriation should be accomplished with the least possible delay after conclusion of peace (Art. 75)); P[]aust, Judicial Power to Determine the Status and Rights of Persons Detained without Trial, 44 Harv. Int'l L. J. 503, 510–511 (2003) (prisoners of war "can be detained during an armed conflict, but the detaining country must release and repatriate them 'without delay after the cessation of active hostilities,' unless they are being lawfully prosecuted or have been lawfully convicted of crimes and are serving sentences" (citing Arts. 118, 85, 99, 119, 129, Geneva Convention (III), 6 T. I .A. S., at 3384, 3392, 3406, 3418)).

Hamdi contends that the AUMF [a 2001 joint congressional resolution titled, Authorization for the Use of Military Force] does not authorize indefinite or perpetual detention. Certainly, we agree that indefinite detention for the purpose of interrogation is not authorized. Further, we understand Congress' grant of authority for the use of "necessary and appropriate force" to include the authority to detain for the duration of the relevant conflict, and our understanding is based on longstanding law-of-war principles. If the practical circumstances of a given conflict are entirely unlike those of the conflicts that informed the development of the law of war, that understanding may unravel. But that is not the situation we face as of this date. Active combat operations against Taliban fighters apparently are ongoing in Afghanistan. See, *e.g.*, Constable, U. S. Launches New Operation in Afghanistan, Washington Post, Mar. 14, 2004, p. A22 (reporting that 13,500 United States troops remain in Afghanistan, including several thousand new arrivals); J. Abizaid, Dept. of Defense, Gen. Abizaid Central Command Operations Update Briefing, Apr. 30, 2004, http://www.defenselink.mil/transcripts/2004/tr200404301402.html (as visited June 8, 2004, and available in the Clerk of Court's case file) (media briefing describing ongoing operations in Afghanistan involving 20,000 United States troops). The United States may detain, for the duration of these hostilities, individuals legitimately determined to be Taliban combatants who "engaged in an armed conflict against the United States." If the record establishes that United States troops are still involved in active combat in Afghanistan, those detentions are part of the exercise of "necessary and appropriate force," and therefore are authorized by the AUMF.

Armed conflict, therefore, is characterized by exchange of hostilities of an intense nature of some duration. Armed conflict is most often initiated by an armed attack that gives rise to a right of self-defense by the state attacked. In the excerpt below, the International Court of Justice discusses the nature of armed attack and other "less grave forms of the use of force" that do not give rise to the right to use armed force in self-defense. The excerpt provides further insight into the kinds of action that come within the subject "use of force."

Military and Paramilitary Activities in and Against Nicaragua

(Nicaragua v. U.S.), 1986 I.C.J. 14, 101–03 (June 27).

191.   As regards certain particular aspects of the principle in question, it will be necessary to distinguish the most grave forms of the use of force (those constituting an armed attack) from other less grave forms. In determining the legal rule which applies to these latter forms, the Court can again draw on the formulations contained in the Declaration on Principles of International Law concerning Friendly Relations and Co-operations among States in accordance with the Charter of the United Nations (General Assembly resolution 2625 (XXV), referred to above). As already observed, the adoption by States of this text affords an indication of their *opinio juris* as to customary international law on the question. Alongside certain descriptions which may refer to aggression, this text includes others which refer only to less grave forms of the use of force. In particular, according to this resolution:

> "Every State has the duty to refrain from the threat or use of force to violate the existing international boundaries of another State or as a means of solving international disputes, including territorial disputes and problems concerning frontiers of States.

States have a duty to refrain from acts of reprisal involving the use of force.

Every state has the duty to refrain from any forcible action which deprives peoples * * * of the * * * right to self-determination and freedom and independence.

Every State has the duty to refrain from organizing or encouraging the organization of irregular forces or armed bands, including mercenaries, for incursion into the territory of another State.

Every State has the duty to refrain from organizing, instigating, assisting or participating in acts of civil strife or terrorist acts in another State or acquiescing in organized activities within its territory directed towards the commission of such acts, when the acts referred to in the present paragraph involve a threat or use of force."

192.   Moreover, in the part of this same resolution devoted to the principle of non-intervention in matters within the national jurisdiction of States, a very similar rule is found:

"Also no State shall organize, assist, foment, finance, incite or tolerate subversive, terrorist or armed activities directed towards the violent overthrow of the régime of another State, or interfere in civil strife in another State."

In the context of the inter-American system, this approach can be traced back at least to 1928 (Convention on the Rights and Duties of States in the Event of Civil Strife, Art. 1 (1)); it was confirmed by resolution 78 adopted by the General Assembly of the Organization of American States on 21 April 1972. The operative part of this resolution reads as follows:

"The General Assembly Resolves:

1.   To reiterate solemnly the need for the member states of the Organization to observe strictly the principles of nonintervention and self-determination of peoples as a means of ensuring peaceful coexistence among them and to refrain from committing any direct or indirect act that might constitute a violation of those principles.

2.   To reaffirm the obligation of those states to refrain from applying economic, political, or any other type of measures to coerce another state and obtain from it advantages of any kind.

3.   Similarly, to reaffirm the obligation of these states to refrain from organizing, supporting, promoting, financing, instigating, or tolerating subversive, terrorist, or armed

activities against another state and from intervening in a
civil war in another state or in its internal struggles."

* * *

195.   In case of individual self-defence, the exercise of this right is
subject to the State concerned having been the victim of an armed
attack. Reliance on collective self-defence of course does not remove the need for this. There appears now to be general agreement on the nature of the acts which can be treated as constituting armed attacks. In particular, it may be considered to be agreed
that an armed attack must be understood as including not merely
action by regular armed forces across an international border, but
also "the sending by or on behalf of a State of armed bands,
groups, irregulars or mercenaries, which carry out acts of armed
force against another State of such gravity as to amount to" (inter
alia) an actual armed attack conducted by regular forces, "or its
substantial involvement therein". This description, contained in
Article 3, paragraph (g), of the Definition of Aggression annexed to
General Assembly resolution 3314 (XXIX), may be taken to reflect
customary international law. * * * [T]he prohibition of armed
attacks may apply to the sending by a State of armed bands to the
territory of another State, if such an operation, because of its scale
and effects, would have been classified as an armed attack rather
than a mere frontier incident had it been carried out by regular
armed forces. But the Court does not believe that the concept of
"armed attack" includes not only acts by armed bands where such
acts occur on a significant scale but also assistance to rebels in the
form of the provision of weapons or logistical or other support.
Such assistance may be regarded as a threat or use of force, or
amount to intervention in the internal or external affairs of other
States.

* * *

249.   * * * While an armed attack would give rise to an entitlement to collective self-defence, a use of force of a lesser degree of
gravity cannot, as the court has already observed * * * produce
any entitlement to take collective countermeasures involving the
use of force.

In Chapter Seven we discuss in detail the terms "armed attack" and "self-
defense." Note for now that an "armed attack" according to the ICJ is
something distinct from "armed conflict" and both are distinct from "use
of force."

3.   THE MEANING OF THE USE OF FORCE

The use of force is the broadest category related to war. All armed attacks that can give rise to the right of self-defense are uses of force, but as the ICJ explained in the Nicaragua Case, the use of force encompasses more than just such armed attacks. The use of force could reasonably include economic coercion, political coercion, physical force not involving arms, or computer attacks. The use of force mentioned in Article 2(4) is not so broad. The drafting history of the Charter, as well as subsequent interpretation by governments and the International Court of Justice, indicate that the kind of force prohibited in Article 2(4) is armed force rather than every kind of forceful action. The drafters used the broader term to ensure that states would not make their old arguments about what constituted war and what constituted armed action short of war. As the excerpt by Brownlie above explains, these arguments had been used for decades to avoid wartime duties.

Even with respect to armed force, however, it appears that certain minimal uses of force may not be a violation of Article 2(4). Numerous examples of states using armed force can be found that are not treated as violations of Article 2(4). The following excerpt is from a commission of enquiry formed by the United Kingdom and Denmark. It describes a use of armed force that would have been lawful if it had not been excessive. We can conclude that using force in this context—policing a fishery conservation zone—does not violate Article 2(4):

The Red Crusader

Commission of Enquiry (Denmark–United Kingdom), March 23, 1962, 35 I.L.R. 485.

THE FACTS—On May 29, 1961, the British trawler *Red Crusader* was arrested by the Danish authorities off the coast of the Faroe Islands. A Commission of Enquiry was set up by an Exchange of Notes of November 15, 1961, between the Governments of Denmark and the United Kingdom to investigate certain incidents relating to this arrest and to subsequent events.

* * *

"As a result of its investigation in Chapter Two, the Commission finds:

"(1) The *Red Crusader* was arrested. This conclusion is established by Captain Sølling's declarations as well as by the evidence given by Skipper Wood. Even if the Skipper formally denied his guilt, his answers clearly implied that he considered at the time that he had been duly arrested for illegal fishing. Notes made in the Skipper's red pocket-book and the *Red Crusader's* log-book also leave no doubt on that point.

"(2) Skipper Wood, after having obeyed for a certain time the order given him by Captain Sølling, changed his mind during the trip to Thorshavn and put into effect a plan, concerted with his crew, whereby he attempted to escape and to evade the jurisdiction of an authority which he had at first, rightly, accepted.

"(3) During this attempt to escape, the Skipper of the *Red Crusader* took steps to seclude Lieutenant Bech and Corporal Kropp during a certain period and had the intention to take them to Aberdeen.

"(4) In opening fire at 03.22 hours up to 03.53 hours, the Commanding Officer of the *Niels Ebbesen* exceeded legitimate use of armed force on two counts: (a) firing without warning of solid gun-shot; (b) creating danger to human life on board the *Red Crusader* without proved necessity, by the effective firing at the *Red Crusader* after 03.40 hours.

"The escape of the *Red Crusader* in flagrant violation of the order received and obeyed, the seclusion on board the trawler of an officer and rating of the crew of *Niels Ebbesen*, and Skipper Wood's refusal to stop may explain some resentment on the part of Captain Sølling. Those circumstances, however, cannot justify such violent action.

"The Commission is of the opinion that other means should have been attempted, which, if duly persisted in, might have finally persuaded Skipper Wood to stop and revert to the normal procedure which he himself had previously followed.

"(5) The cost of the repair of the damage caused by the firing at and hitting of the *Red Crusader* submitted by the British Government has been considered reasonable by the Danish Agent."

The Corfu Channel Case involves uses of force that come closer to the use of force prohibited in Article 2(4). The ICJ, does not, however, state explicitly that any of the uses of force by either Albania or the United Kingdom violated Article 2(4).

The Corfu Channel Case

(U.K. v. Alb.) 1949 ICJ 4, 27–28, 32–35 (July 9).

On May, 15th, 1946, the British cruisers *Orion* and *Superb*, while passing southward through the North Corfu Channel, were fired at by an Albanian battery in the vicinity of Saranda. It appears from the report of the commanding naval officer dated, May 29th, 1946, that the firing started when the ships had already passed the battery and were moving away from it; that from 12 to 20 rounds were fired; that the firing lasted 12 minutes and ceased only when the ships were out of range: but that the ships were not hit although there were a number of "shorts" and of "overs". An Albanian note of May 21st states that the Coastal Commander ordered a few shots to be fired in the direction of the ships "in accordance with a General Order founded on international law".

The United Kingdom Government at once protested to the Albanian Government, stating that innocent passage through straits is a right recognized by international law. There ensued a diplomatic correspondence in which the Albanian Government asserted that foreign warships and merchant vessels had no right to pass through Albanian territorial waters without prior notification to, and the permission of, the Albanian authorities. This view was put into effect by a communication of the Albanian Chief of Staff, dated May 17th, 1946, which purported to subject the passage of foreign warships and merchant vessels in Albanian territorial waters to previous notification to and authorization by the Albanian Government. The diplomatic correspondence continued, and culminated in a United Kingdom note of August 2nd, 1946, in which the United Kingdom Government maintained its view with regard to the right of innocent passage through straits forming routes for international maritime traffic between two parts of the high seas. The note ended with the warning that if Albanian coastal batteries in the future opened fire on any British warship passing through the Corfu Channel, the fire would be returned.

[On October 22, 1946, British warships again entered the Corfu Channel. Two ships struck mines causing extensive damage and the loss of 17 sailors. The ICJ held Albania responsible for placing the mines and not warning the UK about the mines. This part of the Case is dealt with in our discussion of self-defense below. See p. 240.]

* * *

It is, in the opinion of the Court, generally recognized and in accordance with international custom that States in time of peace have a right to send their warships through straits used for international navigation between two parts of the high seas without the previous authorization of a coastal State, provided that the passage is *innocent*. Unless otherwise prescribed in an international convention, there is no right for a coastal State to prohibit such passage through straits in time of peace.[6]

* * *

---

6. This part of the opinion has been modified by the 1980 United Nations Convention on the Law of the Sea, art. 38. Passage is not required because the Corfu Channel is formed by an island and the mainland and a route of similar convenience is available seaward of the island.

In addition to the passage of the United Kingdom warships on October 22nd, 1946, the second question in the Special Agreement relates to the acts of the Royal Navy in Albanian waters on November 12th and 13th, 1946. This is the minesweeping operation called "Operation Retail" by the Parties during the proceedings. This name will be used in the present Judgment.

After the explosions of October 22nd, the United Kingdom Government sent a note to the Albanian Government, in which it announced its intention to sweep the Corfu Channel shortly. The Albanian reply, which was received in London on October 31st, stated that the Albanian Government would not give its consent to this unless the operation in question took place outside Albanian territorial waters. Meanwhile, at the United Kingdom Government's request, the International Central Mine Clearance Board decided, in a resolution of November 1st, 1946, that there should be a further sweep of the Channel, subject to Albania's consent. The United Kingdom Government having informed the Albanian Government, in a communication of November 10th, that the proposed sweep would take place on November 12th, the Albanian Government replied on the 11th, protesting against this "unilateral decision of His Majesty's Government". It said it did not consider it inconvenient that the British fleet should undertake the sweeping of the channel of navigation, but added that, before sweeping was carried out, it considered it indispensable to decide what area of the sea should be deemed to constitute this channel, and proposed the establishment of a Mixed Commission for the purpose. It ended by saying that any sweeping undertaken without the consent of the Albanian Government outside the channel thus constituted, i.e., inside Albanian territorial waters where foreign warships have no reason to sail, could only be considered as a deliberate violation of Albanian territory and sovereignty.

After this exchange of notes, "Operation Retail" took place on November 12th and 13th. Commander Mestre, of the French Navy, was asked to attend as observer, and was present at the sweep on November 13th. The operation was carried out under the protection of an important covering force composed of an aircraft carrier, cruisers and other war vessels.* * *

[T]he explosions of October 22nd, 1946, in a channel declared safe for navigation, and one which the United Kingdom Government, more than any other government, had reason to consider safe, raised quite a different problem from that of a routine sweep carried out under the orders of the mine clearance organizations. These explosions were suspicious; they raised a question of responsibility.

Accordingly, this was the ground on which the United Kingdom Government chose to establish its main line of defence. According to that Government, the *corpora delicti* must be secured as quickly as possible, for fear they should be taken away, without leaving traces, by the authors of the minelaying or by the Albanian authorities. This justification took two distinct forms in the United Kingdom Government's arguments. It was presented first as a new and special application of the theory of intervention, by means of which the State intervening would secure possession of evidence in the territory of another State, in order to submit it to an international tribunal and thus facilitate its task.

The Court cannot accept such a line of defence. The Court can only regard the alleged right of intervention as the manifestation of a policy of force, such as has, in the past, given rise to most serious abuses and such as cannot, whatever be the present defects in international organization, find a place in international law. Intervention is perhaps still less admissible in the particular form it would take here; for, from the nature of things, it would be reserved for the most powerful States, and might easily lead to perverting the administration of international justice itself.

The United Kingdom Agent, in his speech in reply, has further classified "Operation Retail" among methods of self-protection or self-help. The Court cannot accept this defence either. Between independent States, respect for territorial sovereignty is an essential foundation of international relations. The Court recognizes that the Albanian Government's complete failure to carry out its duties after the explosions, and the dilatory nature of its diplomatic notes, are extenuating circumstances for the action of the United Kingdom Government. But to ensure respect for international law, of which it is the organ, the Court must declare that the action of the British Navy constituted a violation of Albanian sovereignty.

This declaration is in accordance with the request made by Albania through her Counsel, and is in itself appropriate satisfaction.

The method of carrying out "Operation Retail" has also been criticized by the Albanian Government, the main ground of complaint being that the United Kingdom, on that occasion, made use of an unnecessarily large display of force, out of proportion to the requirements of the sweep. The Court thinks that this criticism is not justified. It does not consider that the action of the British Navy was a demonstration of force for the purpose of exercising political pressure on Albania. The responsible naval commander, who kept his ships at a distance from the coast, cannot be reproached for having employed an important covering force in a region where twice within a few months his ships had been the object of serious outrages.

Albania was assessed monetary damages for the loss of life and damage to the two British vessels. The United Kingdom owed no remedy for the unlawful minesweeping. In fact, the ICJ accepted the mines in evidence that the UK had collected through unlawful means.

In addition to states using force below the threshold of armed conflict, non-state actors, such as terrorist organizations, mercenaries, and organized crime groups have long used significant armed force that is nevertheless not characterized as armed conflict. It may become an armed conflict when the armed force is used to control territory or force a government from power. We take up a number of these issues in later chapters.

C. Notes, Questions, and Problems

1. In the Corfu Channel Case, were the United Kingdom and Albania engaged in an armed conflict? Do you detect any action by either side that constituted an "armed attack?" Would you characterize any interactions as an "incident?" Does anything amount to a use of force less grave than an "incident?"

2. Is the fact that terrorists use force intermittently (rather than as sustained armed attacks) fatal to characterizing a terror attack or even a series of attacks as armed conflict? Ingrid Detter DeLupis, Law of War 25 (2 ed., 2000), offers the following conclusion on whether terrorism can ever amount to armed conflict:

> In spite of the obvious problems, a definition may be ventured to cover a somewhat hazy area:
>
> > International terrorism implies the intermittent use or threat of force against person(s) to obtain certain political objectives of international relevance from a third party.
> >
> > But at the same time the intermittent factor, which is a hallmark of terrorism, excludes it from constituting war per se. But as will be shown, terrorist tactics may be adopted in war for the purpose of guerilla warfare.

3. Is there a need for a mutual exchange of armed force for violence to amount to armed conflict? In Madrid, Spain on March 11, 2004, terrorists associated with Al Qaeda planted bombs on two passenger trains killing almost 200 people. Was Spain then in an armed conflict? In common understanding, a fight does not begin until a blow is exchanged for a blow. If someone is hit, but walks away or waits years to hit back, we do not characterize the initial attack as a fight. Is there an armed conflict before a return attack? Do any of the authorities in this Chapter address this question?

4. Some argue that armed conflict must have a territorial dimension and conclude that non-state actors, terrorist groups like Al Qaeda, cannot engage in armed conflict if they do not control territory. *See*, Gabor Rona, *Interesting Times for International Humanitarian Law: Challenges from the 'War on Terror,'* 27 Fletcher Forum of World Affairs 55, 57 (2003);

Christopher Greenwood, *The Concept of War in Modern International Law*, 36 I.C.L.Q. 283 (1987). Must this be so? Why might the control of territory be an important element in the definition of armed conflict?

5. A few definitions also require that fighting be "protracted" to amount to armed conflict. The International Criminal Court has jurisdiction to try war crimes in cases where fighting was "protracted." International Criminal Court Statute, Art. 8.2(f), July 17, 1998, UN Doc. A/CONF.183/9, 37 ILM 999–1019 (1998). Why might the protracted nature of a conflict be significant? Can you think of situations where it would not be significant?

6. Can you think why few governments acknowledge civil unrest as amounting to civil war or internal armed conflict? Why do they prefer to call it "unrest" or criminality. Can you cite an example where you can make the case under the understanding of armed conflict in this chapter that in fact an armed conflict prevails despite the official position of the state involved? Should it matter whether the state itself recognizes fighting as amounting to armed conflict? The Inter–American Court found a violation of the international humanitarian law applicable in civil war despite the fact El Salvador refused to recognize a civil war on its territory at the time. *See* Lucio Parada Cea, et al. v. El Salvador, Case 10.480, Inter–Am. CHR No. 1/99. *See also* Juan Carlos Abella v. Argentina, Case 11.137, Inter–Amer. CHR No. 55/97 (distinguishing "internal disturbances" from armed conflict on the basis of the nature and level of violence.)

7. In the spring of 1994 in Rwanda, officials of the Hutu-controlled government called on Hutus throughout the country to kill all Tutsis. Within a few short months an estimated 800,000 people were killed. It finally ended when a Tutsi rebel army invaded the country and drove the Hutus from power. The UN Security Council formed a court to prosecute individuals who participated in the atrocity. The International Criminal Tribunal for Rwanda had not by 2003 charged anyone with a war crime. Rather, all charges have been for genocide and crimes against humanity. A Swiss military court, however, did charge the mayor of a town in Rwanda with war crimes. *See* Niyonteze, Military Court of Cassation, April 27, 2001. Some national courts may have jurisdiction over war crimes but not other kinds of international crimes—making the determination of whether violence amounts to an "armed conflict" a key issue.

8. If armed conflicts are identifiable today by the actual fact of fighting rather than by formal declarations, what of agreements that end wars? Are peace treaties or armistice agreements any longer of legal importance? In other words, if peace prevails, is the lack of a peace treaty important? *See* YORAM DINSTEIN, WAR, AGGRESSION AND SELF-DEFENCE 33–47 (2003.)

9. After September 11, 2001, when hijacked passenger jets were crashed into buildings and a farm field in the US, President George W. Bush said the United States was in a "war on terror." He said it was a global war that would last "until every terrorist group of global reach has been found, stopped and defeated." *See* George W. Bush, President's Address to the Nation on the Terrorist Attacks, 37 Weekly Comp. Pres. Doc. 1301 (Sept. 11, 2001); President's Address to a Joint Session of Congress on the United

States Response to the Terrorist Attacks of September 11, 37 Weekly Comp. Pres. Doc. 1432 (Sept. 20, 2001); http://www.whitehouse.gov

Was the U.S. in a "global war on terror" in terms of international law on September 11, 2001? Cite the authorities discussed in this Chapter that support the President's claim and those that do not. *See Alain Pellet, No, This is Not War*, EUR. J. INT'L L., Oct. 3, 2001, http://www.ejil.org/forum_WTC/ny-pellet.html

10. Problem: On September 28, 2000, General (later Prime Minister) Ariel Sharon went to the al-Aqsa mosque in Jerusalem. His visit was protested by Palestinians. Israeli authorities fired at the protesters, killing five and wounding hundreds. The shootings triggered further protests, along with rock-throwing and similar violence. Israel responded with helicopters, bombs, tanks, and ground forces across the border with Israel inside the Palestinian Authority. Palestinian groups, in particular, Hamas, a terrorist organization, responded with suicide attacks inside Israel, killing hundreds of people, including children and the elderly. Between September 1993 and September 2000, Israel reported 256 deaths caused by Palestinians. Between September 2000 and July 2004, Israel reports 983 deaths. (http://mfa.gov.il) Between September 2000 and July 2004, the Palestinian Red Cross reported 3064 Palestinian deaths. (The Palestinian Red Cross does not report deaths prior to September 2000, but they were considerably fewer. See http://www.palestinercs.org).

From these facts, can you argue that under international law the situation between Israelis and Palestinians was an armed conflict before 2000? After 2000? At no time? What further information would you like?

CHAPTER TWO

TWO CASE STUDIES ON THE USE OF FORCE

The case studies of war in Iraq that follow are undisputed examples of armed conflict. They provide tangible depictions of the definition discussed in Chapter One from the Tadić Case: "an armed conflict exists whenever there is a resort to armed force between States or protracted armed violence between governmental authorities and organized armed groups or between such groups within a State." (P. 8, above.) In both cases, the fighting reached the level of intensity and duration mentioned in Tadić. In addition to providing a look at two actual armed conflicts, the case studies demonstrate the very real but problematic role of law in controlling armed conflict. As you read further, search for evidence of law. Consider what role law is or is not playing in the unfolding of these conflicts, in how the conflicts are conducted and how they are concluded. Refer back to the case studies as you study the particular rules on the use of force in later chapters. Consider how the rules applied in these actual cases. The questions at the end of the Chapter should help guide your reading. You may wish to turn to those now.

A. THE IRAQI INVASION OF KUWAIT (1990)

The United Nations Security Council is charged with maintaining international peace and security. It is a body in permanent session to react to the world's on-going crises. Under Chapter VII of the United Nations Charter, it has the authority to mandate action by states in response to a threat to the peace, breach of the peace or act of aggression. The Council reacted swiftly to news that Iraq had invaded its neighbor Kuwait. The resolution below was passed as the invasion was in progress.

United Nations   **S**

Security Council

Distr.
General

S/RES/660 (1990)
2 August 1990

Resolution 660 (1990)
of 2 August 1990

The Security Council,

Alarmed by the invasion of Kuwait on 2 August 1990 by the military forces of Iraq.

Determining that there exists a breach of international peace and security as regards the Iraqi invasion of Kuwait;

Acting under Articles 39 and 40 of the Charter of the United States Nations,

1. *Condemns* the Iraqi invasion of Kuwait;

2. *Demands* that Iraq withdraw immediately and unconditionally all its forces to the positions in which they were located on 1 August 1990;

3. *Calls* upon Iraq and Kuwait to begin immediately intensive negotiations for the resolution of their difference and supports all efforts in this regard, and especially those of the League of Arab States;

4. *Decides* to meet again as necessary to consider further steps to ensure compliance with the present resolution.

> *Adopted at the 2932nd meeting by 14 votes to none. One member (Yemen) did not participate in the vote.*

N.Y Times, Aug. 3, 1990, at AI

Invading Iraqis Seize Kuwait and Its Oil; U.S. Condemns Attack, Urges United Action

'NAKED AGGRESSION'

Bush Suggests Action by U.N.—Emir flees to Saudi Arabia Exile

By R. W. Apple Jr.

Special to the New York Times

WASHINGTON, Aug. 2—Iraqi troops stormed into the desert sheikdom of Kuwait today, seizing control of its capital city and its rich oilfields, driving its ruler into exile, plunging the strategic Persian Gulf region into crisis and sending tremors of anxiety around the world.

President Bush condemned the Invasion as "naked aggression" and sought to enlist world leaders to collective action against Iraq.

Faced with dire threat from the truculent Iraqi leader, Saddam Hussein, to a region containing much of the world's oil reserves, and with world financial markets in turmoil, Mr. Bush banned nearly all imports from Iraq and froze the nation's assets in the United States. At a news conference in Woody Creek, Colo., the President and Prime Minister Margaret Thatcher of Britain raised the possibility of economic or even military action by the United Nations.

Iraq Suspends
Payments

In response, Iraq, which had been accusing Kuwait for weeks of stealing its oil and violating production limits set by the Organization of Petroleum Exporting Countries, suspended debt payments to the United States. Western experts asserted that Iraq had been motivated by a financial squeeze that only more oil dollars could ease and by ambitions for regional dominance. Although oil prices rose sharply today, analysts noted that world inventories are unusually high, and they saw no immediate threat to supplies. Witnesses in Kuwait said that hundreds of people were killed or wounded today as Iraqi ground forces, led by columns of tanks, surged into the desert emirate at the head of the gulf. Other troops came by air.

For Mr. Bush, the Invasion posed manifold problems: the difficulty of direct military action despite the huge commitment of money and resources to the gulf in recent years; fear of another surge in oil prices

which could hurt economic growth and rekindle inflation; the potential disruption of fragile budget negotiations between the White House and the Congress, in which a gasoline tax has been considered, and possible damage to the Republican Party in elections this fall.

Reuters reported that the Kuwaiti forces continued to resist tonight in at least one area of the capital at the main military barracks. Earlier reports spoke of explosions and gunfire echoing around the steel-and-glass skyscrapers of the city center in fierce fighting at dawn. But the Iraqi Army, the most powerful in the Arab world, vastly outnumbered the Kuwaiti forces, and 12 hours after the Invasion began the Iraqis were reported in control of the airport, central bank and all key government buildings.

The State Department reported that Iraqi troops had taken six American oilfield workers into custody near the Kuwait–Iraq border. Officials said their whereabouts were unknown.

The President said he could not

confirm that Americans has been seized but that if it were true, "it would affect me in a very dramatic way because I view as a fundamental responsibility of my Presidency protecting American citizens."

Mr. Bush said this morning that American military intervention was not under active consideration, but Lieut. Gen. Howard Graves of the Joint Chiefs of Staff, traveling in Mongolia with Secretary of State James A. Baker III, said the United States was considering "political, military or economic moves" against Iraq. And after flying west to meet Mrs. Thatcher and delivering a speech at the Aspen Institute, the President said, "We're not ruling any options in but we're not ruling any options out."

Warships Head Toward Gulf

An American naval task force, headed by the carrier Independence with 60 fighters and bombers, sailed from the Indian Ocean toward the mouth of the Persian Gulf in a show of strength. The Kuwaiti Ambassador in Washington, a close relative of the Emir, Sheik Jaber al-Ahmed al-Sabah, who is now in Saudi Arabia, pleaded for immediate American military intervention.

At the United Nations, the Security Council issued a unanimous call for an Iraqi withdrawal despite Iraqi assertions, brushed aside by virtually all nations, that Baghdad had been asked to send troops into Kuwait by rebel elements there and that Iraqi forces would be withdrawn from Kuwait within a few weeks.

Mrs. Thatcher called Mr. Hussein's behavior "intolerable" and said that "a collective and effective will of the nations belonging to the U.N." was needed.

United States and British officials referred to Chapter 7 of the United Nations Charter which permits the Security Council to use economic sanctions or military action against any nation that threatens the peace.

Such action was always difficult to take during the cold war because it was very rare to find all five permanent members of the Security Council in agreement on any major dispute.

Soviet Shipments Suspended

But the Soviet Union, a principal arms supplier to Iraq immediately suspended its military shipments to that country, and the United States and the Soviet Union planned a joint statement on Friday after Mr. Baker arrives in Moscow. He hurriedly changed his travel plans after receiving news of the invasion.

Still there seemed to be little practical action that anyone could take in the days immediately ahead to reverse the Iraqi conquest. If Baghdad absorbs Kuwait or sets up a compliant government there, the oil reserves under Iraqi control will be doubled to about 125 billion barrels, making it second only to Saudi Arabia, which has 255 billion barrels.

The invasion appeared to have the potential to shift not only the economic but also the military and political balance in the region.

Moving swiftly today to endorse the President's actions against Iraq, the House voted 416 to 0 to impose trade sanctions and to cut off Export–Import Bank credits.

The Senate unanimously approved a resolution calling for multilateral actions "involving air, sea and land forces" under the United Nations charter to restore international peace and security to the region.

Senator Claiborne Pell of Rhode Island, the Democratic chairman of the Senate Foreign Relations Committee, called Mr. Hussein "the Hitler of the Middle East" and criticized Mr. Bush for not having moved earlier to forestall an invasion. Representative Lee H. Hamilton, Democrat of Indiana, an influential member of the House Foreign Affairs Committee complained that there had been "a kind of inertia" to American policy toward Iraq in recent weeks.

Fears Over Saudi Arabia

Several lawmakers suggested that

Mr. Hussein might now be emboldened to move into neighboring Saudi Arabia. Senator David Boren, Democrat of Oklahoma, who was briefed by the Central Intelligence Agency this morning, noted that the primary Saudi oilfields are only 250 miles from Kuwait, with no terrain "that would impede a rapid movement of forces" by Iraq.

"We have to understand that our national interests are very much at stake," Mr. Boren said. "I think it would be wrong to underestimate the ultimate aims of Saddam Hussein. He really hopes in the long run to put Iraq on a par with the kind of power he sees the Western powers as having."

Judith Kipper, a Middle East specialist at the Brookings Institution, described the conflict in Kuwait as "a war of resources."

"This is the first post cold war crisis in the economically dependent world,"

she said. "With the end of the East–West game, small countries can act with impunity to rearrange the neighborhood. Iraq is a superpower in its own area, but they need cash to service their debt and rebuild their old industry. He gets cash from oil; oil prices are going up. Plus, they have historic claims to Kuwait which Saddam Hussein has chosen to act upon."

Gary Sick, a Middle East expert in the Ford, Carter and Reagan administrations who now teaches at Columbia University, said that condemnations by nations around the world would have "no effect at all."

"Saddam Hussein obviously expected that when he did it," Mr. Sick said, "He can't be surprised by the reaction and he obviously discounted that in advance. Some tangible steps will have to be taken if in fact Saddam Hussein is to be persuaded that this didn't work out to his benefit."

Washington Is Galvanized

The news of the invasion galvanized Washington on Wednesday night and this morning.

Mr. Bush was told of the invasion at 9 p.m. on Wednesday in the residential quarters of the White House, officials said, and was awakened from time to time during the night for briefings by his national security adviser, Brent Scowcroft. He signed his orders on Iraqi assets and trade at 5 a.m., they said.

At 8 this morning, the President met at length with his senior advisers, including the chairman of the Joint Chiefs, Gen. Colin L. Powell. Michael J. Boskin, Mr. Bush's chief economic adviser, said that if oil prices rose 25 percent, and he seemed to consider this plausible, it would have "some deleterious effect on our economy." * * *

Iraq-Kuwait

Border and Territorial Disputes 245–47
(Alan J. Day ed., rev. 2d ed. 1987)*

* * *

* Footnotes omitted.

Historical Background

In the 19th century Kuwait had been administered as part of the Ottoman province of Basra, although the Turks had never occupied or gained full sovereignty over it. In 1896 Shaikh Mubarak the Great seized power in Kuwait after murdering his pro-Turkish half brother, Shaikh Mohammed, and asserted Kuwait's independence from the Ottoman empire, saying that his people owed no allegiance to the Turks. To this end Shaikh Mubarak sought protection from Britain and in 1899, without the approval of the Ottoman Sultan, an agreement was signed under which Britain undertook to give Kuwait protection in return for control over its foreign affairs. Under an Anglo–Turkish convention of July 29, 1913, Britain secured Turkish recognition of Kuwait's autonomy within an area formed by a 40–mile (64–km) radius around the town of Kuwait; however, the outbreak of World War I in 1914 prevented ratification of this agreement. On Nov. 3, 1914, Shaikh Mubarak was promised British recognition as an "independent government under British protection" in return for his co-operation in the capture of Basra from the Turks. Kuwait retained this status until June 19, 1961, when an exchange of notes was signed between Britain and Kuwait which terminated the 1899 agreement between the two countries and provided for British recognition of Kuwait as a sovereign and independent state (although a military assistance agreement remained in force).

Iraq had formerly comprised three Mesopotamian provinces *(vilayet)* of Baghdad, Mosul and Basra and was administered by the Ottoman empire through appointed governors (pashas) answerable to the Sultan–Caliph in Constantinople. After the dissolution of the Ottoman empire in 1918 it was agreed that Mesopotamia should form a self-governing state and on Oct. 20, 1920, Britain accepted a League of Nations mandate for Iraq until it was ready for independence. Under the Treaty of Lausanne of July 24, 1923, Turkey renounced all the territory it had previously possessed outside the borders of present-day Turkey, this renunciation applying also to Kuwait as a part of the former Ottoman province of Basra. After Britain had on Jan. 28,1932, given up its mandate over Iraq, on Oct. 3 of that year Iraq became an independent sovereign state and was admitted to the League of Nations.

The border between Iraq and Kuwait had first been defined in an exchange of letters, dated April 4 and April 19, 1923, between Shaikh Ahmad al Sabah of Kuwait and Maj.-Gen. Sir Percy Cox, then British high commissioner for Iraq. In a subsequent exchange of letters, dated July 21 and Aug. 10, 1932, Shaikh Ahmad and the then Iraqi Prime Minister, Nuri al Said, reaffirmed the "existing frontier between Iraq and Kuwait" on the basis of the 1923 letters * * * However, this early border demarcation was later regarded as invalid by Iraq on the grounds that Iraq had not been an independent state on the date of Nuri al Said's letter of July 21, 1932.

The Iraqi Claim to Kuwait

On June 25, 1961, Gen. Kassem made a claim of Iraqi sovereignty over Kuwait, which he described as an "integral part of Iraq". Gen. Kassem's claim was based on the Iraqi argument that (i) Kuwait had been part of

Basra province in the Ottoman empire, and (ii) that Britain and other powers had recognized Ottoman sovereignty over Kuwait both before and after the signature of the 1899 agreement under which Kuwait became a British protectorate. In addition, Gen. Kassem said that he had issued a decree appointing the Shaikh of Kuwait as *Qaim Maqaam* (prefect) of Kuwait.

Elaborating on Gen. Kassem's assertions, the Iraqi Foreign Ministry in a statement issued on June 26, 1961, said that it recognized neither the "secret agreement" of 1899, as it had been concluded without the authority of the Ottoman Sultan, nor the agreement of 1961, as it aimed "under the new cloak of national independence ... to maintain imperialist influence and to keep Kuwait separate from Iraq". The statement added that formerly the Ottoman Sultan had appointed the Shaikh of Kuwait "by a decree conferring on him the title of *Qaim Maqaam* and making him representative of the governor of Basra in Kuwait", and that the Shaikhs of Kuwait had thus "continued to derive their administrative powers from the Ottoman Sultan until 1914".

Kuwait rejected the Iraqi arguments, asserting that it had never been subject to Turkish sovereignty, that Kuwait had been governed "without direct Turkish interference" by the same dynasty since 1756 and that the title of *Qaim Maqaam* was never used in Kuwait and "never influenced the course of life or the independence of Kuwait from the Turkish empire". (It should be noted in this context, however, that historians of the area have generally taken the view that Shaikh Mubarak—in 1896—was the first Kuwaiti ruler to refuse this title.)

In response to a Kuwaiti request for military assistance, prompted by rumours that Iraq was moving troops southwards in the Basra area (which Iraq denied), forces from Britain and also Saudi Arabia arrived in Kuwait by early July 1961, and Kuwait's own forces were mobilized. Efforts by the UN Security Council in early July to defuse the crisis were unsuccessful and mediation was taken over by the Arab League (which on July 20 admitted Kuwait as a member despite Iraqi opposition). On Aug. 12 the Arab League countries, Iraq alone dissenting, signed an agreement with Kuwait under which British forces were to be replaced by a force from the League itself and under which they also pledged (i) to preserve Kuwait's integrity and independence under her present regime; (ii) to regard any aggression against the shaikhdom as aggression against the League's members; and (iii) in the event of any such aggression, to render Kuwait immediate assistance and, if necessary, repel it with armed force. Notwithstanding this agreement Iraq reiterated its claim to Kuwait and withdrew its representatives from all countries which had recognized that country.

Developments following Iraqi Recognition of Kuwait in 1963

The overthrow of Gen. Kassem on Feb. 3, 1963, led to an easing of the friction between Iraq and Kuwait. Under President Aref, the new Iraqi regime on Oct. 4, 1963 (in the course of a visit to Baghdad by an invited Kuwaiti delegation), entered into an agreement with Kuwait under which

Iraq inter alia "recognized the independence and complete sovereignty of the state of Kuwait with its boundaries as specified in the letter of the Prime Minister of Iraq dated 21.7.1932 and which was accepted by the ruler of Kuwait in his letter dated 10.8.1932". In addition, the two countries agreed to work towards improving relations and establishing co-operation at all levels and to this end decided to establish immediately diplomatic relations at ambassadorial level.

* * *

Talks on the delimitation of the Iraq–Kuwait border made little progress over the following years, despite the formation in 1978 of a joint committee headed by the Interior Ministers of the two countries to work towards resolving outstanding issues. The outbreak of war between Iraq and Iran in September 1980 led to a revival of the Iraqi claim to [the islands of] Warba and Bubiyan in July 1981. * * *

Having become a member of the Gulf Co-operation Council (GCC) on its formation in May 1981 (together with Bahrain, Oman, Qatar, Saudi Arabia and the United Arab Emirates), Kuwait followed the GCC's policy of supporting Arab Iraq's cause against Iran, a non-Arab country which was seen as having expansionist ambitions in the Gulf area. In consequence, relations with Iraq improved in the 1980s, as the Gulf war dragged on and as Kuwaiti installations and ships themselves became the targets of Iranian air attacks. Moreover, with the Iraqi port of Basra on the Shatt al-Arab waterway closed, Iraq became increasingly dependent on Kuwaiti transit facilities for access to the sea.

United Nations   **S**

Security Council

Distr.
General

S/RES/661 (1990)
6 August 1990

Resolution 661 (1990)
of 6 August 1990

The Security Council,

Reaffirming its resolution 660 (1990) of 2 August 1990,

Deeply concerned that that resolution has not been implemented and that the invasion by Iraq of Kuwait continues, with further loss of human life and material destruction,

Determined to bring the invasion and occupation of Kuwait by Iraq to an end and to restore the sovereignty, independence and territorial integrity of Kuwait,

Noting that the legitimate Government of Kuwait has expressed its readiness to comply with resolution 660 (1990),

Mindful of its responsibilities under the Charter of the United Nations for the maintenance of international peace and security,

Affirming the inherent right of individual or collective self-defence, in response to the armed attack by Iraq against Kuwait, in accordance with Article 51 of the Charter,

Acting under Chapter VII of the Charter,

1. *Determines* that Iraq so far has failed to comply with paragraph 2 of resolution 660 (1990) and has usurped the authority of the legitimate Government of Kuwait;

2. *Decides,* as a consequence, to take the following measures to secure compliance of Iraq with paragraph 2 of resolution 660 (1990) and to restore the authority of the legitimate Government of Kuwait;

3. *Decides* that all States shall prevent:

   (a) The import into their territories of all commodities and products originating in Iraq or Kuwait exported therefrom after the date of the present resolution;

[There follows more provisions for a comprehensive economic embargo of Iraq.]

Adopted at the 2933rd meeting by
13 votes to none with 2 abstentions
(Cuba and Yemen).

Address to the Nation Announcing the Deployment of United States Armed Forces to Saudi Arabia

President George H.W. Bush
The Oval Office

August 8, 1990

In the life of a nation, we're called upon to define who we are and what we believe. Sometimes these choices are not easy. But today as President, I ask for your support in a decision I've made to stand up for what's right and condemn what's wrong, all in the cause of peace.

At my direction, elements of the 82d Airborne Division as well as key units of the United States Air Force are arriving today to take up defensive positions in Saudi Arabia. I took this action to assist the Saudi Arabian Government in the defense of its homeland. No one commits America's Armed Forces to a dangerous mission lightly, but after perhaps unparalleled international consultation and exhausting every alternative, it became necessary to take this action. Let me tell you why.

Less than a week ago, in the early morning hours of August 2, Iraqi Armed Forces, without provocation or warning, invaded a peaceful Kuwait. Facing negligible resistance from its much smaller neighbor, Iraq's tanks stormed in blitzkrieg fashion through Kuwait in a few short hours. With more than 100,000 troops, along with tanks, artillery, and surface-to-surface missiles, Iraq now occupies Kuwait. This aggression came just hours after Saddam Hussein [President of Iraq] specifically assured numerous countries in the area that there would be no invasion. There is no justification whatsoever for this outrageous and brutal act of aggression.

A puppet regime imposed from the outside is unacceptable. The acquisition of territory by force is unacceptable. No one, friend or foe, should doubt our desire for peace; and no one should underestimate our determination to confront aggression.

Four simple principles guide our policy. First, we seek the immediate, unconditional and complete withdrawal of all Iraqi forces from Kuwait. Second, Kuwait's legitimate government must be restored to replace the puppet regime. And third, my administration, as has been the case with every President from President Roosevelt to President Reagan, is committed to the security and stability of the Persian Gulf. And fourth, I am determined to protect the lives of American citizens abroad.

Immediately after the Iraqi invasion, I ordered an embargo of all trade with Iraq and, together with many other nations; announced sanctions that both freeze all Iraqi assets in this country and protected Kuwait's assets. The stakes are high. Iraq is already a rich and powerful country that possesses the world's second largest reserves of oil and over a million men under arms. It's the fourth largest military in the world. Our country now imports nearly half the oil it consumes and could face a major threat to its economic independence. Much of the world is even more dependent upon imported oil and is even more vulnerable to Iraqi threats.

We succeeded in the struggle for freedom in Europe because we and our allies remained stalwart. Keeping the peace in the Middle East will require no less. We're beginning a new era. This new era can be full of promise, an age of freedom, a time of peace for all peoples. But if history teaches us anything, it is that we must resist aggression or it will destroy our freedoms. Appeasement does not work. As was the case in the 1930's, we see in Saddam Hussein an aggressive dictator threatening his neighbors. Only 14 days ago, Saddam Hussein promised his friends he would not invade Kuwait. And 4 days ago, he promised the world he would withdraw. And twice we have seen what his promises mean: His promises mean nothing.

In the last few days, I've spoken with political leaders from the Middle East, Europe, Asia, and the Americas; and I've met with Prime Minister Thatcher [of the United Kingdom], Prime Minister Mulroney [of Canada], and NATO Secretary General Woerner. And all agree that Iraq cannot be allowed to benefit from its invasion of Kuwait.

We agree that this is not an American problem or a European problem or a Middle East problem: it is the world's problem. And that's why, soon after the Iraqi invasion, the United Nations Security Council, without dissent, condemned Iraq, calling for the immediate and unconditional withdrawal of its troops from Kuwait. The Arab world, through both the Arab League and the Gulf Cooperation Council, courageously announced its opposition to Iraqi aggression. Japan, the United Kingdom, and France, and other governments around the world have imposed severe sanctions. The Soviet Union and China ended all arms sales to Iraq.

And this past Monday, the United Nations Security Council approved for the first time in 23 years mandatory sanctions under chapter VII of the United Nations Charter. These sanctions, now enshrined in international law, have the potential to deny Iraq the fruits of aggression while sharply limiting its ability to either import or export anything of value, especially oil.

I pledge here today that the United States will do its part to see that these sanctions are effective and to induce Iraq to withdraw without delay from Kuwait.

But we must recognize that Iraq may not stop using force to advance its ambitions. Iraq has massed an enormous war machine on the Saudi border capable of initiating hostilities with little or no additional preparation. Given the Iraqi government's history of aggression against its own citizens as well as its neighbors, to assume Iraq will not attack again would be unwise and unrealistic.

And therefore, after consulting with King Fahd [of Saudi Arabia], I sent Secretary of Defense Dick Cheney to discuss cooperative measures we could take. Following those meetings, the Saudi Government requested our help, and I responded to that request by ordering U.S. air and ground forces to deploy to the Kingdom of Saudi Arabia.

Let me be clear: The sovereign independence of Saudi Arabia is of vital interest to the United States. This decision, which I shared with the congressional leadership, grows out of the longstanding friendship and security relationship between the United States and Saudi Arabia. U.S. forces will work together with those of Saudi Arabia and other nations to preserve the integrity of Saudi Arabia and to deter further Iraqi aggression. Through their presence, as well as through training and exercises, these multinational forces will enhance the overall capability of Saudi Armed Forces to defend the Kingdom.

I want to be clear about what we are doing and why. America does not seek conflict, nor do we seek to chart the destiny of other nations. But America will stand by her friends. The mission of our troops is wholly defensive. Hopefully, they will not be needed long. They will not initiate hostilities, but they will defend themselves, the Kingdom of Saudi Arabia, and other friends in the Persian Gulf.

We are working around the clock to deter Iraqi aggression and to enforce U.N. sanctions. I'm continuing my conversations with world leaders. Secretary of Defense Cheney has just returned from valuable consultations with President Mubarak of Egypt and King Hassan of Morocco. Secretary of State Baker has consulted with his counterparts in many nations, including the Soviet Union, and today he heads for Europe to consult with President Ozal of Turkey, a staunch friend of the United States. And he'll then consult with the NATO Foreign Ministers.

I will ask oil-producing nations to do what they can to increase production in order to minimize any impact that oil flow reductions will have on the world economy. * * *

Thank you, and God bless the United States of America.

United Nations	**S**

Security Council

Distr.
General

S/RES/678 (1990)
29 November 1990

Resolution 678 (1990)
of 29 November 1990

The Security Council,

Recalling and reaffirming its resolutions 660 (1990) of 2 august 1990, 661 (1990) of 6 August 1990, 662 (1990) of 9 August 1990, 64 (1990) of 18 August 1990, 665 (1990) of 25 August 1990, 666 (1990) of 13 September 1990, 667 (1990) of 16 September 1990, 669 (1990) of 24 September 1990, 670 (1990) of 25 September 1990, 674 (1990) of 29 October 1990 and 677 (1990) of 28 November 1990,

Noting that, despite all efforts by the United Nations, Iraq refuses to comply with its obligation to implement resolution 660 (1990) and the above-mentioned subsequent relevant resolutions, in flagrant contempt of the Security Council,

Mindful of its duties and responsibilities under the Charter of the United Nations for the maintenance and preservation of international peace and security,

Determined to secure full compliance with its decisions,

Acting under Chapter VII of the Charter,

1. *Demands* that Iraq comply fully with resolution 660 (1990) and all subsequent relevant resolutions, and decides, while maintaining all its decisions, to allow Iraq one final opportunity, as a pause of goodwill, to do so;

2. *Authorizes* Member States co-operating with the Government of Kuwait, unless Iraq on or before 15 January 1991 fully implements, as set forth in paragraph 1 above, the above-mentioned resolutions, to use all necessary means to uphold and implement resolution 660 (1990) and all subsequent relevant resolutions and to restore international peace and security in the area;

3. *Requests* all States to provide appropriate support for the actions undertaken in pursuance of paragraph 2 above;

4. *Requests* the States concerned to keep the Security Council regularly informed on the progress of actions undertaken pursuant to paragraphs 2 and 3 above;

5. *Decides* to remain seized of the matter.

> *Adopted at the 2963rd meeting, by 12 votes to 2. (Cuba and Yemen), with 1 abstention (China).*

Amnesty International, Iraq/Occupied Kuwait Human Rights Violations Since 2 August, December 19, 1990*

Torture and Ill–Treatment of Detainees

In the period August to November, Amnesty International interviewed scores of detainees who stated that they had been tortured while in the custody *of* Iraqi forces. The majority of the victims were Kuwaiti males between the ages of 16 and 35, some of whom still bore marks of torture on their bodies when interviewed. Amnesty International has also received numerous other testimonies from the families of torture victims, the doctors who examined them and, in the cases of those who died, the people who buried them. Some have also given accounts of the torture and illtreatment of women generally, who are said to have been subjected to beatings and rape. The methods of torture and ill-treatment said to have been used by the Iraqi forces, since 2 August are listed in detail at the end of this section.

Iraqi forces at all levels appear to have been involved in the infliction of torture on detainees. They include ordinary soldiers from Iraq's regular army, senior military personnel, and agents of Iraqi intelligence and the security forces. Based on the information it has received and the interviews it has conducted, Amnesty International believes that torture is being systematically used during interrogation, both in order to extract information and as punishment. It is during this period that torture is described at its most brutal, when the interrogation methods used by Iraqi forces have frequently resulted in permanent physical or mental damage. The condition of detainees under such circumstances is compounded by their deprivation

* Excerpts.

of medical treatment while in custody and, following their release, by the almost total absence of medical facilities.

Two categories of detainees appear to have been targeted for particularly severe torture: actual or suspect members of the Kuwaiti armed forces, National Guard, police and security forces, and individuals suspected of having participated in armed resistance against Iraqi forces. However, others have been tortured for involvement, in non-violent activities such as peaceful demonstrations (in the early days of the invasion), writing anti-Iraq slogans on walls, possessing opposition leaflets and raising the Kuwaiti flag. In large measure, torture in these cases was aimed at extracting information about the identity of persons involved in opposition activities, the locations of such activities, and the whereabouts of individuals or families being sought by the Iraqi authorities. In other cases, the objective was to force detainees to cooperate with the Iraqis after, release by acting as informers. Coupled with that was forcing them to make statements against the Kuwait ruling family and government and making declarations of allegiance to Iraq's President Saddam Hussein. Finally, the sheer brutality of the torture inflicted on detainees was designed to terrorize the population at large and to discourage others from expressing in whatever form their opposition to the Iraqi presence in Kuwait.

Washington Post, Jan. 10, 1991, at A23

Baker, Aziz Describe Six Hours of Talking Past Each Other

By William Drozdiak

Washington Post Foreign Service

GENEVA, Jan. 9— Tariq Aziz slowly scrutinized President Bush's letter, which officials said spelled out in blunt, vivid detail why President Saddam Hussein's forces should leave Kuwait or face the possible destruction of his regime by the collective military power of 28 nations.

The Iraqi foreign minister lowered his glasses, according to participants in the talks today, and handed the letter back to Secretary of State James A. Baker III. "I am sorry, I cannot receive this letter," he said in his own recounting for the press. "The language in this letter is not compatible with the language between heads of state."

Aziz's rebuff, at the outset of the diplomatic showdown in a stark ballroom at the Hotel Intercontinental, symbolized the inability of the United States and Iraq to find common language to bridge differences at their first high-level encounter since the Persian Gulf crisis erupted five months ago. For most of those five months, the United States sought to force Saddam to retreat through pressure tactics, including the largest American military buildup since the Vietnam War and a global economic embargo against Baghdad. The Bush administration eschewed any talks with its adversary in Baghdad until after the United Nations had authorized the use of force.

* * *

As stock and oil prices gyrated and a worldwide audience yearned for a break- through that would defuse a conflict be- tween two foes with more than a million troops poised for war, Baker and Aziz spent three fruitless rounds of discussion talking past each other, mainly repeat- ing old positions.

* * *

N.Y. Times, Jan. 17, 1991, at A1

U.S. and Allies Open Air War on Iraq, Bomb Baghdad and Kuwaiti Targets; 'No Choice' but Force, Bush Declares

By Andrew Rosen- thal

Special to The New York Times

WASHINGTON, Jan., 16—The Unit- ed States and allied forces attacked Iraq today, striking Bagh- dad and other tar- gets in Iraq and Ku- wait with waves of air attacks at the start of the long- threatened war to force President Sad- dam Hussein's army from Kuwait.

"The liberation of Kuwait has be- gun," President Bush said in con- firming the start of the attack with a three-sentence state- ment that was read by his spokesman, Marlin Fitzwater, shortly after the raids began. Later, in a televised address to the nation, Mr. Bush said, "We have no choice but to force Saddam from Kuwait by force. We will not fail."

* * *

N.Y. Times, Feb. 28, 1991 at A1

Bush Calls Halt to Allied Offensive: Declares Kuwait Free, Iraq Beaten; Sets Stiff Terms for Full Cease–Fire

MILITARY AIMS MET

Ground War Suspended, Conditioned on End to Iraqi Attacks

By Andrew Rosen- thal

Special to The New York Times

WASHINGTON, Feb. 27—President Bush, declaring that "Kuwait is li- berated" and "Iraq's Army is de- feated," tonight or- dered the suspen- sion of offensive military operations against President Saddam Hussein's battered army.

Mr. Bush said the suspension, to begin at midnight Eastern time, would continue as long as Iraq did not attack allied forces or launch missile at- tacks on any other country.

For there to be a permanent cease- fire, he said, Iraq must comply with a strict set of demands that require it to honor all 12 United Nations resolutions on Kuwait, free all prisoners of war and detained Kuwaiti citizens, and give the allies the location of all land and sea mines that Iraq had laid in the region.

100 Hours of Offensive

"At midnight tonight, Eastern standard time, exactly 100 hours since ground operations commenced and six weeks since the start of Operation Desert Storm, all United States and coalition forces will suspend offensive combat operation." Mr. Bush said in his third nationally televised speech from the Oval Office since Iraq invaded Kuwait last Aug. 2. * * *

The President, who had brushed aside Iraq's last attempt to win a cease-fire on favorable terms, said: "Iraq's Army is defeated. Our military objectives are met. Kuwait is once more in the hands of Kuwaitis in control of their own destiny." * * *

Baker to Go to Middle East

Declaring an end to the seven-month crisis on which he had staked his Presidency, one that challenged his diplomatic skills by forcing him

to hold together a disparate international coalition, Mr. Bush said he was sending Secretary of State James A. Baker 3d to the Middle East to deal with "the difficult task of securing a potentially historic peace."

Mr. Bush's speech capped a six-week allied military offensive against Iraq in which fewer than 100 Americans were killed, as of the latest report today from the Pentagon, and that astonished even the President's war council with its swiftness.

He spoke only a few hours after his commander in the Persian Gulf, Gen. H. Norman Schwarzkopf, described the last major battle of the war, between allied armored divisions and Iraq's Republican Guard, the last remnants [sic] of what had been Mr. Hussein's huge military machine, near the southern Iraqi city of Basra.

Mr. Bush's speech, scheduled less than three hours before it was delivered at 9 P.M. Eastern time, seemed to represent a balancing of the American position, that Iraq could not get off too easily, with mounting international

pressures to stop the assaults on an obviously defeated army.

The President invited Mr. Hussein to send senior officers to a meeting in the war theater to discuss military terms for a permanent cease-fire with allied commanders.

But with Mr. Hussein still in power in Baghdad, the declaration of victory left major political and diplomatic issues ahead, including the question of a postwar role for Iraq in the region, the durability of Mr. Hussein himself and the inevitable pressure on the United States to take a leading role in resolving the so-far intractable Middle East problems to which the Administration is now turning its attention, including the Israeli–Palestinian dispute.

Before Mr. Bush spoke, it had been a day for optimistic predictions of victory, tough talk against Iraq and the back-and-forth struggle of diplomacy and semantics between Washington and Baghdad.

Defense Secretary Dick Cheney, speaking to the American Legion early this afternoon said, "It looks like what's happened is that the mother of all battles has turned into the mother of all retreats."

Bush Meets Douglas Hurd

Mr. Bush and Foreign Minister Douglas Hurd of Britain began consultations about how to administer the peace in the gulf, including how long the allies would keep the sanctions against Baghdad in place, how they would neutralize Mr. Hussein after the war if he hangs onto his political power and what kind of peacekeeping forces would be needed.

Administration officials said Mr. Hurd, who also met with Secretary Baker, was carrying a British proposal to put all the allies' demands for ending the war into a United Nations Security Council resolution that Iraq would then have to accept formally.

The day began with a message to the United Nations from Baghdad in which Foreign Minister Tariq Aziz of Iraq said his Government, which had promised to heed the United Nations reso-

lution requiring its withdrawal from Kuwait, now "agrees to abide" by two other resolutions. One would nullify Iraq's annexation of the occupied sheikdom, and the other would require Baghdad to pay war reparation.

The alliance held out for Iraq's unconditional acceptance of all 12 United Nations resolutions, the continuation of sanctions beyond the war, and the surrender of all Iraqi tanks and other weapons. It also said its demand for the immediate release of all prisoners would cover an estimated 40,-000 Kuwaitis thought to have been removed from the country by the Iraqi Army in the last week.

Official statements made it clear that the coalition has political and military aims beyond driving the Iraqis out of Kuwait.

Mr. Cheney said, "Even after we've achieved our military objectives, even after we've destroyed his offensive military capability and expelled his forces from Kuwait, liberated Kuwait, the world will still be vitally interested in the future course of events with

respect to the kinds of activities and policies pursued by the Government in Baghdad."

In Riyadh, Gen. H. Norman Schwarzkopf, commander of the allied forces, said, "There's a lot more purpose to this war than just 'Get the Iraqis out of Kuwait.' "

Marlin Fitzwater, the President's spokesman, said the Untied Nations resolutions calling for "peace and stability" in the gulf region authorize the allies to reduce Iraq's military forces. He added, "Assuming that the U.N. resolutions are met, that would require that we continue this effort to degrade his military structure."

The allies also continued to apply pressure that according to American officials, the alliance hopes could lead to Mr. Hussein's overthrow from within Iraq.

Mr. Baker said, "Our position is as long as that particular Government continues in power, we'll want to make certain, at least with respect to arms, that there are some sort of constraints on rearmament and the shipment of arms

into that country   weapons of mass de-
and particularly   struction.

United Nations   **S**

 Security Council

Distr.
General

S/RES/686 (1991)
2 March 1991

Resolution 686 (1991)
of 2 March 1991

The Security Council,

Recalling and reaffirming its resolutions 660 (1990) of 2 August 1990, 661 (1990) of 6 August 1990, 662 (1990) of 9 August 1990, 664 (1990) of 18 August 1990, 665 (1990) of 25 August 1990, 666 (1990) of 13 of September 1990, 667 (1990) of 16 September 1990, 669 (1990) of 24 September 1990, 670 (1990) of September 1990, 674 (1990) of 29 October 1990, 677 (1990) of 28 November 1990 and 678 (1990) of 29 November 1990.

Recalling the obligations of Member States under Article 25 of the Charter of the United Nations,

Recalling also paragraph 9 of resolution 661 (1990) regarding assistance to the Government of Kuwait and paragraph 3 (*c*) of that resolution regarding supplies strictly for medical purposes and, in humanitarian circumstances, foodstuffs,

Taking note of the letters dated 27 February 1991 from the Deputy Prime Minister and Minister for Foreign Affairs of Iraq addressed to the President of the Security Council and to the Secretary–General, confirming Iraq's agreement to comply fully with all of the resolutions noted above, and of his letter of the same date addressed to the President of the Security Council stating Iraq's intention to release prisoners of war immediately.

Noting the suspension of offensive combat operations by the forces of Kuwait and the Member States cooperating with Kuwait pursuant to resolution 678 (1990),

Bearing in mind the need to be assured of Iraq's peaceful intentions, and the objective expressed in resolution 678 (1990) of restoring international peace and security in the region,

Underlining the importance of Iraq taking the necessary measures which would permit a definitive end to the hostilities.

Affirming the commitment of all Member States to the independence, sovereignty and territorial integrity of Iraq and Kuwait, and noting the intention expressed by the Member States cooperating with Kuwait under paragraph 2 of resolution 678 (1990) to bring their military presence in Iraq to an end as soon as possible consistent with achieving the objectives of that resolution,

Acting under Chapter VII of the Charter,

1. *Affirms* that all twelve resolutions noted above continue to have full force and effect;

2. *Demands* that Iraq implement its acceptance of all twelve resolutions noted above and in particular that Iraq:

(*a*) Rescind immediately its actions purporting to annex Kuwait;

(*b*) Accept in principle its liability under international law for any loss, damage or injury arising in regard to Kuwait and third States and their nationals and corporations, as a result of the invasion and illegal occupation of Kuwait by Iraq;

(*c*) Immediately release under the auspices of the International Committee of the Red Cross, Red Cross Societies or Red Crescent Societies all Kuwaiti and third-State nationals detained by Iraq and return the remains of any deceased Kuwaiti and third-State nationals so detained;

(*d*) Immediately begin to return all Kuwaiti property seized by Iraq, the return to be completed in the shortest possible period;

3. *Also demands* that Iraq:

(*a*) Cease hostile or provocative actions by its forces against all Member States, including missile attacks and flights of combat aircraft;

(*b*) Designate military commanders to meet with counterparts from the forces of Kuwait and the Member States cooperating with Kuwait pursuant to resolution 678 (1990) to arrange for the military aspects of a cessation of hostilities at the earliest possible time;

(*c*) Arrange for immediate access to and release of all prisoners of war under the auspices of the International Committee of the Red Cross and return the remains of any deceased personnel of the forces of Kuwait and the Member States cooperating with Kuwait pursuant to resolution 678 (1990);

(*d*) Provide all information and assistance in identifying Iraqi mines, booby traps and other explosives as well as any chemical and biological weapons and material in Kuwait, in areas of Iraq where forces of Member States cooperating with Kuwait pursuant to resolution 678 (1990) are present temporarily, and in the adjacent waters;

4. *Recognizes* that during the period required for Iraq to comply with paragraphs 2 and 3 above, the provisions of paragraph 2 of resolution 678 (1990) remain valid;

5. *Welcomes* the decision of Kuwait and the Member States cooperating with Kuwait pursuant to resolution 678 (1990) to provide access to and commence immediately the release of Iraqi prisoners of war under the auspices of the International Committee of the Red Cross, as required by

the terms of the Geneva Convention relative to the Treatment of Prisoners of War, of 12 August 1949;

6. *Requests* all Member States, as well as the United Nations, the specialized agencies and other international organizations in the United Nations system, to take all appropriate action to cooperate with the Government and people of Kuwait in the reconstruction of their country;

7. *Decides* that Iraq shall notify the Secretary–General and the Security Council when it has taken the actions set out above;

8. *Also decides*, in order to secure the rapid establishment of a definitive end to the hostilities, to remain actively seized of the matter.

Adopted at 2978th meeting by 11 votes to 1 (Cuba), with 3 abstentions (China, India, Yemen).

United Nations

Security Council

S

Distr.
General

S/RES/687 (1991)
3 April 1991

Resolution 687(1991)
of 8 April 1991*

The Security Council,

Recalling its resolutions 660 (1990) of 2 August 1990, 661 (1990) of 6 August 1990, 662 (1990) of 9 August 1990, 664 (1990) of 18 August 1990, 665 (1990) of 25 August 1990, 666 (1990) of 13 September 1990, 667 (1990) of 16 September 1990, 669 (1990) of 24 September 1990, 670 (1990) of 25 September 1990, 674 (1990) of 29 October 1990, 677 (1990) of 28 November 1990, 678 (1990) of 29 November 1990 and 686 (1991) of 2 March 1991,

Welcoming the restoration to Kuwait of its sovereignty, independence and territorial integrity and the return of its legitimate Government,

Affirming the commitment of all Member States to the sovereignty, territorial integrity and political independence of Kuwait and Iraq, and noting the intention expressed by the Member States cooperating with Kuwait under paragraph 2 of resolution 678 (1990) to bring their military presence in Iraq to an end as soon as possible consistent with paragraph 8 of resolution 686 (1991),

Reaffirming the need to be assured of Iraq's peaceful intentions in the light of its unlawful invasion and occupation of Kuwait,

* Footnotes omitted.

Taking note of the letter dated 27 February 1991 from the Deputy Prime Minister and Minister for Foreign Affairs of Iraq addressed to the President of Security Council and of his letters of the same date addressed to the President of the Council and to the Secretary–General, and those letters dated 3 March and 5 March he addressed to them, pursuant to resolution 686 (1991),

Noting that Iraq and Kuwait, as independent sovereign States, signed at Baghdad on October 1963 "Agreed Minutes between the State of Kuwait and the Republic of Iraq regarding the restoration of friendly relations, recognition and related matters", thereby formally recognizing the boundary between Iraq and Kuwait and the allocation of islands, which Agreed Minutes were registered with the United Nations in accordance with Article 102 of the Charter of the United Nations and in which Iraq recognized the independence and complete sovereignty of the State of Kuwait with its boundaries as specified in the letter of the Prime Minister of Iraq dated 21 July 1932 and as accepted by the ruler of Kuwait in his letter dated 10 August 1932,

Conscious of the need for demarcation of the said boundary,

Conscious also of the statements by Iraq threatening to use weapons in violation of its obligations under the Protocol for the Prohibition of the Use in War of Asphyxiating, Poisonous or Other Gases, and of Bacteriological Methods of Warfare, signed at Geneva on 17 June 1925, and of its prior use of chemical weapons, and affirming that grave consequences would follow any further use by Iraq of such weapons,

Recalling that Iraq has subscribed to the Final Declaration adopted by all States participating in the Conference of States Parties to the 1925 Geneva Protocol and Other Interested States, held in Paris from 7 to 11 January 1989, establishing the objective of universal elimination of chemical and biological weapons,

Recalling also that Iraq has signed the Convention on the Prohibition of the Development, Production and Stockpiling of Bacteriological (Biological) and Toxin Weapons and on Their Destruction, of 10 April 1972, * * *

Noting also the importance of all States adhering to the Convention and encouraging its forthcoming review conference to reinforce the authority, efficiency and universal scope of the Convention,

Stressing the importance of an early conclusion by the Conference on Disarmament of its work on a convention on the universal prohibition of chemical weapons and of universal adherence thereto,

Aware of the use by Iraq of ballistic missiles in unprovoked attacks and therefore of the need to take specific measures in regard to such missiles located in Iraq,

Concerned by the reports in the hands of Member States that Iraq has attempted to acquire materials for a nuclear-weapons programme contrary to its obligations under the Treaty on the Non–Proliferation of Nuclear Weapons of 1 July 1968,

Recalling the objective of the establishment of a nuclear-weapon-free zone in the region of the Middle East,

Conscious of the threat that all weapons of mass destruction pose to peace and security in the area and of the need to work towards the establishment in the Middle East of a zone free of such weapons,

Conscious also of the objective of achieving balanced and comprehensive control of armaments in the region,

Conscious further of the importance of achieving the objectives noted above using all available means, including a dialogue among the States of the region,

Noting that resolution 686 (1991) marked the lifting of the measures imposed by resolution 661 (1990) in so far as they applied to Kuwait,

Noting also that despite the progress being made in fulfilling the obligations of resolution 686 (1991), many Kuwaiti and third-State nationals are still not accounted for and property remains unreturned,

Recalling the International Convention against the Taking of Hostages, opened for signature in New York on 18 December 1979, which categorizes all acts of taking hostages as manifestations of international terrorism,

Deploring threats made by Iraq during the recent conflict to make use of terrorism against targets outside Iraq and the taking of hostages by Iraq,

Taking note with grave concern of the reports transmitted by the Secretary–General on 20 March and 28 March 1991, and conscious of the necessity to meet urgently the humanitarian needs in Kuwait and Iraq,

Bearing in mind its objective of restoring international peace and security in the area as set out in its recent resolutions,

Conscious of the need to take the following measures acting under Chapter VII of the Charter,

1. *Affirms* all thirteen resolutions noted above, except as expressly changed below to achieve the goals of the present resolution, including a formal cease-fire;

A

2. *Demands* that Iraq and Kuwait respect the inviolability of the international boundary and the allocation of islands set out in the "Agreed Minutes between the State of Kuwait and the Republic of Iraq regarding the restoration of friendly relations, recognition and related matters", signed by them in the exercise of their sovereignty at Baghdad on 4 October 1963 and registered with the United Nations;

3. *Calls upon* the Secretary–General to lend his assistance to make arrangements with Iraq and Kuwait to demarcate the boundary between Iraq and Kuwait, drawing on appropriate material including the maps transmitted with the letter dated 28 March 1991 addressed to him by the Permanent Representative of the United Kingdom of Great Britain and

Northern Ireland to the United Nations, and to report back to the Council within one month;

4. *Decides* to guarantee the inviolability of the above-mentioned international boundary and to take, as appropriate, all necessary measures to that end in accordance with the Charter of the United States;

B

5. *Requests* the Secretary–General, after consulting with Iraq and Kuwait, to submit within three days to the Council for its approval a plan for the immediate deployment of a United Nations observer unit to monitor the Khawr 'Abd Allah and a demilitarized zone, * * *

6. *Notes* that as soon as the Secretary–General notifies the Council of the completion of the deployment of the United Nations observer unit, the conditions will be established for the Member States cooperating with Kuwait in accordance with resolution 678 (1990) to bring their military presence in Iraq to an end consistent with resolution 686 (1991);

C

7. *Invites* Iraq to reaffirm unconditionally its obligations under the Protocol for the Prohibition of the Use in War of Asphyxiating, Poisonous or Other Gases, and of Bacteriological Methods of Warfare, signed at Geneva on 17 June 1925, and to ratify the Convention on the Prohibition of the Development, Production and Stockpiling of Bacteriological (Biological) and Toxin Weapons and on Their Destruction, of 10 April 1972;

8. *Decides* that Iraq shall unconditionally accept the destruction, removal, or rendering harmless, under international supervision, of:

(*a*) All chemical and biological weapons and all stocks of agents and all related subsystems and components and all research, development, support and manufacturing facilities related thereto;

(*b*) All ballistic missiles with a range greater than one hundred and fifty kilometers, and related major parts and repair and production facilities;

9. *Decides also*, for the implementation of paragraph 8, the following:

(*a*) Iraq shall submit to the Secretary–General, within fifteen days of the adoption of the present resolution, a declaration on the locations, amounts and types of all items specified in paragraph 8 and agree to urgent, on-site inspection as specified below;

(*b*) The Secretary–General, in consultation with the appropriate Governments and, where appropriate, with the Director–General of the World Health Organization, within forty-five days of the adoption of the present resolution shall develop and submit to the Council for approval a plan calling for the completion of the following acts within forty-five days of such approval:

(i) The forming of a special commission which shall carry out immediate on-site inspection of Iraq's biological, chemical and missile capabilities, based on Iraq's declarations and the designation of any additional locations by the special commission itself;

(ii) The yielding by Iraq of possession to the Special Commission for destruction, removal or rendering harmless, taking into account the requirements of public safety, of all items specified under paragraph 8 (*a*), including items at the additional locations designated by the Special Commission under paragraph (i) and the destruction by Iraq, under the supervision of the Special Commission, of all its missile capabilities, including launchers, as specified under paragraph 8 (*b*);

(iii) The provision by the Special Commission to the Director General of the International Atomic Energy Agency of the assistance and cooperation required in paragraphs 12 and 13.

10. *Decides further* that Iraq shall unconditionally undertake not to use, develop, construct or acquire any of the items specified in paragraphs 8 and 9, and requests the Secretary–General, in consultation with the Special Commission, to develop a plan for the future ongoing monitoring and verification of Iraq's compliance with the present paragraph, to be submitted to the Council for approval within one hundred and twenty days of the passage of the present resolution;

11. *Invites* Iraq to reaffirm unconditionally its obligations under the Treaty on the Non–Proliferation of Nuclear Weapons, of 1 July 1968;

12. *Decides* that Iraq shall unconditionally agree not to acquire or develop nuclear weapons or nuclear-weapon-usable material or any subsystems or components or any research, development, support or manufacturing facilities related to the above; to submit to the Secretary–General and the Director General of the International Atomic Energy Agency within fifteen days of the adoption of the present resolution a declaration of the locations, amounts and types of all items specified above; * * *

13. *Requests* the Director General of the International Atomic Energy Agency, through the Secretary–General and with the assistance and cooperation of the Special Commission as provided for in the plan of the Secretary–General referred to in paragraph 9 (*b*), to carry out immediate on-site inspection of Iraq's nuclear capabilities based on Iraq's declarations and the designation of any additional locations by the Special Commission; to develop a plan for submission to the Council within forty-five days calling for the destruction, removal or rendering harmless as appropriate of all items listed in paragraph 12; * * *

14. *Notes* that the actions to be taken by Iraq in paragraphs 8 to 13 represent steps towards the goal of establishing in the Middle East a zone free from weapons of mass destruction and all missiles for their delivery and the objective of a global ban on chemical weapons;

D

15. *Requests* the Secretary–General to report to the Council on the steps taken to facilitate the return of all Kuwaiti property seized by Iraq,

including a list of any property that Kuwait claims has not been returned or which has not been returned intact;

E

16. *Reaffirms* that Iraq, without prejudice to its debts and obligations arising prior to 2 August 1990, which will be addressed through the normal mechanisms, is liable under international law for any direct loss, damage— including environmental damage and the depletion of natural resources—or injury to foreign Governments, nationals and corporations as a result of its unlawful invasion and occupation of Kuwait;

17. *Decides* that all Iraqi statements made since 2 August 1990 repudiating its foreign debt are null and void, and demands that Iraq adhere scrupulously to all of its obligations concerning servicing and repayment of its foreign debt;

18. *Decides also* to create a fund to pay compensation for claims that fall within paragraph 16 and to establish a commission that will administer the fund;

* * *

F

20. *Decides*, effective immediately, that the prohibitions against the sale or supply to Iraq of commodities or products other than medicine and health supplies, and prohibitions against financial transactions related thereto contained in resolution 661 (1990), shall not apply to foodstuffs notified to the Security Council Committee established by resolution 661 (1990) concerning the situation between Iraq and Kuwait or, with the approval of that Committee, under the simplified and accelerated "no-objection" procedure, to materials and supplies for essential civilian needs as identified in the report to the Secretary–General dated 20 March 1991, and in any further findings of humanitarian need by the Committee;

21. *Decides* to review the provisions of paragraph 20 every sixty days in the light of the policies and practices of the Government of Iraq, including the implementation of all relevant resolutions of the Council, for the purpose of determining whether to reduce or lift the prohibitions referred to therein;

22. *Decides also* that upon the approval by the Council of the pro-gramme called for in paragraph 19 and upon Council agreement that Iraq has completed all actions contemplated in paragraphs 8 to 13, the prohibi-tions against the import of commodities and products originating in Iraq and the prohibitions against financial transactions related thereto con-tained in resolution 661 (1990) shall have no further force or effect;

23. *Decides further* that, pending action by the Council under para-graph 22, the Security Council Committee established by resolution 661 (1990) concerning the situation between Iraq and Kuwait shall be empow-ered to approve, when required to assure adequate financial resources on the part of Iraq to carry out the activities under paragraph 20, exceptions

to the prohibition against the import of commodities and products originating in Iraq;

24. *Decides* that, in accordance with resolution 661 (1990) and subsequent related resolutions and until it takes a further decision, all States shall continue to prevent the sale or supply to Iraq, or the promotion or facilitation of such sale or supply, by their nationals or from their territories or using their flag vessels or aircraft, of:

(a) Arms and related *matériel* of all types, specifically including the sale or transfer through other means of all forms of conventional military equipment, including for paramilitary forces, and spare parts and components and their means of production for such equipment;

(b) Items specified and defined in paragraphs 8 and 12 not otherwise covered above;

(c) Technology under licensing or other transfer arrangements used in the production, utilization or stockpiling of items specified in paragraphs (a) and (b);

(d) Personnel or materials for training or technical support services relating to the design, development, manufacture, use, maintenance or support of items specified in paragraphs (a) and (b);

25. *Calls upon* all States and international organizations to act strictly in accordance with paragraph 24, notwithstanding the existence of any contracts, agreements, licenses or any other arrangements;

* * *

G

30. *Decides* that, in furtherance of its commitment to facilitate the repatriation of all Kuwaiti and third-State nationals, Iraq shall extend all necessary cooperation to the International Committee of the Red Cross by providing lists of such persons, facilitating the access of the International Committee to all such persons wherever located or detained and facilitating the search by the International Committee for those Kuwaiti and third-State nationals still unaccounted for;

31. *Invites* the International Committee of the Red Cross to keep the Secretary–General apprised, as appropriate, of all activities undertaken in connection with facilitating the repatriation or return of all Kuwaiti and third-State nationals or their remains present in Iraq on or after 2 August 1990;

H

32. *Requires* Iraq to inform the Council that it will not commit or support any act of international terrorism or allow any organization directed towards commission of such acts to operate within its territory and to condemn unequivocally and renounce all acts, methods and practices of terrorism;

I

33. *Declares* that, upon official notification by Iraq to the Secretary–General and to the Security Council of its acceptance of the above provisions, a formal cease-fire is effective between Iraq and Kuwait and the Member States cooperating with Kuwait in accordance with resolution 678 (1990);

34. *Decides* to remain seized of the matter and to take such further steps as may be required for the implementation of the present resolution and to secure peace and security in the region.

Adopted at the 2981st meeting by 12 Votes to 1 (Cuba) with 2 abstentions (Ecuador, Yemen).

United Nations | **S**

Security Council

Distr.
General

S/RES/688 (1991)
5 April 1991

Resolution 688 (1991)
of 5 April 1991

The Security Council,

Mindful of its duties and its responsibilities under the Charter of the United Nations for the maintenance of international peace and security,

Recalling the provisions of Article 2, paragraph 7, of the Charter of the United States,

Gravely concerned by the repression of the Iraqi civilian population in many parts of Iraq, including most recently in Kurdish populated areas, which led to a massive flow of refugees towards and across international frontiers and to cross border incursions, which threaten international peace and security in the region,

Deeply disturbed by the magnitude of the human suffering involved,

* * *

Reaffirming the commitment of all Member States to the sovereignty, territorial integrity and political independence of Iraq and of all States in the region,

Bearing in mind the Secretary–General's report of 20 March 1991 (S/22366),

1. *Condemns* the repression of the Iraqi civilian population in many parts of Iraq, including most recently in Kurdish-populated areas, the consequences of which threaten international peace and security in the region;

2. *Demands* that Iraq, as a contribution to removing the threat to international peace and security in the region, immediately end this repression, and in the same context expresses the hope that an open dialogue will take place to ensure that the human and political rights of all Iraqi citizens are respected;

3. *Insists* the Iraq allow immediate access by international humanitarian organization to all those in need of assistance in all parts of Iraq and to make available all necessary facilities for their operations;

4. *Requests* the Secretary–General to pursue his humanitarian efforts in Iraq and to report forthwith, if appropriate on the basis of a further mission to the region, on the plight of the Iraqi civilian population, and in particular the Kurdish population, suffering from the repression in all its forms inflicted inflicted by the Iraqi authorities;

5. *Requests* the Secretary–General to use all the resources at his disposal, including those of the relevant United Nations agencies, to address urgently the critical needs of the refugees and displaced Iraqi population;

6. *Appeals* to all Member States and to all humanitarian organizations to contribute to these humanitarian relief efforts;

7. *Demands* that Iraq cooperate with the Secretary–General to these ends;

8. *Decides* to remain seized of the matter.

> *Adopted at the 2982nd meeting by 10 votes to 3 (Cuba, Yemen, Zimbabwe), with 2 abstentions (China, India).*

B. The US–Led Invasion of Iraq (2003)

Ten years after the Security Council adopted Resolution 687, sanctions remained in place against Iraq. A number of states and non-governmental organizations had worked diligently to have them lifted, owing to the widespread suffering of the civilian population in the aftermath of sanctions being imposed. Saddam Hussein, however, had kept UN weapons inspectors out of Iraq in defiance of Resolution 687 and numerous subsequent resolutions. The new United States Administration under the presidency of another George Bush wanted sanctions kept in place. The new Secretary of State, Colin Powell, succeeded after intense negotiations in persuading the Security Council to adopt Resolution 1360. Powell persuaded enough states that Saddam Hussein still posed a danger and that it was Saddam who was responsible for preventing food, medicine and other essentials from reaching the population, while blaming the UN's sanctions.

United Nations   **S**

Security Council

Distr.
General

S/RES/1360 (2001)
3 July 2001

**Resolution 1360 (2001)
of 3 July 2001**

The Security Council,

Recalling its previous relevant resolutions, including its resolution 986 (1995) of 14 April 1995, 1284 (1999) of 17 December 1999, 1330 (2000) of 5 December 2000 and 1352 (2001) of 1 June 2001, as they relate to the improvement of the humanitarian programme for Iraq,

Convinced of the need as a temporary measure to continue to provide for the humanitarian needs of the Iraqi people until the fulfilment by the Government of Iraq of the relevant resolutions, including notably resolution 687 (1991) of 3 April 1991, allows the Council to take further action with regard to the prohibitions referred to in resolution 661 (1990) of 6 August 1990, in accordance with the provisions of those resolutions,

Convinced also of the need for equitable distribution of humanitarian supplies to all segments of the Iraqi population throughout the country,

Determined to improve the humanitarian situation in Iraq,

Reaffirming the commitment of all Member States to the sovereignty and territorial integrity of Iraq,

Acting under Chapter VII of the Charter of the United Nations,

1. *Decides* that the provisions of resolution 986 (1995), except those contained in paragraphs 4, 11 and 12 and subject to paragraph 15 of resolution 1284 (1999), shall remain in force for a new period of 150 days beginning at 00.01 hours, Eastern Daylight Time, on 4 July 2001;

2. *Further decides* that from the sum produced from the import by States of petroleum and petroleum products originating in Iraq, including financial and other essential transactions related thereto, in the 150–day period referred to in paragraph 1 above, the amounts recommended by the Secretary–General in his report of 1 February 1998 (S/1998/90) for the food/nutrition and health sectors should continue to be allocated on a priority basis in the context of the activities of the Secretariat, of which 13 per cent of the sum produced in the period referred to above shall be used for the purposes referred to in paragraph 8 (b) of resolution 986 (1995);

3. *Requests* the Secretary–General to continue to take the actions necessary to ensure the effective and efficient implementation of this resolution, and to continue to enhance as necessary the United Nations observation process in Iraq in such a way as to provide the required assurance to the Council that the goods produced in accordance with this resolution are distributed equitably and that all supplies authorized for procurement, including dual usage items and spare parts, are utilized for the purpose for which they have been authorized, including in the housing sector and related infrastructure development;

4. *Decides* to conduct a thorough review of all aspects of the implementation of this resolution 90 days after the entry into force of paragraph 1 above and again prior to the end of the 150–day period, and expresses its intention, prior to the end of the 150–day period, to consider favourably renewal of the provisions of this resolution as appropriate, provided that the reports referred to in paragraphs 5 and 6 below indicate that those provisions are being satisfactorily implemented;

5. *Requests* the Secretary–General to provide a comprehensive report to the Council 90 days after the date of entry into force of this resolution on its implementation and again at least one week prior to the end of the 150–day period, on the basis of observations of United Nations personnel in Iraq, and of consultations with the Government of Iraq, on whether Iraq has ensured the equitable distribution of medicine, health supplies, foodstuffs, and materials and supplies for essential civilian needs, financed in accordance with paragraph 8 (a) of resolution 986 (1995), including in his reports any observations which he may have on the adequacy of the revenues to meet Iraq's humanitarian needs; * * *

14. *Decides* to remain seized of the matter.

> *Adopted at the 4344nd meeting by*
> *15 votes to none.*

Address to the United Nations General Assembly in New York City

George W. Bush

September 12, 2002

Mr. Secretary–General, Mr. President, distinguished delegates, and ladies and gentlemen: We meet one year and one day after a terrorist attack brought grief to my country and brought grief to many citizens of our world. Yesterday we remembered the innocent lives taken that terrible morning. Today we turn to the urgent duty of protecting other lives, without illusion and without fear.

* * *

The United Nations was born in the hope that survived a world war, the hope of a world moving toward justice, escaping old patterns of conflict and fear. The founding members resolved that the peace of the world must never again be destroyed by the will and wickedness of any man. We created the United Nations Security Council, so that, unlike the League of Nations, our deliberations would be more than talk, our resolutions would be more than wishes. After generations of deceitful dictators and broken treaties and squandered lives, we dedicated ourselves to standards of human dignity shared by all and to a system of security defended by all.

Today, these standards and this security are challenged. Our commitment to human dignity is challenged by persistent poverty and raging disease. The suffering is great, and our responsibilities are clear. The United States is joining with the world to supply aid where it reaches people and lifts up lives, to extend trade and the prosperity it brings, and to bring medical care where it is desperately needed.

* * *

Twelve years ago, Iraq invaded Kuwait without provocation, and the regime's forces were poised to continue their march to seize other countries and their resources. Had Saddam Hussein been appeased instead of stopped, he would have endangered the peace and stability of the world. Yet this aggression was stopped by the might of coalition forces and the will of the United Nations.

To suspend hostilities, to spare himself, Iraq's dictator accepted a series of commitments. The terms were clear to him and to all, and he agreed to prove he is complying with every one of those obligations. He has proven instead only his contempt for the United Nations and for all his pledges. By breaking every pledge, by his deceptions, and by his cruelties—Saddam Hussein has made the case against himself.

In 1991, Security Council Resolution 688 demanded that the Iraqi regime cease at once the repression of its own people, including the systematic repression of minorities, which the Council said threatened international peace and security in the region. This demand goes ignored.

Last year, the U.N. Commission on Human Rights found that Iraq continues to commit extremely grave violations of human rights and that the regime's repression is all pervasive. Tens of thousands of political opponents and ordinary citizens have been subjected to arbitrary arrest and imprisonment, summary execution, and torture by beating and burning, electric shock, starvation, mutilation, and rape. Wives are tortured in front of their husbands, children in the presence of their parents, and all of these horrors concealed from the world by the apparatus of a totalitarian state.

In 1991, the U.N. Security Council, through Resolutions 686 and 687, demanded that Iraq return all prisoners from Kuwait and other lands. Iraq's regime agreed. It broke this promise. Last year, the Secretary General's high-level coordinator for this issue reported that Kuwaiti, Saudi, Indian, Syrian, Lebanese, Iranian, Egyptian, Bahraini, and Omani nationals remain unaccounted for—more than 600 people. One American pilot is among them.

In 1991, the U.N. Security Council, through Resolution 687, demanded that Iraq renounce all involvement with terrorism and permit no terrorist organizations to operate in Iraq. Iraq's regime agreed. It broke this promise. In violation of Security Council Resolution 1373, Iraq continues to shelter and support terrorist organizations that direct violence against Iran, Israel, and Western governments. Iraqi dissidents abroad are targeted for murder. In 1993, Iraq attempted to assassinate the Emir of Kuwait and a former American President. Iraq's Government openly praised the attacks of September the 11th, and Al Qaida terrorists escaped from Afghanistan and are known to be in Iraq.

In 1991, the Iraqi regime agreed to destroy and stop developing all weapons of mass destruction and long-range missiles and to prove to the world it has done so by complying with rigorous inspections. Iraq has broken every aspect of this fundamental pledge.

From 1991 to 1995, the Iraqi regime said it had no biological weapons. After a senior official in its weapons program defected and exposed this lie, the regime admitted to producing tens of thousands of liters of anthrax and other deadly biological agents for use with Scud warheads, aerial bombs, and aircraft spray tanks. U.N. inspectors believe Iraq has produced 2 to 4 times the amount of biological agents it declared and has failed to account for more than three metric tons of material that could be used to produce biological weapons. Right now, Iraq is expanding and improving facilities that were used for the production of biological weapons. United Nations' inspections also revealed that Iraq likely maintains stockpiles of VX, mustard, and other chemical agents, and that the regime is rebuilding and expanding facilities capable of producing chemical weapons.

And in 1995, after 4 years of deception, Iraq finally admitted it had a crash nuclear weapons program prior to the Gulf war. We know now, were it not for that war, the regime in Iraq would likely have possessed a nuclear weapon no later than 1993.

Today, Iraq continues to withhold important information about its nuclear program, weapons design, procurement logs, experiment data, an accounting of nuclear materials, and documentation of foreign assistance. Iraq employs capable nuclear scientists and technicians. It retains physical infrastructure needed to build a nuclear weapon. Iraq has made several attempts to buy high strength aluminum tubes used to enrich uranium for a nuclear weapon. Should Iraq acquire fissile material, it would be able to build a nuclear weapon within a year. And Iraq's state-controlled media has reported numerous meetings between Saddam Hussein and his nuclear scientists, leaving little doubt about his continued appetite for these weapons.

Iraq also possesses a force of Scud-type missiles with ranges beyond the 150 kilometers permitted by the U.N. Work at testing and production facilities shows that Iraq is building more long-range missiles that it can inflict mass death throughout the region.

In 1990, after Iraq's invasion of Kuwait, the world imposed economic sanctions on Iraq. Those sanctions were maintained after the war to compel the regime's compliance with Security Council resolutions. In time, Iraq was allowed to use oil revenues to buy food. Saddam Hussein has subverted this program, working around the sanctions to buy missile technology and military materials. He blames the suffering of Iraq's people on the United Nations, even as he uses his oil wealth to build lavish palaces for himself and to buy arms for his country. By refusing to comply with his own agreements, he bears full guilt for the hunger and misery of innocent Iraqi citizens.

In 1991, Iraq promised U.N. inspectors immediate and unrestricted access to verify Iraq's commitment to rid itself of weapons of mass destruction and long-range missiles. Iraq broke this promise, spending 7 years deceiving, evading, and harassing U.N. inspectors before ceasing cooperation entirely. Just months after the 1991 ceasefire, the Security Council twice renewed its demand that the Iraqi regime cooperate fully with inspectors, condemning Iraq's serious violations of its obligations. The Security Council again renewed that demand in 1994 and twice more in 1996, deploring Iraq's clear violations of its obligations. The Security Council renewed its demand three more times in 1997, citing flagrant violations, and three more times in 1998, calling Iraq's behavior totally unacceptable. And in 1999, the demand was renewed yet again.

As we meet today, it's been almost 4 years since the last U.N. inspectors set foot in Iraq, 4 years for the Iraqi regime to plan and to build and to test behind the cloak of secrecy.

We know that Saddam Hussein pursued weapons of mass murder even when inspectors were in his country. Are we to assume that he stopped when they left? The history, the logic, and the facts lead to one conclusion: Saddam Hussein's regime is a grave and gathering danger. To suggest otherwise is to hope against the evidence. To assume this regime's good faith is to bet the lives of millions and the peace of the world in a reckless gamble. And this is a risk we must not take.

* * *

The United States helped found the United Nations. We want the United Nations to be effective and respectful and successful. We want the resolutions of the world's most important multilateral body to be enforced. And right now those resolutions are being unilaterally subverted by the Iraqi regime. Our partnership of nations can meet the test before us by making clear what we now expect of the Iraqi regime.

* * *

My Nation will work with the U.N. Security Council to meet our common challenge. If Iraq's regime defies us again, the world must move deliberately, decisively to hold Iraq to account. We will work with the U.N. Security

Council for the necessary resolutions. But the purposes of the United States should not be doubted. The Security Council resolutions will be enforced, the just demands of peace and security will be met, or action will be unavoidable. And a regime that has lost its legitimacy will also lose its power.

* * *

* * * We cannot stand by and do nothing while dangers gather. We must stand up for our security and for the permanent rights and the hopes of mankind. By heritage and by choice, the United States of America will make that stand. And delegates to the United Nations, you have the power to make that stand as well.

Thank you very much.

United Nations   **S**

Security Council

Distr.
General

S/RES/1441 (2002)
8 November 2002

Resolution 1441 (2002)
of 8 November 2002

The Security Council,

Recalling all its previous relevant resolutions, in particular its resolutions 661 (1990) of 6 August 1990, 678 (1990) of 29 November 1990, 686 (1991) of 2 March 1991, 687 (1991) of 3 April 1991, 688 (1991) of 5 April 1991, 707 (1991) of 15 August 1991, 715 (1991) of 11 October 1991, 986 (1995) of 14 April 1995, and 1284 (1999) of 17 December 1999, and all the relevant statements of its President,

Recalling also its resolution 1382 (2001) of 29 November 2001 and its intention to implement it fully,

Recognizing the threat Iraq's non-compliance with Council resolutions and proliferation of weapons of mass destruction and long-range missiles poses to international peace and security,

Recalling that its resolution 678 (1990) authorized Member States to use all necessary means to uphold and implement its resolution 660 (1990) of 2 August 1990 and all relevant resolutions subsequent to resolution 660 (1990) and to restore international peace and security in the area,

Further recalling that its resolution 687 (1991) imposed obligations on Iraq as a necessary step for achievement of its stated objective of restoring international peace and security in the area,

Deploring the fact that Iraq has not provided an accurate, full, final, and complete disclosure, as required by resolution 687 (1991), of all aspects of its programmes to develop weapons of mass destruction and ballistic missiles with a range greater than one hundred and fifty kilometers, and of all holdings of such weapons, their components and production facilities and locations, as well as all other nuclear programmes, including any which it claims are for purposes not related to nuclear-weapons-usable material,

Deploring further that Iraq repeatedly obstructed immediate, unconditional, and unrestricted access to sites designated by the United Nations Special Commission (UNSCOM) and the International Atomic Energy Agency (IAEA), failed to cooperate fully and unconditionally with UNSCOM and IAEA weapons inspectors, as required by resolution 687 (1991), and ultimately ceased all cooperation with UNSCOM and the IAEA in 1998,

Deploring the absence, since December 1998, in Iraq of international monitoring, inspection, and verification, as required by relevant resolutions, of weapons of mass destruction and ballistic missiles, in spite of the Council's repeated demands that Iraq provide immediate, unconditional, and unrestricted access to the United Nations Monitoring, Verification and Inspection Commission (UNMOVIC), established in resolution 1284 (1999) as the successor organization to UNSCOM, and the IAEA, and regretting the consequent prolonging of the crisis in the region and the suffering of the Iraqi people,

Deploring also that the Government of Iraq has failed to comply with its commitments pursuant to resolution 687 (1991) with regard to terrorism, pursuant to resolution 688 (1991) to end repression of its civilian population and to provide access by international humanitarian organizations to all those in need of assistance in Iraq, and pursuant to resolutions 686 (1991), 687 (1991), and 1284 (1999) to return or cooperate in accounting for Kuwaiti and third country nationals wrongfully detained by Iraq, or to return Kuwaiti property wrongfully seized by Iraq,

Recalling that in its resolution 687 (1991) the Council declared that a ceasefire would be based on acceptance by Iraq of the provisions of that resolution, including the obligations on Iraq contained therein,

Determined to ensure full and immediate compliance by Iraq without conditions or restrictions with its obligations under resolution 687 (1991) and other relevant resolutions and recalling that the resolutions of the Council constitute the governing standard of Iraqi compliance,

Recalling that the effective operation of UNMOVIC, as the successor organization to the Special Commission, and the IAEA is essential for the implementation of resolution 687 (1991) and other relevant resolutions,

Noting that the letter dated 16 September 2002 from the Minister for Foreign Affairs of Iraq addressed to the Secretary–General is a necessary first step toward rectifying Iraq's continued failure to comply with relevant Council resolutions,

Noting further the letter dated 8 October 2002 from the Executive Chairman of UNMOVIC and the Director–General of the IAEA to General Al–Saadi of the Government of Iraq laying out the practical arrangements, as a follow-up to their meeting in Vienna, that are prerequisites for the resumption of inspections in Iraq by UNMOVIC and the IAEA, and expressing the gravest concern at the continued failure by the Government of Iraq to provide confirmation of the arrangements as laid out in that letter,

Reaffirming the commitment of all Member States to the sovereignty and territorial integrity of Iraq, Kuwait, and the neighbouring States,

Commending the Secretary–General and members of the League of Arab States and its Secretary–General for their efforts in this regard,

Determined to secure full compliance with its decisions,

Acting under Chapter VII of the Charter of the United Nations,

1. *Decides* that Iraq has been and remains in material breach of its obligations under relevant resolutions, including resolution 687 (1991), in particular through Iraq's failure to cooperate with United Nations inspectors and the IAEA, and to complete the actions required under paragraphs 8 to 13 of resolution 687 (1991);

2. *Decides*, while acknowledging paragraph 1 above, to afford Iraq, by this resolution, a final opportunity to comply with its disarmament obligations under relevant resolutions of the Council; and accordingly decides to set up an enhanced inspection regime with the aim of bringing to full and verified completion the disarmament process established by resolution 687 (1991) and subsequent resolutions of the Council;

3. *Decides* that, in order to begin to comply with its disarmament obligations, in addition to submitting the required biannual declarations, the Government of Iraq shall provide to UNMOVIC, the IAEA, and the Council, not later than 30 days from the date of this resolution, a currently accurate, full, and completed declaration of all aspects of its programmes to develop chemical, biological, and nuclear weapons, ballistic missiles, and other delivery systems such as unmanned aerial vehicles and dispersal systems designed for use on aircraft, including any holdings and precise locations of such weapons, components, subcomponents, stocks of agents, and related material and equipment, the locations and work of its research, development and production facilities, as well as all other chemical, biological, and nuclear programmes, including any which it claims are for purposes not related to weapon production or material;

4. *Decides* that false statements or omissions in the declarations submitted by Iraq pursuant to this resolution and failure by Iraq at any time to comply with, and cooperate fully in the implementation of, this resolution shall constitute a further material breach of Iraq's obligations and will be reported to the Council for assessment in accordance with paragraphs 11 and 12 below;

5. *Decides* that Iraq shall provide UNMOVIC and the IAEA immediate, unimpeded, unconditional, and unrestricted access to any and all, including underground, areas, facilities, buildings, equipment, records, and means of transport which they wish to inspect, as well as immediate, unimpeded, unrestricted, and private access to all officials and other persons whom UNMOVIC or the IAEA wish to interview in the mode or location of UNMOVIC's or the IAEA's choice pursuant to any aspect of their mandates; further decides that UNMOVIC and the IAEA may at their discretion conduct interviews inside or outside of Iraq, may facilitate the travel of those interviewed and family members outside Iraq, and that, at the sole discretion of UNMOVIC and the IAEA, such interviews may occur without the presence of observers from the Iraqi Government; and instructs UNMOVIC and requests the IAEA to resume inspections no later than 45 days following adoption of this resolution and to update the Council 60 days thereafter;

* * *

7. *Decides* further that, in view of the prolonged interruption by Iraq of the presence of UNMOVIC and the IAEA and in order for them to accomplish the tasks set forth in this resolution and all previous relevant resolutions and notwithstanding prior understandings, the Council hereby establishes * * * revised or additional authorities, which shall be binding upon Iraq, to facilitate their work in Iraq * * * [The Security Council lists the rights inspectors will have in Iraq to carry out their mission.]

8. *Decides* further that Iraq shall not take or threaten hostile acts directed against any representative or personnel of the United Nations or the IAEA or of any Member State taking action to uphold any Council resolution;

9. *Requests* the Secretary–General immediately to notify Iraq of this resolution, which is binding on Iraq; demands that Iraq confirm within seven days of that notification its intention to comply fully with this resolution; and demands further that Iraq cooperate immediately, unconditionally, and actively with UNMOVIC and the IAEA;

10. *Requests* all Member States to give full support to UNMOVIC and the IAEA in the discharge of their mandates, including by providing any information related to prohibited programmes or other aspects of their mandates, including on Iraqi attempts since 1998 to acquire prohibited items, and by recommending sites to be inspected, persons to be interviewed, conditions of such interviews, and data to be collected, the results of which shall be reported to the Council by UNMOVIC and the IAEA;

11. *Directs* the Executive Chairman of UNMOVIC and the Director–General of the IAEA to report immediately to the Council any interference by Iraq with inspection activities, as well as any failure by Iraq to comply with its disarmament obligations, including its obligations regarding inspections under this resolution;

12. *Decides* to convene immediately upon receipt of a report in accordance with paragraphs 4 or 11 above, in order to consider the

situation and the need for full compliance with all of the relevant Council resolutions in order to secure international peace and security;

13. *Recalls*, in that context, that the Council has repeatedly warned Iraq that it will face serious consequences as a result of its continued violations of its obligations;

14. *Decides* to remain seized of the matter.

> *Adopted at the 1441nd meeting by 15 votes to none.*

———————

United Nations Security Council Fifty-eighth year, 4707th meeting Friday, 14 February 2003, 10 a.m. New York*

The President: I now call on the Minister for Foreign Affairs of France, His Excellency * * *:

Mr. Dominique Galouzeau de Villepin (*spoke in French*): I would like to thank Mr. Blix and Mr. ElBaradei for the information they have just given us on the ongoing inspections in Iraq. I would like to reiterate to them France's confidence in and complete support for their work.

One knows the value France has placed on the unity of the Security Council from the outset of the Iraqi crisis. Today this unity is based on two fundamental elements.

Together we are pursuing the objective of effectively disarming Iraq, and therefore we are obligated to achieve results. We must not call into question our common commitment in this regard. Collectively we bear this onerous responsibility that must leave no room for ulterior motives or assumptions. Let us be clear: none of us feels the least indulgence towards Saddam Hussain and the Iraqi regime.

In unanimously adopting resolution 1441 (2002) we collectively expressed our agreement with the two-stage approach proposed by France: disarmament through inspections and, if this strategy should fail, consideration by the Security Council of all the options, including resorting to force. Clearly, it was in the event that inspections failed, and only in that case, that a second resolution could be justified.

The question today is simple: do we believe in good conscience that disarmament via inspections missions is now a dead end, or do we believe that the possibilities regarding inspections made available in resolution 1441 (2002) have not yet been fully explored?

In response to this question, France believes two things. First, the option of inspections has not been exhausted, and it can provide an effective response to the imperative of disarming Iraq. Secondly, the use of

* UN Doc. S/PV.4707

force would have such heavy consequences for the people, the region and international stability that it should be envisaged only as a last resort.

* * *

Mr. Colin L. Powell, Secretary of State of the United States of America * * *:

* * *

Resolution 1441 (2002) was about the disarmament of Iraq. We worked on that resolution for seven weeks, from the time of President Bush's powerful speech here in the General Assembly on 12 September until the resolution was adopted on 8 November. We had intense discussions. All of you are familiar with that; you participated in those discussions. That was about disarmament.

The resolution began with the clear statement that Iraq had been in material breach of its obligations for the previous 11 years, and remained to that day—the day the resolution was adopted—in material breach. The resolution said that Iraq must now come into compliance; it must disarm. The resolution went on to say that we wanted to see a declaration from Iraq, within 30 days, of all of its activities. "Put it all on the table; let us see what you have been doing. Give us a declaration that we can believe in that is full, complete and accurate"—that is what we said to Iraq on 8 November. And some 29 days later we got 12,000 pages. Nobody in this Council can say that that was a full, complete or accurate declaration.

Now it is several months after that declaration was submitted, and I have heard nothing to suggest that they have filled in the gaps that were in that declaration, or that they have added new evidence that should give us any comfort that we have a full, complete and accurate declaration. You will recall that we put that declaration requirement into the resolution as an early test of Iraq's seriousness. Are they serious? Are they going to disarm? Are they going to comply? Are they going to cooperate? The answer, with that declaration, was, "No—we are going to see what we can get away with* * *."

* * *

We cannot wait for one of these terrible weapons to show up in one of our cities and wonder where it came from after it has been detonated by Al–Qaeda or somebody else. This is the time to go after this source of this kind of weaponry.

* * *

* * * Force should always be a last resort. I have preached this for most of my professional life as a soldier and as a diplomat. But it must be a resort. We cannot allow this process to be endlessly strung out, as Iraq is trying to do right now: "String it out long enough and the world will start looking in other directions. The Security Council will move on. We will get away with it again."

* * *

N.Y. Times, March 11, 2003 at A8

Annan Says U.S. Will Violate Charter if it Acts Without Approval

By PATRICK E. TYLER and FELICITY BARRINGER

UNITED NATIONS, March 10—Secretary General Kofi Annan warned today that if the United States fails to win approval from the Security Council for an attack on Iraq, Washington's decision to act alone or outside the Council would violate the United Nations charter. "The members of the Security Council now face a great choice," Mr. Annan said in The Hague, where he was trying to broker a United Nations deal on Cyprus. "If they fail to agree on a common position and action is taken without the authority of the Security Council, the legitimacy and support for any such action will be seriously impaired."

Mr. Annan's remarks drew a sharp response from Washington, where the Bush administration, like its allies overseas, was engaged in a strong lobbying effort to win the necessary nine votes to pass a resolution this week authorizing war.

The White House spokesman Ari Fleischer in a strongly worded retort said that "from a moral point of view," if the United Nations fails to support the Bush administration's war aims, it will have "failed to act once again," as it did in Kosovo in the face of persecution of the ethnic Albanians by Serbia and earlier in Rwanda in the face of genocidal massacres by Hutus against Tutsis.

Some international legal experts also took issue with Mr. Annan's assertions, that the United States and its coalition partners who ejected Iraqi forces from Kuwait in 1991 retained the legal authority to take additional action against Baghdad for its failures to live up to the United Nations resolutions that authorized that Persian Gulf war.

Others said that President Bush has nonetheless muddied the legal picture by returning to the Security Council now for a final resolution authorizing war. In this circumstance, they said, it is difficult for Mr. Bush and the international community to ignore a negative vote by the Security Council or a veto by one of its permanent members.

"I just disagree with the secretary general's legal view because there are fundamental Security Council resolutions that underlie this," said Ruth Wedg[]wood, professor of international law at Johns Hopkins University.

Richard N. Gardner, professor of international law at Columbia University, said that since Saddam Hussein has repeatedly violated the conditions of the 1991 cease-fire, "the United States and other countries revert to their rights to restore peace and security in the area" under the resolution authorizing that war, passed in 1990.

Mr. Annan, whose trip to The Hague also includes presiding over the investiture of the International Criminal Court, which has been opposed by Washington, insisted that "the United Nations—founded to save succeeding generations from the scourge of war—has a duty to search until the very end for the peaceful resolution of conflicts."

Responding to a question on the United Nations Charter, Mr. Annan said the charter is "very clear on circumstances under which force can be used. If the U.S. and others were to go outside the Council and take military action, it would not be in conformity with the charter."

United Nations officials said that Mr. Annan planned his remarks today to signal to Washington that it needed to consider a compromise that would draw more support on the 15–member Council.

Lawyers here scrambled to support Mr. Annan's remarks, pointing to Chapter 1 of the charter, which says that all members

should refrain from the use of force in international relations. These lawyers also argued that America's new doctrine to make preemptive strikes against perceived threats does not conform with Chapter 7, which recognizes the "right of individual or collective" self-defense.

Referring to Mr. Annan, William H. Luers, a former American diplomat who heads the United Nations Association, said, "His job is to defend the U.N. Charter" because it "best defines how nations should behave when it comes to the use of force."

Professor Wedg[]wood said that even if the United States loses the final vote and proceeds to war, "the failure of this particular resolution" does "not obviate the prior ones," especially since the prior resolutions gave the United States and its allies special authority to disarm Iraq for the sake of the peace and security of the region.

The main point, she said, "is that we've been there before." She cited the case of Kosovo, when the Clinton administration bypassed the

Security Council— where Russia was threatening to veto any military action— and used NATO as its instrument to lead the bombing of Yugoslavia.

Professor Gardner agreed that the authority existed in previous resolutions and said he is confident as an international lawyer that Mr. Bush has the authority he needs, "but we are now in a situation where there are certain ambiguities."

He continued, "I am very uneasy about going to war at this stage without authority from the Council" because the Council is divided on the question of whether all efforts by the United Nations weapons inspectors to disarm Iraq peacefully have been exhausted.

At the same time, Professor Gardner said that Mr. Bush had engendered a great deal of confusion by asserting American rights under a new national security doctrine of pre-emptive attack.

"Of course this sounds good," he said. "But it leaves us in a world where every country is self-judging what it does, and that leads to world anarchy. Hitler used national security when he invaded Czechoslo-

vakia, and Russia did the same in its aggressions. I am not one of these

purists on this subject, but the search for legitimacy has to be taken seriously."

N.Y. Times, March 20, 2003 at A1

U.S. Begins Attack With Strike at Baghdad After Deadline for Hussein to Go Runs Out

BLASTS IN CAPITAL

Bush Orders an Assault and Says Americans Will Disarm Foe

By DAVID E. SANGER with JOHN F. BURNS

WASHINGTON, March 19—President Bush ordered the beginning of a war on Iraq tonight, and his spokesman, Air Fleischer, said at about 9:45 p.m. that American forces had begun to disarm Iraq and would depose Saddam Hussein.

The announcement came just 10 minutes after word from Baghdad, where the American attack began, just before first light at 5:35 a.m. The first signs were an air raid siren followed by antiaircraft fire and loud explosions over the city that appeared to be ineffective, striking at low altitude over the city.

At least one impact was visible about a half mile from the Rashid Hotel in central Baghdad, throwing a great cloud of dust into the air.

The initial round of explosions took place about 10 minutes and was followed by a lull. The first traffic of the day racing down the highway appeared to be drivers fleeing the attack.

"The opening stages of the disarmament of the Iraqi regime have begun," Mr. Fleischer said in a brief news conference on television tonight.

The deadline for President Saddam Hussein to leave Iraq expired as American troops massed on Iraq's southern border, awaiting the order for the invasion plan that Mr. Bush and his war council completed only this afternoon.

Mr. Bush formally informed Congress, and then

world leaders, that he was ready to depose Mr. Hussein by force. In a seven-page message to Congress, he argued that force was now the only way to "adequately protect the national security of the United States" and that toppling the Iraqi government was "a vital part" of a broader war against terrorism. The message was required under a statute passed last fall explicitly authorizing war against Iraq that the president determined that a diplomatic solution was impossible.

As he completed the legal formalities, Mr. Bush was clearly embarked on one of the country's most ambitious military ventures since Vietnam, and on a war his administration began planning over a year ago. "There are a lot of us," said one of his more hawkish senior advisers, "who have been waiting for this day of liberation for years."

Mr. Bush had given Mr. Hussein and members of his family until shortly after 8 p.m. today to leave the country in order to forestall an American-led attack. But there was no discernible sign that the Iraqi leader was even thinking of leaving, despite an offer of asylum from Bahrain.

As the deadline passed tonight, Mr. Bush was eating dinner in the living room of the White House residence with his wife, Laura. He received a call from Andrew H. Card, the White House chief of staff, and asked Mr. Card if there was any evidence that Mr. Hussein had left Iraq. There was none, Mr. Card told him, according to Mr. Fleischer.

"The disarmament of the Iraqi regime," Mr. Fleischer told reporters tonight, "will begin at a time of the president's choosing."

Even as punishing sandstorms swirled around the Army troops massed in Kuwait, the engineering battalions that will be in the vanguard of the invasion force—breaching berms and clearing minefield—were already on the move. Special Operations forces were reportedly already deployed inside Iraq, shaping the battlefield for the larger invasion force to come.

American and British warplanes flew bombing missions tonight against a dozen Iraqi artillery and surface-to-surface missile positions in southern Iraq, wiping out placements that could threaten advancing troops.

Roughly 17 Iraqi border troops surrendered along the border, and were taken into custody by Kuwaiti forces. A few administration officials seized on the defections as an early indicator of the mass defections they hope to see when the fighting begins.

But others in the administration warned against overconfidence, cautioning that toppling Mr. Hussein and the protective apparatus that has kept him in power for more than three decades is a far riskier enterprise than was ousting his forces from Kuwait 12 years ago in the Persian Gulf war.

Mr. Fleischer cautioned that "Americans ought to be prepared for loss of life." He noted that while the White House sought "as precise, short a conflict as possible," the unknowns—from how American, British and Australian troops would be received to the elements of weather, accident and so-called friendly fire—were numerous.

The notification to Congressional leaders, sent to Capitol Hill late on Tuesday night, provided the most detailed legal justification yet for military action.

Mr. Bush stayed largely out of sight today, save for a brief meeting this morning with Mayor Michael R. Bloomberg and the secretary of homeland security, Tom Ridge, to review New York City's needs to prepare for any new terrorist attacks. The White House later said it would go to Congress for a special appropriation bill to pay for the war and homeland security.

Washington was eerily quiet, but there were isolated voices of dissent. "Today, I weep for my country," Senator Robert C. Byrd, the West Virginia Democrat and the war's biggest critic in the Senate said. "No more is the image of America one of strong, yet benevolent, peacekeeper. Around the globe, our friends mistrust us, our word is disputed, our intentions are questioned."

The breach with Europe continued to widen. As Mr. Bush tried to convince Congress that the attack on Iraq would advance the war on terror, France's foreign minister, Dominique de Villepin, said the war would spawn more terrorism. The German foreign minister, Joschka Fischer, said, "Germany emphatically rejects the impending war."

But while Germany allowed American troops to fly over its territory, Turkey was still arguing about opening its airspace. Turkey further said it would not allow United States forces to use its air bases to refuel—a remarkable slap from a NATO ally. Mr. Fleischer made clear that the $30 billion in proposed aid and loans to Turkey—dangled when it seemed as if the country would allow American and

British forces to use its territory to invade Iraq from the north—is "no longer on the table."

Mr. Fleischer disputed the view of Europeans and others who argue that the pending invasion is a violation of the United Nations Charter. He cited three Security Council resolutions that he said provided all of the authorization Mr. Bush needed. But he also likened the current preparations to the Cuban missile crisis in 1962, arguing that just as President Kennedy imposed a quarantine around Cuba— "an act of war," Mr. Fleischer said—to force it to remove nuclear missiles, Mr. Bush is acting to protect the United States from a threat that it would never see coming.

Several scholars have disputed that view, noting that in the case of the missile crisis, the Soviet missiles could have easily reached the United States, and the weapons clearly put Americans at peril.

Mr. Bush argued on Monday night that waiting for the Iraq threat to develop was tantamount to "suicide." The president's definition

seemed to fit what scholars say is the classic war of prevention.

"We choose to meet that threat now, where it arises, before it can appear suddenly in our skies and cities," the president said then.

The document submitted to Congress laid out yet another argument— Iraq's current links to terrorists, an area in which the administration's evidence has been scanty, and its potential for greater links in the future.

"Both because Iraq harbors terrorists and because Iraq could share weapons of mass destruction with terrorist who seek them for use against the United States, the use of force to bring Iraq into compliance with its obligations under United Nations Security Council resolutions would be a significant contribution to the war on terrorists of global reach," the report to Congress said.

"A change in the current Iraqi regime would eliminate an important source of support for international terrorist activities," it said. "It would likely also assist efforts to disrupt terrorist networks and capture terrorists around the globe. United States government personnel operating in Iraq may discover information through Iraqi government documents and interviews with detained Iraqi officials that would identify individuals currently in the United States and abroad who are linked to terrorist organizations."

That rationale would seem, on its face, to support military action against many nations, from Pakistan to Indonesia. But Mr. Fleischer insisted that the conditions surrounding Iraq's defiance were "unique."

As the 48–hour ultimatum to Mr. Hussein to leave Iraq expired, Pentagon officials were deliberately vague on when American forces might strike. While it seemed unlikely that they could gain much tactical surprise at this late date, some officials said keeping Iraqi soldiers on edge would increase their anxiety, fuel their thoughts of defection and perhaps fill them with dread.

Their potential use of chemical weapons remains one of the biggest worries. Hans Blix, one of the chief United Nations weapons inspector, said that "if they have any still, and that's a big if, I would doubt that they would use it, because a lot of countries and people in the world are negative to the idea of waging war," adding, "And if the Iraqis were to use any chemical weapons then, I think, the public opinion around the world will immediately turn against the Iraqis."

Operation Iraqi Freedom

President George W. Bush Addresses the Nation
   The Oval Office
   March 19, 2003

THE PRESIDENT: My fellow citizens, at this hour, American and coalition forces are in the early stages of military operations to disarm Iraq, to free its people and to defend the world from grave danger.

On my orders, coalition forces have begun striking selected targets of military importance to undermine Saddam Hussein's ability to wage war. These are opening stages of what will be a broad and concerted campaign. More than 35 countries are giving crucial support—from the use of naval and air bases, to help with intelligence and logistics, to the deployment of combat units. Every nation in this coalition has chosen to bear the duty and share the honor of serving in our common defense.

To all the men and women of the United States Armed Forces now in the Middle East, the peace of a troubled world and the hopes of an oppressed people now depend on you. That trust is well placed.

The enemies you confront will come to know your skill and bravery. The people you liberate will witness the honorable and decent spirit of the American military. In this conflict, America faces an enemy who has no regard for conventions of war or rules of morality. Saddam Hussein has placed Iraqi troops and equipment in civilian areas, attempting to use innocent men, women and children as shields for his own military—a final atrocity against his people.

I want Americans and all the world to know that coalition forces will make every effort to spare innocent civilians from harm. A campaign on the harsh terrain of a nation as large as California could be longer and more difficult than some predict. And helping Iraqis achieve a united, stable and free country will require our sustained commitment.

We come to Iraq with respect for its citizens, for their great civilization and for the religious faiths they practice. We have no ambition in Iraq, except to remove a threat and restore control of that country to its own people.

I know that the families of our military are praying that all those who serve will return safely and soon. Millions of Americans are praying with you for the safety of your loved ones and for the protection of the innocent. For your sacrifice, you have the gratitude and respect of the American people. And you can know that our forces will be coming home as soon as their work is done.

Our nation enters this conflict reluctantly—yet, our purpose is sure. The people of the United States and our friends and allies will not live at the mercy of an outlaw regime that threatens the peace with weapons of mass murder. We will meet that threat now, with our Army, Air Force, Navy, Coast Guard and Marines, so that we do not have to meet it later with armies of fire fighters and police and doctors on the streets of our cities.

Now that conflict has come, the only way to limit its duration is to apply decisive force. And I assure you, this will not be a campaign of half measures, and we will accept no outcome but victory.

My fellow citizens, the dangers to our country and the world will be overcome. We will pass through this time of peril and carry on the work of peace. We will defend our freedom. We will bring freedom to others and we will prevail.

May God bless our country and all who defend her.

———————

United Nations   **S/2003/350**

 Security Council

Distr.
General

Original: English

Letter dated 20 March 2003 from the Permanent Representative of the United Kingdom of Great Britain and Northern Ireland to the United Nations addressed to the President of the Security Council

I have the honour to inform you on behalf of my Government that the Armed Forces of the United Kingdom—in association with those of the United States and Australia—engaged in military action in Iraq on 20 March 2003. The action is continuing.

The action follows a long history of non-cooperation by Iraq with the United Nations Special Commission (UNSCOM), the United Nations Monitoring, Verification and Inspection Commission (UNMOVIC) and the International Atomic Energy Agency (IAEA) and numerous findings by the Security Council that Iraq has failed to comply with its disarmament obligations under Security Council resolutions. In its resolution 1441 (2002), the Council recognized that Iraq's possession of weapons of mass destruction constitutes it threat to international peace and security, that Iraq has failed, in clear violation of its obligations, to disarm and that in consequence Iraq is in material breach of the conditions for the ceasefire at the end of hostilities in 1991 laid down by the Council in its resolution 687 (1991). Military action was undertaken consistent with resolutions 678 (1990), 687 (1991) and 1441 (2002) only when it became apparent that there was no other way of achieving compliance by Iraq.

The objective of the action is to secure compliance by Iraq with its disarmament obligations as laid down by the Council. All military action will be limited to the minimum measures necessary to secure this objective. Operations will be conducted in accordance with the international laws of armed conflict. Targets have been carefully chosen to avoid civilian casualties.

I would be grateful if you could circulate the text of the present letter as a document of the Security Council.

(*Signed*) Jeremy Greenstock*

---

* *See also* Letter dated 20 March 2003 from the Permanent Representative of Australia to the United Nations addressed to the President of the Security Council, U.N.Doc. S/2003/352 (2003).

United Nations   **S/2003/350**

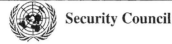 **Security Council**

Distr.
General

Original: English

Letter dated 20 March 2003 from the Permanent Representative of the United States of America to the United Nations addressed to the President of the Security Council

Coalition forces have commenced military operations in Iraq. These operations are necessary in view of Iraq's continued material breaches of its disarmament obligations under relevant Security Council resolutions, including resolution 1441 (2002). The operations are substantial and will secure compliance with those obligations. In carrying out these operations, our forces will take all reasonable precautions to avoid civilian casualties.

The actions being taken are authorized under existing Council resolutions, including its resolutions 678 (1990) and 687 (1991). Resolution 687 (1991) imposed a series of obligations on Iraq, most importantly, extensive disarmament obligations, that were conditions of the ceasefire established under it. It has been long recognized and understood that a material breach of these obligations removes the basis of the ceasefire and revives the authority to use force under resolution 678 (1990). This has been the basis for coalition use of force in the past and has been accepted by the Council, as evidenced, for example, by the Secretary–General's public announcement in January 1993 following Iraq's material breach of resolution 687 (1991) that coalition forces had received a mandate from the Council to use force according to resolution 678 (1990).

Iraq continues to be in material breach of its disarmament obligations under resolution 687 (1991), as the Council affirmed in its resolution 1441 (2002). Acting under the authority of Chapter VII of the Charter of the United Nations, the Council unanimously decided that Iraq has been and remained in material breach of its obligations and recalled its repeated warnings to Iraq that it will face serious consequences as a result of its continued violations of its obligations. The resolution then provided Iraq a "final opportunity" to comply, but stated specially that violations by Iraq of its obligations under resolution 1441 (2002) to present a currently accurate, full and completed declaration of all aspects of its weapons of mass destruction programmes and to comply with and cooperate fully in the implementation of the resolution would constitute a further material breach.

The Government of Iraq decided not to avail itself of its final opportunity under resolution 1441 (2002) and has clearly committed additional violations. In view of Iraq's material breaches, the basis for the ceasefire has been removed and use of force is authorized under resolution 678 (1990).

Iraq repeatedly has refused, over a protracted period of time, to respond to diplomatic overtures, economic sanctions and other peaceful means, designed to help bring about Iraqi compliance with its obligations to disarm and to permit full inspection of its weapons of mass destruction and related programmes. The actions that coalition forces are undertaking are an appropriate response. They are necessary steps to defend the United States and the international community from the threat posed by Iraq and to restore international peace and security in the area. Further delay would simply allow Iraq to continue its unlawful and threatening conduct.

It is the Government of Iraq that bears full responsibility for the serious consequences of its defiance of the Council's decisions.

I would be grateful if you could circulate the test of the present letter as a document of the Security Council.

(Signed) John D. Negroponte

Houston Chronicle, March 26, 2003, at A2

Pentagon Warns Iraq Not to Harm Prisoners

By JULIE MASON, Houston Chronicle

WASHINGTON, March 26—Pentagon officials warned Iraq on Tuesday not to mistreat coalition prisoners of war, but came under harsh international criticism for their treatment of prisoners in U.S. custody.

At least seven U.S. military personnel have been captured in Iraq and the U.S. government has alleged mistreatment by Iraqi captors.

"Their treatment of coalition POWs is a violation of the Geneva Conventions," Defense Secretary Donald Rumsfeld said at the Pentagon.

At the White House, spokesman Ari Fleischer echoed the concern, saying Iraqi leader Saddam Hussein "better not" harm coalition prisoners.

"As President Bush stated, in the conflict with Iraq, war crimes will be prosecuted, war criminals will be punished. And we are seeing a pattern of war crimes," Fleischer said.

But several human rights organizations are criticizing American military tactics regarding prisoners, even while raising alarms about potential abuses by Iraq.

"American POWs in Iraqi custody need all the help they can get to secure their Geneva Convention rights," said Kenneth Roth, executive director of Human Rights Watch. "It's unfortunate that the United States hasn't been a more staunch defender of the Geneva Conventions in its own recent conduct."

Rumsfeld said there are now more than 3,500 Iraqi prisoners of war being detailed as part of the nearly week-old Operation Iraqi Freedom.

At issue for several groups are the hundreds of detainees from the action in Afghanistan still in custody at Guantanamo Bay.

The same day Iraqi television showed American soldiers being questioned after capture, 30 new detainees were flown from Afghanistan to the U.S. Navy base in Cuba, according to Amnesty International.

When the first prisoners were brought to Guantanamo last year, the Pentagon released photographs showing them kneeling and shackled, in orange jumpsuits and goggles.

Several organizations contend that a number of the prisoners are being held illegally, that their treatment violates the Geneva Conventions, and that interrogation tactics being used against them may be legally construed as torture.

Asked about the apparent discrepancy, Fleischer said U.S. officials have treated Guantanamo detainees "humanely."

"There are two different situations. You have the war against terrorism and then you have this conflict, which is much more of a traditional conflict," he

said. "And we have always treated people humanely consistent with international agreements."

In addition, the Bush administration early on deemed the Guantanamo prisoners captured in Afghanistan "unlawful combatants," arguing that they are not entitled to the usual protections afforded prisoners of war—a claim that has been challenged by legal scholars and human rights groups.

Eighteen Afghan men were freed Tuesday from the Guantanamo camp. They told reporters they were generally well fed and given medical care, but housed in cramped cells and sometimes shackled, hit and humiliated.

Some flashed medical records showing extensive care by American military doctors, while others complained that American soldiers insulted Islam by sitting on the Koran or dumping their sacred text into a toilet.

Overseas, assurances by American officials have been branded as hypocrisy by several organizations in the world press, who note that

the International Red Cross has not been permitted to meet with either Iraqi or American prisoners in the current conflict.

It was unclear where the thousands of Iraqi prisoners of war were being held, although Pentagon officials said international law was being closely followed in their handling and treatment.

In addition to the thousands already captured, Rumsfeld said Iraqi soldiers were "capitulating by the hundreds."

Air Force Gen. Richard Myers, chairman of the Joint Chiefs of Staff, said he anticipated negotiating access for the Red Cross to Iraqi prisoners by Wednesday.

"We expect the same thing," he said.

In the last Gulf War, American prisoners were beaten, several were tortured, and at least one female soldier was raped while in Iraqi custody.

"It's Saddam Hussein's regime that better not harm our prisoners. The president has made that clear," Fleischer said.

United Nations   **S**

Security Council

Distr.
General

S/RES/1483 (2003)
22 May 2003

Resolution 1483
of 22 May 2003

The Security Council,

Recalling all its previous relevant resolutions, *Reaffirming* the sovereignty and territorial integrity of Iraq,

Reaffirming also the importance of the disarmament of Iraqi weapons of mass destruction and of eventual confirmation of the disarmament of Iraq,

Stressing the right of the Iraqi people freely to determine their own political future and control their own natural resources, *welcoming* the commitment of all parties concerned to support the creation of an environment in which they may do so as soon as possible, and *expressing* resolve that the day when Iraqis govern themselves must come quickly,

Encouraging efforts by the people of Iraq to form a representative government based on the rule of law that affords equal rights and justice to all Iraqi citizens without regard to ethnicity, religion, or gender, and, in this connection, *recalls* resolution 1325 (2000) of 31 October 2000,

Welcoming the first steps of the Iraqi people in this regard, and *noting* in this connection the 15 April 2003 Nasiriyah statement and the 28 April 2003 Baghdad statement,

Resolved that the United Nations should play a vital role in humanitarian relief, the reconstruction of Iraq, and the restoration and establishment of national and local institutions for representative governance,

Noting the statement of 12 April 2003 by the Ministers of Finance and Central Bank Governors of the Group of Seven Industrialized Nations in which the members recognized the need for a multilateral effort to help rebuild and develop Iraq and for the need for assistance from the International Monetary Fund and the World Bank in these efforts,

Welcoming also the resumption of humanitarian assistance and the continuing efforts of the Secretary–General and the specialized agencies to provide food and medicine to the people of Iraq,

Welcoming the appointment by the Secretary–General of his Special Adviser on Iraq,

Affirming the need for accountability for crimes and atrocities committed by the previous Iraqi regime,

Stressing the need for respect for the archaeological, historical, cultural, and religious heritage of Iraq, and for the continued protection of archaeological, historical, cultural, and religious sites, museums, libraries, and monuments,

Noting the letter of 8 May 2003 from the Permanent Representatives of the United States of America and the United Kingdom of Great Britain and Northern Ireland to the President of the Security Council (S/2003/538) and recognizing the specific authorities, responsibilities, and obligations under applicable international law of these states as occupying powers under unified command (the "Authority"),

Noting further that other States that are not occupying powers are working now or in the future may work under the Authority,

Welcoming further the willingness of Member States to contribute to stability and security in Iraq by contributing personnel, equipment, and other resources under the Authority,

Concerned that many Kuwaitis and Third–State Nationals still are not accounted for since 2 August 1990,

Determining that the situation in Iraq, although improved, continues to constitute a threat to international peace and security,

Acting under Chapter VII of the Charter of the United Nations,

1. *Appeals* to Member States and concerned organizations to assist the people of Iraq in their efforts to reform their institutions and rebuild their country, and to contribute to conditions of stability and security in Iraq in accordance with this resolution;

2. *Calls upon* all Member States in a position to do so to respond immediately to the humanitarian appeals of the United Nations and other international organizations for Iraq and to help meet the humanitarian and other needs of the Iraqi people by providing food, medical supplies, and resources necessary for reconstruction and rehabilitation of Iraq's economic infrastructure;

3. *Appeals* to Member State to deny safe haven to those members of the previous Iraqi regime who are alleged to be responsible for crimes and atrocities and to support actions to bring them to justice;

4. *Calls upon* the Authority, consistent with the Charter of the United Nations and other relevant international law, to promote the welfare of the Iraqi people through the effective administration of the territory, including in particular working towards the restoration of conditions of security and stability and the creation of conditions in which the Iraqi people can freely determine their own political future;

5. *Calls upon* all concerned to comply fully with their obligations under international law including in particular the Geneva Conventions of 1949 and the Hague Regulations of 1907;

6. *Calls upon* the Authority and relevant organizations and individuals to continue efforts to locate, identify, and repatriate all Kuwaiti and

Third–State Nationals or the remains of those present in Iraq on or after 2 August 1990, as well as the Kuwaiti archives, that the previous Iraqi regime failed to undertake, and, in this regard, *directs* the High–Level Coordinator, in consultation with the International Committee of the Red Cross and the Tripartite Commission and with the appropriate support of the people of Iraq and in coordination with the Authority, to take steps to fulfill his mandate with respect to the fate of Kuwaiti and Third–State National missing persons and property;

7. *Decides* that all Member States shall take appropriate steps to facilitate the safe return to Iraqi institutions of Iraqi cultural property and other items of archaeological, historical, cultural, rare scientific, and religious importance illegally removed from the Iraq National Museum, the National Library, and other locations in Iraq since the adoption of resolution 661 (1990) of 6 August 1990, including by establishing a prohibition on trade in or transfer of such items and items with respect to which reasonable suspicion exists that they have been illegally removed, and *calls upon* the United Nations Educational, Scientific, and Cultural Organization, Interpol, and other international organizations, as appropriate, to assist in the implementation of this paragraph;

8. *Requests* the Secretary–General to appoint a Special Representative for Iraq whose independent responsibilities shall involve reporting regularly to the Council on his activities under this resolution, coordinating activities of the United Nations in post-conflict processes in Iraq, coordinating among United Nations and international agencies engaged in humanitarian assistance and reconstruction activities in Iraq, and, in coordination with the Authority, assisting the people of Iraq through [a variety of efforts, coordinated with the Authority], * * *;

9. *Supports* the formation, by the people of Iraq with the help of the Authority and working with the Special Representative, of an Iraqi interim administration as a transitional administration run by Iraqis, until an internationally recognized, representative government is established by the people of Iraq and assumes the responsibilities of the Authority;

10. *Decides* that, with the exception of prohibitions related to the sale or supply to Iraq of arms and related materiel other than those arms and related materiel required by the Authority to serve the purposes of this and other related resolutions, all prohibitions related to trade with Iraq and the provision of financial or economic resources to Iraq established by resolution 661 (1990) and subsequent relevant resolutions, including resolution 778 (1992) of 2 October 1992, shall no longer apply;

11. *Reaffirms* that Iraq must meet its disarmament obligations, *encourages* the United Kingdom of Great Britain and Northern Ireland and the United States of America to keep the Council informed of their activities in this regard, and *underlines* the intention of the Council to revisit the mandates of the United Nations Monitoring, Verification, and Inspection Commission and the International Atomic Energy Agency as set forth in resolutions 687 (1991) of 3 April 1991, 1284 (1999) of 17 December 1999, and 1441 (2002) of 8 November 2002;

12. *Notes* the establishment of a Development Fund for Iraq to be held by the Central Bank of Iraq and to be audited by independent public accountants * * *;

13. *Notes further* that the funds in the Development Fund for Iraq shall be disbursed at the direction of the Authority, in consultation with the Iraqi interim administration, for the purposes set out in paragraph 14 below;

14. *Underlines* that the Development Fund for Iraq shall be used in a transparent manner to meet the humanitarian needs of the Iraqi people, for the economic reconstruction and repair of Iraq's infrastructure, for the continued disarmament of Iraq, and for the costs of Iraqi civilian administration, and for other purposes benefiting the people of Iraq;

15. *Calls upon* the international financial institutions to assist the people of Iraq in the reconstruction and development of their economy and to facilitate assistance by the broader donor community, and *welcomes* the readiness of creditors, including those of the Paris Club, to seek a solution to Iraq's sovereign debt problems;

16. *Requests* also that the Secretary–General, in coordination with the Authority, continue the exercise of his responsibilities under Security Council resolution 1472 (2003) of 28 March 2003 and 1476 (2003) of 24 April 2003, for a period of six months following the adoption of this resolution, and terminate within this time period, in the most cost effective manner, the ongoing operations of the "Oil-for-Food" Programme (the "Programme"), both at headquarters level and in the field, transferring responsibility for the administration of any remaining activity under the Programme to the Authority, * * *;

17. *Requests further* that the Secretary–General transfer as soon as possible to the Development Fund for Iraq 1 billion United States dollars from unencumbered funds in the accounts established pursuant to * * * of resolution 986 (1995), restore Government of Iraq funds that were provided by Member States to the Secretary–General as requested in paragraph 1 of resolution 778 (1992), * * *;

18. *Decides* to terminate effective on the adoption of this resolution the functions related to the observation and monitoring activities undertaken by the Secretary–General under the Programme, including the monitoring of the export of petroleum and petroleum products from Iraq;

19. *Decides* to terminate the Committee established pursuant to paragraph 6 of resolution 661 (1990) at the conclusion of the six month period called for in paragraph 16 above and *further decides* that the Committee shall identify individuals and entities referred to in paragraph 23 below;

20. *Decides* that all export sales of petroleum, petroleum products, and natural gas from Iraq following the date of the adoption of this resolution shall be made consistent with prevailing international market best practices, to be audited by independent public accountants reporting to the International Advisory and Monitoring Board referred to in paragraph

12 above in order to ensure transparency, and *decides further* that, except as provided in paragraph 21 below, all proceeds from such sales shall be deposited into the Development Fund for Iraq until such time as an internationally recognized, representative government of Iraq is properly constituted;

21. *Decides further* that 5 per cent of the proceeds referred to in paragraph 20 above shall be deposited into the Compensation Fund established in accordance with resolution 687 (1991) and subsequent relevant resolutions and that, unless an internationally recognized, representative government of Iraq and the Governing Council of the United Nations Compensation Commission [for the compensation of victims of the 1990 invasion of Kuwait], in the exercise of its authority over methods of ensuring that payments are made into the Compensation Fund, decide otherwise, this requirement shall be binding on a properly constituted, internationally recognized, representative government of Iraq and any successor thereto;

22. *Noting* the relevance of the establishment of an internationally recognized, representative government of Iraq and the desirability of prompt completion of the restructuring of Iraq's debt as referred to in paragraph 15 above, further *decides* that, until December 31, 2007, unless the Council decides otherwise, petroleum, petroleum products, and natural gas originating in Iraq shall be immune, until title passes to the initial purchaser from legal proceedings against them and not be subject to any form of attachment, garnishment, or execution, and that all States shall take any steps that may be necessary under their respective domestic legal systems to assure this protection, and that proceeds and obligations arising from sales thereof, as well as the Development Fund for Iraq, shall enjoy privileges and immunities equivalent to those enjoyed by the United Nations except that the above mentioned privileges and immunities will not apply with respect to any legal proceeding in which recourse to such proceeds or obligations is necessary to satisfy liability for damages assessed in connection with an ecological accident, including an oil spill, that occurs after the date of adoption of this resolution;

23. *Decides* that all Member States in which there are:

(a) funds or other financial assets or economic resources of the previous Government of Iraq or its state bodies, corporations, or agencies, located outside Iraq as of the date of this resolution, or

(b) funds or other financial assets or economic resources that have been removed from Iraq, or acquired, by Saddam Hussein or other senior officials of the former Iraqi regime and their immediate family members, including entities owned or controlled, directly or indirectly, by them or by persons acting on their behalf or at their direction,

shall freeze without delay those funds or other financial assets or economic resources and, unless these funds or other financial assets or economic resources are themselves the subject of a prior judicial, administrative, or arbitral lien or judgement, immediately shall cause their transfer to the

Development Fund for Iraq, it being understood that, unless otherwise addressed, claims made by private individuals or non-government entities on those transferred funds or other financial assets may be presented to the internationally recognized, representative government of Iraq; and *decides further* that all such funds or other financial assets or economic resources shall enjoy the same privileges, immunities, and protections as provided under paragraph 22;

24. *Requests* the Secretary–General to report to the Council at regular intervals on the work of the Special Representative with respect to the implementation of this resolution and on the work of the International Advisory and Monitoring Board and *encourages* the United Kingdom of Great Britain and Northern Ireland and the United States of America to inform the Council at regular intervals of their efforts under this resolution;

25. *Decides* to review the implementation of this resolution within twelve months of adoption and to consider further steps that might be necessary;

26. *Calls upon* Member States and international and regional organizations to contribute to the implementation of this resolution;

27. *Decides* to remain seized of this matter.

> *Adopted at the 4761st meeting by 14 votes to none, with 1 non-voting.*

Houston Chronicle, December 16, 2003, at A16.

Saddam: The Capture/Saddam Trial/Iraqis Eye Quick Execution, but Others Not So Sure

By Niko Price Associated Press

BAGHDAD, Iraq—Their exuberance over his capture still fresh, Iraqi leaders said Monday they want to send Saddam Hussein to a quick trial with an eye toward executing him by summer. But U.S. officials signaled the Iraqis may have to wait.

U.N. Secretary–General Kofi Annan said the world body would not support bringing Saddam before a tribunal that might sentence him to death.

"The U.N. does not support death penalty. In all the courts we have set up, (U.N. officials) have not included death penalty," Annan said Monday at the United Nations. "And so as secretary-general and the U.N. as an organization are not going to turn around and support a death penalty."

Members of the U.S.-appointed Iraq Governing Council said Monday the trial would be televised in the interest of exposing Saddam's atrocities and beginning a process of national healing. But some couldn't hold back from declaring the verdict a done deal.

"This man has killed hundreds of thousands of people. If he has to be killed once, I think he has to be resurrected hundreds of times and killed again," said council member Mouwafak al-Rabii, a human rights activist who was imprisoned under Saddam.

Al–Rabii and other council members met with what they described as an unrepentant Saddam on Sunday, hours after his capture by U.S. troops. They said proceedings against the deposed dictator would begin soon in an Iraqi special tribunal written into law last week.

"Very soon. In the next few weeks," al-Rabii said. "We passed the law. We have almost agreed on most of the judges and prosecutors.

We're almost there. I can tell you, he's going to be the first."

Council member Adnan Pachachi said he expected the trial would begin "sometime in March." A third council member, Kurdish judge Dara Noor al-Din, offered a more conservative estimate: "Maybe four to six months."

But U.S. officials were just beginning to interrogate their captive on a laundry list of subjects, including the insurgency that has killed hundreds of U.S. troops and his alleged weapons of mass destruction, the main rationale for the U.S.-led war.

Appearing to contradict earlier U.S. statements that officials would leave it to Iraqis to work out the details of

their special tribunal, State Department spokesman Richard Boucher indicated the U.S. government now planned to play a major role in crafting the court.

Boucher said the State Department would send Pierre–Richard Prosper, its ambassador at large for war crime issues, to Baghdad early next year to work on setting up a court.

Human rights activists said they were shocked at the timeline outlined by the Iraqi leaders.

"I find that extremely disturbing and distressing," said Susannah Sirkin of Physicians for Human Rights in Boston. "It's virtually unthinkable, and it would be a shame in terms of justice possibly being served."

Report of the International Committee of the Red Cross (ICRC) on the Treatment By the Coalition Forces of Prisoners of War and Other Protected Persons By the Geneva Conventions in Iraq During Arrest, Internment and Interrogation

FEBRUARY 2004*

* * *

EXECUTIVE SUMMARY

In its "Report on the Treatment by the Coalition Forces of Prisoners of War and other protected persons in Iraq", the International Committee of the Red Cross (ICRC) draws the attention of the Coalition Forces (hereafter called "the CF") to a number of serious violations of International Human-

* Available at www.icrC.org.

itarian Law. These violations have been documented and sometimes observed while visiting prisoners of war, civilian internees and other protected persons by the Geneva Conventions (hereafter called persons deprived of their liberty when their status is not specifically mentioned) in Iraq between March and November 2003. During its visits to places of internment of the CF, the ICRC collected allegations during private interviews with persons deprived of their liberty relating to the treatment by the CF of protected persons during their capture, arrest, transfer, internment and interrogation.

The main violations, which are described in the ICRC report and presented confidentially to the CF, include:

- Brutality against protected persons upon capture and initial custody, sometimes causing death or serious injury
- Absence of notification of arrest of persons deprived of their liberty to their families causing distress among persons deprived of their liberty and their families
- Physical or psychological coercion during interrogation to secure information
- Prolonged solitary confinement in cells devoid of daylight
- Excessive and disproportionate use of force against persons deprived of their liberty resulting in death or injury during their period of internment

Serious problems of conduct by the CF affecting persons deprived of their liberty are also presented in the report:

- Seizure and confiscation of private belongings of persons deprived of their liberty
- Exposure of persons deprived of their liberty to dangerous tasks
- Holding persons deprived of their liberty in dangerous places where they are not protected from shelling

According to allegations collected by ICRC delegates during private interviews with persons deprived of their liberty, ill-treatment during capture was frequent. While certain circumstances might require defensive precautions and the use of force on the part of battle group units, the ICRC collected allegations of ill-treatment following capture which took place in Baghdad, Basrah, Ramadi and Tikrit, indicating a consistent pattern with respect to times and places of brutal behavior during arrest. The repetition of such behavior by CF appeared to go beyond the reasonable, legitimate and proportional use of force required to apprehend suspects or restrain persons resisting arrest or capture, and seemed to reflect a usual modus operandi by certain CF battle group units.

According to the allegations collected by the ICRC, ill-treatment during interrogation was not systematic, except with regard to persons arrested in connection with suspected security offences or deemed to have an "intelligence" value. In these cases, persons deprived of their liberty under supervision of the Military Intelligence were at high risk of being subjected to a variety of harsh treatments ranging from insults, threats and humiliations to both physical and psychological coercion, which in some cases was tantamount to torture, in order to force cooperation with their interrogators.

The ICRC also started to document what appeared to be widespread abuse of power and ill-treatment by the Iraqi police which is under the responsibility of the Occupying Powers, including threats to hand over persons in their custody to the CF so as to extort money from them, effective hand over of such persons to the custody of the CF on allegedly fake accusations, or invoking CF orders or instructions to mistreat persons deprived of their liberty during interrogation.

In the case of the "High Value Detainees" held in Baghdad International Airport, their continued internment, several months after their arrest, in strict solitary confinement in cells devoid of sunlight for nearly 23 hours a day constituted a serious violation of the Third and Fourth Geneva Conventions.

The ICRC was also concerned about the excessive and disproportionate use of force by some detaining authorities against persons deprived of their liberty involved during their internment during periods of unrest or escape attempts that caused death and serious injuries. The use of firearms against persons deprived of their liberty in circumstances where methods without using firearms could have yielded the same result could amount to a serious violation of International Humanitarian Law. The ICRC reviewed a number of incidents of shootings of persons deprived of their liberty with live bullets, which have resulted in deaths or injuries during periods of unrest related to conditions of internment or escape attempts. Investigations initiated by the CF into these incidents concluded that the use of firearms against persons deprived of their liberty was legitimate. However, non-lethal measures could have been used to obtain the same results and quell the demonstrations or neutralize persons deprived of their liberty trying to escape.

Since the beginning of the conflict, the ICRC has regularly brought its concerns to the attention of the CF. The observations in the present report are consistent with those made earlier on several occasions orally and in writing to the CF throughout 2003. In spite of some improvements in the materials conditions of internment, allegations of ill-treatment perpetrated by members of the CF against persons deprived of their liberty continued to be collected by the ICRC and thus suggested that the use of ill-treatment against persons deprived of their liberty went beyond exceptional cases and might be considered as a practice tolerated by the CF.

The ICRC report does not aim to be exhaustive with regard to breaches of International Humanitarian Law by the CF in Iraq. Rather, it illustrates priority areas that warrant attention and corrective action on the part of CF, in compliance with their International Humanitarian Law obligations.

Consequently the ICRC asks the authorities of the CF in Iraq:

— to respect at all times the human dignity, physical integrity and cultural sensitivity of the persons deprived of their liberty held under their control

— to set up a system of notifications of arrest to ensure quick and accurate transmission of information to the families of persons deprived of their liberty

— to prevent all forms of ill-treatment, moral or physical coercion of persons deprived of their liberty in relation to interrogation

— to set up an internment regime which ensures the respect of the psychological integrity and human dignity of the persons deprived of their liberty

— to ensure that all persons deprived of their liberty are allowed sufficient time every day outside in the sunlight, and that they are allowed to move and exercise in the outside yard

— to define and apply regulations and sanctions compatible with International Humanitarian Law and to ensure that persons deprived of their liberty are fully informed upon arrival about such regulations and sanctions to thoroughly investigate violations of International Humanitarian Law in order to determine responsibilities and prosecute those found responsible for violations of International Humanitarian Law

— to ensure that battle group units arresting individuals and staff in charge of internment facilities receive adequate training enabling them to operate in a proper manner and fulfill their responsibilities as arresting authority without resorting to ill-treatment or making excessive use of force.

* * *

C. Notes and Questions

1. Identify the initial use of force in each of the case studies of war in Iraq. Can you find more than one possibility? Why is it important to correctly identify the first use of force? What legal arguments do you find in the materials to justify any of the initial uses? What counter-arguments do you find? What sources of law and types of evidence have you relied on in identifying the first uses of force and the legal arguments for and against the legality of those first uses?

2. Even if an initial resort to armed force is lawful, can you argue that the way a conflict is conducted is equally important, as a matter of law, to the justification for war? Do you find any problems described in the materials respecting the conduct of either the Gulf War or the Iraq War? What sources of law and types of evidence did you find in the materials to support your arguments on the conduct of these conflicts?

3. Consider the range of actors involved in each of the armed conflicts. What are their roles with respect to the law relevant to the conflicts?

Where do they look for the law to guide their own conduct or to make claims regarding the unlawful conduct of others?

4. Can you identify how international law is enforced from these case studies? How does enforcement of international law compare with enforcing national law?

5. The fact that these armed conflicts occurred at all means the international legal system for peace and security failed. What weaknesses in the system in terms of either substantive rules or institutions do the case studies reveal? What strengths? How can the system be improved? What aspects of the system seem to be working well?

6. Are there times you think the law should be ignored to accomplish a greater good? What is the potential impact on the law of tolerating law violations on the basis of moral or policy arguments? Is the potential harm to international law of such tolerance possibly greater than tolerating law violations in national legal systems? Isn't the international legal system a far more fragile system, less able to withstand disrespect than national law? It lacks a regular court system, for example, so the decision on whether to violate the law in preference to a moral argument will be made by the law-breaker. Or is that very fragility a basis for arguing international law violations should be more readily tolerated than national law violations? Do either of the cases presented in the case studies present a possible example where force should have been used despite the fact doing so would violate international law? For further discussion of these issues, see *Iraq: One Year Later*, 2004 Proc. Am. Soc'y Int'l L. 261 and Right v. Might, International Law and the Use of Force (Louis Henkin et al., eds. 2d ed. 1991).

7. For more on the international law issues presented in the case studies, see Sean Murphy, *Assessing the Legality of Invading Iraq*, 92 Geo. L. Rev. 173 (2004); *Agora: Future Implications of the Iraq Conflict*, 97 Am. J. Int'l L. 553 (2003); *Agora: The Gulf Crisis in International & Foreign Relations Law*, 85 Am. J. Int'l L. (1991); Mary Ellen O'Connell, *Enforcing the Prohibition on the Use of Force: The U.N.'s Response to Iraq's Invasion of Kuwait*, 15 S. Ill. U. L.J. 453 (1991).

CHAPTER THREE

WHAT IS THE ROLE OF LAW IN THE USE OF FORCE?

Through the ages law has played two primary roles relative to the use of force. It has regulated when leaders may resort to war, and it has regulated how individuals engaged in armed conflict must conduct themselves. The law governing when force is used and how it is used have grown into two large and separate bodies of law commonly known by the Latin terms: the *jus ad bellum* (law to war) and *jus in bello* (law in war). These categories are typically studied separately—the first being most important to governments and other leaders of armed groups; the second to people actually engaged in fighting. But they have important overlaps—both practical and theoretical. Leaders who decide for war are ultimately responsible for how their armed forces actually fight. At Nuremberg, Germany's high political leaders were charged with war crimes and crimes against humanity as well as crimes against the peace. The rank and file of the German armed forces were not held legally responsible for their leaders' decisions to wage unlawful war, but neither were they honored for having fought in such a war. After the war, the heroes were those who joined the resistance.

It is also important to study both aspects of the law because there is not, in fact, such an easy division between them. Throughout this book you will finds areas where *ad bellum* and *in bello* rules overlap and influence each other. These can be seen by studying both topics together. For example, the principle of necessity is a core concept in both the *jus ad bellum* and the *jus in bello*. In the *jus ad bellum* the principle of necessity restricts the use of force to an option of last resort. In the *jus in bello*, force is only permitted when it is necessary to accomplish a military objective. We will discuss in future chapters whether necessity is really the same concept in both cases. If it is, then court cases or scholarly analysis of necessity in decisions to go to war can be cited in understanding the use of force during combat, and vice versa. It may also be the case that while the concepts were once separate, the two branches of the law on the use of force are growing more intertwined, eliminating past divisions.

Before turning to the law on the use of force proper, however, we will deal with another aspect of the role of law on the use of force. Despite the long pedigree of this law and the many rules and institutions associated with it, there are those who insist that law plays no role relative to the use of force. It is a view associated, as indicated in the Introduction, with Cicero's famous adage, "in war law is silent." As promised, we return to that existential challenge in this chapter. We will look at four arguments against the possibility of law on war. The first two are arguments that apply to both the *jus ad bellum* and the *jus in bello*—they have to do with the nature of war and the nature of international law. Some see war as the antithesis of law. Neither the decision for war, nor how it is conducted, can be subject to law. The second general argument is that international law is not law and since it is international law that we look to for regulation of the use of force, no law regulates it. The other two arguments are less extreme variations of the "no law" argument. A handful of scholars perennially raise the challenge that while international law may be real law, it has not developed viable rules to regulate either the decision for war or the conduct of war.

All of these arguments point to important weaknesses in the law on the use of force, but are they persuasive that international law is not playing a role in regulating the use of force? The general answer to the critics is that, while the law on the use of force is clearly not as robust as we would like, we nevertheless have strong evidence that it does indeed play a role, or more accurately, a variety of roles in regulating the use of force.

A. IS LAW ON FORCE POSSIBLE?

In addition to Cicero's, we find other famous rejections of law on war:

Carl Von Clausewitz, The Maximum Use of Force

ON WAR 75–77 (Michael Howard and Peter Par eds. & trans., 1984).

Kind-hearted people might of course think there was some ingenious way to disarm or defeat an enemy without too much bloodshed, and might imagine this is the true goal of the art of war. Pleasant as it sounds, it is a fallacy that must be exposed: war is such a dangerous business that the mistakes which come from kindness are the very worst. The maximum use of force is in no way incompatible with the simultaneous use of the intellect. If one side uses force without compunction, undeterred by the bloodshed it involves, while the other side refrains, the first will gain the upper hand. That side will force the other to follow suit; each will drive its opponent toward extremes, and the only limiting factors are the counterpoises inherent in war.

This is how the matter must be seen. It would be futile—even wrong—to try and shut one's eyes to what war really is from sheer distress at its brutality.

If wars between civilized nations are far less cruel and destructive than wars between savages, the reason lies in the social conditions of the states themselves and in their relationships to one another. These are the forces that give rise to war; the same forces circumscribe and moderate it. They themselves however are not part of war; they already exist before fighting starts. To introduce the principle of moderation into the theory of war itself would always lead to logical absurdity.

Two different motives make men fight one another: *hostile feelings* and *hostile intentions*. Our definition is based on the latter, since it is the universal element. Even the most savage, almost instinctive, passion of hatred cannot be conceived as existing without hostile intent; but hostile intentions are often unaccompanied by any sort of hostile feelings—at least by none that predominate. Savage peoples are ruled by passion, civilized peoples by the mind. The difference, however, lies not in the respective natures of savagery and civilization, but in their attendant circumstances, institutions, and so forth. The difference, therefore, does not operate in every case, but it does in most of them. Even the most civilized of peoples, in short, can be fired with passionate hatred for each other.

Consequently, it would be an obvious fallacy to imagine war between civilized peoples as resulting merely from a rational act on the part of their governments and to conceive of war as gradually ridding itself of passion, so that in the end one would never really need to use the physical impact of the fighting forces—comparative figures of their strength would be enough. That would be a kind of war by algebra.

Theorists were already beginning to think along such lines when the recent wars taught them a lesson. If war is an act of force, the emotions cannot fail to be involved. War may not spring from them, but they will still affect it to some degree, and the extent to which they do so will depend not on the level of civilization but on how important the conflicting interests are and on how long their conflict lasts.

If, then, civilized nations do not put their prisoners to death or devastate cities and countries, it is because intelligence plays a larger part in their methods of warfare and has taught them more effective ways of using force than the crude expression of instinct.

The invention of gunpowder and the constant improvement of firearms are enough in themselves to show that the advance of civilization has done nothing practical to alter or deflect the impulse to destroy the enemy, which is central to the very idea of war.

The thesis, then, must be repeated: war is an act of force, and there is no logical limit to the application of that force. Each side, therefore, compels its opponent to follow suit; a reciprocal action is started which must lead, in theory, to extremes.

Michael Howard, Constraints on Warfare

THE LAWS OF WAR 1–2 (Michael Howard et al., eds., 1994).

There is a crude assumption that in war societies act as if all is fair, that all normal moral constraints are suspended, and that they consider themselves entitled to do any damage necessary to destroy the enemy. Clausewitz gave currency to this view when he wrote: "War is an act of force to compel our enemy to do our will.... [A]ttached to force are certain self-imposed, imperceptible limitations hardly worth mentioning, known as international law and custom, but they scarcely weaken it."[a] He knew very well, however, that the conduct of war was subject to considerably greater and more perceptible limitations in his own time than it had been in the days of, say, Genghis Khan. He explained this by saying that "if wars between civilized nations are far less cruel and destructive than wars between savages, the reason lies in the social conditions of the states themselves and in their relationship to one another."[b] Restraints on war grew out of the cultures of the war-making societies, rather than being imposed on them by some transcendent moral order.

In fact, "savages," as Clausewitz described them (a word habitually employed during the era of the Enlightenment), are not more cruel and destructive in war than civilized peoples.[c] Anthropological studies show that although war in some form was endemic in most primitive societies, it was often highly ritualized and sometimes almost bloodless. It could be a *rite de passage* for adolescents, a quasi-religious ceremonial substituting for legal process, or a legitimized form of violent competition comparable to team sports in contemporary societies. Clausewitz's definition of war as an instrument of *Staatspolitik* was one that would not have been widely accepted, or indeed understood, in Europe before the fifteenth century, and perhaps even less in the rest of the world. There is no contribution in this volume on primitive warfare, and we would probably need a great many to cover it adequately. But our Western classical and medieval examples show the extent to which wars even in those societies were ritual or agonistic and, as such, subject to strict and generally recognized regulation.[d]

Quincy Wright, Law, War, and Peace

A STUDY OF WAR 173–74 (1964).

Among the hypotheses suggested to explain the recurrence of war was the inadequacy of the sources and sanctions of international law continually to keep that law an effective analysis of the changing interests of states and the changing values of humanity.

a. Carl von Clausewitz, *On War*, trans. Michael Howard and Peter Paret (Princeton: Princeton University Press, 1976), 75.

b. Ibid., 76.

c. See, e.g., Harry H. Turney–High, *Primitive War* (Columbia: University of South Carolina Press, 1949). For a full bibliography, see William T. Divale, *War in Prim-itive Socieites* (Santa Barbara, Calif.: Clio Press, 1973).

d. For the agonistic element in war, see Robert E. Osgood and Robert Tucker, Force, Order and Justice (Baltimore: Johns Hopkins University Press, 1967).

Although certain branches of law have as their end the definition and regulation of permissible violence (laws of war and of military occupation) and the organization of collective violence (military law and martial law) and all systems of law tolerate certain kinds of violence under certain circumstances (right of self-defense and police action), the normal end of law—the maintenance of order and justice—is hostile to violence. When Cicero wrote, *Inter arma silent legis*, he emphasized this generally accepted antithesis between law and violence. Political philosophers have emphasized the same antithesis when they have posited the social contract, establishing law and society, as the process of man's nature, which, if not a perpetual *bellum omnium contra omnes*, was at least a condition in which each man judged his own case, and violence was frequent. Violence has been considered synonymous with disorder and injustice, both of which are eliminated in the ideal legal community. The concept of war has included both law and violence. The same is true of the concept of peace, which, according to Augustine, is "tranquility in order." But order has never been maintained in practice without occasional violence against the evil doer. Peace may, then, be defined as the condition of a community in which order and justice prevail, internally among its members and externally in its relations with other communities.

It is the function of law to produce this condition—of municipal law to maintain internal peace in each state and of international law to maintain external peace among all states. As crime, rebellion, and insurrection are evidences of the imperfection of municipal law, so interventions, reprisals, and wars are evidences of the imperfection of international law. This proposition is not denied by the existence of abnormal law to regulate these conditions. Just as remedial medicine is necessary to rectify the imperfections of preventive medicine, so abnormal law is necessary to remedy the imperfections of normal law, or, if not to remedy them, at least to ameliorate their resulting evils.

———

Skepticism about law and war grew in the United States after the Second World War, especially among political scientists. Some were skeptical about law and war because they were skeptical of all international law. They have been dubbed international law "deniers." And, of course, if there is no international law, there can be no international law on the use of force—*ad bellum* or *in bello*. The American diplomat (trained in law), George Kennan, was apparently such a denier—he compared international law to a "strait jacket" on the running of foreign affairs.[1] Former US Secretary of

1. George Kennan, American Diplomacy, 1900–1950, 95–99 (1951). For a more compli-   cated view of international law, but ultimately one that denies law can constrain a

State Dean Acheson, also a lawyer, said, "Law simply does not deal with such questions of ultimate power...."[2]

The eminent international law scholar, Louis Henkin, has written that Kennan probably had in mind the international law on the use of force rather than all international law. Henkin, who served four years in combat during the Second World War, replied as follows to Kennan (and Acheson):

> ... [Y]ears of experience with the law of the Charter do not support the assertion that nations will not accept this law on the conclusion that it cannot work. All nations have appeared willing, even eager, to adhere to the United Nations Charter: they have found it at least desirable, perhaps necessary, to outlaw force as an instrument of change; and they have largely abided by this law.[3]

John Bolton, another American diplomat and lawyer, also generally denies that international law is law. With regard to the use of force, he wrote the following on NATO's bombing of Yugoslavia in 1999:

John R. Bolton, Clinton Meets "International Law" in Kosovo

WALL ST. J., April 5, 1999, at A23.

Criticism of the Clinton administration's decision to bomb Yugoslavia has been loudly accompanied by doubts about the legality of the military action. Some of the legal criticism has rested on constitutional objections to the president's actions, with opponents arguing that it's Congress's job to declare war. Other opponents have questioned whether the attacks can be justified in "international law." In fact, both arguments stem from the basic misconception that bad policy is also necessarily bad law.

As terribly misconceived as I believe the president's actions to be, there is little doubt that the U.S. and its NATO allies are acting lawfully in the international arena. Indeed, the "legal" arguments raised by Mr. Clinton's critics are fundamentally political and their purported legal bases ephemeral indeed.

* * *

The real lesson of Kosovo is that "international law" in political and military matters is increasingly exposed as an academic sham. While Mr. Clinton's policy is wrong, he has complete justification for NATO's actions, and neither he nor his supporters need to resort to exotic legal theories to find the requisite authority. If nothing else beneficial emerges from this crisis, perhaps it will at

---

nation's pursuit of power, see HANS MORGENTHAU, POLITICS AMONG NATIONS (1948); Morgenthau's followers have included such international law deniers as Kenneth Walz.

2. Remarks of Dean Acheson, (57 ASIL PROC 14 C1963).

3. Louis Henkin, How Nations Behave 325 (2d ed. 1979).

least give us a more realistic sense of the limits and inadequacies of the chimera of international legal theorizing.

Four years later, Bolton was a US Under Secretary of State, in charge of preventing proliferation of weapons of mass destruction. The following is an account of one of Mr. Bolton's encounters with international law as a government official.

Mary Ellen O'Connell, Search and Seizure v. The Proliferation Security Initiative

Ad Hoc War, in Krisensicherung Und Humänitarerer Schultz—Crisis Management and Humanitarian Protection 405, 418–20 (Horst Fischer et al, eds., 2004).

* * *

* * * President Bush announced the Proliferation Security Initiative (PSI) on May 31, 2003, during a speech in Poland.[a] The President called for "partnerships of states working in concert, employing their national capabilities to develop a broad range of legal, diplomatic, economic, military, and other tools to interdict threatening shipments of WMD and missile related equipment and technologies."[b] Apparently the Administration developed PSI to make similar seizures at sea like the one in December.

Spain hosted the first meeting to discuss the PSI in Madrid in June 12, 2003. The eleven participants included Australia, France, Germany, Italy, Japan, the Netherlands, Poland, Portugal, Spain, the United Kingdom, and the U.S.[c] In Madrid, the eleven participants unanimously agreed that there was a need to take active measures to control the flow of weapons of mass destruction (chemical, biological and nuclear weapons—WMD), missiles and related items. The participants emphasized the importance of preventing these weapons from falling into the hands of terrorists.

Shortly after the meeting, U.S. officials acknowledged in answer to media questions that some interceptions the group would like to make would require Security Council authorization.[d] By the time of the second PSI meeting in Brisbane, July 9–10, 2003, no request

---

a. Speech by Hon. Alexander Downer, M.P. Address at the Proliferation Security Inlitiative, Brisbane (July 9, 2003), *available at* www.foreignminister.gov.au/speeches/2003/030709_wmd.html

b. Rebecca Weiner, *Proliferation Security Initiative to Stem Flow of WMD Material* (July 16, 2003), *available at* http://cns.miis.edu/pubs/week/030716.htm

c. Chairman's Statement on the Proliferation Security Initiative, Brisbane Meeting (July 9–10, 2003), *available at* http://www.dfat.gov.au/globalissues/psi/chair_statement_0603.html.

d. Matt Kelley, *Admiral Says War With Korea Unlikely*, AP Online, June 26, 2003, *available at* 2003 WL 57826213.

for authorization had been made. Rather, John Bolton, Under–Secretary of State for Arms Control and International Security, said, "We are prepared to undertake interdictions right now and, if that opportunity arises, if we had actionable intelligence and it was appropriate, we would do it now." Bolton added, "There is broad agreement within the group that we have that authority." British diplomatic sources were said to be taken aback by Mr. Bolton's interpretation. A Foreign Office Spokesman said, "All 11 participants agreed that any action that might be taken would have to be consistent with international law."[e]

Within nine months of the Brisbane meeting, Mr. Bolton signed treaties with Liberia and Panama to get the consent of these states to search vessels flying their flags. His negotiation of bilateral treaties—international law in one of its most basic forms—could be interpreted by some as a reversal of his earlier position that international law on the use of force constitutes an "academic sham."

Statement by President: Panama's Signing of Ship Boarding Agreement

The United States welcomes Panama's signing today of a ship-boarding agreement that supports the efforts of the Proliferation Security Initiative (PSI) to stop the trade in deadly weapons and materials.

The agreement establishes streamlined procedures for American officials to request and board ships registered to Panama if those ships are suspected of carrying weapons of mass destruction, their delivery systems, or related materials. More ships sail under the Panamanian flag than that of any other nation. This agreement sends a strong signal to proliferators that the free nations of the world are determined to protect their people and preserve the peace.

This is the second bilateral ship-boarding agreement signed to support PSI. The United States and the Government of Liberia signed a similar agreement on February 11, 2004. Together, Panama and Liberia account for roughly 30 percent of the world's commercial shipping tonnage. We welcome this historic decision by the Government of Panama. And we urge other nations with large commercial shipping registries to follow the lead of Panama and Liberia to make a stand against proliferation.

---

e. Michael Evans, *U.S. Plans to Seize Suspects at Will*, THE TIMES (London), July 11, 2003, at 23.

In addition to these treaties, we have other indications that as a high US official, Mr. Bolton treats international law seriously. On May 6, 2002, he sent an unprecedented formal request to the United Nations Secretary General to indicate the US wished to terminate any legal obligation incurred by President Clinton when President Clinton signed the Rome Statute of the International Criminal Court. The US had no intention of ratifying the treaty, but Mr. Bolton's letter recognized that just signing a treaty can result in legal obligations. On December 13, 2001, the US also sent a formal notice to Russia as required to withdraw from the bilateral Anti–Ballistic Missile Treaty.[4]

In the minds of some, trying to control the use of force by law seems strange.[5] Aren't force and law antithetical? Isn't the use of force a sign that the legal regime has failed? The premise of these materials is that law and force must be mutually reinforcing on the international scene, just as on the domestic scene. More importantly, law should have an impact on national and international decision-making concerning vital issues of war and peace, just as on other major public issues. This view is not shared by all—not even by all international lawyers. But there is a wealth of experience that makes the position persuasive.

In domestic affairs, whether public or private, clients want their lawyers to help both in deciding what to do and in enabling the clients to do what they want to do with maximum benefits and minimum costs. Those are two closely related, though not identical, aims. Law is often directly relevant to both, but is almost never controlling. Most often, non-legal issues are the primary ones, whether the question is a contract and the primary concern is price, or a divorce and the principal concern is custody of children.

Similarly, in matters of international affairs, law is often a key factor, but rarely the decisive one. In the same sense, issues of when and under what circumstances it is lawful for an individual or State to use force are important domestic law questions in both the criminal law and civil law contexts.

This similarity between use of force and the role of law at the national and international levels holds true despite the significant differences that exist between the national and international communities. We think of our domestic legal system—in terms both of rules and institutions that apply those rules—as having the potential to cover all possible issues, with a legislature available to make law, administrative bodies to make regulations, an executive to implement the laws and regulations, and a judicial system to adjudicate disputes. International law, however, is more analogous to numerous islands in a sea of non-law—not lawlessness, but non-law in the sense that the international legal system simply has not addressed

---

4. *See* State Department press releases and documents, May 6, 2002 (letter of Mr. John Bolton to UN Secretary Genderal Kofi Ammar); Steven Mufson, *ABM Treaty May Be History, But Deterrence Doctrine Lives*, Wash. Post, Dec. 16, 2001, at A37.

5. Adapted from Thomas Ehrlich and Mary Ellen O'Connell, International Law and the Use of Force, 3–5 (1993).

most matters, at least not yet. At the same time, those who consider the matter for the first time are often struck by how much international law exists. The economics sphere is most obvious. One cannot send a letter, make a telephone call, buy a product from abroad, or do scores of other commonplace activities without bringing into play one of the many thousands of international agreements to which the United States is a party. Prior to World War I, the United States had entered into about 700 such agreements. Between the two world wars, another 600 were executed. In the 45 years since then, about 8,000 more were concluded and the United States joined several hundred international organizations.

A primary thesis of these materials is that law can and should have an impact on decision-making concerning vital issues of war and peace, just as law has an impact on decision-making relating to the domestic scene. During much of the 1980's, this view was opposed by influential members of the Reagan administration and supporters of that administration. As stated by Jeanne Kirkpatrick, then United States ambassador to the United Nations, "We cannot permit ourselves to feel bound by unilateral compliance with obligations which do in fact exist under the [United Nations] Charter, but are renounced by others. This is not what the rule of law is all about." Robert Bork, rejected nominee to the United States Supreme Court, put the matter more sharply: "By eliminating morality from its calculus, international law actually makes moral action appear immoral."

It can hardly be doubted that, in the American view, it would be a moral act to help a people overthrow a dictatorship that had replaced a government by force, thereby restoring democracy and freedom. Yet when our leaders act for such moral reasons, they are forced into continued explanation by international law. Many other commentators, particularly from abroad, were sharply critical of this approach. Commentator Lars–Eric Nelson, writing in 1989, was one example: "Since the Bork view appears to be prevailing, America's message to the world is that we are good, we are moral, and we will do what we think is right. Most Americans probably will agree. Just don't be surprised if nobody else does."

The conclusion of the Cold War, as Ambassador Kirkpatrick has written, offered a renewed opportunity to develop standards of multilateral compliance with international law that avoided the concerns that troubled her previously. This approach requires a central role for international law.

It is important, however, not to overstate the thesis that law can and should have a major impact on issues of war and peace. The thesis is not that law can or should be involved in any "but for" sense—"but for" legal considerations, decisions would necessarily be different. Rather, those considerations constitute one of several clusters of considerations, along with political, social, and economic concerns.

B.   RESORT TO FORCE: *JUS AD BELLUM*

A more persistent critique of law on war, one that comes from within the ranks of international law, is the argument that the widespread use of force means that states do not support the *ad bellum* rules. At various times since the adoption of the Charter, scholars have taken stock of the state of international relations and have concluded that there are, in reality, no rules restricting the use of armed force.

Thomas M. Franck, Who Killed Article 2(4)?

64 Am. J. Int'l L. 809–810 (1970)*

Twenty-five years ago, the Allied nations gathered at San Francisco in the warming glow of victory and signed a solemn treaty giving effect to their determination "to save succeeding generations from the scourge of war ..." and "to ensure, by the acceptance of principles and the institution of methods, that armed force shall not be used, save in the common interest...." Specifically, they undertook in Article 2(4) to "refrain in their international relations from the threat or use of force against the territorial integrity or political independence of any state...." They also committed themselves to "settle their international disputes by peaceful means...."

Yet today the high-minded resolve of Article 2(4) mocks us from its grave. That the rules against the use of force should have had so short a life appears due to various factors. The rules, admirable in themselves, were seemingly predicated on a false assumption: that the wartime partnership of the Big Five would continue, providing the means for policing the peace under the aegis of the United Nations. They appeared to address themselves to preventing conventional military aggression at the very moment in history when new forms of attack were making obsolete all prior notions of war and peace strategy. And the Charter itself provided enough exceptions and ambiguities to open the rules to deadly erosion.

But if the rules prohibiting recourse to force were imperfect and, to some extent, already obsolescent by the time the Charter came into operation, this does not alone account for the demise of Article 2(4). Blame for this must be shared by powerful, and even some not-so-powerful, states which, from time to time over the past twenty-five years, have succumbed to the temptation to settle a score, to end a dispute or to pursue their national interest through the use of force.

The practice of these states has so severely shattered the mutual confidence which would have been the *sine qua non* of an operative rule of law embodying the precepts of Article 2(4) that, as with Ozymandias, only the words remain. Perhaps the nations, given the changed realities of the postwar quarter-century, could not realistically have been expected to live with Article 2(4). But its demise does raise a serious question for the nations: Having

* Footnotes omitted.

violated it, ignored it, run roughshod over it, and explained it away, can they live without it?

Louis Henkin, The Reports of the Death of Article 2(4) Are Greatly Exaggerated

65 Am. J. Int'l L. 544, 544–45 (1971)*

Dr. Thomas Franck, pathologist for the ills of the international body politic, has pronounced the death of the heart of the United Nations Charter, and proceeded to tell us who killed it. In my view, the death certificate is premature and the indictment for legicide must be redrawn to charge lesser though aggravated degrees of assault. Article 2(4) lives and, while its condition is grave indeed, its maladies are not necessarily terminal. There is yet time to prescribe, transplant, salvage, to keep alive at all cost the principal norm of international law in our time.

It is difficult to quarrel with Dr. Franck's diagnosis of the ills of the Charter, congenital, hereditary, acquired, and induced: the mistaken original assumption of Big–Power unanimity; the changing character of war; the loopholes for "self-defense" and "regional" action; the lack of impartial means to find and characterize facts; the disposition of nations to take law into their own hands and distort and mangle it to their own purpose. Distracted and distraught by these ills, one can indeed fall into the conclusion that Article 2(4) is virtually dead, but that, I believe, would mistake the lives and the ways of the law.

My principal difference with Dr. Franck's diagnosis is that it judges the vitality of the law by looking only at its failures. The purpose of Article 2(4) was to establish a norm of national behavior and to help deter violation of it. Despite common misimpressions, Article 2(4) has indeed been a norm of behavior and has deterred violations. In inter-state as in individual penology, deterrence often cannot be measured or even proved, but students of politics agree that traditional war between nations has become less frequent and less likely. The sense that war is not done has taken hold, and nations more readily find that their interests do not in fact require the use of force after all. Expectations of international violence no longer underlie every political calculation of every nation, and war plans lie buried deep in national files. Even where force is used, the fact that it is unlawful cannot be left out of account and limits the scope, the weapons, the duration, the purposes for which force is used. Of the "some one hundred separate outbreaks of hostilities" to which Dr. Franck refers, less than fingers-full became "war" or successful conquest, and hundreds of other instances of conflict of interest and tension have not produced even an international shot: cold war has remained cold,

* Footnotes omitted.

threats to the peace have remained threats, issues have remained only issues, for peaceful settlement or non-settlement (as in Cyprus, Kashmir, Berlin).

Many will refuse credit to Article 2(4), attributing the lack of traditional war to other factors—to nuclear weapons and the changing character of war to greater territorial stability, to other changes in national interests reducing national temptation to use force. If it were so, Article 2(4) would not be the less a norm: law often reflects dispositions to behavior as much as it shapes them. Like others, Dr. Franck concludes that, by the time the Charter came, "new forms of attack were making obsolete all prior notions of war and peace strategy." If it were so, one might yet conclude that that development reflected and supported Article 2(4) and made it viable. In fact, nothing, alas, has rendered war obsolete— between India and Pakistan, India and China, Turkey and Greece, Honduras and El Salvador, Egypt and Israel. The occasions and the causes of war remain. What has become obsolete is the notion that nations are as free to indulge it as ever, and the death of that notion is accepted in the Charter.

Despite Henkin's insight into the actual vitality of the norm prohibiting force, Jean Combacau, writing in 1986, concluded:

> [T]he international community no longer believes in the system of the Charter, because the collective guarantee, in exchange for which its members had renounced their individual right to resort to force, does not work, and no real substitute for it has been found. In any society a collective system of guarantees protects the interests, rightful or not, of the members; when the authority which has the sole legal power to make this system work fails to do so, States will take back their individual means of protecting their own interests because they are no longer receiving that for which they had exchanged their freedom of action; that is, they will take back these means *de facto*, while still paying limited and derisory lip service, traces of which are to be found in U.N. practice. But whatever the official pretense, and perhaps the legal situation, the international community is in fact back where it was before 1945: in the state of nature; and as is well-known, the notion of self-defence makes no sense there.[6]

In the International Court of Justice (ICJ) in a case involving the use of force brought by Nicaragua against the United States had this to say about the frequent uses of force in violation of the prohibition on the use of force:

---

6. Jean Combacau, *The Exception of Self–Defense in U.N. Practice, in* THE CURRENT LEGAL REGULATION OF THE USE OF FORCE 9, 32 (A. Cassese ed., 1986) (footnotes omitted).

Military and Paramilitary Activities in and Against Nicaragua

(Nicaragua v. U.S.), 1986 I.C.J. 14, paras. 184–186 (June 27).

* * *

184.   The mere fact that States declare their recognition of certain rules is not sufficient for the Court to consider these as being part of customary international law, and as applicable as such to those States. Bound as it is by Article 38 of its Statute to apply, *inter alia*, international custom "as evidence of a general practice accepted as law", the Court may not disregard the essential role played by general practice. Where two States agree to incorporate a particular rule in a treaty, their agreement suffices to make that rule a legal one, binding upon them; but in the field of customary international law, the shared view of the Parties as to the content of what they regard as the rule is not enough. The Court must satisfy itself that the existence of the rule in the *opinio juris* of States is confirmed by practice.

185.   In the present dispute, the Court, while exercising its jurisdiction only in respect of the application of the customary rules of non-use of force and non-intervention, cannot disregard the fact that the Parties are bound by these rules as a matter of treaty law and of customary international law. Furthermore, in the present case, apart from the treaty commitments binding the Parties to the rules in question, there are various instances of their having expressed recognition of the validity thereof as customary international law in other ways. It is therefore in the light of this "subjective element"—the expression used by the Court in its 1969 Judgment in the North Sea Continental Shelf cases (*I.C.J. Reports 1969*, p. 44)—that the Court has to appraise the relevant practice.

186.   It is not to be expected that in the practice of States the application of the rules in question should have been perfect, in the sense that States should have refrained, with complete consistency, from the use of force or from intervention in each other's internal affairs. The Court does not consider that, for a rule to be established as customary, the corresponding practice must be in absolutely rigorous conformity with the rule. In order to deduce the existence of customary rules, the Court deems it sufficient that the conduct of States should, in general, be consistent with such rules, and that instances of State conduct inconsistent with a given rule should generally have been treated as breaches of that rule, not as indications of the recognition of a new rule. If a State acts in a way prima facie incompatible with a recognized rule, but defends its conduct by appealing to exceptions or justifications contained within the rule itself, then whether or not the State's

conduct is in fact justifiable on that basis, the significance of that attitude is to confirm rather than to weaken the rule.

Nevertheless, in 2002, the rules were declared dead again, this time by Michael Glennon:

> [S]ince 1945, dozens of member states have engaged in well over 100 inter-state conflicts that have killed millions of people. This record of violation is legally significant. The international legal system is voluntary and states are bound only by rules to which they consent. A treaty can lose its binding effect if a sufficient number of parties engage in conduct that is at odds with the constraints of the treaty. The consent of United Nations member states to the general prohibition against the use of force, as expressed in the Charter, has in this way been supplanted by a changed intent as expressed in deeds.... It seems the Charter has, tragically, gone the way of the 1928 Kellogg–Briand Pact which purported to outlaw war and was signed by every major belligerent in World War II.[7]

In the 2000 edition of her book, *International Law and the Use of Force*, Christine Gray had already responded to arguments like Glennon's, pointing out that such arguments were based only on actual uses of force, and

> discount what states say in reaction to the use of force by other states; they claim that the absence of a Security Council or General Assembly resolution or of any sanctions against the state using force means that its behaviour should be seen not as a breach of international law but as the emergence of a new right to use force.
>
> The effect of this argument is compounded by the fact that some of these writers also discount what the states using force actually say in justification of their use of force and try to extract new rights to use force on the basis of the actions of the states using force. That is, they ignore the fact that states generally do not claim revolutionary new rights to use force, but try to defend their use of force by claiming self-defence or other legal justifications.[8]

In 2003, the International Court of Justice was called upon again to decide another case on the use of force, this one brought by Iran against the United States. It found, as it had in the Nicaragua Case, that the United States used force against Iran in violation of international law rules.

---

7. Michael J. Glennon, *How War Left the Law Behind*, NY Times, Nov. 21, 2002, at A33; *see also* Michael J. Glennon, *Preempting Terrorism: The Case for Anticipatory Self–Defense*, Weekly Standard, Jan. 28, 2002, at 24.

8. Christine Gray, International and the Use of Force 18 (2000); *see also* Mary Ellen O'Connell, *Releasing the Dogs of War, Review of Christine Gray's International Law and the Use of Force*, 97 Am. J. Int'l L. 446, 446–49 (2003).

Only Judge Simma, in a separate opinion, spoke to the viability of law on the use of force:

Oil Platforms Case

(Iran v. US) 2003 ICJ (Sep. Op. Judge Simma)

6.   * * * I find it regrettable that the Court has not mustered the courage of restating, and thus reconfirming, more fully fundamental principles of the law of the United Nations as well as customary international law (principles that in my view are of the nature of *jus cogens*) on the use of force, or rather the prohibition on armed force, in a context and at a time when such a reconfirmation is called for with the greatest urgency. * * * Everybody will be aware of the current crisis of the United Nations system of maintenance of peace and security, of which Articles 2(4) and 51 are cornerstones. We currently find ourselves at the outset of an extremely controversial debate on the further viability of the limits on unilateral military force established by the United Nations Charter. In this debate, "supplied" with a case allowing it to do so, the Court ought to take every opportunity to secure that the voice of the law of the Charter rise above the current cacophony.* * *[T]he present Judgment is an exercise in inappropriate self-restraint.

C.   THE APPLICATION OF FORCE: *JUS IN BELLO*

Despite the intense doctrinal debate that has lasted for decades over the existence of law to restrain resort to force, we have seen less debate about the existence of law restraining how force is used, but it does exist:

Geoffrey Best, The *Jus In Bello* Vindicated

HUMANITY IN WARFARE 10–15 (1980)(footnotes omitted).

Skepticism about the value of the law of war is nothing new. Anyone who writes or thinks about it has to make up his mind whether the idea that it is one of civilization's triumphs is a boon or a bane to mankind. The changing terms of its justification from time to time are part of its history, and will be included below. But something ought to be said about it in these opening pages.

There seem to me to be two skeptical criticisms which need to be met: first, that while it does no particular harm, the law of war does no particular good either, and may therefore be discounted as a standing failure; second, that it does positive harm, and had therefore better be abolished as a standing nuisance.

The first line of skepticism has this much firmly to be said for it, that the law of war is obviously more liable than any other branch of law to fall short of its goal. Its mission, strictly speaking, is impossible. It seeks to introduce moderation and restraint into a medium peculiarly insusceptible to those qualities. Definitions and descriptions of war alike agree that parts at least of its essence are passion, violence, and unpredictability. Even the most self-consciously controlled, chivalrous, entirely professional wars have their moments of confusion and nastiness, and most campaigns and wars are nothing like that anyway. Is it reasonable, for example, to get cross when a thirsty, sleepless, over-worked, anxious young officer with death in the air all round him fails to keep sedulously 'within the law' when we know very well that much lighter pressures bend the law-abidingness of even the most respectable pillars of our communities, not to mention their less respectable flying-buttresses? No one should be surprised that the law of war is at the best of times never more than imperfectly observed, and at worse times is very poorly observed indeed.

But this line of criticism goes deeper. At least, it may argue, the codes and systems of law which your accountants, garage owners and dons are expected to observe are generally accepted; no one makes radical criticisms of them, they are in quite good working order, it is clearly in almost everybody's interest to observe them almost all the time, and there is an effective machinery of detection, enforcement and punishment waiting in the wings to help concentrate the minds of possible deviants at critical moments of temptation. Such can be said of any healthy branch of law or legal system. The requirements of the law and the sanction of the law go together. How different, however, must appear the system of international law, especially the branch of it with which we are concerned! The great difference between international law and any system of national law lies in the reality and effectiveness of the sanctions attending breaches of the latter. One famous school of jurisprudence maintains that there is simply no law where there is no sovereign power to enforce it. Anyone can understand that laws without reliable means of enforcement lack much of their value and force. International law by definition has no means of enforcement other than what its participants agree to submit to. There is no international, or rather *supra*national, sovereign. The International Court of The Hague only handles those limited classes of disputes which States choose to allow it to handle. It suits those States' interests to submit thus far to its judgments. The European Court at Luxembourg has gone further. The member States of the European Community have accepted quite a large obligation to conform to its common law; but this expressly excludes matters of national defence and security. When it comes to matters with a military aspect, States are normally at their most sovereign; the attempt to institute an international criminal court, capable of enforcing among other things the law of war, has so far utterly failed, nor is there any present prospect that things will change. Whatever may be the sanctions of the law of war, they do not include a known and inescapable court with some sovereign power behind it. One of Britain's greatest experts on the law of war, Thomas Erskine Holland, a man who as a matter of fact believed profoundly in it and fought for it nobly, nevertheless thought it proper in 1880 to describe international law as 'the vanishing point of jurisprudence'; an exercise in legal perspective to which his no less distinguished successor Hersh Lauterpacht has added the observation, that 'If international law is, in some ways, at the vanishing point of law, the law of war is, perhaps even more conspicuously, at the vanishing point of international law.'

Such judgments, even from such men, being possible, we should perhaps not so much complain that the law of war does not work well, as marvel that it works at all. And yet it does work. Almost all international wars, and some major civil wars, since the eighteenth century have been softened by the operation of the law of war. There has often been room for further softening. Even vestigial recollections of the law seem to have disappeared at some bad moments and on some dark fronts. Beastliness occurred even where everyone had apparently been trying to behave well. But the weight of the evidence is unmistakable, that the law of war has done nothing but good, and the implication is clear, that wars where it was not enforced, known, or even dimly apprehended, were the more horrible for their lack of it. Legal precisians who are reluctant to grant this, fail to note how much the extreme weakness of formal sanctions is compensated by ordinary muddled human sentiment and sentimentality; the personal paradox of man's mixed nature within the social paradox of war.

The second line of criticism, the more worried one that the law of war actually does harm, has to be answered in different terms. What is thought (by the critics answered in the preceding paragraph—not by me) to do neither much harm nor much good may at any rate be left where it is. What is alleged to do positive harm had better be abolished. This charge, which has turned up in one form or another throughout the centuries and has obvious attractions for people with particularly passionate or absolute casts of mind, was put by just such a person, Tolstoy, into the mouth of Prince Andrew Bolkhonsky in a celebrated passage in *War and Peace*. It came when he was discussing the war—and war in general—with Pierre Bezhukov.

> 'Not take prisoners,' continued Prince Andrew, 'that by itself would quite change the whole war and make it less cruel. As it is we have played at war.... We play at magnanimity and all that stuff. Such magnanimity and sensibility are like the magnanimity and sensibilities of a lady who faints when she sees a calf being killed; she is so kind-hearted that she can't look at blood, but enjoys eating the calf served up with sauce. They talk to us of the rules of war, of chivalry, of flags of

truce, of mercy to the unfortunate and so on. It's all rubbish. I saw chivalry and flags of truce in 1805. They humbugged us and we humbugged them. They plunder other peoples' houses, issue false paper money, and worst of all they kill my children and my father, and then talk of rules of war and magnanimity to foes! Take no prisoners but kill and be killed! ... If there was none of this magnanimity in war, we should go to war only when it was worth while going to certain death, as now.... War is not courtesy but the most horrible thing in life; and we ought to understand that, and not play at war.... The air of war is murder; the methods of war are spying, treachery, and their encouragement, the ruin of a country's inhabitants, robbing them or stealing to provision the army, and fraud and falsehood termed military craft....'

This is strong stuff, and anyone who has got far enough outside his conventionally patriotic and aggressive self to be able to look at war dispassionately knows it is 'true'; as also is 'true' so much of what Tolstoy wrote, both in that epic and later, about patriotism and militarism. Yet one is not bound to be persuaded by it. Tolstoy probably put it more fiercely than anyone else; but the argument was not new when he took it up, and as good an answer to it as any I have read had in fact been given, about the time Tolstoy was getting his first direct military experiences, by the British radical MP, John Roebuck. In the course of a searching review of *Napier's Peninsular War*, he thus met Prince Andrew's argument:

It has indeed been said that, in those who wish to diminish strife, it is unwise to render the intercourse of warring armies less ferocious and destructive. By stripping war of its horrors, it is supposed that we foster a warlike spirit, and invest the horrible business of slaughter with an attractive and deceiving character. If, indeed, we could hope to put an end to all war, by making it terrible, then we might admit the justice of this argument; but of this happy state of universal peace we have no expectation; neither do we believe that we should conduce to its attainment by creating and increasing ferocious habits amongst opposing nations. Cruelty begets cruelty—one atrocity creates another, by way of reprisal—and national animosity is kept alive and heightened by a desire to gratify personal hatred and revenge.

Tolstoy himself evidently came later to similar conclusions. Through Prince Andrew he aired some of his strong thoughts about the war problem, and one cannot doubt that they appealed strongly to the violent and aggressive aspects of his personality. But in the long run he turned away from that radical solution and adopted instead the equally radical pacifist one; no less absolute, and (as those of his admirers who retained some critical faculties at once recognized) no less satisfying to his will towards moral domination, since like the Prince Andrew solution it also disposed, god-like, of the powers of life and death. Most varieties of pacifism are less life-denying than that ruthless form of it espoused by the aged Tolstoy, which, taken seriously, is a way of death rather than life. But Tolstoy's pacifism, like other pacifisms, at any rate contains a solution to the war problem, namely, the belief that the appetite for war will diminish and shrivel in proportion as people offer not resistance and counter-violence but love and nonresistance to those who threaten them. Whether one's admiring respect for this belief and so many of those who adhere to it leads one to be a pacifist or not depends first, I suppose, on whether one thinks this a plausible estimate of probabilities, and second, on how much one thinks it matters if the estimate turns out to be mistaken. "The pacifist argument that it pays everyone not to have wars runs up against the fact that it would pay some people, in a world where others are pacifist, to make war on the pacifists."

In between the positions of unrestrained and absolute violence on the one hand, unresisting and absolute non-violence on the other—which are, in not wholly dissimilar ways, consistent responses to the question what to do about the horrors of war—comes the position described in this book: accepting war as a more or less regrettable recurrence in the mixed moral experience of mankind, without abandoning hope of sooner or later reducing its incidence to near-vanishing-point; in the meantime, restricting the extent of its horrors by observing the laws and rules of war, appealing partly to the softer side of human nature, partly to plain self-interest (which may or may not be thought the worse side). Those who adopt this standpoint are fortified by a belief that the law of war has on balance done more good than harm. By definition, they do not expect too much. Richard Falk, one of the United States' most powerful writers about the contemporary law of war, has wisely remarked upon 'an ironic tendency for people to expect law in international affairs to do more for the order and welfare of the community than it does in domestic affairs. Perhaps', he speculates, 'law is given special duties in world affairs to compensate for the weak international social structure; when these extravagant expectations are disappointed, the contributions actually made by law to world order are extravagantly neglected.'

* * *

D.   THE INTERCONNECTIONS OF *JUS AD BELLUM* AND *JUS IN BELLO*

At the outset of this Chapter, we spoke of the interconnections that you will see between the *jus ad bellum* and the *jus in bello* throughout this book. Here is an excerpt from an important article describing those intersections:

Christopher Greenwood, The Relationship Between Ius Ad Bellum and Ius In Bello

9 Rev. Int'l Stud. 221, 232–33 (1983).

Ius ad bellum and *ius in bello* are closer today than they have been for over two centuries. Both are aspects of the same problem in that both seek to impose legal restraints upon international violence. Whereas in the past they operated at different stages, they now apply simultaneously so that international law now applies to all aspects of armed conflict. Nevertheless, they remain distinct branches of international law, not merely for historical reasons but because they are logically independent of each other, operate in different ways, with different degrees of precision and different sanctions. They are separate but complementary systems of rules, which are capable of being studied and applied separately but which must both be considered in evaluating the legality of a state's use of force. To regard them as being in competition is nonsense. Of course one can say that if the *ius ad bellum* were respected by all, the *ius in bello* would be superfluous; but the *ius ad bellum* is not respected by all and is unlikely to be so respected unless there is a major restructuring of international society. The argument that the existence of the *ius in bello* merely encourages conflict by displaying a lack of confidence in the *ius ad bellum* and by making war more palatable simply does not hold good. It is not the existence of rules for the conduct of war which causes states to resort to force but more fundamental factors in international relations. Nor is there any evidence that if there were no humanitarian restraints on war states would be more likely to avoid it— there has, after all, been no shortage in this century of wars of the most horrific savagery. Both *ius ad bellum* and *ius in bello*, therefore, remain essential parts of international law and an understanding of their distinct, yet closely related characters is crucial to any discussion of the use of force in international relations.

E.   Notes, Questions, and Problems

1. Judging by the evidence you found in the case studies, which of the scholars briefly mentioned in the Chapter, in your view, provides the most persuasive argument about the existence (or lack thereof) of a rule prohibiting the use of armed force: Franck, Henkin, Combacau, Glennon, Gray, or Simma? Would you change your view if you knew Professor Franck in 2001–2002 wrote that the Charter rules applied to the US/UK use of force against Afghanistan? *See* Thomas Franck, *Terrorism and the Right of Self-Defense*, 95 AJIL 839 (2001); *see also* Thomas Franck, What Happens Now? The United Nations After Iraq 97 AJIL 607 (2003). Thomas Franck, Recourse to Force: State Action Against Threats and Armed Attacks (2002).

2. All of the scholars mentioned in Note 1 have concerns about the current health of law on the use of force. What would it take, do you think, to improve the effectiveness of law on the use of force? In considering this question, think first about what this law is for. What do you think we hope to accomplish by having law on the use of force? Consider as you read further in this book what it would take to improve the law. Or do you agree with Cicero and von Clausewitz?

3. If you believe that law on the use of force is a contradiction in terms, how would you advise a national policy maker as his or her international law expert? What would you advise regarding your own country's decisions to use force? How would you advise that your country react to other countries' use of force? What about training your country's military regarding law on the use of force? Would you advise pulling out of the many ongoing efforts to further develop this law in international organizations, international tribunals, the academy and among governments? What about the observation of Professor Barbara Stark: "It may be that, '[i]f law does not recognize power it will be marginalized,' but if power does not recognize law it will be despised."[9]

4. Why do you imagine that the military of most countries and through time have been among the strongest supporters of law on the use of force? Can you think of practical as well as normative reasons why this might be so? Consider these questions as well as the role of the military in the development of law on the use of force as you read the material in the next Chapter on the historical development of law on the use of force.

5. In addition, as you consider the historical development of the law on the use of force, think about the goals various actors had in promoting law on the use of force. Notice when they succeeded and when they failed. Can you see patterns or themes through history in the development of law on the use of force? Do those give you ideas about how this law can be improved, if you are one of those who believe improvement is possible?

6. Problem: The former leader of Iraq, Saddam Hussein, was charged in June 2004, with, among other crimes, the invasion of Kuwait and war crimes (*in bello* violations). If you were his court-appointed defense counsel, would you argue that there is no law prohibiting the use of force, citing, for example, Bolton or Glennon? Would you argue that there is no law prohibiting *in bello* crimes? Consider the arguments for that position in the excerpt by Best. Consider also the arguments that no international law exists or none on the use of force. Would you have any concerns in the area of professional ethics in making these arguments? *See Iraqi Special Tribunal Head Discusses Saddam Trial with Kuwaitis*, AGENCE FR-PRESSE, July 8, 2004 WL 85340233.

---

9. Barbara Stark, *What We Talk About When We Talk About War*, 32 STAN. J. INT'L L. 91 (1996) (reviewing THOMAS EHRLICH AND MARY ELLEN O'CONNELL, INTERNATIONAL LAW AND THE USE OF FORCE (1993)).

PART II

The Historic Development of International Law on the Use of Force

CHAPTER FOUR

RESTRICTING THE RESORT TO FORCE

This chapter traces the development of limits on resort to force from the rise of modern international law to the adoption of the United Nations Charter.

A. FROM ROME TO THE HAGUE

The origins of contemporary law *ad bellum* can be traced to Roman law and beyond. St. Augustine (354–430) drew on the Greeks and Romans to persuade pacifist early Christians that using limited force in a just cause could be consistent with Christian values. International law still permits the use of coercion in a limited way to achieve certain permitted ends. Thus, Augustine's just war doctrine remains at the foundation of contemporary thinking about the resort to war.

Augustine is unquestionably one of the great thinkers on the question of whether a society should use armed force, and, if so, when and how. Histories of the international law on the use of force inevitably make reference to Augustine's just war doctrine as an important milestone on the road to the contemporary rules regulating resort to force and the conduct of war.[1] Educated in the early Christian pacifist tradition, Augustine, nevertheless, responded to the use of violence against his own community with a doctrine of justifiable war.[2] His doctrine not only permitted Christians to protect themselves against marauding bandits, but also opened the way to justifying force in response to a broad array of provocations. Eventually Augustine's followers built the just war doctrine to the point it could justify war to create the Holy Roman Empire.

Before Augustine, many early Christians would not become soldiers, would not fight back when attacked, and did not consider the use of coercion appropriate for establishing order in community life. Even among the earliest Christians, however, not all accepted strict pacifism. One sect, the Donatists, actually embraced violence.[3] They preyed on pacifist Christians,

---

1. *See, e.g.,* Benedetto Conforti, *The Doctrine of "Just War" and Contemporary International Law,* 2002 IT. YBK. INT'L L. 3, 3–4; YORAM DINSTEIN, WAR, AGGRESSION, AND SELF-DEFENCE 59–61 (3d ed. 2001).

2. WILHELM G. GREWE, THE EPOCHS OF INTERNATIONAL LAW 108–111 (Michael Byers trans. & rev'd, 2000); ARTHUR NUSSBAUM, A CONCISE HISTORY OF THE LAW OF NATIONS 35 (rev'd ed., 1962).

3. *See Donatists* in THE CATHOLIC ENCYCLOPEDIA, *available at* http://www.newadvent.org/cathen/05121a.htm. The Donatists

and were a primary inducement for Augustine in considering how a Christian could use force while remaining true to the Gospel values of peace and non-violence. Drawing on Greek and Roman just war thinking as a foundation, Augustine added Christian elements to produce a hybrid doctrine. The Romans, and prominently Cicero, taught that war could only be used to fight for a just cause, eventually to achieve peace. Aristotle had similarly taught that peace was the ultimate just cause of war.[4] Peace was also among the highest Christian values, so Augustine reasoned that achieving peace could be a just cause of war for Christians as it had been for Cicero and Aristotle. Augustine concluded that using limited war when necessary as "a means of preserving or restoring peace" was both a moral and an acceptable action for faithful Christians.[5] In a letter to St. Boniface, he wrote:

> Peace should be the object of your desire; war should be waged only as a necessity and waged only that God may by it deliver men from the necessity and preserve them peace. For peace is not sought in order to [be] the kindling of war, but war is waged in order that peace may be obtained.[6]

Within this broader category of fighting to restore peace, Augustine included fighting to restore what was stolen, be it land, people, or property. It is also just to respond to wrongdoing in an attempt to prevent future wrongs. War simply in the pursuit of power or revenge is unjust,[7] but war to implement the Gospel is arguably consistent with the Gospel.

Augustine introduced limits to both when and how force might be used. He presented his conception as a set of rules borrowing the Roman law format and infusing it with the substance of Christian moral teaching.[8]

Despite the limits Augustine placed on the causes and conduct of war, after him the idea of fighting in a just cause transformed the place of war in Christian thinking. Fighting to preserve and promote the Church became a noble and virtuous thing,[9] and from that conception the just war doctrine created the philosophical conditions to establish a Christian empire. Once all the world was converted to Christianity, peace would prevail and all fighting would end. These ideas, combined with more secular human ambitions, resulted in the Holy Roman Empire that lasted from the

---

interpreted Christ's words to Peter, that Peter put away his sword the night of the arrest by the Romans, to mean literally "put away swords." They did not understand this as a teaching against the use of violence. They substituted clubs, knives, stones and other weapons as alternatives to the forbidden sword in conducting frenzies of violence. *Id.,* at 7. *See also* GREWE, *supra* note 2, at 108–11.

4. Joachim von Elbe, *The Evolution of the Concept of the Just War in International Law,* 33 AJIL 665, 666,n.9 (1939); *citing* the *Nicomachean Ethics,* Book X, Ch. VI XVII, 6 and; *Politics,* VII, 14.

5. GREWE, *supra* note 2, at 107. (Latin re-phrasing omitted).

6. THE LAW OF WAR: A DOCUMENTARY HISTORY 7 (Leon Friedman ed., 1972).

7. NUSSBAUM, *supra* note 2, at 35.

8. Von Elbe *supra* note 4, at 665.

9. Geoffrey Parker, *Early Modern Europe, in* THE LAWS OF WAR, CONSTRAINTS ON WARFARE IN THE WESTERN WORLD 40, 43 (Michael Howard ed., 1994).

crowning of Charlemagne in 800[10] to the end of the Thirty Years' War with the signing of the Peace of Westphalia in 1648.

During this long period, scholars continued to develop the just war doctrine. The most influential just war scholar of the Middle Ages, Thomas Aquinas (1225–1274), is credited with systematizing Augustine's work. This systematization, while not adding much of substance, gave the doctrine more of a law-like form, one that Aquinas's successors invariably followed.[11] Aquinas set three core conditions for a just war. He required: 1.) a declaration of war by a person with authority; 2.) a just cause, and 3.) the right intention by those waging the war.[12] After Aquinas, scholars developed lists of just causes including violations of sovereign territory, treaty breaches, breaches of diplomatic immunity, and other wrongs. Many of these would come to form the core of international law. Aquinas did add the new idea that "war should pursue the general interest, the common good...."[13] In addition to looking at Aquinas, just war scholars also returned to Augustine, the Canon Law, the Romans and the Bible. They looked to the military codes (codes of chivalry) and actual practice of warring parties to develop ever-more sophisticated versions of the doctrine.[14]

Beside these scholarly endeavors aimed at regulating war, popular movements sought to preserve to some extent the early Christian ideal of pacifism. For example, the "Peace of God" movement, begun in 11th century France sought to protect the weak in time of war and to limit the days for warfare to Mondays through Wednesdays.[15] Some of these efforts to limit war, scholarly and popular, met with success—certainly in cases where a leader had deep religious faith. Church teaching to respect the limits on war could be enforced when necessary against these individuals through various sanctions. Bishops could compel obedience through the threat of excommunication or the withholding of sacraments. "[W]e know, by the example of Henry IV, who knelt upon the snowy ground at Canoss before [Pope] Gregory VII, how heavily such sanctions could weigh upon a rebel."[16] "[T]his powerful combination of natural divine law, ecclesiastical precept, military law, common custom, and self-interest ... coalesced to impart a new and enduring consistency in the principles regulating when and how war could be conducted between 1550 and 1700."[17]

The form was consistent perhaps, but elements within the structure of what was becoming known as the law of war was changing. All agreed that war required a just cause, but the list of just causes steadily expanded from the few important causes identified by Augustine to very different causes, including the Crusades, fighting for Papal lands, imposing punishment, and

---

10. NUSSBAUM, *supra* note 2, at 20.

11. *Id.*, at 37.

12. GREWE *supra* note 2, at 109; *see also* Von Elbe, *supra* note, at 669.

13. Conforti, *supra* note 1, at 5.

14. Parker, *supra* note 9, at 41.

15. *Id.*, at 41; *see also* NUSSBAUM, *supra* note 2, at 17–18.

16. Jacque Dumas, *Sanctions of International Arbitration*, 5 AJIL 934, 937 (1911).

17. Parker, *supra* note 9, at 42.

so on—all very different from the early pacifism. For those cases where a prince did not have a just cause even under the expanded list of causes, legal scholars counseled the use of measures short of war, i.e., reprisals. Reprisals were not governed by the just war doctrine. The Pope or Emperor might restrain their use, but as papal and imperial authority declined, princes engaged in reprisals and feuds without acknowledging restraint on their right to do so. The reprisal, "although originally designed as a means for settling private claims, was frequently resorted to by independent princes and communities to vindicate their injured rights after the paramount power of the Emperor had *de facto* vanished."[18] Conditions in Italy reached a point of chaos that inspired Bartolus (1314–1357) to seek some sort of legal restraint on reprisals since neither military nor moral constraints from the Church or Empire were effective. Looking to the Roman *Corpus Juris*, Bartolus extended just war restraints to the use of the reprisal. This move flowed naturally from Bartolus's view that all human activity must be subject to some superior law.[19] It could not be the case that violent reprisals were unregulated.

Belli (1502–1575), too, contributed to the conception of a superior law. In his *Treatise on Military Matters and Warfare* published in 1536, Belli wrote that legal rules could restrain even in the absence of a personal authority to implement them, and a defensive war could be lawful even if someone in authority had not authorized it. Belli continued to support the requirement of right intention—thus a war in a just cause could become unjust if fought for revenge or to achieve gains beyond the righting of the original wrong.[20] Belli's ideas are important for extending just war constraints to all armed force and for the view that even those who had rejected the authority of the Pope or Emperor must still respect the constraints. Yet, eliminating those authorities introduced another problem. How could a fair determination be made between competing parties as to who had the just cause? By Belli's time, Europeans accepted normative constraint on violence, but the institutions of the Papacy and Holy Roman Empire to implement the constraints were not being replaced as they faded from authority.

The great Spanish scholastics, Vitoria (1480–1546), Suarez (1548–1617), and others, also contributed to the idea of the law itself as the ultimate governor of human action as opposed to a human authority. They, too, promoted the just war doctrine to constrain the use of war between societies. They did not, however, contribute to closing the implementation gap.[21] Vitoria championed the position that the just war doctrine extended to non-Christians.[22] Vitoria also introduced the concept of proportionality in warfare.

> For him, the resort to war becomes unjust if it is not proportionate to the aims pursued, if there is not a correct balance between the

---

18. Von Elbe, *supra* note 4, at 671–72 (footnotes omitted).

19. *Id.*, at 673.

20. *Id.*, at 673–74 (footnotes omitted); Nussbaum, *supra* note 2, at 91–93.

21. Von Elbe, *supra* note 4, at 674–75; Nussbaum, *supra* note 2, at 79–91.

22. Nussbaum, *supra* note 2, at 81.

use of force and the utility sought (a balance, it must be clear, between the use of force and the utility sought, not between the war and the injustice suffered). He says textually:

> If the recovery of one town entails heavy damages such as the devastation of other[']s towns, the justification for other wars, the death of numerous persons, the irritation of other rules ("irritatio principum") ... then the ruler must give up his right and abstain from the use of force.[23]

Vitoria, along with Suarez, and others, also began thinking about the possibility of a secular law, based on reason to intermediate between divine law and municipal law. In addition to these concepts considered progressive today, however, Vitoria introduced a decidedly unprogressive idea—a notion that almost proved the undoing of the just war doctrine. Vitoria taught that opposing sides in the same conflict could both be waging a just war, so long as their intentions were just. He understood that while only one party could objectively have a just cause, the other could make a good faith mistake and believe it was acting in a just cause, too. Good faith could absolve the party of any wrongdoing in waging an objectively unjust war.[24] Another Spaniard, Ayala, went even further. He believed that while the formalities must be kept as the Romans had taught, the reasons for going to war are not relevant to its legality. Suarez considered this absurd, but Suarez still insisted on the ultimate authority of the Pope to decide between competing claims of justice.[25] Suarez had no ready solution for those who rejected Papal authority. Some were advocating arbitration, but Suarez did not support secular arbitration.[26]

Without an authority over the parties, the Italian protestant, Alberico Gentili, writing in 1593, argued strenuously that all sides may have a just cause in the same conflict. He wrote that while

> [i]t is true, the prince is still considered as bound to examine the justice of his cause before he engages in war; ... whatever the result of his decision may be, it never affects the legality of his action, since war is nothing more than a procedural device that may be resorted to even for the redress of a probable wrong without exposing either party to the blame of injustice.[27]

For Gentili, the decision to use force was solely a matter for the ruler's personal conscience. The problem of telling any particular sovereign ruler

---

23. Conforti, *supra* note 1, *citing* Francisco De Vitoria, *De Indis, Sive de Jure Belli Hispanorum in Barbaros—Relectio Posterior, in* THE CLASSICS OF INTERNATIONAL LAW 445 (James Brown Scott ed., no. 7, 1917).

24. This argument arose in Vitoria's defense of the Native Americans. He argued that in their fear and ignorance they misunderstood the intentions of the Spaniards and attacked them. The Spaniards used force in response in justifiable self-defense. This argu-

ment was considered highly progressive when contrasted with the argument that non-European people were barbarians not entitled to the constraints of the just war doctrine. *See* NUSSBAUM, *supra* note 2, at 80. *See also,* Conforti, *supra* note 1 at 6.

25. NUSSBAUM, *supra* note 2, at 87–90.

26. Von Elbe, *supra* note 4, at 675–76; NUSSBAUM, *supra* note 2, at 92–93.

27. Von Elbe, *supra* note 4, at 678.

that he or she is acting unjustly had emerged full blown. Hugo Grotius, however, disliked the results of leaving matters to the consciences of European leaders of his day. The devastating Thirty Year's War (1618–1648) was at least partly a result of clashing consciences. Protestant rulers challenged Catholic ones for the right to practice their religion and to impose it on their subjects. Everyone was fighting in a subjectively just cause. In this context, Grotius argued, in distinction to Gentili, that the cause must be objectively just, and not just only in the mind of a prince about his own cause. Grotius, thereby, preserved the just war doctrine, at least in theory. According to Von Elbe, "The demise of the concept of the just war to which the idea of the *bellum justum ex utraque parte* seemed to lead was averted by Grotius who made of it an issue of modern international law."[28]

Grotius made his just war argument in his seminal work, *On the Law and War and Peace* (1625). He wrote the book hoping to contribute to ending the Thirty Years' War. He wanted to inspire greater humanity in the conduct of the war and encourage the establishment of a legal order for Western Europe after the war.[29] Building on the Spanish Scholastics, he adopted a secular basis for law, eschewing the religious controversies fueling the war. Rather than rely on divine revelation as the primary source of law, he offered a natural law vision based on human reason rather than wholly on divine will. Law's origin remained divine—Grotius understood law to be superior to the wishes of individuals or communities—but it may be understood through human reason. Both divine law and human reason ordained for Grotius that war be fought only in a just cause. The following is an excerpt from *The Law of War and Peace* setting out the three just causes of war.

Hugo Grotius, The Law of War and Peace

II De Jure Belle ac pacis Libri Tres 171–
72 (Francis W. Kelsey trans., 1964).

The Causes of War: First, Defense of Self and Property

I—*What causes of war may be called justifiable*

1. Let us proceed to the causes of war—I mean justifiable causes; for there are also other causes which influence men through regard for what is expedient and differ from those that influence men through regard for what is right.

The two kinds of causes Polybius accurately distinguishes from each other and from beginnings of war, such as the [wounding of the] stag was in the war between Aeneas and Turnus. Although the distinction between these matters is clear, nevertheless the words applied to them are often confused. For what we call

---

28. Von Elbe, *supra* note 4, at 678. "*Ex utraque parte*" referred to all sides in a conflict potentially having a just cause.

29. Nussbaum, *supra* note 2, at 105.

justifiable causes Livy, in the speech of the Rhodians, called beginnings: 'You certainly are Romans who claim that your wars are so fortunate because they are just, and pride yourselves not so much on their outcome, in that you gain the victory, as upon their beginnings, because you do not undertake wars without cause.'

In the same sense also Aelian (in Book XII, chapter liii) speaks of the beginnings of wars, and Diodorus Siculus (Book XIV), giving an account of the war of the Lacedaemonians against the Eleans, expresses the same idea by using the words 'pretexts' and 'beginnings'.

2.   These justifiable causes are the special subject of our discussion. Pertinent thereto is the famous saying of Coriolanus quoted by Dionysius of Halicarnassus: 'This, I think, ought to be your first concern, that you have a cause for war which is free from reproach and just.' Similarly Demosthenes says: 'As the substructures of houses, the framework of ships, and similar things ought to be most firm, so, in the case of actions, the causes and fundamental reasons ought to be in accord with justice and truth.' Equally pertinent is the statement of Dio Cassius: [101] 'We must give the fullest consideration to justice. With justice on your side, military prowess warrants good hope; without it, we have nothing sure, even if the first successes equal our desires.' Cicero also says, 'Those wars are unjust which have been undertaken without cause;' and in another passage he criticizes Crassus because Crassus had determined to cross the Euphrates without any cause for war.

3.   What has been said is no less true of public than of private wars. Hence the complaint of Seneca:

> We try to restrain murders and the killing of individuals. Why are wars and the crime of slaughtering nations full of glory? Avarice and cruelty know no bounds. In accordance with decrees of the Senate and orders of the people atrocities are committed, and actions forbidden to private citizens are commanded in the name of the state.

Wars that are undertaken by public authority have, it is true, in some respects a legal effect, as do judicial decisions, which we shall need to discuss later; but they are not on that account more free from wrong if they are undertaken without cause. Thus Alexander, if he commenced war on the Persians and other peoples without cause, was deservedly called a brigand by the Scythians, according to Curtius, as also by Seneca; likewise by Lucan he was styled a robber, and by the sages of India 'a man given over to wickedness,' while a pirate once put Alexander in the same class with himself. Similarly, Justin tells how two kings of Thrace were deprived of their royal power by Alexander's father, Philip, who exemplified the deceit and wickedness of a brigand. In this connexion belongs the saying of Augustine: 'If you take away justice, what are empires if not vast robberies?' In full accord with such expressions is the statement of Lactantius: 'Ensnared by the appearance of empty glory, men give to their crimes the name of virtue.'

4.   No other just cause for undertaking war can there be excepting injury received. 'Unfairness of the opposing side occasions just wars,' said the same Augustine, using 'unfairness' when he meant 'injury,' as if he had confused the Greek words for these two concepts. In the formula used by the Roman fetial are the words, 'I call you to witness that that people is unjust and does not do what is right in making restitution.'

II—*Justifiable causes include defence, the obtaining of that which belongs to us or is our due, and the inflicting of punishment.*

1.   It is evident that the sources from which wars arise are as numerous as those from which lawsuits spring; for where judicial settlement fails, war begins. Actions, furthermore, lie either for wrongs not yet committed, or for wrongs already done.

An action lies for a wrong not yet committed in cases where a guarantee is sought against a threatened wrong, or security against an anticipated injury, or an interdict of a different sort against the use of violence. An action for a wrong committed lies where a reparation for injury, or the punishment of the wrong-doer, is sought.

These two sources of legal obligations were rightly distinguished by Plato, in the ninth book of the *Laws*. Reparation is concerned either with what is or has been ours, giving rise to actions involving property interests, and certain personal actions; or with what is owed to us by contract, or in consequence of a criminal act; or by operation of law, a category to which must be referred also cases arising from implied contracts and constructive crimes. Under these subdivisions the rest of the personal actions fail. An act deserving punishment opens the way to accusation and public trial.

2.   Authorities generally assign to wars three justifiable causes, defence, recovery of property, and punishment. All three you may find in Camillus's declaration with reference to the Gauls: 'All things which it is right to defend, to recover, and to avenge.' In this enumeration the obtaining of what is owed to us was omitted, unless the word 'recover' is used rather freely. But this was not omitted by Plato when he said that wars are waged not only in case one is attacked, or despoiled of his possessions, but also if one has been deceived. In harmony with this is a sentence of Seneca: 'Perfectly fair, and in complete accord with the law of nations, is the maxim, "Pay what you owe," ' The thought was expressed also in the formula of the fetial: 'Things which they have not given, nor paid, nor done, which things ought to have been given, to have been done, to have been paid'; in the words of Sallust, in his

Histories: 'I demand restitution in accordance with the law of nations'

Whenever, however, Augustine said, 'Those wars are wont be defined as just which avenge wrongs,' he used the word 'avenge' in a rather general way [102] to mean 'exact requital for'. This is shown by what follows, for therein we find not a logical subdivision but a citation of examples: 'War, then, ought to be undertaken against that people and state which has either neglected to exact punishment for wrongs done by its members, or to return what has been wrongfully taken away.'

3.   It was in accordance with this natural principle that a king of India, according to Diodorus, brought against Semiramis the charge 'that she commenced war without having suffered any wrong'. So also the Romans demanded of the Senones that they should not attack people at whose hands they had received no injury. Aristotle in his *Analytics*, Book II, Chapter II, says: 'It is customary to make war on those who were the first to inflict injury.' * * * 'It was agreed that of barbarians they were the most just; they refrained from war unless attacked.'

The first cause of a justifiable war, then, is an injury not yet inflicted, which menaces either person or property.

––––––––––

The Peace of Westphalia of 1648 finally ended the Thirty Years' War, more than twenty years after Grotius wrote *The Law of War and Peace*. The treaties making up the Peace were negotiated over three years in the "first European Congress."[30] In addition to providing substantive principles aimed at resolving the causes of the long war, the Peace also contained enforcement mechanisms.

The Peace was essentially a move away from the Holy Roman Empire toward a community of formally equal and sovereign states. The Peace prohibited the resort to force by one state to dominate others. The 300 members of the Empire could join alliances, ensuring independence from the Emperor and other sovereigns seeking new empires. Should disputes arise, the offended party was required to first try "amicable settlement of legal discussion."[31] After three years, if the disputants failed to reach settlement, all other parties to the Treaty "shall take up arms with all council and might in order to subdue the offender." Nussbaum calls this the "first attempt at international organization for peace."[32] Leo Gross, too, pointed out Westphalia's orientation toward achieving peace through collective security: "Another aspect of the Peace of Westphalia which exercised considerable influence on future developments relates to the

30. NUSSBAUM, *supra* note 2, at 115.

31. ARTHUR NUSSBAUM, A CONCISE HISTORY OF THE LAW OF NATIONS 117 (1953).

32. *Id.* at 113.

guarantee of the peace itself.... For the first time Europe thus received 'what may fairly be described as an international constitution, which gave to all its adherents the right of intervention to enforce its engagements.' "[33]

The basic concepts in the Peace of Westphalia reflected Grotian ideas about limitation on the use of force for just causes only, including on behalf of the community. Forceful action may only aim at a wrong-doer; the purpose of action must be to right the wrong and not for vengeance. An enforcement action must be proportional to the wrong; third states may assist the injured in serious cases, and attempts to right a wrong through peaceful means are preferred and sometimes required.

The Articles of the Treaty of Peace, Sign'd and Seal'd at Munster, in Westphalia, October the 24th, 1648

By the Ambassadors Plenipotentiarys of their Sacred, Imperial, and Most Christian Majestys, and Extraordinary Deputys, Electors, Princes, and States of the Sacred *Roman* Empire.

Article I. That there shall be a Christian and Universal Peace, and a perpetual, true, and sincere Amity, between his Sacred Imperial Majesty, and his most Christian Majesty; as also, between all and each of the Allies, and Adherents of his said Imperial Majesty, the *House of Austria*, and its Heirs, and Successors; but chiefly between the Electors, Princes, and States of the Empire on the one side; and all and each of the Allies of his said Christian Majesty, and all their Heirs and Successors, chiefly between the most Serene Queen and Kingdom of *Swedeland*, the Electors respectively, the Princes and States of the Empire, on the other part. That this Peace and Amity be observ'd and cultivated with such a Sincerity and Zeal, that each Party shall endeavour to procure the Benefit, Honor and Advantage of the other; that thus on all sides they may see this Peace and Friendship in the *Roman* Empire, and the Kingdom of *France* flourish, by entertaining a good and faithful Neighborhood.

II. That there shall be on the one side and the other a perpetual Oblivion, Amnesty, or Pardon of all that has been committed since the beginning of these Troubles, in what place, or what manner soever the Hostilitys have been practis'd, in such a manner, that no body, under any pretext whatsoever, shall practice any Acts of Hostility, entertain any Enmity, or cause any Trouble to each other; neither as to Persons, Effects and Securitys, neither of themselves or by others, neither privately nor openly, neither directly nor indirectly, neither under the colour of Right, nor by the way of Deed, either within or without the extent of the Empire, notwithstanding all Cove-

---

33. Leo Gross, The Peace of Westphalia *in* I Essays on International Law and Organization 3, 7 (1984), *citing* David Jayne Hill, II A History of Diplomacy in the International Development of Europe 602 (1925).

nants made before to the contrary: That they shall not act, or permit to be acted, any wrong or injury to any whatsoever; but that all that has pass'd on the side, and the other, as well before during the War, in Words, Writings, and outrageous Actions, in Violences, Hostilitys, Damages and Expences, without any respect to Persons or Things, shall be entirely abolish'd in such a manner, that all that might be demanded of or pretended to, by each other on that behalf, shall be bury'd in eternal Oblivion.

III.

And that reciprocal Amity between the Emperor and the Most Christian King, the Electors, Princes and States of the Empire, may be maintain'd so much the more firm and sincere (to say nothing at present of the Article of Security, which will be mention'd hereafter) the one shall never assist the present or future Enemys of the other, under any Title or Pretense whatsoever, either with Arms, Money, Soldiers, or any sort of Ammunition; nor no one, who is a Member of this Pacification, shall suffer any Enemys Troops to retire thro' or sojourn in his Country.

* * *

CXXII.

That he who by his Assistance or Counsel shall contravene this Transaction or Publick Peace, or shall oppose its Execution and the above said Restitution, or who shall have endeavour'd, after the Restitution has been lawfully made, and without exceeding the manner agreed on before, without a lawful Cognizance of the Cause, and without the ordinary Course of Justice, to molest those that have been restor'd, whether Ecclesiasticks or Laymen; he shall incur the Punishment of being an Infringer of the publick Peace, and Sentence given against him according to the Constitutions of the Empire, so that the Restitution and Reparation may have its full effect.

CXXIII.

That nevertheless the concluded Peace shall remain in force, and all Partys in this Transaction shall be oblig'd to defend and protect all and every Article of this Peace against any one, without distinction of Religion; and if it happens any point shall be violated, the Offended shall before all things exhort the Offender not to come to any Hostility, submitting the Cause to a friendly Composition, or the ordinary Proceedings of Justice.

CXXIV.

Nevertheless, if for the space of three years the Difference cannot be terminated by any of those means, all and every one of those concerned in this Transaction shall be oblig'd to join the injur'd Party, and assist him with Counsel and Force to repel the Injury, being first advertis'd by the injur'd that gentle Means and Justice prevailed nothing; * * * And it shall not be permitted to any State of the Empire to pursue his Right by Force and Arms; but if any difference has happen'd or happens for the future, every one shall try the means of ordinary Justice, and the Contravener shall be regarded as an Infringer of the Peace. That which has been determin'd by Sentence of the Judge, shall be put in execution, without distinction of Condition, as the Laws of the Empire enjoin touching the Execution of Arrests and Sentences.

CXXV.   And that the publick Peace may be so much the better preserv'd intire, the Circles shall be renew'd; and as soon as any Beginnings of Troubles are perceiv'd, that which has been concluded in the Constitutions of the Empire, touching the Execution and Preservation of the publick Peace, shall be observ'd.

CXXVI.   And as often as any would march Troops thro' the others Territorys, this Passage shall be done at the charge of him whom the Troops belong to, and that without burdening or doing any harm or damage to those whose Countrys they march thro'. In a word, all that the Imperial Constitutions determine and ordain touching the Preservation of the publick Peace, shall be strictly observ'd.

Done, pass'd, and concluded at *Munster* in *Westphalia*, the 24th Day of *October*, 1648.

———

Vattel, writing a century after Grotius, failed to see a community of states, but rather saw a world of unrivaled sovereigns whose decisions on war and peace could not be ultimately subjected to law. After Grotius, Vattel has arguably had the greatest influence on international law. His principle work was a widely read book: *The Law of Nations* (1758). Vattel was a professional diplomat and wrote the book out of very different motivations to those of Grotius. While Grotius wrote in reaction to the horrors of the Thirty Years' War, Vattel wrote in service to "sovereigns and their ministers."[34] Vattel's book is based on his experiences and is filled with real world examples and practical advice. He shared with Grotius an understanding that a higher law governed human affairs than the law created by humans themselves.[35] On the other hand, he elevated the state and the will of the state to the point that positivism—the doctrine that law is made from the positive acts of states—was the natural development in the wake of his ideas.[36] In particular, by leaving normative issues to the private conscience of sovereigns, Vattel limited the right of co-equal sovereigns to

34. NUSSBAUM, *supra* note 2, at 156.

35. EMMERICH DE VATTEL, THE LAW OF NATIONS OR THE PRINCIPLES OF NATURAL LAW, APPLIED OT THE CONDUCT AND TO THE AFFAIRS OF NATIONS AND OF SOVEREIGNS 189–192 (Charles G. Fenwick trans., 1758 ed.)

36. GROSS, *supra* note 33, at 17. The American Founding Fathers especially liked Vattel's emphasis on sovereignty. NUSSBAUM, *supra* note 2, at 161–62.

sit in judgment of each other. Little was left of international law derived from the divine or reason—it became a matter of what the sovereigns willed.[37]

Vattel's heightened sovereignty became yet more vaunted when it combined with ideas of nationalism during the French revolution.[38] To prevent states from intervening in the Revolution, Robespierre and other French thinkers advocated non-intervention and collective war against states intervening to "oppress a nation."[39] But then, imbued with the superiority of their ideas, defensive war evolved to offensive war, ever justified as for the common good. France declared it was intervening to spread self-determination and liberation. Its leaders continued making these attractive declarations even as Napoleon was intervening for purposes quite the opposite of self-determination. Napoleon fought for empire. When he was finally defeated Europe had seen two decades of lawlessness and violence. Europeans were ready to try to control once again the lawful resort to armed force. "European nations resumed the traditions of the law of nations, influenced by changed conditions and on the basis of a new stabilised political balance of power."[40]

The Final Act of the Congress of Vienna, signed on June 9, 1815, aimed in general at preserving the peace.[41] The treaty made territorial dispositions—settling boundaries, transferring regions, clarifying rights of passage, and the like. The treaty also stated principles for the cooperative use of rivers; it granted amnesties; resolved the issue of funds on deposit in third states, and provided for the conduct of diplomacy. Great Britain, Austria, France and Russia guaranteed a cession of territory by Saxony to Prussia.[42] Arbitration was to be used to resolve potential disputes respecting Luxemburg's boundaries. A mixed boundary commission of professional members was called for to draw-up the boundaries between Prussia and The Netherlands.[43] The Vienna Treaty had no overall enforcement provisions, however, in distinction to the Peace of Westphalia, it did not restrict the unilateral use of force through collective enforcement. Yet, "[i]n the nineteenth century, after the Napoleonic wars, there may be discerned in the Congress and Concert system the beginning of a conscious effort to establish a community of states based on the will of all states or at least on the will of the Great Powers. The Hague Peace Conferences, the League of Nations ... [were] further stages in this development cognizable by positive international law."[44]

---

37. Von Elbe, *supra* note 4, at 682–83 (footnotes omitted); *see also* PHILIP ALLOTT, THE HEALTH OF NATIONS 56–62 (2002), on Vattel's role in the rise of sovereignty.

38. GREWE, *supra* note, at 414–16.

39. *Id.*, at 416–18.

40. *Id.*, at 424.

41. Vienna Congress Treaty, *reprinted in* Key Treaties for the Great Powers, 1814–1914, 41 (Michael Hurst, ed. 1972); *see also* Nussbaum, *supra* note 2, at 186.

42. Vienna Congress Treaty at art. XVII & LXIX.

43. Vienna Congress Treaty LXVI.

44. GROSS, *supra* note 33, at 19.

Vienna Congress Treaty

KEY TREATIES FOR THE GREAT POWERS 1814–1914 (Michael Hurst ed., 1972).

GENERAL TREATY between Great Britain, Austria, France, Portugal, Prussia, Russia, Spain, and Sweden.

—Signed at Vienna, 9th June, 1815, and ratified on the same date.

In the Name of the Most Holy and Undivided Trinity.

The Powers who signed the Treaty concluded at Paris on the 30th of May, 1814, having assembled at Vienna, in pursuance of Article XXXII of that Act, with the Princes and States their Allies, to complete the provisions of the said Treaty, and to add to them the arrangements rendered necessary by the state in which Europe was left at the termination of the last war; being now desirous to embrace, in one common transaction, the various results of their negotiations, for the purpose of confirming them by their reciprocal Ratifications, have authorised their Plenipotentiaries to unite, in a general Instrument, the regulations of superior and permanent interest, and to join to that Act, as integral parts of the arrangements of Congress, the Treaties, Conventions, Declarations, Regulations, and other particular Acts, as cited in the present Treaty.

* * *

Part of Duchy of Warsaw to be united to Russia. Title of King of Poland to be borne by the Czar.

Art. I. The Duchy of Warsaw, with the exception of the provinces and districts which are otherwise disposed of by the following Articles, is united to the Russian Empire. It shall be irrevocably attached to it by its Constitution, and be possessed by His Majesty the Emperor of all the Russias, his heirs and successors in perpetuity. His Imperial Majesty reserves to himself to give to this State, enjoying a distinct administration, the interior improvement which he shall judge proper. He shall assume with his other titles that of Czar, King of Poland, agreeably to the form established for the titles attached to his other possessions.

Poles to receive Representative and National Institutions.

The Poles, who are respective subjects of Russia, Austria, and Prussia, shall obtain a Representation and National Institutions, regulated according to the degree of political consideration, that each of the Governments to which they belong shall judge expedient and proper to grant them.

* * *

Ratification of the Treaty and Deposition of the Original in the Archives of the Court and State of Vienna.

Art. CXXI. The present Treaty shall be ratified, and the Ratifications exchanged in six months, and by the Court of Portugal in a year, or sooner, if possible.

A copy of this General Treaty shall be deposited in the Archives of the Court and State of His Imperial and Royal Apostolic Majesty, at Vienna, in case any of the Courts of Europe shall think proper to consult the original text of this Instrument.

In faith of which the respective Plenipotentiaries have signed this Act, and have affixed thereunto the Seals of their Arms.

Done at Vienna, the 9th of June, in the year of Our Lord, 1815.

—(The Signatures follow in the Alphabetical Order of the Courts.)

Throughout the 19th century European states continued to act through congresses like the Vienna Congress to resolve issues. The Paris Congress drew-up the Treaty of Paris of 1856 to settle the Crimean War. It also established the International Commission of the Danube and included Turkey, as a dramatic extension of cooperation under international law beyond Europe. According to Nussbaum, the Treaty of Paris is "second only to the treaties of Westphalia and Vienna in its importance for the history of international law."[45] After the Paris Congress, the next most important meeting for the development of international law was the Berlin Congress of 1878. This time the parties attempted to resolve the Balkans problem. The Berlin Congress of 1885 divided Africa among the Europeans settling a problem at least for them.[46] Vattel had encouraged the use of Congresses and their use might well have prevented some armed conflict, yet the 19th century was violent. European states fought around the world to build colonial empires and to check the growing power of any rival. The 19th century was the era of "cabinet" wars, wars fought to balance power through shifting alliances. Wars were fought to acquire colonies either against indigenous people or against external competitors. None of these reasons for war could be justified under the Grotian just war doctrine.

Despite the growing inconsistencies between actual practice and the just war doctrine, states did, in fact, continue to proclaim the justice of their causes.[47] States attempted to avoid the implications of formally declaring war by engaging in force short of war or reprisals.[48] In reality, however, the growing sense of equality among states, along with the ascendance of the view that the positive acts of states formed the only source of law began to eliminate the just war doctrine. Positivism resulted in the exclusion of divine or natural law sources, and the important protections derived from declaring neutrality, all but eliminated the idea that a state could only lawfully fight a war if the war met the criteria of a just war. Still, the 19th

---

45. NUSSBAUM, *supra* note 2, at 190.

46. *Id.*, at 193.

47. Von Elbe, *supra* note 4, at 684.

48. GREWE, *supra* note 2, at 367–69.

century is called by some the "Golden Age" of international law when states went into great detail about the rules governing neutrality,[49] reprisals, treaty-making, diplomatic law, and so on. It was the era of the multi-party treaty to regulate international conduct, and it was the era that gave rise to international organizations. The Paris Declaration on Maritime Law of 1856 had provisions regulating the conduct of maritime warfare, including the outlawing of privateering.[50] It is considered the first "law-making treaty."[51] The Paris Declaration was followed in 1864 by the first of the Geneva Conventions devoted to humanizing the conduct of land warfare.

The famous exchange of correspondence between Britain's Lord Ashburton and the US Secretary of State Webster in the *Caroline* Case is an example of 19th century attention to legal detail in a use of force short of war:

The Caroline

CHARLES CHENEY HYDE, INTERNATIONAL LAW 239 (1945).

[During an insurrection in Canada in 1837, the insurgents secured recruits and supplies from the American side of the border. There was an encampment of one thousand armed men organized at Buffalo, and located at Navy Island in Upper Canada; there was another encampment of insurgents at Black Rock, on the American side. The Caroline was a small steamer employed by these encampments. On December 29, 1837, while moored at Schlosser, on the American side of the Niagara River, and while occupied by some thirty-three American citizens, the steamer was boarded by an armed body of men from the Canadian side, who attacked the occupants. The latter merely endeavored to escape. Several were wounded; one was killed on the dock; only twenty-one were afterwards accounted for. The attacking party fired the steamer and set her adrift over Niagara Falls. In 1841, upon the arrest and detention of one Alexander McLeod, in New York, on account of his alleged participation in the destruction of the vessel, Lord Palmerston avowed responsibility for the destruction of the Caroline as a public act of force in self-defense, by persons in the British service. He therefore demanded McLeod's release. McLeod was, however, tried in New York, and acquitted. In 1842 the two Governments agreed on principle that the requirements of self-defense might necessitate the use of force. Mr. Webster, Secretary of State, denied, however, that the necessity existed in this particular case, while Lord Ashburton, the British Minister, apologized for the invasion of American territory. Said Mr. Webster in the course of a communication to the British Minister, August 6, 1842:]

---

49. GREWE, *supra* note 2, at 533–539. (The United States was a leading proponent of neutrality law in the 19th century.)

50. NUSSBAUM, *supra* note 2, at 192.

51. *Id.,* at 198.

The President sees with pleasure that your Lordship fully admits those great principles of public law, applicable to cases of this kind, which this government has expressed; and that on your part, as on ours, respect for the inviolable character of the territory of independent states is the most essential foundation of civilization. And while it is admitted on both sides that there are exceptions to this rule, he is gratified to find that your Lordship admits that such exceptions must come within the limitations stated and the terms used in a former communication from this department to the British plenipotentiary here. Undoubtedly it is just, that, while it is admitted that exceptions growing out of the great law of self-defense do exist, those exceptions should be confined to cases in which the "necessity of that self-defence is instant, overwhelming, and leaving no choice of means, and no moment for deliberation."

In an earlier letter to the British authorities, Mr. Webster included a requirement of proportionality: "It will be for [Her Majesty's Government] to show, also, that the local authorities of Canada, even supposing the necessity of the moment authorized them to enter territories of the United States at all, did nothing unreasonable or excessive; since the act, justified by the necessity of self-defence, must be limited by that necessity, and kept clearly within it." Mr. Webster to Mr. Fox (April 24, 1841), 29 British and Foreign State Papers 1129, 1138 (1857).

* * *

The *Caroline* Case also demonstrates that while Britain was the dominant power, it did not seek hegemony against its rival powers as had the Holy Roman Emperors or Napoleon or as German leaders would seek to do.[52] Without a hegemon, international law could play a role coordinating the relations among states on the basis of formal equality and positivism.[53]

Lassa Oppenheim, a German who became professor of international law in Cambridge University, was very much the positivist. He belonged among those scholars who saw no ultimate legal prohibition on war. The 1906 edition of his influential treatise contains the following passage:

[F]anatics of international peace, as well as those innumerable individuals who cannot grasp the idea of a law between Sovereign States, frequently consider war and law inconsistent. They quote the fact that wars are frequently waged by States as a proof against the very existence of an International Law. It is not difficult to show the absurdity of this opinion. As States are Sovereign, as consequently no central authority can exist above them able to enforce compliance with its demands, war cannot

---

52. Niall Ferguson, *Hegemony or Empire?*, 82 FOREIGN AFF. 154 (2003).

53. GREWE, *supra* note 2, at 462.

always be avoided. International Law recognizes this fact but at the same time provides regulations with which the belligerents have to comply....[54]

Many international lawyers came to share Oppenheim's view that the decision to go to war was the ultimate prerogative of the state and beyond legal regulation.[55] Yet at the same time they viewed measures short of war and the conduct of war itself to be subject to extensive legal conditions.[56] From quite the opposite perspective, even Oppenheim's "fanatics of international peace" held views that coincided with Oppenheim in that they, too, did not see war as the proper tool of a legal system. They wanted arbitration in place of war. For the last several decades of the 19th century and the first decade of the 20th, popular movements for peace advocated the use of arbitration in place of armed force. The idea of peaceful settlement appealed to foreign policy makers in the United States, too. Prominent among them was Elihu Root (1845–1937) who became convinced of the value of courts and tribunals for the settlement of international disputes. Before he became Secretary of War after the Spanish–American War of 1898 and later Secretary of State, Root had pursued a successful legal practice in New York City. He was a practitioner, not an academic. He did not advocate particular theories but rather actively promoted what he saw as practical solutions. He was not an anti-war advocate. He apparently agreed with Oppenheim that law could not ultimately outlaw war. Oppenheim was in fact highly influential among American international lawyers at the turn of the century.[57] Root, however, saw war as rarely a rational option, when a court or tribunal could resolve a dispute.[58] He did advocate war against Germany in 1914 believing Germany could not be persuaded through legal or any means to give up its plan of hegemony. After the war, Root continued his advocacy of courts for the settlement of most international disputes and was part of the drafting committee for the Permanent Court of International Justice.

Root came from the world of courts and understandably preferred them. His preference also coincided with an older trend in the U.S. Vattel had been particularly influential in the United States at the time of the nation's founding.[59] Vattel had advocated arbitration and arbitration was included in Jay Treaty of 1794 that settled issues between the United States and United Kingdom following the Revolutionary War. Arbitration had worked well for the fledgling state that could not possibly challenge militarily Britain, France or the other 19th century Great Powers. The U.S. and U.K. conducted a number of arbitrations under the Jay Treaty starting with the

54. LASSA OPPENHEIM, II INTERNATIONAL LAW 55–57 (1905–06).

55. Indeed, some saw it as "a natural and physiological event within the international community." Conforti, *supra* note 1, at 7.

56. GREWE, *supra* note, at 525, *citing* A. Bulmerincq, *Die Staatsstreitigkeiten und ihre*

Entscheidung ohne Krieg, in 4 HOTZENDORFFS HANDBUCH DES VÖLKERRCHTS 85, 87 (1889).

57. FRANCIS ANTHONY BOYLE, FOUNDATIONS OF WORLD ORDER, THE LEGALIST APPROACH TO INTERNATIONAL RELATIONS 11 (1999).

58. Mary Ellen O'Connell, *Elihu Root and Conflict Prevention*, 2000 PROC. ASIL 115.

59. NUSSBAUM, *supra* note 2, at 161.

St. Croix River Arbitration of 1798, in which arbitrators settled much of the boundary between present-day Canada and the United States.[60] They also established claims commissions to settle property disputes between American and British claimants, but with less success.[61] Nevertheless, the idea of arbitration gained ground. Arbitration clauses were included in 59 treaties between 1823 and 1898.[62] Hundreds of arbitral awards were made.[63] It was, however, the Alabama Claims Arbitration of 1871–1872, also originating under the Jay Treaty, that particularly inspired various peace advocates and movements to start lobbying for permanent machinery for the peaceful settlement of disputes.[64]

The 1898 Spanish–American War galvanized these efforts. The war had been a bloody conflict in which Spain lost most of its remaining overseas colonies to the United States. The popular view of the day was that the war began due to the mistaken belief of U.S. officials that Spanish agents had sunk a United States naval vessel, the *Maine*, in the Port of Havana.[65] The peace movements adhered to the theory that the ship sank due to accidental causes. They believed mechanisms of peaceful settlement could have clarified the true cause of the Maine disaster, avoiding the war.

The Russian Tsar was sympathetic to the goals of the peace movements and called a peace conference for The Hague in 1899. The Tsar was interested in pursuing ways to avoid war, not only to gain the benefits of peace, but in the interest of Russian security. Russia was not keeping pace with other world powers in acquiring the new technology of war, so rather than continue to try to compete, Russia saw a limitation on war as the better course. In other words, Russia sought alternatives to wars it feared it could not win.[66]

During the First Hague Peace Conference, delegates from 26 countries drafted a convention defining and setting out rules and procedures for good offices, mediation, inquiry and arbitration. The British delegation had formally proposed an international court for the settlement of disputes during the conference, but was unable to get sufficient support for the idea. The closest the delegates came to creating a court was the Permanent Court of Arbitration (PCA). The PCA is a list of available arbitrators, a set of arbitration rules and a small secretariat in The Hague.[67] No state is

---

60. GREWE, *supra* note 2, at 366.

61. *Id.*, at 365–66.

62. *Id.*, at 521.

63. GREWE cites counts of 177, 330 and 537 for the period of the 19th century—varying apparently by differing classification criteria. "The boundary between arbitration and conciliation is frequently ambiguous, and this can make the classification of some cases controversial. However, there is not doubt that there were hundreds of arbitral awards...." *Id.* at 519.

64. David Caron, *War and International Adjudication: Reflections on the 1899 Peace Conference*, 94 AM J. INT'L L. 4 (2000).

65. *Id.* at 7; *see also* RICHARD W. LEOPOLD, HISTORY OF AMERICAN FOREIGN POLICY 180 (1962).

66. Leila Nadya Sadat, *The Establishment of the International Criminal Court: From The Hague to Rome and Back Again*, 8 J. INT'L L. & PRAC. 97, n. 1 (1999) (citing, WILLIAM I. HULL, THE TWO HAGUE CONFERENCES AND THEIR CONTRIBUTIONS TO INTERNATIONAL LAW 3 (1908)).

67. *See* the website of the Permanent Court of Arbitration, *at* http://www.pca-cpa.

bound to have resort to it. The discussions for a real court and the first steps toward one in the form of the PCA, inspired the U.S. delegation to resolve to make further efforts toward creating a real court as it left The Hague.

The use of inquiry in 1906 to resolve the Dogger Bank dispute that nearly resulted in a war between Russia and Britain added to the enthusiasm for methods of peaceful settlement.[68] Delegates to the Second Hague Peace Conference in 1907 added more rules for inquiry, and the arbitration rules were modified and improved. Elihu Root at the head of the U.S. delegation tried diligently to get agreement on a permanent international court. Again the idea failed, owing largely to German opposition. The delegates in 1907 did agree to the first multilateral treaty outlawing the use of force for a particular class of disputes: The Convention of 1907 Respecting the Limitation of the Employment of Force for the Recovery of Contract Debts.[69] The delegates also agreed to form a permanent prize court, though that court was never established.[70]

The Hague Convention of 1907 for the Pacific Settlement of International Disputes

CONVENTION (I) for the pacific settlement of international disputes.—Signed at The Hague, October 18, 1907.

* * *

PART I. THE MAINTENANCE OF GENERAL PEACE

Article 1. With a view to obviating as far as possible recourse to force in the relations between states, the *Contracting* Powers agree to use their best efforts to insure the pacific settlement of international differences.

PART II. GOOD OFFICES AND MEDIATIONS

Article 2. In case of serious disagreement or dispute, before an appeal to arms, the *Contracting* Powers agree to have recourse, as far as circumstances allow, to the good offices or mediation of one or more friendly powers.

Article 3. Independently of this recourse, the *Contracting* Powers deem it expedient *and desirable* that one or more powers, strangers to the dispute, should, on their own initiative and as far as circumstances may allow, offer their good offices or mediation to the states at variance.

org. *See also*, P. Hamilton et al, The Permanent Court of Arbitration: International Arbitration and Dispute Settlement, Summaries of Awards, Settlement Agreements and Reports (1999).

68. Richard Ned Lebow, *Accidents and Crises: The Dogger Bank* Affair 31 Nav. War. Col. Rev., 66 (1978).

69. 1907 Stat. 36: 2241, Malloy's T.S. 2:2248.

70. Hans-Jürgen Schlochauer, *Permanent Court of International Justice*, 1 Encyclopedia of Public International Law 163–164 (Rudolf Bernhardt ed., 1981) [hereinafter EPIL].

> Powers strangers to the dispute have the right to offer good offices or mediation even during the course of hostilities.
>
> The exercise of this right can never be regarded by either of the parties in dispute as an unfriendly act.

* * *

By 1914 Root believed forceful action needed to be taken against Germany, but not in response to a legal wrong. America's most prominent international lawyer and founder of the American Society of International Law held firmly to his view that the U.S. needed to go to war against Germany to join in common cause with England and put a stop to German imperial designs. German intentions had been clear enough for Root at the Hague Peace Conference. The German government did not share the Anglo–American enthusiasm for third-party settlement.[71] German legal scholars were generally lukewarm at best about international law methods for promoting peace.[72] Some German scholars were plainly suspicious of the barriers to war being created by British and American scholars and officials. They were seen as a means to preventing Germany from acquiring an empire while preserving the British one. Britain had used war to conquer extensive colonies, and now was happy to declare a prohibition on the use of force by others.

B.   FROM THE HAGUE TO NUREMBERG

After Germany was defeated in the First World War, it was no longer an obstacle to further development of peaceful means of dispute settlement. U.S. President Woodrow Wilson arrived in Paris with an ambitious plan for a world organization to ensure peace and justice. Such an organization was foreseen in the Treaty of Versailles that formally ended the war. The organization itself was formed under the Covenant of the League of Nations, adopted on April 28, 1919.[73] The League Covenant grew out of Wilson's plan and other proposals and draft texts prepared before and during the early stages of the Paris Peace Conference. Neither Root nor any of the other Americans long involved in promoting peace through law were part of the American delegation to the Conference.[74] Philip Jessup has noted that President Woodrow Wilson, an academic and Democrat, disliked lawyers and that he wanted no prominent Republicans like Root in the delegation. More importantly, Root had a different vision from Wilson for the post-war order. Root wanted an assembly to discuss issues and use

---

71.   BOYLE, *supra* note 57, at 28.

72.   MARTTI KOSKENNIEMI, THE GENTLE CIVILIZER OF NATIONS: THE RISE AND FALL OF INTERNATIONAL LAW 1870–1960 213 (2001).

73.   I.F.P. WALTERS, A HISTORY OF THE LEAGUE OF NATIONS 4, 38–39 (1952).

74.   *See* Philip C. JESSUP, 2 ELIHU ROOT AND THE CONSERVATIVE TRADITION 380 (1954); *see also* MICHAEL DUNNE, THE UNITED STATES AND THE WORLD COURT, 1920–1935, 20–21 (1988).

negotiation to settle them. He also very much wanted a court with compulsory jurisdiction. He did not, however, support Wilson's idea that the collective use of force be made available to enforce the peaceful settlement of disputes. Root's opposition played a significant role in the U.S. Senate's decision not to give its consent to the adoption of the Covenant.

Nevertheless, the League was established in Geneva, composed of an Assembly, Council and Secretariat.

The Covenant of the League of Nations

THE HIGH CONTRACTING PARTIES, In order to promote international co-operation and to achieve international peace and security by the acceptance of obligations not to resort to war by the prescription of open, just and honourable relations between nations by the firm establishment of the understandings of international law as the actual rule of conduct among Governments, and by the maintenance of justice and a scrupulous respect for all treaty obligations in the dealings of organised peoples with one another Agree to this Covenant of the League of Nations.

* * *

ARTICLE 8

The Members of the League recognise that the maintenance of peace requires the reduction of national armaments to the lowest point consistent with national safety and the enforcement by common action of international obligations. The Council, taking account of the geographical situation and circumstances of each State, shall formulate plans for such reduction for the consideration and action of the several Governments. * * *

* * *

ARTICLE 10.

The Members of the League undertake to respect and preserve as against external aggression the territorial integrity and existing political independence of all Members of the League. In case of any such aggression or in case of any threat or danger of such aggression the Council shall advise upon the means by which this obligation shall be fulfilled.

ARTICLE 11.

Any war or threat of war, whether immediately affecting any of the Members of the League or not, is hereby declared a matter of concern to the whole League, and the League shall take any action that may be deemed wise and effectual to safeguard the peace of nations. In case any such emergency should arise the Secretary General shall on the request of any Member of the League forthwith summon a meeting of the Council. It is also declared to be the friendly right of each Member of the League to bring to the attention of the Assembly or of the Council any circumstance whatever affecting international relations which threatens to disturb international peace or the good understanding between nations upon which peace depends.

ARTICLE 12.

The Members of the League agree that if there should arise between them any dispute likely to lead to a rupture, they will submit the matter either to arbitration or to inquiry by the Council, and they agree in no case to resort to war until three months after the award by arbitrators or the report by the Council. In any case under this Article the award of the arbitrators shall be made within a reasonable time, and the report of the Council shall be made within six months after the submission of the dispute.

ARTICLE 13.

The Members of the League agree that whenever any dispute shall arise between them which they recognise to be suitable for submission to arbitration and which cannot be satisfactorily settled by diplomacy, they will submit the whole subject-matter to arbitration. * * *

ARTICLE 14.

The Council shall formulate and submit to the Members of the League for adoption plans for the establishment of a Permanent Court of International Justice. The Court shall be competent to hear and determine any dispute of an international character which the parties thereto submit to it. The Court may also give an advisory opinion upon any dispute or question referred to it by the Council or by the Assembly.

ARTICLE 15.

If there should arise between Members of the League any dispute likely to lead to a rupture, which is not submitted to arbitration in accordance with Article 13, the Members of the League agree that they will submit the matter to the Council. * * *

ARTICLE 16.

Should any Member of the League resort to war in disregard of its covenants under Articles 12, 13, or 15, it shall ipso facto be deemed to have committed an act of war against all other Members of the League, which hereby undertake immediately to subject it to the severance of all trade or financial relations, the prohibition of all intercourse between their nations and the nationals of the covenant-breaking State, and the prevention of all financial, commercial, or personal intercourse between the national of the covenant-breaking State and the nationals of any other State, whether a Member of the League or not. It shall be the duty of the Council in such case to recommend to the several Governments concerned what effective military, naval, or air force the Members of the League shall severally contribute to the armed forces to be used to protect the covenants of the League. The Members of the League agree, further, that they will mutually support one another in the financial and economic measures which are taken under this Article, in order to minimise the loss and inconvenience resulting from the above measures, and that they will mutually support one another in resisting any special measures aimed at one of their number by the covenant breaking State, and that they will take the necessary steps to afford passage through their territory to the forces of any of the Members of the League which are co-operating to protect the covenants of the League. Any Member of the League which has violated any covenant of the League may be declared to be no longer a Member of the League by a vote of the Council concurred in by the Representatives of all the other Members of the League represented thereon.

ARTICLE 17.

In the event of a dispute between a Member of the League and a State which is not a Member of the League, or between States not Members of the League, the State or States, not Members of the League shall be invited to accept the obligations of membership in the League for the purposes of such dispute, upon such conditions as the Council may deem just. * * *

In addition to the League, the Treaty of Versailles called for other progressive steps, such as individual accountability. The delegations to the Paris Peace Conference agreed that the Kaiser should be tried before a special international tribunal. He should not simply be exiled as Napoleon had been. This agreement became Article 227 of the treaty of Versailles:

ARTICLE 227

The Allied and Associated Powers publicly arraign William II of Hohenzollern, formerly German Emperor, for a supreme offence against international morality and the sanctity of treaties.

A special tribunal will be constituted to try the accused, thereby assuring him the guarantees essential to the right of defence. It will be composed of five judges, one appointed by each of the following Powers: namely, the United States of America, Great Britain, France, Italy and Japan.

In its decision the tribunal will be guided by the highest motives of international policy, with a view to vindicating the solemn obligations of international undertakings and the validity of international morality. It will be its duty to fix the punishment which it considers should be imposed.

The Allied and Associated Powers will address a request to the Government of the Netherlands for the surrender to them of the ex-Emperor in order that he may b[e] put on trial.

But the ex-Emperor never was surrendered. James Brown Scott describes the position of the Dutch:

* * * [T]he Dutch Government[] called attention to the fact that Holland was not a party to the Treaty of Versailles; that Article 228 of the treaty did not impose a duty upon Holland; that it looked at this question, therefore, from its own conception of its duty. It was not connected with the outbreak of the war; it was not a party to it; it was a neutral, and in no way bound "to associate itself with this act of high international policy of the powers."

Then follows a very important suggestion which Holland took the opportunity of making, and which will be referred to later. "If in the future there should be instituted by the society of nations an international jurisdiction, competent to judge in case of war deeds qualified as crimes and submitted to its jurisdiction by statute antedating the acts committed, it would be fit for Holland to associate herself with the new regime." In the absence of an international duty which would be created in this manner, the case was to be decided by "the laws of the kingdom and national tradition."

* * * "[N]either the constituent laws of the kingdom, which are based upon the principles of law universally recognized, nor the age-long tradition which has made this country always a ground of refuge for the vanquished in international conflicts, permit the Government of Holland to defer to the desire of the powers by withdrawing from the former Emperor the benefit of its laws and this tradition."[75]

Willis provides the political background.[76]

Even if the Allies had agreed on punishment for Wilhem II, it is unlikely that the ex-kaiser would ever have appeared before a tribunal. Recognizing his peril, the kaiser prepared to disappear into hiding and even considered suicide. In the end, he did not

---

75. *The Trial of the Kaiser, in* WHAT REALLY HAPPENED IN PARIS? 243–44 (Edward Mandell House & Charles Seymour eds., 1921).

76. JAMES F. WILLIS, PROLOGUE TO NUREMBERG, THE POLITICS AND DIPLOMACY OF PUNISHING WAR CRIMINALS OF THE FIRST WORLD WAR 98 (1982).

have to resort to such desperate measures. The government of the Netherlands learned from various sources that the Allies lacked determination and concluded that it could safely reject any request for the surrender of the kaiser. Lloyd George remained committed to the idea of a trial for Wilhelm II, but other British officials, respecting the wishes of their royal family, virtually forced him to abandon efforts to bring the kaiser before a court. Lloyd George eventually was willing to settle for interment of Wilhelm II on an island under Allied supervision, much in the way Britain had confined Napoleon to Saint Helena, but failed to secure even that solution. The Dutch remained true to their tradition of providing refuge for the vanquished and would not agree, to such an arrangement. Dutch intransigence was made possible, in part, because British diplomats unsympathetic with Lloyd George's wishes sabotaged his efforts. Other Allied governments also let the Dutch know that the scheme did not have their approval. Italian and French leaders would not even help force the exile of the kaiser to the Dutch East Indies. Instead, the Allies accepted Dutch settlement of the kaiser in the Netherlands with assurances that he would not be permitted to carry on political intrigues.

Some trials of German military officers were held, however. Those are discussed in the next chapter.

In addition to the trial of the Kaiser, the Versailles Treaty and the Covenant called for major efforts at disarmament. Here the United States played a large role, calling a conference in Washington for general disarmament that resulted in the Treaty for the Limitation of Naval Armaments, February 6, 1922.[77] A subsequent conference called in 1927, however, made little additional progress nor did states agree to a general disarmament treaty. Between the U.S. failure to join the League and the failure to achieve general disarmament, Americans, especially in the peace movements, were becoming increasingly bitter. Led by such prominent peace and social justice activists as Jane Addams, who, as the first president of the Women's International League for Peace and Freedom, won the Nobel Peace Prize in 1919, pressure was put on the U.S. government to do something tangible for the cause of peace.

In response to this popular pressure, the U.S. concluded the Kellogg–Briand Pact of 1928.[78] The parties to the Pact renounced war and committed themselves to seeking the peaceful settlement of disputes. The Pact, unlike the League, however, had no enforcement provisions. It was a simple declaration against the use of war as an instrument of national policy.

77. 43 Stat. 1655, 2 Bevans 351.

78. *See also* IAN BROWNLIE, INTERNATIONAL AND THE USE OF FORCE BY STATES 57 (1963).

Treaty Providing for the Renunciation of War as an Instrument of National Policy

August 27, 1928, 46 Stat. 2343 T.S. No. 796, 2 Bevans 732.*

ARTICLE I

The High Contracting Parties solemnly declare in the names of their respective peoples that they condemn recourse to war for the solution of international controversies, and renounce it, as an instrument of national policy in their relations with one another.

ARTICLE II

The High Contracting Parties agree that the settlement or solution of all disputes or conflicts of whatever nature or of whatever origin they may be, which may arise among them, shall never be sought except by pacific means.

Article III

The present Treaty shall be ratified by the High Contracting Parties named in the Preamble in accordance with their respective constitutional requirements and shall take effect as between them as soon as all their several instruments of ratification shall have been deposited at Washington.

This Treaty shall, when it has come into effect as prescribed in the preceding paragraph, remain open as long as may be necessary for adherence by all the other Powers of the world. Every instrument evidencing the adherence of a Power shall be deposited at Washington and the Treaty shall immediately upon such deposit become effective as; between the Power thus adhering and the other Powers parties hereto.

It shall be the duty of the Government of the United States to furnish each Government named in the Preamble and every Government subsequently adhering to this Treaty with a certified copy of the Treaty and of every instrument of ratification or adherence. It shall also be the duty of the Government of the United States telegraphically to notify such Governments immediately upon the deposit with it of each instrument of ratification or adherence.

The Pact, however, did not eliminate the right to use force in self-defense, nor was it clear that the Pact was meant to prohibit the use of force for the enforcement of legal rights.[79] In addition to the Covenant and the Pact, a

---

* (Also known as the Kellogg–Briand Pact or Pact of Paris).

79. BROWNLIE, *supra* note 78, at 89. Accord Röling: " '[S]elf-defence' was regarded

as embracing defence against nonviolent illegal impairment of interests." Bert V.A. Röl-

number of other bilateral and regional agreements for the renunciation of war were adopted.[80] A number of constitutions also placed limits on war.[81] Even in these cases, however, many governments understood they retained the right to use force in self-defense or to enforce legal rights.

Where it was clear that the right to resort to war to enforce legal rights was no longer permitted, many scholars believed the right to take reprisals remained. Legal opinion was mixed as to whether the Kellogg–Briand Pact or the Covenant prohibited *armed* reprisals.[82] Armed reprisals continued to be used for various purposes, principally enforcing rights. The Naulilaa Case (p. 5, above) arose before the adoption of the Covenant but was decided years after and gave the impression that armed reprisals to enforce legal rights continued to be a lawful form of enforcement, if strict procedures were followed.

Despite the limits on war, if the legal requirements for taking reprisals were met, many considered them a lawful use of armed force to enforce rights. Nevertheless, Brownlie points out that after the adoption of the Kellogg–Briand Pact—the same year as the Naulilaa arbitration—the use of armed reprisals practically ended.[83]

The use of war, however, did not. Japan, a member of the League of Nations, invaded Manchuria in 1931–33. The League failed to respond to the invasion despite the fact that Article 10 of the Covenant mandated action.[84] The United States having just championed the Kellogg–Briand Pact with its total renunciation of war (and total lack of enforcement provisions), felt it had to make some reaction to the invasion for the Pact to be taken at all seriously. Secretary of State Henry L. Stimson announced the policy of refusing to grant legal recognition to "any situation, treaty or agreement which may be brought about contrary to the covenants and obligations of the Pact of Paris."[85] The League passed a similar resolution, but the resolution did not induce Japan to comply with the Covenant or the Pact, nor did the resolutions prevent another armed conflict in breach of international law, the Chaco War between Paraguay and Bolivia in 1934.[86] The terminal event for the League came just one year later. In 1935 Italy invaded Abyssinia, present day Ethiopia. The League again failed to apply either military or economic sanctions. The limited sanctions that were applied were organized outside the League[87] and were abandoned once Italy gained control of Ethiopia in order to avoid encouraging Mussolini to form

---

ing, *The Ban on the Use of Force and the U.N. Charter, in* THE CURRENT LEGAL REGULATION OF THE USE OF FORCE 5 (A. Cassese ed., 1986).

80. *See, e.g.,* Locarno Treaty of Mutual Guarantee, Oct. 16, 1925, 54 LNTS 289.

81. BROWNLIE, *supra* note 78, at 27.

82. Alexandrov believes that measures short of force were generally considered to be subject to the Covenant, too, although there was some unclarity. STANIMER ALEXANDROV,

SELF-DEFENSE AGAINST THE USE OF FORCE IN INTERNATIONAL LAW 38 (1996).

83. BROWNLIE, *supra* note 78, at 222.

84. NUSSBAUM, *supra* note 78, at 252.

85. JAMES L. BRIERLY, THE LAW OF NATIONS 171–73 (6th ed. Waldock ed.); *see also* NUSSBAUM, *supra* note 2, at 254.

86. NUSSBAUM, *supra* note 2, at 253.

87. KOSKENNIEMI, *supra* note 73, at 239.

an alliance with Hitler.[88] Mussolini formed an alliance anyway and the world was plunged, once again, into war.

At the end of the war, the victorious Allies—the United States, Great Britain, the Soviet Union and France—held Germany's high political and military leaders responsible for war crimes, crimes against humanity and crimes against the peace. In this Chapter we consider the charges of crimes against the peace against Hermann Göring and Joachim von Ribbentrop. They were accused of "crimes against the peace" for violating the *jus ad bellum* in existence in 1939 when Germany first used force against a neighbor. Similar charges were brought against Japanese leaders in the Tokyo Trials.[89] In the next Chapter we consider the *jus in bello* charges brought against both German and Japanese political officials and military officers.

Trial of the Major War Criminals Before the International Military Tribunal

Nuremberg
14 November 1945–1 October 1946

* * *

Judgment

On 8 August 1945, the Government of the United Kingdom of Great Britain and Northern Ireland, the Government of the United States of America, the Provisional Government of the French Republic, and the Government of the Union of Soviet Socialist Republics entered into an Agreement establishing this Tribunal for the Trial of War Criminals whose offenses have no particular geographical location. In accordance with Article 5, the following Governments of the United Nations have expressed their adherence to the Agreement:

Greece, Denmark, Yugoslavia, the Netherlands, Czechoslovakia, Poland, Belgium, Ethiopia, Australia, Honduras, Norway, Panama, Luxemburg, Haiti, New Zealand, India, Venezuela, Uruguay, and Paraguay.

By the Charter annexed to the Agreement, the constitution, jurisdiction, and functions of the Tribunal were defined.

The Tribunal was invested with power to try and punish persons who had committed Crimes against Peace, War Crimes, and Crimes against Humanity as defined in the Charter.

The Charter also provided that at the Trial of any individual member of any group or organization the Tribunal may declare (in connection with any act of which the individual may be convicted)

---

88. *Id.*, at 239; *see also* NUSSBAUM, *supra* note at 253–54.

89. *See*, e.g. TIM MAGA, JUDGMENT AT TOKYO (2001).

that the group or organization of which the individual was a member was a criminal organization.

In Berlin, on 18 October 1945, in accordance with Article 14 of the Charter, an Indictment was lodged against the defendants named in the caption above, who had been designated by the Committee of the Chief Prosecutors of the signatory Powers as major war criminals.

A copy of the Indictment in the German language was served upon each defendant in custody, at least 30 days before the Trial opened.

This Indictment charges the defendants with Crimes against Peace by the planning, preparation, initiation, and waging of wars of aggression, which were also wars in violation of international treaties, agreements, and assurances; with War Crimes; and with Crimes Against Humanity. The defendants are also charged with participating in the formulation or execution of a common plan or conspiracy to commit all these crimes. The Tribunal was further asked by the Prosecution to declare all the named groups or organizations to be criminal within the meaning of the Charter.

The Defendant Robert Ley committed suicide in prison on 25 October 1945. On 15 November 1945 the Tribunal decided that the Defendant Gustav Krupp von Bohlen und Halbach could not then be tried because of his physical and mental condition, but that the charges against him in the Indictment should be retrained for trial thereafter, if the physical and mental condition of the defendant should permit. On 17 November 1945 the Tribunal decided to try the Defendant Bormann in his absence under the provisions of Article 12 of the Charter. After argument, and consideration of full medical reports, and as statement from the defendant himself, the Tribunal decided on 1 December 1945 that no grounds existed for a postponement of the Trial against the Defendant Hess because of his mental condition. A similar decision was made in the case of the Defendant Streicher.

In accordance with Articles 16 and 23 of the Charter, Counsel were either chosen by the defendants in custody themselves, or at their request were appointed by the Tribunal. In his absence the Tribunal appointed Counsel for the Defendant Bormann, and also assigned Counsel to represent the named groups or organizations.

The Trial, which was conducted in four languages—English, Russian, French, and German—began on 20 November 1945, and pleas of "Not Guilty" were made by all the defendants except Bormann.

The hearing of evidence and the speeches of Counsel concluded on 31 August 1946.

Four hundred and three open sessions of the Tribunal have been held. Thirty-three witnesses gave evidence orally for the

Prosecution against the individual defendants and 61 witnesses, in addition to 19 of the defendants, gave evidence for the Defense.

A further 143 witnesses gave evidence for the Defense by means of written answers to interrogatories.

The Tribunal appointed Commissioners to hear evidence relating to the organizations, and 101 witnesses were heard for the Defense before the Commissioners, and 1,809 affidavits from other witnesses were submitted. Six reports were also submitted, summarizing the contents of a great number of further affidavits.

Thirty-eight thousand affidavits, signed by 155,000 people, were submitted on behalf of the Political Leaders, 136,213 on behalf of the SS, 10,000 on behalf of the SA, 7,000 on behalf of the SD, 3,000 on behalf of the General Staff and OKW, and 2,000 on behalf of the Gestapo.

The Tribunal itself heard 22 witnesses for the organizations. The documents tendered in evidence for the Prosecution of the individual defendants and the organizations numbered several thousands. A complete stenographic record of everything said in Court has been made, as well as an electrical recording of all the proceedings.

Copies of all the documents put in evidence by the Prosecution have been supplied to the Defense in the German language.

* * *

Violations of International Treaties

The Charter defines as a crime the planning or waging of war that is war of aggression or a war in violation of international treaties. The Tribunal has decided that certain of the defendants planned and waged aggressive wars against 12 nations, and were therefore guilty of this series of crimes. This makes it unnecessary to discuss the subject in further detail, or even to consider at any length the extent to which these aggressive wars were also "wars in violation of international treaties, agreements, or assurances."

These treaties are set out in Appendix C of the Indictment. Those of principal importance are the following.

Hague Conventions

In the 1899 Convention the signatory powers agreed: "before an appeal to arms...to have recourse, as far as circumstances allow, to the good offices or mediation of one or more friendly powers." As similar clause was inserted in the Convention for Pacific Settlement of International Disputes of 1907. In the accompanying Convention Relative to Opening of Hostilities, Article I contains this far more specific language: "The Contracting Powers recognize that hostilities between them must not commence without a previous and explicit warning, in the form of either a declaration of war, giving reasons, or an ultimatum with a conditional declaration of war." Germany was a party to these conventions.

Versailles Treaty

Breaches of certain provisions of the Versailles Treaty are also relied on by the Prosecution—Not to fortify the left bank of the Rhine (Articles 42–44); to "respect strictly the independence of Austria" (Article 80); renunciation of any rights in Memel (Article 99) and the Free City of Danzig (Article 100); the recognition of the independence of the Czechoslovak State; and the military, naval, and air clauses against German rearmament found in Part V. There is no doubt that action was taken by the German Government contrary to all these provisions * * *.

* * *

Treaties of Mutual Guarantee, Arbitration, and Non–Aggression

It is unnecessary to discuss in any detail the various treaties entered into by Germany with other Powers. Treaties of mutual guarantee were signed by Germany at Locarno in 1925, with Belgium, France, Great Britain, and Italy, assuring the maintenance of the territorial *status quo*. Arbitration treaties were also executed by Germany at Locarno with Czechoslovakia, Belgium, and Poland.

Article I of the latter treaty is typical, providing: "All disputes of every kind between Germany and Poland ... which it may not be possible to settle amicably by the normal methods of diplomacy, shall be submitted for decision to an arbitral tribunal...."

Conventions of Arbitration and Conciliation were entered into between Germany, the Netherlands, and Demark in 1926; and between Germany and Luxembourg in 1929. Non-aggression treaties were executed by Germany with Denmark and Russia in 1939.

Kellogg–Briand Pact

The Pact of Paris was signed on 27 August 1928 by Germany, the United States, Belgium, France, Great Britain, Italy, Japan, Poland, and other countries; and subsequently by other Powers. The Tribunal has made full reference to the nature of this Pact and its legal effect in another part of this judgment. It is therefore not necessary to discuss the matter further here, save to state that in the opinion of the Tribunal this Pact was violated by Germany in all the cases of aggressive war charged in the Indictment. It is to be noted that on 26 January 1934 Germany signed a Declaration for the Maintenance of Permanent Peace with Poland, which was explicitly based on the Pact of Paris, and in which the use of force was outlawed for a period of 10 years.

The Tribunal does not find it necessary to consider any of the other treaties referred to in the Appendix, or the repeated agreements and assurances of her peaceful intentions entered into by Germany.

The Law of the Charter

The jurisdiction of the Tribunal is defined in the Agreement and Charter, and the crimes coming within the jurisdiction of the Tribunal, for which there shall be individual responsibility, are set out in Article 6. The law of the Charter is decisive, and binding upon the Tribunal.

The making of the Charter was the exercise of the sovereign legislative power by the countries to which the German Reich unconditionally surrendered; and the undoubted right of these countries to legislate for the occupied territories has been recognized by the civilized world. The Charter is not an arbitrary exercise of power on the part of the victorious Nations, but in the view of the Tribunal, as will be shown, it is the expression of international law existing at the time of its creation; and to that extent is itself a contribution to international law.

The Signatory Powers created this Tribunal, defined the law it was to administer, and made regulations for the proper conduct of the Trial. In doing so, they have done together what any one of them might have done singly; for it is not to be doubted that any nation has the right thus to set up special courts to administer law. With regard to the constitution of the Court, all that the defendants are entitled to ask is to receive a fair trial on the facts and law.

The Charter makes the planning or waging of a war of aggression or a war in violation of international treaties a crime; and it is therefore not strictly necessary to consider whether and to what extent aggressive war was a crime before the execution of the London Agreement. But in view of the great importance of the questions of law involved, the Tribunal has heard full argument from the Prosecution and the Defense, and will express its view on the matter.

It was urged on behalf of the defendants that a fundamental principle of all law—international and domestic—is that there can be no punishment of crime without a pre-existing law. *"Nullum crimen sine lege, nulla poena sine lege."* It was submitted that *ex post facto* punishment is abhorrent to the law of all civilized nations, that no sovereign power had made aggressive war a crime at the time that the alleged criminal acts were committed, that no statute had defined aggressive war, that no penalty had been fixed for its commission, and no court had been created to try and punish offenders.

In the first place, it is to be observed that the maxim *nullum crimen sine lege* is not a limitation of sovereignty, but is in general a principle of justice. To assert that it is unjust to punish those who in defiance of treaties and assurances have attacked neighboring states without warning is obviously untrue, for in such circumstances the attacker must know that he is doing wrong, and so far from it being unjust to punish him, it would be unjust if his wrong were allowed to go unpunished. Occupying the positions they did in the Government of Germany, the defendants, or at least some of them must have known of the treaties signed by Germany, outlawing recourse to war for the settlement of international disputes; they must have known that they were acting in defiance of all international law when in complete deliberation they carried out their designs of invasion and aggression. On this view of the case alone, it would appear that the maxim has no application to the present facts.

This view is strongly reinforced by a consideration of the state of international law in 1939, so far as aggressive war is concerned. The General Treaty for the Renunciation of War of 27 August 1928, more generally known as the Pact of Paris or the Kellogg–Briand Pact, was binding on 63 nations, including Germany, Italy, and Japan at the outbreak of war in 1939.* * *

The question is, what was the legal effect of this Pact? The nations who signed the Pact or adhered to it unconditionally condemned recourse to war for the future as an instrument of policy, and expressly renounced it. After the signing of the Pact, any nation resorting to war as an instrument of national policy breaks the Pact. In the opinion of the Tribunal, the solemn renunciation of war was an instrument of national policy necessarily involves the proposition that such a war is illegal in international law; and that those who plan and wage such a war, with its inevitable and terrible consequences, are committing a crime in so doing. War for the solution of international controversies undertaken as an instrument of national policy certainly includes a war of aggression, and such a war is therefore outlawed by the Pact. As Mr. Henry L. Stimson, then Secretary of State of the United States, said in 1932:

> "War between nations was renounced by the signatories of the Kellogg–Briand Treaty. This means that it has become throughout practically the entire world ... an illegal thing. Hereafter, when nations engage in armed conflict, either one or both of them must be termed violators of this general treaty law.... We denounce them as law breakers."

But it is argued that the Pact does not expressly enact that such wars are crimes, or set up courts to try those who make such wars. To that extent the same is true with regard to the laws of war contained in the Hague Convention. The Hague Convention of 1907 prohibited resort to certain methods of waging war. These included the inhumane treatment of prisoners, the employment of poisoned weapons, the improper use of flags of truce, and similar matters. Many of these prohibitions had been enforced long before the date of the Convention; but since 1907 they have certainly been crimes, punishable as offenses against the laws of war; yet the Hague Convention nowhere designates such practices as criminal, nor is any sentence prescribed, nor any mention made of a court to try and punish offenders. For many years past, however, military tribunals have tried and punished individuals guilty of violating the rules of land warfare laid down by this Convention. In the opinion of the Tribunal, those who wage aggressive war are doing that which is equally illegal, and of much greater moment than a breach of one of the rules of the Hague Convention. In interpreting the words of the Pact, it must be remembered that international law is not the product of an international legislature, and that such international agreements as the Pact of Paris have to deal with general principles of law, and not with administrative matters of procedure. The law of war is to be found not only in treaties, but with general principles of law, and not with administrative matters of procedure. The law of war is to be found not only in treaties, but in the customs and practices of states which gradually obtained universal recognition, and from the general principles of justice applied by jurists and practiced by military courts. This law is not static, but by continual adaptation follows the needs of a changing world. Indeed, in may cases treaties do no more than express and define for more accurate reference the principles of law already existing.

The view which the Tribunal takes of the true interpretation of the Pact is supported by the international history which preceded it. In the year 1923 the draft of a Treaty of Mutual Assistance was sponsored by the League of Nations. In Article I the Treaty declared "that aggressive war is an international crime", and that the parties would "undertake that no one of them will be guilty of its commission". The draft treaty was submitted to 29 states, about half of whom were in favor of accepting the text. The principal objection appeared to be in the difficulty of defining the acts which would constitute "aggression", rather than any doubt as to the criminality of aggressive war. The preamble to the League of Nations 1924 Protocol for the Pacific Settlement of International Disputes ("Geneva Protocol"), after "recognizing the solidarity of the members of the international community", declared that "a war of aggression constitutes a violation of this solidarity and is an international crime." It went on to declare that the contracting parties were "desirous of facilitating the complete application of the system provided in the Covenant of the League of Nations for the pacific settlement of disputes between the States and of ensuring the repression of international crimes." The Protocol was recommended to the members of the League of Nations by a unanimous resolution in the assembly of the 48 members of the League. These members included Italy and Japan, but Germany was not then a member of the League.

Although the Protocol was never ratified, it was signed by the leading statesmen of the world, representing the vast majority of the civilized states and peoples, and may be regarded as strong evidence of the intention to brand aggressive war as an international crime.

At the meeting of the Assembly of the League of Nations on 24 September 1927, all the delegations then present (including the German, the Italian, and the Japanese), unanimously adopted a declaration concerning wars of aggression. The preamble to the declaration stated:

"The Assembly:

Recognizing the solidarity which unites the community of nations;

Being inspired by a firm desire for the maintenance of general peace;

Being convinced that a war of aggression can never serve as a means of settling international disputes, and is in consequence an international crime . . ."

The unanimous resolution of 18 February 1928 of 21 American republics at the Sixth (Havana) Pan–American Conference, declared that "war of aggression constitutes an international crime against the human species".

All these expressions of opinion, and others that could be cited, so solemnly made, reinforce the construction which the Tribunal placed upon the Pact of Paris, that resort to a war of aggression is not merely illegal, but is criminal. The prohibition of aggressive war demanded by the conscience of the world, finds its expression in the series of pacts and treaties to which the Tribunal has just referred.

It is also important to remember that Article 227 of the Treaty of Versailles provided for the constitution of a special Tribunal, composed of representatives of five of the Allied and Associated Powers which had been belligerents in the first World War opposed to Germany, to try the former German Emperor "for a supreme offense against international morality and the sanctity of treaties." The purpose of this trial was expressed to be "to vindicate the solemn obligations of international undertakings, and the validity of international morality". In Article 228 of the Treaty, the German Government expressly recognized the right of the Allied Powers "to bring before military tribunals persons accused of having committed acts in violation of the laws and customs of war".

It was submitted that international law is concerned with the actions of sovereign States, and provides no punishment for individuals; and further, that where the act in question is an act of State, those who carry it out are not personally responsible, but are protected by the doctrine of the sovereignty of the State. In the opinion of the Tribunal, both these submissions must be rejected. That international law imposes duties and liabilities upon individuals as well as upon States has long been recognized. In the recent case of Ex Parte Quirin (1942 317 U.S. 1), before the Supreme Court of the United States, persons were charged during the war with landing in the United States for purposes of spying and sabotage. The late Chief Justice Stone, speaking for the Court, said:

> "From the very beginning of its history this Court has applied the law of war as including that part of the law of nations which prescribes for the conduct of war, the status, rights, and duties of enemy nations as well as enemy individuals."

He went on to give a list of cases tried by the Courts, where individual offenders were charged with offenses against the laws of nations, and particularly the laws of war. Many other authorities could be cited, but enough has been said to show that individuals can be punished for violations of international law. Crimes against international law are committed by men, not by abstract entities, and only by punishing individuals who commit such crimes can the provisions of international law be enforced.

The provisions of Article 228 of the Treaty of Versailles already referred to illustrate and enforce this view of individual responsibility.

The principle of international law, which under certain circumstances, protects the representatives of a state, cannot be applied to acts which are condemned as criminal by international law. The authors of these acts cannot shelter themselves behind their official position in order to be freed from punishment in appropriate proceedings. Article 7 of the Charter expressly declares:

> "The official position of Defendants, whether as heads of State, or responsible officials in Government departments, shall not be considered as freeing them from responsibility, or mitigating punishment."

On the other hand the very essence of the Charter is that individuals have international duties which transcend the national obligations of obedience imposed by the individual state. He who violates the laws of war cannot obtain immunity while acting in pursuance of the authority of the state if the state in authorizing action moves outside its competence under international law.

It was also submitted on behalf of most of these defendants that in doing what they did they were acting under the orders of Hitler, and therefore cannot be held responsible for the acts committed by them in carrying out these orders. The Charter specifically provides in Article 8:

> "The fact that the Defendant acted pursuant to order of his Government or of a superior shall not free him from responsibility, but may be considered in mitigation of punishment."

The provisions of this article are in conformity with the law of all nations. That a soldier was ordered to kill or torture in violation of the international law of war has never been recognized as a defense to such acts of brutality, though, as the Charter here provides, the order may be urged in mitigation of the punishment. The true test, which is found in varying degrees in the criminal law of most nations, is not the existence of the order, but whether moral choice was in fact possible.

* * *

GÖRING

Göring is indicted on all four Counts. The evidence shows that after Hitler he was the most prominent man in the Nazi regime. He was Commander-in-Chief of the Luftwaffe, Plenipotentiary for the Four Year Plan, and had tremendous influence with Hitler, at least until 1943 when their relationship deteriorated, ending in his arrest in 1945. He testified that Hitler kept him informed of all important military and political problems.

Crimes against Peace

From the moment he joined the Party in 1922 and took command of the street-fighting organization, the SA, Göring was the adviser, the active agent of Hitler, and one of the prime leaders of the Nazi movement. As Hitler's political deputy he was largely instrumental in bringing the national Socialists to power in 1933, and was charged with consolidating this power and expanding German armed might. He developed the Gestapo, and created the first concentration camps, relinquishing them to Himmler in 1934, conducted the Röhm purge in that year, and engineered the sordid proceedings which resulted in the removal of Von Blomberg and Von Fritsch from the Army. In 1936 he became Plenipotentiary for the Four Year Plan, and in theory and in practice was the economic dictator of the Reich. Shortly after the Pact of Munich, he announced that he would embark on a five-fold expansion of the Luftwaffe, and speed rearmament with emphasis on offensive weapons.

Göring was one of the five important leaders present at the Hossbach Conference of 5 November 1937, and he attended the other important conferences already discussed in this Judgment. In the Austrian Anschluss, he was indeed the central figure, the ringleader. He said in Court: "I must take 100 per cent responsibility.... I even overruled objections by the Führer and brought everything to its final development." In the seizure of the Sudetenland, he played his role as Luftwaffe chief by planning an air offensive which proved unnecessary, and his role as politician by lulling the Czechs with false promises of friendship. The night before the invasion of Czechoslovakia and the absorption of Bohemia and Moravia, at a conference with Hitler and President Hacha he threatened to bomb Prague if Hacha did not submit. This threat he admitted in his testimony.

Göring attended the Reich Chancellery meeting in 23 May 1939 when Hitler told his military leaders "there is, therefore, no question of sparing Poland," and was present at the Obersalzber briefing of 22 August 1939. And the evidence shows he was active in the diplomatic maneuvers which followed. With Hitler's connivance, he used the Swedish businessman, Dahlerus, as a go-between to the British, as described by Dahlerus to this Tribunal, to try to prevent the British Government from keeping its guarantee to the Poles.

He commanded the Luftwaffe in the attack on Poland and throughout the aggressive wars which followed.

Even if he opposed Hitler's plans against Norway and the Soviet Union, as he alleged, it is clear that he did so only for strategic reasons; once Hitler had decided the issue, he followed him without hesitation. He made it clear in his testimony that these differences were never ideological or legal. He was "in a rage" about the invasion of Norway, but only because he had not received sufficient warning to prepare the Luftwaffe offensive. He admitted he approved of the attack: "My attitude was perfectly positive." He was active in preparing and executing the Yugoslavian and Greek campaigns, and testified that "Plan Marita," the attack on Greece, had been prepared long beforehand. The Soviet Union he regarded as the "most threatening menace to Germany," but said there was no immediate military necessity for the attack. Indeed, his only objection to the war of aggression against the U.S.S.R. was its timing; he wished for strategic reasons to delay until Britain was conquered. He testified: "My point of view was decided by political and military reasons only."

After his own admissions to this Tribunal, from the positions which he held, the conferences he attended, and the public words he uttered, there can remain no doubt that Göring was the moving force for aggressive war, second only to Hitler. He was the planner and prime mover in the military and diplomatic preparation for war which Germany pursued.

* * *

VON RIBBENTROP

Von Ribbentrop is indicted under all four Counts. He joined the Nazi Party in 1932. By 1933 he had been made Foreign Policy Adviser to Hitler, and in the same year the representative of the Nazi Party on foreign policy. In 1934 he was appointed Delegate for Disarmament Questions, and in 1935 Minister Plenipotentiary at Large, a capacity in which he negotiated the Anglo–German Naval Agreement in 1935 and the Anti–Comintern Pact in 1936. On 11 August 1936 he was appointed Ambassador to England. On 4 February 1938 he succeeded Von Neurath as Reichsminister for Foreign Affairs as part of the general reshuffle which accompanied the dismissal of Von Fritsch and Von Blomberg.

Crimes Against Peace

Von Ribbentrop was not present at the Hossbach Conference held on 5 November 1937, but on 2 January 1938, while still Ambassador to England, he sent a memorandum to Hitler indicating his opinion that a change in the *status quo* in the East in the German sense could only be carried out by force and suggesting methods to prevent England and France from intervening in a European war fought to bring about such a change. When Von Ribbentrop became Foreign Minister Hitler told him that Germany still had four problems to solve, Austria, Sudetenland, Memel, and Danzig, and mentioned the possibility of "some sort of a showdown" or "military settlement" for their solution.

On 12 February 1938 Von Ribbentrop attended the conference between Hitler and Schuschnigg at which Hitler, by threats of invasion, forced Schuschnigg to grant a series of concessions designed to strengthen the Nazis in Austria, including the appointment of Seyss–Inquart as Minister of Security and Interior, with control over the police. Von Ribbentrop was in London when the occupation of Austria was actually carried out and, on the basis of information supplied him by Göring, informed the British Government that Germany had not presented Austria with an ultimatum, but had intervened in Austria only to prevent civil war. On 13 March 1938 Von Ribbentrop signed the law incorporating Austria into the German Reich.

Von Ribbentrop participated in the aggressive plans against Czechoslovakia. Beginning in March 1938, he was in close touch with the Sudeten German Party and gave the instructions which had the effect of keeping the Sudeten German question a live issue which might serve as an excuse for the attack which Germany was planning against Czechoslovakia. In August 1938 he participated in a conference for the purpose of obtaining Hungarian support in the event of a war with Czechoslovakia. After the Munich Pact he continued to bring diplomatic pressure with the object of occupying the remainder of Czechoslovakia. He was instrumental in inducing the Slovaks to proclaim their independence. He was present at the conference of 14–15 March 1939 at which Hitler, by threats of invasion, compelled President Hacha to consent to the German occupation of Czechoslovakia. After the German troops had marched in, Von Ribbentrop signed the law establishing a protectorate over Bohemia and Moravia.

Von Ribbentrop played a particularly significant role in the diplomatic activity which led up to the attack on Poland. He participated in a conference held on 12 August 1939, for the purpose of obtaining Italian support if the attack should lead to a general European war. Von Ribbentrop discussed the German demands with respect to Danzig and the Polish Corridor with the British Ambassador in the period from 25 August to 30 August 1939, when he knew that the German plans to attack Poland had merely been temporarily postponed in an attempt to induce the British to abandon their guarantee to the Poles. The way in which he carried out these discussions makes it clear that he did not enter them in good faith in an attempt to reach a settlement of the difficulties between Germany and Poland.

Von Ribbentrop was advised in advance of the attack on Norway and Denmark and of the attack on the Low Countries, and prepared the official Foreign Office memoranda attempting to justify these aggressive actions.

Von Ribbentrop attended the conference on 20 January 1941, at which Hitler and Mussolini discussed the proposed attack on Greece, and the conference in January 1941, at which Hitler obtained from Antonescu permission for German troops to go through Rumania for this attack. On 25 March 1941, when Yugoslavia adhered to the Axis Tri-partite Pact, Von Ribbentrop had assured Yugoslavia that Germany would respect its sovereignty and territorial integrity. On 27 March 1941 he attended the meeting, held after the *coup d'etat* in Yugoslavia, at which plans were made to carry out Hitler's announced intention to destroy Yugoslavia.

Von Ribbentrop attended a conference in May 1941 with Hitler and Antonescu relating to Rumanian participation in the attack on the U.S.S.R. He also consulted with Rosenberg in the preliminary planning for the political exploitation of Soviet territories and in July 1941, after the outbreak of war, urged Japan to attack the Soviet Union.

* * *

Von Ribbentrop's defense to the charges made against him is that Hitler made all the important decisions and that he was such a great admirer and faithful follower of Hitler that he never questioned Hitler's repeated assertions that he wanted peace or the truth of the reasons that Hitler gave in explaining aggressive action. The Tribunal does not consider this explanation to be true. Von Ribbentrop participated in all of the Nazi aggressions from the occupation of Austria to the invasion of the Soviet Union. Although he was personally concerned with the diplomatic rather than the military aspect of these actions, his diplomatic efforts were so closely connected with war that he could not have remained unaware of the aggressive nature of Hitler's actions. In the administration of territories over which Germany acquired control by illegal invasion Von Ribbentrop also assisted in carrying out criminal policies, particularly those involving the extermination of the Jews. There is abundant evidence, moreover, that Von Ribbentrop was in complete sympathy with all the main tenets of the National Socialist creed, and that his collaboration with Hitler and with other defendants in the commission of Crimes against Peace, War Crimes, and Crimes against Humanity was whole-hearted. It was because Hitler's policy and plans coincided with his own ideas that Von Ribbentrop served him so willingly to the end.

Conclusion

The Tribunal finds that Von Ribbentrop is guilty on all four Counts.

* * *

C. Notes, Questions, and Problems

1. As long as humanity has waged war it has sought to restrain it. What accounts for this contradictory human struggle? Can you detect recurrent influences in history toward strengthening or weakening legal restraints on the use of force? Do you see patterns in humanity's attempts at legal restraint?

2. Is there a role for the just war doctrine in evaluating contemporary uses of force? Conforti suggests that we should indeed assess uses of force on normative grounds and might come to evaluate them differently than on strictly legal grounds. This might be the case for uses of force with Security Council authorization, in self-defense, for humanitarian purposes and against terrorism. He writes, "* * * I wonder whether the reaction against the crime of terrorism can consist in the use of force against States, involving the death of innocent people instead of the adoption of all the appropriate preventive and repressive measures against the individuals committing such crimes." Conforti, *supra* note 1, at 10. Consider the restatement of Aquinas just war criteria at p. 108, above. Can you argue that a use of force against terrorists could be consistent with the just war doctrine? *See also* Joseph Sweeney, *The Just War Ethic in International Law*, 27 Fordham Int'l L.J. 1865 (2004); National Conference of Catholic Bishops, The Challenge of Peace (1983); Michael Walzer, Just and Unjust Wars, A Moral Argument with Historical Illustrations (1977).

3. Is it clear to you that the positive legal rules for prohibiting force somehow lack normative content? While it is true that positivism seeks to make the source of legal rules an objective one, subject to rules of recognition, consider the rules on the use of force that were agreed at the Hague Conferences and the Paris Peace Conference. In what ways are they different from or similar to the rules that Grotius purported to find through reason in the natural order of things?

4. Japan was a member of the League of Nations when it invaded Manchuria in 1931. Review the excerpts from the League Covenant. (pp. 127–129, above.) How should the League have reacted when the invasion occurred? Why do you think it did not? The United States did react invoking the Kellogg–Briand Pact. The Pact, however, had no enforcement measures. Can you argue that the U.S., nevertheless, had the right to take coercive action in response to a breach of the Pact?

5. *Nullum crimen sine lege, nulla poena sine lege.* No punishment without a crime—no criminal liability *ex post facto*—after the fact. These maxims lie at the heart of the chief criticism of the Nuremberg and Tokyo Trials. It was *ex post facto* law, victor's justice. In fact, the treaties cited at Nuremberg do not include provisions for trial and punishment of individuals for crimes against the peace. Review the reasoning of the International Military Tribunal as to this criticism. Are you persuaded that the *ex post facto* prohibition was not violated? Can you add to the Tribunal's reasoning from other examples in this Chapter? If trials did violate the *ex post facto* rule, what alternatives did the Allies have with respect to the German, Japanese and other Axis leaders in their custody?

6. Would the IMT reasoning as to individual accountability have been more persuasive if any of the political or military leaders of any of the victorious Allies had faced any charge at all for international law violations during the war? Presumably, they would not have been subject to the charge crimes against the peace, the subject of this Chapter, but we debate to this day whether Allied leaders did not order the commission of war crimes and even crimes against humanity. These debates will be discussed in the next Chapter. *See* pp. 205–207 below.

7. Did you note that Ribbentrop was found guilty of preparing the legal defense for invading Denmark and Norway? Do you think lawyers advising governments on international law are aware of this? If so, would you expect to see more resignations by lawyers? One British government lawyer did resign because she felt the use of force against Iraq in 2003 was unlawful. *See* Vikram Dodd, *Iraq War Illegal, Says Former Adviser Who Quit,*

Guardian, June 14, 2004, at 4. Presumably several hundred international lawyers work in the American, Australian, British and Polish governments. What is a government lawyer's ethical duty when a government ignores his or her advice that a use of armed force will violate international law? For a discussion of the role of international lawyers, including academic international lawyers, in justifying the actions of the Third Reich and more recent violations of international law, *see* Detlev Vagts, *Hegemonic International Law*, 95 Am. J. Int'l L. 843 (2001). For more on the professional ethics of international lawyers in the U.S. State Department, see Joint Committee of the ASIL & American Branch of the ILA, *The Role of the Legal Adviser of the Department of State*, 85 Am. J. Int'l L. 358 (1991).

8. **Problem**: The victorious World War I Allies made little effort to bring the Kaiser to trial, despite Article 227 of the Treaty of Versailles. This irritated a group of American soldiers, led by one Colonel Luke Lee. In 1919, he hatched a plan to grab the Kaiser in The Netherlands and drive him to Paris for trial. A group of seven managed to drive near the estate where the Kaiser was staying but abandoned their kidnap plan owing to a washed out bridge. Instead, they bluffed their way into the house with the intention of persuading the Kaiser to come with them voluntarily. The Kaiser would not see them. After a two-hour stand off, with Dutch forces by then surrounding the house, the Americans departed—Kaiser-less. *See* James F. Willis, Prologue to Nuremberg 100–01 (1982).

If the Americans had succeeded, and you were appointed to prosecute the Kaiser, what were the *ad bellum* rules in existence in 1914 that were arguably binding on the Kaiser? Would those be the same or different from rules binding on Germany? What would you argue in the Kaiser's defense?

CHAPTER FIVE

Regulating the Application of Force

Restrictions on the actual use of force, like restrictions on the resort to force, date from earliest times and are found in all regions of the world.[1] In this Chapter we trace the general development of the law *in bello* from Augustine to the trials of war criminals in Tokyo after World War II. The *jus in bello* contains far more rules and far more detailed rules than the *jus ad bellum*. Rather than try to deal with these rules comprehensively, we will look at some of the overarching principles here as well as specific rules in the areas of who may be targeted in armed conflict; the rules regarding detention, and the rules on military occupation. These three broad categories have arguably given rise to more litigation than other categories and so are also the focus of later chapters on the current law.

A. From Rome (Again) to The Hague (Again)

The early Christian scholar Augustine not only restricted when force should be used but also how. Just as he had done in developing his doctrine of the just causes of war, Augustine drew on the Greeks, Romans, and Hebrews for model principles on how warfare should be conducted. These ancient communities promoted mercy in wartime especially towards defenseless persons, including enemy prisoners.[2] Augustine counseled fighting war always with an eye on winning the peace. Even wars fought against evil men to stop them from committing further evil had to be done in a way that did not reduce the enemy to an outlaw. Augustine understood that cruelty in warfare could be the cause of the next conflict. People treated inhumanely often sought revenge. Since Augustine taught that war could only be just if it ultimately brought peace, he also taught that the conduct of war had to be carried out in such a way that allowed for future trust and minimized the desire for revenge.[3]

---

1. The literature on the history of the *jus in bello* is large. *See e.g.*, Yoram Distein, The Conduct of Hostilities Under the Law of International Armed Conflict (2004); Frits Kalshoven & Liesbeth Zegveld, Constraints on the Waging of War 3d ed. (2001); L.C. Green, The Contemporary Law of Armed Conflict (2000); The Handbook of Humanitarian Law (Dieter Fleck ed., 1995); Assisting the Victims of Armed Conflict and Other Disasters (Frits Kalshoven ed., 1989); Geoffrey Best, Humanity in Warfare 290 (1980).

2. Green, *supra* note 1, at 21–22; The Law of War: A Documentary History 4–5 (Leon Friedman ed., 1972).

3. Wilhelm G. Grewe, The Epochs of International Law 107–08 (trans. & rev'd, Michael Byers 2000); Arthur Nussbaum, A Concise History of the Law of Nations 35 (rev'd ed., 1962).

Thus in a letter to Boniface, Augustine wrote:

> Therefore it ought to be necessity, and not your will, that destroys an enemy who is fighting you. And just as you use force against the rebel or opponent, so you ought now to use mercy towards the defeated or the captive, and particularly so when there is no fear that peace will be disturbed.*

Following Augustine, the Catholic Church in the Middle Ages regulated some aspects of the conduct of war, just as it did the decision to resort to war.[4] In addition to Church teaching, unwritten codes—codes of chivalry—also carried forward to modern international law principles on the conduct of war.[5]

Geoffrey Parker, Extending the Laws of War**

Early Modern Europe, in The Laws of War (Michael
Howard et al, eds., 40, 51–55 (1994.))

* * *

[A]s time passed, the range of military misconduct condoned by military authorities and by public opinion steadily narrowed. Taking and killing hostages or perpetrating exemplary atrocities, which Vitoria and Gentili had tolerated in the sixteenth century, came to be execrated by writers such as Johann Justus Moser and Emerich de Vattel in the eighteenth; while today some theorists condemn even sieges and economic blockades as a species of terrorism because they intentionally inflict harm on innocent civilians in order to force governments to capitulate.

Moreover, in most of the wars waged in Europe since the sixteenth century, breaches of the norms for military conduct laid down in treatises (and more recently in treaties) have been condemned and chastised with increasing rigor. Individual soldiers faced trial and punishment by special military tribunals for crimes committed against either fellow soldiers or civilians.[a] Thus in 1574 Philip II ordered a judicial enquiry into accusations that the duke of Alba had used disproportionate force in his conduct of the war against the Dutch rebels, and although Alba himself was acquitted, several of his senior officials were banished from Court. After the brutal sack of Antwerp by the Spanish army in 1576, a full judicial

---

* Augustine: Political Writings 217 (E.M. Atkins & R.J. Dodaro eds., 2001).

4. Green, *supra* note 1, at 24.

5. *Id.*, at 24–25.

** (Most footnotes omitted.)

a. Two published fragments of seventeenth-century court-martial records give some idea of their work: J. Adair, "The Court Martial Papers of Sir William Waller's Arm, 1644," *Journal of the Society for Army Historical Research* 44 (1966: 205–23); Godfrey Davis, ed., "Dundee Court–Martial Records, 1651," *Scottish Historical Society Miscellany*, vol. 3, Scottish History Society, 2d ser., vol. 19 (Edinburgh 1919) 3–67. For the Spanish Arem of Flanders see also Licienne van Meerbeeck, *Inventaire des Archives des tribunaux militaries* (Glembloux, 1939).

enquiry was held to determine responsibility for the atrocities which left eight thousand citizens dead and one thousand houses destroyed; and in Ireland after the trauma of the civil war and the Cromwellian occupation, a court of claims was established in 1662 specifically to examine charges against those accused of war crimes.

This development constituted a significant and lasting extension in the application of the laws of war and it was paralleled by another: conventions previously applied selectively during the early modern period gradually came to be enforced almost universally. In a sense this process merely represented a stage in a longer evolution. Many tribal societies equated mankind with members of their own tribe and regarded all others as nonhumans to be treated—or, rather, mistreated—as animals. Even in medieval Europe the laws of war only governed "the conduct of men who fought to settle by arms quarrels which were in nature private, and whose importance was judged by the social status of the principals involved." They therefore affected only equals. In the sixteenth century, however, starting in Spain's war against the Dutch, the same rules began to be applied to all combatants, whatever their social status.

Even as Balthasar Ayala composed his uncompromising treatise on the need to wage a war to the death against all rebels, his commanding officer (Alessandro Faroese, duke of Parma) negotiated generous terms for the return of rebellious cities to the king's obedience and for the exchange and ransom of captured soldiers in enemy hands. Soon afterward the regular exchange of prisoners of war became standard practice: by 1599, if not before, Spain and the Dutch Republic had concluded a formal convention—the *cuartel general*—stipulating that every captain should ransom all his captured men within twenty-five days. First, prisoners of equal rank on each side were to be exchanged free of charge; thereafter, a ransom appropriate to the soldier's rank (usually the equivalent of one month's pay) was due, plus an agreed per diem "entertainment" for time spent in captivity. The convention was reissued every few years, with the schedule of payments revised upward to take account of inflation. In 1637 and again in 1643 the Dutch–Spanish protocol was translated and published in English; and from 1639 the same system was introduced into the war between Spain and France. Likewise, agreement was reached that sick and injured soldiers who fell into enemy hands should be placed under a special safeguard and repatriated with a minimum of formality. Thus matters which had previously been subject to private contract now came under state regulation; and the available evidence suggests that exchanges were effected fairly and fast—even if the prisoners were released "from the most remote parts, as usual, so that they will not find it easy to return home."

Simultaneously, new regulations began to limit the violence and plunder of unpaid soldiery at the expense of noncombatants. Both sides in the Low Countries' Wars began to accept prearranged sums of protection money from individual communities based on mutual guarantees that they would neither engage in hostilities nor be subjected to further extortions from those whom they paid. Parties of troops took up station specifically to enforce the agreements. Once again, the idea was not new: during the Hundred Years' War most local commanders had issued letters of protection to a community in return for financial contributions, but each safeguard only bound the party that issued it—a community was still liable to depredations from the troops of other commanders even when they were on the same side. In the Low Countries' Wars, however, the growing power of the state made the system binding on all troops, and its effectiveness may be judged from a letter written by a Spanish field officer to his superiors in 1640: "The majority of the villages [near the enemy frontier] ... contain enemy 'protection troops.' ... [This] gives rise to many inconveniences for His Majesty's service. One is that our own men cannot go there to collect information about the enemy, because they are immediately arrested as spies by the protection troops. And, thanks to their presence, the peasants are able to bring in their crops safely and provide full aid and assistance to the enemy."

Four factors explain the new restraint in war. First, the composition of armies underwent a major change: the contingents hired and maintained via military contractors gave way to units raised and sustained directly by the state.

* * *

A second reason favoring greater restraint in the conduct of war in the West was a steady process of deconfessionalization. By 1650 the religious frontiers of Europe had largely stabilized, for the religious rebels had either succeeded in gaining recognition as a state (as with the Dutch Republic) or had been forced either to conform or leave (as in the Spanish Netherlands). Furthermore, the calamitous changes of fortune experienced by each creed during the period seem to have dented the absolute certainty of many participants that they served as agents of God's purpose: a sense of resignation often replaced the dynamic providentialism that had led men to fight to the death with a clear conscience. Almost simultaneously, after the Peace of Westphalia in 1648 religion ceased to be an issue for which most states were prepared to go to war.

* * *

Alongside this gradual intellectual process lay another: a general feeling that in the wars of the mid-seventeenth century Europe had come perilously close to self-destruction.

* * *

A fourth and final explanation for the growth of restraint in early modern European warfare lay in the steady spread of reciprocity. During the Middle Ages honor and reputation had to some extent ensured observance of the conventions, but they were always reinforced by the threat of vengeance: the kin of a knight slain by treachery would normally seek revenge, creating a blood feud. And where this sanction was lacking, restraint diminished. Thus encounters between knights and members of the lower social orders normally turned into bloodbaths, whoever won: witness the carnage after the various victories of the Swiss or after the defeat of peasant armies. Restraint only appeared in such unequal conflicts when they became protracted: barbarous behavior by one side, confident of the righteousness of its own cause and its own invulnerability, changed dramatically when the other side acquired the capacity to retaliate. Thus in the early stages of the Dutch revolt, according to the duke of Alba himself, it was Spain's strict policy to hang all prisoners. But this changed abruptly in the autumn of 1573 when the Dutch captured one of Alba's most capable subordinates, the count of Bossu. The Dutch leaders made it clear that, unless the systematic execution of Dutch prisoners ceased, Bossu would be hanged. The Spaniards reluctantly agreed, and negotiations began for the release of Bossu and other Spaniards in exchange for certain rebels in Spanish hands. Enemy troops came to be accepted as soldiers first and rebels second. Likewise, during the civil war in England, although the king's provost marshal initially treated captured parliamentarians as rebels and traitors, Parliament's threats to hang all their royalist prisoners in retaliation caused a notable reduction in severity.

* * *

It took a little longer for the same principle to be accepted in the war at sea. As late as 1622–25 the crews of Flemish privateers were either hanged or thrown overboard ("foot watering" as it was known) when captured by their Dutch adversaries; but when the Dunkirkers captured no fewer than fifteen hundred Dutch prisoners the foot watering abruptly ceased.

Grotius, also supported this trend toward restraint, devoting considerable space in *The Law of War and Peace* to the proper conduct of armed conflict. He wrote in detail on the use of reprisals, the treatment of property, treatment of the sick and wounded, burial rights, and much more. Among the most important principles he includes is the basic requirement that the manner of waging of war is not unlimited.

Hugo Grotius, The Law of War and Peace

III De Jure Belle ac pacis Libri 722 (Francis W. Kelsey trans. 1964).

Moderation with Respect to the Right of Killing in a Lawful War

I.—*In a lawful war certain acts are devoid of moral justice; a condition which is explained*

I.   Not even in a lawful war ought we to admit that which is said in the line,

> He, who refuses what is just, yields all.

Cicero's point of view is better: 'There are certain duties which must be performed even toward those from whom you have received an injury. There is in fact a limit to vengeance and to punishment.' The same writer praises the ancient days of Rome, when the issues of wars were either mild or in accordance with necessity.

Seneca calls those persons cruel who 'have a reason for punishing, but observe no limit'. Aristides, in his second speech *On Leuctra*, says: 'Men may indeed be unjust in avenging themselves, if they carry vengeance beyond measure. He, who in punishing goes so far as to do what is unjust, becomes a second wrongdoer.' Thus, in the judgement of Ovid, a certain king,

> Avenging himself to excess,
> And slaughtering the guilty, guilty himself became.

––––––––––––

Grotius then goes on to list those who should not be killed even in a lawful war, including children, academics and clergy, farmers, and merchants. Women, the elderly and prisoners of war should not be killed unless they have done something criminal.[6] Grotius had seen the violation of these principles and more in the brutal Thirty Years' War. When that war ended with the Peace of Westphalia "the nature of relations between fighting men had changed."[7] The system of chivalry faded out as professional officer corps replaced knights in the new military organizations of sovereign states.[8] Lawful war became "a hostile contention by means of armed forces carried on between states."[9] As Parker describes above, this professionali-

---

6.   Hugo Grotius, III De Jure Belle ac pacis Libri 722–744 (Francis W. Kelsey, trans. 1964).

7.   Green, *supra* note 1, at 28.

8.   Robert C. Stacy, *The Age of Chivalry*, *in* The Laws of War, 27, 39 (Michael Howard et al, eds. 1994).

9.   Green, *supra* note 1, at 28–29.

zation and the deconfessionalization that occurred at the same time, made the possibility of law restricting excesses in war possible.

Vattel, always thinking in terms of what would serve his sovereign master best, warned against punishing opponents too severely for the practical reasons pointed out by Augustine. The consequences of doing so could be worse than the original wrong—as the Duke of Alba learned after executing 20,000 citizens of The Netherlands. The backlash led to Spain eventually losing The Netherlands. Vattel recommended granting amnesties, showing mercy. Similarly, in the conduct of war, principles of humanity, forbearance, truthfulness and honor apply to both sides.[10] Complying with the law of war, according to Vattel, would diminish the interest in retaliation and foster trust, which is needed to eventually reach an agreement on peace.

Vattel's book on international law was well-known to America's Founding Fathers. Benjamin Franklin not only read but distributed copies of it.[11] In 1785, Franklin concluded with Frederick the Great of Prussia a treaty of friendship and commerce that also codified principles for the humane treatment of prisoners of war. The treaty is credited with being one of the first international agreements to include principles on the law *in bello* in written form.[12] The first multinational treaty would not follow for seventy years.

In the meantime, with advances in technology, civilians and soldiers alike began suffering the effects of war in ways that led to demands for safeguards. Florence Nightingale, who nursed the sick and wounded in the Crimean War (1853–56) pioneered medical and nursing services for wartime.[13] Her advances were adopted in the United States during the American Civil War. The Civil War was particularly brutal and induced President Lincoln to approve the drafting of "General Orders No. 100" by Francis Lieber, a German–American professor of international law at Columbia College, now Columbia University. The result was a detailed manual for Union forces to guide their conduct in the war. "Lieber's Code was the first attempt to set down, in a single set of instructions for forces in the field, the laws and customs of war."[14] Lieber had himself fought in Europe before emigrating to the United States. He lost one son fighting for the confederacy and had two other sons who fought for the Union.[15] He was uniquely qualified to produce a manual that rapidly won wide acceptance. By the end of the 19th century, the leading western military powers had generally adapted Lieber's Code for their own militaries.

---

10. EMMERICH DE VATTEL, THE LAW OF NATIONS OR THE PRINCIPLES OF NATURAL LAW, APPLIED TO THE CONDUCT AND TO THE AFFAIRS OF NATIONS AND OF SOVEREIGNS 338 (Charles G. Fenwick trans. of 1758 ed.).

11. NUSSBAUM, *supra* note, at 161.

12. THE HANDBOOK OF HUMANITARIAN LAW, *supra* note 1, at 17.

13. *Id.*

14. *Id.* at 18.

15. RICHARD SHELLY HARTIGAN, LIEBER'S CODE OF THE LAW OF WAR, 5–7, 15 (1983).

The Lieber Code

Washington, D.C., April 24, 1863

Instructions for the Government of Armies of the United States
in the Field by Order of the Secretary of War:

* * *

Article XIV

Military necessity, as understood by modern civilized nations,
consists in the necessity of those measures which are indispensable
for securing the ends of the war, and which are lawful according to
the modern law and usages of war.

Article XV

Military necessity admits of all direct destruction of life or limb of
armed enemies, and of other persons whose destruction is incidentally *unavoidable* in the armed contests of the war; it allows of the
capturing of every armed enemy, and every enemy of importance
to the hostile government, or of peculiar danger to the captor; it
allows of all destruction of property, and obstruction of the ways
and channels of traffic, travel, or communication, and of all
witholding of sustenance or means of life from the enemy; of the
appropriation of whatever an enemy's country affords necessary
for the subsistence and safety of the army, and of such deception
as does not involve the breaking of good faith either positively
pledged, regarding agreements entered into during the war, or
supposed by the modern law of war to exist. Men who take up
arms against one another in public war do not cease on this
account to be moral beings, responsible to one another and to God.

Article XVI

Military necessity does not admit of cruelty—that is, the infliction
of suffering for the sake of suffering or for revenge, nor of
maiming or wounding except in fight, nor of torture to extort
confessions. It does not admit of the use of poison in any way, nor
of the wanton devastation of a district. It admits of deception, but
disclaims acts of perfidy; and, in general, military necessity does
not include any act of hostility which makes the return to peace
unnecessarily difficult.

* * *

Article XXIX

Peace is their normal condition; war is the exception. The ultimate
object of all modern war is a renewed state of peace.

The more vigorously wars are pursued, the better it is for humanity. Sharp wars are brief.

* * *

ARTICLE XXXVII

The United States acknowledge and protect, in hostile countries occupied by them, religion and morality; strictly private property; the persons of the inhabitants, especially those of women; and the sacredness of domestic relations. Offenses to the contrary shall be rigorously punished.

This rule does not interfere with the right of the victorious invader to tax the people or their property, to levy forced loans, to billet soldiers, or to appropriate property, especially houses, lands, boats or ships, and churches, for temporary and military uses.

ARTICLE XXXVIII

Private property, unless forfeited by crimes or by offenses of the owner, can be seized only by way of military necessity, for the support or other benefit of the army or of the United States.

If the owner has not fled, the commander officer will cause receipts to be given, which may serve the spoliated owner to obtain indemnity.

* * *

ARTICLE XLIV

All wanton violence committed against persons in the invaded country, all destruction of property not commanded by the authorized officer, all robbery, all pillage or sacking, even after taking a place by main force, all rape, wounding, maiming, or killing of such inhabitants, are prohibited under the penalty of death, or such other severe punishment as may seem adequate for the gravity of the offense.

A soldier, officer or private, in the act of committing such violence, and disobeying a superior ordering him to abstain from it, may be lawfully killed on the spot by such superior.

* * *

ARTICLE XLIX

A prisoner of war is a public enemy armed or attached to the hostile army for active aid, who has fallen into the hands of the captor, either fighting or wounded, on the field or in the hospital, by individual surrender, or by capitulation.

All soldiers, of whatever species of arms; all men who belong to the rising *en masse* of the hostile country; all those who are attached to the army for its efficiency and promote directly the object of the war, except such as are hereinafter provided for; all disabled men or officers on the field or elsewhere, if captured; all enemies who have thrown away their arms and ask for quarter, are prisoners of war, and as such exposed to the inconveniences as well as entitled to the privileges of a prisoner of war.

ARTICLE L

Moreover, citizens who accompany an army for whatever purpose, such as sutlers, editors, or reporters of journals, or contractors, if captured, may be made prisoners of war, and be detained as such.

The monarch and members of the reigning hostile family, male or female, the chief, and chief officers of the hostile government, its diplomatic agents, and all persons who are of particular and singular use and benefit to the hostile army or its government, are, if captured, on belligerent ground, and if unprovided with a safe conduct granted by the captor's government, prisoners of war.

ARTICLE LI

If the people of that portion of an invaded country which is not yet occupied by the enemy, or of the whole country, at the approach of a hostile army, rise, under a duly authorized levy, *en masse* to resist the invader, they are now treated as public enemies, and, if captured, are prisoners of war.

ARTICLE LII

No belligerent has the right to declare that he will treat every captured man in arms of a levy *en masse* as a brigand or bandit.

If, however, the people of a country, or any portion of the same, already occupied by an army, rise against it, they are violators of the laws of war, and are not entitled to their protection.

* * *

ARTICLE LVI

A prisoner of war is subject to no punishment for being a public enemy, nor is any revenge wreaked upon him by the intentional infliction of any suffering, or disgrace, by cruel imprisonment, want of food, by mutilation, death, or any other barbarity.

ARTICLE LVII

So soon as a man is armed by a sovereign government and takes the soldier's oath of fidelity, he is a belligerent; his killing, wounding, or other warlike acts are not individual crimes or offenses. No belligerent has a right to declare that enemies of a certain class, color, or condition, when properly organized as soldiers, will not be treated by him as public enemies.

ARTICLE LVIII

The law of nations knows of no distinction of color, and if an enemy of the United States should enslave and sell any captured persons of their army, it would be a case for the severest retaliation, if not redressed upon complaint.

The United States cannot retaliate by enslavement; therefore death must be the retaliation for this crime against the law of nations.

ARTICLE LIX

A prisoner of war remains answerable for his crimes committed against the captor's army or people, committed before he was captured, and for which he has not been punished by his own authorities.

All prisoners of war are liable to the infliction of retaliatory measures.

* * *

ARTICLE LXVIII

Modern wars are not internecine wars, in which the killing of the enemy is the object. The destruction of the enemy in modern war, and indeed, modern war itself, are means to obtain that object of the belligerent which lies beyond the war.

Unnecessary or revengeful destruction of life is not lawful.

* * *

ARTICLE LXXI

Whoever intentionally inflicts additional wounds on an enemy already wholly disabled, or kills such an enemy, or who orders or encourages soldiers to do so, shall suffer death, if duly convicted, whether he belongs to the Army of the United States, or is an enemy captured after having committed his misdeed.

* * *

The case that follows is one of a number dealt with by United States courts arising out of the American Civil War. In this case, the United States Supreme Court explains when military law and military courts will oust the civilian courts and peacetime rules. It is a case dealing with similar issues to those raised in Chapter One. It is also a case that demonstrates how the *jus in bello* was applied and enforced by national courts in the 19th century.

Ex Parte Milligan

4 Wall. 2 (1866)

MR. JUSTICE DAVIS delivered the opinion of the court.

On the 10th day of May, 1865, Lambdin P. Milligan presented a petition to the Circuit Court of the United States for the District of Indiana, to be discharged from an alleged unlawful imprisonment. The case made by the petition is this: Milligan is a citizen of the United States; has lived for twenty years in Indiana; and, at the time of the grievances complained of, was not, and never had been in the military or naval service of the United States. On the 5th day of October, 1864, while at home, he was arrested by order of General Alvin P. Hovey, commanding the military district of Indiana; and has ever since been kept in close confinement.

* * *

The controlling question in the case is this: Upon the *facts* stated in Milligan's petition, and the exhibits filed, had the military commission mentioned in it *jurisdiction*, legally, to try and sentence him? Milligan, not a resident of one of the rebellious states, or a prisoner of war, but a citizen of Indiana for twenty years past, and never in the military or naval service, is, while at his home, arrested by the military power of the United States, imprisoned, and, on certain criminal charges preferred against him, tried, convicted, and sentenced to be hanged by a military commission, organized under the direction of the military commander of the military district of Indiana. Had this tribunal the *legal* power and authority to try and punish this man?

No graver question was ever considered by this court, nor one which more nearly concerns the rights of the whole people; for it is the birthright of every American citizen when charged with crime, to be tried and punished according to law. The power of punishment is, alone through the means which the laws have provided for that purpose, and if they are ineffectual, there is an immunity from punishment, no matter how great an offender the individual may be, or how much his crimes may have shocked the sense of justice of the country, or endangered its safety. By the protection of the law human rights are secured; withdraw that protection, and they are at the mercy of wicked rulers, or the clamor of an excited people. If there was law to justify this military trial, it is not our province to interfere; if there was not, it is our duty to declare the nullity of the whole proceedings. The decision of this question does not depend on argument or judicial precedents, numerous and highly illustrative as they are. These precedents inform us of the extent of the struggle to preserve liberty and to relieve those in civil life from military trials. The founders of our government were familiar with the history of that struggle; and secured in a written constitution every right which the people had wrested from power during a contest of ages. By that Constitution and the laws authorized by it this question must be determined. The provisions of that instrument on the administration of criminal justice are too plain and direct, to leave room for misconstruction or doubt of their true meaning. Those applicable to this case are found in the clause of the original Constitution which says, "That the trial of all crimes, except in case of impeachment, shall be by jury;" and in the fourth, fifth, and sixth articles of the amendments. * * *

* * *

Time has proven the discernment of our ancestors; for even these provisions, expressed in such plain English words, that it would seem the ingenuity of man could not evade them, are *now*, after the lapse of more than seventy years, sought to be avoided. Those great and good men foresaw that troublous times would arise, when rulers and people would become restive under restraint, and seek by sharp and decisive measures to accomplish ends deemed just and proper; and that the principles of constitutional liberty would be in peril, unless established by irrepealable law. The history of the world had taught them that what was done in the past might be attempted in the future. The Constitution of the United States is a law for rulers and people, equally in war and in peace, and covers with the shield of its protection all classes of men, at all times, and under all circumstances. No doctrine, involving more pernicious consequences, was ever invented by the wit of man than that any of its provisions can be suspended during any of the great exigencies of government. Such a doctrine leads directly to anarchy or despotism, but the theory of necessity on which it is based is false; for the government, within the Constitution, has all the powers granted to it, which are necessary to preserve its existence; as has been happily proved by the result of the great effort to throw off its just authority.

* * *

[T]he "laws and usages of war" * * * can never be applied to citizens in states which have upheld the authority of the government, and where the courts are open and their process unobstructed. This court had judicial knowledge that in Indiana the Federal authority was always unopposed, and its courts always open to hear criminal accusations and redress grievances; and no usage of war could sanction a military trial there for any offence whatever of a citizen in civil life, in nowise connected with the military service. Congress could grant no such power; and to the honor of our national legislature be it said, it has never been provoked by the state of the country even to attempt its exercise. One of the plainest constitutional provisions was, therefore, infringed when

Milligan was tried by a court not ordained and established by Congress, and not composed of judges appointed during good behavior.

* * *

It follows, from what has been said on this subject, that there are occasions when martial rule can be properly applied. If, in foreign invasion or civil war, the courts are actually closed, and it is impossible to administer criminal justice according to law, *then*, on the theatre of active military operations, where war really prevails, there is necessity to furnish a substitute for the civil authority, thus overthrown, to preserve the safety of the army and society; and as no power is left but the military, it is allowed to govern by martial rule until the laws can have their free course. As necessity creates the rule, so it limits its duration; for, if this government is continued *after* the courts are reinstated, it is a gross usurpation of power. Martial rule can never exist where the courts are open, and in the proper and unobstructed exercise of their jurisdiction. It is also confined to the locality of actual war. Because, during the late Rebellion it could have been enforced in Virginia, where the national authority was overturned and the courts driven out, it does not follow that it should obtain in Indiana, where that authority was never disputed, and justice was always administered. And so in the case of foreign invasion, marital rule may become a necessity in one state, when, in another, it would be "mere lawless violence."

We are not without precedents in English and American history illustrating our views of this question; but it is hardly necessary to make particular reference to them.

From the first year of the reign of Edward the Third, when the Parliament of England reversed the attainder of the Earl of Lancaster, because he could have been tried by the courts of the realm, and declared, "that in time of peace no man ought to be adjudged to death for treason or any other offence without being arraigned and held to answer; and that regularly when the king's courts are open it is a time of peace in judgment of law," down to the present day, martial law, as claimed in this case, has been condemned by all respectable English jurists as contrary to the fundamental laws of the land, and subversive of the liberty of the subject.

* * *

So sensitive were our Revolutionary fathers on this subject, although Boston was almost in a state of siege, when General Gage issued his proclamation of martial law, they spoke of it as an "attempt to supersede the course of the common law, and instead thereof to publish and order the use of martial law." The Virginia

Assembly, also, denounced a similar measure, on the part of Governor Dunmore "as an assumed power, which the king himself cannot exercise; because it annuls the law of the land and introduces the most execrable of all systems, martial law."

In some parts of the country, during the war of 1812, our officers made arbitrary arrests and, by military tribunals, tried citizens who were not in the military service. These arrests and trials, when brought to the notice of the courts, were uniformly condemned as illegal. The cases of *Smith v. Shaw* and *McConnell v. Hampton* (reported in 12 Johnson), are illustrations, which we cite, not only for the principles they determine, but on account of the distinguished jurists concerned in the decisions, one of whom for many years occupied a seat on this bench.

* * *

It is proper to say, although Milligan's trial and conviction by a military commission was illegal, yet, if guilty of the crimes imputed to him, and his guilt had been ascertained by an established court and impartial jury, he deserved severe punishment. Open resistance to the measures deemed necessary to subdue a great rebellion, by those who enjoy the protection of government, and have not the excuse even of prejudice of section to plead in their favor, is wicked; but that resistance becomes an *enormous crime* when it assumes the form of a secret political organization, armed to oppose the laws, and seeks by stealthy means to introduce the enemies of the country into peaceful communities, there to light the torch of civil war, and thus overthrow the power of the United States. Conspiracies like these, at such a juncture, are extremely perilous; and those concerned in them are dangerous enemies to their country, and should receive the heaviest penalties of the law, as an example to deter others from similar criminal conduct. It is said the severity of the laws caused them; but Congress was obliged to enact severe laws to meet the crisis; and as our highest civil duty is to serve our country when in danger, the late war has proved that rigorous laws, when necessary, will be cheerfully obeyed by a patriotic people, struggling to preserve the rich blessings of a free government.

* * *

It is not easy to see how he can be treated as a prisoner of war, when he lived in Indiana for the past twenty years, was arrested there, and had not been, during the late troubles, a resident of any of the states in rebellion. If in Indiana he conspired with bad men to assist the enemy, he is punishable for it in the courts of Indiana; but, when tried for the offence, he cannot plead the rights of war; for he was not engaged in legal acts of hostility against the government, and only such persons, when captured, are prisoners of war. If he cannot enjoy the immunities attaching to the character of a prisoner of war, how can he be subject to their pains and penalties?

This case, as well as the kindred cases of Bowles and Horsey, were disposed of at the last term, and the proper orders were entered of record. There is, therefore, no additional entry required.

Not long after the Lieber Code was drafted, the first multinational treaty for limiting the conduct of war was concluded. The Geneva Convention for the Amelioration of the Condition of the Wounded in Armies in the Field was the result of the efforts of Henri Dunant. Dunant had observed the grave suffering of the wounded left on the battlefield after the Battle of Solferino in 1859. He formed an organization prepared to help such victims in the future, the International Committee of the Red Cross, in 1863. The 1864 Convention codified protections for the wounded as well as Red Cross and other humanitarian personnel seeking to assist them.[16]

In 1868, Czar Alexander II of Russia called a conference in St. Petersburg to prohibit the exploding bullet. The Czar called another conference with more general aims in 1874 in Brussels. Though not enough states ratified the final result of the Brussels conference, the conference did pave the way for another conference in 1880 in Oxford that resulted in the *Manual of the Laws of War on Land*.[17] The Lieber Code, the Geneva Convention, the Declaration of St. Petersburg and the *Oxford Manual* were all important precursors to the Hague Peace Conferences of 1899 and 1907.[18] Among the most important results of the two conferences were agreements on the conduct of war, agreements that remain binding law today. The 1899 Conference adopted various declarations prohibiting the use of certain weapons as well as Convention (II) with Respect to the Laws and Customs of War on Land with an annex of regulations on the conduct of warfare on land. In 1907, the 1899 Conventions were modified and ten additional conventions were added. The annex on land warfare became part of Hague Convention IV of 1907. The preamble of both Hague II of 1899 and Hague IV of 1907 contains what is known as the "Martens Clause:"[19]

> [I]n cases not included in the Regulations adopted [by the parties], the inhabitants and the belligerents remain under the protection and the rule of the principles of the law of nations, as they result from the usages established among civilized peoples, from the laws of humanity, and the dictates of the public conscience.

---

16. The Handbook of Humanitarian Law, *supra* note 1, at 18; Green, *supra* note 1, at 30.

17. Green, *supra* note 1, at 31–32.

18. *See* Symposium: The Hague Peace Conferences, 94 Am. J. Int'l L. 1 (2000).

19. *See* Theodor Meron, *The Martens Clause, Principles of Humanity, and Dictates of Public Conscience*, 94 Am. J. Int'l L. 78 (2000).

Annex to the Convention

Regulations Respecting the Laws and Customs of War on Land

SECTION I—ON BELLIGERENTS

CHAPTER I—*The Qualifications of Belligerents*

Article 1

The laws, rights, and duties of war apply not only to armies, but also to militia and volunteer corps fulfilling the following conditions:

1. To be commanded by a person responsible for his subordinates;

2. To have a fixed distinctive emblem recognizable at a distance;

3. To carry arms openly; and

4. To conduct their operations in accordance with the laws and customs of war.

In countries where militia or volunteer corps constitute the army, or form part of it, they are included under the denomination 'army'.

Article 2

The inhabitants of territory which has not been occupied, who, on the approach of the enemy, spontaneously take up arms to resist the invading troops without having had time to organize themselves in accordance with Article 1, shall be regarded as belligerents if they carry arms openly and if they respect the laws and customs of war.

Article 3

The armed forces of the belligerent parties may consist of combatants and non-combatants. In the case of capture by the enemy, both have a right to be treated as prisoners of war.

CHAPTER II—*Prisoners of War*

Article 4

Prisoners of war are in the power of hostile Government, but not of the individuals or corps who capture them.

They must be humanely treated.

All their personal belongings, except arms, horses, and military papers, remain their property.

Article 5

Prisoners of war may be interned in a town, fortress, camp, or other place, and bound not to go beyond certain fixed limits; but they can not be confined except as an indispensable measure of safety and only while the circumstances which necessitate the measure continue to exist.

* * *

Article 7

The Government into whose hands prisoners of war have fallen is charged with their maintenance.

In the absence of a special agreement between the belligerents, prisoners of war shall be treated as regards board, lodging, and clothing on the same footing as the troops of the Government who captured them.

Article 8

Prisoners of war shall be subject to the laws, regulations, and orders in force in the army of the State in whose power they are. Any act of insubordination justifies the adoption towards them of such measures of severity as may be considered necessary.

Escaped prisoners who are retaken before being able to rejoin their own army or before leaving the territory occupied by the army which captured them are liable to disciplinary punishment.

Prisoners who, after succeeding in escaping, are again taken prisoners, are not liable to any punishment on account of the previous flight.

Article 9

Every prisoner of war is bound to give, if he is questioned on the subject, his true name and rank, and if he infringes this rule, he is liable to have the advantages given to prisoners of his class curtailed.

* * *

Article 14

An inquiry office for prisoners of war is instituted on the commencement of hostilities in each of the belligerent States, * * *

* * *

Section II—Hostilities

Chapter I—*Means of Injuring the Enemy, Sieges, and Bombardments*

Article 22

The right of belligerents to adopt means of injuring the enemy is not unlimited.

Article 23

In addition to the prohibitions provided by special Conventions, it is especially forbidden—

(a) To employ poison or poisoned weapons;

(b) To kill or wound treacherously individuals belonging to the hostile nation or army;

(c) To kill or wound an enemy who, having laid down his arms, or having no loner means of defence, has surrendered at discretion;

(d) To declare that no quarter will be given;

(e) To employ arms, projectiles, or material calculated to cause unnecessary suffering;

(f) To make improper use of a flag of truce, of the national flag or the military insignia and uniform of the enemy, as well as the distinctive badges of the Geneva Convention;

(g) To destroy or seize the enemy's property, unless such destruction or seizure be imperatively demanded by the necessities of war;

(h) To declare abolished, suspended, or inadmissible in a court of law the rights and actions of the nationals of the hostile party.

A belligerent is likewise forbidden to compel the nationals of the hostile party to take part in the operations of war directed against their own country, even if they were in the belligerent's service before the commencement of the war.

Article 24

Ruses of war and the employment of measures necessary for obtaining information about the enemy and the country are considered permissible.

Article 25

The attack or bombardment, by whatever means, of towns, villages, dwellings, or buildings which are undefended is prohibited.

Article 26

The officer in command of an attacking force must, before commencing a bombardment, except in cases of assault, do all in his power to warn the authorities.

Article 27

In sieges and bombardments all necessary steps must be taken to spare, as far as possible, buildings dedicated to religion, art, science, or charitable purposes, historic monuments, hospitals, and places where the sick and wounded are collected, provided they are not being used at the time for military purposes.

It is the duty of the besieged to indicate the presence of such buildings or places by distinctive and visible signs, which shall be notified to the enemy beforehand.

Article 28

The pillage of a town or place, even when taken by assault, is prohibited.

* * *

SECTION III—MILITARY AUTHORITY OVER THE TERRITORY OF THE HOSTILE STATE

Article 42

Territory is considered occupied when it is actually placed under the authority of the hostile army.

The occupation extends only to the territory where such authority has been established and can be exercised.

Article 43

The authority of the legitimate power having in fact passed into the hands of the occupant, the latter shall take all the measures in his power to restore, and ensure, as far as possible, public order and safety,* while respecting, unless absolutely prevented, the laws in force in the country.

Article 44

A belligerent is forbidden to force the inhabitants of territory occupied by it to furnish information about the army of the other belligerent, or about its means of defense.

Article 45

It is forbidden to compel the inhabitants of occupied territory to swear allegiance to the hostile Power.

Article 46

Family honor and rights, the lives of persons, and private property, as well as religious convictions and practice, must be respected.

Private property cannot be confiscated.

Article 47

Pillage is formally forbidden.

* * *

B. From The Hague to Tokyo

The Hague Peace Conferences did not prevent the First World War nor apparently mitigate the suffering significantly of the military or civilians. The parties to the conflict did accept the Hague Conventions as applicable to the conflict. The Allies had wanted to try the Kaiser for waging an unlawful war, in violation of the Hague Conventions and other treaties.

---

* Footnote omitted.

You will recall from Chapter Four that they did not succeed in that. The Allies also included in the Treaty of Versailles a requirement for trials of persons committing war crimes. They made no similar commitments regarding their own nationals.

The Treaty of Versailles

ARTICLE 228.

The German Government recognises the right of the Allied and Associated Powers to bring before military tribunals persons accused of having committed acts in violation of the laws and customs of war. Such persons shall, if found guilty, be sentenced to punishments laid down by law. This provision will apply notwithstanding any proceedings or prosecution before a tribunal in Germany or in the territory of her allies.

The German Government shall hand over to the Allied and Associated Powers, or to such one of them as shall so request, all persons accused of having committed an act in violation of the laws and customs of war, who are specified either by name or by the rank, office or employment which they held under the German authorities.

ARTICLE 229.

Persons guilty of criminal acts against the nationals of one of the Allied and Associated Powers will be brought before the military tribunals of that Power.

Persons guilty of criminal acts against the nationals of more than one of the Allied and Associated Powers will be brought before military tribunals composed of members of the military tribunals of the Powers concerned.

In every case the accused will be entitled to name his own counsel.

ARTICLE 230.

The German Government undertakes to furnish all documents and information of every kind, the production of which may be considered necessary to ensure the full knowledge of the incriminating acts, the discovery of offenders and the just appreciation of responsibility.

Willis summarizes events around the few trials the Germans held at Leipzig of officers accused of war crimes.[20]

The German war crimes trials at Leipzig proved unsatisfactory to the Allies, and the measures the French took against the Germans

20.   JAMES F. WILLIS, PROLOGUE TO NUREMBERG: THE POLITICS AND DIPLOMACY OF PUNISHING   WAR CRIMINALS OF THE FIRST WORLD WAR 126 (1982).

in retaliation disturbed Franco–German relations throughout the 1920s. The Allies believed, with good reason, that the Germans did not fully carry out their pledge to punish their own war criminals. There was a long delay before they began proceedings. The Reichsgericht handed down few convictions. Those found guilty received light sentences, and the two most notorious war criminals soon escaped from prison and disappeared. Subsequently, in secret session, the Reichsgericht reversed itself and found even those two men innocent. The British preferred to allow the issue to fade away, for they adopted a policy of reconciliation with Germany. The French and Belgians did not.

Upon the insistence of the French, the Allies in 1922 repudiated the compromise arrangement for German trials and reserved all formal rights under articles 228, 229, and 230 of the Versailles treaty. The French and Belgians subsequently tried hundreds of accused Germans *par contumace* and attempted to use the war crimes issue as a diplomatic weapon to force compliance with other provisions of the treaty, particularly the articles on reparations. The French and Belgians stopped their trials only after the Locarno treaty of 1925 improved relations with Germany. The French, nonetheless, continued a discriminatory policy toward Germans who had been convicted, denying them entry into France until 1929. Many Germans bitterly resented the humiliation of having their soldiers branded as war criminals and did everything possible to erase what they saw as a stain on their national honor.

The following is an account of one of the Leipzig trials. The British referred the case and supplied evidence. British observers were at the trial. The excerpt below was prepared from a British observer's record.[21]

* * *

Captain Emil Müller.

The case was more serious than either of the other prison-camp cases. In the first place, the cruelty inflicted upon the unfortunate prisoners resulted in a heavy death-roll; secondly, Müller was a man of education, and an officer. In civil life he was a barrister, living at Karlsruhe.

In April, 1918, Müller was a Captain in the Reserve, and was appointed to take command of the prison camp of Flavy-le-Martel shortly after the neighbourhood had passed under German control. To quote the judgment of the Court:

21. CLAUD MULLINS, THE LEIPZIG TRIALS 67–87 (1921).

The duties of the Company Commanders consisted solely in housing, feeding and supervising their prisoners, and in arranging, day by day, to provide the troops requisitioned for outside work. They had nothing to do with the regulation of this work itself or settling the hours of labour. This was the business of the Commander of the Battalion.

*The Company Commanders took over a camp which was found empty. The camp had shortly before been taken from the English during the March offensive, and had previously been used by them as a camp for the temporary reception of German prisoners of war. It was in a wretched condition. It lay in a marshy and completely devastated district, immediately behind the fighting line, where everything was still in constant movement. During the time the English had been in possession of it, it was unfit for human occupation. The witness Roeder, who at the end of January and beginning of February, 1918, had taken part in the war on the English side, and had often come there as interpreter gave evidence that the accommodation had been defective in the extreme. In the two residential barracks, which together afforded room for some three hundred prisoners only, double that number had been quartered. These barracks had a muddy, unboarded floor. There were no beds, but only some rotten wood-wool, which was infected with vermin. Windows and roofing were leaky. There were but two small so-called trench stoves, so the German prisoners suffered from the cold in winter. The latrines were as primitive and unwholesome as can be imagined. There was a complete absence of sanitary arrangements, and [an] * * * absence of facilities for cooking and washing as well as of rugs. As a consequence of all this, numerous prisoners had become sick with influenza and intestinal troubles, especially with dysentery. Many had died. All had complained of the plague of lice. Even the English guard had suffered heavily. An English doctor had endeavoured in vain to remove these defects.*

It is desirable to set out this finding at the outset because the appalling sufferings of the British prisoners at this camp were primarily due to its physical conditions, and one of the principal questions in the trial was the extent to which Captain Müller was responsible for the suffering and the death-roll that resulted. The evidence of Roeder had great weight with the Court, but the most important part of his evidence was that, when this camp was under British control "as a rule men were only three or four days there; occasionally a fortnight." Roeder added that "the British commandant behaved very well."

There is an enormous difference between using a camp as a temporary "cage" where three hundred to six hundred prisoners were housed for a few days, and using the same camp, without alterations, as a semi-permanent camp for well over one thousand men who were doing heavy work. The outside fence of the camp was only about two hundred yards in circumference, and the whole area of the camp soon became one large cesspool. The men rapidly got into a filthy and verminous condition and became afflicted with sores. The accommodation was utterly insufficient. The thousand men were herded in three huts, the approximate dimensions of which were sixty feet by twenty feet. There were no floor boards, and no bedding or camp utensils were supplied. The men had to sleep on the wet ground, and so crowded were the huts that there was not room for all to lie down. One witness (Higginbotham) told the Court that "each hut could at most hold one hundred men. We slept on the earth. We could not all get into the huts, but were driven in by sentries. All could not lie down."

The Court found that:

The accused found the camp in precisely this condition, and had to do his best with it. The position was rendered more difficult for him because he was obliged to quarter over one thousand men in the barracks, as fresh prisoners were constantly arriving. Further, all the wells round about were ruined. The food allotted was insufficient, and during the first days he had no medical assistance. Finally, he was obliged to detail daily very many men for heavy outside work, and the prisoners were already in a quite exhausted condition when they came under him. They were inadequately equipped with uniforms on arrival, as also with underclothes, rugs, and so on.

* * *

The Court would not hold Müller in any way responsible for the physical conditions of this camp.

The accused at once set energetically to work to effect an improvement. On the one hand he sent many memoranda to his superiors in order to draw their attention to the conditions, and he made emphatic demands for what was wanting. By urgent representations, both verbal and in writing, he in fact obtained many things. For example, medical assistance was allotted to him as early as the third day. Furthermore, he himself took in hand the improvement of the camp as far as was possible. He formed a working parity from what labour was left in the camp. He had wells sunk, stoves installed, proper latrines laid out, cooking and washing places provided, and he fought the plague of lice first by means of powder and finally by getting a disinfecting station set up. He also succeeded in getting some improvement in the food, and occasionally he got the outside work made easier. On one occasion he procured soap as well as extra food and luxuries from Belgium. On another he managed to get hold of some clothing which was not intended for his men at all. Several times he procured some horseflesh, and he detailed those prisoners who were particularly weak for duty in the kitchens and bakeries, where they could get more food. He thus showed that he had sympathy with his prisoners and that he was not insensible to their real needs.

In spite of all this the position of the prisoners became continuously worse.

* * *

So far, therefore, as the general conditions in the prisoners' camp at Flavy-le-Martel are concerned the accused must not only be acquitted of any blame, but it should be placed on record that the zeal with which he carried out his duties deserves high praise.

* * *

Though the Court acquitted Müller of any responsibility for the conditions of the camp, it severely denounced him for many acts of individual brutality. The Court found:

His attitude towards the prisoners was hard and over severe, sometimes even brutal, and in other cases it was at least contrary to regulations. He treated them not as subordinates, and it was as such that he ought to have regarded his prisoners, but he treated them more like convicts or inmates of penitentiaries. His methods were those of the convict prison or such like institutions, although even on this standard his conduct could not be tolerated. The Court has heard of his ill-treating prisoners by hitting and kicking them. He allowed his staff to treat them in the same manner. Insults were hurled at the prisoners and there was other ill-treatment which was contrary to the regulations. He habitually struck them when he was on horseback, using a riding cane or a walking stick.

There has been an accumulation of offences which show an almost habitually harsh and contemptuous, and even a frankly brutal, treatment of prisoners entrusted to his care. His conduct has sometimes been unworthy of a human being. These factors the Court considers decisive. When he mixed with the prisoners there was seldom anything but angry words, attempts to ride them down, blows and efforts to push them out of his way; he never listened patiently to their grievances and complaints; he had no eyes for their obvious sufferings; he cared little for the individual if only he could secure order among the prisoners collectively. It is impossible to consider his conduct as a number of separate instances of rash actions which he regretted; it appears rather as a deliberate practice of domineering disregard for other men's feelings. It is no justification that his methods were intended to secure discipline. It is also no excuse that the conditions had been brutalised by war.

The accused should have avoided being unduly severe; and above all he ought not to have indulged in such reprehensible means of punishment as blows, kicks, tying-up and such like. Such conduct dishonours our army, and is singularly unfitting in a man of his education and military as well as civilian position.

* * *

A few instances of Müller's brutality must suffice. The following cases were accepted as proved by the Court:

The accused while on horseback struck a prisoner who was suffering from a bad foot. At roll-call this prisoner had raised his leg to show it to the accused, but the accused hit him across his leg with his riding cane. The man cried out, fell down and had to be carried into barracks.

He thrashed the prisoner Batey with his walking stick. This man became ill while at work outside the camp and, although violently attacked by the sentries who did not believe in his inability to work, he refused to work any further. The sentries reported him to the accused on their return and Batey repeated that he was ill and emphatically asked for a doctor. The accused got furious over this, as he thought that Batey was a malingerer; he then belaboured him.

The accused admits that he liked, as soon as he appeared at roll-call, to ride quite quickly up to the ranks. He thought this was a suitable way of ensuring proper respect for himself and of making the prisoners attentive. According to the evidence of almost all the English, and also of some German, witnesses he frequently rode so far into the ranks that the ranks were broken. The prisoners scattered on all sides and many who could not get out of the way quickly enough were thrown down by the horse. Such excesses when riding up to a body of men are altogether contrary to regulations and are to be condemned. This is also the opinion of the military expert, General von Fransecky.

The accused once struck Drewcock at roll-call. He struck him across his wounded knee with his riding cane so hard that an abscess developed and later had to be cut. The accused could not have foreseen this, for the wounds on Drewcock's knee were not visible to him. But the blow must have been a heavy one.

In general the accused has admitted that it was his practice to enforce discipline, in cases of irregular behaviour, by means of light blows. He will not as a rule tax his memory about the details. He explains, however, that it would have been impossible to attain rigid discipline if he had tolerated any lengthy explanations, especially as he and the prisoners could not understand each other's language. There may be some truth in this and there were no doubt serious difficulties in commanding such a camp. But nevertheless the accused never had any right to get over these difficulties by means of endless acts of violence.

* * *

The only possible excuse for him was that he was over-excited; that he feared disorder, and that he did not know how to handle men. But even so, it must be recalled that he had under him prisoners who were peculiarly unfortunate, sick and suffering men who deserved protection. When these prisoners offended against the regulations, the cause for the most part lay in their miserable condition. Such men in such conditions were not likely to be really refractory.

He has been an able officer who faithfully tried to do his duty, who always strove to win the appreciation of his superiors, and who had hitherto secured appreciation in full measure through his long years of war service. Then, however, he was suddenly confronted with an unusually difficult situation. He was obliged to take over the to him novel position of commandant of prisoners of war, and this in one of the most disturbed battle areas, close up against the front, in a devastated and unhealthy neighborhood and at a time of most severe scarcity of all necessaries of life. The accused had, so to speak, to create out of nothing a camp to house the unending stream of prisoners. All these burdens were placed upon him at a time when he was already almost breaking down as a result of war strain and an old heart complaint, and when he was afflicted with serious nerve trouble.

But none the less the Court was of opinion that Müller "showed himself, generally speaking, equal to his task." It found, further, that:

His excesses were only due to that military enthusiasm which worked him up to an exaggerated conception of military necessity and discipline. He made insufficient allowance for the special conditions in which prisoners in war-time find themselves. He showed himself severe and lacking in consideration, but not deliberately cruel. His acts originated, not in any pleasure in persecution, or even in any want of feeling for the sufferings of the prisoners; but in a conscious disregard of the general laws of humanity.

* * *

The final judgment of the Court was that nine instances of deliberate personal cruelty had been proved; that in addition there was one case in which he had allowed one of his subordinates to ill-treat a prisoner; that there were also four instances of minor breaches of the regulations, and two cases of insults. A sentence of six months' imprisonment was passed, the period of detention pending and during trial to be considered as part of the term awarded.

* * *

No sooner was the First World War over, then new efforts began to improve the law regulating conduct of war. In 1922, states agreed to the first phase of naval disarmament in the Washington Convention.[22] In 1925, states adopted the Geneva Protocol for the Prohibition of the Use in War of Asphyxiating, Poisonous or Other Gases, and of Bacteriological Methods of Warfare.

Protocol for the Prohibition of the Use in War of Asphyxiating, Poisonous or Other Gases, and of Bacteriological Methods of Warfare

Done at Geneva June, 17, 1925.

THE UNDERSIGNED PLENIPOTENTIARIES, in the name of their respective Governments:

Whereas the use in war of asphyxiating, poisonous or other gases, and of all analogous liquids materials or devices, has been justly condemned by the general opinion of the civilized world; and

Whereas the prohibition of such use has been declared in Treaties to which the majority of Powers of the world are Parties; and

To the end that this prohibition shall be universally accepted as a part of International Law, binding alike the conscience and the practice of nations;

DECLARE:

> That the High Contracting Parties, so far as they are not already Parties to Treaties prohibiting such use, accept this prohibition, agree to extend this prohibition to the use of bacteriological methods of warfare and agree to be bound as between themselves according to the terms of this declaration.

* * *

In 1929 states adopted a convention on the treatment of prisoners of war at Geneva, the Convention Relative to the Treatment of Prisoners, Geneva, July 27, 1929.

> Admittedly, rules relating to the status of prisoners of war did already exist: having initially developed as rules of customary law, they had been incorporated in 1899 in the Hague Regulations on Land Warfare * * *. Yet the First World War, with its long duration and huge numbers of prisoners of war on both sides, had

22. Treaty for the Limitation of Naval Armaments, Feb. 6, 1922, 43 Stat. 1655, 2 Bevans 351. *See also*, Detlev Vagts, *The Hague Conventions and Arms Control*, 94 AM. J. INT'L L. 31, 37 (2000).

brought to light the need for more detailed regulations for the protection of this category of war victims. The Convention of 1929 achieved this goal; as particularly important improvements on the old law could be mentioned: the far greater clarity and completeness of the rules and principles on capture and captivity of prisoners of war; introduction of a categorical ban on reprisals against such persons, and acceptance of the principle that application of the agreed rules would be open to international scrutiny.[23]

The International Committee of the Red Cross also began work after the First World War on a convention aimed at protecting civilians in time of war.[24] It built on the experience of the Committee for the Relief of Belgium that had been formed during the war to relieve the suffering of millions of persons in occupied Belgium and northern France.[25] Civilians had been in need of food, fuel, shelter, clothes, and medicine owing to the disruption to industry, trade, and agriculture as a result of the German occupation and requisitioning of supplies, as well as the Allied blockade of the North Sea ports. The final draft of a convention to aid civilian victims was approved at the 1934 Tokyo International Conference of the Red Cross, but the Second World War broke out before the Tokyo draft could be submitted to a diplomatic conference.

Nevertheless, military and political leaders of the Axis powers were found criminally liable for their treatment of civilians during the war, as well as for crimes against prisoners of war. During the course of the war, the United States Supreme Court heard the case of a group of German saboteurs. The central question was whether the process of a military tribunal was appropriate for adjudicating the case, but the Supreme Court also touched on several substantive principles of the law governing combatants. The case has been cited in subsequent trials enforcing the international law on the use of force following the war, including by the International Military Tribunal at Nuremberg.

Ex Parte Quirin

317 U.S. 1 (1942).*

MR. CHIEF JUSTICE STONE delivered the opinion of the Court.

These cases are brought here by petitioners' several applications for leave to file petitions for habeas corpus in this Court, and by their petitions for certiorari to review orders of the District

---

23. KALSHOVEN (1987), *supra* note 1, at 10.

24. Mary Ellen O'Connell, *Humanitarian Assistance in Non–International Armed Conflict, The Fourth Wave of Rights, Duties and Remedies*, 31 ISRAEL YBK. ON HUMAN RIGHTS 183 (2000).

25. PETER MACALISTER-SMITH, INTERNATIONAL HUMANITARIAN ASSISTANCE, DISASTER RELIEF ACTIONS IN INTERNATIONAL LAW AND ORGANIZATION 11–12 (1985); *see also*, COMMENTARY TO THE 1949 GENEVA CONVENTION IV, 3–9 (Jean Pictet ed., 1958).

* Footnotes omitted.

Court for the District of Columbia, which denied their applications for leave to file petitions for habeas corpus in that court.

The question for decision is whether the detention of petitioners by respondent for trial by Military Commission, appointed by Order of the President of July 2, 1942, on charges preferred against them purporting to set out their violations of the law of war and of the Articles of War, is in conformity to the laws and Constitution of the United States.

The following facts appear from the petitions or are stipulated. Except as noted they are undisputed.

All the petitioners were born in Germany; all have lived in the United States. All returned to Germany between 1933 and 1941. All except petitioner Haupt are admitted citizens of the German Reich, with which the United States is at war. Haupt came to this country with his parents when he was five years old; it is contended that he became a citizen of the United States by virtue of the naturalization of his parents during his minority and that he has not since lost his citizenship. The Government, however, takes the position that on attaining his majority he elected to maintain German allegiance and citizenship, or in any case that he has by his conduct renounced or abandoned his United States citizenship. * * * For reasons presently to be stated we do no find it necessary to resolve these contentions.

After the declaration of war between the United States and the German Reich, petitioners received training at a sabotage school near Berlin, Germany, where they were instructed in the use of explosives and in methods of secret writing. Thereafter petitioners, with a German citizen, Dasch, proceeded from Germany to a seaport in Occupied France, where petitioners Burger, Geinck and Quirin, together with Dasch, boarded a German submarine which proceeded across the Atlantic to Amagansett Beach on Long Island, New York. The four were landed from the submarine in the hours of darkness, on or about June 13, 1942, carrying with them a supply of explosives, fuses, and incendiary and timing devices. While landing they wore German Marine Infantry uniforms or parts of uniforms. Immediately after landing they buried their uniforms and the other articles mentioned, and proceeded to civilian dress to New York City.

The remaining petitioners at the same French port boarded another German submarine, which carried them across the Atlantic to Ponte Vedra Beach, Florida. On or about June 17, 1942, they came ashore during the hours of darkness, wearing caps of the German Marine Infantry and carrying with them a supply of explosives, fuses, and incendiary and timing devices. They immediately buried their caps and the other articles mentioned, and proceeded in civilian dress to Jacksonville, Florida, and thence to various points in the United States. All were taken into custody in

New York or Chicago by agents of the Federal Bureau of Investigation. All had received instructions from Germany from an officer of the German High Command to destroy war industries and war facilities in the United States, for which they or their relatives in Germany were to receive salary payments from the German Government. They also had been paid by the German Government during their course of training at the sabotage school and had received substantial sums in United States currency, which were in their possession when arrested. The currency had been handed to them by an officer of the German High Command, who had instructed them to wear their German uniforms while landing in the United States.

The President, as President and Commander in Chief of the Army and Navy, by Order of July 2, 1942, appointed a Military Commission and directed it to try petitioners for offenses against the law of war and the Articles of War, and prescribed regulations for the procedure on the trial and for review of the record of the trial and of any judgment or sentence of the Commission. On the same day, by Proclamation, the President declared that "all persons who are subjects, citizens or residents of any nation at war with the United States or who give obedience to or act under the direction of any such nation, and who during the time of war enter or attempt to enter the United States ... through coastal or boundary defenses, and are charged with committing or attempting or preparing to commit sabotage, espionage, hostile or warlike acts, or violations of the law of war, shall be subject to the law of war and to the jurisdiction of military tribunals."

* * *

We are not here concerned with any question of the guilt or innocence of petitioners. * * * Constitutional safe-guards for the protection of all who are charged with offenses are not to be disregarded in order to inflict merited punishment on some who are guilty. *Ex parte Milligan, supra*, 119, 132; *Tumey v. Ohio*, 273 U.S. 510, 535; *Hill v. Texas*, 326 U.S. 400,406. But the detention and trial of petitioners—ordered by the President in the declared exercise of powers as Commander in Chief of the Army in time of war and of grave public danger—are not to be set aside by the courts without the clear conviction that they are in conflict with the Constitution or laws of Congress constitutionally enacted.

* * *

An important incident to the conduct of war is the adoption of measures by the military command not only to repel and defeat the enemy, but to seize and subject to disciplinary measures those enemies who in their attempt to thwart or impede our military effort have violated the law of war.

* * *

We are concerned only with the question whether it is within the constitutional power of the National Government to place petitioners upon trial before a military commission for the offenses with which they are charged. We must therefore first inquire whether any of the acts charged is an offense against the law of war cognizable before a military tribunal, and if so whether the Constitution prohibits the trial.

* * *

It is no objection that Congress is providing for the trial of such offenses has not itself undertaken to codify that branch of international law or to mark its precise boundaries, or to enumerate or define by statute all the acts which that law condemns. An Act of Congress punishing "the crime of piracy, as defined by the law of nations" is an appropriate exercise of its constitutional authority, Art.I, § 8, cl.10, "to define and punish" the offense, since it has adopted by the reference the sufficiently precise definition of international law. *United States v. Smith*, 5 Wheat. 153; see *The Marianna Flora*, 11 Wheat. 1, 40–41; *United States v. Brig Malek Adhel*, 2 How. 210, 232; *The Ambrose Light*, 25 F. 408, 423–28; 18 U.S.C. § 481.

* * *

By universal agreement and practice, the law of war draws a distinction between the armed forces and the peaceful populations of belligerent nations and also between those who are lawful and unlawful combatants. Lawful combatants are subject to capture and detention as prisoners of war by opposing military forces. Unlawful combatants are likewise subject to capture and detention, but in addition they are subject to trial and punishment by military tribunals for acts which render their belligerency unlawful. The spy who secretly and without uniform passes the military lines of a belligerent in time of war, seeking to gather military information and communicate it to the enemy, or an enemy combatant who without uniform comes secretly through the lines for the purpose of waging war by destruction of life or property, are familiar examples of belligerents who are generally deemed not to be entitled to the status of prisoners of war, but to be offenders against the law of war subject to trial and punishment by military tribunals. See Winthrop, Military Law, 2d ed., pp. 1196–97, 1219–21; Instructions for the Government of Armies of the United States in the Field, approved by the President, General Order No. 100, April 24, 1863, §§ IV and V.

Such was the practice of our own military authorities before the adoption of the Constitution, and during the Mexican and Civil Wars. The definition of lawful belligerents * * * is that adopted by Article 1, Annex to Hague Convention No. IV of October 18, 1907, to which the United States was a signatory and which was ratified by the Senate in 1909. 36 State. 2295. The preamble to the Convention declares: "Until a more complete code of the laws of war has been issued, the High Contracting Parties deem it expedient to declare that, in cases not included in the Regulations adopted by them, the inhabitants and the belligerents remain under the protection and the rule of the principles of the law of nations, as they result from the usages established among civilized peoples, from the laws of humanity, and the dictates of the public conscience."

Our Government, by thus defining lawful belligerents entitled to be treated as prisoners of war, has recognized that there is a class of unlawful belligerents not entitled to that privilege, including those who, though combatants, do not wear "fixed and distinctive emblems."

* * *

By a long course of practical administrative construction by its military authorities, our Government has likewise recognized that those who during time of war pass surreptitiously from enemy territory into our own, discarding their uniforms upon entry, for the commission of hostile acts involving destruction of life or property, have the status of unlawful combatants punishable as such by military commission. This precept of the law of war has been so recognized in practice both here and abroad, and has so generally been accepted as valid by authorities on international law that we think it must be regarded as rule or principle of the law of war recognized by this Government.

* * *

Nor are petitioners any the less belligerents if, as they argue, they have not actually committed or attempted to commit any act or depredation or entered the theater or zone of active military operations. The argument leaves out of account the nature of the offense which the Government charges and which the Act of Congress, by incorporating the law of war, punishes. It is that each petitioner, in circumstances which gave him the status of an enemy belligerent, passed our military and naval lines and defenses or went behind those lines, in civilian dress and with hostile purpose. The offense was complete when with that purpose they entered—or, having so entered, they remained upon—our territory in time of war without uniform or other appropriate means of identification.

* * *

Petitioners, and especially petitioner Haupt, stress the pronouncement of this Court in the *Milligan case, supra,* p. 121, that the law of war "can never be applied to citizens in states which have upheld the authority of the government, and where the courts are open and their process unobstructed." Elsewhere in its opinion, at pp. 118, 121–22 and 131, the Court was at pains to point out that Milligan, a citizen twenty years resident in Indiana, who had never been a resident of any of the states in the rebellion, was not an enemy belligerent either entitled to the status of a prisoner of war or subject to the penalties imposed upon unlawful belligerents. We construe the Court's statement as to the inapplicability of the law of war to Milligan's case as having particular reference to the facts before it. From them the Court concluded that Milligan, not being a part of or associated with the armed forces of the enemy, was a non-belligerent, not subject to the law of war save as—in circumstances found not there to be present, and not involved here—martial law might be constitutionally established.

The Court's opinion is inapplicable to the case presented by the present record. We have no occasion now to define with meticulous care the ultimate boundaries of the jurisdiction of military tribunals to try persons according to the law of war. It is enough that petitioners here, upon the conceded facts, were plainly within those boundaries, and were held in good faith for trial by military commission, charged with being enemies who, with the purpose of destroying war materials and utilities, entered, or after entry remained in, our territory without uniform—an offense against the law of war. We hold only that those particular acts constitute an offense against the law of war which the Constitution authorizes to be tried by military commission.

* * *

At the end of the war, at Nuremberg, Germany see p. 134, above, German political and military leaders were charged with *in bello* as well as *ad bellum* crimes. The first excerpt below is a continuation of the International Military Tribunal's decision in the case of Göring. In this part the tribunal considers war crimes and crimes against humanity. The excerpt that follows is from the decision in the case of Admiral Dönitz, who through much of the war had been a commander in and then the commander of the German navy.

The Trial of Hermann Göring,
cont'd*

* * *

War Crimes and Crimes against Humanity

The record is filled with Göring's admissions of his complicity in the use of slave labor.

> "We did use this labor for security reasons so that they would not be active in their own country and would not work against us. On the other hand, they served to help in the economic war."

And again:

> "Workers were forced to come to the Reich. That is something I have not denied."

The man who spoke these words was Plenipotentiary for the Four Year Plan charged with the recruitment and allocation of manpower. As Luftwaffe Commander-in-Chief he demanded from Himmler more slave laborers for his underground aircraft factories: "That I requested inmates of concentration camps for the armament of the Luftwaffe is correct and it is to be taken as a matter of course."

As Plenipotentiary, Göring signed a directive concerning the treatment of Polish workers in Germany and implemented it by regulations of the SD, including "special treatment." He issued directives to use Soviet and French prisoners of war in the armament industry; he spoke of seizing Poles and Dutch and making them prisoners of war if necessary, and using them for work. He agrees Russian prisoners of war were used to man anti-aircraft batteries.

As Plenipotentiary, Göring was the active authority in the spoliation of conquered territory. He made plans for the spoliation of Soviet territory long before the war on the Soviet Union. Two months prior to the invasion of the Soviet Union, Hitler gave Göring the over-all direction for the economic administration in the territory. Göring set up an economic staff for this function. As Reichsmarshal of the Greater German Reich, "the orders of the Reich Marshal cover all economic fields, including nutrition and agriculture." His so-called "Green" folder, printed by the Wehrmacht, set up an "Economic Executive Staff, East." This directive contemplated plundering and abandonment of all industry in the food deficit regions and, from the food surplus regions, a diversion of food to German needs. Göring claims its purposes have been misunderstood but admits "that as a matter of course and a

* *See* pp. 143–145, above.

matter of duty we would have used Russia for our purposes,'' when conquered.

And he participated in the conference of 16 July 1941 when Hitler said the National Socialists had no intention of ever leaving the occupied countries, and that "all necessary measures—shooting, desettling, etc." should be taken.

Göring persecuted the Jews, particularly after the November 1938 riots * * *. His own utterances then and his testimony now shows this interest was primarily economic—how to get their property and how to force them out of the economic life of Europe. As these countries fell before the German Army, he extended the Reich's anti-Jewish laws to them; the *Reichsgesetzblatt* for 1939, 1940, and 1941 contains several anti-Jewish decrees signed by Göring. Although their extermination was in Himmler's hands, Göring was far from disinterested or inactive, despite his protestations in the witness box. By decree of 31 July 1941 he directed Himmler and Heydrich to "bring about a complete solution of the Jewish question in the German sphere of influence in Europe."

There is nothing to be said in mitigation. For Göring was often, indeed almost always, the moving force, second only to his leader. He was the leading war aggressor, both as political and as military leader; he was the director of the slave labor program and the creator of the oppressive program against the Jews and other races, at home and abroad. All of these crimes he has frankly admitted. On some specific cases there may be conflict of testimony but in terms of the broad outline, his own admissions are more than sufficiently wide to be conclusive of his guilt. His guilt is unique in its enormity. The record disclosed no excuses for this man.

Conclusion

The Tribunal finds the Defendant Göring guilty on all four Counts of Indictment.

The Trial of Karl Dönitz

International Military Tribunal, Nuremberg, Nov. 14, 1945–Oct. 1, 1946.

Dönitz is indicted on Counts One, Two, and Three. In 1935 he took command of the first U-boat flotilla commissioned since 1918, became in 1936 commander of the submarine arm, was made Vice-Admiral in 1940, Admiral in 1942, and on 30 January 1943 Commander-in-Chief of the German Navy. On 1 May 1945 he became the Head of State, succeeding Hitler.

Crimes against Peace

Although Dönitz built and trained the German U-boat arm, the evidence does not show he was privy to the conspiracy to wage aggressive wars or that he prepared and initiated such wars. He was a line officer performing strictly tactical duties. He was not present at the important conferences when plans for aggressive wars were announced, and there is no evidence he was informed about the decisions reached there. Dönitz did, however, wage aggressive war within the meaning of that word as used by the Charter. Submarine warfare which began immediately upon the outbreak of war, was fully coordinated with the other branches of the Wehrmacht. It is clear that his U-boats, few in number at the time, were fully prepared to wage war.

It is true that until his appointment in January 1943 as Commander-in-Chief he was not an "Oberbefehlshaber". But this statement underestimates the importance of Dönitz' position. He was no mere army or division commander. The U-boat arm was the principal part of the German fleet and Dönitz was its leader. The High Seas fleet made a few minor, if spectacular, raids during the early years of the war, but the real damage to the enemy was done almost exclusively by his submarines as the millions of tons of Allied and neutral shipping sunk will testify. Dönitz was solely in charge of this warfare. The Naval War Command reserved for itself only the decision as to the number of submarines in each area. In the invasion of Norway, for example, Dönitz made recommendations in October 1939 as to submarine bases, which he claims were no more than a staff study, and in March 1940 he made out the operational orders for the supporting U-boats, as discussed elsewhere in this Judgement.

That his importance to the German war effort was so regarded is eloquently proved by Raeder's recommendation of Dönitz as his successor and his appointment by Hitler on 30 January 1943 as Commander-in-Chief of the Navy. Hitler, too, knew that submarine warfare was the essential part of Germany's naval warfare.

From January 1943, Dönitz was consulted almost continuously by Hitler. The evidence was that they conferred on naval problems about 120 times during the course of the war.

As late as April 1945, when he admits he knew the struggle was hopeless, Dönitz as its Commander-in-Chief urged the Navy to continue its fight. On 1 May 1945 he became the Head of State and as such ordered the Wehrmacht to continue its war in the East, until capitulation on 9 May 1945. Dönitz explained that his reason for these orders was to insure that the German civilian population might be evacuated and the Army might make an orderly retreat from the East.

In the view of the Tribunal, the evidence shows that Dönitz was active in waging aggressive war.

War Crimes

Dönitz is charged with waging unrestricted submarine warfare contrary to the Naval Protocol of 1936, to which Germany acceded, and which reaffirmed the rules of submarine warfare laid down in the London Naval Agreement of 1930.

The Prosecution has submitted that on 3 September 1939 the German U-boat arm began to wage unrestricted submarine warfare upon all merchant ships, whether enemy or neutral, cynically disregarding the Protocol; and that a calculated effort was made throughout the war to disguise this practice by making hypocritical references to international law and supposed violations by the Allies.

Dönitz insists that at all times the Navy remained within the confines of international law and of the Protocol. He testified that when the war began, the guide to submarine warfare was the German Prize Ordinance taken almost literally from the Protocol, that pursuant to the German view, he ordered submarines to attack all merchant ships in convoy, and all that refused to stop or used their radio upon sighting a submarine. When his reports indicated that British merchant ships were being used to give information by wireless, were being armed, and were attacking submarines on sight, he ordered his submarines on 17 October 1939 to attack all enemy merchant ships without warning on the ground that resistance was to be expected. Orders already had been issued on 21 September 1939 to attack all ships, including neutrals, sailing at night without lights in the English Channel.

On 24 November 1939 the German Government issued a warning to neutral shipping that, owing to the frequent engagements taking place in the waters around the British Isles and the French Coast between U-boats and Allied merchant ships which were armed and had instructions to use those arms as well as to ram U-boats, the safety of neutral ships in those waters could no longer be taken for granted. On 1 January 1940 the German U-boat Command, acting on the instructions of Hitler, ordered U-boats to attack all Greek merchant ships in the zone surrounding the British Isles which was banned by the United States to its own ships and also merchant ships of every nationality in the limited area of the Bristol Channel. Five days later a further order was given to U-boats to "make immediately unrestricted use of weapons against all ships" in an area of the North Sea, the limits of which were defined. Finally on 18 January 1940, U-boats were authorized to sink, without warning, all ships "in those waters near the enemy coasts in which the use of mines can be pretended". Exceptions were to be made in the cases of United States, Italian, Japanese, and Soviet ships.

Shortly after the outbreak of war the British Admiralty, in accordance with its *Handbook of Instructions* of 1938 to the

Merchant Navy, armed its merchant vessels, in many cases convoyed them with armed escort, gave orders to send position reports upon sighting submarines, thus integrating merchant vessels into the warning network of naval intelligence. On 1 October 1939 the British Admiralty announced that British merchant ships had been ordered to ram U-boats if possible.

In the actual circumstances of this case, the Tribunal is not prepared to hold Dönitz guilty for his conduct of submarine warfare against British armed merchant ships.

However, the proclamation of operational zones and the sinking of neutral merchant vessels which enter those zones presents a different question. This practice was employed in the war of 1914–18 by Germany and adopted in retaliation by Great Britain. The Washington Conference of 1922, the London Naval Agreement of 1930, and the Protocol of 1936 were entered into with full knowledge that such zones had been employed in the first World War. Yet the Protocol made no exception for operational zones. The order of Dönitz to sink neutral ships without warning when found within these zones was therefore, in the opinion of the Tribunal, a violation of the Protocol.

It is also asserted that the German U-boat arm not only did not carry out the warning and rescue provisions of the Protocol but that Dönitz deliberately ordered the killing of survivors of shipwrecked vessels, whether enemy or neutral. The Prosecution has introduced much evidence surrounding two orders of Dönitz—War Order Number 154, issued in 1939, and the so-called "Laconia" Order of 1942. The Defense argues that these orders and the evidence supporting them do not show such a policy and introduced much evidence to the contrary. The Tribunal is of the opinion that the evidence does not establish with the certainty required that Dönitz deliberately ordered the killing of shipwrecked survivors. The orders were undoubtedly ambiguous, and deserve the strongest censure.

The evidence further shows that the rescue provisions were not carried out and that the Defendant ordered that they should not be carried out. The argument of the Defense is that the security of the submarine is, as the first rule of the sea, paramount to rescue, and that the development of aircraft made rescue impossible. This may be so, but the Protocol is explicit. If the commander cannot rescue, then under its terms he cannot sink a merchant vessel and should allow it to pass harmless before his periscope. These orders, then, prove Dönitz is guilty of a violation of the Protocol.

In view of all of the facts proved and in particular of an order of the British Admiralty announced on 8 May 1940, according to which all vessels should be sunk at night in the Skagerrak, and the answers to interrogatories by Admiral Nimitz stating that unrestricted submarine warfare was carried on in the Pacific Ocean by the United States from the first day that Nation entered the war, the sentence of Dönitz is not assessed on the ground of his breaches of the international law of submarine warfare.

Dönitz was also charged with responsibility for Hitler's Commando Order of 18 October 1942. Dönitz admitted he received and knew of the order when he was Flag Officer of U-boats, but disclaimed responsibility. He points out that the order by its express terms excluded men captured in naval warfare, that the Navy had no territorial commands on land, and that submarine commanders would never encounter commandos.

In one instance, when he was Commander-in-Chief of the Navy, in 1943, the members of the crew of an Allied motor torpedo boat were captured by German Naval Forces. They were interrogated for intelligence purposes on behalf of the local Admiral, and then turned over by his order to the SD and shot. Dönitz said that if they were captured by the Navy their execution was a violation of the Commando Order, that the execution was not announced in the Wehrmacht communiqué, and that he was never informed of the incident. He pointed out that the Admiral in question was not in his chain of command, but was subordinate to the Army general in command of the Norway occupation. But Dönitz permitted the order to remain in full force when he became Commander-in-Chief, and to that extent he is responsible.

Dönitz, in a conference of 11 December 1944, said, "12,000 concentration camp prisoners will be employed in the shipyards as additional labor". At this time Dönitz had no jurisdiction over shipyard construction, and claims that this was merely a suggestion at the meeting that the responsible officials do something about the production of ships, that he took no steps to get these workers since it was not a matter for his jurisdiction and that he does not know whether they ever were procured. He admits he knew of concentration camps. A man in his position must necessarily have known that citizens of occupied countries in large numbers were confined in the concentration camps.

In 1945 Hitler requested the opinion of Jodl and Dönitz whether the Geneva Convention should be denounced. The notes of the meeting between the two military leaders on 20 February 1945 show that Dönitz expressed his view that the disadvantages of such an action outweighed the advantages. The summary of Dönitz' attitude shown in the notes taken by an officer, included the following sentence: "It would be better to carry out the measures considered necessary without warning, and at all costs to save face with the outer world."

The Prosecution insisted that "the measures" referred to meant the Convention should not be denounced, but should be broken at will. The Defense explanation is that Hitler wanted to break the Convention for two reasons: to take away from German troops the protection of the Convention, thus preventing them from continuing to surrender in large groups to the British and Americans, and also to permit reprisals against Allied prisoners of war because of Allied bombing raids. Dönitz claims that what he meant by "measures" were disciplinary measures against German troops to prevent them from surrendering, and that his words had no reference to measures against the Allies; moreover that this was merely a suggestion, and that in any event no such measures were ever taken, either against Allies or Germans. The Tribunal, however, does not believe this explanation. The Geneva Convention was not, however, denounced by Germany. The defense has introduced several affidavits to prove that British naval prisoners of war in camps under Dönitz' jurisdiction were treated strictly according to the Convention, and the Tribunal takes this fact into consideration, regarding it as a mitigating circumstance.

Conclusion

The Tribunal finds Dönitz is not guilty on Count One of the Indictment, and is guilty on Counts Two and Th[ree].

* * *

The International Military Tribunal for the Far East (IMTFE) was created by order of U.S. General Douglas MacArthur, Supreme Commander for Allied Powers in Japan on January 19, 1946. The Tribunal had similar objectives to the more famous Nuremberg Tribunal, though there are some notable differences in its procedural and substantive design. Article 5 of the IMTFE Charter divided offenses prosecuted into 3 main categories: Class A, Class B, and Class C. Class A offenses were crimes against peace, or, conspiracy, preparation, initiation and waging of an aggressive war or war that violated international law; Class B offenses were conventional war crimes (violations of customs of war); and Class C offenses were crimes against humanity. The prosecution of the Class A "major offenses," became known as the Tokyo Trials.

Unlike the Nuremberg Trials, the IMTFE Charter provided jurisdiction only in the case of persons charged with offenses that included crimes against peace. Persons charged only with conventional war crimes or crimes against humanity were to be tried by national or other courts, including military tribunals. Also unlike the Nuremberg Trials that involved only four Western countries, the Tokyo Trials involved eleven states, including non-Western countries, each having a judge on the court panel. They were Australia, Canada, China, France, Great Britain, India, the Philippines, the Netherlands, the Soviet Union, the United States and New Zealand. In addition, to these eleven, evidence was also submitted from six other countries and territories: Manchuria, Mongolia, Thailand, Cambodia, Burma and Portugal.

Twenty-eight Japanese leaders were charged with 56 counts. The final judgment resulted in seven hangings, sixteen life imprisonments, one twenty-year prison term and a seven-year prison term. Two of those charged died during the course of the trials. No one charged was acquitted of all charges brought against him.

There were three fundamental issues at Tokyo: first, whether aggressive war was a crime in international law; second, whether there could be individual responsibility assigned for international crimes; and third, whether killing in the course of an aggressive war constituted murder.

The prosecution made its case and the Court agreed that as a matter of customary international law, the Japanese had been put on sufficient notice that they could be held criminally accountable for their actions in waging a war of aggression. The prosecution cited the Hague Convention of 1907, the Geneva Conventions of 1925 and 1929 and the Kellogg–Briand Pact of 1928 as customary international law. In addition, not only was the Japanese government on notice but also prior to the war Japan had actually agreed to, signed or taken part in many of the treaties, pacts and conferences cited. The prosecution wanted to establish that their jurisdiction to try such cases was founded well before the 1945 Potsdam Declaration—the agreement signed by Japanese officials that articulated the right to hold trials and punish Japanese war criminals. The tribunal agreed that the Japan had launched aggressive wars against certain Allied Powers. While they did not previously define aggressive war, the judges concluded that whatever the definition, Japan's actions would obviously constitute one form of aggressive war, i.e. "unprovoked attacks prompted by the desire to seize the possessions of these nations."

Like the Nuremberg Trials, it was not a sufficient defense from individual responsibility for those charged to claim that they were acting under the orders of superiors or government officials, though these factors could be mitigating. Nor could individuals in roles of responsibility as military officers or governmental ministers and officials protect themselves from prosecution by characterizing their actions as actions of state.

The Trials in Tokyo attempted to go further than Nuremberg by alleging that persons responsible for planning, preparation, initiation and waging a war of aggression could be found guilty of murder because their illegal actions led directly to the death of both combatants and non-combatants. Ultimately, the tribunal sidestepped this issue in its final judgment.

Little scholarship, especially legal scholarship, has been done regarding the Tokyo Trials. One of the best-known trials from the Far East was not even heard by the IMTFE. A military tribunal heard the case of General Tomoyuki Yamashita. He appealed to the United States Supreme Court, challenging the legality of both the process used to try him and the charges against him.

Yamashita v. Styer

327 U.S. 1 (1946).

MR. CHIEF JUSTICE STONE delivered the opinion of the Court.

* * *

From the petitions and supporting papers it appears that prior to September 3, 1945, petitioner was the Commanding General of the Fourteenth Army Group of the Imperial Japanese Army in the Philippine Islands. On that date he surrendered to and became a prisoner of war of the United States Army Forces in Baguio, Philippine Islands. On September 25th, by order of respondent, Lieutenant General Wilhelm D. Styer, Commanding General of the United States Army Forces, Western Pacific, which command embraces the Philippine Islands, petitioner was served with a charge prepared by the Judge Advocate General's Department of the Army, purporting to charge petitioner with a violation of the law of war. On October 8, 1945, petitioner, after pleading not guilty to the charge, was held for trial before a military commission of five Army officers appointed by order of General Styer. The order appointed six Army officers, all lawyers, as defense counsel. Throughout the proceedings which followed, including those before this Court, defense counsel have demonstrated their professional skill and resourcefulness and their proper zeal for the defense with which they were charged.

On the same date a bill of particulars was filed by the prosecution, and the commission heard a motion made in petitioner's behalf to dismiss the charge on the ground that it failed to state a violation of the law of war. On October 29th the commission was reconvened, a supplemental bill of particulars was filed, and the motion to dismiss was denied. The trial then proceeded until its conclusion on December 7, 1945, the commission hearing two hundred and eighty-six witnesses, who gave over three thousand pages of testimony. On that date petitioner was found guilty of the offense as charged and sentenced to death by hanging.

The petitions for habeas corpus set up that the detention of petitioner for the purpose of the trial was unlawful for reasons which are now urged as showing that the military commission was without lawful authority or jurisdiction to place petitioner on trial, as follows:

(a) That the military commission which tried and convicted petitioner was not lawfully created, and that no military commission to try petitioner for violations of the law of war could lawfully be convened after the cessation of hostilities between the armed forces of the United States and Japan;

(b) that the charge preferred against petitioner fails to charge him with a violation of the law of war;

(c) that the commission was without authority and jurisdiction to try and convict petitioner because the order governing the procedure of the commission permitted the admission in evidence of depositions, affidavits and hearsay and opinion evidence, and because the commission's rulings admitting such evidence were in violation of the 25th and 38th Articles of War (10 U.S.C. §§ 1496, 1509, 10 U.S.C.A. §§ 1496, 1509) and the Geneva Convention (47 Stat. 2021), and deprived petitioner of a fair trial in violation of the due process clause of the Fifth Amendment;

(d) that the commission was without authority and jurisdiction in the premises because of the failure to give advance notice of petitioner's trial to the neutral power representing the interests of Japan as a belligerent as required by Article 60 of the Geneva Convention, 47 Stat. 2021, 2051.

On the same grounds the petitions for writs of prohibition set up that the commission is without authority to proceed with the trial.

The Supreme Court of the Philippine Islands, after hearing argument, denied the petition for habeas corpus presented to it, on the ground, among others, that its jurisdiction was limited to an inquiry as to the jurisdiction of the commission to place petitioner on trial for the offense charged, and that the commission, being validly constituted by the order of General Styer, had jurisdiction over the person of petitioner and over the trial for the offense charged.

[1]   In Ex parte Quirin, 317 U.S. 1, 63 S.Ct. 2, 87 L.Ed. 3, we had occasion to consider at length the sources and nature of the authority to create military commissions for the trial of enemy combatants for offenses against the law of war. We there pointed out that Congress, in the exercise of the power conferred upon it by Article I, § 8, Cl. 10 of the Constitution to "define and punish * * * Offenses against the Law of Nations * * *," of which the law of war is a part, had by the Articles of War (10 U.S.C. §§ 1471–1593, 10 U.S.C.A. §§ 1471–1593) recognized the "military commission" appointed by military command, as it had previously existed in United States Army practice, as an appropriate tribunal for the trial and punishment of offenses against the law of war. Article 15 declares that "the provisions of these articles conferring jurisdiction upon courts-martial shall not be construed as depriving military commissions * * * or other military tribunals of concurrent jurisdiction in respect of offenders of offenses that by statute or by the law of war may be triable by such military commissions * * * or other military tribunals." See a similar provision of the Espionage Act of 1917, 50 U.S.C. § 38, 50 U.S.C.A. § 38. Article 2 includes among those persons subject to the Articles of War the personnel of our own military establishment. But this, as Article 12 indicates, does not exclude from the class of

persons subject to trial by military commissions "any other person who by the law of war is subject to trial by military tribunals," and who, under Article 12, may be tried by court martial, or under Article 15 by military commission.

* * *

The Congressional recognition of military commissions and its sanction of their use in trying offenses against the law of war to which we have referred, sanctioned their creation by military command in conformity to long established American precedents. Such a commission may be appointed by any field commander, or by any commander competent to appoint a general court martial, as was General Styer, who had been vested with that power by order of the President. 2 Winthrop, Military Law and Precedents, 2d Ed., *1302; cf. Article of War 8.

* * *

The trial and punishment of enemy combatants who have committed violations of the law of war is thus not only a part of the conduct of war operating as a preventive measure against such violations, but is an exercise of the authority sanctioned by Congress to administer the system of military justice recognized by the law of war. That sanction is without qualification as to the exercise of this authority so long as a state of war exists—from its declaration until peace is proclaimed. See United States v. Anderson, 9 Wall. 56, 70, 19 L.Ed. 615; The Protector, 12 Wall. 700, 702, 20 L.Ed. 463; McElrath v. United States, 102 U.S. 426, 438, 26 L.Ed. 189; Kahn v. Anderson, 255 U.S. 1, 9, 10, 41 S.Ct. 224, 226, 65 L.Ed. 469. The war power, from which the commission derives its existence, is not limited to victories in the field, but carries with it the inherent power to guard against the immediate renewal of the conflict, and to remedy, at least in ways Congress has recognized, the evils which the military operations have produced. See Stewart v. Kahn, 11 Wall. 493, 507, 20 L.Ed. 176.

[12] We cannot say that there is no authority to convene a commission after hostilities have ended to try violations of the law of war committed before their cessation, at least until peace has been officially recognized by treaty or proclamation of the political branch of the Government. In fact, in most instances the practical administration of the system of military justice under the law of war would fail if such authority were thought to end with the cessation of hostilities. For only after their cessation could the greater number of offenders and the principal ones be apprehended and subjected to trial.

No writer on international law appears to have regarded the power of military tribunals, otherwise competent to try violations of the law of war, as terminating before the formal state of war has ended. In our own military history there have been numerous instances in which offenders were tried by military commission after the cessation of hostilities and before the proclamation of peace, for offenses against the law of war committed before the cessation of hostilities.

[13] The extent to which the power to prosecute violations of the law of war shall be exercised before peace is declared rests, not with the courts, but with the political branch of the Government, and may itself be governed by the terms of an armistice or the treaty of peace. Here, peace has not been agreed upon or proclaimed. Japan, by her acceptance of the Potsdam Declaration and her surrender, has acquiesced in the trials of those guilty of violations of the law of war. The conduct of the trial by the military commission has been authorized by the political branch of the Government, by military command, by international law and usage, and by the terms of the surrender of the Japanese government.

The Charge. Neither Congressional action nor the military orders constituting the commission authorized it to place petitioner on trial unless the charge preferred against him is of a violation of the law of war. The charge, so far as now relevant, is that petitioner, between October 9, 1944 and September 2, 1945, in the Philippine Islands, "while commander of armed forces of Japan at war with the United States of America and its allies, unlawfully disregarded and failed to discharge his duty as commander to control the operations of the members of his command, permitting them to commit brutal atrocities and other high crimes against people of the United States and of its allies and dependencies, particularly the Philippines; and he * * * thereby violated the laws of war."

Bills of particulars, filed by the prosecution by order of the commission, allege a series of acts, one hundred and twenty-three in number, committed by members of the forces under petitioner's command, during the period mentioned. The first item specifies the execution of "a deliberate plan and purpose to massacre and exterminate a large part of the civilian population of Batangas Province, and to devastate and destroy public, private and religious property therein, as a result of which more than 25,000 men, women and children, all unarmed noncombatant civilians, were brutally mistreated and killed, without cause or trial, and entire settlements were devastated and destroyed wantonly and without military necessity." Other items specify acts of violence, cruelty and homicide inflicted upon the civilian population and prisoners of war, acts of wholesale pillage and the wanton destruction of religious monuments.

[14] It is not denied that such acts directed against the civilian population of an occupied country and against prisoners of

war are recognized in international law as violations of the law of war. Articles 4, 28, 46, and 47, Annex to Fourth Hague Convention, 1907, 36 Stat. 2277, 2296, 2303, 2306, 2307. But it is urged that the charge does not allege that petitioner has either committed or directed the commission of such acts, and consequently that no violation is charged as against him. But this overlooks the fact that the gist of the charge is an unlawful breach of duty by petitioner as an army commander to control the operations of the members of his command by "permitting them to commit" the extensive and widespread atrocities specified. The question then is whether the law of war imposes on an army commander a duty to take such appropriate measures as are within his power to control the troops under his command for the prevention of the specified acts which are violations of the law of war and which are likely to attend the occupation of hostile territory by an uncontrolled soldiery, and whether he may be charged with personal responsibility for his failure to take such measures when violations result. That this was the precise issue to be tried was made clear by the statement of the prosecution at the opening of the trial.

[15] It is evident that the conduct of military operations by troops whose excesses are unrestrained by the orders or efforts of their commander would almost certainly result in violations which it is the purpose of the law of war to prevent. Its purpose to protect civilian populations and prisoners of war from brutality would largely be defeated if the commander of an invading army could with impunity neglect to take reasonable measures for their protection. Hence the law of war presupposes that its violation is to be avoided through the control of the operations of war by commanders who are to some extent responsible for their subordinates.

This is recognized by the Annex to Fourth Hague Convention of 1907, respecting the laws and customs of war on land. Article I lays down as a condition which an armed force must fulfill in order to be accorded the rights of lawful belligerents, that it must be "commanded by a person responsible for his subordinates." 36 Stat. 2295. Similarly Article 19 of the Tenth Hague Convention, relating to bombardment by naval vessels, provides that commanders in chief of the belligerent vessels "must see that the above Articles are properly carried out." 36 Stat. 2389. And Article 26 of the Geneva Red Cross Convention of 1929, 47 Stat. 2074, 2092, for the amelioration of the condition of the wounded and sick in armies in the field, makes it "the duty of the commanders-in-chief of the belligerent armies to provide for the details of execution of the foregoing articles (of the convention), as well as for unforeseen cases." And, finally, Article 43 of the Annex of the Fourth Hague Convention, 36 Stat. 2306, requires that the commander of a force occupying enemy territory, as was petitioner, "shall take all the measures in his power to restore, and ensure, as far as possible, public order and safety, while respecting, unless absolutely prevented, the laws in force in the country."

[16] These provisions plainly imposed on petitioner, who at the time specified was military governor of the Philippines, as well as commander of the Japanese forces, an affirmative duty to take such measures as were within his power and appropriate in the circumstances to protect prisoners of war and the civilian population. This duty of a commanding officer has heretofore been recognized, and its breach penalized by our own military tribunals. A like principle has been applied so as to impose liability on the United States in international arbitrations. Case of Jenaud, 3 Moore, International Arbitrations, 3000; Case of "The Zafiro," 5 Hackworth, Digest of International Law, 707.

[17][18] We do not make the laws of war but we respect them so far as they do not conflict with the commands of Congress or the Constitution. There is no contention that the present charge, thus read, is without the support of evidence, or that the commission held petitioner responsible for failing to take measures which were beyond his control or inappropriate for a commanding officer to take in the circumstances. We do not here appraise the evidence on which petitioner was convicted. We do not consider what measures, if any, petitioner took to prevent the commission, by the troops under his command, of the plain violations of the law of war detailed in the bill of particulars, or whether such measures as he may have taken were appropriate and sufficient to discharge the duty imposed upon him. These are questions within the peculiar competence of the military officers composing the commission and were for it to decide. See Smith v. Whitney, 116 U.S. 167, 178, 6 S.Ct. 570, 576, 29 L.Ed. 601. It is plain that the charge on which petitioner was tried charged him with a breach of his duty to control the operations of the members of his command, by permitting them to commit the specified atrocities. This was enough to require the commission to hear evidence tending to establish the culpable failure of petitioner to perform the duty imposed on him by the law of war and to pass upon its sufficiency to establish guilt.

* * *

Petitioner argues as ground for the writ of habeas corpus, that Article 25 of the Articles of War prohibited the reception in evidence by the commission of depositions on behalf of the prosecution in a capital case, and that Article 38 prohibited the reception of hearsay and of opinion evidence.

* * *

[21] * * * Petitioner, an enemy combatant, is therefore not a person made subject to the Articles of War by Article 2, and the military commission before which he was tried, though sanctioned,

and its jurisdiction saved, by Article 15, was not convened by virtue of the Articles of War, but pursuant to the common law of war. It follows that the Articles of War, including Articles 25 and 38, were not applicable to petitioner's trial and imposed no restrictions upon the procedure to be followed. The Articles left the control over the procedure in such a case where it had previously been, with the military command.

[22]   Petitioner further urges that by virtue of Article 63 of the Geneva Convention of 1929, 47 Stat. 2052, he is entitled to the benefits afforded by the 25th and 38th Articles of War to members of our own forces. Article 63 provides: "Sentence may be pronounced against a prisoner of war only by the same courts and according to the same procedure as in the case of persons belonging to the armed forces of the detaining Power." Since petitioner is a prisoner of war, and as the 25th and 38th Articles of War apply to the trial of any person in our own armed forces, it is said that Article 63 requires them to be applied in the trial of petitioner. But we think examination of Article 63 in its setting in the Convention plainly shows that it refers to sentence "pronounced against a prisoner of war" for an offense committed while a prisoner of war, and not for a violation of the law of war committed while a combatant.

* * *

* * * For reasons already stated we hold that the commission's rulings on evidence and on the mode of conducting these proceedings against petitioner are not reviewable by the courts, but only by the reviewing military authorities. From this viewpoint it is unnecessary to consider what, in other situations, the Fifth Amendment might require, and as to that no intimation one way or the other is to be implied. Nothing we have said is to be taken as indicating any opinion on the question of the wisdom of considering such evidence, or whether the action of a military tribunal in admitting evidence, which Congress or controlling military command has directed to be excluded may be drawn in question by petition for habeas corpus or prohibition.

[23]   Effect of failure to give notice of the trial to the protecting power. Article 60 of the Geneva Convention of July 27, 1929, 47 Stat. 2051, to which the United States and Japan were signatories, provides that "At the opening of a judicial proceeding directed against a prisoner of war, the detaining Power shall advise the representative of the protecting Power thereof as soon as possible, and always before the date set for the opening of the trial." Petitioner relies on the failure to give the prescribed notice to the protecting power to establish what of authority in the commission to proceed with the trial. For reasons already stated we conclude that Article 60 of the Geneva Convention, which appears in part 3,

Chapter 3, Section V, Title III of the Geneva Convention, applies only to persons who are subjected to judicial proceedings for offenses committed while prisoners of war. It thus appears that the order convening the commission was a lawful order, that the commission was lawfully constituted, that petitioner was charged with violation of the law of war, and that the commission had authority to proceed with the trial, and in doing so did not violate any military, statutory or constitutional command. We have considered, but find it unnecessary to discuss other contentions which we find to be without merit. We therefore conclude that the detention of petitioner for trial and his detention upon his conviction, subject to the prescribed review by the military authorities were lawful, and that the petition for certiorari, and leave to file in this Court petitions for writs of habeas corpus and prohibition should be, and they are

Denied.

Writs denied.

MR. JUSTICE JACKSON took no part in the consideration or decision of these cases.

MR. JUSTICE MURPHY, dissenting.

The significance of the issue facing the Court today cannot be overemphasized. An American military commission has been established to try a fallen military commander of a conquered nation for an alleged war crime. The authority for such action grows out of the exercise of the power conferred upon Congress by Article I, § 8, Cl. 10 of the Constitution to "define and punish * * * Offenses against the Law of Nations * * *." The grave issue raised by this case is whether a military commission so established and so authorized may disregard the procedural rights of an accused person as guaranteed by the Constitution, especially by the due process clause of the Fifth Amendment.

The answer is plain. The Fifth Amendment guarantee of due process of law applies to "any person" who is accused of a crime by the Federal Government or any of its agencies. No exception is made as to those who are accused of war crimes or as to those who possess the status of an enemy belligerent. Indeed, such an exception would be contrary to the whole philosophy of human rights which makes the Constitution the great living document that it is. The immutable rights of the individual, including those secured by the due process clause of the Fifth Amendment, belong not alone to the members of those nations that excel on the battlefield or that subscribe to the democratic ideology. They belong to every person in the world, victor or vanquished, whatever may be his race, color or beliefs. They rise above any status of belligerency or outlawry. They survive any popular passion or frenzy of the moment. No court or legislature or executive, not even the mightiest army in the world, can ever destroy them. Such is the universal and indestructible nature of the rights which the due process clause of the Fifth Amendment recognizes and protects when life or liberty is threatened by virtue of the authority of the United States.

The existence of these rights, unfortunately, is not always respected. They are often trampled under by those who are motivated by hatred, aggression or fear. But in this nation individual rights are recognized and protected, at least in regard to governmental action. They cannot be ignored by any branch of the Government, even the military, except under the most extreme and urgent circumstances.

The failure of the military commission to obey the dictates of the due process requirements of the Fifth Amendment is apparent in this case. The petitioner was the commander of an army totally destroyed by the superior power of this nation. While under heavy and destructive attack by our forces, his troops committed many brutal atrocities and other high crimes. Hostilities ceased and he voluntarily surrendered. At that point he was entitled, as an individual protected by the due process clause of the Fifth Amendment, to be treated fairly and justly according to the accepted rules of law and procedure. He was also entitled to a fair trial as to any alleged crimes and to be free from charges of legally unrecognized crimes that would serve only to permit his accusers to satisfy their desires for revenge.

A military commission was appointed to try the petitioner for an alleged war crime. The trial was ordered to be held in territory over which the United States has complete sovereignty. No military necessity or other emergency demanded the suspension of the safeguards of due process. Yet petitioner was rushed to trial under an improper charge, given insufficient time to prepare an adequate defense, deprived of the benefits of some of the most elementary rules of evidence and summarily sentenced to be hanged. In all this needless and unseemly haste there was no serious attempt to charge or to prove that he committed a recognized violation of the laws of war. He was not charged with personally participating in the acts of atrocity or with ordering or condoning their commission. Not even knowledge of these crimes was attributed to him. It was simply alleged that he unlawfully disregarded and failed to discharge his duty as commander to control the operations of the members of his command, permitting them to commit the acts of atrocity. The recorded annals of warfare and the established principles of international law afford not the slightest precedent for such a charge. This indictment in effect permitted the military commission to make the crime whatever it willed, dependent upon its biased view as to petitioner's duties and his disregard thereof, a practice reminiscent of that pursued in certain less respected nations in recent years.

In my opinion, such a procedure is unworthy of the traditions of our people or of the immense sacrifices that they have made to advance the common ideals of mankind. The high feelings of the moment doubtless will be satisfied. But in the sober afterglow will come the realization of the boundless and dangerous implications of the procedure sanctioned today. No one in a position of command in an army, from sergeant to general, can escape those implications. Indeed, the fate of some future President of the United States and his chiefs of staff and military advisers may well have been sealed by this decision. But even more significant will be the hatred and ill-will growing out of the application of this unprecedented procedure. That has been the inevitable effect of every method of punishment disregarding the element of personal culpability. The effect in this instance, unfortunately, will be magnified infinitely for here we are dealing with the rights of man on an international level. To subject an enemy belligerent to an unfair trial, to charge him with an unrecognized crime, or to vent on him our retributive emotions only antagonizes the enemy nation and hinders the reconciliation necessary to a peaceful world.

That there were brutal atrocities inflicted upon the helpless Filipino people, to whom tyranny is no stranger, by Japanese armed forces under the petitioner's command is undeniable. Starvation, execution or massacre without trial, torture, rape, murder and wanton destruction of property were foremost among the outright violations of the laws of war and of the conscience of a civilized world. That just punishment should be meted out to all those responsible for criminal acts of this nature is also beyond dispute. But these factors do not answer the problem in this case. They do not justify the abandonment of our devotion to justice in dealing with a fallen enemy commander. To conclude otherwise is to admit that the enemy has lost the battle but has destroyed our ideals.

War breeds atrocities. From the earliest conflicts of recorded history to the global struggles of modern times inhumanities, lust and pillage have been the inevitable by-products of man's resort to force and arms. Unfortunately, such despicable acts have a dangerous tendency to call forth primitive impulses of vengeance and retaliation among the victimized peoples. The satisfaction of such impulses in turn breeds resentment and fresh tension. Thus does the spiral of cruelty and hatred grow.

* * *

It is important, in the first place, to appreciate the background of events preceding this trial. From October 9, 1944, to September

2, 1945, the petitioner was the Commanding General of the 14th Army Group of the Imperial Japanese Army, with headquarters in the Philippines. The reconquest of the Philippines by the armed forces of the United States began approximately at the time when the petitioner assumed this command. Combined with a great and decisive sea battle, an invasion was made on the island of Leyte on October 20, 1944. "In the six days of the great naval action the Japanese position in the Philippines had become extremely critical. Most of the serviceable elements of the Japanese Navy had become committed to the battle with disastrous results. The strike had miscarried, and General MacArthur's land wedge was firmly implanted in the vulnerable flank of the enemy * * *. There were 260,000 Japanese troops scattered over the Philippines but most of them might as well have been on the other side of the world so far as the enemy's ability to shift them to meet the American thrusts was concerned. If General MacArthur succeeded in establishing himself in the Visayas where he could stage, exploit, and spread under cover of overwhelming naval and air superiority, nothing could prevent him from overrunning the Philippines." Biennial Report of the Chief of Staff of the United States Army, July 1, 1943, to June 30, 1945, to the Secretary of War, p. 74.

By the end of 1944 the island of Leyte was largely in American hands. And on January 9, 1945, the island of Luzon was invaded. "Yamashita's inability to cope with General MacArthur's swift moves, his desired reaction to the deception measures, the guerrillas, and General Kenney's aircraft combined to place the Japanese in an impossible situation. The enemy was forced into a piecemeal commitment of his troops." Ibid, p. 78. It was at this time and place that most of the alleged atrocities took place. Organized resistance around Manila ceased on February 23. Repeated land and air assaults pulverized the enemy and within a few months there was little left of petitioner's command except a few remnants which had gathered for a last stand among the precipitous mountains.

As the military commission here noted, "The Defense established the difficulties faced by the Accused with respect not only to the swift and overpowering advance of American forces, but also to the errors of his predecessors, weaknesses in organization, equipment, supply with especial reference to food and gasoline, training, communication, discipline and morale of his troops. It was alleged that the sudden assignment of Naval and Air Forces to his tactical command presented almost insurmountable difficulties. This situation was followed, the Defense contended, by failure to obey his orders to withdraw troops from Manila, and the subsequent massacre of unarmed civilians, particularly by Naval forces. Prior to the Luzon Campaign, Naval forces had reported to a separate ministry in the Japanese Government and Naval Commanders may not have been receptive or experienced in this instance with respect to a joint land operation under a single commander who was designated from the Army Service.''

The day of final reckoning for the enemy arrived in August, 1945. On September 3, the petitioner surrendered to the United States Army at Baguio, Luzon. He immediately became a prisoner of war and was interned in prison in conformity with the rules of international law. On September 25, approximately three weeks after surrendering, he was served with the charge in issue in this case. Upon service of the charge he was removed from the status of a prisoner of war and placed in confinement as an accused war criminal. Arraignment followed on October 8 before a military commission specially appointed for the case. Petitioner pleaded not guilty. He was also served on that day with a bill of particulars alleging 64 crimes by troops under his command. A supplemental bill alleging 59 more crimes by his troops was filed on October 29, the same day that the trial began. No continuance was allowed for preparation of a defense as to the supplemental bill. The trial continued uninterrupted until December 5, 1945. On December 7 petitioner was found guilty as charged and was sentenced to be hanged. The petitioner was accused of having "unlawfully disregarded and failed to discharge his duty as commander to control the operations of the members of his command, permitting them to commit brutal atrocities and other high crimes.'' The bills of particular further alleged that specific acts of atrocity were committed by "members of the armed forces of Japan under the command of the accused.'' Nowhere was it alleged that the petitioner personally committed any of the atrocities, or that he ordered their commission, or that he had any knowledge of the commission thereof by members of his command.

The findings of the military commission bear out this absence of any direct personal charge against the petitioner. The commission merely found that atrocities and other high crimes "have been committed by members of the Japanese armed forces under your command * * * that they were not sporadic in nature but in many cases were methodically supervised by Japanese officers and noncommissioned officers * * * that during the period in question you failed to provide effective control of your troops as was required by the circumstances.''

In other words, read against the background of military events in the Philippines subsequent to October 9, 1944, these charges amount to this: "We, the victorious American forces, have done everything possible to destroy and disorganize your lines of communication, your effective control of your personnel, your ability to wage war. In those respects we have succeeded. We have defeated and crushed your forces. And now we charge and condemn you for having been inefficient in maintaining control of your troops during the period when we were so effectively beseiging and eliminating your forces and blocking your ability to maintain effective control. Many terrible atrocities were committed by your disorganized troops. Because these atrocities were so widespread we will not bother to charge or prove that you committed, ordered or condoned any of them. We will assume that they must have resulted from your inefficiency and negligence as a commander. In short, we charge you with the crime of inefficiency in controlling your troops. We will judge the discharge of your duties by the disorganization which we ourselves created in large part. Our standards of judgment are whatever we wish to make them."

Nothing in all history or in international law, at least as far as I am aware, justifies such a charge against a fallen commander of a defeated force. To use the very inefficiency and disorganization created by the victorious forces as the primary basis for condemning officers of the defeated armies bears no resemblance to justice or to military reality.

International law makes no attempt to define the duties of a commander of an army under constant and overwhelming assault; nor does it impose liability under such circumstances for failure to meet the ordinary responsibilities of command. The omission is understandable. Duties, as well as ability to control troops, vary according to the nature and intensity of the particular battle. To find an unlawful deviation from duty under battle conditions requires difficult and speculative calculations. Such calculations become highly untrustworthy when they are made by the victor in relation to the actions of a vanquished commander. Objective and realistic norms of conduct are then extremely unlikely to be used in forming a judgment as to deviations from duty. The probability that vengeance will form the major part of the victor's judgment is an unfortunate but inescapable fact. So great is that probability that international law refuses to recognize such a judgment as a basis for a war crime, however fair the judgment may be in a particular instance. It is this consideration that undermines the charge against the petitioner in this case. The indictment permits, indeed compels, the military commission of a victorious nation to sit in judgment upon the military strategy and actions of the defeated enemy and to use its conclusions to determine the criminal liability of an enemy commander. Life and liberty are made to depend upon the biased will of the victor rather than upon objective standards of conduct.

The Court's reliance upon vague and indefinite references in certain of the Hague Conventions and the Geneva Red Cross Convention is misplaced. Thus the statement in Article 1 of the Annex to Hague Convention No. IV of October 18, 1907, 36 Stat. 2277, 2295, to the effect that the laws, rights and duties of war apply to military and volunteer corps only if they are "commanded by a person responsible for his subordinates," has no bearing upon the problem in this case. Even if it has, the clause "responsible for his subordinates" fails to state to whom the responsibility is owed or to indicate the type of responsibility contemplated. The phrase has received differing interpretations by authorities on international law. In Oppenheim, International Law (6th ed., rev. by Lauterpacht, 1940, vol. 2, p. 204, fn. 3) it is stated that "The meaning of the word 'responsible' * * * is not clear. It probably means 'responsible to some higher authority,' whether the person is appointed from above or elected from below; * * *." Another authority has stated that the word "responsible" in this particular context means "presumably to a higher authority," or "possibly it merely means one who controls his subordinates and who therefore can be called to account for their acts." Wheaton, International Law (14th ed., by Keith, 1944, p. 172, fn. 30). Still another authority, Westlake, International Law (1907, Part II, p. 61), states that "probably the responsibility intended is nothing more than a capacity of exercising effective control." Finally, Edwards and Oppenheim, Land Warfare (1912, p. 19, par. 22) state that it is enough "if the commander of the corps is regularly or temporarily commissioned as an officer or is a person of position and authority." It seems apparent beyond dispute that the word "responsible" was not used in this particular Hague Convention to hold the commander of a defeated army to any high standard of efficiency when he is under destructive attack; nor was it used to impute to him any criminal responsibility for war crimes committed by troops under his command under such circumstances.

* * *

C. NOTES, QUESTIONS, AND PROBLEMS

1. Can you see a danger for the viability of rules *in bello* in the concept of just war?

2. Why do you think wars of religion and civil wars have tended to be even more brutal than wars waged for other reasons, such as acquiring territory or enforcing legal rights?

3. Augustine, Grotius and Vattel all urged respecting basic principles of humanity in the waging of war in order to have a chance at peace. How does the failure to respect basic principle threaten the peace? Why did Lincoln have General Orders No. 100 drafted?

4. Can your think of other reasons a military would train its members in the law of armed conflict besides assuring the future peace? Does the military have the same interest in training its members in the *jus ad bellum* as in the *jus in bello*?

5. Identify some of the general principles governing the conduct of armed force in existence by the outbreak of the Second World War. What *in bello* principles remained identifiable from the time of Augustine until the

Second World War? Why do you think these principles have withstood the test of time? No high-ranking political or military leader from among the Allies in World War II faced any criminal charges at the end of the war. Only the Axis leaders were tried and punished. Considering in particular the trial of Admiral Dönitz, however, can you argue that in fact Allied war crimes and treaty violations did receive some scrutiny? See also the Problem below on the bombing of Dresden, Germany.

6.   Justice Murphy's powerful and famous dissent is the Yamashita case predicts that the majority decision will spark a cycle of revenge. He speaks in terms reminiscent of Augustine, Grotius, Vattel, and others about the importance of treating an enemy with humanity, eschewing revenge. Consider U.S.-Japanese relations after the Second World War. Did the case spark a cycle of revenge and bitterness? Did it possibly have other negative consequences? Even if it did not, is Justice Murphy's dissent still valuable? The topic of command responsibility in contemporary law is taken up again in Chapter 11. Consider there whether the majority decision Yamashita is today a precedent.

7.   In addition to the publications referred to in the Chapter's notes, see also the following on the historical development of war crimes tribunals, GARY JONATHAN BASS, STAY THE HAND OF VENGEANCE: THE POLITICS OF WAR CRIMES TRIBUNALS (2000).

8.   Problem: Over the years, at least two Allied decisions in World War II have received particularly close and persistent scrutiny: The British decision to bomb the German city of Dresden and the American decision to drop atomic bombs on the Japanese cities of Hiroshima and Nagasaki. The following excerpt presents some of the pertinent facts of the Dresden case:

> On a clear February night in 1945, a first wave of Allied bombers struck at Dresden in eastern Germany. By the following evening, British and American warplanes had dropped 4,500 tons of incendiaries and high explosives on Saxony's ancient capital. Some 20 square kilometers of the city center, previously untouched by the bombers, was leveled, and some of Europe's finest baroque architechture collapsed into rubble. Up to 40,000 civilians lay dead. * * *
>
> [Dresden] had good reason to hope it might escape devastation. At the time of the attack, the war's outcome was in little doubt. Dresden was a city of exceptional beauty—"Florence on the Elbe"—far richer in culture than in industry. Unlike the much-bombed industrial centers of the Ruhr, the city made little contribution to the German war effort. Indeed, it was packed with refugees who believed in its safety. * * *
>
> [However,] the city's manufacturers had retooled to produce military equipment. Factories that once turned out sewing machines and cameras were making gun sights and bullets. For the German Army, Dresden was also an important road and rail center. * * * Allied commanders had little reason to believe that

the German Army was on its knees. Only two months earlier a counterattack in the Ardennes had punched a hole in the American lines. * * * In any case, it's beyond dispute that the British were interested in more than a city's military significance. As far back as 1942, Churchill had instructed the RAF's Bomber Command: "The primary object of your operations should now be focused on the morale of the enemy civilian population." William Underhill, *Justifying the Means; A New Book Makes a Case for the Dresden Bombing*, NEWSWEEK INTERNATIONAL, Mar. 8, 2004, at 58, 2004 WL 65299427.

Relying on the materials in this Chapter and these minimal facts, develop arguments for and against the legality of bombing Dresden. See also the non-binding Hague Rules of Air Warfare of 1923.

*

PART III

THE CONTEMPORARY INTERNATIONAL LAW ON THE USE OF FORCE

CHAPTER SIX

THE BASIC INTERNATIONAL LAW AND INSTITUTIONS ON RESORT TO FORCE

This Chapter presents the basic framework of law and institutions on resort to force. This is the framework that emerged after the Second World War and forms the foundation of today's law. New substantive rules and new institutions replaced many of the treaties and institutions of the inter-war period. We will look at what emerged that remains relevant today—the United Nations Organization, its Charter, and various regional security arrangements, including the North Atlantic Treaty Organization (NATO).[1]

The United Nations Charter is a binding, multilateral treaty that opened for signature on June 26, 1945. It provides for the establishment of the United Nations Organization and substantive rules of conduct for the UN's members. Most importantly, it prohibits the use of force by its members except in self-defense or with the authorization of the UN Security Council. The Charter does more, however. It also provides principles designed to eliminate the causes of war by mandating respect for human rights and promotion of economic development. This Chapter will touch only tangentially on the Charter's response to the causes of war. It focuses more directly on how the UN was originally organized to address uses of force and the substantive Charter rules on the use of force. Chapters Seven and Eight consider how these rules have evolved over time and consider the rules on resort to force that are now part of customary international law.

The core rules on the use of force are found in Chapters I and VII of the Charter. Chapter I's Article 2(4) is a general prohibition on the use of force by states. It is at the heart of the Charter scheme for regulating force, but is accompanied by a number of related rules, such as the self-defense exception found in Chapter VII Article 51. These rules and their interconnections are discussed in Section B. below. In Section C. we will consider the Charter's various organs for the use of force and preservation of peace. The most important institutional arrangement is the UN Security Council, a body with the power to determine and act in response to "any threat to the peace, breach of the peace, or and act of aggression...." Various other

---

1. On the United Nations, see, THE CHARTER OF THE UNITED NATIONS: A COMMENTARY (Bruno Simma et al. eds., 2d ed. 2002) [hereinafter UN CHARTER COMMENTARY]; UNITED NA-TIONS: LAW, POLICIES, AND PRACTICE (Rudiger Wolfrum ed., 1995); UNITED NATIONS LEGAL ORDER (Oscar Schachter & Christopher Joyner eds., 1995).

UN organs play a role as well, including the General Assembly, the Secretary General, and the International Court of Justice. Regional arrangements are allowed in the Charter and in discussing those provisions we will take a brief look at NATO.

We start, however, with a look at the drafting of the Charter. The Vienna Convention on the Law of Treaties indicates that to understand a treaty— to properly interpret it—requires looking at its objects and purposes, its context, and, if necessary, to its drafting history.[2] We introduce here all of these elements relevant to the United Nations Charter as to its provisions on the use of force.

A. THE CHARTER'S HISTORY

The drafting of the United Nations Charter began well before the end of the Second World War. The planning for a post-war organization designed to keep the peace was largely a U.S. effort.[3] From the underlying concepts to the Organization's name, American officials took the lead. United States President Franklin Roosevelt gave the Organization its name when he coined the term "United Nations" to describe the countries that came together to fight the Axis powers. The reference to "United Nations" was then used officially in the "Declaration of the United Nations" on January 1, 1942, a pledge by 26 countries to continue the common fight against the Axis. The name remained for the new body that would maintain the post-war peace.

During the period August to October 1944, representatives of the United States, Soviet Union, United Kingdom and China met at Dumbarton Oaks, a private foundation near Washington, D.C. to draft a plan for a new organization and a new strategy for maintaining the peace. Then in February 1945, in the town of Yalta in the Soviet Union, Roosevelt, Stalin and Churchill met to agree on further aspects of the new organization, including a place and time for a multilateral conference to negotiate the final treaty text. From April 25 to June 26, 1945, delegates from fifty countries met in San Francisco. What emerged was the United Nations Charter, a plan for world order that has remained largely unchanged for sixty years. The Charter came into force on October 24, 1945, after ratification by the four principle drafters and a majority of the original signatories.[4]

---

2. Vienna Convention on the Law of Treaties, May 23, 1969, arts. 31 & 32, 1155 UNTS 331.

3. *See* STEPHEN C. SCHLESINGER, ACT OF CREATION: THE FOUNDING OF THE UNITED NATIONS, A STORY OF SUPERPOWERS, SECRET AGENTS, WARTIME ALLIES AND ENEMIES, AND THEIR QUEST FOR A PEACEFUL WORLD (2003). *See also,* WILHELM GREWE & DANIEL-ERASMUS KHAN, *DRAFTING HISTORY, IN* UN CHARTER COMMENTARY 1–12, *supra*

note 1. EVAN LUARD, A HISTORY OF THE UNITED NATIONS (1982).

4. Basic Facts about the United Nations 2000, Sales No. E.00.I.21. (The Charter is considered to have 51 original signatories. Poland did not have a representative in San Francisco, but signed later. Its signature is counted as an original signature.)

Stephen C. Schlesinger, Act of Creation: The Founding of the United Nations

A Story of Superpowers, Secret Agents, Wartime Allies and
Enemies, and Their Quest for a Peaceful World 33–34,
37, 47–51, 57, 58–59, 64, 72 (2003).*

By the fall of 1939, the State Department had already started to prepare secret plans for the postwar period. Acting in response to President Roosevelt's cautionary words to the American people about a possible war and the need for a "final peace," Secretary of State Cordell Hull proposed an in-house research team on a global security plan. Roosevelt consented to this proposition because, unlike President Wilson, he wanted to keep all postwar blueprints within his administration to avoid the confusion that had led to the defeat of the League of Nations. Roosevelt also sought to keep postwar planning under wraps for fear of stirring up the isolationists and diverting focus from the war. To lead the planning, Hull chose his long-time personal assistant, Leo Pasvolsky, a Russian-born economist, as special aide for the problems of peace and gave him the authority to direct a departmental operational group.

* * *

[Pasvolsky] possessed formidable and indefatigable work habits. For the seven years between 1939 and 1945—under two presidents, three secretaries of state, and three undersecretaries of state—he directed most of the department's committees preparing an international charter, immersed himself in every facet of the review process inside and outside the government, assisted in resolving disputes over the organization, and continuously briefed U.S. and foreign officials about the progress on the assembly's construction. He was a brilliant negotiator. Observers called him "the chess player in operation." He nurtured the organization's first seeds in Washington and, by 1945, presided over its full flowering in San Francisco.

* * *

In mid-August 1941, President Roosevelt's dramatic meeting at sea with British Prime Minister Winston Churchill, in Argentia Bay off the coast of Newfoundland, brought new attention to a world organization. Roosevelt first demurred from Churchill's suggestion that the two men issue a proclamation, known later as the Atlantic Charter, that would refer to the setting up of an "effective international organization." Under pressure from his aides, including Harry Hopkins and Sumner Welles, as well as from Churchill himself, Roosevelt finally embraced a somewhat different if muddier formulation, calling for the disarmament of the aggressors

---

* Footnotes omitted.

"pending the establishment of a wider and permanent system of general security." This latter statement, relatively innocuous at the time, soon became the key intellectual underpinning for the State Department's covert labors.

* * *

* * * Roosevelt, Hull, and Pasvolsky had gained agreement with the Big Four on a late August 1944 conclave. There was one hitch—the Russians objected to sitting down with the Chinese because they had not yet declared war on Japan. Consequently, Roosevelt consented to two successive meetings: the first with the British and Russians, a later one with the British and the Chinese. But neither the British, the Russians, nor the Chinese seemed to take the preparatory work very seriously. Each of the governments sent Roosevelt some general thoughts on a global body, but, except for some lengthy British notations titled "Future World Organization," nothing of serious consequence. The result was that, as Robert Hilderbrand, author of the standard work on Dumbarton Oaks, later wrote, the Pasvolsky proposal, "which was by far the most complete and detailed of the three, became—albeit unofficially—the basic frame of reference for building a plan of world organization." Another U.N. specialist, Edward Luard, also concluded after an exhaustive analysis of the meeting that the U.S. proposal "to a large extent, formed the basis for discussions" at the conference. So, too, Hull himself observed in his memoirs that "all the essential points in the tentative draft" that he had originally handed to the Russians and the British before the conference "were incorporated in the draft now accepted by the conference."

* * *

The Big Three nations early on accepted the basic framework for the world organization inherited from the League of Nations, including an eleven-member Security Council (with five permanent seats), a General Assembly, a Secretariat, and various subagencies—as well as a Military Staff Committee composed of officers from the five permanent states to direct all U.N. enforcement actions.

The discussions in the meetings mainly centered on how to distribute powers among the various branches. Pasvolsky tried to persuade the Russians to accept an Economic and Social Council to deal with the causes of war, such as poverty and famine, arguing, though, that it should remain separate from the already overburdened Security Council. The British liked the idea. Eventually the Soviets agreed.

Next, the British and Americans reached a compromise (later accepted by the Russians) on the question of regionalism based on a paper presented by Pasvolsky titled "Role of Local and Regional Agencies." Pasvolsky had originally emphasized the subordination of regional groupings to the Security Council, but the U.S. delegation finally gave way somewhat to the British position, which favored a higher profile for regional assemblies. It accepted language stating that "nothing in the Charter should preclude the existence of regional arrangements or agencies." Washington, struggling to accommodate to its own regional Pan–American Congress, was, in any event, in an ambivalent frame of mind about the matter. In acquiescing to the amended phraseology, it was, in effect, mildly discouraging regional bodies but also somewhat enhancing their autonomy.

On the matter of the Security Council, Pasvolsky played a significant role in helping to define that body's responsibilities. He persuaded Undersecretary Stettinius to oppose the designation of Brazil as the sixth permanent member of the Security Council, a cause pressed by Roosevelt to quell impending Latin American discontent over representation. Stettinius used many of the arguments in Pasvolsky's memo, including the question of whether Brazil really amounted to a Great Power, to convince Roosevelt ultimately to drop the notion of Brazil. And Pasvolsky argued successfully for the council to stay in continuous session at the U.N. to handle crises.

Third, he aggressively fought a Russian proposal to give an absolute veto to the five permanent members, a posture that would have allowed them to block attempts at discussion of an issue or peacefully settling disputes in which they themselves were involved. This was a viewpoint that his own boss, Cordell Hull, had at first supported. Pasvolsky regarded such an outsized veto as giving the Big Nations far too much power, much of which could probably be abused by the Soviets; and, as well, it would place the major states unfairly on a higher plane than smaller nations regarding conflict settlement. Eventually, Hull changed his mind, as Hilderbrand put it, worn down by Pasvolsky's sheer "perseverance." On September 13, along with his two junior counterparts, Gladwyn Jebb of Great Britain and Arkadei Sobelov of the USSR, Pasvolsky developed a tentative compromise formula whereby the veto could be used only on enforcement or "substantive" issues, not on matters of discussion or peaceful settlement, which were viewed as "procedural" issues. However, when this notion was presented to Stalin, the Soviet leader stuck unswervingly to his original stand; he was later joined by Churchill, further complicating the U.S. position.

Toward the end of the conference, the Soviets suddenly demanded that all sixteen Soviet republics become members. The Russian representative, Andrei Gromyko, pressed this proposal, apparently because of Stalin's fear that the Western powers, with their fellow democracies, would always outvote the USSR. Taken aback by the suggestion, and fearful that it would damage the U.N.'s chances in the Senate, Roosevelt instructed Stettinius to give the Russians the impression that the United States would give their idea serious consideration; but privately he would attempt to derail it. Stettinius swore the U.S. delegation to secrecy about the Roosevelt strategy, informing no other official but Pasvolsky and another fellow operative on the Joint Steering Committee. Gromyko eventually withdrew his notion temporarily, hoping for unspecified future action on it. Pasvolsky later circulated a list of proposed states for U.N. membership (excluding the sixteen Soviet republics) that left Gromyko disgruntled again. He opposed including nations that had not yet declared war on the Axis, such as Argentina. Pasvolsky's initiative only increased the Soviet resistance to any deal.

Pasvolsky did not succeed in persuading the Soviets to reconsider their stance on either the extra votes or on the veto. For all his remarkable talents, there were certain questions that he (and the U.S. mission) was simply unable to resolve at Dumbarton Oaks. The lingering issues were the absolute veto; the membership list; further delineation of the authority of the Economic and Social Council, and more broadly, the General Assembly; the role of regional groups; congressional authorization of U.S. troops under U.N. command; the creation of a Trusteeship council (a subject not brought up because of U.S. military opposition); the statute of the World Court; a site for the U.N. headquarters; the transfer of League of Nations property to the U.N.; and a budget for the new body. By the end of the conference, although it was clear that much had been accomplished at Dumbarton Oaks, there was an evident consensus that the host of undecided issues must now be bucked up to the highest authorities in the United States, Great Britain, and the Soviet Union for resolution. (This same conclusion was strengthened later in the second China phase of the meeting.) On September 21, at a White House meeting with Roosevelt, the president asked his officials to bring Dumbarton Oaks to a close and hold all unsettled questions in abeyance until his own get-together with Stalin and Churchill. Pasvolsky returned to his research position in the State Department.

* * *

* * * [A]s the meeting among the three major powers drew nearer, there began to be misgivings on the U.S. and British sides over the choice of Yalta for the conference. Stalin had begged off Roosevelt's suggestion of meeting in the Mediterranean, preferably Sicily, because, as he wrote, "I still have to pay heed to my doctors' warning of the risk involved in long journeys." He preferred instead the Soviet Black Sea coast. In retrospect, this choice seems singularly ironic; it was clearly Roosevelt, crippled and sickly, who would have to forgo the cautions of his doctors and make a journey that was far more arduous, Yalta being thousands of miles from the United States. Roosevelt was, in this tiring foray, taking a heavy risk with his health. *New York Times* columnist Anne O'Hare McCormick, an intimate of Roosevelt's who interviewed him days before he died, wrote that it was primarily because of the United Nations that he made "the hard, perhaps fatal, trip to Yalta.... [T]his was the thing he was straining his strength to accomplish."

* * *

* * * [At Yalta, the] leaders haggled over military strategy in the first few days. On the third day, February 6, they began to focus on the United Nations. That afternoon, Secretary of State Stettinius presented the U.S. position on the voting formula to Stalin and Churchill. Roosevelt discussed the proposed U.S. formula at some length. At one point, Stalin referred back to the USSR's ouster from the League of Nations in 1939, after it had invaded Finland, and wanted to know whether the veto would not protect his nation against such action in the future. Anthony Eden, the British foreign secretary, assured him it would. Eventually, Stalin suggested that the U.S. proposal be put under study, to which Roosevelt and Churchill consented. There was some foreboding that the issue might now linger past Yalta, placing the U.N. Conference in jeopardy; but Foreign Minister Molotov appeared next afternoon and said that, because the Soviet side now had a clearer understanding of the Roosevelt plan and that his country felt it would keep the unity of the Major Powers, Moscow now found it "acceptable." Such a rapid turnaround in the Russian position came as a welcome surprise to the Americans, especially to Stettinius, who grinned broadly.

* * *

[Upon his return to Washington, Roosevelt addressed Congress.]

His speech was not so much a report on Yalta as it was a plea to Congress—his final plea, as it turned out—to rally around the creation of the United Nations. His thinking clearly reflected a personal determination to avoid the errors of the League of Nations battle of 1919–1920. The Yalta accords, he promised his audience, "ought" to spell the end of unilateral actions, spheres of influence, balances of power, and exclusive alliances that "have been tried for centuries—and have always failed." He wanted the U.N. established right away. As he said, "This time we shall not make the mistake of waiting until the end of the war to set up the machinery of peace. This time, as we fight together to get the war over quickly, we work together to keep it from happening again."

* * *

Four days later, Great Britain, the United States, and the USSR, as well as China, acting as the sponsoring powers, issued the formal invitations to San Francisco—initially to the thirty-seven nations that had, by March 1, declared war on one or more of the Axis enemy.

* * *

Just thirteen days before his rendezvous with San Francisco, he died.

Richard C. Edis, A Job Well Done: The Founding of the United Nations Revisited

6 Cambridge Rev. Int'l Aff. 29, 35–38 (1992).*

San Francisco

The San Francisco conference which was to finalise the drafting of the United Nations Charter opened on April 25th 1945 and was attended by the fifty countries who were signatories of the UN Declaration or "associated powers." Although states such as Spain, Eire and initially Argentina, who were regarded as having been less then helpful in the conflict were excluded, as were ex-enemy states even if they had subsequently declared war on Germany, such as Italy, Finland, Hungary, Rumania and Bulgaria, along with some persistent neutrals such as Switzerland and Sweden, the conference was widely representative. The submission by the Great Powers of their proposals to detailed scrutiny by such a large group of smaller states was unprecedented. * * * [T]his was motivated by pragmatic as well as idealistic considerations. If the new system was to work, it had to engage the willing participation of nations as a whole and this would be more readily attracted if they were actively engaged in the formulation process. To emphasise this, decisions at the conference were made by a two-thirds majority vote.

* * *

While participants in the conference agreed to take the Dumbarton Oaks proposals as the basis of their deliberations, these were not in charter language and significant areas of the new organisation's activities remained to be filled in. In addition, the non-sponsoring powers sought to re-open or redefine some of the Dumbarton Oaks proposals. The main issues at the conference were:

— the position of the Permanent Members in the Security Council and in particular the scope of the veto;

---

* *See also*, Documents of the United Nations Conference on International Organiza- tion (United Nations Information Organization 1945).

— the role of the General Assembly and of the Economic and Social Council;

— the status of bilateral and regional arrangements;

— the question of domestic jurisdiction;

— the handling of Trusteeship and colonial matters.

The non-great powers accepted, albeit somewhat grudgingly, the basic concept that the leading powers in the victorious Allied coalition should be accorded a special position in the new international security system. However, they subjected the proposed veto power to detailed scrutiny and applied considerable ingenuity to efforts to whittle it down, as well as to accord themselves a greater influence. Their attempt to clarify the proposed extent of the application of the veto provoked a split among the sponsoring powers with the Russians re-opening the Yalta agreement in this respect, necessitating a direct appeal to Stalin.

The onslaught by the non-great powers on the veto privilege took a number of forms. A move to take away it applicability from the pacific settlements of disputes procedure was only voted down fairly narrowly after the sponsoring powers mustered every effort to defeat it. There was a proposal to increase the number of non-Permanent Members on the Security Council and also to give a vote to parties to a dispute. There was even an idea of adding new Permanent Members such as Brazil. Another line of attack was to limit the duration of the veto privilege for a fixed period of time and, allied to this, to set a date by which the whole system would be subject to review.

While ready to make concessions in other areas, the sponsoring powers were adamant in opposing any significant lessening of the veto power and in the end made it clear that without the veto there would be no United Nations. Nor would they see their hands tied in maintaining international peace and security by attempts to define what constituted "aggression" or to go down the road of expanding on concepts of "justice." However, there was one significant change to the proposed security system as a result of the discussion at San Francisco, which was the addition to the enforcement procedure of a range of measures falling short of the use of force, i.e. economic and diplomatic sanctions, military demonstrations and blockade.

Other issues which reflected the particular concerns of the non-great powers related to the powers of the Security Council were the status of existing and future regional arrangements and the protection of national sovereignty. The Latin Americans were anxious to protect the inter-American system that had been developed, most recently through the Act of Chapultepec. The Arab countries had also just set up the Arab League. These concerns chimed in with Soviet and French desires to maintain bilateral alliances that had been concluded as a precaution against a revival of German power. The outcome was some primarily cosmetic changes to the existing regional provisions of the draft but much more significantly the addition of a new article which reserved the right of individual and collective defence.

A similarly important addition was a clause designed to protect domestic jurisdiction. This was a general concern of the medium and smaller powers since unlike the Great Powers they were not protected by the veto. However it was the Australians and South Africans who took a lead on the issue because of their fears of attacks on their racial policies. In fact the lack of definition in the drafting of the article left scope for subsequent erosion of its force.

Foiled in their attempt to diminish the position of the Great Powers in the Security Council, the other states were more successful in extending the status and responsibilities of those parts of the organisation in which all members were on the same footing. The right of the General Assembly to discuss all matters within the scope of the Charter, including those relating to international peace and security unless the Security Council was formally seized of the issue, was established. And the Economic and Social Council's role was enhanced. It was given the status of a principal organ and ambitious hopes were entertained for its activities in the economic and social field. Greater prominence was also attached to human rights and to social issues such as the status of women.

* * *

In the judicial area, the existing Permanent Court of International Justice was effectively maintained under a new name as the International Court of Justice, although its role in the new security system was less than that under the League. Finally, Russian attempts to neuter the Secretary General's independence were unsuccessful.

Despite the length and intensity of debate on many issues, and indication of the overall acceptability of the outcome was that the Charter was signed by all states participating in the conference without reservations on 26 June 1945.

B. CHARTER RULES

The motivations of states for founding the United Nations are spelled out eloquently in the Charter Preamble:

Preamble

WE THE PEOPLES OF THE UNITED NATIONS DETERMINED

- to save succeeding generations from the scourge of war, which twice in our lifetime has brought untold sorrow to mankind, and
- to reaffirm faith in fundamental human rights, in the dignity and worth of the human person, in the equal rights of men and women and of nations large and small, and
- to establish conditions under which justice and respect for the obligations arising from treaties and other sources of international law can be maintained, and
- to promote social progress and better standards of life in larger freedom,

AND FOR THESE ENDS

- to practice tolerance and live together in peace with one another as good neighbors, and
- to unite our strength to maintain international peace and security, and
- to ensure, by the acceptance of principles and the institution of methods, that armed force shall not be used, save in the common interest, and
- to employ international machinery for the promotion of the economic and social advancement of all peoples,

HAVE RESOLVED TO COMBINE OUR EFFORTS TO ACCOMPLISH THESE AIMS

Accordingly, our respective Governments, through representatives assembled in the city of San Francisco, who have exhibited their full powers found to be in good and due form, have agreed to the present Charter of the United Nations and do hereby establish an international organization to be known as the United Nations.

As with the Preamble, the Charter's Chapter I on purposes and principles emphasizes the UN's purpose of preserving the peace as well the promotion of human rights and economic development. Article 2(4) is at the heart of the legal strategy to maintain peace. Note, however, Article 2(7) as well.

UN Charter, Chapter I Purposes and Principles

Article 1

The Purposes of the United Nations are:

1. To maintain international peace and security, and to that end: to take effective collective measures for the prevention and removal of threats to the peace, and for the suppression of acts of aggression or other breaches of the peace, and to bring about by peaceful means, and in conformity with the principles of justice

and international law, adjustment or settlement of international disputes or situations which might lead to a breach of the peace;

2.   To develop friendly relations among nations based on respect for the principle of equal rights and self-determination of peoples, and to take other appropriate measures to strengthen universal peace;

3.   To achieve international cooperation in solving international problems of an economic, social, cultural, or humanitarian character, and in promoting and encouraging respect for human rights and for fundamental freedoms for all without distinction as to race, sex, language, or religion; and

4.   To be a center for harmonizing the actions of nations in the attainment of these common ends.

Article 2

The Organization and its Members, in pursuit of the Purposes stated in Article 1, shall act in accordance with the following Principles:

1.   The Organization is based on the principle of the sovereign equality of all its Members.

2.   All Members, in order to ensure to all of them the rights and benefits resulting from membership, shall fulfill in good faith the obligations assumed by them in accordance with the present Charter.

3.   All Members shall settle their international disputes by peaceful means in such a manner that international peace and security, and justice, are not endangered.

4.   All Members shall refrain in their international relations from the threat or use of force against the territorial integrity or political independence of any state, or in any other manner inconsistent with the Purposes of the United Nations.

5.   All Members shall give the United Nations every assistance in any action it takes in accordance with the present Charter, and shall refrain from giving assistance to any state against which the United Nations is taking preventive or enforcement action.

* * *

7.   Nothing contained in the present Charter shall authorize the United Nations to intervene in matters which are essentially within the domestic jurisdiction of any state or shall require the Members to submit such matters to settlement under the present Charter; but this principle shall not prejudice the application of enforcement measures under Chapter VII.

The wording of Article 2(4) could be interpreted as limiting all force, not just armed force. The records from San Francisco, as well as subsequent interpretation by governments and the International Court of Justice make clear that despite the general reference to "force" in Article 2(4) the kind of force prohibited is armed force, and not other kinds of forceful action. "Force,"[5] could reasonably prohibit economic coercion,[6] political coercion,[7] physical force not involving arms,[8] computer attacks,[9] and much else. These, however, are typically regulated under the customary principle of non-intervention or the law of countermeasures and not the Charter rules governing the use of force.

Article 2(4) is understood to prohibit the use of armed force. Further, the drafters intended it to have wide application. The references in the Article to "territorial integrity" and "political independence" of states may read like qualifications, but all indications are that they are not intended to restrict the scope of the Article. The objects and purposes of the Charter, the structure, the drafting history, subsequent resolutions of the General Assembly and statements by governments and the International Court of Justice, consistently interpret 2(4) as banning any use of armed force by states except those in self-defense (and possibly those of a very limited or *de minimis* nature).

The scope of Article 2(4) was discussed at San Francisco. A U.S. delegate stated in response to the Brazilian delegation that "the intention of the authors of the original text was to state in the broadest terms an absolute all-inclusive prohibition; the phrase 'or in any other manner' was designed to insure that there should be no loopholes."[10] The final structure of the Charter that emerged in San Francisco underscores the broad scope of Article 2(4). The Security Council was given explicit, broad authority in Articles 39 and 42 to use armed force against threats to the peace, breaches of the peace and acts of aggression. By contrast, states acting without Security Council authority received only a narrow, explicit right to use force in Article 51. Article 51 permits force in individual and collective self-defense when an armed attack occurs until the Security Council takes action. Further, if Article 2(4) only prohibited force aimed at territorial

---

5. *See* Albrecht Randelzhofer, *Article 2(4), in* UN CHARTER COMMENTARY, *supra* note 1, at 112–136.

6. Examples of economic coercion include economic embargoes, the termination of aid or contracts of sale.

7. Political coercion can take innumerable forms. The most common examples may be terminating diplomatic relations or official statements in denunciation.

8. Physical coercion not involving arms may include the interdicting a river to a downstream state, deliberating setting force to cross a border, or cutting fishing nets.

9. *See, e.g.,* George K. Walker, *Information Warfare and Neutrality*, 33 VAND. J.

TRANSNAT'L L. 1079 (2000); Michael Schmitt, *Computer Network Attack and the Use of Force in International Law*, 37 COLUM. J. TRANSNAT'L L. 885 (1999).

10. 6 UNITED NATIONS CONFERENCE ON INTERNATIONAL ORGANIZATION 334–35 (United Nations Information Office, 1945). Brownlie concludes that at the San Francisco conference to draft the Charter, "[t]here was a presumption against self-help and even action in self-defence within Article 51 was made subject to control by the Security Council." IAN BROWNLIE, INTERNATIONAL LAW AND THE USE OF FORCE BY STATES 275 (1968) and references therein.

integrity and political independence, Article 51 might be redundant since few would view defending against an unlawful attack to be interference with the attacking state's territorial integrity or political independence.

In addition to the prohibition on force and the institutions designed to ensure peace and security, the Charter also promotes the principles of peaceful settlement of dispute. In a sense, peaceful settlement receives less emphasis in the Charter than it did in the League Covenant. The Covenant did not directly prohibit the use of force but rather required states to try peaceful settlement first. Because the Charter generally prohibits armed force, there was less need to mandate dispute resolution as a means to delay resort to force. The Charter's Chapter VI requires only that if parties seek to resolve disputes they must do so peacefully. The Charter does not take the next logical step beyond the Covenant—it does not create a system of compulsory dispute resolution.

UN Charter, Chapter VI Pacific Settlement of Disputes

Article 33

1.   The parties to any dispute, the continuance of which is likely to endanger the maintenance of international peace and security, shall, first of all, seek a solution by negotiation, enquiry, mediation, conciliation, arbitration, judicial settlement, resort to regional agencies or arrangements, or other peaceful means of their own choice.

2.   The Security Council shall, when it deems necessary, call upon the parties to settle their dispute by such means.

Article 34

The Security Council may investigate any dispute, or any situation which might lead to international friction or give rise to a dispute, in order to determine whether the continuance of the dispute or situation is likely to endanger the maintenance of international peace and security.

Article 35

1.   Any Member of the United Nations may bring any dispute, or any situation of the nature referred to in Article 34, to the attention of the Security Council or of the General Assembly.

* * *

3.   The proceedings of the General Assembly in respect of matters brought to its attention under this Article will be subject to the provisions of Articles 11 and 12.

Article 36

1.   The Security Council may, at any stage of a dispute of the nature referred to in Article 33 or of a situation of like nature, recommend appropriate procedures or methods of adjustment.

* * *

Article 37

1. Should the parties to a dispute of the nature referred to in Article 33 fail to settle it by the means indicated in that Article, they shall refer it to the Security Council.

2. If the Security Council deems that the continuance of the dispute is in fact likely to endanger the maintenance of international peace and security, it shall decide whether to take action under Article 36 or to recommend such terms of settlement as it may consider appropriate.

* * *

While still extolling peaceful settlement of disputes, the Charter's larger focus is on responding to violations of the prohibition on the use of force. The Charter provides unprecedented authority to the Security Council to enforce the peace when the Council finds a threat to the peace, breach of the peace or act of aggression. The Council may then mandate action, including the use of armed force, by UN members in response. Thus, the core conception of the Charter for the maintenance of peace in the short term is a prohibition on force backed up by an institution authorized to enforce the prohibition. Chapter VII spells out the Council's authority to act for the maintenance of peace and security.

UN Charter, Chapter VII Action with Respect to Threats to the Peace, Breaches of the Peace, and Acts of Aggression

Article 39

The Security Council shall determine the existence of any threat to the peace, breach of the peace, or act of aggression and shall make recommendations, or decide what measures shall be taken in accordance with Articles 41 and 42, to maintain or restore international peace and security.

* * *

Article 41

The Security Council may decide what measures not involving the use of armed force are to be employed to give effect to its decisions, and it may call upon the Members of the United Nations to apply such measures. These may include complete or partial interruption of economic relations and of rail, sea, air, postal, telegraphic, radio, and other means of communication, and the severance of diplomatic relations.

Article 42

Should the Security Council consider that measures provided for in Article 41 would be inadequate or have proved to be inadequate, it may take such action by air, sea, or land forces as may be necessary to maintain or restore international peace and security. Such action may include demonstrations, blockade, and other operations by air, sea, or land forces of Members of the United Nations.

* * *

Article 48

1. The action required to carry out the decisions of the Security Council for the maintenance of international peace and security shall be taken by all the Members of the United Nations or by some of them, as the Security Council may determine.

The United Nations operates under different rules on the use of force than do states. The Security Council was given broader authority to use force: it may respond to threats to the peace and acts of aggression as well as to breaches of international peace.[11] The Council was given broad discretion to determine what a breach to international peace is.[12] Nevertheless, the drafters understood breach of the peace or threats to the peace to mean the use of organized force between states. Violence within states was not considered within the scope of Article 39. Nor did the drafters have in mind some of the more expansive meanings of breach of international peace that have been proposed from time to time, such as violations of human rights within a state.

Article 39 sets out the parameters of Security Council action: the Council may make recommendations or take measures (per articles 41 and 42) to maintain or restore international peace and security when there is a threat to the peace, breach of the peace or act of aggression. Thus, as stated above, the Security Council's authority to use force is broader than that of individual states. It has the right to respond to threats to as well as to actual breaches of "international peace" and acts of aggression.

In addition to specifying "international peace," article 39 also refers to "threats," "breaches" and "acts of aggression." Breach of the peace, is "characterized by hostilities between armed units of two states."[13] Aggression is "the direct or indirect application of the use of force; thus, it is always a breach of peace."[14] As for threats to the peace, this concept is not so easily defined.[15] The Council plainly has wide discretion to determine what a threat to the peace is.

---

11. The General Assembly granted itself in the Uniting for Peace Resolution authority to recommend action in cases of threats or breaches of the peace where the Security Council has failed to act. G.A. Res. 377(V) (1950).

12. Joachin Frowein & Nico Krisch, *Article 39, in* UN CHARTER COMMENTARY, *supra* note 1, at 717, 720–29.

13. *Id.,* at 721.

14. *Id.,* at 722.

15. *Id.*

Article 39's reference to the Council's authority to maintain "international" peace and security, however, may be an additional limitation on Security Council action. This reference recalls Article 2(7) and the reservation of domestic affairs as beyond the scope of the Charter. While Article 2(7) does not seek to limit Chapter VII, Article 39, in turn, indicates Chapter VII authority was not originally intended to reach non-international peace and security issues.

These provisions also reveal that the Security Council was not originally authorized to use force to enforce general international law or even the most important rules of international law. As discussed above, the Security Council is authorized to enforce the peace. Nevertheless, the meaning of "international peace" has come in for re-interpretation. These developments will be discussed in Chapter Eight.

When acting under Article 39, the Security Council has the authority to order UN members to take action per Articles 41 and 42. Article 41 refers to non-military enforcement. Should those prove inadequate, the Council may order member states to use military force. In addition to the use of combat forces, Article 42 contemplates demonstrations and blockades—meaning the sealing off of territory of forceful inspection of shipping. To carry out these activities, the Council was to form agreements with member states under Article 43(1). These agreements were never formed and to the extent the UN has relied on armed forces it has been on an *ad hoc* basis. In many cases, the UN has provided a mandate only. The command of the forces has remained with national states or regional organizations. Some of these cases are discussed in Chapter Eight.

Article 51

Nothing in the present Charter shall impair the inherent right of individual or collective self-defense if an armed attack occurs against a Member of the United Nations, until the Security Council has taken measures necessary to maintain international peace and security. Measures taken by Members in the exercise of this right of self-defense shall be immediately reported to the Security Council and shall not in any way affect the authority and responsibility of the Security Council under the present Charter to take at any time such action as it deems necessary in order to maintain or restore international peace and security.

Article 51 permits force in individual and collective self-defense when an armed attack occurs until the Security Council takes action. As discussed above in Section A., Latin American delegates at San Francisco particularly wanted Article 51 included—something of a last-minute effort. They were concerned that regional arrangements for collective self-defense would be eliminated by Article 2(4). To clarify that Article 2(4) did not prohibit either the right of individual *or* collective self-defense, the delegates added Article 51. It is a limited exception to Article 2(4) allowing self-defense in a situation where it can be shown by the tangible evidence of an armed attack that a state may respond. The response is limited to defense and lasts only until the Security Council acts or the defense is achieved.

Two phrases in Article 51 have engendered debate since the Charter's adoption. Writers have questioned whether the drafters intended for the phrase "if an armed attack occurs" to be taken literally or if the customary law understanding of self-defense continued because Article 51 uses the term "inherent" right of self-defense. This debate will be considered in Chapter Seven.

The final important substantive principle of the Charter relevant to the use of force is Article 103. As we shall see in future Chapters, when the Security Council mandates action by UN members that mandate pre-empts even contrary treaty obligations.

UN Charter, Chapter XVI Miscellaneous Provisions

* * *

Article 103

In the event of a conflict between the obligations of the Members of the United Nations under the present Charter and their obligations under any other international agreement, their obligations under the present Charter shall prevail.

C. UN Organs[22]

In addition to the core legal prohibition on the use of armed force in Article 2(4), the drafters of the Charter aimed to improve the institutional design for enforcing the prohibition over that of the League. This section reviews the main UN organs and their role in preserving peace and security.

UN Charter, Chapter III Organs

Article 7

1. There are established as the principal organs of the United Nations: a General Assembly, a Security Council, an Economic and Social Council, a Trusteeship Council, an International Court of Justice, and a Secretariat.

2. Such subsidiary organs as may be found necessary may be established in accordance with the present Charter.

---

22. Adapted from Thomas Ehrlich & the Use of Force (1993). Mary Ellen O'Connell, International Law and

1. The Security Council

As the drafting history in Section A above reveals, the principal focus in organizing the UN was on the Security Council. The founding members agreed, after some struggle, to give the Council great authority, but also great responsibility to ensure that the substantive rules on peace were enforced.

UN Charter, Chapter V The Security Council

Article 23

1. The Security Council shall consist of fifteen Members of the United Nations. The Republic of China, France, the Union of Soviet Socialist Republics, the United Kingdom of Great Britain and Northern Ireland, and the United States of America shall be permanent members of the Security Council. The General Assembly shall elect ten other Members of the United Nations to be non-permanent members of the Security Council, due regard being specially paid, in the first instance to the contribution of Members of the United Nations to the maintenance of international peace and security and to the other purposes of the Organization, and also to equitable geographical distribution.

2. The non-permanent members of the Security Council shall be elected for a term of two years. * * *

Article 24

1. In order to ensure prompt and effective action by the United Nations, its Members confer on the Security Council primary responsibility for the maintenance of international peace and security, and agree that in carrying out its duties under this responsibility the Security Council acts on their behalf.

2. In discharging these duties the Security Council shall act in accordance with the Purposes and Principles of the United Nations. The specific powers granted to the Security Council for the discharge of these duties are laid down in Chapters VI, VII, VIII, and XII.

* * *

Article 25

The Members of the United Nations agree to accept and carry out the decisions of the Security Council in accordance with the present Charter.

* * *

Article 27

1.   Each member of the Security Council shall have one vote.

2.   Decisions of the Security Council on procedural matters shall be made by an affirmative vote of nine members.

3.   Decisions of the Security Council on all other matters shall be made by an affirmative vote of nine members including the concurring votes of the permanent members; provided that, in decisions under Chapter VI, and under paragraph 3 of Article 52, a party to a dispute shall abstain from voting.

* * *

Article 31

Any Member of the United Nations which is not a member of the Security Council may participate, without vote, in the discussion of any question brought before the Security Council whenever the latter considers that the interests of that Member are specially affected.

In addition to these powers and procedures, the Security Council may call on regional arrangements for assistance, per Chapter VII, Article 53, set out below. The Council has been expanded from its original nine members to fifteen. Otherwise, no major changes have been made to the text of the Charter relative to the Security Council.

It is often said that the Security Council's design was based on the assumption that the anti-Axis alliance of the United States, United Kingdom, the Soviet Union, China and France would remain united. The drafting history, however, indicates these states had serious differences throughout the war and with respect to the UN design. Rather than assuming great power cooperation, the underlying assumption may have been the far more pragmatic one that the Security Council design was the best that could be achieved in the circumstances. The Soviet Union would only join the organization if it had the veto power in the Security Council. The United States was at least able to keep the veto restricted to substantive matters and not procedural ones. The veto and other compromises that made up the final agreement are certainly open to criticism. On the other hand, unlike the more ideal League of Nations, the United Nations did not fall apart after less than twenty years. The permanent members of the Security Council accepted that they would have special responsibility to act in matters of peace and security. As a quid pro quo of that special responsibility, they expected to have the right to veto proposals when they could not support such action.

Some early issues as to voting procedure are taken up here. Other developments in Security Council practice more specifically related to the use of force are reviewed in Chapter Eight. In January 1950, the Council considered whether it could function in the absence of a permanent member. The Soviet Union was boycotting the Council because a representative of Nationalist China held China's permanent seat in the Council instead of a representative of the People's Republic of China. The United States position was that

The absence of the Soviet Union will not prevent us from conducting the business to which we are pledged. It is the view of my Government that the absence of a permanent member from a meeting of the Security Council in no way diminishes its powers or its authority to act. The Charter provides in Article 28 that "The Security Council shall be so organized as to be able to function continuously." We cannot allow this arbitrary action of our Soviet Union colleagues to prevent us from fulfilling our obligation to the Charter.[24]

This view was accepted by the other Council members and was the procedure in place when North Korea invaded South Korea in June 1950. The Council was able to take action, authorizing a UN force to support South Korea because the Soviet Union was not present to veto the measures.

Another voting issue concerned whether the determination that a matter was substantive or procedural needed the concurring votes of all permanent members. The answer to this question given at San Francisco was that

[i]t will be unlikely there will arise in the future any matters of great importance on which a decision will have to made as to whether a procedural vote would apply. Should, however, such a matter arise, the decision regarding the preliminary question as to whether or not such a matter is procedural must be taken by a vote of nine members of the Security Council, including the concurring votes of the permanent members.[25]

The Council at first followed this procedure, allowing a double veto on some matters—first a veto of the matter being procedural, then a veto of the matter as substantive. The impact of the double-veto was soon diminished by other procedural moves. An early president of the Council made a presidential decision as to the procedural or substantive nature of a matter and insisted that any question as to his decision follow the procedure for overruling a presidential ruling, by precedent a procedural matter. The General Assembly also became involved passing a resolution that the double veto should not apply to 35 categories of questions.

2.   The General Assembly

The General Assembly, like the League of Nations Assembly, was to be first and foremost a place for discussion. It could take up matters of peace and security and make recommendations but only if the Security Council was not already seized of the matter, and only the Council may mandate action. On the other hand, the General Assembly was given sole authority and control in the area of the UN's budget. And, unlike the League Assembly, the UN General Assembly makes decisions by majority and two-thirds votes, not unanimity.

24. *Id.,* at 208.   **25.** *Id.,* at 209.

UN Charter, Chapter IV The General Assembly

Article 9

1.   The General Assembly shall consist of all the Members of the United Nations.

2.   Each member shall have not more than five representatives in the General Assembly.

Article 10

The General Assembly may discuss any questions or any matters within the scope of the present Charter or relating to the powers and functions of any organs provided for in the present Charter, and, except as provided in Article 12, may make recommendations to the Members of the United Nations or to the Security Council or to both on any such questions or matters.

Article 11

1.   The General Assembly may consider the general principles of cooperation in the maintenance of international peace and security, including the principles governing disarmament and the regulation of armaments, and may make recommendations with regard to such principles to the Members or to the Security Council or to both.

2.   The General Assembly may discuss any questions relating to the maintenance of international peace and security brought before it by any Member of the United Nations, or by the Security Council, * * *, and, except as provided in Article 12, may make recommendations with regard to any such questions to the state or states concerned or to the Security Council or to both. Any such question on which action is necessary shall be referred to the Security Council by the General Assembly either before or after discussion.

3.   The General Assembly may call the attention of the Security Council to situations which are likely to endanger international peace and security.

4.   The powers of the General Assembly set forth in this Article shall not limit the general scope of Article 10.

Article 12

1.   While the Security Council is exercising in respect of any dispute or situation the functions assigned to it in the present Charter, the General Assembly shall not make any recommendation with regard to that dispute or situation unless the Security Council so requests.

2.   The Secretary–General, with the consent of the Security Council, shall notify the General Assembly at each session of any matters relative to the maintenance of international peace and

security which are being dealt with by the Security Council and shall similarly notify the General Assembly, or the Members of the United Nations if the General Assembly is not in session, immediately the Security Council ceases to deal with such matters.

Article 13

1.   The General Assembly shall initiate studies and make recommendations for the purpose of:

> a.   promoting international cooperation in the political field and encouraging the progressive development of international law and its codification;

> b.   promoting international cooperation in the economic, social, cultural, educational, and health fields, and assisting in the realization of human rights and fundamental freedoms for all without distinction as to race, sex, language, or religion.

* * *

Article 14

Subject to the provisions of Article 12, the General Assembly may recommend measures for the peaceful adjustment of any situation, regardless of origin, which it deems likely to impair the general welfare or friendly relations among nations, including situations resulting from a violation of the provisions of the present Charter setting forth the Purposes and Principles of the United Nations.

* * *

Article 17

1.   The General Assembly shall consider and approve the budget of the Organization.

2.   The expenses of the Organization shall be borne by the Members as apportioned by the General Assembly.

* * *

Article 18

1.   Each member of the General Assembly shall have one vote.

2.   Decisions of the General Assembly on important questions shall be made by a two-thirds majority of the members present and voting. These questions shall include: recommendations with respect to the maintenance of international peace and security, the election of the non-permanent members of the Security Council, * * *.

3.   Decisions on other questions, including the determination of additional categories of questions, to be decided by a two-thirds majority, shall be made by a majority of the members present and voting.

Article 19

A Member of the United Nations which is in arrears in the payment of its financial contributions to the Organization shall have no vote in the General Assembly if the amount of its arrears equals or exceeds the amount of the contributions due from it for the preceding two full years. The General Assembly may, nevertheless, permit such a Member to vote if it is satisfied that the failure to pay is due to conditions beyond the control of the Member.

Article 20

The General Assembly shall meet in regular annual sessions and in such special sessions as occasion may require. Special sessions shall be convoked by the Secretary–General at the request of the Security Council or of a majority of the Members of the United Nations.

Article 21

The General Assembly shall adopt its own rules of procedure. It shall elect its President for each session.

* * *

The Charter provisions on the General Assembly have remained basically the same since 1945. The Assembly is in session for only part of the year. It conducts its formal work in plenary sessions but most of the body's real work is carried on in its seven committees of the whole: two for political affairs, two for economic and social affairs, one for trusteeship affairs, one for administrative and budgetary questions, and one for legal matters. In addition, the Assembly has created numerous subsidiary bodies concerned with matters related to peace and security such as arms control, peaceful uses of outspace, and conflict prevention.

The General Assembly has adopted important resolutions on peace and security and regularly debates particular uses of force. It will often vote to condemn unlawful uses. These resolutions, discussions and votes are a rich source of states' legal positions that can be assessed for the practice and *opinio juris* that make up customary international law.

3. The Secretariat

Again, like the League, the United Nations has a chief administrative officer. In addition to administering the UN staff and implementing the resolutions of the Security Council and the General Assembly, the Secretary General may bring matters of peace and security to the attention of the Council.

UN Charter Chapter XV The Secretariat

Article 97

The Secretariat shall comprise a Secretary–General and such staff as the Organization may require. The Secretary–General shall be appointed by the General Assembly upon the recommendation of the Security Council. He shall be the chief administrative officer of the Organization.

* * *

Article 99

The Secretary–General may bring to the attention of the Security Council any matter which in his opinion may threaten the maintenance of international peace and security.

The practice grew up of selecting the Secretary General from different regions of the world on a rotating basis. Secretary Generals have traditionally served two five year terms. It is also a practice not to select a Secretary General from the Security Council's permanent members.

4.   The International Court of Justice

Probably no other peace and security institution has remained as unchanged from the League period to the UN era as the World Court. Its name changed from the Permanent Court of International Justice to the International Court of Justice, but its statute was modified in only limited ways. The UN itself, however, has a much different relationship to the Court as did the League.

UN Charter Chapter XIV The International Court of Justice

Article 92

The International Court of Justice shall be the principal judicial organ of the United Nations. It shall function in accordance with the annexed Statute, which is based upon the Statute of the Permanent Court of International Justice and forms an integral part of the present Charter.

Article 93

1.   All Members of the United Nations are *ipso facto* parties to the Statute of the International Court of Justice.

* * *

Article 94

1. Each Member of the United Nations undertakes to comply with the decision of the International Court of Justice in any case to which it is a party.

2. If any party to a case fails to perform the obligations incumbent upon it under a judgment rendered by the Court, the other party may have recourse to the Security Council, which may, if it deems necessary make recommendations or decide upon measures to be taken to give effect to the judgment.

* * *

Article 96

1. The General Assembly or the Security Council may request the International court of Justice to give an advisory opinion on any legal question.

2. Other organs of the United Nations and specialized agencies, which may at any time be so authorized by the General Assembly, may also request advisory opinions of the Court on legal questions arising within the scope of their activities.

The Statute of the International Court was adapted from that of its predecessor. Under Article 34 of the Statute, "[o]nly states may be parties in cases before the Court." And Article 38 provides that, in deciding "in accordance with international law such disputes as are submitted to it," the Court shall apply:

> a. international conventions, whether general or particular, establishing rules expressly recognized by the contesting states;

> b. international custom, as evidence of a general practice accepted as law;

> c. the general principles of law recognized by civilized nations;

> d. subject to the provisions of Article 59, judicial decisions and the teachings of the most highly qualified publicists of the various nations, as subsidiary means for the determination of rules of law.

Unlike the League system, however, the International Court is an organ of the United Nations. Under Article 93 of the Charter, all United Nations members are parties to the Court's Statute. However, states are subject to the jurisdiction of the Court only to the extent that have given their consent under one of the provisions of Article 36 of the Court's Statute. One of the few major questions raised at San Francisco concerning the Court was whether and to what extent its jurisdiction should be compulsory. A majority of the smaller countries wanted some kind of compulsory jurisdiction, but both the United States and the Soviet Union quashed the idea. Instead, the Court's jurisdiction in contentious cases is limited, like that of the Permanent Court, to cases in which the parties consent. States many submit to the Court's jurisdiction in several ways. First, they may file a unilateral declaration, as provided in Article 36(2) of the Statute. Second, states may submit to the Court's jurisdiction in advance through provisions in bilateral or multilateral treaties. Finally, states may conclude a *compromis* relating specifically to the submission of a particular case to the Court.

The ICJ may issue provisional measures during the pendancy of a case. These bind the parties and generally require them not to exacerbate a situation—such as armed conflict—while the court works.

In addition to deciding contentious disputes between parties, the Court is empowered by Charter Article 96 to give advisory opinions "on any legal question" put to it by the General Assembly, the Security Council, or any other organ or specialized agency of the United Nations authorized by the General Assembly to request advisory opinions.

The Statute of the Court provides that candidates for election to the Court must obtain an absolute majority in both the General Assembly and the Security Council. Under Article 2, judges must "possess the qualifications required in their respective countries for appointment to the highest judicial offices, or ... [be] jurisconsults of recognized competence in international law." Each must, under Article 20, "make a solemn declaration in open court that he will exercise his power impartially and conscientiously."

5.   Regional Arrangements

UN Charter, Chapter VIII Regional Arrangements

Article 52

1.   Nothing in the present Charter precludes the existence of regional arrangements or agencies for dealing with such matters relating to the maintenance of international peace and security as are appropriate for regional action, provided that such arrangements or agencies and their activities are consistent with the Purposes and Principles of the United Nations.

* * *

Article 53

1.   The Security Council shall, where appropriate, utilize such regional arrangements or agencies for enforcement action under its authority. But no enforcement action shall be taken under regional arrangements or by regional agencies without the authorization of the Security Council * * *.

* * *

Article 54

The Security Council shall at all times be kept fully informed of activities undertaken or in contemplation under regional arrangements or by regional agencies for the maintenance of international peace and security.

NATO, the North Atlantic Treaty Organization,[26] and the now defunct Warsaw Treaty Organization were formed under the terms of Article 51's reference to collective self-defense and not under Chapter VIII.[27] Thus, the operative provision of the original North Atlantic Treaty (which is similar to Article 4 of the old Warsaw Treaty) contemplated that NATO would act in collective self-defense and would not take on other types of missions. Article 5 states:

> The Parties agree that an armed attack against one or more of them in Europe or North America shall be considered an attack against them all and consequently they agree that, if such an armed attack occurs, each of them, in exercise of the right of individual or collective self-defense recognized by Article 51 of the Charter of the United Nations will assist the Party or Parties so attacked by taking forthwith, individually, and in concert with the other parties, such action as it deems necessary, including the use of armed force, to restore and maintain the security of the North Atlantic area.
>
> Any such armed attack and all measures taken as a result thereof shall immediately be reported to the Security Council. Such measures shall be terminated when the Security Council has taken the measures necessary to restore and maintain international peace and security.

Being formed on the basis of Article 51 and not Chapter VIII was also believed to free both organizations from Chapter VIII's Article 54 which requires that "[t]he Security Council shall at all times be kept fully informed of activities undertaken or in contemplation under regional arrangements or by regional agencies for the maintenance of international peace and security."

Organizations which have expressly declared themselves Chapter VIII organizations include: the Organization of American States (OAS), the Organization for Security and Cooperation in Europe, and the Commonwealth of Independent States (CIS).[28]

---

26. North Atlantic Treaty, 34 U.N.T.S. 243, 246, 43 Am. J. Int'l L. Supp. 159 (1949).

27. *Id., see also* Treaty of Friendship, Co-operation and Mutual Assistance ("Warsaw Pact"), 14 May 1955, 219 U.N.T.S. 3, 24.

28. *See* Englebert Theuermann, *Regionale Friedenssicherung im Lichter von Kapitel VIII der Satzung der Vereinten Nationen: Juristische und Politisische Proleme in* Blauhelme in Einer Turbulenten Welt 245 (Winrich Kühne ed. 1993).

D.   NOTES, QUESTIONS, AND PROBLEMS

1.   The Charter allows for amendment in Article 108: "Amendments to the present Charter shall come into force for all Members of the United Nations when they have been adopted by a vote of two thirds of the members of the General Assembly and ratified in accordance with their respective constitutional processes by two thirds of the Members of the United Nations, including all the permanent members of the Security Council."

Do the terms of this Article suggest why the Charter has rarely been amended? With respect to the provisions we have considered in this Chapter, the size of the Council has been increased through formal amendment. Other than the terms of Article 108, can you think of reasons that an organization formed in 1945 has remained virtually unchanged after decades?

2.   In what ways did the original concept of the United Nations improve on the League of Nations? Are there respects in which the League was the better organization?

What should the delegates at San Francisco have included in the Charter that they did not? What should they have left out of the provisions you have just studied?

3.   As the readings show the UN was largely an American creation. Since the presidency of Ronald Reagan in the 1980s, the United States has been a vocal critique of the UN, often refusing to pay assessed dues. Does America's role in the design of the UN give it any more or less responsibility to address problems US politicians see? Or does it depend on what the nature of the criticism is?

The literature on the question of UN reform and the US position vis-à-vis the UN is extensive. *See, e.g.* DOCUMENTS ON REFORM OF THE UNITED NATIONS (Paul Taylor, et al. eds., 1997). Very often it is a complaint that the UN Charter, both its substantive rules and organs, limit America's freedom of action too much, especially to use force. Is that a legitimate criticism for the UN's chief founder?

4.   In July 2004 armed clashes occurred in the Darfur region of Sudan among local militias and government forces resulting in a serious humanitarian crisis for the civilian population. Human rights groups called on the UN Security Council to "fulfill its purpose" by protecting the human rights of civilians in Sudan. What was the purpose of the Security Council when it was founded? What was the purpose of the UN as a whole? Consider as you read on in this book whether those purposes have changed.

5.   Has NATO outgrown its usefulness as a collective self-defense organization for the North Atlantic area? It was founded to respond to the threat posed by the Soviet Union which had formed its own defensive alliance, the Warsaw Treaty Organization. The Soviet Union and the Warsaw Pact dissolved in the early 1990s. Why didn't NATO? For more on NATO, *see,* NATO HANDBOOK 2001.

6. Problem: You are a member of the Secretary General's High Level Panel formed in 2003 to provide proposals for United Nations reform. You have the job of developing proposals for the better maintenance of peace and security in the 21st century. What would you propose? Bear in mind that any proposals requiring Charter amendment must meet the terms of Article 108. *See* The High Level Panel, Terms of Reference, http://www.un.org/apps/news/infocusRel.asp?infocusID=84 & Body=xxxxx & Body1; *see also*, The Annual Report of the Secretary–General on the Work of the Organization, UN Doc. A/58/1 (2003), available at www.un.org/documents/secretariat.htm.

CHAPTER SEVEN

UNILATERAL ACTION

As you saw in the last chapter, the United Nations Charter generally prohibits the use of force with two exceptions: force may be used by states acting in individual and collective self-defense and force may be used when authorized by the Security Council. We take up the self-defense exception here since that is the primary basis stated explicitly in the Charter upon which states may take action unilaterally. The Chapter also looks at another basis often invoked by states to justify unilateral uses of force: intervention in internal conflicts or crises. This basis is not explicitly found in the Charter. Nevertheless, we will see in Section C below that governments have regularly argued they have the right to intervene in internal armed conflict (civil war) when requested to do so by a government with authority. Scholars have also argued that states may intervene unilaterally, even without a request, to end a humanitarian crisis. The law governing the right to take collective action in similar circumstances is discussed in Chapter Eight.

A.   SELF DEFENSE

As we saw in the last chapter, the aim of the Charter drafters was to generally prohibit force in Article 2(4), allowing only a narrow exception to states in Article 51. The exception in Article 51 is for self-defense. The force exercised must have the purpose of defense. In the Corfu Channel Case, the ICJ's first case on the use of force decided in 1949, the court underscored the broad prohibition on force, even deciding that certain actions taken for the purpose of defense might be lawful if taken for a different purpose.

1.   THE PURPOSE OF DEFENSE

The Corfu Channel Case arose when on May 15, 1946, Albanian shore batteries fired on British warship passing through the north end of the Corfu Channel, formed by the Greek island of Corfu and the Albanian mainland. The British sent four more warships through the Channel on October 22, 1946, prepared to return fire. Two of the British vessels struck mines, causing damage and loss of life. Three weeks later, in what they called, "Operation Retail" the British sent minesweepers, protected by warships, back to the Channel where they collected 22 mines.

The Corfu Channel Case
(UK v. Alb.) 1949 ICJ 4, 29–35 (Dec. 15).

* * *

Having regard to these various considerations, the Court has arrived at the conclusion that the North Corfu Channel should be considered as belonging to the class of international highways through which passage cannot be prohibited by a coastal State in time of peace.

On the other hand, it is a fact that the two coastal States did not maintain normal relations, that Greece had made territorial claims precisely with regard to a part of Albanian territory bordering on the Channel, that Greece had declared that she considered herself technically in a state of war with Albania, and that Albania, invoking the danger of Greek incursions, had considered it necessary to take certain measures of vigilance in this region. The Court is of opinion that Albania, in view of these exceptional circumstances, would have been justified in issuing regulations in respect of the passage of warships through the Strait, but not in prohibiting such passage or in subjecting it to the requirement of special authorization.

For these reasons the Court is unable to accept the Albanian contention that the Government of the United Kingdom has violated Albanian sovereignty by sending the warships through the Strait without having obtained the previous authorization of the Albanian Government.

In these circumstances, it is unnecessary to consider the more general question, much debated by the Parties, whether States under international law have a right to send warships in time of peace through territorial waters not included in a Strait.

The Albanian Government has further contended that the sovereignty of Albania was violated because the passage of the British warships on October 22nd, 1946, was not an *innocent passage*. The reasons advanced in support of this contention may be summed up as follows: The passage was not an ordinary passage, but a political mission; the ships were manoeuvring and sailing in diamond combat formation with soldiers on board; the position of the guns was not consistent with innocent passage; the vessels passed with crews at action stations; the number of the ships and their armament surpassed what was necessary in order to attain their object and showed an intention to intimidate and not merely pass; the ships had received orders to observe and report upon the coastal defences and this order was carried out.

It is shown by the Admiralty telegram of September 21st, cited above, and admitted by the United Kingdom Agent, that the object of sending the warships through the Strait was not only to carry out a passage for purposes of navigation, but also to test Albania's attitude. As mentioned above, the Albanian Government, on May 15th, 1946, tried to impose by means of gunfire its view with regard to the passage. As the exchange of diplomatic notes did not lead to any clarification, the Government of the United

Kingdom wanted to ascertain by other means whether the Albanian Government would maintain its illegal attitude and again impose its view by firing at passing ships. The legality of this measure taken by the Government of the United Kingdom cannot be disputed, provided that it was carried out in a manner consistent with the requirements of international law. The "mission" was designed to affirm a right which had been unjustly denied. The Government of the United Kingdom was not bound to abstain from exercising its right of passage, which the Albanian Government had illegally denied.

It remains, therefore, to consider whether the *manner* in which the passage was carried out was consistent with the principle of innocent passage and to examine the various contentions of the Albanian Government in so far as they appear to be relevant.

When the Albanian coastguards at St. George's Monastery reported that the British warships were sailing in combat formation and were manoeuvring, they must have been under a misapprehension. It is shown by the evidence that the ships were not proceeding in combat formation, but in line, one after the other, and that they were not manoeuvring until after the first explosion. Their movements thereafter were due to the explosions and were made necessary in order to save human life and the mined ships. It is shown by evidence of witnesses that the contention that soldiers were on board must be due to a misunderstanding probably arising from the fact that the two cruisers carried their usual detachment of marines.

It is known from the above-mentioned order issued by the British Admiralty on August 10th, 1946, that ships, when using the North Corfu Strait, must pass with armament in fore and aft position. That this order was carried out during the passage on October 22nd is stated by the Commander-in-Chief, Mediterranean, in a telegram of October 26th to the Admiralty. The guns were, he reported, "trained fore and aft, which is their normal position at sea in peace time, and were not loaded". It is confirmed by the commanders of *Saumarez* and *Volage* that the guns were in this position before the explosions. The navigating officer on board *Mauritius* explained that all guns on that cruiser were in their normal stowage position. The main guns were in the line of the ship, and the anti-aircraft guns were pointing outwards and up into the air, which is the normal position of these guns on a cruiser both in harbour and at sea. In the light of this evidence, the Court cannot accept the Albanian contention that the position of the guns was inconsistent with the rules of innocent passage.

In the above-mentioned telegram of October 26th, the Commander-in-Chief reported that the passage "was made with ships at action stations in order that they might be able to retaliate quickly if fired upon again". In view of the firing from the

Albanian battery on May 15th, this measure of precaution cannot, in itself, be regarded as unreasonable. But four warships—two cruisers and two destroyers—passed in this manner, with crews at action stations, ready to retaliate quickly if fired upon. They passed one after another through this narrow channel, close to the Albanian coast, at a time of political tension in this region. The intention must have been, not only to test Albania's attitude, but at the same time to demonstrate such force that she would abstain from firing again on passing ships. Having regard, however, to all the circumstances of the case, as described above, the Court is unable to characterize these measures taken by the United Kingdom authorities as a violation of Albania's sovereignty.

Admiralty Chart, Annex 21 to the Memorial, shows that coastal defences in the Saranda region had been observed and reported. In a report of the commander of *Volage*, dated October 23rd, 1946—a report relating to the passage on the 22nd—it is stated: "The most was made of the opportunities to study Albanian defences at close range. These included, with reference to XCU..."—and he then gives a description of some coastal defences.

In accordance with Article 49 of the Statute of the Court and Article 54 of its Rules, the Court requested the United Kingdom Agent to produce the documents referred to as XCU for the use of the Court. Those documents were not produced, the Agent pleading naval secrecy; and the United Kingdom witnesses declined to answer questions relating to them. It is not therefore possible to know the real content of these naval orders. The Court cannot, however, draw from this refusal to produce the orders any conclusions differing from those to which the actual events gave rise. The United Kingdom Agent stated that the instructions in these orders related solely to the contingency of shots being fired from the coast—which did not happen. If it is true, as the commander of *Volage* said in evidence, that the orders contained information concerning certain positions from which the British warships might have been fired at, it cannot be deduced there from that the vessels had received orders to reconnoitre Albanian coastal defences. Lastly, as the Court has to judge of the innocent nature of the passage, it cannot remain indifferent to the fact that, though two warships struck mines, there was no reaction, either on their part or on that of the cruisers that accompanied them.

With regard to the observations of coastal defences made after the explosions, these were justified by the fact that two ships had just been blown up and that, in this critical situation, their commanders might fear that they would be fired on from the coast, as on May 15th.

Having thus examined the various contentions of the Albanian Government in so far as they appear to be relevant, the Court has arrived at the conclusion that the United Kingdom did not violate the sovereignty of Albania by reason of the acts of the British Navy in Albanian waters on October 22nd, 1946.

* * *

In addition to the passage of the United Kingdom warships on October 22nd, 1946, the second question in the Special Agreement relates to the acts of the Royal Navy in Albanian waters on November 12th and 13th, 1946. This is the minesweeping operation called "Operation Retail" by the Parties during the proceedings. This name will be used in the present Judgment.

* * *

The United Kingdom Government does not dispute that "Operation Retail" was carried out against the clearly expressed wish of the Albanian Government. It recognizes that the operation had not the consent of the international mine clearance organizations, that it could not be justified as the exercise of a right of innocent passage, and lastly that, in principle, international law does not allow a State to assemble a large number of warships in the territorial waters of another State and to carry out minesweeping in those waters. The United Kingdom Government states that the operation was one of extreme urgency, and that it considered itself entitled to carry it out without anybody's consent.

The United Kingdom Government put forward two reasons in justification. First, the Agreement of November 22nd, 1945, signed by the Governments of the United Kingdom, France, the Soviet Union and the United States of America, authorizing regional mine clearance organizations, such as the Mediterranean Zone Board, to divide the sectors in their respective zones amongst the States concerned for sweeping. Relying on the circumstance that the Corfu Channel was in the sector allotted to Greece by the Mediterranean Zone Board on November 5th, i.e., before the signing of the above-mentioned Agreement, the United Kingdom Government put forward a permission given by the Hellenic Government to resweep the navigable channel.

The Court does not consider this argument convincing.

It must be noted that, as the United Kingdom Government admits, the need for resweeping the Channel was not under consideration in November 1945; for previous sweeps in 1944 and 1945 were considered as having effected complete safety. As a consequence, the allocation of the sector in question to Greece, and therefore, the permission of the Hellenic Government which is relied on, were both of them merely nominal. It is also to be remarked that Albania was not consulted regarding the allocation to Greece to the sector in question, despite the fact that the Channel passed through Albanian territorial waters.

But, in fact, the explosions of October 22, 1946, in a channel declared safe for navigation, and one which the United Kingdom Government, more than any other government, had reason to consider safe, raised quite a different problem from that of a routine sweep carried out under the orders of the mine clearance organizations. These explosions were suspicious; they raised a question of responsibility.

Accordingly, this was the ground on which the United Kingdom Government chose to establish its main line of defence. According to that Government, the *corpora delicti* must be secured as quickly as possible, for fear they should be taken away, without leaving traces, by the authors of the minelaying or by the Albanian authorities. This justification took two distinct forms in the United Kingdom Government's arguments. It was presented first as a new and special application of the theory of intervention, by means of which the State intervening would secure possession of evidence in the territory of another State, in order to submit it to an international tribunal and thus facilitate its task.

The Court cannot accept such a line of defence. The Court can only regard the alleged right of intervention as the manifestation of a policy of force, such as has, in the past, given rise to most serious abuses and such as cannot, whatever be the present defects in international organization, find a place in international law. Intervention is perhaps still less admissible in the particular form it would take here; for, from the nature of things, it would be reserved for the most powerful States, and might easily lead to perverting the administration of international justice itself.

The United Kingdom Agent, in his speech in reply, has further classified "Operation Retail" among methods of self-protection or self-help. The Court cannot accept this defence either. Between independent States, respect for territorial sovereignty is an essential foundation of international relations. The Court recognizes that the Albanian Government's complete failure to carry out its duties after the explosions, and the dilatory nature of its diplomatic notes, are extenuating circumstances for the action of the United Kingdom Government. But to ensure respect for international law, of which it is the organ, the Court must declare that the action of the British Navy co[n]stituted a violation of Albanian sovereignty.

This declaration is in accordance with the request made by Albania through her Counsel, and is in itself appropriate satisfaction.

The method of carrying out "Operation Retail" has also been criticized by the Albanian Government, the main ground of complaint being that the United Kingdom, on that occasion, made use of an unnecessarily large display of force, out of proportion to the requirements of the sweep. The Court thinks that this criticism is not justified. It does not consider that the action of the British Navy was demonstration of force for the purpose of exercising political pressure on Albania. The responsible naval commander, who kept his ships at a distance from the coast, cannot be reproached for having employed an important covering force in a region where twice within a few months his ships had been the object of serious outrages.

2.   ARMED ATTACK

Following the Corfu Channel Case, the next significant debate on the right of states to use armed force broke out in connection with the Suez Canal Crisis of 1954–56. Professor Henkin relates that the argument that the pre-Charter rules on self-defense survived the adoption of the Charter surfaced during the Suez crisis.[1] Britain argued during the crisis that Israel had the right to use force in lawful self-defense against Egypt even before Egypt attacked it. Egypt was in the midst of a massive military build-up and had already indicated its hostile intent toward Israel. Britain argued this was enough to justify an Israeli preemptive strike on Egypt before Egypt had the opportunity to develop a military force that could overwhelm Israel. States generally rejected the argument that Israel could use force before Egypt attacked. The use of force by all parties in the Suez crisis was widely condemned, including by both the United States and Soviet Union.

Israel again attacked Egypt on June 5, 1967. The Six Day War is widely cited as an example to support the principle that a state may use force in anticipation of an armed attack even where one has not yet occurred. In reporting on its initial use of force to the Security Council, however, Israel did not argue that it acted in anticipation of an attack, but rather that Egyptian forces had actually crossed into Israeli-held territory. By June 17, when the General Assembly began its debate on the conflict, Israel's foreign minister no longer spoke of actual Egyptian attacks, but only of Egyptian forces approaching Israel's borders.[2] Following the Six Day War, a number of scholars began to interpret Article 51 as allowing force in anticipatory self-defense, where an attack was imminent or occurring, even if it had not yet occurred. The 1981 Security Council debated on Israel's bombing of a nuclear reactor in Iraq, turned very much on the requirement of "imminence":

Security Counsel Consideration of a Complaint by Iraq, 8 June 1981

36 UN SCOR, 2280–2288 mtgs (1981).

Mr. Blum (Israel):

57.   On Sunday, 7 June 1981, the Israeli Air Force carried out an operation against the Iraqi atomic reactor called "Osirak". That

---

1. LOUIS HENKIN, *Use of Force: Law and U.S. Policy, in* MIGHT V. RIGHT, INTERNATIONAL LAW AND THE USE OF FORCE 45 (Louis Henkin et al. eds., 1989).

2. 1967 U.N.Y.B 175–77, 196.

reactor was in its final stages of construction near Baghdad. The pilots' mission was to destroy it. They executed their mission successfully.

58.   In destroying Osirak, Israel performed an elementary act of self-preservation, both morally and legally. In so doing, Israel was exercising its inherent right of self-defence as understood in general international law and as preserved in Article 51 of the Charter of the United Nations.

59.   A threat of nuclear obliteration was being developed against Israel by Iraq, one of Israel's most implacable enemies. Israel tried to have the threat halted by diplomatic means. Our efforts bore no fruit. Ultimately we were left with no choice. We were obliged to remove that mortal danger. We did it cleanly and effectively. The Middle East has become a safer place. We trust that the international community has also been given pause to make the world a safer place.

60.   Those facts and the potentials for a safer world are widely recognized. Several States in the Middle East and beyond are sleeping more easily today in the knowledge that Saddam Hussein's nuclear-arms potential has been smashed.

* * *

97.   The Government of Israel, like any other Government, has the elementary duty to protect the lives of its citizens. In destroying Osirak last Sunday, Israel was exercising its inherent and natural right to self-defence, as understood in general international law and well within the meaning of Article 51 of the Charter of the United Nations.

98.   Commenting on the meaning of Article 51 of the Charter, Sir Humphrey Waldock, now President of the International Court of Justice, stated in a lecture delivered at The Hague Academy of International Law in 1952 that

"it would be a travesty of the purposes of the Charter to compel a defending State to allow its assailant to deliver the first and perhaps fatal blow. . . . To read Article 51 otherwise is to protect the aggressor's right to the first strike."

99.   In a similar vein, Professor Morton Kaplan and Nicholas de B. Katzenbach wrote in their book, *The Political Foundations of International Law*:

"Must a state wait until it is too late before it may defend itself? Must it permit another the advantages of military build-up, surprise attack, and total offense, against which there may be no defense? It would be unreasonable to expect any State to permit this—particularly when given the possibility that a surprise nuclear blow might bring about total destruction, or at least total subjugation, unless the attack were forestalled.''

100.   Professor Derek Bowett of Cambridge University, in his authoritative work on *Self-Defense in International Law*, observed:

> ''No state can be expected to await an initial attack, which in the present state of armaments, may well destroy the state's capacity for further resistance and so jeopardize its very existence.''

101.   So much for the legalities of the case. Still, we have been accused of acting unlawfully. Presumably it is lawful for a sovereign State to create an instrument capable of destroying several hundred thousand Israelis; it is unlawful to halt that fatal process before it reaches completion.

102.   The decision taken by my Government in the exercise of its right of self-defence, after the unusual international procedures and avenues had proven futile, was one of the most agonizing we have ever had to take. We sought to act in a manner which would minimize the danger to all concerned, including a large segment of Iraq's population. We waited until the eleventh hour after the diplomatic clock had run out hoping against hope that Iraq's nuclear arms project would be brought to a halt. Our Air Force was only called in when, as I have said, we learned on the basis of completely reliable information that there was less than a month to go before Osirak might have become critical. Our Air Force's operation was consciously launched on a Sunday, and timed for late in the day, the assumption that the workers on the site, including foreign experts employed at the reactor, would have left. That assumption proved correct, and the loss of human life, which we sincerely regret, was minimal.

103.   I should add that those same considerations worked in the opposite direction as regards Iraq's other nuclear facilities and constrained Israel from taking action against the smaller Western-supplied research reactor, as well as a small Soviet research reactor. Both of those facilities are operational and if attacked, could release substantial amounts of radiation.

104.   In this connection, I wish to deny in the most categorical terms the false allegation made here by the Minister for Foreign Affairs of Iraq—who had the courtesy to leave the Chamber when I started my statement—that Iraq's nuclear installations were attacked by Israel on a date prior to 7 June.

105.   With regard to the statement of the Foreign Minister of Baghdad as a whole, let me just observe that he added yet another tale to the *Tales of 1,001 Nights*, which, if I am not mistaken, were all written, like his statement, in Baghdad.

* * *

118.   MR. CAID ESSEBSI (Tunisia) (*interpretation from French*): Since the announcement of the atrocious act committed on Sunday, 7 June, against one of our Member States, Iraq, the eyes of the world have turned to the United Nations and to this supreme body entrusted with the task of maintaining international peace and security, as well as respect for the fundamental principles of the Charter. * * *

129.   I need hardly recall here that, according to the Definition of Aggression contained in the annex to resolution 3314 (XXIX) adopted by the General Assembly on 14 December 1974, bombardment by the armed forces of a State against the territory of another State, regardless of a declaration of war, constitutes an act of aggression. I need hardly recall article 5 of the Definition of Aggression, which states:

> "1.   No consideration of whatever nature, whether political, economic, military or otherwise, may serve as a justification for aggression.
>
> "2.   A war of aggression is a crime against international peace. Aggression gives rise to international responsibility."

130.   In our view that is the only appropriate response to Israel's quibbling. We refuse to give undue weight to considerations not founded on generally accepted international rules that are based on principle and law.

* * *

MR. PARSONS (UNITED KINGDOM):

> "The Government have already made plain their view that armed attack in such circumstances cannot be justified. It represents a grave breach of international law."

Mrs. Thatcher was asked about the fact that, whereas Iraq has signed the nuclear Non–Proliferation Treaty and accepted IAEA safeguards, Israel has not. She replied:

> "The Government firmly support the Non–Proliferation Treaty and wish that more countries would become signatories."

She went on to say:

> "A tragedy of this case was that Iraq was a signatory to the Agreement and had been inspected, but neither of these facts protected her. It was an unprovoked attack, which we must condemn. Just because a country is trying to manufacture energy from nuclear sources, it must not be believed that she is doing something totally wrong."

It has been argued that the Israeli attack was an act of self-defence. But it was not a response to an armed attack on Israel by Iraq. There was no instant or overwhelming necessity for self-defence. Nor can it be justified as a forcible measure of self-protection. The Israeli intervention amounted to a use of force which cannot find a place in international law or in the Charter and which violated the sovereignty of Iraq.

It has also been argued that, whatever the legal rights and wrongs of the matter, the international community privately breathed a sigh of relief after the Israeli raid, the suggestion being that the Iraqi Government will not now have a nuclear-weapon potential for some further time to come. That is certainly not the case so far as my Government is concerned. We do not believe that Iraq had the capacity to manufacture fissile material for nuclear weapons. Answering an assertion of this kind in the House of Commons, my Prime Minister replied:

> "Had there been such an attack on Israel of the kind that there has just been on Iraq, I should totally and utterly have condemned it. I therefore totally and utterly condemn the attack on Iraq."

* * *

151.   The PRESIDENT (*interpretation from Spanish*): I shall now put to the vote the draft resolution in document S/14556.

A vote was taken by show of hands.

The draft resolution was adopted unanimously.*

152.   The PRESIDENT (*interpretation from Spanish*): I shall now call on those members of the Council who have asked to be allowed to speak following the vote.

* * *

156.   Mrs. KIRKPATRICK (United States of America): Like other members of the Council, the United States does not regard the resolution just adopted as a perfect one.

157.   With respect to the resolution, I must point out that my country voted against the resolution of IAEA which is referred to in the present resolution. We continue to oppose it. In addition, our judgement that Israeli actions violated the Charter of the United Nations is based solely on the conviction that Israel failed to exhaust peaceful means for the resolution of this dispute. Finally, we also believe that the question of appropriate redress must be understood in the full legal context of the relationships that exist in the region.

158.   Nothing in this resolution will affect my Government's commitment to Israel's security and nothing in these reservations affects my Government's determination to work with all Govern-

---

* Resolution 487 (1981), see p. 252, be-low.

ments of the region willing to use appropriate means to enhance the peace and security of the area.

* * *

197.   Mr. AL–QAYSI (Iraq): I apologize to you, Mr. President, and the members of the Council for having asked to be allowed to speak for a few minutes in this late hour.

198.   My purpose in doing so is to recall that the representative of Israel at the end of his statement called this a moment of truth for all of us. Let us see how he has abided by that motto of his statement.

199.   The representative of Israel saw fit in his statement of 12 June [*2280th meeting*] before the Council and in his statement today to quote from an article by Sir Humphrey Waldock, the President of the International Court of Justice. He has also quoted from other sources in a vain attempt to substantiate his allegations. Let us see what the truth of that quotation was.

200.   Sir Humphrey Waldock said exactly the following:

> "The Charter prohibits the use of force except in self-defence. The Charter obliges Members to submit to the Council or Assembly any dispute dangerous to peace which they cannot settle. Members have therefore an imperative duty to invoke the jurisdiction of the United Nations whenever a grave menace to their security develops carrying the probability of armed attack. But, if the action of the United Nations is obstructed, delayed or inadequate and the armed attack becomes manifestly imminent, then it would be a travesty of the purposes of the Charter to compel a defending State to allow its assailant to deliver the first and perhaps fatal blow. If an armed attack is imminent within the strict doctrine of the *Caroline*, then it would seem to bring the case within Article 51. To read Article 51 otherwise is to protect the aggressor's right to the first stroke."

201.   That is what was said by Sir Humphrey Waldock in the article referred to by the representative of Israel. Yet, the representative of Israel on two occasions deemed it fit to quote Sir Humphrey Waldock as having said:

> "It would be a travesty of the purposes of the Charter to compel a defending State to allow its assailant to deliver the first and perhaps fatal blow. . . . To read Article 51 otherwise is to protect the aggressor's right to the first strike." [*Para.* 81 above.]

S

 Security Council

Distr.
General

S/RES/487 (1981)
19 June 1981

**Resolution 487 (1981)
of 19 June 1981***

The Security Council,

Having considered the agenda contained in document S/Agenda/2280,

Having noted the contents of the letter dated 8 June 1981 from the Minister for Foreign Affairs of Iraq,

Having heard the statements made on the subject at its 2280th through 2288th meetings,

Taking note of the statement made by the Director–General of the International Atomic Energy Agency to the Agency's Board of Governors on the subject on 9 June 1981 and his statement to the Security Council at its 2288th meeting on 19 June 1981,

* * *

Fully aware of the fact that Iraq has been a party to the Treaty on the Non–Proliferation of Nuclear Weapons since it came into force in 1970, that in accordance with that Treaty Iraq has accepted the Agency safeguards on all its nuclear activities, and that the Agency has testified that these safeguards have been satisfactorily applied to date,

Noting furthermore that Israel has not adhered to the Treaty on the Non–Proliferation of Nuclear Weapons,

Deeply concerned about the danger to international peace and security created by premeditated Israeli air attack on Iraqi nuclear installations on 7 June 1981, which could at any time explode the situation in the area, with grave consequences for the vital interests of all States,

Considering that, under the terms of Article 2, paragraph 4, of the Charter of the United Nations, "all members shall refrain in their international relations from the threat or use of force against the territorial integrity or political independence of any State, or

* Footnotes omitted.

in any other manner inconsistent with the purposes of the United Nations,"

1. *Strongly condemns* the military attack by Israel in clear violation of the Charter of the United Nations and the norms of international conduct;

2. *Calls upon* Israel to refrain in the future from any such acts or threats thereof;

3. *Further considers* that the said attack constitutes a serious threat to the entire safeguards régime of the International Atomic Energy Agency, which is the foundation of the Treaty on the Non–Proliferation of Nuclear Weapons;

4. *Fully recognizes* the inalienable sovereign right of Iraq and all other States, especially the developing countries, to establish programmes of technological and nuclear development to develop their economy and industry for peaceful purposes in accordance with their present and future needs and consistent with the internationally accepted objectives of preventing nuclear-weapons proliferation;

5. *Calls upon* Israel urgently to place its nuclear facilities under the safeguards of the International Atomic Energy Agency;

6. *Considers* that Iraq is entitled to appropriate redress for the destruction it has suffered, responsibility for which has been acknowledged by Israel;

7. *Requests* the Secretary–General to keep Security Council regularly informed of the implementation of the present resolution.

Adopted unanimously at the 2288th meeting.

––––––––––

The International Court of Justice, in a case brought by Nicaragua against the United States in 1986 also dealt with the requirement of an armed attack. The United States had maintained in the preliminary stages of the case that Nicaragua had attacked El Salvador (as well as Costa Rica and Honduras) by supplying rebels fighting El Salvador's government. The US joined in collective self-defense with El Salvador in defending against these shipments, the US characterizing the shipments as constituting an armed attack. Once the Court found it had jurisdiction in the case (at least on questions of customary international law) the United States refused to proceed further. The Court has no default judgment authority and had to ascertain for itself as best it could the law and the facts to reach a judgment. The Court found that the low level shipments of weapons about which it had evidence did not amount to an armed attack that could trigger the right of self-defense. Owing to the basis of jurisdiction, the Court could consider only the customary law on the use of force.

Case Concerning Military and Paramilitary Activities in and Against Nicaragua

(Nic. *v*. U.S.), 1986 ICJ 14 (June 27).

193. The general rule prohibiting force allows for certain exceptions. In view of the arguments advanced by the United States to justify the acts of which it is accused by Nicaragua, the Court must express a view on the content of the right of self-defence, and more particularly the right of collective self-defence. First, with regard to the existence of this right, it notes that in the language of Article 51 of the United Nations Charter, the inherent right (or "droit naturel") which any State possesses in the event of an armed attack, covers both collective and individual self-defence. Thus, the Charter itself testifies to the existence of the right of collective self-defence in customary international law. Moreover, just as the wording of certain General Assembly declarations adopted by States demonstrates their recognition of the principle of the prohibition of force as definitely a matter of customary international law, some of the wording in those declarations operates similarly in respect of the right of self-defence (both collective and individual). Thus, in the declaration quoted above on the Principles of International Law concerning Friendly Relations and Co-operation among States in accordance with the Charter of the United Nations, the reference to the prohibition of force is followed by a paragraph stating that:

> "nothing in the foregoing paragraphs shall be construed as enlarging or diminishing in any way the scope of the provisions of the Charter concerning cases in which the use of force is lawful".

This resolution demonstrates that the States represented in the General Assembly regard the exception to the prohibition of force constituted by the right of individual or collective self-defence as already a matter of customary international law.

194. With regard to the characteristics governing the right of self-defence, since the Parties consider the existence of this right to be established as a matter of customary international law, they have concentrated on the conditions governing its use. In view of the circumstances in which the dispute has arisen, reliance is placed by the Parties only on the right of self-defence in the case of an armed attack which has already occurred, and the issue of the lawfulness of a response to the imminent threat of armed attack has not been raised. Accordingly the Court expresses no view on that issue. The Parties also agree in holding that whether the response to the attack is lawful depends on observance of the criteria of the necessity and the proportionality of the measures taken in self-defence. Since the existence of the right of collective self-defence is established in customary international law, the

Court must define the specific conditions which may have to be met for its exercise, in addition to the conditions of necessity and proportionality to which the Parties have referred.

195.   In the case of individual self-defence, the exercise of this right is subject to the State concerned having been the victim of an armed attack. Reliance on collective self-defence of course does not remove the need for this. There appears now to be general agreement on the nature of the acts which can be treated as constituting armed attacks. In particular, it may be considered to be agreed that an armed attack must be understood as including not merely action by regular armed forces across an international border, but also "the sending by or on behalf of a State of armed bands, groups, irregulars or mercenaries, which carry out acts of armed force against another State of such gravity as to amount to" (*inter alia*) an actual armed attack conducted by regular forces, "or its substantial involvement therein". This description, contained in Article 3, paragraph (*g*), of the Definition of Aggression annexed to General Assembly resolution 3314 (XXIX), may be taken to reflect customary international law. The Court sees no reason to deny that, in customary law, the prohibition of armed attacks may apply to the sending by a State of armed bands to the territory of another State, if such an operation, because of its scale and effects, would have been classified as an armed attack rather than as a mere frontier incident had it been carried out by regular armed forces. But the Court does not believe that the concept of 'armed attack' includes not only acts by armed bands where such acts occur on a significant scale but also assistance to rebels in the form of the provision of weapons or logistical or other support. Such assistance may be regarded as a threat or use of force, or amount to intervention in the internal or external affairs of other States. It is also clear that it is the State which is the victim of an armed attack which must form and declare the view that it has been so attacked. There is no rule in customary international law permitting another State to exercise the right of collective self-defence on the basis of its own assessment of the situation. Where collective self-defence is invoked, it is to be expected that the State for whose benefit this right is used will have declared itself to be the victim of an armed attack.

* * *

227.   The Court will first appraise the facts in the light of the principle of the non-use of force, examined in paragraphs 187 to 200 above. What is unlawful, in accordance with that principle, is recourse to either the threat or the use of force against the territorial integrity or political independence of any State. For the most part, the complaints by Nicaragua are of the actual use of force against it by the United States. Of the acts which the Court

has found imputable to the Government of the United States, the following are relevant in this respect:

— the laying of mines in Nicaraguan internal or territorial waters in early 1984 (paragraph 80 above);

— certain attacks on Nicaraguan ports, oil installations and a naval base (paragraphs 81 and 86 above).

These activities constitute infringements of the principle of the prohibition of the use of force, defined earlier, unless they are justified by circumstances which exclude their unlawfulness, a question now to be examined. The Court has also found (paragraph 92) the existence of military manoeuvres held by the United States near the Nicaraguan borders; and Nicaragua has made some suggestion that this constituted a "threat of force", which is equally forbidden by the principle of non-use of force. The Court is however not satisfied that the manoeuvres complained of, in the circumstances in which they were held, constituted on the part of the United States a breach, as against Nicaragua, of the principle forbidding recourse to the threat or use of force.

228.   Nicaragua has also claimed that the United States has violated Article 2, paragraph 4, of the Charter, and has used force against Nicaragua in breach of its obligation under customary international law in as much as it has engaged in

"recruiting, training, arming, equipping, financing, supplying and otherwise encouraging, supporting, aiding, and directing military and paramilitary actions in and against Nicaragua" (Application, para. 26 (a) and (c)).

So far as the claim concerns breach of the Charter, it is excluded from the Court's jurisdiction by the multilateral treaty reservation. As to the claim that United States activities in relation to the *contras* constitute a breach of the customary international law principle of the non-use of force, the Court finds that, subject to the question whether the action of the United States might be justified as an exercise of the right of self-defence, the United States has committed a prima facie violation of that principle by its assistance to the *contras* in Nicaragua, by "organizing or encouraging the organization of irregular forces or armed bands ... for incursion into the territory of another State", and "participating in acts of civil strife ... in another State", in the terms of General Assembly resolution 2625 (XXV). According to that resolution, participation of this kind is contrary to the principle of the prohibition of the use of force when the acts of civil strife referred to "involve a threat or use of force". In the view of the Court, while the arming and training of the *contras* can certainly be said to involve the threat or use of force against Nicaragua, this is not necessarily so in respect of all the assistance given by the United States Government. In particular, the Court considers that the mere supply of funds to the *contras*, while undoubtedly an act of intervention in the internal affairs of Nicaragua, as will be explained below, does not in itself amount to a use of force.

229. The Court must thus consider whether, as the Respondent claims, the acts in question of the United States are justified by the exercise of its right of collective self-defence against an armed attack. The Court must therefore establish whether the circumstances required for the exercise of this right of self-defence are present and, if so, whether the steps taken by the United States actually correspond to the requirements of international law. For the Court to conclude that the United States was lawfully exercising its right of collective self-defence, it must first find that Nicaragua engaged in an armed attack against El Salvador, Honduras or Costa Rica.

230. As regards El Salvador, the Court has found (paragraph 160 above) that it is satisfied that between July 1979 and the early months of 1981, an intermittent flow of arms was routed via the territory of Nicaragua to the armed opposition in that country. The Court was not however satisfied that assistance has reached the Salvadorian armed opposition, on a scale of any significance, since the early months of 1981, or that the Government of Nicaragua was responsible for any flow of arms at either period. Even assuming that the supply of arms to the opposition in El Salvador could be treated as imputable to the Government of Nicaragua, to justify invocation of the right of collective self-defence in customary international law, it would have to be equated with an armed attack by Nicaragua on El Salvador. As stated above, the Court is unable to consider that, in customary international law, the provision of arms to the opposition in another State constitutes an armed attack on that State. Even at a time when the arms flow was at its peak, and again assuming the participation of the Nicaraguan Government, that would not constitute such armed attack.

* * *

237. Since the Court has found that the condition *sine qua non* required for the exercise of the right of collective self-defence by the United States is not fulfilled in this case, the appraisal of the United States activities in relation to the criteria of necessity and proportionality takes on a different significance. As a result of this conclusion of the Court, even if the United States activities in question had been carried on in strict compliance with the canons of necessity and proportionality, they would not thereby become lawful. If however they were not, this may constitute an additional ground of wrongfulness. On the question of necessity, the Court observes that the United States measures taken in December 1981 (or, at the earliest, March of that year—paragraph 93 above)

cannot be said to correspond to a "necessity" justifying the United States action against Nicaragua on the basis of assistance given by Nicaragua to the armed opposition in El Salvador. First, these measures were only taken, and began to produce their effects, several months after the major offensive of the armed opposition against the Government of El Salvador had been completely repulsed (January 1981), and the actions of the opposition considerably reduced in consequence. Thus it was possible to eliminate the main danger to the Salvadorian Government without the United States embarking on activities in and against Nicaragua. Accordingly, it cannot be held that these activities were undertaken in the light of necessity. Whether or not the assistance to the *contras* might meet the criterion of proportionality, the Court cannot regard the United States activities summarized in paragraphs 80, 81 and 86, i.e., those relating to the mining of the Nicaraguan ports and the attacks on ports, oil installations, etc., as satisfying that criterion. Whatever uncertainty may exist as to the exact scale of the aid received by the Salvadorian armed opposition from Nicaragua, it is clear that these latter United States activities in question could not have been proportionate to that aid. Finally on this point, the Court must also observe that the reaction of the United States in the context of what it regarded as self-defence was continued long after the period in which any presumed armed attack by Nicaragua could reasonably be contemplated.

238.   Accordingly, the Court concludes that the plea of collective self-defence against an alleged armed attack on El Salvador, Honduras or Costa Rica, advanced by the United States to justify its conduct toward Nicaragua, cannot be upheld; and accordingly that the United States has violated the principle prohibiting recourse to the threat or use of force by the acts listed in paragraph 227 above, and by its assistance to the *contras* to the extent that this assistance "involve[s] a threat or use of force" (paragraph 228 above).

The United States government presented a new view of the need for an armed attack as a basis for self-defense following the terrorist attacks of September 11. The 2002 National Security Strategy contains the following passage relevant to requirement of an armed attack.

The National Security Strategy of the United States of America, September 2002

http://www.whitehouse.gov/nsc/nss.html at 15.

For centuries, international law recognized that nations need not suffer an attack before they can lawfully take action to defend themselves against forces that present an imminent danger of attack. Legal scholars and international jurists often conditioned the legitimacy of preemption on the existence of an imminent threat—most often a visible mobilization of armies, navies, and air forces preparing to attack.

We must adapt the concept of imminent threat to the capabilities and objectives of today's adversaries. Rogue states and terrorists do not seek to attack us using conventional means. They know such attacks would fail. Instead, they rely on acts of terror and, potentially, the use of weapons of mass destruction—weapons that can be easily concealed, delivered covertly, and used without warning.

The targets of these attacks are our military forces and our civilian population, in direct violation of one of the principal norms of the law of warfare. As was demonstrated by the losses on September 11, 2001, mass civilian casualties is the specific objective of terrorists and these losses would be exponentially more severe if terrorists acquired and used weapons of mass destruction.

The United States has long maintained the option of preemptive actions to counter a sufficient threat to our national security. The greater the threat, the greater is the risk of inaction—and the more compelling the case for taking anticipatory action to defend ourselves, even if uncertainty remains as to the time and place of the enemy's attack. To forestall or prevent such hostile acts by our adversaries, the United States will, if necessary, act preemptively.

The United States will not use force in all cases to preempt emerging threats, nor should nations use preemption as a pretext for aggression. Yet in an age where the enemies of civilization openly and actively seek the world's most destructive technologies, the United States cannot remain idle while dangers gather.

Extract from Debate in the British House of Lords, April 21 2004

Apr. 21, 2004, cols. 369–371.

The Attorney–General (Lord Goldsmith): My Lords, I also congratulate the noble Lord, Lord Thomas of Gresford, on having secured the debate. He asks Her Majesty's Government.

"whether they accept the legitimacy of pre-emptive armed attack as a constituent of the inherent right of individual or collective self-defense under Article 51 of the United Nations Charter; and, if so, whether they will define the principles upon which it will be excercised".

Despite the discouragement from the noble Lord opposite, I shall answer the Question, although I will go further—he need have no doubt about that.

Article 51 of the charter provides that,

> "Nothing in the present Charter shall impair the inherent right of individual or collective self-defence if an armed attack occurs against a Member of the United Nations".

It is argued by some that the language of Article 51 provides for a right of self-defence only in response to an actual armed attack. However, it has been the consistent position of successive United Kingdom Governments over many years that the right of self-defence under international law includes the right to use force where an armed attack is imminent.

It is clear that the language of Article 51 was not intended to create a new right of self-defence. Article 51 recognises the inherent right of self-defence that states enjoy under international law. That can be traced back to the "Caroline" incident in 1837. If the noble lord, Lord Henley, will not accept the description "distinguished lawyer", he can at least accept "accurate lawyer". It is not a new invention. The charter did not therefore affect the scope of the right of self-defence existing at that time in customary international law, which included the right to use force in anticipation of an imminent armed attack.

The Government's position is supported by the records of the international conference at which the UN charter was drawn up and by state practice since 1945. It is therefore the Government's view that international law permits the use of force to mount a pre-emptive strike against a threat that is more remote. However, those rules must be applied in the context of the particular facts of each case. That is important.

The concept of what constitutes an "imminent" armed attack will develop to meet new circumstances and new threats. For example, the resolutions passed by the Security Council in the wake of 11 September 2001 recognised both that large-scale terrorist action could constitute an armed attack that will give rise to the right of self-defense and that force might, in certain circumstances, be used in self-defence against those who plan and perpetrate such acts and against those harbouring them, if that is necessary to avert further such terrorist acts. It was on that basis that United Kingdom forces participated in military action against Al'Qaeda and the Taliban in Afghanistan.

It must be right that states are able to act in self-defence in circumstances where there is evidence of further imminent attacks by terrorist groups, even if there is no specific evidence of where such an attack will take place or of the precise nature of the attack.

Two further conditions apply where force is to be used in self-defense in anticipation of an imminent armed attack. First, military action should be used only as a last resort. It must be necessary to use force to deal with the particular threat that is faced. Secondly, the force used must be proportionate to the threat faced and must be limited to what is necessary to deal with the threat.

In addition, Article 51 of the charter requires that if a state resorts to military action in self-defence, the measures it has taken must be immediately reported to the Security Council. The right to use force in self-defense continues until the Security Council has taken measures necessary to maintain international peace and security. That is the answer to the Question as posed.

But I go further, particularly because it has been suggested that the military action taken against Iraq was based on an alleged right of pre-emptive action against Saddam's possession of weapons of mass destruction. Perhaps I may say very clearly that that is not the case. It has never been the position of the Government that the military action against Iraq was legally justified on grounds of "pre-emptive self defence".

The next case concerns the construction of a security barrier by Israel to protect itself from terrorist attacks originating in the Occupied Palestinian Territories. The case is dealt with more fully in Chapter Ten. Here we focus on the ICJ statement regarding the right of self-defense being linked to an armed attack that is attributable to a state before Israel would have the right to invoke self-defense per Article 51.

Legal Consequences of the Construction of a Wall in the Occupied Palestinian Territory

(Advisory Opinion) 2004 ICJ (July 9)

138. * * * Annex I to the report of the Secretary–General states that, according to Israel: "the construction of the Barrier is consistent with Article 51 of the Charter of the United Nations, its inherent right to self-defence and Security Council resolutions 1368 (2001)". More specifically, Israel's Permanent Representative to the United Nations asserted in the General Assembly on 20 October 2003 that "the fence is a measure wholly consistent with the right of States to self-defence enshrined in Article 51 of the Charter"; the Security Council resolutions referred to, he continued, "have clearly recognized the right of States to use force in self-defence against terrorist attacks", and therefore surely recognize the right to use non-forcible measures to that end (A/ES–10/PV.21, p. 6).

139. * * * Article 51 of the Charter thus recognizes the existence of an inherent right of self-defence in the case of armed attack by one State against another State. However, Israel does not claim that the attacks against it are imputable to a foreign State.

The Court also notes that Israel exercises control in the Occupied Palestinian Territory and that, as Israel itself states, the threat which it regards as justifying the construction of the wall originates within, and not outside, that territory. The situation is thus different from that contemplated by Security Council resolutions 1368 (2001) and 1373 (2001), and therefore Israel could not in any event invoke those resolutions in support of its claim to be exercising a right of self-defence.

Consequently, the Court concludes that Article 51 of the Charter has no relevance in this case.

140. The Court has, however, considered whether Israel could rely on a state of necessity which would preclude the wrongfulness of the construction of the wall. In this regard the Court is bound to note that some of the conventions at issue in the present instance include qualifying clauses of the rights guaranteed or provisions for derogation (see paragraphs 135 and 136 above). Since those treaties already address considerations of this kind within their own provisions, it might be asked whether a state of necessity as recognized in customary international law could be invoked with regard to those treaties as a ground for precluding the wrongfulness of the measures or decisions being challenged. However, the Court will not need to consider that question. As the Court observed in the case concerning the *Gabcíkovo-Nagymaros Project (Hungary/Slovakia)*, "the state of necessity is a ground recognized by customary international law" that "can only be accepted on an exceptional basis"; it "can only be invoked under certain strictly defined conditions which must be cumulatively satisfied; and the State concerned is not the sole judge of whether those conditions have been met" *(I.C.J. Reports 1997,* p. 40, para. 51). One of those conditions was stated by the Court in terms used by the International Law Commission, in a text which in its present form requires that the act being challenged be "the only way for the State to safeguard an essential interest against a grave and imminent peril" (Article 25 of the International Law Commission's Articles on Responsibility of States for Internationally Wrongful Acts; see also former Article 33 of the Draft Articles on the International Responsibility of States, with slightly different wording in the English text). In the light of the material before it, the Court is not convinced that the construction of the wall along the route chosen was the only means to safeguard the interests of Israel against the peril which it has invoked as justification for that construction.

141. The fact remains that Israel has to face numerous indiscriminate and deadly acts of violence against its civilian population. It has the right, and indeed the duty, to respond in order to protect the life of its citizens. The measures taken are

bound nonetheless to remain in conformity with applicable international law.

142. In conclusion, the Court considers that Israel cannot rely on a right of self-defence or on a state of necessity in order to preclude the wrongfulness of the construction of the wall resulting from the considerations mentioned in paragraphs 122 and 137 above. The Court accordingly finds that the construction of the wall, and its associated regime, are contrary to international law.

Separate Opinion of Judge Higgins

* * *

33. I do not agree with all that the Court has to say on the question of the law of self-defence. In paragraph 139 the Court quotes Article 51 of the Charter and then continues "Article 51 of the Charter thus recognizes the existence of an inherent right of self-defence in the case of armed attack by one State against another State." There is, with respect, nothing in the text of Article 51 that *thus* stipulates that self-defence is available only when an armed attack is made by a State. *That* qualification is rather a result of the Court so determining in *Military and Paramilitary Activities in and against Nicaragua (Nicaragua* v. *United States of America) (Merits, Judgment, I.C.J. Reports 1986,* p. 14). It there held that military action by irregulars could constitute an armed attack if these were sent by or on behalf of the State and if the activity "because of its scale and effects, would have been classified as an armed attack ... had it been carried out by regular armed forces" *(ibid.,* p. 103, para. 195). While accepting, as I must, that this is to be regarded as a statement of the law as it now stands, I maintain all the reservations as to this proposition that I have expressed elsewhere (R. Higgins, *Problems and Process: International Law and How We Use It,* pp. 250–251).

34. I also find unpersuasive the Court's contention that, as the uses of force emanate from occupied territory, it is not an armed attack "by one State against another". I fail to understand the Court's view that an occupying Power loses the right to defend its own civilian citizens at home if the attacks emanate from the occupied territory—a territory which it has found not to have been annexed and is certainly "other than" Israel. Further, Palestine cannot be sufficiently an international entity to be invited to these proceedings, and to benefit from humanitarian law, but not sufficiently an international entity for the prohibition of armed attack on others to be applicable. This is formalism of an unevenhanded sort. The question is surely where responsibility lies for the sending of groups and persons who act against Israeli civilians and the cumulative severity of such action.

35. In the event, however, these reservations have not caused me to vote against subparagraph (3) (A) of the *dispositif,*

for two reasons. First, I remain unconvinced that non-forcible measures (such as the building of a wall) fall within self-defence under Article 51 of the Charter as that provision is normally understood. Second, even if it were an act of self-defence, properly so called, it would need to be justified as necessary and proportionate. While the wall does seem to have resulted in a diminution on attacks on Israeli civilians, the necessity and proportionality for the particular route selected, with its attendant hardships for Palestinians uninvolved in these attacks, has not been explained.

Some scholars suggest the rescue of nationals is an exception to the requirement of armed attack. Kidnapping nationals is not an armed attack. But when Israel used minimal armed force to rescue hostages held by terrorists at the airport at Entebbe, Uganda, in 1976, while many countries criticized it, many other countries supported the action. Kenya even allowed Israel to refuel its planes there.[3] Israeli commandos flew to the airport solely for the purpose of plucking hostages out of a life-threatening situation. The hostage-takers and some Uganda soldiers aiding them were killed in the action. Some Ugandan planes were destroyed to prevent pursuit. Rather than an exercise of self-defense, however, it may be more accurate to characterize the rescue as a de minimis use of force not rising to the level of a breach of Article 2(4). See p. 222, above.

3.   AGAINST THE RESPONSIBLE PARTY

At the time the ICJ rendered its decision in the Nicaragua case, a war was raging in the Persian Gulf between Iran and Iraq. The conflict ended only in 1988, two short years before Iraq's invasion of Kuwait, one of the case studies in Chapter Two. The next excerpt is a case that arose in the Iran–Iraq war involving a United States use of force against Iran. The ICJ reached its judgment in the case only in 2003. The decision re-affirms the requirement of an armed attack to act in self-defense, but it focuses on the need to direct any response at the responsible party.

Case Concerning Oil Platforms

(Iran v. U.S.), 2003 ICJ (Nov. 6).

23.   * * * The actions giving rise to both the claim and the counter-claim occurred in the context of the general events that took place in the Persian Gulf between 1980 and 1988, in particular the armed conflict that opposed Iran and Iraq. That conflict began on 22 September 1980, when Iraqi forces advanced into the western areas of Iranian territory, and continued until the bellig-

---

3. A. MARK WEISBURD, USE OF FORCE: THE PRACTICE OF STATES SINCE WORLD WAR II 276–77 (1997).

erent parties accepted a ceasefire in the summer of 1988, pursuant to United Nations Security Council resolution 598 (1987) of 20 July 1987. During the war, combat occurred in the territories of both States, but the conflict also spread to the Persian Gulf— which is an international commercial route and line of communication of major importance—and affected commerce and navigation in the region. From the very beginning of the conflict, on 22 September 1980, Iran established a defence exclusion zone around its coasts; shortly after, in early October 1980, Iraq declared a "prohibited war zone" and later established a "naval total exclusive zone" in the northern area of the Persian Gulf. In 1984, Iraq commenced attacks against ships in the Persian Gulf, notably tankers carrying Iranian oil. These were the first incidents of what later became known as the "Tanker War": in the period between 1984 and 1988, a number of commercial vessels and warships of various nationalities, including neutral vessels, were attacked by aircraft, helicopters, missiles or warships, or struck mines in the waters of the Persian Gulf. Naval forces of both belligerent parties were operating in the region, but Iran has denied responsibility for any actions other than incidents involving vessels refusing a proper request for stop and search. The United States attributes responsibility for certain incidents to Iran, whereas Iran suggests that Iraq was responsible for them.

24. A number of States took measures at the time aimed at ensuring the security of their vessels navigating in the Persian Gulf. In late 1986 and early 1987, the Government of Kuwait expressed its preoccupation at Iran's alleged targeting of its merchant vessels navigating in the Persian Gulf. It therefore requested the United States, the United Kingdom and the Soviet Union to "reflag" some of these vessels to ensure their protection. Following this request, the Kuwaiti Oil Tanker Company was able to charter a number of Soviet vessels, and to flag four ships under United Kingdom registry and 11 ships under United States registry. In addition, the Government of the United States agreed to provide all United States-flagged vessels with a naval escort when transiting the Persian Gulf, in order to deter further attacks; these escort missions were initiated in July 1987, under the designation "Operation Earnest Will". Other foreign Powers, including Belgium, France, Italy, the Netherlands and the United Kingdom, took parallel action, sending warships to the region to protect international shipping. Despite these efforts, a number of ships, including reflagged Kuwaiti vessels, merchant tankers carrying Kuwaiti oil and warships participating in "Operation Earnest Will", suffered attacks or struck mines in the Persian Gulf between 1987 and the end of the conflict.

25. Two specific attacks on shipping are of particular relevance in this case. On 16 October 1987, the Kuwaiti tanker *Sea Isle City*, reflagged to the United States, was hit by a missile near

Kuwait harbour. The United States attributed this attack to Iran, and three days later, on 19 October 1987, it attacked Iranian offshore oil production installations, claiming to be acting in self-defence. United States naval forces launched an attack against the Reshadat ["Rostam"] and Resalat ["Rakhsh"] complexes; the R–7 and R–4 platforms belonging to the Reshadat complex were destroyed in the attack. On 14 April 1988, the warship USS *Samuel B. Roberts* struck a mine in international waters near Bahrain while returning from an escort mission; four days later the United States, again asserting the right of self-defence, employed its naval forces to attack and destroy simultaneously the Nasr ["Sirri"] and Salman ["Sassan"] complexes.

* * *

34. * * * [T]he Court has had occasion, in the case concerning Military and Paramilitary Activities in and against Nicaragua (Nicaragua v. United States of America), to examine a provision in another treaty concluded by the United States, of which the text is substantially identical to that of Article XX, paragraph 1 (d). This was Article XXI, paragraph 1 (d), of the 1956 Treaty of Friendship, Commerce and Navigation between the United States and Nicaragua. In its decision in that case, the Court observed that since that provision

"contains a power for each of the parties to derogate from the other provisions of the Treaty, the possibility of invoking the clauses of that Article must be considered once it is apparent that certain forms of conduct by the United States would otherwise be in conflict with the relevant provisions of the Treaty" (I.C.J. Reports 1986, p. 117, para. 225).

* * *

37. * * * [The United States] gave notice of its action to the Security Council under Article 51 of the United Nations Charter.

* * *

40. * * * When Article XX, paragraph 1 (*d*), is invoked to justify actions involving the use of armed force, allegedly in self-defence, the interpretation and application of that Article will necessarily entail an assessment of the conditions of legitimate self-defence under international law.

* * *

43. * * * As the Court emphasized, in relation to the comparable provision of the 1956 USA/Nicaragua Treaty in the case concerning Military and Paramilitary Activities in and against Nicaragua, "the measures taken must not merely be such as tend

to protect the essential security interests of the party taking them, but must be 'necessary' for that purpose"; and whether a given measure is "necessary" is "not purely a question for the subjective judgment of the party" (I.C.J. Reports 1986, p. 141, para. 282), and may thus be assessed by the Court. In the present case, the question whether the measures taken were "necessary" overlaps with the question of their validity as acts of self-defence. As the Court observed in its decision of 1986 the criteria of necessity and proportionality must be observed if a measure is to be qualified as self-defence (see I.C.J. Reports 1986, p. 103, para. 194, and paragraph 74 below).

44. In this connection, the Court notes that it is not disputed between the Parties that neutral shipping in the Persian Gulf was caused considerable inconvenience and loss, and grave damage, during the Iran–Iraq war. It notes also that this was to a great extent due to the presence of mines and minefields laid by both sides. The Court has no jurisdiction to enquire into the question of the extent to which Iran and Iraq complied with the international legal rules of maritime warfare. It can however take note of these circumstances, regarded by the United States as relevant to its decision to take action against Iran which it considered necessary to protect its essential security interests. Nevertheless, the legality of the action taken by the United States has to be judged by reference to Article XX, paragraph 1 (*d*), of the 1955 Treaty, in the light of international law on the use of force in self-defence.

45. The United States has never denied that its actions against the Iranian platforms amounted to a use of armed force. Some of the details of the attacks, so far as established by the material before the Court, may be pertinent to any assessment of the lawfulness of those actions. As already indicated, there were attacks on two successive occasions, on 19 October 1987 and on 18 April 1988. The Court will examine whether each of these met the conditions of Article XX, paragraph 1 (*d*), as interpreted by reference to the relevant rules of international law.

46. The first installation attacked, on 19 October 1987, was the Reshadat complex, which consisted of three drilling and production platforms—R–3, R–4 and R–7—linked to a total of 27 oil wells. * * * At the time of the United States attacks, these complexes were not producing oil due to damage inflicted by prior Iraqi attacks in October 1986, July 1987 and August 1987. Iran has maintained that repair work on the platforms was close to completion in October 1987. The United States has however challenged this assertion * * *.

47. On 19 October 1987, four destroyers of the United States Navy, together with naval support craft and aircraft, approached the Reshadat R–7 platform. Iranian personnel was warned by the United States forces via radio of the imminent attack and aban-

doned the facility. The United States forces then opened fire on the platform; a unit later boarded and searched it, and placed and detonated explosive charges on the remaining structure. The United States ships then proceeded to the R–4 platform, which was being evacuated; according to a report of a Pentagon spokesman, cited in the press and not denied by the United States, the attack on the R–4 platform had not been included in the original plan, but it was seen as a "target of opportunity". After having conducted reconnaissance fire and then having boarded and searched the platform, the United States forces placed and detonated explosive charges on this second installation. As a result of the attack, the R–7 platform was almost completely destroyed and the R–4 platform was severely damaged. While the attack was made solely on the Reshadat complex, it affected also the operation of the Resalat complex. Iran states that production from the Reshadat and Resalat complexes was interrupted for several years.

48.   The nature of this attack, and its alleged justification, was presented by the United States to the United Nations Security Council in the following terms (letter from the United States Permanent Representative of 19 October 1987, S/19219):

> "In accordance with Article 51 of the Charter of the United Nations, I wish, on behalf of my Government, to report that United States forces have exercised the inherent right of self-defence under international law by taking defensive action in response to attacks by the Islamic Republic of Iran against United States vessels in the Persian Gulf.
>
> At approximately 11 p.m. Eastern Daylight Time on 16 October 1987, a Silkworm missile fired by Iranian forces from Iranian-occupied Iraqi territory struck the *Sea Isle City*, a United States flag vessel, in the territorial waters of Kuwait. This is the latest in a series of such missile attacks against United States flag and other non-belligerent vessels in Kuwaiti waters in pursuit of peaceful commerce. These actions are, moreover, only the latest in a series of unlawful armed attacks by Iranian forces against the United States, including laying mines in international waters for the purpose of sinking or damaging United States flag ships, and firing on United States aircraft without provocation.
>
> At approximately 7 a.m. Eastern Daylight Time on 19 October 1987, United States naval vessels destroyed the Iranian military ocean platform at Rashadat [sic] (also known as Rostam) in international waters of the Persian Gulf. The military forces stationed on this platform have engaged in a variety of actions directed against United States flag and other non-belligerent vessels and aircraft. They have monitored the movements of United States convoys by radar and other means; co-ordinated minelaying in the path of our convoys;

assisted small-boat attacks against other non-belligerent ship-ping; and fired at United States military helicopters, as oc-curred on 8 October 1987. Prior warning was given to permit the evacuation of the platform."

49. In its Counter–Memorial, the United States linked its previous invocation of the right of self-defence with the application of Article XX, paragraph 1 (d), of the 1955 Treaty. It argued that Iranian actions during the relevant period constituted a threat to essential security interests of the United States, inasmuch as the flow of maritime commerce in the Persian Gulf was threatened by Iran's repeated attacks on neutral vessels; that the lives of United States nationals were put at risk; that United States naval vessels were seriously impeded in their security duties; and that the United States Government and United States nationals suffered severe financial losses. According to the United States, it was clear that diplomatic measures were not a viable means of deterring Iran from its attacks: "Accordingly, armed action in self-defense was the only option left to the United States to prevent additional Iranian attacks".

50. The Court will thus first concentrate on the facts tending to show the validity or otherwise of the claim to exercise the right of self-defence. In its communication to the Security Council, cited above, the United States based this claim on the existence of

"a series of unlawful armed attacks by Iranian forces against the United States, including laying mines in inter-national waters for the purpose of sinking or damaging United States flag ships, and firing on United States aircraft without provocation";

it referred in particular to a missile attack on the *Sea Isle City* as being the specific incident that led to the attack on the Iranian platforms. Before the Court, it has based itself more specifically on the attack on the *Sea Isle City*, but has continued to assert the relevance of the other attacks (see paragraph 62 below). To justify its choice of the platforms as target, the United States asserted that they had "engaged in a variety of actions directed against United States flag and other non-belligerent vessels and aircraft". Iran has denied any responsibility for (in particular) the attack on the *Sea Isle City*, and has claimed that the platforms had no military purpose, and were not engaged in any military activity.

51. Despite having thus referred to attacks on vessels and aircraft of other nationalities, the United States has not claimed to have been exercising collective self-defence on behalf of the neutral States engaged in shipping in the Persian Gulf; this would have required the existence of a request made to the United States "by the State which regards itself as the victim of an armed attack" (I.C.J. Reports 1986, p. 105, para. 199). Therefore, in order to establish that it was legally justified in attacking the Iranian

platforms in exercise of the right of individual self-defence, the United States has to show that attacks had been made upon it for which Iran was responsible; and that those attacks were of such a nature as to be qualified as "armed attacks" within the meaning of that expression in Article 51 of the United Nations Charter, and as understood in customary law on the use of force. As the Court observed in the case concerning *Military and Paramilitary Activities in and against Nicaragua*, it is necessary to distinguish "the most grave forms of the use of force (those constituting an armed attack) from other less grave forms" (*I.C.J. Reports 1986*, p. 101, para. 191), since "In the case of individual self-defence, the exercise of this right is subject to the State concerned having been the victim of an armed attack" (*ibid.*, p. 103, para. 195). The United States must also show that its actions were necessary and proportional to the armed attack made on it, and that the platforms were a legitimate military target open to attack in the exercise of self-defence.

52.   Since it was the missile attack on the *Sea Isle City* that figured most prominently in the United States contentions, the Court will first examine in detail the evidence relating to that incident. The *Sea Isle City* was a Kuwaiti tanker reflagged to the United States; on 16 October 1987 it had just ended a voyage under "Operation Earnest Will" (see paragraph 24 above), when it was hit by a missile near Kuwait's Al–Ahmadi Sea Island (or Mina al-Ahmadi) terminal. This incident, which caused damage to the ship and injury to six crew members, was claimed by the United States to be the seventh involving Iranian anti-ship cruise missiles in the area in the course of 1987. The United States asserts that the missile that struck the *Sea Isle City* was launched by Iran from a facility located in the Fao area. It recalls that in February 1986 Iran had taken control of a large part of the Fao peninsula and had captured three formerly Iraqi missile sites in the area, which it held at the time of the attack. It also maintains that there was an additional active cruise missile staging facility on Iranian territory near the Fao peninsula.

53.   The evidence produced by the United States includes images, taken by satellite or aerial reconnaissance aircraft, of the Fao area and of the four alleged missile sites under Iranian control at the time of the attack, as well as a complementary expert report describing and examining this imagery. Although the United States has indicated that it was unable to recover and examine fragments of the specific missile that hit the *Sea Isle City*, it has produced, in the present proceedings, a statement by an independent expert, dated 27 March 1997, based on a previous examination by United States military analysts of fragments retrieved from other similar incidents in early 1987. That evidence shows, in the United States submission, that the specific missile was a land-launched HY–2 cruise missile of Chinese manufacture (also known

as the "Silkworm" missile). The United States has also produced the testimony, dated 21 May 1997, of two Kuwaiti officers, to the effect that military personnel stationed on Kuwaiti islands had witnessed, in January, September and October 1987, the launching of six missiles from Iranian-controlled territory in the Fao area; in addition, one of these officers asserts that he personally observed the path of the missile that struck the *Sea Isle City* on 16 October 1987.

54. Iran suggests that no credible evidence has been produced that there were operational Iranian missile sites in the Fao area; it acknowledges that it had captured three Iraqi missile sites in 1986, but these "were heavily damaged during the fighting with Iraq" and "were inoperative throughout the period that Iranian forces held Fao". It therefore denies that the missile that struck the *Sea Isle City* was launched from those sites, or from an additional Iranian Silkworm missile site that the United States claims to have identified in the area, the existence of which Iran denies. Iran observes that the satellite images produced by the United States are not very clear, and appeals to its own experts' opinion to prove that the installations shown therein "bear no resemblance to a normal Silkworm missile site". Moreover, according to Iran, other United States evidence would show that, at the time of the attack, Iran had operative missile sites only in the Strait of Hormuz. Iran maintains that the statement of Kuwaiti officers produced by the United States is unconvincing since it is largely based on hearsay and is in part inconsistent.

55. Iran also suggests the alternative theory that the missile that hit the *Sea Isle City* was fired by Iraq, which, it contends, had both the appropriate missile capabilities, and an interest in internationalizing the conflict with Iran. According to Iran, the missile could have been launched by Iraq either from an aircraft, from a naval vessel or from an "operational missile site located at a position on Fao just to the west of areas occupied by Iran". Iran alleges that, while the maximum range of the standard HY–2 (Silkworm) missile is 95 km, Iraq was in possession of modified versions of that missile that could cover ranges up to 150 or even 200 km. Moreover, according to an expert report produced by Iran, a missile of this kind does not necessarily travel in a straight line and could have been heading in the direction observed by the witnesses invoked by the United States even if it had not been launched from Iranian-held territory in the Fao area.

56. The United States claims that its satellite imagery shows that there was no Iraqi missile launching facility in the Fao area at the time. It also affirms, on the basis of an independent expert's opinion, that HY–2 missiles are not equipped with a system capable of guiding them along a circuitous path, as contended by Iran. Finally, the United States rejects the Iranian theory that the

missile was launched from air or sea, both because the fragments of missiles launched against Kuwaiti territory at the same period indicated a land-launched missile, and because United States AWACS radar planes did not detect any Iraqi military aircraft aloft in the northern Persian Gulf at the time of the attacks.

57.   For present purposes, the Court has simply to determine whether the United States has demonstrated that it was the victim of an "armed attack" by Iran such as to justify it using armed force in self-defence; and the burden of proof of the facts showing the existence of such an attack rests on the United States. The Court does not have to attribute responsibility for firing the missile that struck the *Sea Isle City*, on the basis of a balance of evidence, either to Iran or to Iraq; if at the end of the day the evidence available is insufficient to establish that the missile was fired by Iran, then the necessary burden of proof has not been discharged by the United States.

58.   As noted above, the United States claims that the missile that struck the *Sea Isle City* was a ground-launched HY–2 anti-ship missile of the type known as the "Silkworm", but it has not been able to produce physical evidence of this, for example in the form of recovered fragments of the missile. The Court will however examine the other evidence on the hypothesis that the missile was of this type. The United States contends that the missile was fired from Iranian-held territory in the Fao area, and it has offered satellite pictures and expert evidence to show that there was, at the time, Iranian missile-firing equipment present there. Even with the assistance of the expert reports offered by both Parties, the Court does not however find the satellite images sufficiently clear to establish this point. The evidence that the particular missile came from the Fao direction is the testimony, mentioned above, of a Kuwaiti military officer, who claims to have observed the flight of the missile overhead, and thus to be able to identify the approximate bearing on which it was travelling. However, this testimony was given ten years after the reported events; and the officer does not state that he observed the launch of the missile (and the alleged firing point was too remote for this to have been possible), nor that he saw the missile strike the *Sea Isle City*, but merely that he saw a missile passing "overhead", and that that vessel was struck by a missile "minutes later". In sum, the witness evidence cannot be relied upon. Furthermore, the Court notes that there is a discrepancy between the English and Arabic texts of the statement produced before the Court, both of which were signed by the witness; the Arabic version lacks any indication of the bearing on which the observed missile was traveling.

59.   There is a conflict of evidence between the Parties as to the characteristics of the Silkworm missile, in particular its maximum range, and whether or not when fired it always follows a

straight-line course. According to the United States, the maximum range of the missile is of the order of 105 km, and this type of missile always follows a straight course until it approaches its objective, when its on-board guidance equipment causes it to lock on to a target which may be up to 12 degrees on either side of its course. Iran however contends that the missile may also be set to follow either a curved or dog-leg path, and that its maximum range is less, 95 km at the most. The Court does not consider that it is necessary for it to decide between the conflicting expert testimony. It appears that at the time different models of the missile existed, with differing programming characteristics and maximum ranges. There is however no direct evidence at all of the type of missile that struck the *Sea Isle City*; the evidence as to the nature of other missiles fired at Kuwaiti territory at this period is suggestive, but no more. In considering whether the United States has discharged the burden of proof that Iranian forces fired the missile that struck the *Sea Isle City*, the Court must take note of this deficiency in the evidence available.

60. In connection with its contention that the *Sea Isle City* was the victim of an attack by Iran, the United States has referred to an announcement by President Ali Khameini of Iran some three months earlier, indicating that Iran would attack the United States if it did not "leave the region". This however is evidently not sufficient to justify the conclusion that any subsequent attack on the United States in the Persian Gulf was indeed the work of Iran. The United States also observes that, at the time, Iran was blamed for the attack by "Lloyd's Maritime Information Service, the General Council of British Shipping, Jane's Intelligence Review and other authoritative public sources". These "public sources" are by definition secondary evidence; and the Court has no indication of what was the original source, or sources, or evidence on which the public sources relied. In this respect the Court would recall the caveat it included in its Judgment in the case concerning Military and Paramilitary Activities in and against Nicaragua, that "Widespread reports of a fact may prove on closer examination to derive from a single source, and such reports, however numerous, will in such case have no greater value as evidence than the original source." (I.C.J. Reports 1986, p. 41, para. 63.)

61. In short, the Court has examined with great care the evidence and arguments presented on each side, and finds that the evidence indicative of Iranian responsibility for the attack on the *Sea Isle City* is not sufficient to support the contentions of the United States. The conclusion to which the Court has come on this aspect of the case is thus that the burden of proof of the existence of an armed attack by Iran on the United States, in the form of the missile attack on the *Sea Isle City*, has not been discharged.

* * *

64. On the hypothesis that all the incidents complained of are to be attributed to Iran, and thus setting aside the question, examined above, of attribution to Iran of the specific attack on the *Sea Isle City*, the question is whether that attack, either in itself or in combination with the rest of the "series of . . . attacks" cited by the United States can be categorized as an "armed attack" on the United States justifying self-defence. The Court notes first that the *Sea Isle City* was in Kuwaiti waters at the time of the attack on it, and that a Silkworm missile fired from (it is alleged) more than 100 km away could not have been aimed at the specific vessel, but simply programmed to hit some target in Kuwaiti waters. Secondly, the Texaco Caribbean, whatever its ownership, was not flying a United States flag, so that an attack on the vessel is not in itself to be equated with an attack on that State. As regards the alleged firing on United States helicopters from Iranian gunboats and from the Reshadat oil platform, no persuasive evidence has been supplied to support this allegation. There is no evidence that the minelaying alleged to have been carried out by the Iran Ajr, at a time when Iran was at war with Iraq, was aimed specifically at the United States; and similarly it has not been established that the mine struck by the Bridgeton was laid with the specific intention of harming that ship, or other United States vessels. Even taken cumulatively, and reserving, as already noted, the question of Iranian responsibility, these incidents do not seem to the Court to constitute an armed attack on the United States, of the kind that the Court, in the case concerning Military and Paramilitary Activities in and against Nicaragua, qualified as a "most grave" form of the use of force (see paragraph 51 above).

* * *

67. The nature of the attacks on the Salman and Nasr complexes, and their alleged justification, was presented by the United States to the United Nations Security Council in the following terms (letter from the United States Permanent Representative of 18 April 1988, S/19791):

> "In accordance with Article 51 of the Charter of the United Nations, I wish, on behalf of my Government, to report that United States forces have exercised their inherent right of self-defence under international law by taking defensive action in response to an attack by the Islamic Republic of Iran against a United States naval vessel in international waters of the Persian Gulf. The actions taken are necessary and are proportionate to the threat posed by such hostile Iranian actions."

* * *

68. The Court notes that the attacks on the Salman and Nasr platforms were not an isolated operation, aimed simply at the oil installations, as had been the case with the attacks of 19 October 1987; they formed part of a much more extensive military action, designated "Operation Praying Mantis", conducted by the United States against what it regarded as "legitimate military targets"; armed force was used, and damage done to a number of targets, including the destruction of two Iranian frigates and other Iranian naval vessels and aircraft.

69. The USS *Samuel B. Roberts* was a warship returning to Bahrain on 14 April 1988, after escorting a convoy of United States-flagged merchant ships in the context of "Operation Earnest Will", when it hit a mine near Shah Allum Shoal in the central Persian Gulf. The United States reports that, in the days following the attack, Belgian and Dutch mine-clearing forces and its own navy discovered several mines bearing Iranian serial numbers in the vicinity and it concludes therefore that the mine struck by the USS *Samuel B. Roberts* was laid by Iran. It also adduces other discoveries of Iranian mining activities at the time (including the boarding by United States forces of the Iranian vessel Iran Ajr, said to have been caught in the act of laying mines, referred to in paragraph 63 above), contemporary statements by Iranian military leaders and conclusions of the international shipping community (see paragraph 60 above), all allegedly demonstrating that Iran made a general practice of using mines to attack neutral shipping.

70. Iran denies that it had systematic recourse to minelaying in the Persian Gulf and suggests that evidence produced by the United States is unpersuasive. Furthermore, it contends that the United States has submitted no independent evidence that the laying of the mine that hit the USS *Samuel B. Roberts* is attributable to Iran. Iran also suggests that the mine may have been laid by Iraq, a hypothesis that the United States rejects.

71. As in the case of the attack on the *Sea Isle City*, the first question is whether the United States has discharged the burden of proof that the USS *Samuel B. Roberts* was the victim of a mine laid by Iran. The Court notes that mines were being laid at the time by both belligerents in the Iran–Iraq war, so that evidence of other minelaying operations by Iran is not conclusive as to responsibility of Iran for this particular mine. In its communication to the Security Council in connection with the attack of 18 April 1988, the United States alleged that "The mines were laid in shipping lanes known by Iran to be used by U.S. vessels, and intended by them to damage or sink such vessels" (paragraph 67 above). Iran has claimed that it laid mines only for defensive purposes in the Khor Abdullah Channel, but the United States has submitted evidence suggesting that Iran's mining operations were

more extensive. The main evidence that the mine struck by the USS *Samuel B. Roberts* was laid by Iran was the discovery of moored mines in the same area, bearing serial numbers matching other Iranian mines, in particular those found aboard the vessel *Iran Ajr* (see paragraph 63 above). This evidence is highly suggestive, but not conclusive.

72.   The Court notes further that, as on the occasion of the earlier attack on oil platforms, the United States in its communication to the Security Council claimed to have been exercising the right of self-defence in response to the "attack" on the USS *Samuel B. Roberts*, linking it also with "a series of offensive attacks and provocations Iranian naval forces have taken against neutral shipping in the international waters of the Persian Gulf" (paragraph 67 above). Before the Court, it has contended, as in the case of the missile attack on the *Sea Isle City*, that the mining was itself an armed attack giving rise to the right of self-defence and that the alleged pattern of Iranian use of force "added to the gravity of the specific attacks, reinforced the necessity of action in self-defense, and helped to shape the appropriate response" (see paragraph 62 above). No attacks on United States-flagged vessels (as distinct from United States-owned vessels), additional to those cited as justification for the earlier attacks on the Reshadat platforms, have been brought to the Court's attention, other than the mining of the USS *Samuel B. Roberts* itself. The question is therefore whether that incident sufficed in itself to justify action in self-defence, as amounting to an "armed attack". The Court does not exclude the possibility that the mining of a single military vessel might be sufficient to bring into play the "inherent right of self-defence"; but in view of all the circumstances, including the inconclusiveness of the evidence of Iran's responsibility for the mining of the USS *Samuel B. Roberts*, the Court is unable to hold that the attacks on the Salman and Nasr platforms have been shown to have been justifiably made in response to an "armed attack" on the United States by Iran, in the form of the mining of the USS *Samuel B. Roberts*.

* * *

Note on Terrorism and Self-Defense:

Evidence of responsibility was the main issue in the Oil Platforms Case. Evidence of responsibility is usually the main issue in cases of terror attacks. States and non-state actors have for centuries carried out clandestine, violent attacks against civilian targets to punish or intimidate. Because the attacks are clandestine, a state that wishes to respond may not have solid evidence of who is responsible. If the victim states learns that a terrorist group as opposed to another state has attacked, an additional issue of responsibility arises. If the state or states where the terrorist group is found happens to be making a good faith effort to stop the terrorist group and has some basic ability to do so, then the victim state cannot hold the territorial state responsible for the acts of terrorism and may not respond with armed force on the territory of that state.

In addition to responsibility, another issue making it difficult to fit terrorism in the self-defense category, is the problem of the one-off attack. If a state experiences a single attack on its territory and has no evidence of future attacks, then it has no case for military force for the purpose of self-defense against attacks. For both reasons—state responsibility and purpose of defense—terrorist acts are classically treated as crimes and not armed attacks giving rise to the right of self-defense.

The first issue, responsibility, is demonstrated in a 1988 incident. Israel sent a commando team to Tunisia to kill the PLO's number two, Khalil Wazir, also known as Abu Jihad. The PLO had undoubtedly carried out numerous terror attacks against Israel. Yet, the Security Council condemned the killing of Abu Jihad as an "assassination" in Resolution 611 (April 25, 1988). The United States abstained rather than vetoing the resolution. Presumably the U.S. did not hold Tunisia responsible for the acts of the PLO. Nor did the United States see the attack in Tunisia as a lawful military action against terrorism. The U.S. representative to the UN at the time, Ambassador Herbert Okun, "referred to Tunisia as a friend of the United States and said 'the perpetration of political assassination on Tunisian soil stands in stark contrast to Tunisia's longstanding tradition of non-violence.' "[4] The U.S. position regarding this incident is now supported by the Wall Case, p. 261, above.

As to the second issue, armed attack, we find that most countries do not treat single terrorist attacks as armed attacks. Consider, for example, the Madrid train bombing that killed 200 on March 11, 2004 or the bombing of a discotheque in Bali, Indonesia that also killed about 200 in 2002. On the other hand, in cases where a an attack has occurred and the victim state has clear and convincing evidence that more such attacks are planned and the attacks are either sponsored by a state or a state cannot or will not stop them, states have claimed the right to use force in self-defense. Important cases include the United States armed force against Libya (1986); Israeli armed force against Lebanon (1980s), and Turkish armed force against Iraq (1990s).

In all of these cases, the use of force was criticized by other states. However, it is difficult to pin down exactly what was being criticized. In each case, states pointed particularly to the loss of innocent civilian lives. It is, therefore, difficult to separate this criticism from any criticism of the claims to exercise self-defense in the circumstances. The Wall Case explains that where a state is not responsible for terrorist attacks, Article 51 may not be invoked to justify measures in self-defense. Implicit in this formula-

---

4. Candice Hughes, *Security Council Condemns Wazir Slaying, U.S. Abstains,* As- soc. Pr., April 25, 1988, available at 1988 WL 3779956.

tion is the argument that where a state *is* responsible for terrorist attacks, a state *may* act in self-defense. The defending state's measures in self-defense must, nevertheless, be necessary and proportional for the purpose of defense, which is our next topic.[5] Whether the current law of self-defense is adequate to meet the challenge posed by terrorism is discussed in Chapter 12.

4.   NECESSITY AND PROPORTIONALITY

The ICJ refers to the need to respect the principles of necessity and proportionality in both the Corfu Channel and Nicaragua Cases. It dealt with these principles in greater detail in its Advisory Opinion on Nuclear Weapons and in the Oil Platforms Case, both excerpted here.

Legality of the Threat or Use of Nuclear Weapons

(Advisory Opinion) 1996 ICJ 226 (July 8).

37.   The Court will now address the question of the legality or illegality of recourse to nuclear weapons in the light of the provisions of the Charter relating to the threat or use of force.

38.   The Charter contains several provisions relating to the threat and use of force. In Article 2, paragraph 4, the threat or use of force against the territorial integrity or political independence of another State or in any other manner inconsistent with the purposes of the United Nations is prohibited. That paragraph provides:

> "All Members shall refrain in their international relations from the threat or use of force against the territorial integrity or political independence of any State, or in any other manner inconsistent with the Purposes of the United Nations."

This prohibition of the use of force is to be considered in the light of other relevant provisions of the Charter. In Article 51, the Charter recognizes the inherent right of individual or collective self-defence if an armed attack occurs. A further lawful use of force is envisaged in Article 42, whereby the Security Council may take military enforcement measures in conformity with Chapter VII of the Charter.

39.   These provisions do not refer to specific weapons. They apply to any use of force, regardless of the weapons employed. The Charter neither expressly prohibits, nor permits, the use of any

---

5. Mary Ellen O'Connell, *Lawful Self-Defense to Terrorism*, 63 U. PITT. L. REV. 889 (2002); *but see* Michael Reisman, *Internation-* *al Legal Responses to Terrorism*, 22 HOUSTON J. INT'L L. 4, 17–18 (1999).

specific weapon, including nuclear weapons. A weapon that is already unlawful per se, whether by treaty or custom, does not become lawful by reason of its being used for a legitimate purpose under the Charter.

40.   The entitlement to resort to self-defence under Article 51 is subject to certain constraints. Some of these constraints are inherent in the very concept of self-defence. Other requirements are specified in Article 51.

41.   The submission of the exercise of the right of self-defence to the conditions of necessity and proportionality is a rule of customary international law. As the Court stated in the case concerning Military and Paramilitary Activities in and against Nicaragua (Nicaragua v. United States of America): there is a "specific rule whereby self-defence would warrant only measures which are proportional to the armed attack and necessary to respond to it, a rule well established in customary international law" (I.C.J. Reports 1986, p. 94, para. 176). This dual condition applies equally to Article 51 of the Charter, whatever the means of force employed.

42.   The proportionality principle may thus not in itself exclude the use of nuclear weapons in self-defence in all circumstances. But at the same time, a use of force that is proportionate under the law of self-defence, must, in order to be lawful, also meet the requirements of the law applicable in armed conflict which comprise in particular the principles and rules of humanitarian law.

43.   Certain States have in their written and oral pleadings suggested that in the case of nuclear weapons, the condition of proportionality must be evaluated in the light of still further factors. They contend that the very nature of nuclear weapons, and the high probability of an escalation of nuclear exchanges, mean that there is an extremely strong risk of devastation. The risk factor is said to negate the possibility of the condition of proportionality being complied with. The Court does not find it necessary to embark upon the quantification of such risks; nor does it need to enquire into the question whether tactical nuclear weapons exist which are sufficiently precise to limit those risks: it suffices for the Court to note that the very nature of all nuclear weapons and the profound risks associated therewith are further considerations to be borne in mind by States believing they can exercise a nuclear response in self-defence in accordance with the requirements of proportionality.

Case Concerning Oil Platforms,
Cont'd*

73. As noted above (paragraph 43), in the present case a question of whether certain action is "necessary" arises both as an element of international law relating to self-defence and on the basis of the actual terms of Article XX, paragraph 1 (*d*), of the 1955 Treaty, already quoted, whereby the Treaty does "not preclude ... measures ... necessary to protect [the] essential security interests" of either party. In this latter respect, the United States claims that it considered in good faith that the attacks on the platforms were necessary to protect its essential security interests, and suggests that "A measure of discretion should be afforded to a party's good faith application of measures to protect its essential security interests". Iran was prepared to recognize some of the interests referred to by the United States—the safety of United States vessels and crew, and the uninterrupted flow of maritime commerce in the Persian Gulf—as being reasonable security interests of the United States, but denied that the United States actions against the platforms could be regarded as "necessary" to protect those interests. The Court does not however have to decide whether the United States interpretation of Article XX, paragraph 1 (d), on this point is correct, since the requirement of international law that measures taken avowedly in self-defence must have been necessary for that purpose is strict and objective, leaving no room for any "measure of discretion". The Court will therefore turn to the criteria of necessity and proportionality in the context of international law on self-defence.

74. In its decision in the case concerning *Military and Paramilitary Activities in and against Nicaragua*, the Court endorsed the shared view of the parties to that case that in customary law "whether the response to the [armed] attack is lawful depends on observance of the criteria of the necessity and the proportionality of the measures taken in self-defence" (*I.C.J. Reports 1986*, p. 103, para. 194). One aspect of these criteria is the nature of the target of the force used avowedly in self-defence. In its communications to the Security Council, in particular in that of 19 October 1987 (paragraph 46 above), the United States indicated the grounds on which it regarded the Iranian platforms as legitimate targets for an armed action in self-defence. In the present proceedings, the United States has continued to maintain that they were such, and has presented evidence directed to showing that the platforms collected and reported intelligence concerning passing vessels, acted as a military communication link co-ordinating Iranian naval forces and served as actual staging bases to launch helicopter and small boat attacks on neutral commercial shipping. The United

---

* See pp. 264–276, above.

States has referred to documents and materials found by its forces aboard the vessel *Iran Ajr* (see paragraph 63 above), allegedly establishing that the Reshadat platforms served as military communication facilities. It has also affirmed that the international shipping community at the time was aware of the military use of the platforms, as confirmed by the costly steps commercial vessels took to avoid them, and by various witness reports describing Iranian attacks. The United States has also submitted expert analysis of the conditions and circumstances surrounding these attacks, examining their pattern and location in the light of the equipment at Iran's disposal. Finally, the United States has produced a number of documents, found on the Reshadat complex when it was attacked, allegedly corroborating the platforms' military function. In particular, it contends that these documents prove that the Reshadat platforms had monitored the movements of the *Sea Isle City* on 8 August 1987. On the other hand, the forces that attacked the Salman and Nasr complexes were not able to board the platforms containing the control centres, and did not therefore seize any material (if indeed such existed) tending to show the use of those complexes for military purposes.

75. Iran recognizes the presence of limited military personnel and equipment on the Reshadat platforms, but insists that their purpose was exclusively defensive and justified by previous Iraqi attacks on its oil production facilities. Iran further challenges the evidence adduced by the United States in this regard. It alleges that documents found aboard the *Iran Ajr* and the Reshadat platforms are read out of their proper context, incorrectly translated and actually consistent with the platforms' purely defensive role; and that military expert analysis relied on by the United States is hypothetical and contradictory. Iran asserts further that reports and testimony referred to by the United States are mostly non-specific about the use of the platforms as staging bases to launch attacks, and that the equipment at its disposal could be used from mainland and offshore islands, without any need to have recourse to the platforms.

76. The Court is not sufficiently convinced that the evidence available supports the contentions of the United States as to the significance of the military presence and activity on the Reshadat oil platforms; and it notes that no such evidence is offered in respect of the Salman and Nasr complexes. However, even accepting those contentions, for the purposes of discussion, the Court is unable to hold that the attacks made on the platforms could have been justified as acts of self-defence. The conditions for the exercise of the right of self-defence are well settled: as the Court observed in its Advisory Opinion on *Legality of the Threat or Use of Nuclear Weapons*, "The submission of the exercise of the right of self-defence to the conditions of necessity and proportionality is a rule of customary international law" (*I.C.J. Reports 1996* (I), p.

245, para. 41); and in the case concerning *Military and Paramilitary Activities* in and against Nicaragua, the Court referred to a specific rule "whereby self-defence would warrant only measures which are proportional to the armed attack and necessary to respond to it" as "a rule well established in customary international law" (*I.C.J. Reports 1986*, p. 94, para. 176). In the case both of the attack on the *Sea Isle City* and the mining of the USS *Samuel B. Roberts*, the Court is not satisfied that the attacks on the platforms were necessary to respond to these incidents. In this connection, the Court notes that there is no evidence that the United States complained to Iran of the military activities of the platforms, in the same way as it complained repeatedly of minelaying and attacks on neutral shipping, which does not suggest that the targeting of the platforms was seen as a necessary act. The Court would also observe that in the case of the attack of 19 October 1987, the United States forces attacked the R–4 platform as a "target of opportunity", not one previously identified as an appropriate military target (see paragraph 47 above).

77.   As to the requirement of proportionality, the attack of 19 October 1987 might, had the Court found that it was necessary in response to the *Sea Isle City* incident as an armed attack committed by Iran, have been considered proportionate. In the case of the attacks of 18 April 1988, however, they were conceived and executed as part of a more extensive operation entitled "Operation Praying Mantis" (see paragraph 68 above). The question of the lawfulness of other aspects of that operation is not before the Court, since it is solely the action against the Salman and Nasr complexes that is presented as a breach of the 1955 Treaty; but the Court cannot assess in isolation the proportionality of that action to the attack to which it was said to be a response; it cannot close its eyes to the scale of the whole operation, which involved, *inter alia*, the destruction of two Iranian frigates and a number of other naval vessels and aircraft. As a response to the mining, by an unidentified agency, of a single United States warship, which was severely damaged but not sunk, and without loss of life, neither "Operation Praying Mantis" as a whole, nor even that part of it that destroyed the Salman and Nasr platforms, can be regarded, in the circumstances of this case, as a proportionate use of force in self-defence.

----

5. REPORTING

A final, formal requirement for all states acting in self-defense is a report to the Security Council. We have seen examples of these reports in the case study of the invasion of Iraq (pp. 68–70) and in the Oil Platforms, (p. 264). In addition to reporting, the ICJ explained in The Nicaragua Case that states acting in collective self-defense with the victim of an armed attack must have an invitation from the victim.

Military and Paramilitary Activities, Cont'd*

232. The exercise of the right of collective self-defence presupposes that an armed attack has occurred; and it is evident that it is the victim State, being the most directly aware of that fact, which is likely to draw general attention to its plight. It is also evident that if the victim State wishes another State to come to its help in the exercise of the right of collective self-defence, it will normally make an express request to that effect. Thus in the present instance, the Court is entitled to take account, in judging the asserted justification of the exercise of collective self-defence by the United States, of the actual conduct of El Salvador, Honduras and Costa Rica at the relevant time, as indicative of a belief by the State in question that it was the victim of an armed attack by Nicaragua, and of the making of a request by the victim State to the United States for help in the exercise of collective self-defence.

233. The Court has seen no evidence that the conduct of those States was consistent with such a situation, either at the time when the United States first embarked on the activities which were allegedly justified by self-defence, or indeed for a long period subsequently. So far as El Salvador is concerned, it appears to the Court that while El Salvador did in fact officially declare itself the victim of an armed attack, and did ask for the United States to exercise its right of collective self-defence, this occurred only on a date much later than the commencement of the United States activities which were allegedly justified by this request. The Court notes that on 3 April 1984, the representative of El Salvador before the United Nations Security Council, while complaining of the "open foreign intervention practised by Nicaragua in our internal affairs" (S/PV.2528, p. 58), refrained from stating that El Salvador had been subjected to armed attack, and made no mention of the right of collective self-defence which it had supposedly asked the United States to exercise. Nor was this mentioned when El Salvador addressed a letter to the Court in April 1984, in connection with Nicaragua's complaint against the United States. It was only in its Declaration of Intervention filed on 15 August 1984, that El Salvador referred to requests addressed at various dates to the United States for the latter to exercise its right of collective self-defence (para. XII), asserting on this occasion that it had been the victim of aggression from Nicaragua "since at least 1980". In that Declaration, El Salvador affirmed that initially it had "not wanted to present any accusation or allegation [against

---

* See pp. 254–258, above.

Nicaragua] to any of the jurisdictions to which we have a right to apply", since it sought "a solution of understanding and mutual respect" (para. III).

234.   As to Honduras and Costa Rica, they also were prompted by the institution of proceedings in this case to address communications to the Court; in neither of these is there mention of armed attack or collective self-defence. As has already been noted (paragraph 231 above), Honduras in the Security Council in 1984 asserted that Nicaragua had engaged in aggression against it, but did not mention that a request had consequently been made to the United States for assistance by way of collective self-defence. On the contrary, the representative of Honduras emphasized that the matter before the Security Council "is a Central American problem, without exception, and it must be solved regionally" (S/PV.2529, p. 38), i.e., through the Contadora process. The representative of Costa Rica also made no reference to collective self-defence. Nor, it may be noted, did the representative of the United States assert during that debate that it had acted in response to requests for assistance in that context.

235.   There is also an aspect of the conduct of the United States which the Court is entitled to take into account as indicative of the view of that State on the question of the existence of an armed attack. At no time, up to the present, has the United States Government addressed to the Security Council, in connection with the matters the subject of the present case, the report which is required by Article 51 of the United Nations Charter in respect of measures which a State believes itself bound to take when it exercises the right of individual or collective self-defence. The Court, whose decision has to be made on the basis of customary international law, has already observed that in the context of that law, the reporting obligation enshrined in Article 51 of the Charter of the United Nations does not exist. It does not therefore treat the absence of a report on the part of the United States as the breach of an undertaking forming part of the customary international law applicable to the present dispute. But the Court is justified in observing that this conduct of the United States hardly conforms with the latter's avowed conviction that it was acting in the context of collective self-defence as consecrated by Article 51 of the Charter. This fact is all the more noteworthy because, in the Security Council, the United States has itself taken the view that failure to observe the requirement to make a report contradicted a State's claim to be acting on the basis of collective self-defence (S/PV.2187).

236.   Similarly, while no strict legal conclusion may be drawn from the date of El Salvador's announcement that it was the victim of an armed attack, and the date of its official request addressed to the United States concerning the exercise of collective

self-defence, those dates have a significance as evidence of El Salvador's view of the situation. The declaration and the request of El Salvador, made publicly for the first time in August 1984, do not support the contention that in 1981 there was an armed attack capable of serving as a legal foundation for United States activities which began in the second half of that year. The states concerned did not behave as though there were an armed attack at the time when the activities attributed by the United States to Nicaragua, without actually constituting such an attack, were nevertheless the most accentuated; they did so behave only at a time when these facts fell furthest short of what would be required for the Court to take the view that an armed attack existed on the part of Nicaragua against El Salvador.

B.   INTERVENTION

Since the end of the Cold War, internal armed conflict or civil wars have been a particularly acute problem as the break-up of Yugoslavia, the Kurdish uprising in Iraq, El Salvador, Congo, Somalia, Colombia, Sudan, Liberia, Sierre Leone, Indonesia (East Timor), Russia (Chechnya), Cambodia and other cases demonstrate. Many of these conflicts have been transformed from largely internal conflicts to international ones by the intervention of outside parties. In a number of these conflicts the justification for intervention has been a request by a government or government official deemed to have authority to request outside assistance. In other cases, scholars have argued that third parties had the right or even the duty to intervene to end humanitarian crises, regardless of authorization by a government or the Security Council.

1.   INTERNAL CONFLICTS

In the view of a number of scholars and governments, intervening on the side of a government in effective control to assist that government in putting down a violent rebel movement is lawful. The first excerpt below is from a study of state practice before the end of the Cold War that raises doubts as to whether international law really does allow intervention by invitation. The excerpts that follow concern two cases of such intervention, the US intervention in Panama in 1989 and the French intervention in Ivory Coast in 2003.

Louise Doswald–Beck, The Legal Validity of Military Intervention By Invitation of the Government

56 Brit. Ybk. Int'l L. 189, 251–252 (1985).*

It is submitted that there is, at the least, a very serious doubt whether a State may validly aid another government to suppress a

----

* Footnotes omitted.

rebellion, particularly if the rebellion is widespread and seriously aimed at the overthrow of the incumbent regime. The combination of Resolutions 2131 (XX) and 2625 (XXV), taking into account the motivation behind these resolutions, of the fact that States justify such interventions on the basis of prior outside intervention, and of the number of statements stressing true independence, self-determination and non-intervention in internal affairs, provides substantial evidence to support a theory that intervention to prop up a beleaguered government is illegal. Although it is true that occasions have occurred in which States have given such aid, the reaction to such interventions indicates the need to show effective involvement by a third State. In the case of Afghanistan in particular, States were unconvinced that substantial subversion was proved, mere propaganda or the obtaining of arms in third countries not being, it seems, enough. This is supported by the example of US action in the Lebanon in 1958 when the members of the Security Council were interested in establishing whether men and arms were being infiltrated from Syria into Lebanon. The same would be true of the other fact situations reviewed. An alternative defence to intervention would be the assertion by the intervening State that aid is limited to arms and/or advice and that it does not involve direct action against the rebels. This was stated to be the case by France when giving military aid to the Government of Chad. In this context, it is to be noted that there appears to be no prohibition against States providing governments with weapons and other military supplies during a civil war, and thus the norm of non-intervention does not put governments and rebels on exactly the same footing.

It might be argued that States justify their interventions on the basis of self-defence in order to provide an extra excuse and thus be more acceptable politically. It is submitted, however, that the consistency of this practice has by now hardened into a legal requirement and the view that self-defence is the only justification for the individual use of force in the Charter is strengthened by the new customary norm of non-intervention in internal affairs. Another possible objection could be the view that statements by States are a less secure basis for international customary law than their actions. This assertion must be viewed in the light of the fact that events are very differently perceived by different observers. As international law is principally auto interpretative, each State will act according to its own perception of the facts, which may be very different from that of another State. Statements as to the law, however, provide a more secure basis for an identifiable norm provided that such statements are made as assertions of *lex lata* rather than *lex ferenda*. The latter category would include standards which are vaguely agreed to be striven for, such as certain human rights and especially those pertaining to economic development. So-called "soft law" and "lip-service" can be distinguished from *opinio juris* in that the latter relates to rights and duties immediately applicable and having concrete legal effects. Further, some violations of the law are not going to eliminate the existence of that law, whereas consistent opposite behaviour will render the alleged norm "lip service" rather than customary law. Much human rights "law" is unfortunately in the former category, whereas it is submitted that States are not in practice supporting tottering governments as a pattern of normal behaviour and the weight of normative statements against such behaviour would indicate the existence of a customary law to that effect.

With regard to the origin of the norm of non-intervention in internal affairs, this can best be seen, in this author's opinion, in the *travaux préparatoires* to Resolution 2131. The ideological differences between the East and West blocs and the support by the former of rebel movements attempting to reject the yoke of colonialism gave rise to an interest in the 1950s and 1960s in seeing the success of certain rebellions against established governments. The principle of nonintervention in internal affairs is, in effect, an attempt to limit outside neo-colonial attempts to influence events in other countries for the interests of the intervening country. The policy behind the norm is a recognition that countries intervene in practice for their own benefit and major powers have an interest in not allowing the influence of an adversary power to be strengthened in this way. The policy interest of weaker countries is self-evident as well as the general wish to avoid the escalation of violence. It is to be expected, however, that these norms will be broken when a State considers it imperative to do so in certain circumstances, or when it considers that it can be got away with, but this is quite normal with any legal system and does not in itself derogate from the norm when that norm is clearly expressed and not in doubt. It is submitted that this is the case with the law of non-intervention in internal affairs.

The effect of this new customary law is to revolutionize the traditional law, which held that a State can intervene to help a government suppress a rebellion unless belligerency is declared. It has already been argued that the doctrine of belligerency may well have fallen into desuetude and in this author's opinion, the old formulation has been totally replaced by the new law of non-intervention in internal affairs. It is this that now regulates intervention in civil war and represents the modern law.

DISCUSSION OF THE PANAMA INVASION AT THE 84TH ANNUAL MEETING OF THE AMERICAN SOCIETY OF INTERNATIONAL LAW

84 Proc. Am. Soc. Int'l L. 182–89 (1990).

Panel: The Panamanian Revolution: Diplomacy, War and Self–Determination in Panama, *Remarks by Abraham D. Sofaer***

Statement of Judge Abraham Sofaer, Legal Adviser to the United States Department of State:

The use of force by the United States has traditionally evoked vigorous public debate. The U.S. action in Panama is no exception to this pattern. Public debate is not only proper, it is healthy and helpful. But as I have said on other occasions to this distinguished association, the disagreements publicly expressed over the legitimacy of uses of force are so extreme and intemperate that the public must feel—as some scholars and commentators have concluded—that international law is purely subjective and political, and has no useful contribution to make in the search for a world that is both peaceful and free.

The United States believes that international law plays an indispensable role in the world on countless issues including the use of force. The UN Charter makes clear, in our view, that threat or use of force by states or their surrogates is a great step which should be undertaken only when necessary and for strong and legitimate reasons. At the same time, however, we believe that the threat or use of force is not inherently wrong. A willingness and ability to use force effectively against all serious forms of aggression is an essential component of a stable world in which states retain the right to conduct their own affairs through democratic institutions. The law should be applied in a manner that avoids undermining the legitimate scope of the threat and use of force.

The Bush administration used force in Panama for several compelling and legitimate reasons: the Noriega regime's escalating attacks against U.S. soldiers and civilians; the unique status accorded the United States in Panama by the Canal Treaties; the illegitimacy of the rule of Manuel Noriega; and the support and cooperation extended to the U.S. action by the duly elected President of Panama, Guillermo Endara.

HOSTILE ACTS AGAINST THE UNITED STATES

For many months, the Noriega regime conducted a calculated program of forcible actions and harassment against the U.S. armed forces and U.S. nationals. On December 15, 1989, this program escalated dramatically. Noriega's National Assembly declared "the

---

** Note in original: "Mr. Sofaer spoke in his personal capacity."

Republic of Panama in a state of war for the duration of the aggression unleashed against the Panamanian people by the U.S. Government." This statement, though baseless in its description of the consequences of purely economic and diplomatic sanctions, was a seriously intended threat. The resolution containing the statement specifically noted the National Assembly's constitutional authority "to declare war"; and "to face this state of war," the Assembly bestowed on Noriega "the position as maximum leader of the struggle for national liberation."

Noriega responded to this assignment by promising to go beyond resistance and to "advance toward an offensive of creativity." He promised that "we, the Panamanians, will sit along the banks of the Canal to watch the dead bodies of our enemies pass by."

Noriega's inflammatory address had the effect he no doubt intended. Brutal acts against U.S. personnel and dependents occurred on the very next day. On December 16, a U.S. Marine Lieutenant, Lt. Paz was killed without justification by Panamanian Defense Force (P.D.F.) personnel. On the same day, other P.D.F. elements viciously beat U.S. Navy Lt. Curtis and unlawfully detained, physically abused and threatened to rape his wife. Significantly, the Noriega regime offered no apology or statement of regret concerning these incidents. Whereas Noriega had attempted, after prior incidents, to satisfy U.S. concerns, in this instance the killing was falsely portrayed as a response to shooting and "terrorism" by drunken "gringos". The assault and threatened rape were denied by the P.D.F., which claimed the couple had been "courteously" treated. These blatant lies convinced U.S. diplomats and military officials in Panama that further attacks were certain to follow.

Given the pattern and increasing severity of these incidents, President Bush concluded that the attacks of December 16 were "enough"—the last straw in a deliberate and escalating pattern designed to intimidate the United States into accepting Noriega or losing its rights. These hostile acts of the Noriega regime—in fact followed by further acts of hostility on December 18—constituted a form of aggression against the United States serious enough to justify appropriate defensive action. The President would have been held responsible for the consequences for failing to act.

Now some international lawyers argue that self-defense may be exercised only in response to an "attack" upon the territory of the state taking such action. The United States rejects this notion, and has since the UN Charter was written. The United States believes that it has the right to defend its nationals from attacks anywhere launched upon them simply because they are Americans.

U.S. Rights under the Panama Canal Treaties

The hostile acts of Noriega against the United States had special legal significance because of the unique and extensive rights accorded the United States under the Panama Canal Treaties. In exchange for recognizing Panamanian sovereignty over the Panama Canal in the 1977 Treaties, the United States retained the right and the obligation to ensure continued operation of the Canal, not only in connection with external threats to the canal, but also with respect to the internal threats. The Treaties prohibit the United States interfering in the internal affairs of Panama. But this limitation was not intended to prevent the exercise of any U.S. rights conferred in the Canal Treaties. The Office of Legal Counsel explained to the Senate Committee on Foreign Relations during the Senate's consideration of the Treaties that "[a]ction conforming with the proposed treaty would not be interference with the *internal* affairs of Panama because being the subject of a treaty obligation, the matters embraced by the Neutrality Treaty are not the internal affairs of either State party to that treaty."

The Noriega regime's conduct and policies posed a serious threat to U.S. rights. Noriega had consistently failed to carry out treaty obligations essential to the operation of the Canal. He had failed to maintain roads and other important facilities, or to provide basic services required by the Canal Commission and its employees. During the months preceding the U.S. action, members of the U.S. forces and of the Canal work force were unlawfully detained, threatened and otherwise deprived of Treaty protections. On December 15, 1989, Noriega explicitly claimed the United States had no right to defend the canal, because it could not effectively do so, and he called for the end of all U.S. rights in Panama. As he put it: "only one territory and only one flag."

President Bush was justified in taking these circumstances into account in deciding whether to use force to ensure the continued safe and efficient operation of the canal. He was not required to wait until the canal was under physical attack before protecting U.S. rights.

Support of the Legitimate Government of Panama

In authorizing the U.S. action in Panama, President Bush also relied on Noriega's illegitimacy, and President Endara's approval and cooperation. The United States does not accept the notion that a state is entitled to use force to overthrow the dictator of another state, however mad or cruel. The substantial respect accorded the doctrine of humanitarian intervention, however, reflects the fact that the advancement of human rights and of democratic self-determination are legitimate objectives of our international system. Panama presented a strong case for humanitarian intervention. Noriega agreed in 1989 to hold an election, which he lost decisively in the opinion of all international observers. He nonetheless nullified the election, and continued to rule Panama through the PDF and his Dignity Battalions, which physically assaulted Endara and other opposition candidates and suppressed all dissent.

For its part, the United States consistently refused to accept the Noriega regime as a legitimate government of Panama. To the United States, moreover, Noriega was an indicted drug dealer who used his power to prevent Panama's compliance with narcotics conventions requiring his prosecution or extradition. As the situation in Panama deteriorated, the U.S. government decided it should seek President-elect Endara's cooperation in any military action eventually undertaken, and should support him in obtaining the office to which he was morally and legally entitled.

When informed of the impending arrival of U.S. troops in Panama on December 19, 1989, Endara decided to be sworn in as President. He welcomed the United States action, presented his views as to the proper objectives of U.S. efforts, and immediately began to cooperate fully in their implementation. He appealed to the Panamanian forces "not to resist" the U.S. action, which he said was unavoidable and "seeks to end the Noriega dictatorship and reestablish democracy, justice and freedom."

The cooperation and support of President Endara lends substantial weight to the legitimacy of the U.S. action in Panama. Had Endara controlled Panamanian territory and been able to exercise governmental powers prior to December 19, the U.S. action would have been lawful on this ground alone. That he lacked such clear control, however, does not deprive his consent of legal significance. He was not a U.S. puppet, but the chosen President of the people of Panama. His wide spread acceptance by the Panamanian people after the U.S. action reflects his continuing legitimacy. Obtaining Endara's formal approval for the U.S. action before a firm decision had been made to proceed would have exposed him to unjustifiable political and physical risk.

The U.S. Action was Necessary and Proportionate

President Bush reasonably concluded that Operation Just Cause was both necessary and proportionate under international law. By December 20, 1989, Noriega had declared as his objective, "only one territory and only one flag," and had repudiated the U.S. right to protect the canal. He regarded Panama as in a state of war with the United States, and had crossed the line from harassment to homicide in the escalation of hostilities. The United States had attempted to negotiate Noriega's voluntary surrender of power, had protested Noriega's violations of the Canal Treaties and his violence against U.S. forces, and had invoked all available forms of diplomatic and economic sanctions. All these efforts failed.

Under these circumstances, ousting Noriega was a legitimate and necessary objective of any military action in Panama; only that result could end the attacks on Americans, preserve U.S. (and

Panamanian) rights under the Canal Treaties, restore the legitimate democratic government, selected by the people of Panama, and end Noriega's alleged involvement in international drug violations.

Having properly determined to remove Noriega from authority in Panama, the substantial military action designed to achieve that result was fully warranted. The Joint Chiefs of Staff recommended, and the President adopted, a plan designed to employ a swift, overpowering force, on the belief that far fewer casualties would result than if any less intensive effort were implemented. U.S. diplomats and military officials on the scene emphatically concurred in this strategy, as did the democratically-elected Panamanian leadership. Without total victory, the PDF and/or Noriega would have utilized their massive store of weapons to make democratic government impossible. A protracted operation would have been a tactical disaster, and would have exposed U.S. civilians to continuing danger.

International law, and international lawyers, should avoid utilizing the doctrine of proportionality as a vehicle for second guessing tactical judgments as to what form a military action should take to achieve an objective that is legitimate. The military judgment President Bush accepted was reasonable in light of the continuing danger that otherwise would have existed for U.S. forces, for U.S. rights concerning the canal and for President Endara's capacity to govern.

Conclusion

The U.S. action in Panama violated neither Article 2(4) of the UN Charter, nor Articles 18 or 20 of the OAS Charter. The United States acted only after Noriega's regime had begun to murder Americans, and had declared its intention to deprive the United States of its rights and to sabotage the canal; all measures short of the use of force had been invoked without success; and the duly elected President of Panama had welcomed and made common cause with the U.S. action.

In this context, the action in Panama cannot fairly be viewed as having been intended to compromise the territorial integrity or political independence of Panama. Rather, it protected the lives of U.S. troops and citizens, preserved a treaty relationship that recognized Panamanian sovereignty over the canal and installed the government democratically elected by Panamanian people. Use-of-force rules should not be applied mechanically, like what Julius Stone called a "juristic push-button device," but with an appreciation for all the relevant circumstances of each special case. The relevant circumstances here make clear that, by undertaking the action in Panama the United States does not indicate a willingness or claim a right to use force merely to replace regimes in this hemisphere that it opposes on policy grounds. The action in Panama was no return to "gunboat diplomacy." It was based on several legitimate considerations and valid international objectives. It was a Just—and a lawful—Cause.

John Quigley:* In presentations before the OAS and the United Nations, representatives of the United States relied on two arguments to justify the Panama invasion, namely, the first two that you mentioned, self-defense and the Panama Canal Treaties. You have mentioned two other matters that were stated by President Bush and Secretary of State Baker at the time as objectives of the invasion, but that were not put forward to the OAS or the United Nations as legal justifications. The first matter is the illegitimacy of the Noriega Government, and the second is that Mr. Endara welcomed the invasion. Are you saying that these circumstances provide independent legal justification?

Mr. Sofaer: I am not saying that anything provides an independent legal justification. I am not required as Legal Adviser to preach about independent justifications. I am required to look at all the circumstances of a given situation, describe those circumstances and to make the judgment of what the effect of all those circumstances is. The effect here is that this action should be considered a reasonable utilization of the use of force under the UN Charter and the OAS Charter in light of all the circumstances that were presented.

One of the circumstances was Endara's formal welcoming of the United States. This came very close to the intervention, it is true, but it was not a bolt out of the blue. We were well aware of his attitude and well aware that it was inconceivable politically to take a stand on what his position would be formally before we were committed to act. It would have exposed him to the fickleness of American politics, and it would have been irresponsible to put him in that position. But once we decided that we were prepared to go ahead, we did consult with him and he did formally welcome the action. Indeed, he went further and made common cause with it. By instructing the U.S. officials who communicated with him as to the appropriate objectives of that action. I do not have the statements made in the OAS and the United Nations, and I do not know what reliance was placed on this specific factor. I can tell you that long before the action, this was identified as a relevant factor and was included in legal memoranda presented to all relevant administrative personnel, and discussed with congressional leaders. It was no surprise to us that President-elect Endara was consulted before the planes arrived in Panama. The lawyers in the

* Ohio State University

administration had asked for that to occur and it was properly implemented by the diplomats on the spot.

* * *

Roundtable Discussion

* * *

Tom Farer: Listening to the Legal Adviser, I could not think of a better historical position for him than as a courtier in the palace of that famous emperor who, having put on his invisible cloths, emerges from his closet. The first courtier to greet him is the Legal Advisor. When the emperor said, "How do I look?" the Legal Adviser observed him closely and replied, "Marvelous, marvelous, a post modern-costume."

* * * Although the Charter says nothing about the defense of nationals as a legitimate use of force, I am prepared to argue that practice and expectations have reached a point where there is a sufficient expectation that powers will rescue their citizens and that we probably should regard this as a gloss on the Charter. Therefore, if there were a legitimate threat to American citizens in Panama, and there were no alternative means of avoiding that threat, the United States had a strong argument. The difficulty is that the increasing harassment of U.S. citizens related directly to our attempts to overthrow the de facto government of Panama and to remove its head, that is Mr. Noriega, to the United States. There is a perfect correlation between the two. In other words, it would seem to follow that if we had decided to desist from our policy of seeking to overthrow Noriega, to remove him from the country and prosecute him, he would then have desisted from the calculated harassment of U.S. personnel, which was clearly a bargaining chip in his negotiations with his former employer, the U.S. government.

Therefore, in order to satisfy the condition of necessity, we must move from the question of the necessity to protect U.S. citizens to examine an implicitly claimed other right, namely, the right to overthrow the de facto government of the country. To be honest, I felt quite ambivalent about the removal of Noriega. I have met the gentleman. You would not want to meet him in a dark alley unless you were armed with an AK47 and he with a twig. Be that as it may, he was in effective control of the country, and for the most part, for the last hundred years, or indeed, the past millennium, a group of people in effective control of a state has been regarded as forming the legitimate government of the state. Therefore, there is a case to be made for the proposition that one state may invade another in order to remove or alter the political arrangements in that other country for reasons other than the need to protect one's own citizens.

The only argument here, it seems to me, is that participation in the hurling of narcotics into the United States is equivalent to participation in the sending of troops into the United States under the Charter. That is not an argument that can be made quickly, but it is one that needs to be examined. Are there acts by states (such as narcotics trafficking or counterfeiting currency) that, although not constituting an armed attack in any literal sense of that term, are sufficiently threatening to the interests of the target State to activate its right to self-defense under Article 51? Again, you would have to apply the conditions of necessity and proportionality. That poses the appropriate structure of analysis.

Resolutions adopted without reference to a Main Committee

44/240. *Effects of the military intervention by the United States of America in Panama on the situation in Central America*

Date: 29 December 1989 Vote: 75–20–40 (recorded)

The General Assembly
Meeting: 89
Draft: A/44/L.63 and Add.1

Taking note of the statements made in the General Assembly and the Security Council regarding the invasion of Panama,

Reaffirming the sovereign and inalienable right of Panama to determine freely its social, economic and political system and to develop its international relations without any form of foreign intervention, interference, subversion, coercion or threat,

Recalling that, in accordance with Article 2, paragraph 4, of the Charter of the United Nations, all Member States shall refrain in their international relations from the threat or use of force against the territorial integrity or political independence of any State, or in any other manner inconsistent with the purposes of the United Nations,

Reaffirming the need to restore conditions which will guarantee the full exercise of the human rights and fundamental freedoms of the Panamanian people,

Expressing its profound concern at the *serious* consequences the armed intervention by the United States of America in Panama might have for peace and security in the Central American region,

1. *Strongly* deplores the intervention in Panama by the armed forces of the United States of America, which constitutes a flagrant violation of international law and of the independence, sovereignty and territorial integrity of States;

2. *Demands* the immediate cessation of the intervention and the withdrawal from Panama of the armed invasion forces of the United States;

3. *Demands* as to full respect for and strict observance of the letter and spirit of the Torrijos–Carter Treaties;

4. *Calls* upon all States to uphold and respect the sovereignty, independence and territorial integrity of Panama;

5. Requests the Secretary–General to monitor the developments in Panama and to report to the General Assembly within twenty-four hours after the adoption of the present resolution.

France has a long history of intervening militarily in its former colonies. Such interventions have attracted little protest when France had a request to do so and the situation was one of unrest or other disorder short of civil war.

> * * * France intervened at the request of the government of Gabon to protect it against an army mutiny in 1964; it invoked a defence treaty which allowed force not only against external attack but also against domestic unrest, and sent extra troops to supplement those French forces already in Gabon. Its justification was that it had been invited to re-establish the elected government and to prevent disorder. There was no discussion in the UN. France also used this justification in 1968 when its troops in Chad were strengthened by reinforcements from outside to "re-establish order" at the request of the government under a 1960 defence treaty. Its troops remained until 1972. Again when the French intervened to overthrow Emperor Bokassa in the Central African Republic in 1979 they claimed that they had been invited in by the new ruler to ensure order; in fact the French forces and the new President arrived together. In 2002 when French troops were ostensibly supporting the democratically-elected government of Côte d'Ivoire against a military threat, there were suspicions that France was actually putting pressure on the government to come to terms with the rebels. The Security Council nevertheless welcomed its intervention.[1]

Within a year of France's intervention in Ivory Coast, however, as the two media reports that follow indicate, it became difficult to tell if France was there with the permission of a government in effective control or not. It may well be that the legal basis of French intervention was no longer invitation but Security Council authorization. Without Security Council support, query whether France would have had the legal right to remain in Ivory Coast.

UN Takes over Peacekeeping in Volatile Ivory Coast

Agence-France Presse, April 5, 2004

ABIDJAN, April 5 (AFP)—The United Nations envoy in Ivory Coast struck a note of optimism here Monday as UN peacekeepers formally took up duty in the divided, volatile west African country.

---

1. CHRISTINE GRAY, INTERNATIONAL LAW AND THE USE OF FORCE 72 (2d ed., 2004).

"This day that comes after so many ordeals is a day of hope for all Ivorians and for the international community," said Albert Tevoedjre, the special representative of UN Secretary General Kofi Annan.

"Do not disappoint the people of Ivory Coast, do not disappoint the world which supports you and is watching you," he told government leaders and former rebels now in the government, at a ceremony to mark the handover to UN troops.

"Nothing has been lost, everything is still possible," added Tevoedjre.

The changeover began with the transfer to UN command of 1,300 west African troops, who are already in Ivory Coast manning a buffer zone between the rebel-held north and government forces in the south.

It came just over a week after clashes between anti-government protestors and security forces left at least 37 people dead, according to the government.

The opposition said up to 500 were killed.

The opposition had called for a peaceful march in Abidjan on March 25 to protest at president Laurent Gbagbo's failure to respect the terms of a peace pact signed last year.

But Gbagbo banned demonstrations and the army, on presidential orders, cordoned off the port city and violently quashed the protest.

Ivory Coast's security minister said Thursday there was "incontestable evidence" that atrocities were committed after the protest, but blamed them on "parallel forces."

Tevoedjre also read out a statement at Monday's ceremony from Kofi Annan urging Gbagbo to fully cooperate with an international committee set up to investigate the violence surrounding the demonstration.

Annan called on Gbagbo to "guarantee that civil and political freedoms are restored without delay."

Ivory Coast's human rights minister, meanwhile, accused the UN of making a biased and ethnic-based interpretation of the rights situation in the country.

"It has been noted that certain attitudes and written statements by the UN tend to encourage defiance of the Ivorian authorities," said Victorine Wodie in a statement published Monday in Notre Voie, a daily newspaper close to Gbagbo's Ivorian Popular Front party.

"In the same vein, a biased and sometime ethnic interpretation of the human rights situation in Ivory Coast can be seen in the activities of the UN organs in Ivory Coast," she added.

The African force that on Monday became a UN force has been in Ivory Coast since early 2003, under the command of the Economic Community of West African States.

Nearly 5,000 more UN soldiers are due to deploy between now and July, from countries such as Bangladesh, Morocco, Pakistan and Ukraine.

The UN Operation in Ivory Coast (UNOCI) is tasked with overseeing a disarmament and reconciliation process in a country divided since September 2002, when rebels rose up against Gbagbo and plunged the nation into civil war.

The UN troops will operate alongside 4,000 French soldiers, who are in the country on the authorisation of the UN but remain a separate force. France is the former colonial power in Ivory Coast.

The rebels have said the aim of their uprising was to defend the rights of Ivory Coast's Muslims and ethnic minorities, both of whom, they insist, have been marginalised by Gbagbo's government.

Annan called on Gbagbo to "present the National Assembly with bills provided for in the Linas–Marcoussis (peace) pact without delay."

The French-brokered peace pact, signed in January 2003 in the Paris suburb of Marcoussis, called on Gbagbo to cede some executive powers to a prime minister and brought the political opposition and rebels into a reconciliation government.

Seven opposition groups, including the former rebels, walked out of the interim government to protest at the quashing of last month's anti-Gbagbo demonstration.

Annan urged them to return, and exhorted all sides to disarm and demobilise their fighters.

Leave Now, French Troops are Told by Government Supporters in Ivory Coast

Agence–France Presse, June 10, 2004.

ABIDJAN, June 10 (AFP)—Anti–French vitriol rocked the Ivory Coast main city Abidjan again Thursday as hundreds of young government supporters clogged the entrance to the French military base in a peaceful demonstration.

The 4,000 French troops patrolling their former colony since last year have worn out their welcome, firebrand "Young Patriots" leader Charles Ble Goude said.

He and other hardline partisans of President Laurent Gbagbo have repeatedly accused France of betraying the country with its perceived support for rebels whose failed coup bid in September 2002 plunged the west African state into war.

The "Patriots" also demanded that UN peacekeepers who have been in Ivory Coast since April stay home until Gbagbo returns Wednesday from a private trip to the United States.

Tight security nearly matched one security officer to each of the 300 or so demonstrators to thwart violence from erupting outside the military base as it has in past protests by the hardliners.

A wave of anti-French violence washed over Abidjan earlier this week in the aftermath of tit-for-tat breaches of the confidence zone stretching 400 kilometers (250 miles) across Ivory Coast, the world's top cocoa producer.

The Ivorian armed forces targeted a rebel convoy with an air strike in retaliation for an incursion into the confidence zone that has been blamed on "renegade elements" of the rebel forces who were trying to steal weapons from a military post operated jointly by French, Ivorian and UN troops.

Ble Goude, the self-proclaimed "Youth General," demanded a full accounting of the incident in the farming village of Gohitafla tucked into the confidence zone that left 22 dead including five Ivorian soldiers.

More than 100 black clad Gbagbo supporters pelted the French embassy with stones and set alight pyres of tires and wooden stakes in response to the rebel strike in Gohitafla.

* * *

Once a beacon of stability and economic prosperity for a restive and impoverished region, Ivory Coast has been flattened by 20 months of political and military conflict spawned by the rebel uprising.

* * *

2. Humanitarian Crises

Ian Brownlie, Humanitarian Intervention

Law and Civil War in the Modern World 217–228 (J.N. Moore ed. 1974).*

1. Introduction

In the recent literature of the law, proposals have been made to the effect that forcible intervention in human rights situations is lawful and, further, that the present need is to clarify the criteria by which the legitimacy of such action may be judged. My purpose is to subject these proposals to a critique. The critique will relate particularly to the views of Richard Lillich and the Interim Report of the Sub–Committee of the Committee on Human Rights of the

---

* Footnotes omitted.

International Law Association. The Interim Report was based upon two articles published previously by Lillich.

It is as well if I point out that I share the objectives of the principal Committee in shifting the emphasis from definition to implementation in matters of human rights * * *. The issue, of course, is to discover the best means of implementation acceptable to the majority of states. While publicists and experts can take the initiative in prompting states to action, they cannot afford to ignore the expectations, attitudes and aptitudes of governments when formulating proposals.

Unless the context clearly requires a different interpretation, "humanitarian intervention" in my usage is the threat or use of armed force by a state, a belligerent community, or an international organization, with the object of protecting human rights. It must be emphasized that this usage begs the question of legality and stresses function or objective. In diplomatic usage, the term "humanitarian intervention" has been used more widely to describe diplomatic intervention *de bene esse* on behalf of non-nationals or on behalf of nationals in matters which are in law within the domestic jurisdiction of the state of their residence or sojourn.

2. The Legal Context

* * * It is clear to the present writer that a jurist asserting a right of forcible humanitarian intervention has a very heavy burden of proof. Few writers familiar with the modern materials of state practice and legal opinion on the use of force would support such a view. In the first place. it is significant that the very small number of writers cited in support of this view by Lillich include two, McDougal and Reisman, who lean heavily on a flexible and teleological interpretation of treaty texts. Leading modern authorities who either make no mention of humanitarian intervention and whose general position militates against its legality, or expressly deny its existence include Brierly, Castren, Jessup, Jimenez de Arechaga, Briggs, Schwarzenberger, Goodrich, Hambro and Simons, Skubiszewski, Friedmann, Waldock, Bishop, Sørensen, and Kelsen. In the lengthy discussions over the years in United Nations bodies of the definition of aggression and the principles of international law concerning international relations and cooperation among states, the variety of opinions canvassed has not revealed even a substantial minority in favor of the legality of humanitarian intervention. *The Repertory of Practice of United Nations Organs* provides no support; nor does the International Law Commission's Draft Declaration of the Rights and Duties of States. The voluminous materials in Whiteman's *Digest* lack even a passing reference to humanitarian intervention. Counting heads is not, of course, a sound way of resolving issues of principle. However, quite apart from the weight of the opinion of experts

cited above, it is the writer's view that these authorities are reporting and reflecting the universal consensus of government opinion and the practice of states since 1945. Their views thus combine both policy in the sense of the reasonable expectations of states and the normative quality of rules based on *consensus*. With due respect to Lillich, it must be said that, if a new view is to be put forward, either it should be based on a much more substantial exposition of the practice, doctrine, and general development of the law relating to the use of force by states or the view should be offered *tout court* as a proposal to change the existing law. * * * Even those prone to give a broad definition of self-defense do not, in general support the view that humanitarian intervention is lawful. The minority who would support the legality of intervention to protect the lives of nationals rely significantly on the category of self-defense: and humanitarian intervention is not a form of self-help by definition, whereas self-defense is a legitimate form of self-help. The minority who argue that Article 51 reserves without transformation the right of self-defense in customary law rely on the category of self-defense and do not suggest that the erratic "rights of intervention" variously propounded by pre–1928 writers survive * * *.

3.   State Practice

* * * The ILA Report and Lillich's articles on humanitarian intervention are almost entirely devoid of any serious examination of the practice in the period of "customary international law," apparently pre–1945. Reference is made to Turkish treatment of Christians and Russian treatment of Jews—instances of diplomatic intervention. The other pre–1914 references are to the collective intervention in Greece in 1827 and American action in Cuba in 1898. Both these cases can only be recruited as examples by "ex post factoism." The governments of the time did not use a legal justification in the case of the Greek insurgency. Jurists classify the intervention in Cuba in 1898 in various ways, and the Joint Resolution of Congress justified the intervention in terms of American interests. An examination of the practice provides one possibly genuine example of altruistic action, namely, the intervention of 1860 in Syria to prevent the recurrence of massacres of Maronite Christians. The only approximation to use of the justification between 1913 and 1945 was the Proclamation on the German occupation of Bohemia and Moravia, made by Hitler on March 15, 1939. In this, he referred to "assaults on the life and liberty of minorities, and the purpose of disarming Czech troops and terrorist bands threatening the lives of minorities."

The period of the United Nations Charter is totally lacking in practice on the point. However, the ILA Report holds out the Stanleyville operation of 1964 and the initial introduction of troops into the Dominican Republic as instances of permissible intervention to protect human rights. The Stanleyville operation took place with the authorization of the Government of the Congo, which, both legally and otherwise, makes a great deal of difference. * * *

4.   The Arguments for Legality of Intervention to Protect Human Rights

My examination * * * leads to three, conclusions. First, the role of humanitarian intervention, even before the first attempt at regulating resort to war in the League Covenant, was dubious, and the practice probably did not present a constant and uniform usage. Secondly, the practice of the League period cannot be said to assist the somewhat derelict doctrine, although a number of writers, especially prior to the Kellogg–Briand Pact, continued to give it support. Thirdly, the practice in the period of the United Nations Charter is totally inadequate to the task of establishing an interpretation in terms of subsequent conduct of the parties favorable to intervention to protect human rights.

There are two points remaining for consideration. First, how is the "protection of human rights" to be defined? This point will be reserved, partly because the issue of definition is not necessarily identical with the substance of the matter—the existence of the particular legal title to act. Secondly, apart from the subsequent conduct of the parties as a guide to interpretation, what is the proper interpretation of the Charter provisions? The approach to the Charter of the ILA subcommittee is curious to a degree since, in contrast to most lawyers they place customary law and the charter in opposition. * * * For most lawyers the principles of the Charter are the customary law, * * * governing use of force by states. This is especially the case after twenty-five years of state practice based upon the Charter.

The ILA subcommittee's remark that the drafters of the Charter "paid no attention to whether these doctrines [of humanitarian intervention] were to survive the Charter" is simply not true. The participating governments took a view of the legal regime as a whole and because they made no reference to what statesmen would have regarded as a non-issue, it can hardly be said that they were reserving their position on the point.

The ILA subcommittee produced two other points. The first was to cite Professors Reisman and Thomas for the view that intervention which does not impair the "territorial integrity or political independence" of a state is not prohibited by Article 2(4). This argument is used by very few lawyers and has long been discredited. If there is an ambiguity, then, according to ordinary principles of interpretation, one has recourse to the preparatory materials. These make it clear that the phrase "against the territorial integrity" was added at San Francisco at the behest of small states wanting a stronger guarantee against intervention. Of course, the states taking action within the territory of other states commonly attempt to mitigate their policies by assertions that their motives are limited or even benevolent. The other legal argument in the sub-committee's Report is irrelevant to the present issue. This asserts, correctly, that the United Nations can intervene, if the state violating human rights causes an actual threat to peace.

5. Policy Issues

My own assumption is that, basically, Professor Lillich is intent on making lawyers look afresh at humanitarian intervention and that it is constructive to look at his views on their merits as a legislative proposal. A preliminary point to be made is the unprepossessing character of the historical evidence: the near impossibility of discovering an aptitude of governments in general for carefully moderated, altruistic, and genuine interventions to protect human rights. What follows is concerned with humanitarian intervention *as it would be practiced* on the basis of existing evidence of behavior patterns. Naturally, the moral setting, even in genuine cases, is far from simple. There is a moral and legislative problem of the type raised by euthanasia, itself a form of "humanitarian intervention." Euthanasia is unlawful, but doctors on occasion commit technical breaches of the law, for example, by administering massive drug dosages which accelerate coma and death. It is very generally assumed that legalizing euthanasia would alter the moral climate and produce harmful abuse.

Particularly when considering policy issues, attention should be paid to the actual behavior of states. Reference to the behavior of states before 1920, or 1945, on the premise that in the practice of that time one can find models of humanitarian intervention, involves a failure to see the development of the law as a whole. Before 1945, matters of human rights were, apart from treaty, within the domestic jurisdiction of states. When the League Covenant was drafted, modest Japanese proposals concerning racial and religious discrimination received no support. Guarantees concerning minorities were imposed only on defeated states and new states, such as Poland, as the price of recognition. It is surprising to expect a worthwhile doctrine of intervention to protect human rights at a time when the most modest proposals not for implementing but for merely setting of standards were struck down as threats to domestic jurisdiction. * * * [D]omestic jurisdiction is much less of a shield than it was in 1920 in matters of human rights. The question remains whether state conduct in administering intervention unilaterally has improved since the period before the League and the United Nations. Is it the case that the performance of individual states is and would be better than the centralized enforcement and other measures available to the United Nations? The latter is certainly unreliable, but is the alternative more reliable? I am accused of "throwing the baby out with the bath water" by adopting a cautious attitude to intervention to protect human rights, but my view is that those making novel proposals need to produce more evidence. What is the price in *human terms* of intervention? What were the casualty ratios in the Stanleyville operation in 1964, the Dominican Republic in 1965, and other possible examples? How many were killed in order to "save lives?" To what extent does the typical intervention cause collateral harms by exacerbating a civil war, introducing indiscriminate use of air power in support operations, and so on? Was there a policy of pacification and general involvement, together with extraction of concessions by treaty or otherwise as the price of withdrawal?

Since a part of Lillich's argument is based on the *essence* of state practice, *i.e.*, on what it was really about, aside from the existence of some formal title to intervention, one can also look at the evidence in his way. The *general* picture, as others may see it, is not encouraging. In the years of Stanleyville and the landings in the Dominican Republic, there were far more serious and persistent threats to human rights which were ignored. In 1965, not less than 300,000 persons of Chinese origin were murdered in Indonesia. The facts were well reported in the world press. The regime responsible received massive material support from several governments, including a million-pound-sterling credit from the United Kingdom. The whole field is driven by political expediency and capriciousness. One area of human rights in which there is a strong consensus in the United Nations is racial discrimination and especially the practice of *apartheid*. The United States has shown caution in supporting even mandatory economic sanctions against South Africa through the Security Council. Moreover, human rights is a category which can provide good public relations for national policies. In the Western Hemisphere, concern for human rights sharpened considerably after the change of regime in Cuba in 1959.

There are other, more precise, considerations of policy. A major issue, unexplored by the ILA subcommittee, is the whole question of the use of force in community relations. The situation in Ulster, the desegregation issue in the United States, and comparable problems in many countries, cannot be "solved" by a use of force. Community relations can be policed in a crude sense; massacres can be prevented. The wrong kind of intervention and the drawing of police lines, however, may increase alienation, worsen community relations, and produce new problems. A further point of great importance is the extent to which the position of minorities is hazarded by foreign protection or sponsorship. There is a good deal of literature, ignored by the ILA subcommittee, on the working of the League of Nations machinery for the protection of minorities. Even when the supervision was through international machinery and was not very demanding, it was felt by many commentators that the position of "minority" groups within the state was invidious by reason of their partly externalized status.

6. The Value of Proto–Legal Guidelines

The ILA subcommittee's Report recapitulates five standards formulated by Professor John Norton Moore which can be used in evaluating the legitimacy of a putative humanitarian intervention. They are as follows: "(1) An immediate and extensive threat to fundamental human rights, particularly a threat of widespread loss of human life; (2) A proportional use of forces which does not threaten greater destruction of values than the human rights at stake; (3) A minimal effect on authority structures; (4) A prompt disengagement, consistent with the purpose of the action; and (5) Immediate full reporting to the Security Council and appropriate regional organizations." Nanda and Lillich have offered criteria which are similar but include the existence of an invitation by the recognized government and the relative disinterestedness of the intervening state or states. If an invitation to intervene has been made, then the action would be lawful on any view. Apart from that and consistent with my own view of the law, I would regard such criteria as of value, as providing (a) good criteria should humanitarian intervention become a part of the law, and (b) a fine basis for a political plea in mitigation in parliaments, U.N. organs, and regional organizations. My e[u]thanasia parallel applies here: a defense lawyer and a court still need to distinguish the false from the genuine case, as a matter of mitigation.

7. Definition of Intervention to Protect Human Rights

A subject not taken up by the ILA subcommittee is the isolation of "intervention situations." Obviously, they do not extend to all violations. Professor Moore refers to "an immediate and extensive threat to fundamental human rights, particularly a widespread loss of human life." Oppenheim (edited by Hersch Lauterpacht) gives apparent approbation to intervention "when a state renders itself guilty of cruelties against and persecution of its nationals in such a way as to deny their fundamental human rights and to shock the conscience of mankind." Since a good number of states qualify in this way every decade, the opportunities for intervention will be very many. It is also the case that only a few powerful states will have a choice of voluntary intervention of this kind. Nearly every legal issue may raise a problem of definition, but few are on this scale. It is significant that governments are commonly more cautious than writers in giving currency to vaguely formulated and easily abused excuses for unilateral action. In the Cuban missile crisis, the United States Department of State avoided reference to the somewhat fugitive concept of anticipatory self-defense and chose to use a justification related to the Organization of American States as a regional arrangement. Various states have neighbors playing host to intermediate-range ballistic missiles, just as they may have neighbors guilty of cruelties which may shock the conscience of mankind. "Realism" in the sphere of policy includes restraint and caution in state policy * * *.

9.   Concluding Remarks

My general position is clear and general recapitulation is unhelpful. But a few points may be made by way of emphasis. The position taken up by Lillich is completely outside the general consensus of state practice and the opinion of experts of various nationalities. In the Sixth Committee of the General Assembly, when Spiropoulos once stated that intervention to prevent genocide against a racially related minority in a neighboring state should be lawful, the reaction from other delegates, including those of Israel, Nationalist China, and Panama, was unfavorable. A development proximate to a concept of humanitarian intervention is the support by some members of the United Nations, including most members of the O.A.U., for the view that intervention against a liberation movement is unlawful and assistance to such a movement is lawful. It is common knowledge that there is no consensus on this as yet in the United Nations.

I am in favor of humanitarian intervention, *i.e.*, effective implementation of human rights, in conditions in which this can occur within the law and when the methods and circumstances of the operation do not lead to results which bear no positive relation to the original objective, even assuming it to be genuine. What I find depressing is the absence of evidence that proponents of humanitarian intervention and other very plastic doctrines have spent much time examining state practice in detail. This should be essential for those concerned with policy. * * *

Richard Lillich, Humanitarian Intervention: A Reply to Ian Brownlie and a Plea for Constructive Alternatives

LAW AND CIVIL WAR IN MODERN WORLD 229–
233, 235–251 (J.N. Moore, ed. 1974).*

The preceding [essay] by Ian Brownlie represents another welcomed contribution to the current debate on the contemporary relevance of the doctrine of humanitarian intervention. As could be expected of one of the leading advocates of the view that Article 2(4) of the United Nations Charter absolutely prohibits forcible self-help by States, save in cases of individual or collective self-defense against armed attack authorized by Article 51, [Brownlie] . . . reaches the categorical conclusion that "unilateral action by a State in the territory of another State on the ground that human rights require protection, or a threat of force against a State for

* Footnotes omitted.

this reason, is unlawful." Somewhat unexpectedly, however, he finds the present writer's criteria for judging the legitimacy of a state's use of forcible self-help for humanitarian purposes of some value, if only "as providing a fine basis for a political plea in mitigation in parliaments, U.N. organs, and regional organizations." Indeed, by twice citing a supposed parallel between euthanasia and humanitarian intervention, a parallel one hopes he will develop more fully in his subsequent writings, Brownlie seems to suggest that some such interventions, while technically breaches of Article 2(4), might be condoned, if not actually approved, by the world community.

I. Pre–Charter Practice

* * *

A cursory perusal of Chapter I ("Humanitarian Intervention") of Dean Ganji's *International Protection of Human Rights*, standard work not included in Brownlie's references, reveals many cases where interventions occurred for humanitarian purposes. In addition to the intervention of 1860 by Austria, France, Great Britain, Prussia, and Russia in Syria, acknowledged somewhat grudgingly by Brownlie as "one possibly genuine example of altruistic action," Ganji lists the following instances:

1. The intervention of France, Great Britain, and Russia against the Turkish massacres and suppression of the Greeks, which resulted in the independence of Greece in 1830;

2. The peremptory demands of Austria, France, Italy, Prussia, and Russia (during the years 1866–68) on the Ottoman Empire for the institution of positive action leading to the betterment of the lot of the persecuted Christian population of Crete;

3. The Russian intervention against Turkey (1877–78) on the occasion of insurrections resulting from Turkish misrule and from the outrageous persecutions of the Christian populations of Bosnia, Herzegovina, and Bulgaria; and

4. The intervention of Austria, Russia, Great Britain, Italy, and France in Turkey as a result of insurrections and misrule in Macedonia (1903–8).

Moreover, to these cases of humanitarian intervention he adds "many instances of humanitarian protest and representation by one or more states on behalf of the citizens of other states." While apparently ignoring the implications of his own investigations, Ganji surprisingly concludes that "the doctrine of humanitarian intervention *does not seem* [emphasis added] to claim the authority of a customary rule of international law," he frankly concedes that this view is a minority one by acknowledging that the doctrine "claims the authority of such jurists as Grotius, Vattel, Wheaton,

Heiberg, Woolsey, Bluntschli, Westlake, Rougeer, Arntz, Winfield, Stowell, Borchard and many others."

* * *

II.   Post–Charter Practice * * *

While the Charter contains no provision authorizing unilateral or collective humanitarian intervention by States, neither does it specifically abolish the traditional doctrine. Actually, despite Dr. Brownlie's vigorous objection, it warrants reiteration that "[t]he drafters of the Charter ... paid no attention to whether these doctrines [of protection of nationals and humanitarian intervention] were to survive the *Charter*...." One therefore may accept as common ground Brownlie's contention "that it is impossible to place any form of intervention in the context of the law without examining the legal regime *as a whole*," while rejecting his conclusion that the Charter and subsequent practice thereunder absolutely forbids intervention for humanitarian purposes by a state or a group of states.

Examining the United Nations Charter "as a whole," it is apparent that its two major purposes are the maintenance of peace and the protection of human rights. Article 2(4), the Charter provision relevant to both these purposes, prohibits "the threat or use of force against the territorial integrity or political independence of any State, or in any other manner inconsistent with the Purposes of the United Nations." Since humanitarian interventions by states, far from being inconsistent with Charter purposes, actually may further one of the world organization's major objectives in many situations, such interventions run afoul of Article 2(4) only if they are thought to affect the "territorial integrity" or "political independence" of the state against which they are directed. Brownlie, adopting what one commentator has called "an arid textualist approach," considers all humanitarian interventions by States to have such an effect and hence to violate the Charter. Taking what Professor Stone has labeled "the extreme view" of Article 2(4), Brownlie rejects out-of-hand Stone's argument that what the article prohibits is not all threats or uses of force, but only those actions specifically directed against "the territorial integrity" or "political independence" of a state. "This argument," Brownlie states, "is used by very few lawyers and has long been discredited."

Stone's view is a minority one, admittedly, but, far from being "discredited," it seems to be gaining new recruits annually, at least insofar as humanitarian intervention is concerned. While the present writer agrees with Brownlie that "[c]ounting heads is not, of course, a sound way of resolving issues of principle" in view of the thirteen authorities Brownlie cites in his attempt to demonstrate that humanitarian intervention by states violates the United Nations Charter, a few contrary authorities should be mentioned here. First and foremost among these scholars is McDougal who, several years ago, reassessing his earlier position, acknowledged that

> I'm ashamed to confess that at one time I lent my support to the suggestion that article 2(4) and the related articles did preclude the use of self-help less than self-defense. On reflection, I think this was a very grave mistake, that article 2(4) and article 51 must be interpreted differently.... In the absence of collective machinery to protect against attack and deprivation, I would suggest that the principle of major purposes requires an interpretation which would honor self-help against prior unlawfulness. The principle of subsequent conduct certainly confirms this. Many states of the world have used force in situations short of the requirements of self-defense to protect their national interests.

In collaboration with Reisman, he subsequently utilized this revised approach to justify non-United Nations intervention to prevent serious human rights deprivations. Brownlie casually dismisses their conclusions on the ground that McDougal and Reisman "lean heavily on a flexible and teleological interpretation of treaty texts," but surely the convincing arguments they marshall, and which Brownlie in large measure chooses to ignore, deserve consideration.

In the first place, it should be noted that the above approach to humanitarian intervention is conditioned upon "the absence of collective machinery" to protect human rights, not upon a preference for unilateral over collective intervention. Effective United Nations action remains everyone's goal. The real issue, which Brownlie largely ignores, ... is whether, absent such action in serious human-rights deprivation cases, states today must sit by and do nothing merely because Article 2(4) arguably was intended by its drafters in 1945 to preclude unilateral humanitarian interventions. Doctrinal analysis of Article 2(4), much of it written shortly after the Charter's adoption or based upon attitudes and expectations formed during the immediate post-war period, frequently fails to mention that, to the extent that states consciously relinquished the right to use forcible self-help, they took such action under the assumption that the collective implementation measures envisaged by Chapter VII soon would be available. Yet even staunch supporters of the collective approach, such as Judge Jessup, admitted that unilateral humanitarian interventions might be permissible if the United Nations lacked the capacity to act speedily * * *.

Reisman, who accepts the Stone thesis that the United Nations Charter does not absolutely rule out forcible self-help, acknowledges however, that, as a historical interpretation, the contrary view espoused by Brownlie and other writers is "quite accurate."

> From the standpoint of the contemporary needs of the international community, however, it is clearly outmoded. Only in the most exceptional cases will the United Nations be capable of functioning as an international enforcer; in the vast majority of cases, the conflicting interests of diverse public order systems will block any action. A rational and contemporary interpretation of the Charter must conclude that article 2(4) suppresses self-help insofar as the organization can assume the role of enforcer. When it cannot, self-help prerogatives revive.

As the above extract reveals * * * Reisman regards the right as conditional. Hence his statement that, given the present status of the United Nations, "self-help prerogatives revive," and his correlative comment elsewhere about "the partial suspension of the full thrust of Article 2(4)." * * * Reisman's approach ... clearly contemplates the gradual phasing out of the doctrine as the United Nations develops the capacity and the will to act in such situations.

In addition to being conditional, the McDougal–Reisman approach to humanitarian intervention relies upon a major-purposes construction of the Charter, under which the protection of human rights is accorded equal weight with the maintenance of peace. As mentioned above, this construction would permit humanitarian intervention by states despite Article 2(4) when such intervention was consistent with human rights objectives. "A close reading of [Article 2(4)] will indicate that the prohibition is not against the use of coercion per se," Reisman * * * has observed, "but rather the use of force for specified unlawful means. . . ." He continues:

> Since a humanitarian intervention seeks neither a territorial change nor a challenge to the political independence of the state involved and is not only not inconsistent with the Purposes of the United Nations but is rather in conformity with the most fundamental peremptory norms of the Charter, it is distortion to argue that it is precluded by Article 2(4). Insofar as it is precipitated by intense human rights deprivations and conforms to the general international legal regulations governing the use of force—economy, timeliness, commensurance, lawfulness of purpose and so on—it represents a vindication of international law, and is, in fact, substitute or functional enforcement.

Although this construction of Article 2(4) has been called an exercise in "doctrinal manipulation" by Farer, it at least merits more examination than it has received from Brownlie.

The latter * * * adopts a rather fatalistic attitude toward the human-rights deprivations his rigid construction of Article 2(4) tolerates. * * * Unlike Friedmann, who comes to the same result but finds it "a painful conclusion to reach," there is little evidence that Brownlie has contemplated the costs in terms of life and dignity his construction of the Charter demands. Other authorities, including several cited by Brownlie to support his absolute view of Article 2(4), have made careful cost-benefit analyses, and have concluded that Article 2(4) does not constitute an absolute prohibition against all unilateral humanitarian interventions. Among the contemporary commentators taking this position, in addition to McDougal, Reisman, Stone, and the present writer, are the following: Alford, Goldie, Lauterpacht, J. N. Moore, Nanda, Perez–Vera, Roling, Thapa, and Verzijl.

Finally, the McDougal–Reisman approach to humanitarian intervention, conditioned upon the absence of collective action and otherwise consistent with major purposes of the Charter, receives substantial support from the conduct of states and the response of the United Nations itself during the post-Charter period. Granted that this pattern of conduct falls far short of a consensus approving the doctrine, neither is it "totally inadequate to the task of establishing an interpretation in terms of subsequent conduct of the parties favorable to intervention to protect human rights." Indeed, only one holding an exceptionally narrow view of international law and relations would conclude, as Brownlie does, that "[t]he period of the United Nations Charter is totally lacking in practice on the point." By ruling arbitrarily that certain state conduct does not constitute practice and by ignoring completely the implications to be drawn from certain decisions (or non-decisions) of the United Nations during the past decade, he adopts the posture commonly attributed to the ostrich.

Without examining once again the Stanleyville rescue operation * * * it is worth considering what that operation and the ensuing United Nations debate generated by it reveal about the world community's attitude toward humanitarian intervention claims twenty years after the Charter's enactment. While African accusations in the United Nations against the intervening states—Belgium, Britain, and the United States—occasionally bordered on the slanderous, they generally were grounded upon the political rather than the legal aspects of the case. Thus even the Sudanese representative observed that "[i]n normal circumstances, it would be difficult to oppose a rescue operation for humanitarian purposes." The debate does show, as Higgins concludes, that "the international community is reluctant to approve such interventions," but it also is noted that, in the vague Resolution finally adopted by the Security Council "*[d]eploring* the recent events in [the Democratic Republic of the Congo], [t]he concept of humanitarian intervention was not mentioned, and Belgium, and the

United States received no official condemnation." Indeed, a recent student notewriter suggests that the Resolution constitutes an implied if not an express approval of the operation: "After the Congo debates, the legal principle of Article 2(4) remains, but what that Article means has been altered by political evolution. There is now an unwillingness on the part of the world community to read Article 2(4) as an absolute prohibition on the use of force in humanitarian intervention."

One must be careful, of course, not to overclarify the outcome of the above decision (or non-decision) of the United Nations. Moreover, other actions of the United Nations, such as the adoption of a broad non-intervention principle in the recently-adopted Declaration on Principles of International Law Concerning Friendly Relations and Co–Operation among States in Accordance with the Charter of the United Nations, cut against the implied approval thesis advanced by the above notewriter. Nevertheless, the fact that neither the Stanleyville rescue operation nor any other claimed humanitarian intervention has been condemned by the United Nations as a violation of Article 2(4), in marked contrast to its repeated condemnation of claims to use forcible self-help by way of reprisals, throws considerable light upon the world community's attitude toward humanitarian interventions today. At the very least, this practice shows that such interventions might be considered condonable in appropriate instances, a view kited by Brownlie that warrants serious study.

III.   A Plea for Constructive Alternatives

It is common ground between Brownlie and most authorities, including the present writer, that humanitarian interventions by the United Nations are preferable to such interventions by individual states. As he rightly observes, "[u]nder Chapter VII of the Charter, action may be taken in instances of violations of human rights which give rise to a threat to the peace." Moreover, other authorities, such as Ermacora, contend that, under recent United Nations resolutions, gross or consistent patterns of violations of human rights "are no longer essentially within the domestic jurisdiction of States, and therefore the principle of non-intervention is not applicable." Unfortunately, despite the fact that these jurisdictional bases for remedial action by the world organization exist, "[a] model which accords primary competence to the United Nations to intervene for humanitarian purposes does not ... reflect the present conditions of the [international] system." A combination of the failure to establish a permanent international military force and the existence of the veto power, records Friedmann, has "effectively destroyed the power of the United Nations to act as an organ of enforcement of international law against a potential lawbreaker." He thus reaches the pessimistic conclusion that, like it or not, in the immediate future "the effective power of using military or lesser forms of coercion in international affairs essentially remains with the nation States."

Brownlie, apparently living in what Reisman has dubbed "the paper world of the Charter," considers humanitarian interventions by the United Nations to be more reliable than such interventions by individual states. It is difficult, if not impossible, to find support for this view in the events of the past decade. In the case of the Stanleyville rescue operation, for example, the United Nations failed to take effective action during a four-month period between the seizure of the hostages and the airdrop by the intervening states. At about the same time, as Brownlie himself points out, "there were far more serious and persistent threats to human rights which were ignored. In 1965, not less than 300,000 persons of Chinese origin were murdered in Indonesia." Yet the United Nations and its Member States, supporting his observation that "[t]he whole field is driven by political expediency and capriciousness," did nothing. The dismal failure of the United Nations with respect to Bangladesh is too recent to need recounting. From these instances and others one is compelled to conclude that, at the very least, "the prospects for effective United Nations actions are presently weak." Indeed, without overstatement, they may be said to be almost nonexistent.

Given this bleak outlook, one would have thought that Brownlie and other proponents of the view that humanitarian interventions are permissible only when undertaken by the United Nations would have turned their attention to strengthening its capacity to respond in such situations. At the very least, one would have expected from them a body of literature canvassing the difficulties and suggesting possible solutions to the obvious procedural defects, such as the absence of a standby international expeditionary force, and the presence of the veto power, both of which must be remedied before effective and uniform humanitarian interventions by the United Nations can become a reality. One especially would have welcomed serious examination of the conventional wisdom which places collective interventions in a preferred position over unilateral ones. Yet the writings of Brownlie and like-minded authorities make no mention of these problems. Likewise, they are wholly devoid of constructive alternatives to the admittedly "unreliable" response by the United Nations. Brownlie's message in the preceding chapter, for instance, amounts to no more than a plea to keep the "faith in collective action. * * *"

If, as Falk has remarked, "the renunciation of intervention does not substitute a policy of nonintervention; it involves the development of some form of collective intervention," then concomitantly the failure to develop effective international machinery to facilitate humanitarian interventions arguably permits a state to intervene unilaterally in appropriate situations. Writing a decade ago, Ronning wisely observed that "it is as useless to outlaw intervention without providing a satisfactory substitute as it was to outlaw war when no satisfactory substitute was available...."

If, as seems to be the case, "a simple prohibition to intervene is unable to cope with the problem of intervention," then surely, as the present writer noted some years ago, the most important task confronting international lawyers is "to clarify the various criteria by which the legitimacy of a state's use of forcible self-help in human rights situations can be judged." Nanda, taking this approach, has suggested five such criteria: (1) a specific limited purpose; (2) an invitation by the recognized government; (3) a limited duration of the mission; and (4) a limited use of coercive measures; and (5) a lack of any other recourse. Occasionally overlapping these criteria but also including several additional ones, the present writer has recommended elsewhere his own five tests by which a unilateral humanitarian intervention should be judged: (1) the immediacy of the violation of human rights; (2) the extent of the violation of human rights; (3) the existence of an invitation by appropriate authorities; (4) the degree of coercive measures employed; and (5) the relative disinterestedness of the state invoking the coercive measures. Moreover, Moore has suggested three further criteria: "a minimal effect on authority structures, a prompt disengagement consistent with the purpose of the action, and immediate full reporting to the Security Council and appropriate regional organizations."

Brownlie, invoking an analogy to euthanasia, the legalizing of which he assumes "would alter the moral climate and pro[duce] harmful abuse," rejects the above criteria as determinants of legitimacy, but accepts them as

> a fine basis for a political plea in mitigation in parliaments, U. N. organs, and regional organizations. My euthanasia parallel applies here: a defence lawyer and a court still need to distinguish the false from the genuine case, as a matter of mitigation.

* * * Brownlie [thus] seems to have reached the camp of those authors who, "deny the legality of humanitarian intervention in law, but who condone it to a greater or less degree in practice." Whether one regards humanitarian interventions as legal if they meet the various criteria recommended above, or whether one considers them illegal de jure, yet condonable de facto, if they satisfy the selfsame criteria, seems to the present writer of more jurisprudential than practical importance. Like Falk, who while condemning reprisals nevertheless has worked out a systematic framework for the assessment of claims to use retaliatory force, Brownlie apparently believes that the above criteria, largely based upon the traditional doctrine of humanitarian intervention, are acceptable illustrations of "a kind of second-order level of legal

inquiry that is guided by the more permissive attitudes toward the use of force to uphold national interests that is contained in customary international law." Under this highly sophisticated approach, subsequently adopted and developed by Bowett, numerous criteria are formulated which, when met by a state taking unilateral action, may prevent its running afoul of the United Nations Security Council. The Security's Council's recent resolution which avoids condemning India for its invasion of East Pakistan (now Bangladesh) might be considered an example of this "second-order legality" approach. The parallel to Brownlie's euthanasia analogy is obvious.

If the present writer has not overclarified Brownlie's position, it would appear that, at least as to outcome, there is actually little difference between their views. While this writer prefers a doctrinal approach which forthrightly sanctions unilateral humanitarian interventions when they meet detailed criteria to one which unqualifiedly proscribes such interventions but condones them when compatible with the selfsame criteria, he nevertheless welcomes Brownlie's tentative contribution to the current debate on humanitarian intervention. Hopefully, in his subsequent writings, Brownlie will give serious consideration not only to refining the above criteria, for whatever purposes they may be of use, but also to establishing procedures under which humanitarian interventions through the United Nations someday may take place. Both Reisman's Protocol of Procedure for Humanitarian Intervention and Senator Edward Kennedy's proposal for an Emergency Relief Force may be too ambitious for today's fragmented world community, but these and other innovative recommendations certainly deserve more attention than they have received to date. Granted that most international lawyers have been remiss in their failure to address such procedural problems, Brownlie and other authorities critical of unilateral humanitarian intervention have a special obligation to respond to this plea for constructive alternatives.

Nehal Bhuta, "Paved with Good Intentions..."— Humanitarian War, the New Interventionism and Legal Regulation of the Use of Force

Review Essay, 25 MELB. U. L. REV. 843 (2001).*

* * *

Dr Chesterman [contends in *Just War or Just Peace? Humanitarian Intervention and International Law* (2001)] * * * that the collective security framework of the UN Charter should be defend-

---

* *Reviewing* SIMON CHESTERMAN, JUST WAR INTERNATIONAL LAW (2001).
OR JUST PEACE? HUMANITARIAN INTERVENTION AND

ed, precisely because it seems ultimately more likely to preserve a thin rule of law in international affairs than any "right" of unilateral intervention wielded selectively by powerful states.

* * *

Article 2(4) of the UN Charter proscribes the threat or use of force against the territorial integrity or political independence of states, or in any other manner inconsistent with the purposes of the United Nations, subject only to the inherent right of self-defence. Chapters VI and VII of the Charter confer primary (if not exclusive) authority to authorise non-defensive uses of force on the Security Council, which is charged with supervising the maintenance of international peace and security. The Charter framework is accepted as inaugurating a new era in the legal regulation of the use of force, and would seem to resolve the ambiguity of unilateral "humanitarian intervention" on the side of illegality: unless defensive or authorised by the Security Council, an armed attack against a state's territorial integrity or political sovereignty is prohibited. This reading of the plain words of the Charter was confirmed by the International Court of Justice in the Corfu Channel and Nicaragua cases. In Corfu Channel, the Court rejected any right of unilateral intervention (even as a reprisal), while in Nicaragua it opined that the prohibition on the use of force was a jus cogens norm, violation of which

> could not be the appropriate method to monitor or ensure [respect for human rights]. * * * The Court concludes that the argument derived from the preservation of human rights in Nicaragua cannot afford a legal justification for the conduct of the United States * * *.

Some of the closest legal argument in Dr Chesterman's work is his convincing refutation of scholars who propound a narrow reading of article 2(4) in an effort to render it compatible with a purported right of humanitarian intervention. Put simply, their contention is that article 2(4) does not prohibit force which is not used to usurp another state's territory or impose alien rule upon its peoples, or which is used to promote one of the purposes of the United Nations. The argument has a superficial attraction, but is a specious reading of the relevant Charter provisions. As Dr Chesterman demonstrates, the intention of the drafters as discerned from the travaux préparatories was to prohibit the use of force in the broadest possible terms, so as to render trans-border armed attacks illegal. To suggest that armed attacks which do not seize territory or colonise a state are not against that state's "territorial integrity nor political independence" is to adopt a construction worthy of Orwellian Newspeak. Similarly, the words "or in any other manner inconsistent with the Purposes of the United Nations" is revealed to have been inserted not to create new exceptions to the prohibition of the use of force, but as a residual phrase to ensure an "absolute all-inclusive prohibition; the phrase 'or in any other manner' was designed to insure that there should be no loopholes." In any event, while the promotion of human rights through "international cooperation" is to be found among the purposes of the United Nations, the first listed purpose in article 1 is the maintenance of international peace and security through the prevention and removal of threats to the peace, the suppression of breaches of the peace, and the peaceful settlement of disputes. While it is uncontestable that violations of internationally recognised human rights cannot be claimed to fall exclusively within the domestic jurisdiction of states, it does not follow that hortatory statements concerning human rights protection within the Charter provide any legal basis for the unilateral use of force to prevent human rights abuses. In the absence of a Security Council resolution authorising force under Chapter VII, the Charter envisages the promotion of human rights protection through the monitoring function of various subsidiary organs, such as the Economic and Social Council and the Commission on Human Rights.

The post-Charter state practice and opinio juris reviewed by Dr Chesterman also appear to lack the "consistent and widespread" character required by prevailing theories to establish a new norm of customary international law. Indeed, the three conflicts most commonly cited as clear instances of bona fide humanitarian intervention—Indian intervention in East Pakistan, Vietnamese intervention in Kampuchea and Tanzanian intervention in Uganda—are shown to have been justified by the intervening state as cases of self-defence or protection of nationals. The international community's reaction to the Indian and Tanzanian interventions was to affirm their respective rights to self-defence while calling for a cessation of hostilities; in neither case was there approval for a "right" to use force to stop grave human rights abuses.

In the case of Vietnam's invasion of Kampuchea, international reaction (led by the United States and China) was positively hostile. While proposed Security Council resolutions condemning Vietnam failed due to a Soviet veto, numerous states condemned the action as an illegal use of force in violation of the principle of non-intervention. States uniformly rejected the argument that ending the Khmer Rouge's genocide could have justified the invasion (although Vietnam never expressly relied upon this rationale), with the United Kingdom, for example, stating, "[w]hatever may be said about human rights in Kampuchea, it cannot excuse Viet Nam, whose own human rights record is deplorable, for violating the territorial integrity of Democratic Kampuchea." The General Assembly refused to recognise the representative of the Vietnamese-installed regime, allowing the Khmer Rouge to continue to occupy Kampuchea's seat in the Assembly until 1990.

Genuinely "humanitarian" interventions, then, are difficult to find: where states expressly profess humanitarian intentions, non-humanitarian reasons seem more significant; where interventions actually do terminate genocide or crimes against humanity, they are not justified, or accepted, as evincing a "right" to do so. A cautious analysis of the state practice and opinio juris leads Dr Chesterman to conclude that unilateral "humanitarian intervention" remains an inchoate principle, occasionally tolerated by states without being endorsed. In the cases of Tanzania and India, the international community reacted consistently with the norm of non-intervention, but imposed no countermeasures, which suggests one way of understanding humanitarian intervention is not so much as a "right", but as illegal conduct which is tolerated by the international community in extreme circumstances.

C.   NOTES, QUESTIONS, AND PROBLEMS

1.   In requiring that a use of force be for defense international law seems to return to the just war doctrine where a "right intention" was a requirement. The ICJ in the Corfu Channel Case does indeed consider the purpose or intention of the acts of the UK and Albania. What is the role of intention according to the Oil Platforms Court? What difficulty is presented by a requirement of right intention in the law of self-defense? Can you think of a way to manage the problem and still ensure that the lawful use of force in self-defense is for defense and not other purposes rejected by society?

2.   If force in self-defense may be used for defense only, it follows that force used for other purposes, even after an armed attack would be unlawful. The General Assembly has in fact prohibited the use of armed reprisals. Reprisals are armed attacks for punishment, revenge, or even deterrence rather than self-defense. According to General Assembly Declaration on Principles of International Law Concerning Friendly Relations and Cooperation Among States in Accordance with the Charter of the United Nations 1970, "States have a duty to refrain from acts of reprisal involving the use of force." GA Res. 2625 (XXV), U.N. GAOR, 25th Sess., Supp. No. 28, XXV, U.N. Doc. A/8018 (1970). *See also* the Corfu Channel Case (U.K. v. Alb.), 1949 I.C.J. 4, 108–09.

3.   On September 11, 2001, hijackers commandeered three commercial passenger jets and flew or attempted to fly them against targets in the United States. The World Trade Center in New York and the Pentagon were struck. Were these "armed attacks" that could give rise to the right of self-defense? What further facts must you have to answer the question? Where can you find these facts? Refer again to the Notes and Questions at the end of Chapter One. Does the discussion of self-defense help you answer the question whether war can lawfully be waged against terrorism?

4.   The requirement that a state take action only against the responsible party raises the issue of evidence. In some cases a state may have only a certain amount of evidence of who the responsible party is, rather than actual knowledge. Must a state have actual knowledge? If not, how good must the evidence be? Beyond a reasonable doubt? Clear and convincing? Or just enough to carry the burden of persuasion? What evidentiary standard was the ICJ imposing in Corfu Channel, Nicaragua and Oil Platforms? For an argument that clear and convincing evidence is crystallizing as the standard in international law, *see,* Mary Ellen O'Connell, *Evidence of Terror,* 7 J. OF CONFLICT & SEC'Y L. 19 (2002). For more on the Oil Platforms Case, see *Symposium: Reflections on the ICJ's Oil Platform Decision,* 29 YALE J. INT'L L. 291 (2004).

5. If a state is using its best effort to stop terrorists on its territory, it should not be held responsible for their attacks. If it is not responsible for the attacks, the territorial state should not be the target of armed measures of self-defense. Do you agree? What else can a state do when it is the victim of a terrorist attack but has no right to respond in self-defense?

6. Is it consistent with the United Nations Charter to create a treaty giving one state the right to use force against another regardless of armed attack, Security Council authorization, or consent at the time? Consider the following case:

> * * * Violence exploded throughout Cyprus on Christmas Eve 1963 * * *. The Turkish Prime Minister responded to the Cyprus crisis by announcing that Turkey would intervene unilaterally under article IV of the Treaty of Guarantee between Cyprus, Greece, Turkey and the United Kingdom. By that treaty—one of the package of accords concluded in 1960 when Cyprus became independent—Cyprus undertook to ensure "respect for its Constitution"; and Greece, Turkey, and the United Kingdom "recognized and guaranteed" not only "the independence, territorial integrity and security of the Republic of Cyprus," but also the "state of affairs established by the basic Articles of the [Cypriot] Constitution." Intervention in the wake of the Turkish Prime Minister's announcement was confined to a single warning flight of jet fighters. On March 12, 1964, Turkey again threatened to invade Cyprus under article IV unless "all . . . assaults . . . against the Turkish community in Cyprus . . . [are] stopped . . . [and] an immediate cease-fire . . . [is] established. . . ." Turkey backed away from that threat under strong Security Council pressure. But she refused to be restrained five months later when Cypriot Government forces attacked several Turkish Cypriot villages in the northwest corner of the Island. On August 7 and 8, 1964, the Turkish Air Force bombed the attackers, causing substantial loss of life to many unarmed civilians as well as to Greek Cypriot forces.
>
> From the outset, the Turkish legal case for intervention in Cyprus was based on a key sentence in article IV of the Treaty of Guarantee: "In so far as common or concerted action may not prove possible, each of the three guaranteeing Powers reserves the right to take action with the sole aim of re-

establishing the state of affairs created by the present Treaty."

Thomas Ehrlich, *The Measuring Line of Occasion*, *in* 2 THE VIETNAM WAR AND INTERNATIONAL LAW 1050 (Richard Falk ed., 1968)(footnotes omitted.)

7. Consider the pros and cons of permitting intervention in internal armed conflict by invitation. Consider such issues as what impact might such a rule have on the Charter regime regulating resort to force? If such intervention is permitted, who should have the authority to issue the invitation? If it is a government in effective control of territory, how much territory must it control? What if effective control of most territory is lost while the outside intervenor is participating in the conflict? Must it leave? For further reading on intervention in internal armed conflict, see QUINCY WRIGHT, THE INTERNATIONAL LAW OF CIVIL WAR (Richard A. Falk ed., 1971).

8. Consider the pros and cons of permitting unilateral intervention in humanitarian crises. Again, what impact will such a rule have on the Charter regime for regulating resort to force? Do you think Lillich's approach is workable? Can you identify any successful examples of unilateral humanitarian intervention? If so, how do you define success in such a case? Few if any authors consider the potential success of humanitarian intervention, though much has been written on the general subject. For further reading on humanitarian intervention, see SEAN MURPHY, HUMANITARIAN INTERVENTION: THE UNITED NATIONS IN AN EVOLVING WORLD (1996); Dino Kritsiotis, *Reappraising Policy Objections to Humanitarian Intervention*, 19 MICH. J. INT'L LAW 1005 (1998); FERNANDO R. TESÓN, HUMANITARIAN INTERVENTION: AN INQUIRY INTO LAW AND MORALITY 151 (2d ed., 1996); ANTHONY CLARK AREND AND ROBERT J. BECK, INTERNATIONAL LAW AND THE USE OF FORCE: BEYOND THE UN CHARTER PARADIGM (1993).

9. **Problem**: In the Nicaragua Case, the ICJ said it would not address the question of the right to use force in the face of an imminent threat, because it was called upon to consider only actual armed attacks. Thus, it left open a much debated question, whether Article 51 permits the use of force in self-defense when an armed attack is imminent or only when it is actually occurring. Greenwood writes, "Academic opinion on this question is divided. Brownlie, Gray and Henkin, among others, have argued that there is no right of self-defense until an armed attack has actually commenced. Dinstein also rejects anticipatory self-defense but accepts that there is a right of 'interceptive self-defense', where a State has 'committed itself to an armed attack in an ostensibly irrevocable way', an approach that differs but little from that in the Caroline case. On the other hand, * * * Franck * * *, Waldock, Fitzmaurice, Bowett, Schwebel, and Jennings and Watts have all argued that there is a right of anticipatory self-defense against an imminent armed attack." Christopher Greenwood, *International Law and the Pre–Emptive Use of Force: Afghanistan, Al–Qaida, and Iraq*, 4 SAN DIEGO INT'L L.J. 7 (2003).

Review the Caroline Case (pp. 121–123), the drafting history of the Charter in Chapter Six, the Charter text, and the cases in this Chapter. Develop arguments for and against the right of anticipatory self-defense. Consult the Vienna Convention on the Law of Treaties on how to interpret a treaty.

CHAPTER EIGHT

COLLECTIVE ACTION

In discussing unilateral action, we also discussed a few types of related collective action, including collective self-defense and intervention by invitation. In this Chapter we turn to collective action by previously organized groups. We start with the form of collective action envisaged in the UN Charter—action mandated by the Security Council. We will see that the Charter's plan for Security Council responses to threats to the peace, breaches of the peace and acts of aggression has never been fully implemented. Rather, the Security Council has reacted to various crisis situations in ways either approximating the Charter provisions (Korea and the Gulf War) or in innovative ways, extrapolating from the Charter (peace-keeping and peace enforcement.)

In addition to collective action through the United Nations, we also look at various security arrangements that have responded to security threats and humanitarian crises. In all cases included here, the group taking action did not have Security Council authorization. We will look at the legal arguments about the legality of the Organization of American States (OAS) role in the Cuban Missile Crisis; the role of the Organization of Eastern Caribbean States in the Grenada Intervention (OECS), the role of the Economic Cooperation Organization of West African States (ECOWAS) in Liberia, and the role of the North Atlantic Treaty Organization (NATO) in the Kosovo Crisis.[1]

A. UNITED NATIONS COLLECTIVE ACTION

The Security Council was organized as a standing body with clear responsibility to act on behalf of all victims of unlawful force. It may mandate action by members when it adopts a resolution by nine affirmative votes, if no permanent members vetoes the resolution. And, as mentioned, the Council was to have troops available with which to act. It could also call on regional agencies to act on its behalf. Thus, the Council was to be a uniquely powerful organization in the area of peace and security. Recall, however, the circumstances of the drafting of the Charter and the concerns of non-great powers that the Security Council and, in particular, the permanent members of the Council not be granted unlimited power.

Recall, too, that the Charter calls for member states to make agreements with the United Nations to provide troops for use by the Council when acting under Article 39 to respond to threats to or breaches of the peace. These agreements were never formed. Instead, when the UN has called on

---

1. See generally on this subject, COLLECTIVE SECURITY LAW (Nigel D. White ed., 2003).

armed forces it has done so on an *ad hoc* basis. In 1948 and 1949 it sent truce observers to the Middle East and to the border area between India and Pakistan. Then in 1950 North Korea invaded South Korea with the aim of unifying the peninsula. The Security Council authorized a United Nations force under the command of the United States to intervene and push North Korea back. The authorization was only possible because the Soviet Union was boycotting the Council at the time in protest over the failure to seat a representative of the People's Republic of China in place of the Nationalist Chinese representative.

When the Soviet Union returned to the Council, the U.S. tried to devise an alternative to Security Council authorization for the use of force by going to the General Assembly, where, in those days, it could count on a majority of countries to support its position. In November 1950, the Assembly adopted the "Uniting for Peace" Resolution, setting out that the Assembly had the power to discuss and make recommendations on matters of peace and security if the Council found itself deadlocked. Members were also to hold armed forces ready in the event that the Council failed to act. The Uniting for Peace Resolution was first used in 1956 when Britain and France vetoed Security Council resolutions during the Suez crisis. The General Assembly demanded that the two countries withdraw their troops from Egypt, and they did. The Soviet Union, however, paid no attention at all to a similar demand when it invaded Hungary also in 1956.

The Uniting for Peace Resolution has played a limited role since its adoption, the use of UN members' military forces for UN peacekeeping missions is now a permanent and important feature of the Organization.

1. PEACEKEEPING

The term peacekeeping does not appear in the Charter. The Council has no express authority to send peacekeepers. But UN lawyers have always argued that as long as peacekeeping actions have the consent of all the parties to the particular conflict, peacekeepers act impartially, carry only defensive weapons, and intervene only following a cease-fire, there could be no real legal challenge to their deployment.[2] Under Chapter VI of the Charter, the Security Council has authority to recommend to states a variety of measures for peaceful settlement of disputes and under Chapter VII it can send troops of the member states to conflict areas. Putting these provisions together, international lawyers believe the necessary charter authority can be found. If the peacekeepers have the consent of all parties, following a ceasefire and use limited force, the UN would be able to avoid interfering in the political struggle underlying such conflicts.

Before the end of the Cold War, seventeen peacekeeping missions were organized. These missions aided compliance with cease-fires by literally imposing blue-helmeted soldiers between warring factions or setting up observer posts to report breaches of the cease-fire. Peacekeepers were not,

---

2. Carl-August Fleischhauer, *Remarks* 86 PROC. AM. SOC. INT'L LAW 586–88 (1992); *see* *also*, TREVOR FINDLAY, THE USE OF FORCE IN UN PEACE OPERATIONS (2002).

however, peace enforcers—they did not take coercive action to compel compliance with a cease-fire. This factor was key to a decision by the International Court of Justice that the General Assembly—and not just the Security Council—had the authority to organize peacekeeping missions.

During the complicated Congo Crisis of 1960, the General Assembly, acting under the Uniting for Peace Resolution called for troops to go to support the newly-independent Congolese government. France and the Soviet Union opposed the intervention and refused to pay the expenses associated with it. The General Assembly asked the International Court of Justice for an advisory opinion regarding the obligation of UN members to pay for peacekeeping expenses incurred by the General Assembly.

Certain Expenses of the United Nations,

(Advisory Opinion) 1962 I.C.J 151–156, 162–170, 179 (July 20).

* * *

The power of the Court to give an advisory opinion is derived from Article 65 of the Statute. The power granted is of a discretionary character. In exercising its discretion, the International Court of Justice, like the Permanent Court of International Justice, has always been guided by the principle which the Permanent Court stated in the case concerning the Status of Eastern Carelia on 23 July 1923: "The Court, being a Court of Justice, cannot, even in giving advisory opinions, depart from the essential rules guiding their activity as a Court" (P.C.I.J., Series B, No. 5, p. 29). Therefore, and in accordance with Article 65 of its Statute, the Court can give an advisory opinion only on a legal question. If a question is not a legal one, the Court has no discretion in the matter; it must decline to give the opinion requested. But even if the question is a legal one, which the Court is undoubtedly competent to answer, it may nonetheless decline to do so. As this Court said in its Opinion of 30 March 1950, the permissive character of Article 65 "gives the Court the power to examine whether the circumstances of the case are of such a character as should lead it to decline to answer the Request" (*Interpretation of Peace Treaties with Bulgaria, Hungary and Romania (First Phase), I.C.J. Reports 1950, p. 72*). But, as the Court also said in the same Opinion, "the reply of the Court, itself an 'organ of the United Nations', represents its participation in the activities of the Organization, and, in principle, should not be refused" (*ibid.*, p. 71). Still more emphatically, in its Opinion of 23 October 1956, the Court said that only "compelling reasons" should lead it to refuse to give a requested advisory opinion (*Judgments of the Administrative Tribunal of the I.L.O. upon complaints made against the Unesco, I.C.J. Reports 1956, p. 86*).

The Court finds no "compelling reason" why it should not give the advisory opinion which the General Assembly requested by its resolution 1731 (XVI). It has been argued that the question put to the Court is intertwined with political questions, and that for this reason the Court should refuse to give an opinion. It is true that most interpretations of the Charter of the United Nations will have political significance, great or small. In the nature of things it could not be otherwise. The Court, however, cannot attribute a political character to a request which invites it to undertake an essentially judicial task, namely, the interpretation of a treaty provision.

In the preamble to the resolution requesting this opinion, the General Assembly expressed its recognition of "its need for authoritative legal guidance". In its search for such guidance it has put to the Court a legal question-a question of the interpretation of Article 17, paragraph 2, of the Charter of the United Nations. In its Opinion of 28 May 1948, the Court made it clear that as "the principal judicial organ of the United Nations", it was entitled to exercise in regard to an article of the Charter, "a multilateral treaty, an interpretative function which falls within the normal exercise of its judicial powers" (*Conditions of Admission of a State to Membership in the United Nations (Article 4 of the Charter), I.C.J. Reports 1947–1948, p. 61*).

The Court, therefore, having been asked to give an advisory opinion upon a concrete legal question, will proceed to give its opinion.

The question on which the Court is asked to give its opinion is whether certain expenditures which were authorized by the General Assembly to cover the costs of the United Nations operations in the Congo (hereinafter referred to as ONUC) and of the operations of the United Nations Emergency Force in the Middle East (hereinafter referred to as UNEF), "constitute 'expenses of the Organization' within the meaning of Article 17, paragraph 2, of the Charter of the United Nations".

* * *

The general purposes of Article 17 are the vesting of control over the finances of the Organization, and the levying of apportioned amounts of the expenses of the Organization in order to enable it to carry out the functions of the Organization as a whole acting through its principal organs and such subsidiary organs as may be established under the authority of Article 22 or Article 29.

Article 17 is the only article in the Charter which refers to budgetary authority or to the power to apportion expenses, or otherwise to raise revenue, except for Articles 33 and 35, paragraph 3, of the Statute of the Court which have no bearing on the point here under discussion. Nevertheless, it has been argued before the Court that one type of expenses, namely those resulting from operations for the maintenance of international peace and security, are not "expenses of the Organization" within the meaning of Article 17, paragraph 2, of the Charter, inasmuch as they fall to be dealt with exclusively by the Security Council, and more especially through agreements negotiated in accordance with Article 43 of the Charter.

The argument rests in part upon the view that when the maintenance of international peace and security is involved, it is only the Security Council which is authorized to decide on any action relative thereto. It is argued further that since the General Assembly's power is limited to discussing, considering, studying and recommending, it cannot impose an obligation to pay the expenses which result from the implementation of its recommendations. This argument leads to an examination of the respective functions of the General Assembly and of the Security Council under the Charter, particularly with respect to the maintenance of international peace and security.

Article 24 of the Charter provides:

"In order to ensure prompt and effective action by the United Nations, its Members confer on the Security Council primary responsibility for the maintenance of international peace and security . . ."

The responsibility conferred is "primary", not exclusive. This primary responsibility is conferred upon the Security Council, as stated in Article 24, "in order to ensure prompt and effective action". To this end, it is the Security Council which is given a power to impose an explicit obligation of compliance if for example it issues an order or command to an aggressor under Chapter VII. It is only the Security Council which can require enforcement by coercive action against an aggressor.

* * *

"The General Assembly may discuss any questions relating to the maintenance of international peace and security brought before it by any Member of the United Nations, or by the Security Council, or by a State which is not a Member of the United Nations in accordance with Article 35, paragraph 2, and, except as provided in Article 12, may make recommendations with regard to any such question to the State or States concerned or to the Security Council, or to both. Any such question on which action is necessary shall be referred to the Security Council by the General Assembly either before or after discussion."

The Court considers that the kind of action referred to in Article 11, paragraph 2, is coercive or enforcement action. This paragraph, which applies not merely to general questions relating to peace and security, but also to specific cases brought before the General Assembly by a State under Article 35, in its first sentence empowers the General Assembly, by means of recommendations to States or to the Security Council, or to both, to organize peace-keeping operations, at the request, or with the consent, of the States concerned. This power of the General Assembly is a special power which in no way derogates from its general powers under Article 10 or Article 14, except as limited by the last sentence of Article 11, paragraph 2. This last sentence says that when "action" is necessary the General Assembly shall refer the question to the Security Council. The word "action" must mean such action as is solely within the province of the Security Council. It cannot refer to recommendations which the Security Council might make, as for instance under Article 38, because the General Assembly under Article 11 has a comparable power. The "action" which is solely within the province of the Security Council is that which is indicated by the title of Chapter VII of the Charter, namely "Action with respect to threats to the peace, breaches of the peace, and acts of aggression". If the word "action" in Article 11, paragraph 2, were interpreted to mean that the General Assembly could make recommendations only of a general character affecting peace and security in the abstract, and not in relation to specific cases, the paragraph would not have provided that the General Assembly may make recommendations on questions brought before it by States or by the Security Council. Accordingly, the last sentence of Article 11, paragraph 2, has no application where the necessary action is not enforcement action.

The practice of the Organization throughout its history bears out the foregoing elucidation of the term "action" in the last sentence of Article 11, paragraph 2. Whether the General Assembly proceeds under Article 11 or under Article 14, the implementation of its recommendations for setting up commissions or other bodies involves organizational activity—action—in connection with the maintenance of international peace and security. Such implementation is a normal feature of the functioning of the United Nations. Such committees, commissions or other bodies or individuals, constitute, in some cases, subsidiary organs established under the authority of Article 22 of the Charter. The functions of the General Assembly for which it may establish such subsidiary organs include, for example, investigation, observation and supervision, but the way in which such subsidiary organs are utilized depends on the consent of the State or States concerned.

The Court accordingly finds that the argument which seeks, by reference to Article 11, paragraph 2, to limit the budgetary authority of the General Assembly in respect of the maintenance of international peace and security, is unfounded.

It has further been argued before the Court that Article 43 of the Charter constitutes a particular rule, a *lex specialis*, which derogates from the general rule in Article 17, whenever an expenditure for the maintenance of international peace and security is involved. Article 43 provides that Members shall negotiate agreements with the Security Council on its initiative, stipulating what "armed forces, assistance and facilities, including rights of passage, necessary for the purpose of maintaining international peace and security", the Member state will make available to the Security Council on its call. According to paragraph 2 of the Article:

> "Such agreement or agreements shall govern the numbers and types of forces, their degree of readiness and general location, and the nature of the facilities and assistance to be provided."

The argument is that such agreements were intended to include specifications concerning the allocation of costs of such enforcement actions as might be taken by direction of the Security Council, and that it is only the Security Council which has the authority to arrange for meeting such costs.

With reference to this argument, the Court will state at the outset that, for reasons fully expounded later in this Opinion, the operations known as UNEF and ONUC were not *enforcement* actions within the compass of Chapter VII of the Charter and that therefore Article 43 could not have any applicability to the cases with which the Court is here concerned. However, even if Article 43 were applicable, the Court could not accept this interpretation of its text for the following reasons.

There is nothing in the text of Article 43 which would limit the discretion of the Security Council in negotiating such agreements. It cannot be assumed that in every such agreement the Security Council would insist, or that any Member State would be bound to agree, that such State would bear the entire cost of the "assistance" which it would make available including, for example, transport of forces to the point of operation, complete logistical maintenance in the field, supplies, arms and ammunition, etc. If, during negotiations under the terms of Article 43, a Member State would be entitled (as it would be) to insist, and the Security Council would be entitled (as it would be) to agree, that some part of the expense should be borne by the Organization, then such expense would form part of the expenses of the Organization and would fall to be apportioned by the General Assembly under Article 17. It is difficult to see how it could have been contemplated that all potential expenses could be envisaged in such agreements concluded perhaps long in advance. Indeed, the difficulty or impossibility of anticipating the entire financial impact of enforcement measures on Member States is brought out by the terms of Article 50 which provides that a State, whether a Member of the

United Nations or not, "which finds itself confronted with special economic problems arising from the carrying out of those [preventive or enforcement] measures, shall have the right to consult the Security Council with regard to a solution of those problems". Presumably in such a case the Security Council might determine that the overburdened State was entitled to some financial assistance; such financial assistance, if afforded by the Organization, as it might be, would clearly constitute part of the "expenses of the Organization". The economic problems could not have been covered in advance by a negotiated agreement since they would be unknown until after the event and in the case of non-Member States, which are also included in Article 50, no agreement at all would have been negotiated under Article 43.

Moreover, an argument which insists that all measures taken for the maintenance of international peace and security must be financed through agreements concluded under Article 43, would seem to exclude the possibility that the Security Council might act under some other Article of the Charter. The Court cannot accept so limited a view of the powers of the Security Council under the Charter. It cannot be said that the Charter has left the Security Council impotent in the face of an emergency situation when agreements under Article 43 have not been concluded.

Articles of Chapter VII of the Charter speak of "situations" as well as disputes, and it must lie within the power of the Security Council to police a situation even though it does not resort to enforcement action against a State. The costs of actions which the Security Council is authorized to take constitute "expenses of the Organization within the meaning of Article 17, paragraph 2".

The Court has considered the general problem of the interpretation of Article 17, paragraph 2, in the light of the general structure of the Charter and of the respective functions assigned by the Charter to the General Assembly and to the Security Council, with a view to determining the meaning of the phrase "the expenses of the Organization". The Court does not find it necessary to go further in giving a more detailed definition of such expenses. The Court will, therefore, proceed to examine the expenditures enumerated in the request for the advisory opinion. In determining whether the actual expenditures authorized constitute "expenses of the Organization within the meaning of Article 17, paragraph 2, of the Charter", the Court agrees that such expenditures must be tested by their relationship to the purposes of the United Nations in the sense that if an expenditure were made for a purpose which is not one of the purposes of the United Nations, it could not be considered an "expense of the Organization".

The purposes of the United Nations are set forth in Article 1 of the Charter. The first two purposes as stated in paragraphs 1 and 2, may be summarily described as pointing to the goal of international peace and security and friendly relations. The third purpose is the achievement of economic, social, cultural and humanitarian goals and respect for human rights. The fourth and last purpose is: "To be a center for harmonizing the actions of nations in the attainment of these common ends."

The primary place ascribed to international peace and security is natural, since the fulfillment of the other purposes will be dependent upon the attainment of that basic condition. These purposes are broad indeed, but neither they nor the powers conferred to effectuate them are unlimited. Save as they have entrusted the Organization with the attainment of these common ends, the Member States retain their freedom of action. But when the Organization takes action which warrants the assertion that it was appropriate for the fulfillment of one of the stated purposes of the United Nations, the presumption is that such action is not *ultra vires* the Organization.

If it is agreed that the action in question is within the scope of the functions of the Organization but it is alleged that it has been initiated or carried out in a manner not in conformity with the division of functions among the several organs which the Charter prescribes, one moves to the internal plane, to the internal structure of the Organization. If the action was taken by the wrong organ, it was irregular as a matter of that internal structure, but this would not necessarily mean that the expense incurred was not an expense of the Organization. Both national and international law contemplate cases in which the body corporate or politic may be bound, as to third parties, by an *ultra vires* act of an agent.

In the legal systems of States, there is often some procedure for determining the validity of even a legislative or governmental act, but no analogous procedure is to be found in the structure of the United Nations. Proposals made during the drafting of the Charter to place the ultimate authority to interpret the Charter in the International Court of Justice were not accepted; the opinion which the Court is in course of rendering is an *advisory* opinion. As anticipated in 1945, therefore, each organ must, in the first place at least, determine its own jurisdiction. If the Security Council, for example, adopts a resolution purportedly for the maintenance of international peace and security and if, in accordance with a mandate or authorization in such resolution, the Secretary–General incurs financial obligations, these amounts must be presumed to constitute "expenses of the Organization".

* * *

The obligation is one thing: the way in which the obligation is met—that is from what source the funds are secured—is another. The General Assembly may follow any one of several alternatives:

it may apportion the cost of the item according to the ordinary scale of assessment; it may apportion the cost according to some special scale of assessment; it may utilize funds which are voluntarily contributed to the Organization; or it may find some other method or combination of methods for providing the necessary funds. In this context, it is of no legal significance whether, as a matter of book-keeping or accounting, the General Assembly chooses to have the item in question included under one of the "standard" established sections of the "regular" budget or whether it is separately listed in some special account or fund. The significant fact is that the item is an expense of the Organization and under Article 17, paragraph 2, the General Assembly therefore has authority to apportion it.

At the outset of this opinion, the Court pointed out that the text of Article 17, paragraph 2, of the Charter could lead to the simple conclusion that "the expenses of the Organization" are the amounts paid out to defray the costs of carrying out the purposes of the Organization. It was further indicated that the Court would examine the resolutions authorizing the expenditures referred to in the request for the advisory opinion in order to ascertain whether they were incurred with that end in view. The Court has made such an examination and finds that they were so incurred. The Court has also analyzed the principal arguments which have been advanced against the conclusion that the expenditures in question should be considered as "expenses of the Organization within the meaning of Article 17, paragraph 2, of the Charter of the United Nations", and has found that these arguments are unfounded. Consequently, the Court arrives at the conclusion that the question submitted to it in General Assembly resolution 1731 (XVI) must be answered in the affirmative.

Following the Certain Expenses Case there were years more of negotiation before a separate account for peacekeeping expenses was established, to be paid voluntary. The financing of the Congo operation was not the only contentious issue. The UN troops that went to the Congo were supposed to intervene to counter Belgian intervention on the eve Congolese independence. The UN, however, ended up fighting alongside the central government against the people of Katanga province who were attempting to secede. The UN strove to remain neutral but could not and, thus, tipped the political balance.[3] Future peacekeeping missions for the remainder of the Cold War were established only where both the U.S. and the Soviet Union agreed.

---

3. *See* FINDLAY *supra* note 2, at 51–86; N.D. WHITE, THE UNITED NATIONS AND THE MAINTENANCE OF INTERNATIONAL PEACE AND SECURITY 50–51 (1990); GEORGES ABI-SAAB, INTERNATIONAL CRISES AND THE ROLE OF LAW: THE UNITED NATIONS OPERATION IN THE CONGO 1960–1964 (1978).

2. Peace Enforcement

With the end of the Cold War, the Superpower stand-off and, thus, the veto ceased to be a problem. The UN Security Council was able to respond more closely to the original plan of the Charter when, by unanimous vote, it found that Iraq had violated Article 2(4) by its invasion of Kuwait. The Council did not, however, authorize its own force, but rather, akin to the action in Korea, it authorized a coalition of national forces under United States command to compel Iraq back into compliance with the Charter.

Following the successful enforcement in the Gulf War (one of the case studies in Chapter Two), Security Council members and the UN Secretary General, began to think more expansively about the UN's role in world peace.[4] The Council began to authorize missions to respond to human rights crises, crises that had not traditionally been interpreted as violations of "international peace."[5] The missions themselves were given authority to use force to actually enforce the peace or end the crisis in contrast with traditional peacekeeping missions that could only use force in personal self-defense. The new missions have come to be called "peace enforcement." The Security Council typically refers to "Chapter VII" of the Charter in authorizing them and it usually states the mission has the right to use "all necessary means" to carry out their actions. Despite these significant changes, the troops in the field carrying out the missions still wear the UN blue helmet and are usually still referred to as "peacekeepers."

The first departure from traditional peacekeeping toward peace enforcement can be traced to the establishment of the Iraqi Exclusion Zone in April 1991 just at the end of major fighting in the Gulf War. As the fighting to liberate Kuwait was ending, the Kurds of northern Iraq and the Shia in the south began rebellions against the Iraqi government, apparently either to secede from Iraq or at least to establish an autonomous regions.[6] This development seems to have caught the UN and the coalition off guard. Both resisted initial calls for intervention. The United States took the position that it could not intervene militarily to support the uprisings because intervention would be unlawful interference in Iraq's internal affairs. The French agreed with this legal assessment, yet argued that "[t]he law is one thing, but the safeguard of a population is another, quite as precious, to which humanity cannot be indifferent."[7]

France could not, however, persuade the other permanent members of the Security Council to authorize force to liberate the Kurds or Shia. Instead, the Council ordered only humanitarian aid on the Kurds' behalf. In

---

4. *See* the Secretary General's Agenda for Peace, U.N. Doc. S/24111–A/47/277 (1992).

5. The Security Council took measures with regard to Rhodesia in the 1960s and South Africa in the 1970s. S. C. Res. 418 (1977). While the real motive for action may not have been international peace, the Council found breaches of the peace before issuing resolutions. *Id.* at 609. Thus, it behaved consistently with a legal requirement to respond only to violations of international peace.

6. For a detailed account of these events, *see* Mary Ellen O'Connell, *Continuing Limits on UN Intervention in Civil War*, 67 Ind. L.J. 903, 904–09 (1992).

7. Fin. Times, April 5, 1991, at 4 (Statement of French Foreign Minister Roland Dumas).

Resolution 688, the Council found that Iraqi attacks on the Kurds constituted a threat to peace in the region. In the subsequent operative paragraphs of the resolution, the Council called on Iraq to end its repression of the Kurds and to allow international humanitarian assistance to reach northern Iraq. This was as far as the Council could go without inviting a Chinese veto or failing to get the required two-thirds vote of the fifteen-member Council. As it was, China and India abstained from supporting the resolution, while Cuba, Yemen and Zimbabwe voted against it. All stated they believed the resolution interfered in Iraq's internal affairs.[8]

Providing humanitarian aid was arguably not interference with internal affairs and therefore is not unlawful. Creating the protective zone, however, went well beyond distributing humanitarian aid. There is a question whether such a move was really authorized by the Security Council. The British have argued that Resolution 688, read together with Resolution 678 (which authorized all means to bring peace to the region), did provide authority to create the zone as part of the response to Iraq's violation of international peace.[9] It appears that Iraq gave consent to the establishment of the zone in May 1991. It was then that Coalition forces left the area and United Nations "police" entered.[10]

In mid-summer 1991, fighting broke out in Yugoslavia between the province of Croatia, which had declared its independence, and the Yugoslav federal government. This conflict also raised the question of UN intervention in civil war.

In the early months of the war, the UN played no role. The European Community (EC) wished to mediate the conflict, declaring it a European matter. But the EC had not succeeded in getting a cease-fire by mid-September. The Security Council then became involved, beginning with Resolution 713, which imposed an arms embargo on the entire territory of the former Yugoslavia. This embargo had the consent of Belgrade, and thus avoided a Chinese veto. In November 1991, Zagreb and Belgrade agreed to the formation of a peacekeeping force, the United Nations Protection Force (UNPROFOR), to act as a buffer under Resolution 743.

In July 1995, UNPROFOR was supposed to be policing a ceasefire in the town of Srebrenica between Bosnian Muslims and Bosnian Serbs. As the ceasefire brokedown, UNPROFOR did not prevent it, but did continue to give Muslims the illusion they would be protected. The following is an excerpt from a Report by the UN Secretary General to the General Assembly.

Report of the Secretary–General Pursuant to General Assembly Resolution 53/35 The Fall of Srebrenica
UN Doc. A/54/549 (15 Nov. 1999).

* * *

2. On 16 November 1995, the International Tribunal for the Former Yugoslavia indicted Radovan Karadžić ("President of the

8. O'Connell, *Continuing Limits on UN Intervention, supra* note 6, at 905–06.

9. *Id*. at 906–07.

10. *Id*. at 909.

Republika Srpska") and Ratko Mladić, (Commander of the Bosnian Serb Army) for their alleged, direct responsibility for the atrocities committed in July 1995 against the Bosnian Muslim population of the United Nations-designated safe area of Srebrenica. After a review of the evidence submitted by the Prosecutor, Judge Riad confirmed the indictment, stating that:

> "After Srebrenica fell to besieging Serbian forces in July 1995, a truly terrible massacre of the Muslim population appears to have taken place. The evidence tendered by the Prosecutor describes scenes of unimaginable savagery: thousands of men executed and buried in mass graves, hundreds of men buried alive, men and women mutilated and slaughtered, children killed before their mothers' eyes, a grandfather forced to eat the liver of his own grandson. These are truly scenes from hell, written on the darkest pages of human history."

3. The United Nations had a mandate to "deter attacks" on Srebrenica and five other "safe areas" in Bosnia and Herzegovina. Despite that mandate, up to 20,000 people, overwhelmingly from the Bosnian Muslim community, were killed in and around the safe areas. In addition, a majority of the 117 members of the United Nations Protection Force (UNPROFOR) who lost their lives in Bosnia and Herzegovina died in or around the safe areas.

* * *

11. Following the declaration of independence by Slovenia, fighting broke out between Slovenian forces and predominantly Serb forces of the Yugoslav People's Army (JNA). The fighting, however, lasted for only 10 days, with light casualties on both sides. The conflict ended with the Brioni agreement of 7 July 1991, and was followed, over the coming months, by the withdrawal of JNA forces and de facto independence for Slovenia. In Croatia, the fighting was much more serious. The declaration of independence led to an increase in the armed clashes which had been taking place for several months, pitting Croatian forces against both the JNA and Croatian Serb militias. These clashes descended into full-scale warfare in August 1991 and continued until 2 January 1992, when a ceasefire was signed in Sarajevo under the auspices of the United Nations. Shortly thereafter, the parties to the conflict in Croatia "fully and unconditionally" accepted the "concept for a United Nations peacekeeping operation in Yugoslavia" presented by the Personal Envoy of the Secretary–General, Cyrus Vance ("the Vance Plan"). At the end of this phase of the fighting in Croatia, Serb forces remained in de facto control of approximately one third of the Republic of Croatia.

12. On 25 September 1991, when the fighting in Croatia was at its height, the Security Council, by its resolution 713 (1991), decided that "all States shall, for purposes of establishing peace and stability in Yugoslavia, immediately implement a general and complete embargo on all deliveries of weapons and military equipment to Yugoslavia until the Security Council decides otherwise". The resolution was adopted unanimously, though several observers noted at the time that the major effect of the embargo would be to freeze the military holdings of each of the parties—a move which would overwhelmingly benefit the Serbs, who were dominant both in the Yugoslav military and, to a lesser extent, in the arms industry.

13. On 15 February 1992, the then Secretary–General, Boutros Boutros–Ghali (who served in this position from 1 January 1992 to 31 December 1996), submitted a report to the Security Council proposing the establishment of a peacekeeping force to implement the Vance Plan. He made the following observation:

> "If it is only now that I am proposing such a force, it [is] because of the complexities and dangers of the Yugoslav situation and the consequent need to be as sure as possible that a United Nations force would succeed in consolidating the ceasefire and thus facilitate the negotiation of an overall political settlement. As has been repeatedly stated, this requires not only a working ceasefire but also clear and unconditional acceptance of the plan by all concerned, with equally clear assurances of their readiness to cooperate in its implementation ... I have come to the conclusion that the danger that a United Nations peace operation will fail because of lack of cooperation of the parties is less grievous than the danger that delay in its dispatch will lead to a breakdown of the ceasefire and to a new conflagration in Yugoslavia." (S/23592, para. 28)

14. The Security Council approved the Secretary–General's report and, on 21 February, decided, by resolution 743 (1992), to establish a United Nations Protection Force to assist in the implementation of the Vance Plan. UNPROFOR headquarters was established in Sarajevo on 13 March 1992. Sarajevo was seen, at that time, as a neutral location, and it was hoped that the presence of UNPROFOR in Bosnia and Herzegovina would prove a stabilizing factor amid the increasing tensions in the country. Although resolution 743 (1992) provided for United Nations military observers to patrol certain limited areas in Bosnia and Herzegovina, this was to take place after the demilitarization of the United Nations Protected Areas in Croatia, which did not occur. Until June 1992, the Force had no other mandate in Bosnia and Herzegovina.

* * *

15.   The independence of the Republic of Bosnia and Herzegovina was recognized by the European Community on 6 April 1992 and by the United States of America the following day. At the same time, the sporadic fighting which had taken place in a number of areas began to intensify. This was exacerbated by the JNA withdrawal from Croatia under the terms of the Vance Plan, which had involved the relocation of substantial amounts of *matériel*, particularly heavy weapons, into Bosnia and Herzegovina. Much of this *matériel* later passed into the hands of the Bosnian Serbs.

16.   The International Committee of the Red Cross (ICRC) viewed the conflict that had erupted in Bosnia and Herzegovina as having elements both of an international armed conflict (invasion of that country by the Federal Republic of Yugoslavia) and of an internal armed conflict. In its international aspect, the conflict represented a war between the JNA (later known as the Army of Yugoslavia, or VJ) on one side, against both the Army of the Republic of Bosnia and Herzegovina (ARBiH) and the Croatian Defence Council (HVO) on the other. Later in the conflict, another foreign force, the Croatian Army (HV), was also involved in the fighting. In its internal aspect, the war represented a conflict between armed forces associated with the major nationalities of Bosnia and Herzegovina.

17.   Bosniacs (known until 1993 as "Muslims" or "Bosnian Muslims"), who represented 44 per cent of Bosnia and Herzegovina's population of 4.4 million, were dominant in the Army of the Republic of Bosnia and Herzegovina. The ARBiH, officially established on 15 April 1992, was made up, *ab initio*, of a number elements: territorial defence units, police forces, paramilitary forces and criminal elements. It enjoyed an advantage in manpower over the other forces in the conflict, but was poorly equipped and largely untrained. Prior to April 1993, when fighting broke out between Bosniacs and Croats, the ARBiH was able to secure a limited amount of military *matériel* from foreign supporters via Croatia. The Croats, who constituted 17 percent of the population, were dominant in the HVO. This force also brought together territorial defence units, police forces, paramilitaries and certain prominent criminals. Unlike the ARBiH, however, the HVO enjoyed the backing of the Republic of Croatia, which provided a broad range of support.

18.   Ranged against these forces were the rump JNA (the regular army of the Socialist Federal Republic of Yugoslavia), the "Army of Republika Srpska", known to the international community as the Bosnian Serb Army (BSA), and their paramilitary associates. All of these forces were dominated by Serbs, who constituted 31 percent of the population of Bosnia and Herzegovina. The JNA officially withdrew from Bosnia and Herzegovina to the Federal Republic of Yugoslavia under international pressure on 10 May

1992. In fact, however, the withdrawal was largely cosmetic since the JNA "left behind" those units whose members were nationals of Bosnia and Herzegovina. General Mladić, Commander of JNA forces in Bosnia and Herzegovina, was restyled Commander of the BSA. Throughout the war that was to follow, the BSA remained closely associated with the JNA/VJ and with the Federal Republic of Yugoslavia, on which the BSA relied for *matériel*, intelligence, funds and other forms of support. The Serb paramilitary groups, which included a substantial criminal element, often operated in close cooperation with the regular armies of Yugoslavia and the Bosnian Serbs.

19.   The conflict between these forces differed from conventional warfare in important ways. First, much of the fighting was local, involving regular and irregular fighters operating close to their homes. Second, a central objective of the conflict was the use of military means to terrorize civilian populations, often with the goal of forcing their flight in a process that came to be known as "ethnic cleansing". Third, although several hundred thousand men were engaged for three and a half years, and although several tens of thousands of combatants were killed, the conflict was more often one of attrition, terror, gangsterism and negotiation than it was of high-intensity warfare.

* * *

26.   The Secretary–General concluded as follows:

"The situation in Bosnia and Herzegovina is tragic, danger-ous, violent and confused. I do not believe that in its present phase this conflict is susceptible to the United Nations peace-keeping treatment. Any successful peacekeeping operation has to be based on some agreement between the hostile parties. Such an agreement can range from a simple ceasefire to a comprehensive settlement of their dispute. Without an agree-ment of some sort, a workable mandate cannot be defined and peacekeeping is impossible. . . .

"It also has to be observed that a successful peacekeeping operation requires the parties to respect the United Nations, its personnel and its mandate. One of the more distressing features of the current situation in Bosnia and Herzegovina is that, for all their fair words, none of the parties there can claim to satisfy that condition. . . . These are not the condi-tions which permit a United Nations peacekeeping operation to make an effective contribution." (S/23900, paras. 25–26)

27.   The Security Council then asked the Secretary–General to take on some limited functions in the Sarajevo area. In resolution 757 (1992) of 30 May 1992, by which it also imposed sweeping economic sanctions on the Federal Republic of Yugoslavia, the Council requested the Secretary–General to continue to use his

good offices in order to achieve the conditions for unimpeded delivery of humanitarian supplies to Sarajevo and elsewhere, including the establishment of a security zone encompassing Sarajevo and its airport. The Secretary–General reported to the Security Council on 6 June that UNPROFOR had negotiated an agreement, the previous day, on the reopening of Sarajevo airport for humanitarian purposes. Under the terms of the agreement, UNPROFOR was asked to take on full operational responsibility for the functioning and security of Sarajevo airport. The Secretary–General expressed the view that the agreement represented a "significant breakthrough" in the tragic conflict in Bosnia and Herzegovina, although it was only a first step, and added:

> "It is my view that the opportunity afforded by the willingness of the parties to conclude the present agreement should be seized.... Given that heavy weapons will remain in the hills overlooking Sarajevo and its airport, albeit supervised by UNPROFOR, the viability of the agreement will depend on the good faith of the parties, and especially the Bosnian Serb party, in scrupulously honouring their commitments....
>
> "I accordingly recommend to the Security Council that it take the necessary decision to enlarge the mandate and strength of UNPROFOR, as proposed in the present report. It is to be hoped that this will be the first stage of a process that will restore peace to the long-suffering Republic of Bosnia and Herzegovina." (S/24075, paras. 11 and 13)

28.   The Secretary–General proposed the immediate deployment of United Nations military observers to the airport, to be followed by an UNPROFOR infantry battalion. This was approved by the Security Council in its resolution 758 (1992) of 8 June, marking the formal beginning of the UNPROFOR mandate in Bosnia and Herzegovina.

* * *

41.   As the situation in Bosnia and Herzegovina deteriorated, the activity of the Security Council increased. During the 18–month period from the opening of full-scale hostilities in Bosnia and Herzegovina on 6 April 1992 to 5 October 1993, 47 Security Council resolutions were adopted and 42 statements of the President of the Council were issued on matters relating to the conflict in the former Yugoslavia. The majority of them dealt directly with the conflict in Bosnia and Herzegovina. To this date, no issue in the history of the Security Council has engendered more resolutions and statements over comparable period.

43.   Relatively early in the conflict, a discernible pattern of decision-making emerged in the Security Council. Those countries which opposed lifting the arms embargo committed increasing numbers of troops to UNPROFOR, but resisted efforts to expand

the UNPROFOR mandate in such a way as to bring the Force into direct military confrontation with the Bosnian Serbs. Those countries which favoured more robust action, but which did not have troops on the ground, sought progressively to expand the UNPROFOR mandate and to use the Force directly to confront the Serbs. The result was the deployment by France, the United Kingdom of Great Britain and Northern Ireland and others of forces which were largely configured and equipped for traditional peacekeeping duties rather than enforcement action. At the same time, in an effort to find some consensus in the Council, resolutions were adopted in which some of the more robust language favoured by non-troop-contributing nations was accommodated. Chapter VII of the Charter was invoked with increasing frequency, though often without specifying what that implied in terms of UNPROFOR operations. In this way, the efforts of Member States to find compromise between divergent positions led to the UNPROFOR mandate becoming rhetorically more robust than the Force itself. During the 18–month period of maximum Security Council activity on this issue, Bosnian Serb forces operated almost unchecked; by the time the confrontation line stabilized, in mid–1993, approximately 2 million people, or one half of the total population of Bosnia and Herzegovina, had fled their homes or been expelled.

* * *

45.   One of the proposals which emerged during this search for compromise within the Security Council was to establish "security zones", "safe havens" and "protected areas" for the Bosniac population. In his remarks to the London Conference of 26 and 27 August 1992, the President of the International Committee of the Red Cross, Cornelio Sommaruga, stated that the international community had a vital role to play. "Forced transfers, harassment, arrests and killings must cease at once", he stated. He added that a haven would have to be found for some 10,000 detainees already visited by ICRC in northern and eastern Bosnia. He then asked delegates whether or not they would consider establishing "protected zones" as one of several options for addressing the humanitarian crisis in Bosnia and Herzegovina. In October 1992 ICRC issued a paper in which it stated: "The present situation calls for the creation of zones ... which need international protection". ICRC spoke of the need to protect threatened communities in their places of residence. "For this protection to be effective, the parties to the conflict must facilitate the deployment of UNPROFOR contingents, and the United Nations forces' mandate must be expanded."

51.   The Force Commander of UNPROFOR opposed the concept of establishing safe areas other than by agreement between the belligerents. He was concerned that the nature of the safe area mandate which was being proposed would be inherently incompati-

ble with peacekeeping. He did not oppose the principle of protecting the Bosnian Government and its armed forces against Serb attack, but opined that there could be no role for peacekeepers in such an operation. Protecting the safe areas, in his view, was a job for a combat-capable, peace-enforcement operation. He summarized his position in a communication to the Secretariat, stating, "one cannot make war and peace at the same time".

* * *

55. * * * After extended debate, the Council on 16 April adopted a draft resolution tabled by the non-aligned members, as resolution 819 (1993) in which it demanded that "all parties and others treat Srebrenica and its surroundings as a safe area which should be free from any armed attack or any other hostile act". It also demanded "the immediate cessation of armed attacks by Bosnian Serb paramilitary units against Srebrenica and their immediate withdrawal from the areas surrounding Srebrenica", and further demanded that "the Federal Republic of Yugoslavia immediately cease the supply of military arms, equipment and services to the Bosnian Serb paramilitary units in the Republic of Bosnia and Herzegovina". However, no specific restrictions were put on the activities of the Army of the Republic of Bosnia and Herzegovina. Upon learning of the resolution, UNPROFOR expressed concern to the Secretariat that the regime could not be implemented without the consent of both parties which, given Serb dominance, would certainly require Bosnian Government forces to lay down their weapons.

56. The Security Council, although acting under Chapter VII of the Charter, had provided no resources or mandate for UNPROFOR to impose its demands on the parties. Rather, it requested the Secretary–General, "with a view to monitoring the humanitarian situation in the safe area, to take immediate steps to increase the presence of the United Nations Protection Force in Srebrenica and its surroundings".

* * *

58. Following the adoption of resolution 819 (1993), and on the basis of consultations with members of the Council, the Secretariat informed the UNPROFOR Force Commander that, in its view, the resolution, calling as it did for the parties to take certain actions, created no military obligations for UNPROFOR to establish or protect such a safe area.

* * *

221. The military situation in and around Srebrenica had been generally calm since the agreements of 18 April and 8 May 1993.

During the two years between May 1993 and May 1995, neither side had made any significant attempt to capture territory.

* * *

223. In June 1995 the period of relative military inactivity came to an end. On 1 June a Serb raiding party entered the enclave, ambushed and reportedly killed a number of Bosniac civilians. On the same day, the BSA instructed UNPROFOR to move observation post Echo, an UNPROFOR position on the southern boundary of the enclave, in order to give the Serbs unrestricted use of a strategic road just south of the enclave. UNPROFOR refused to relocate, and on 3 June the Serbs attacked the position with hand-held weapons, mortars and anti-tank weapons. OP Echo was surrendered, despite the Dutchbat Commander's request for close air support to defend it. The request did not reach UNPF headquarters in Zagreb, but appears to have been discouraged further down the chain of command, bearing in mind that hundreds of UNPROFOR personnel remained hostage. The Netherlands battalion nevertheless established two new positions, know as OP Sierra and OP Uniform, next to where OP Echo had been located. The Serbs were taken aback by the move. Moreover, following the capture by the Serbs of OP Echo, Dutchbat agreed to certain measures which seemed to acknowledge that the demilitarization agreements of 1993 were no longer functioning. They agreed that the Bosniacs could carry weapons openly and that they could occupy positions between the UNPROFOR observation posts * * *.

* * *

239. The Bosnian Serb Army launched their attack on Srebrenica in the early morning hours of 6 July [1995]. Fighting took place at a number of points on the perimeter of the enclave, and shells exploded at various locations within the enclave. The main axis of attack, however, was from the south.

* * *

304. The advancing Serb forces now entered the town encountering little or no resistance either from UNPROFOR or from the ARBiH. The Serb flag was hoisted above a bakery at the southern end of the town at 1407 hours, according to one individual who was there at the time. The residents of Srebrenica town, including those who had sought refuge at B Company base, began to flee northwards in the direction of Potočari at approximately 1430 hours. Srebrenica, had fallen. Until that point, at least three (but possibly up to five requests for air support by Dutchbat had been turned down at various levels in the chain of command). Dutchbat

had also not fired a single shot directly at the advancing Serb forces.

305. Eighteen NATO aircraft had by now made their way to Srebrenica. Six of them were detailed to attack targets, with the remainder largely designated for the suppression of enemy air defence systems, if required. At approximately 1440 hours, two NATO aircraft dropped a total of two bombs on what were thought to be Serb vehicles advancing towards the town from the south. It was not clear at the time what damage had been done, if any. NATO aircraft also overflew the southern and north-western portions of the enclave, respectively, but were unable to locate targets.

306. Immediately following this first deployment of NATO close air support, the BSA radioed a message to Dutchbat. They threatened to shell the town and the compound where thousands of inhabitants had begun to gather, and to kill the Dutchbat soldiers being held hostage, if NATO continued with its use of air power. The Special Representative of the Secretary–General recalled having received a telephone call from the Netherlands Minister of Defence at this time, requesting that the close air support action be discontinued, because Serb soldiers on the scene were too close to Netherlands troops, and their safety would be jeopardized. The Special Representative considered that he had no choice but to comply with this request. The message was passed to NATO accordingly, and the air action was halted. The Minister made similar calls to the Under–Secretary–General for Peacekeeping Operations in New York and his Military Adviser (a Netherlands Major General) at the same time, which were echoed in démarches by the Permanent Representative of the Netherlands.

* * *

345. In summary, there is strong documentation to suggest that summary executions did take place on 12 July, into the night and early morning hours of 13 July. It does not appear, however, that the largest number of execution had yet been carried out. Information from Serb sources appears to suggest that the decision to kill the men of Srebrenica may have been taken only after the fall of Srebrenica. The decision to assemble a large number of civilian and military vehicles for the deportation process appears to have been taken independently. Information currently available does not suggest that vehicles from the Federal Republic of Yugoslavia were engaged at this stage.

* * *

350. By the end of the day on 13 July, there were virtually no Bosniac males left in the former "safe area" of Srebrenica. Almost all were in one of four categories:

(1) Those alive and making their way through the woods towards Government-held territory;

(2) Those who had been killed on that journey;

(3) Those who had surrendered themselves to the

Serbs in Potocari or on the way to Government-held territory, and who had already been killed;

(4) Those who had surrendered themselves to the Serbs in Potocari or on the way to Government-held territory, and who were being moved to Bratunac, pending relocation to execution and burial sites.

351.   The United Nations military observers and Dutchbat were aware that Bosniac men were being detained in Bratunac, but did not know the precise numbers or locations. There is now strong evidence that between 4,000 and 5,000 Bosniac males were being held there in various locations around town: a warehouse; an old school; three lines of trucks and buses; and a football field. The Dutchbat soldiers being detained in Bratunac, meanwhile, were in different locations (the Hotel Fontana and the Technical School, both of which are close to the football field).

352.   Although the precise details of what happened to the men of Srebrenica on 13 July have been reconstructed only after subsequent enquiry over the past four years, there was concern at the time, and at least five written messages were sent on that day, expressing alarm about potential human rights abuses having been committed or that potentially might be committed.

* * *

361.   It has since been learned that the Bosnian Serbs began the systematic extermination of the thousands of Bosniac males being held in Bratunac in the early morning hours of 14 July. At that time, they began loading the Bosniacs into vehicles and transporting them to different locations in the wider area. Those locations turned out to be extermination sites, where there is strong evidence to suggest that all of those men were executed over the next two to three days (with the exception of a handful of individuals who survived by hiding under or among the dead bodies). * * *

* * *

498.   The fall of Srebrenica is replete with lessons for this Organization and its Member States—lessons that must be learned if we are to expect the peoples of the world to place their faith in the United Nations. There are occasions when Member States cannot achieve consensus on a particular response to active military conflicts, or do not have the will to pursue what many might consider to be an appropriate course of action. The first of the general lessons is that when peacekeeping operations are used as a

substitute for such political consensus they are likely to fail. There is a role for peacekeeping—a proud role in a world still riven by conflict—and there is even a role for protected zones and safe havens in certain situations; but peacekeeping and war fighting are distinct activities which should not be mixed. Peacekeepers must never again be deployed into an environment in which there is no ceasefire or peace agreement. Peacekeepers must never again be told that they must use their peacekeeping tools—lightly armed soldiers in scattered positions—to impose the ill-defined wishes of the international community on one or another of the belligerents by military means. If the necessary resources are not provided—and the necessary political, military and moral judgments are not made—the job simply cannot be done.

499.   Protected zones and safe areas can have a role in protecting civilians in armed conflict, but it is clear that either they must be demilitarized and established by the agreement of the belligerents, as in the case of the "protected zones" and "safe havens" recognized by international humanitarian law, or they must be truly safe areas, fully defended by a credible military deterrent. The two concepts are absolutely distinct and must not be confused. It is tempting for critics to blame the UNPROFOR units in Srebrenica for its fall, or to blame the United Nations hierarchy above those units. Certainly, errors of judgment were made—errors rooted in a philosophy of impartiality and non-violence wholly unsuited to the conflict in Bosnia—but this must not divert us from the more fundamental mistakes. The safe areas were established by the Security Council without the consent of the parties and without the provision of any credible military deterrent. They were neither protected areas nor safe havens in the sense of international humanitarian law, nor safe areas in any militarily meaningful sense. Several representatives on the Council, as well as the Secretariat, noted this problem at the time, warning that, in failing to provide a credible military deterrent, the safe area policy would be gravely damaging to the Council's reputation and, indeed, to the United Nations as a whole.

* * *

Despite the tragedies of Rwanda and Srebrenica, the UN continues to send Blue Helmets to crisis areas of the world. In July 2004, sixteen UN peacekeeping missions were active—three of those having been approved in 2003–04. Some improvements have been made especially within the UN's Department of Peacekeeping Operations. Yet, many of the missions continue to be characterized by too few troops, troops that lack proper training and equipment, unclear mandates, and uncertain exit strategies. The Security Council wants to respond to crises in the Congo, Haiti, Liberia and other places, but it consistently has difficulty getting states to contribute troops and funds for these missions. It nevertheless sends missions and is also open to flexible arrangements, such as authorizing particular willing states to send troops into crisis situations not under the auspices of the UN. The US and France sent troops in this posture to Haiti under Security Council Resolution 1529.

United Nations   **S**

 Security Council

Distr.
General

S/RES/1529 (2004)
29 February 2004

Resolution 1529 (2004)
of 29 February 2004

The Security Council,

* * *

Deeply concerned by the deterioration of the political, security and humanitarian situation in Haiti and *deploring* the loss of life that has already occurred.

* * *

Taking note of the resignation of Jean–Bertrand Aristide as President of Haiti and the swearing-in of President Boniface Alexandre as the acting President of Haiti in accordance with the Constitution of Haiti,

Acknowledging the appeal of the new President of Haiti for the urgent support of the international community to assist in restoring peace and security in Haiti and to further the constitutional political process now under way,

Determined to support a peaceful and constitutional solution to the current crisis in Haiti,

Determining that the situation in Haiti constitutes a threat to international peace and security, and to stability in the Caribbean especially through the potential outflow of people to other States in the subregion,

Acting under Chapter VII of the Charter of the United Nations,

1. *Calls* on Member States to support the constitutional succession and political process now under way in Haiti and the promotion of a peaceful and lasting solution to the current crisis;

2. *Authorizes* the immediate deployment of a Multinational Interim Force for a period of not more than three months from adoption of this resolution:

(a) To contribute to a secure and stable environment in the Haitian capital and elsewhere in the country, as appropriate and as circumstances permit, in order to support Haitian President Alexandre's request for international assistance to support the constitutional political process under way in Haiti;

(b) To facilitate the provision of humanitarian assistance and the access of international humanitarian workers to the Haitian people in need;

(c) To facilitate the provision of international assistance to the Haitian police and the Haitian Coast Guard in order to establish and maintain public safety and law and order and to promote and protect human rights;

(d) To support establishment of conditions for international and regional organizations, including the United Nations and the Organization of American States, to assist the Haitian people;

(e) To coordinate, as needed, with the OAS Special Mission and with the United Nations Special Adviser for Haiti, to prevent further deterioration of the humanitarian situation;

3. *Declares* its readiness to establish a follow-on United Nations stabilization force to support continuation of a peaceful and constitutional political process and the maintenance of a secure and stable environment, and in this regard requests the Secretary–General, in consultation with the Organization of American States, to submit to the Council recommendations, preferably by 30 days from adoption of this resolution, for the size, structure and mandate of such a force, including the role of international police and means of coordination with the OAS Special Mission, and for subsequent deployment of the United Nations force not later than three months from adoption of this resolution;

4. *Welcomes* the Secretary–General's February 27 appointment of a Special Adviser for Haiti, and *requests* the Secretary–General to elaborate a programme of action for the United Nations to assist the constitutional political process and support humanitarian and economic assistance and promote the protection of human rights and the development of the rule of law;

5. *Calls* on Member States to contribute personnel, equipment and other necessary financial and logistic resources on an urgent basis to the Multinational Interim Force and invites contributing Member States to inform the leadership of the force and

the Secretary–General of their intent to participate in the mission; and *stresses* the importance of such voluntary contributions to help defray the expenses of the Multinational Interim Force that participating Member States will bear;

6. *Authorizes* the Member States participating in the Multinational Interim Force in Haiti to take all necessary measures to fulfil its mandate;

7. *Demands* that all the parties to the conflict in Haiti cease using violent means, and reiterates that all parties must respect international law, including with respect to human rights and that there will be individual accountability and no impunity for violators; *further demands* that parties respect the constitutional succession and the political process under way to resolve the current crisis, and enable legitimate Haitian security forces and other public institutions to perform their duties and provide access to humanitarian agencies to carry out their work;

8. *Further calls* on all parties in Haiti and on Member States to cooperate fully with the Multinational Interim Force in Haiti in the execution of its mandate and to respect the security and freedom of movement of the Multinational Interim Force, as well as to facilitate the safe and unimpeded access of international humanitarian personnel and aid to populations in need in Haiti;

9. *Requests* the leadership of the Multinational Interim Force in Haiti to report periodically to the Council, through the Secretary–General, on the implementation of its mandate;

10. *Calls upon* the international community, in particular the United Nations, the Organization of American States, and the Caribbean Community, to work with the people of Haiti in a long-term effort to promote the rebuilding of democratic institutions and to assist in the development of a strategy to promote social and economic development and to combat poverty;

11. *Decides* to remain seized of the matter.

In addition to the problem of resources for peacekeeping, the old problem of the veto continues to be an issue. States have attempted to develop alternatives to Security Council authorization for the use of force in non-self-defense settings. One alternative is authorization through regional groupings. We turn now to several examples where state have sought alternative authorization beginning with the Cuban missile crisis.

B. COLLECTIVE ACTION THROUGH OTHER (NON-UN) ARRANGEMENTS

The examples of action through non-UN arrangements can be divided between those aimed at security threats and those concerned with humanitarian crises. In most cases, the group taking action had wanted the United Nations to intervene or authorize the group's intervention. Consider in each of the cases that follow why Security Council authorization was not forthcoming. Consider whether these refusals or failures to act represent strengths or weaknesses of the Council design and practice.

1.   Security Threats

In October 1962, the United States detected that the Soviet Union was installing missile launchers on the island of Cuba within easy striking distance of the U.S. The Kennedy Administration decided to establish a naval blockade to prevent Soviet ships from reaching Cuba with remaining material to complete the missile launchers. The US called the blockade a "quarantine" to deflect from the fact that a naval blockade is a use of force prohibited under Article 2(4) of the Charter, unless the blockading state has an exception for its use—self-defense or authorization. The U.S. understood changing the term was not enough and also sought a legal justification for the blockade. The U.S. did not want to claim self-defense because then it would have to characterize the missiles as the equivalent of an armed attack. The U.S. itself had missiles in Turkey that the Soviets could equally have characterized as an armed attack. So the U.S. turned to authorization, but with the Soviets possessing the veto, the State Department's lawyers devised an alternative to requesting authorization from the Security Council.

State Department Memorandum Legal Basis for the Quarantine of Cuba, October 23, 1962

> The quarantine against shipments of offensive weapons to Cuba has been imposed by the United States in accordance with a recommendatory resolution of the Organ of Consultation established by the Inter–American Treaty of Reciprocal Assistance (Rio Treaty). The validity of the action in international law depends on affirmative answers to two questions:
>
> (1) Was the action of the Organ of Consultation authorized by the Rio Treaty; and (2) Is the action consistent with the provisions of the UN Charter to which the Rio Treaty is by its own terms and by the terms of the Charter subordinate?
>
> ### 1.   Authorization Under the Rio Treaty
>
> The Rio Treaty, together with related agreements, constitute the Inter–American system. The paramount purpose of this system, as stated in the Treaty, is:
>
> > "to assure peace, through adequate means, to provide for effective reciprocal assistance to meet armed attacks against any American State, and . . . to deal with threats of aggression against any of them."

The Treaty provides for collective action, not only in the case of armed attack, which is covered by Article 3, but also:

> "If the inviolability or the integrity of the territory or the sovereignty or political independence of any American State should be affected by an aggression which is not an armed attack ... or by any other fact or situation that might endanger the peace of America...." (Article 6.)

In such cases, the Organ of Consultation, comprised of the Foreign Ministers of the Member States or representatives specifically designated for the purpose, is to,

> "meet immediately in order to agree on the measures which must be taken in case of aggression to assist the victim of the aggression or, in any case, the measures which should be taken for the common defense and for the maintenance of the peace and security of the Continent." (Article 6.)

The Organ of Consultation acts "by a vote of two-thirds of the Signatory States which have ratified the Treaty." (Article 17.)

The Treaty is equally explicit as to the measures which may be taken by the Organ of Consultation in any case covered by Article 6. These measures are listed in Article 8 and specifically include "use of armed force". Article 20 further specifies that decisions to take any of the measures listed in Article 8 shall be binding except that "no State shall be required to use armed force without its consent."

The action of the OAS in the present case falls readily within the framework of the procedures established by the Treaty. The Inter–American system has long recognized that the adherence by the present Government of Cuba to Sino–Soviet Communism is inconsistent with the principles of the Inter–American system, and has created a situation endangering the peace of the hemisphere. As early as the Seventh Meeting of Foreign Ministers of the Organization of American States in 1960, the Organization "condemned the intervention or the threat of intervention of extra-continental communist powers in the hemisphere...." The Eighth Meeting, at Punta del Este in 1962, went further. It declared that "the continental unity and democratic institutions of the hemisphere are now in danger." The source of that danger was the "subversive offensive of communist Governments." Among the "outstanding facts in this intensified offensive" was "the existence of a Marxist–Leninist government in Cuba which is publicly aligned with the doctrine and foreign policy of the communist powers." (Resolution I, Final Act, Eighth Meeting of Consultation of Ministers of Foreign Affairs Serving as Organ of Consultation in Application of the Inter–American Treaty of Reciprocal Assistance.)

At that meeting, the Organization took the first collective measures designed to deal with the threat. It prohibited all trade in arms with Cuba, and excluded the present government of that country from participation in the organs of the Inter–American system.

'More recently, on October 2 and 3 of this year, the Foreign Ministers of the American States, meeting informally in Washington, reiterated that 'the Soviet Union's intervention in Cuba threatens the unity of the Americas and its democratic institutions'' and that this called for the adoption of special measures, both individual and collective.

Against this background the Council of the Organization of American States met on October 23 and constituted itself as Organ of Consultation in accordance with Article 12 of the Rio Treaty. The Organ considered the evidence before it of the secret introduction of Soviet strategic missiles into Cuba in the face of Soviet and Cuban assurances to the contrary. It concluded that it was confronted with a situation that might endanger the peace of America within the meaning of Article 6. This considered judgment brought into play the authority to take one or more of the measures listed in Article 8. The resolution adopted by the Organ exercises this authority. It recommends

> "that the member states, in accordance with Articles 6 and 8 of the Inter–American Treaty of Reciprocal Assistance, take all measures, individually and collectively including the use of armed force which they may deem necessary to ensure that the Government of Cuba cannot continue to receive from the Sino–Soviet powers military material and related supplies which may threaten the peace and security of the Continent and to prevent the missiles in Cuba with offensive capability from ever becoming an active threat to the peace and security of the Continent."

The recommendation contained in the Resolution for the use of armed force if necessary was thus fully authorized by the terms of the Rio Treaty and adopted in accordance with its procedure. The quarantine being imposed is specifically designed "to ensure that the Government of Cuba cannot continue to receive from the Sino–Soviet powers" the offensive weapons which threaten the peace and security of the Continent. It represents a minimal use of force to achieve the stated objectives. The United States action thus falls within the terms of the OAS Resolution.

2.   *The UN Charter*

(a) *Regional Organizations*

The Resolution of the Organ of Consultation and the quarantine imposed by the United States pursuant to that Resolution are entirely consistent with the Charter of the United Nations.

The Charter specifically recognizes regional organizations and assigns to them an important place in carrying out the purposes of the United Nations. Article 52(1) states that:

"Nothing in the present Charter precludes the existence of regional arrangements or agencies for dealing with such matters relating to the maintenance of international peace and security as are appropriate for regional action, provided that such arrangements or agencies and their activities are consistent with the Purposes and Principles of the United Nations."

Article 52(2) provides that United Nations National Members that have entered into "such arrangements" or who have constituted "such agencies" must "make every effort to achieve pacific settlement of local disputes through such regional arrangements or by such regional agencies before referring them to the Security Council." Paragraph 3 of the same Article requires the Security Council to "encourage the development of pacific settlement of local disputes through such regional arrangements or by such regional agencies...." Article 54 provides that, "The Security Council shall at all times be kept fully informed of activities undertaken or in contemplation under regional arrangements or by regional agencies for the maintenance of international peace and security." In accordance with this provision, the Organ of Consultation provided that the Security Council would be informed of the contents of the Resolution of October 23rd.

The Charter limits the activities of regional organizations only in the Article 52(1) proviso that such activities must be "consistent with the Purposes and Principles of the United Nations." The Rio Treaty plainly meets this requirement. It was enacted by the High Contracting Parties "to improve the procedure for the pacific settlement of their controversies," in full accord with Article 52(2). The High Contracting Parties expressly reiterated "their will to remain united in an Inter–American system consistent with the purposes and principles of the United Nations." The Resolution and its implementation by the quarantine are in complete accordance with those purposes and principles. These measures are designed, in the opening words of the Charter, "to maintain international peace". They represent "effective collective measures for the prevention and removal of threats to the peace." Article I (i).

The importance of regional agencies in the maintenance of peace and security was recognized in the earliest conceptions of the United Nations. The draft proposal which was prepared at the initial conference at Dumbarton Oaks is virtually the same as Chapter VIII of the Charter.

The framers of the Charter met in San Francisco in 1945 after the basic outlines of the most significant regional arrangement, the

Organization of American States, were already established. The meeting was held subsequent to the Conference of the American Republics at which the Act of Chapultepec was approved. This Act recommended the execution of a treaty to establish a regional arrangement, and specifically provided that the "use of armed force to prevent or repel aggression" constituted "regional action which might appropriately be taken by the regional arrangements." The debates at the San Francisco Conference concerning regional organizations were held against this background, and the Organization of American States provided the principal context for the discussions.

When Article 52 was debated at the San Francisco Conference, the Chairman of the committee charged with considering regional arrangements, speaking as the delegate of Colombia, made the following statement concerning the relationship between the Inter–American system and Chapter VIII of the Charter:

> "The Act of Chapultepec provides for the collective defense of the hemisphere and establishes that if an American nation is attacked all the rest consider themselves attacked. Consequently, such action as they may take to repel aggression, authorized by the article which was discussed in the subcommittee yesterday, is legitimate for all of them. Such action would be in accord with the Charter, by the approval of the article, and a regional arrangement may take action, provided it does not have improper purposes as, for example, joint aggression against another state. From this, it may be deduced that the approval of this article implies that the Act of Chapultepec is not in contravention of the Charter."

No delegate disputed this statement and it must be viewed as generally accepted. The very language of the Act of Chapultepec as well as its purposes were adopted by the Rio Treaty. It is evident that the Treaty created the very type of arrangement contemplated by the Charter.

The records of the Conference reveal that a major role was envisaged for regional arrangements under the Charter. Mr. Perez, the Minister of Foreign Affairs of Venezuela, said, "It is in the interests of all that any conflicts which may arise should be solved as quickly as possible in a satisfactory manner, and no one doubts that regional systems are most appropriate to this effect." The delegate from Mexico, Ambassador Najera noted, "In the chapter to which I am referring, the first consideration of the delegations of the American nations was to safeguard their greatest achievement, the most precious flower of cooperation for security through peaceful means." * * *

The history of events since the San Francisco Conference demonstrates the wisdom of the Charter's framers in entrusting to regional organizations the responsibility for handling regional disputes. Such organizations have close contact with the problems within their regions and thus can exercise considered and informed judgment in dealing with these problems. The Organization of American States is the prime example of this. The political process by which it must operate ensures that action will only be taken after careful analysis. Measures to protect peace and security can only be directed or recommended by a vote of two-thirds of the High Contracting Parties. Article 20 of the Treaty expressly provides that no State may be directed to use armed force without its consent. The Organ of Consultation may only recommend but cannot compel the use of armed force. By the presence of such safeguards, this regional organization is able to take effective action with assurance that such action will be consistent with the limitations imposed by the United Nations Charter. It has taken such action in regard to Cuba by its October 23 Resolution, as implemented by the United States quarantine.

(b) Article 53

Article 53(1) of the UN Charter provides:

> "The Security Council shall, where appropriate, utilize such regional arrangements or agencies for enforcement action under its authority. But no enforcement action shall be taken under regional arrangements or by regional agencies without the authorization of the Security Council. . . ."

The quarantine measures here under consideration as approved by the Organ of Consultation do not constitute "enforcement action". Accordingly, these measures do not require Security Council authorization.

Twice before the Security Council has rejected the contention that the activities of a regional organization constituted "enforcement action" within the meaning of Article 53 of the Charter. In September, 1960, the Council met to consider an allegation by the Soviet Union that a decision of the Organ of Consultation to take certain diplomatic and embargo measures against the Government of the Dominican Republic constituted "enforcement action". The Security Council did not accept that allegation. Earlier this year, Cuba asked the Security Council to consider decisions taken by the American Republics at Punta del Este, claiming that they required Security Council authorization. Again the Council disagreed.

Thus, it appears from the practice of the Security Council, that measures taken by a regional organization to deal with a threat to the peace, are not necessarily "enforcement action" even though they are obligatory in character. When, as here, they are recommendatory in character, it is clear that they cannot involve "enforcement action".

The construction of the phrase "enforcement action" is supported by its use elsewhere in the Charter. The expression appears at several places in the Charter in addition to Article 53. For example, Article 2, paragraph 5 obligates the Members of the United Nations to "refrain from giving assistance to any state against which the United Nations is taking preventive or enforcement action". And Article 5 provides that

> "A Member of the United Nations against which preventive or enforcement action has been taken by the Security Council may be suspended from the exercise of the rights and privileges of membership by the General Assembly upon the recommendation of the Security Council."

The "preventive" and "enforcement" action mentioned in these articles refers to action which the Council is authorized to take under Articles 40, 41, and 42. Article 40 provides for taking of "preventive action" in the form of provisional measures. Such measures are orders of the Council with which Member States are bound to comply. Articles 41 and 42 empower the Council to enforce its decisions by calling upon United Nations Members to apply certain measures or by taking action directly through air, sea, or land forces which are at the disposal of the Security Council. Again, in acting under Articles 41 and 42, the Security Council does more than recommend to Members steps which they might take to meet a threat to peace and security. Rather it decides upon measures and issues orders of enforcement which Member States are obligated under the Charter to carry out.

Council actions under Articles 40, 41, and 42 are to be distinguished from recommendations made by the Council under Article 39 or by the General Assembly in the discharge of its responsibilities as set forth in Chapter IV of the Charter. In the exercise of its powers under Article 10 and 11, the General Assembly has on a number of occasions in the past recommended the use of armed force. The actions of the UN to repel aggression in Korea and to maintain order in the Congo are two such occasions. These actions were taken despite the contention made long ago that such measures constituted "action" which could only be taken by the Security Council. Since the Assembly's powers are only recommendatory in the field of peace and security, the exercise of these powers by the Assembly could not be considered either "preventive" or "enforcement" action.

This distinction between a Security Council measure which is obligatory and constitutes "action," on the one hand, and a measure which is recommended either by the Council or by the General Assembly on the other, is supported by the Advisory Opinion of the International Court of Justice, "Certain Expenses of the United Nations" (July 20, 1962). The Court held that the measures taken by the GA and the Security Council in Suez and the Congo were not enforcement action, in part, because they were only recommendatory as to participating States. Specifically, the Court stated:

> "The word (action) must mean such action as is solely within the province of the Security Council. It cannot refer to recommendations which the Security Council might make, as for instance under Article 38, because the General Assembly under Article II has a comparable power. The (action) which is solely within the province of the Security Council is that which is indicated by the title of Chapter VII of the Charter, namely (Action with respect to threats to the peace, breaches of the peace, and acts of aggression). If the word (action) in Article II, paragraph 2, were interpreted to mean that the General Assembly could make recommendations only of a general character affecting peace and security in the abstract, and not in relation to specific cases, the paragraph would not have provided that the General Assembly may make recommendations on questions brought before it by States or by the Security Council. Accordingly, the last sentence of Article II, paragraph 2, has no application where the necessary action is not enforcement action."

Thus, in the context of United Nations bodies, "enforcement action" does not include action by a United Nations body which is not obligatory on all the Members. As used in Article 53(1), "enforcement action" refers to action by a regional organization rather than to action by an organ of the United Nations, but the words must be given the same meaning in this context. It follows that "enforcement action", as the phrase appears in Article 53(1), does not comprehend action taken by a regional organization which is only recommendatory to the Members of the Organization.

As was pointed out above, the Resolution authorizing the quarantine was agreed upon pursuant to Article 6 of the Rio Treaty. As a recommendation of the "use of armed force", it was specifically authorized by Article 8 of that Treaty. And it is, by the express terms of Article 20, the one measure which, when agreed upon by the Organ of Consultation, Member States are not obligated to carry out. Since States signatories of the Rio Treaty are not obligated to carry out the Resolution recommending quarantine, it does not constitute "enforcement action" under Article 53(1), and is therefore not subject to Security Council authorization.

In 1983, the United States invaded the tiny Caribbean Island state of Grenada, removing the island's leader who had just seized power in a coup.

The US gave three legal justifications for the invasion: to protect U.S. nationals on the island, at the invitation of Britain's Governor–General of Grenada, and by the authorization of the Organization of Eastern Caribbean States (OECS). We look at the third reason here.

Christopher C. Joyner, Reflections on the Lawfulness of Invasion

78 Am. J. Int'l L. 131, 131 (1984).*

Grenada is a micro-state located in the southeastern Caribbean Sea, approximately 1600 miles from the United States. Its territory covers some 133 square miles—about twice the size of the District of Columbia—and its citizen population numbers around 110,000. Granted independence from British colonial rule in 1974, Grenada functioned under a parliamentary government until March 1979, when Maurice Bishop's New Joint Endeavor for the Welfare, Education, and Liberation (JEWEL) Movement ousted then Prime Minister Sir Eric Gairy in a near bloodless coup. Since attaining independence, Grenada sought and secured membership in the British Commonwealth, the Organization of American States, the Caribbean Common Market and the United Nations.

On October 25, 1983, United States military forces invaded Grenada. * * *

The facts of the immediate matter are fairly well acknowledged. On October 12, a military coup fostered by Deputy Prime Minister Bernard Coard toppled the pro-Marxist regime of Prime Minister Maurice Bishop. One week later, on October 19, Bishop and at least five other Grenadan Government officials were executed by "revolutionary armed forces." That same day, a 16–member Revolutionary Military Council was formed, Army Commander General Hudson Austin was designated its "nominal head," and a 24–hour, "shoot-on-sight curfew" was imposed against civilians. Reportedly, foreigners were refused permission to use the airport in order to depart from the island. This unstable internal situation in Grenada, coupled with an apprehension that such conditions might spread and thus foment political instability elsewhere in the Caribbean, gave cause for regional concern. To rectify what was seen as an intolerable state of affairs, a multinational invasion was launched against Grenada. Led by 1,900 U.S. Marines and Army airborne Rangers, the invasion force also included 300 troops representing Jamaica, Barbados, Dominica, St. Lucia, Antigua and St. Vincent. By October 30, the invasion had been completed, and the island militarily secured.

The Caribbean states were all members of the OECS, including Grenada. They invoked the following treaty provision as the legal basis for invading:

* Footnotes omitted.

Treaty Establishing the Organization of Eastern Caribbean States

20 I.L.M. 1166 (1981).

Article 8 (4) The Defence and Security Committee shall have responsibility for coordinating the efforts of Member States for collective defence and the preservation of peace and security against external aggression and for the development of close ties among the Member States of the Organisation in matters of external defence and security, including measures to combat the activities of mercenaries, operating with or without the support of internal or national elements, in the exercise of the inherent right of individual or collective self-defence recognised by Article 51 of the Charter of the United Nations.

The United States vetoed a UN Security Council resolution that would have found the invasion in violation of international law. The General Assembly then took up the question.

The Situation in Grenada

The General Assembly,

Considering the statements made before the Security Council in connection with the situation in Grenada,

Recalling the Declaration on Principles of International Law concerning Friendly Relations and Co-operation among States in accordance with the Charter of the United Nations,

Recalling also, the Declaration on Inadmissibility of Intervention and Interference in the Internal Affairs of States,

Reaffirming the sovereign and inalienable right of Grenada freely to determine its own political, economic and social system, and to develop its international relations without outside intervention, interference, subversion, coercion or threat in any form whatsoever,

Deeply deploring the events in Grenada which led to the killing of the Prime Minister, Mr. Maurice Bishop, and other prominent Grenadians,

Bearing in mind * * * Article 2, paragraph 4, of the Charter of the United Nations,

Gravely concerned at the military intervention taking place * * *,

Conscious of the need for States to show consistent respect for the principles of the Charter,

1. *Deeply deplores* the armed intervention in Grenada, which constitutes a flagrant violation of international law and of the independence, sovereignty and territorial integrity of that State;

2. *Deplores* the death of innocent civilians resulting from the armed intervention;

3. *Calls upon* all States to show the strictest respect for the sovereignty, independence and territorial integrity of Grenada;

4. *Calls* for an immediate cessation of the armed intervention and the immediate withdrawal of the foreign troops from Grenada;

5. *Requests* that free elections be organized as rapidly as possible to enable the people of Grenada to choose its governments democratically;

6. *Requests* the Secretary–General as a matter of urgency to assess the situation and to report back to the General Assembly within seventy-two hours.

43rd plenary meeting
2 November 1983

The vote was 108 to 9, with 27 abstentions. Even the United Kingdom voted in favor of the resolution.

2.   Humanitarian Crises

In addition to security threats, non-UN arrangements have acted in response to humanitarian crises. Some such as the intervention in Grenada was justified in part on the basis of security but also rescue of nationals and in support of democracy. It may be that intervention for humanitarian purposes has been the more common justification.

Marco Gestri, The ECOWAS' Operations in Liberia and Sierra Leone: Amnesty for Past Unlawful Acts or Progress towards Future Rules?

Redefining Sovereignty (Michael Bothe et al. eds., forthcoming in 2005).*

ECOWAS was founded in 1975 by 15 West African States, by virtue of the Treaty of Lagos, as a sub-regional organization devoted to promoting "co-operation and development in all fields of economic activity". Very early, the Community expanded its competence to security matters under the assumption that peace and regional security are crucial factors in the socio-economic development of member States.

In 1978, the Heads of State and Government of member States adopted a Protocol on Non–Aggression. With this Protocol,

* Footnotes omitted.

ECOWAS States on the one hand reaffirmed their obligations under the Charters of the UN and the Organization for African Unity (OAU) not to use force as a means of settling their disputes and not to commit or encourage acts of subversion or hostility against any other member State and on the other undertook to refer any dispute among them to a Committee established by the ECOWAS Authority of Heads of State and Government and, in last resort, to the Authority itself.

Three years later, ECOWAS member States signed a Protocol relating to Mutual Assistance on Defence. In the first place, the Protocol constitutes an example of a treaty for the organization of collective self-defence. Indeed, by virtue of the Protocol, member States resolve to provide mutual assistance for defence against any "external" armed threat or aggression coming from a non-ECOW-AS State. The Protocol also lays down the bases for the creation of an ECOWAS multinational force (the "Allied Armed Forces of the Community") subject to a detailed institutional mechanism. These provisions however have never been fully implemented. In the second place, under the 1981 Defence Protocol, member States undertook to take appropriate measures, including intervention of a collective force, "in case of internal armed conflict within any member State engineered and supported actively from outside likely to endanger the security and peace of the entire Communi-ty". Pursuant to the 1981 Protocol, in case of both external aggression and internal conflict supported from outside, military assistance on the part of ECOWAS is subject to a written request of the Head of State or Government of the victim State. Finally, with regard to an armed conflict involving two member States, the 1981 Protocol envisages the possibility of interposing a multina-tional force between the contending parties.

In order to account for the progressive broadening of the fields of interest of the Community, it may be useful to add that ECOWAS Heads of State and Government adopted a Declaration of Political Principles in Abuja on 6 July 1981, asserting in particular the principle of democracy and condemning any seizure of power by force of arms.

* * *

ECOMOG intervention in Liberia

The first operation orchestrated by ECOWAS in the field of the maintenance of peace took place in Liberia.

The civil war in the West African State erupted in December 1989, when a group of rebels, known as the National Patriotic Front of Liberia (NPFL) and commanded by Charles Taylor, entered Liberia from the neighbouring State of Ivory Coast. The NPFL waged a massive offensive against the Government of President Samuel Doe and his military, the Armed Forces of

Liberia (AFL). The invasion ignited a bloody, inter-ethnic civil war, in which a third faction, led by Prince Johnson and known as the Independent National Patriotic Front of Liberia (INPFL), soon became involved. In a short time, rebel forces acquired control of Nimba county and North–Eastern Liberia. In order to counter the insurgency, President Doe's troops launched indiscriminate attacks on villages in Nimba county, with major losses among the civilian population. However, the counter-insurgency campaign was not successful. By summer 1990, rebel forces controlled most of the country, with the sole exception of a small part of the capital, Monrovia.

On 14 July 1990, President Doe addressed a letter to the Chairman of the ECOWAS Standing Mediation Committee. That body had been established in May 1990 by the ECOWAS Authority of Heads of State and Government to promote the amicable settlement of disputes among Member States. In the letter stressing the tragic humanitarian situation of the country, the President stated that he considered it "most expedient ... to introduce an ECOWAS Peace-keeping force into Liberia to forestall increasing terror and tension and to assure a peaceful transitional environment".

On 7 August 1990, the ECOWAS Standing Mediation Committee, purportedly acting on behalf of the ECOWAS Authority, adopted a Decision calling on all the parties to the conflict to observe a cease-fire and establishing at the same time an ECOWAS Cease–Fire Monitoring Group (ECOMOG). ECOMOG was entrusted with powers "to conduct military operations for the purpose of monitoring the cease-fire, restoring law and order to create the necessary conditions for free and fair elections to be held in Liberia". The creation of ECOMOG by the Committee initially encountered strong reservations as to its constitutionality from the viewpoint of the ECOWAS Treaty on the part of some Francophone members of the Community such as Burkina Faso, Ivory Coast and Senegal. Subsequently, the Decision of the Standing Mediation Committee was substantially validated by the Extraordinary Summit of Heads of State and Government held at Bamako on 27–28 November 1990.

It is important to note that, pursuant to the peace plan formulated in August 1990 by the Standing Mediation Committee, an Interim Government was to be established in Liberia, to which power would be transferred. In order to constitute a broad-based Interim Government, the Standing Mediation Committee decided to facilitate the convening of a conference of all Liberian political parties and interest groups. In any case, according to the peace plan, none of the leaders of the warring parties engaged in the conflict, including President Doe, should head the Interim government.

ECOMOG troops, consisting of approximately 3,000 men, landed in Liberia on 24 August 1990. The Secretary General of the United Nations was informed of the formation and deployment of ECOMOG into Liberia. However, there was no prior express authorization of the mission on the part of the Security Council. As a matter of fact, UN political organs neglected the Liberian crisis for some time.

Furthermore, Charles Taylor's NPFL, whose troops were in control of 90 per cent of Liberian territory, did not consent to dispatch of the force. On the contrary, Taylor overtly opposed the operation and immediately launched a military attack against ECOMOG. In fact, he contested ECOMOG's impartiality, considering its intervention an attempt on the part of Nigeria to assist Samuel Doe.

As envisaged in the peace plan, a conference on Liberia's political future was held in Banjul (Gambia), under the auspices of the ECOWAS Standing Mediation Committee, from 27 August to 1 September 1990. The conference was attended by all Liberian political parties and by the INPFL. Noting that there was no government in Liberia, the Conference decided that some portions of the Liberian Constitution should be suspended and an Interim Government organized. Eventually an Interim Government of National Unity, headed by Amos Sawyer, was elected by the Conference.

On 10 September 1990 President Samuel Doe was killed, reportedly by members of the INPFL, on the occasion of a visit to ECOMOG headquarters. This event provoked a wave of criticism *vis-à-vis* ECOMOG and determined a change of attitude on the part of the multinational force. A new Nigerian Commander was appointed, who impressed a shift from a typical peacekeeping posture to peace-enforcement. As a consequence, intense fighting took place in October 1990 between ECOMOG and the NPFL, enabling the multinational force to drive the NPFL out of the capital and to establish a security zone around it. Of note in this connection is that ECOMOG also had recourse to the air force, notably in order to strike crucial NPFL positions outside Monrovia.

The new military situation on the ground made possible the adoption in Bamako (Mali) on 28 November 1990 of a cease-fire agreement that was also accepted by the NPFL. The agreement put a temporary end to the hostilities, apart from periodical clashes between the NPFL and a newly-established faction, the United Liberation Movement of Liberia for Democracy (ULIMO), mostly made up of former AFL soldiers.

The Security Council did not discuss the Liberian situation until January 1991 that is four months after the deployment of ECOMOG forces. On 22 January 1991, the President of the

Security Council issued a statement in which the members of the Security Council commended "the efforts made by the ECOWAS heads of State and Government to promote peace and normalcy in Liberia" and called upon the parties to the conflict to co-operate fully with the ECOWAS.

In October 1991, another peace plan, known as the "Yamoussoukro IV Accord" was adopted under the auspices of ECOWAS. The Accord provided for the encampment and disarmament of all warring factions under ECOMOG supervision. Pursuant to the peace plan, a buffer zone along the Sierra Leone–Liberia border would also be established. These measures were to create the necessary conditions of peace and security conducive to the holding of free, fair and democratic elections in Liberia. Yet the NPFL, which remained in control of the vast majority of Liberian territory, did not comply with the peace plan.

On 7 May 1992, the President of the United Nations Security Council issued a second note on Liberia in which he, on behalf of the Council members, again commended ECOWAS for its untiring efforts to bring the Liberian conflict to a conclusion and expressed support for the Yamoussoukro IV Accord.

The end of Summer 1992 saw the resumption of heavy fighting between ECOMOG and the NPFL. In October 1992, rebel forces launched a vigorous attack on Monrovia and ECOMOG reacted with a massive use of force, ousting the NPFL from the capital.

As the fighting continued, ECOWAS decided to impose economic sanctions against Liberian combatants failing to comply with the implementation of the Yamoussoukro IV Accord, namely the NPFL. This decision was adopted by the First Joint Session of the ECOWAS Standing Mediation Committee and the Committee of Five. In the Final Communiqué issued at the Joint Session, ECOWAS Head of States strongly reaffirmed their trust in ECOMOG, notably "in its absolute neutrality in the performance of its functions in Liberia". They also "reaffirmed the right of ECOMOG, as a peace-keeping force, to defend itself against armed attacks from any quarter".

Against this background, the Security Council adopted the first Resolution on the Liberian situation on 19 November 1992. In particular, Resolution 788 (1992)—after having determined that "the deterioration of the situation in Liberia constitutes a threat to international peace and security, particularly in West Africa" and made reference to Chapter VIII of the UN Charter–called upon all parties to the conflict to respect and implement the various peace accords concluded to date. It must be underscored that the Resolution adopted by the Security Council expressly commended ECOWAS "for its efforts to restore peace, security and stability in Liberia". On the other hand, the Council condemned "the continuing armed attacks against the peace-keeping forces of ECOWAS in Liberia by one of the parties to the conflict".

Further to a specific request on the part of ECOWAS, Resolution 788 (1992) also imposed, under Chapter VII, a general embargo on all deliveries of weapons and military equipment to Liberia. The arms embargo did not, however, apply to weapons and military equipment destined "for the sole use of the peace-keeping forces of ECOWAS in Liberia". It has to be noted in this regard that the sanctions decided by ECOWAS were broader in scope, for they included the duty for States to prohibit the importation into their territories of products originating from the zones controlled in Liberia by the targeted parties.

By way of its Resolution 788 (1992) the Security Council also requested the Secretary General to appoint a Special Representative for Liberia. The nomination of Trevor Gordon–Somers as Special Representative signaled the first significant involvement of the United Nations in the Liberian crisis. Peace talks held in Geneva in July 1993 under UN auspices led to the conclusion of the Cotonou Peace Agreement of 25 July 1993. The Agreement provided for a cease-fire and cessation of hostilities among the parties. Under the Cotonou Agreement, the parties also agreed to form a transitional government, steered by a Council of State made up of representatives of all the warring parties that should exert its authority until the celebration of free general elections. An expanded ECOMOG force, including troops from African non-ECOWAS States, was entrusted with the supervision of the implementation of the Agreement, in parallel with a UN military observer mission to be established. Basically, ECOMOG was to have the primary responsibility of presiding over the implementation of the military provisions of the Agreement, while the United Nations mission would monitor ECOMOG operations in order to ensure its impartiality. In particular, from an operative point of view, ECOMOG troops were to check entry points, airports and seaports to ensure compliance with the arms embargo established by Resolution 788 (1992), create buffer zones along the Liberian borders and supervise the cantonment, disarmament and demobilization of combatants.

In the wake of the Cotonou Agreement, the Security Council adopted Resolution 866 (1993) on 22 September 1993, which commended ECOWAS action in Liberia once again and provided for the establishment of the UN Observer Mission in Liberia (UNOMIL). In the resolution, the Council stressed that this was the first peace-keeping mission undertaken by the United Nations in co-operation with a peacekeeping mission already set up by another organization, in this case a sub-regional organization (ECOWAS).

According to the mandate envisaged by the Resolution, UNOMIL had "without participation in enforcement operations, to co-ordinate with ECOMOG in the discharge of ECOMOG's separate responsibilities both formally and informally".

In the following years, implementation of the Cotonou Agreement encountered major obstacles due to protracted hostilities among the different factions and difficulties in forming the transitional government. After the conclusion of successive unsuccessful peace agreements, on 17 August 1996 the Abuja II Peace Agreement was finally signed. This event opened the way to the holding of general presidential and parliamentary elections on 19 July 1997.

In the presidential elections that followed, Charles Taylor was elected and held power until 2003 when after renewed fighting, he accepted Nigeria's offer of asylum. Taylor was indicted for various crimes by a semi-international war crimes tribunal in Sierre Leone.

The Washington Post, August 2, 2003

Security Council Backs Nigerian–Led Force in Liberia

By Colum Lynch

—The U.N. Security Council voted tonight to adopt a resolution authorizing the intervention of a Nigerian-led West African peacekeeping mission in Liberia to restore peace and facilitate the departure of the country's president, Charles Taylor, from power.

The council's action clears the way for the deployment of the first battalion of hundreds of Nigerian troops into Liberia on Monday and a larger U.N. peacekeeping mission within two months. After the vote, U.N. Secretary General Kofi Annan suggested that President Bush consider approving the first, if limited, intervention by U.S. troops in an African conflict since President George H.W. Bush ordered U.S. Marines into Somalia in the early 1990s.

"Ultimately that is a decision for President Bush to make, but we do have a desperate situation in Liberia," Annan said, noting the decision to station U.S. warships off the coast of Liberia. Despite overwhelming support by the 15–nation council for the mission, the United States faced stiff opposition to a provision in the resolution that would grant blanket immunity from prosecution by foreign courts to international peacekeepers serving in the mission. Germany, France and Mexico abstained from the vote to protest the inclusion of the provision.

The dispute over immunity soured an otherwise concerted effort by the council to move quickly to adopt a new U.N. mandate that could bring security and relief to Liberia, which has been plagued by 14 years of misrule and civil war under Taylor. "We are in favor of the mission; we are in favor of an early vote," said Germany's U.N. ambassador, Gunter Pleuger. "But there is one foreign element in the resolution which has nothing to do with the multinational force."

Pleuger said the resolution's provision went far beyond previous U.S. efforts to seek immunity for its troops from the International Criminal Court, which the United States opposes. He said it would bar states, including Germany or the United States, from prosecuting foreign nationals in the Liberian mission for crimes committed against their own citizens.

"A German court could not prosecute somebody who murders a German citizen" in Liberia, he said. "And that is in contravention of our constitution."

"Mexico cannot support this," added Mexico's ambassador, Adolfo Aguilar Zinser. "The penal code of Mexico states that crimes committed abroad by a foreigner against a Mexican will be prosecuted in Mexico, provided the accused

has not been subject to a final trial in the country concerned."

Zinser said the United States had refused to consider a proposal to vote on the resolution paragraph by paragraph to allow him to express support for the resolution while voicing opposition to the immunity provision.

Despite the reservations, an upsurge in fighting between government and rebel forces over the past month, which has brought a fresh round of killing and cut off water and food to hundreds of thousands, eased the way for the swift passage of the U.S.-drafted resolution.

"We cannot keep fiddling while Monrovia burns," said Heraldo Munoz, Chile's U.N. ambassador.

The Bush administration's sponsorship of the resolution is likely to increase pressure on the United States to send its soldiers to Liberia to support the regional peacekeeping mission. Bush, citing the United States' historical ties with Liberia, which was founded for black Americans more than 175 years ago, has pledged to help the regional peace-

keeping force with financial, political and logistical support, including a possible role for a limited number of U.S. troops in Liberia.

But Bush cautioned this week that any final commitment to send troops to Liberia would require the imposition of a cease-fire and the departure of Taylor, who was indicted by a U.N. war crimes court in Sierre Leone this year. And he noted that any decision to send troops would be limited in duration and size.

"Peacekeepers will safeguard security in the wake of Charles Taylor's departure from the Liberian presidency," said John D. Negroponte, the U.S. ambassador to the United Nations. "I cannot emphasize how crucial it is for Taylor to leave." The resolution adopted today allows the intervention force to use all necessary means, including force, to impose security, permit the resumption of aid deliveries and pave the way for the arrival of a larger U.N. peacekeeping mission by Oct. 1. It also authorizes the United Nations to borrow money from a separate peacekeeping mission in Sierra Leone to underwrite the costs of the West African vanguard forces of more than 2,000 Nigerian, Senegalese, Malian and Ghanaian peacekeepers.

Senior U.N. officials have warned the United States that it will take them three to six months to get the U.N. mission on its feet. But Negroponte and other U.S. officials urged the United Nations to make the deadline.

"This critical deployment of the multinational force and follow-up peacekeeping operation go hand in hand," Negroponte said. "The multinational force is a crucial short-term bridge to our goal of placing U.N. peacekeepers on the ground as soon as possible."

As you learned above, NATO assisted United Nations peacekeepers in Bosnia during fighting there in 1992–1995. Then NATO was designated to supply the peacekeeping troops to implement the Dayton Peace Accords that brought the fighting to an end. NATO's assistance to UNPROFOR was authorized under UN Security Council Resolution 787 (Nov. 16, 1992). The Resolution mentions both UN Charter Chapters VII and VIII. The Resolution authorizing NATO to participate in the IFOR mission in Bosnia mentions only Chapter VII (SC Res. 1031, Dec. 15, 1995). When the human rights situation in yet another part of Yugoslavia, Kosovo, began to break-down in the spring of 1998, the United States wanted NATO to take enforcement action there, too.[11] The Security Council ordered economic sanctions, but never military force. At least two permanent members, Russia and China, did not support the use of military force. Nevertheless, on March 24, 1999, NATO began bombing Serbia for a period lasting 78 days. Finally, Serb leader, Slobodan Milosevic agreed to pull the army out of Kosovo. It was replaced by NATO and other national peacekeepers, authorized by UN Security Council Resolution, 1244 (June 10, 1999).

During the bombing, Yugoslavia brought a case to the International Court of Justice against ten members of NATO. It argued that NATO's use of force was unlawful and wanted the ICJ to issue provisional measures ordering NATO to stop the bombing. What follows is an excerpt of Yugoslavia's argument on the illegality of the bombing and an excerpt from the United Kingdom's response.

Legality of Use of Force

1999 I.C.J. (Yugo. v. Belg., France, Ger., Italy, Netherlands, Port., Spain, U.K., U.S.A)
Argument of Yugoslavia

* * *

---

11. *See* Mary Ellen O'Connell, *The UN, NATO and International Law After Kosovo,* 22 Hum. Rts. Q. 57 (2000).

2.   The use of force against the Federal Republic of Yugoslavia is illegal

The acts of bombing of the Yugoslav territory are in breach of the obligation not to resort to the threat or use of force against another State, which exists as a general rule of customary law and as a basic principle of the Charter of the United Nations and has a nature of *jus cogens*. Bruno Simma is right when he says:

> "In contemporary international law, as codified in the 1969 Vienna Convention on the Law of Treaties (Articles 53 and 64), the prohibition enunciated in Article 2(4) of the Charter is part of *jus cogens*, i.e., it is accepted and recognized by the international community of States as a whole as norm from which no derogation is permitted and which can be modified only by a subsequent norm of general international law having the same peremptory character. Hence, universal *jus cogens*, like the prohibition embodied in Article 2(4), cannot be contracted out of at the regional level. Further, the Charter prohibition of the threat or use of armed force is binding on States both individually and as members of international organizations, such as NATO, as well as on those organizations themselves." (Bruno Simma, *NATO, the UN and the Use of Force: Legal Aspects, EJIL*, 1999, Vol. 10, No. 1.)

2.2   The acts of bombing of the territory of Yugoslavia are not just illegal acts. They constitute a crime against peace and also the crime of genocide.

2.3   The Security Council of the United Nation is exclusively empowered by the United Nations Charter to decide on the use of force, according to provisions of Chapter VII of the Charter. The United Nations Security Council may utilize regional arrangements or agencies for enforcement action. But according to Article 53 of the Charter "no enforcement action shall be taken under regional arrangements or by regional agencies without the authorization of the Security Council...." NATO and its member States are without authorization of the Security Council for the use of force against the Federal Republic of Yugoslavia.

* * * Article 103 of the Charter of the United Nations:

> "In the event of a conflict between the obligations of the Members of the United Nations under the present Charter and their obligations under any other international agreement, their obligations under the present Charter shall prevail."

And second, Article 7 of the 1949 North Atlantic Treaty, which is quite in harmony with Article 103 of the Charter and reads as follows:

> "The Treaty does not affect, and shall not be interpreted as affecting, in any way the rights and obligations under the

Charter of the Parties which are Members of the United Nations, or the primary responsibility of the Security Council for the maintenance of international peace and security."

2.4   By bombing civilian targets the Respondents are in breach of the obligations established by the 1949 Geneva Convention relative to the Protection of Civilian Persons in Time of War and by the 1977 Protocol I to the Convention.

2.5   By destroying oil refineries and chemical plants, the Respondents caused large pollution of soil, air and water endangering the basic conditions of survival of the nation. They have bombed several times the oil refineries in Pancevo, near Belgrade, in Novi Sad, the chemical plants for production of fertilizers in Pancevo, the nitrogen factory in Pancevo, the chemical company "Prvaiskra" in Baric, close to Belgrade and others. A large part of the population of Pancevo have left their flats to protect themselves.

2.6   By using cluster bombs and weapons containing depleted uranium, the Respondents are in breach of the obligation not to use prohibited weapons, i.e., weapons calculated to cause unnecessary suffering, established as a principle of law of armed conflicts. It is estimated that the Respondents used about 15,000 cluster bombs. As many as 3,600 cluster bombs were used in the attacks against towns in Kosovo and Metohija—Pristina, Uroseva, Djakovica, Prizren and other cities.

* * *

3.   Nothing can justify use of force against the Federal Republic of Yugoslavia

The Declaration on Principles of International Law concerning Friendly Relations and Co-operation among States in accordance with the Charter of the United Nations, adopted by consensus in the General Assembly as resolution 2625 (XXV) of 24 October 1970, says:

> "No state or group of States has the right to intervene, directly or indirectly, for any reason whatever, in the internal or external affairs of any other State. Consequently, armed intervention and all other forms of interference or attempted threats against the personality of the State or against its political, economic and cultural elements, are in violation of international law."

The International Court of Justice has strictly applied this fundamental principle. It made clear its legal understanding of the principle in the *Nicaragua* case as follows:

> "The Court also notes that Nicaragua is accused by the 1985 finding of the United States Congress of violating human rights...while the United States might form its own appraisal of the situation as to respect for human rights in Nicaragua,

the use of force could not be the appropriate method to monitor or ensure such respect. With regard to the steps actually taken, the protection of human rights, a strictly humanitarian objective, cannot be compatible with the mining of ports, the destruction of oil installations, or again with the training, arming and equipping of the *contras*. The Court concludes that the argument derived from the preservation of human rights in Nicaragua cannot afford a legal justification for the conduct of the United States, and cannot in any event be reconciled with the legal strategy of the respondent State, which is based on the right of collective self-defense." *(Military and Paramilitary Activities in and against Nicaragua (Nicaragua v. United States of America), Merits, Judgment, I.C.J. Reports 1986,* pp. 134–135, paras. 267 and 268.)

Professor Schachter is quite clear in his "International Law in Theory and Practice", published in 1991. On page 128, he says:

"International law does not, and should not, legitimize the use of force across national lines except for self-defence (including collective self-defence) and enforcement measures ordered by the Security Council. Neither human rights, democracy or self-determination are acceptable legal grounds or waging war, nor for that matter, are traditional just causes for righting wrongs. This conclusion is not only in accord with the UN Charter as it was originally understood; it is also in keeping with the interpretation adopted by the great majority of States at the present time."

The VICE–PRESIDENT, acting President: Thank you, Mr. Etinski. I give the floor now to Mr. Brownlie.

Mr. BROWNLIE: Mr. President, distinguished Members of the Court,

I have the privilege to represent the Federal Republic of Yugoslavia. My task in the first round is to review the legal issues concerning the use of force by the respondent States.

I. Propositions

In the first place I would like to present a set of propositions.

First: The attack on the territory of Yugoslavia involves a continuing breach of Article 2, paragraph 4, of the United Nations Charter.

Secondly: The attack cannot be justified as individual or collective self-defence and is not authorized by any Security Council resolution.

Thirdly: Humanitarian intervention, the justification belatedly offered by the respondent States, has no legal authenticity whatsoever.

Fourthly: The reliance upon humanitarian intervention is in any case—in any case—invalidated by the unlawful modalities of the aerial bombardment, and the means adopted by the respondent States are extremely disproportionate to the declared aims of the action.

Fifthly: The few exponents of humanitarian intervention invest the doctrine with a profile which is totally unlike this bombing campaign.

Sixthly: The command structure of NATO constitutes an instrumentality of the respondent States, acting as their agent.

That completes my series of propositions.

II.   Article 2, paragraph 4, of the United Nations Charter

And so the attack on the territory of Yugoslavia involves continuing breach of Article 2, paragraph 4, of the Charter.

In my submission, the principle of Article 2, paragraph 4, stated in 1945 remains unqualified. As Professor Virally, amongst others, has pointed out, the preparatory work of the Charter indicates unequivocally that intervention for special motives was ruled out by the inclusion of the phrase "against the territorial integrity or political independence of any State". (See Cot and Pellet, *La Charte des Nations Unies*, 1985, p. 114.) That is the contribution by Professor Virally.

The subsequent practice of the member states of the United Nations has not produced a departure in general international law. Such a departure would, in principle, be a major aberration and would require consistent and substantial evidence. Such a change in customary law has not been asserted to exist, much less proved, by a single member State of NATO.

III.   Confirmation of this position

The position of the Charter was confirmed, 25 years later, in 1970, in the Declaration on Principles of International Law concerning Friendly Relations and Co-operation. As the Court will readily appreciate, the Declaration provides evidence of the consensus among States on the meaning of the principles of the Charter. In particular, the Declaration confirmed:

"The principle concerning the duty not to intervene in matters within the domestic jurisdiction of any State, in accordance with the Charter."

The document then has an official commentary:

"No State or group of States has the right to intervene, directly or indirectly, for any reason whatever, in the internal or external affairs of any other State. Consequently, armed intervention and all other forms of interference or attempted threats against the personality of the State or against its political, economic and cultural elements, are in violation of international law.

No State may use or encourage the use of economic, political or any other type of measures to coerce another State in order to obtain from it the subordination of the exercise of its sovereign rights and to secure from it advantages of any kind. Also, no State shall organize, assist, foment, finance, incite or tolerate subversive, terrorist or armed activities directed towards the violent overthrow of the regime of another State, or interfere in civil strife in another State.

The use of force to deprive peoples of their national identity constitutes a violation of their inalienable rights and of the principle of non-intervention.

Every State has an inalienable right to choose its political, economic, social and cultural systems, without interference in any form by another State.

Nothing in the foregoing paragraphs shall be construed as affecting the relevant provisions of the Charter relating to the maintenance of international peace and security."

The general legal regime of the Charter was affirmed by Professor Schwebel, as he then was, in his Hague lectures delivered in 1972 under the heading "Aggression, Intervention and Self-defence in Modern International Law" (*Recueil des Cours*, Vol. II (1972), pp. 413–497).

The basic principles of the legal regime relating to the use of force were also reaffirmed in the Definition of Aggression adopted by the General Assembly on 14 December 1974 (resolution 3314 (XXIX)). Article 5 of the definition provides that: "No consideration of whatever nature, whether political, economic, military or otherwise, may serve as a justification for aggression."

IV. Reliable sources give no recognition to the doctrine of humanitarian intervention

In my submission, the respondent States cannot rely upon the alleged doctrine of humanitarian intervention. There is no evidence of such a development in customary international law. Moreover, officials of the respondent States have, in fact, sought to rely upon resolutions of the Security Council, and not a doctrine of humanitarian intervention. I refer to the expression viewed by the Foreign Secretary of the United Kingdom, Mr. Robin Cook, on 19 October 1998, and the speech in Parliament by Mr. Blair, Prime Minister, on 23 March this year.

Reliable authority covering a period of 30 years has failed to recognize a principle of humanitarian intervention.

I shall review the relevant authorities in chronological order.

The first is that of Dr. Marjorie Whiteman, editing the famous *Digest of International Law* in accordance with United States practice (Vol. 12, pp. 204–215 (1971) (Tab 3.)) It is of course an official publication of the United States Department of State. Dr. Whiteman sets out various opinions—some in favour, some against—but she offers no endorsements of the principle by the United States Government. That is in 1971.

Secondly, there are the views of Professor Schwebel, as he then was, in the *Hague Academy Lectures* of 1972. In his substantial review of the subjects of aggression and intervention, Mr. Schwebel did not make a single reference to humanitarian intervention. That is in 1972.

Thirdly, there is the view of Professor Oscar Schachter, which appears in the *Michigan Law Review* (Vol. 82 (1984), p. 1629). Professor Schachter wrote that "governments by and large (and most jurists) would not assert a right to forcible intervention to protect the nationals of another country from atrocities carried out in that country".

Fourthly, there is the British Foreign Office view expressed in Foreign Policy Document No. 148. This is set out in full in the *British Year Book of International Law,* Volume 57 (1986), beginning at page 614.

The key passage reads thus:

"II.22. In fact, the best case that can be made in support of humanitarian intervention is that it cannot be said to be unambiguously illegal. To make that case, it is necessary to demonstrate, in particular by reference to Article 1(3) of the UN Charter, which includes the promotion and encouragement of respect for human rights as one of the Purposes of the United Nations, that paragraphs 7 and 4 of Article 2 do not apply in cases of flagrant violations of human rights. But the overwhelming majority of contemporary legal opinion comes down against the existence of a right of humanitarian intervention, for three main reasons: first, the UN Charter and the corpus of modern international law do not seem specifically to incorporate such a right; secondly, state practice in the past two centuries, and especially since 1945, at best provides only a handful of genuine cases of humanitarian intervention, and, on most assessments, none at all; and finally, on prudential grounds, that the scope for abusing such a right argues strongly against its creation. As Akehurst argues, 'claims by some states that they are entitled to use force to prevent violations of human rights may make other states reluctant to accept legal obligations concerning human rights'. In essence, therefore, the case against making humanitarian intervention an exception to the principle of non-intervention is that its doubtful benefits would be heavily outweighed by its costs in terms of respect for international law." (Footnote omitted.) (P. 619.)

I next come to the opinion of Professor Yoram Dinstein, in his monograph on *War, Aggression and Self–Defence* (CUP, 1988, at p. 89 (Tab 4)). Professor Dinstein concluded that: "Nothing in the Charter substantiates the right of one State to use force against another under the guise of ensuring the implementation of human rights." (*Ibid.* p. 89)

There is then the view of Professor Randelzhofer of Germany, in the volume edited by Bruno Simma, the *Charter of the United Nations, A Commentary* (OUP, 1994, (Tab 6) at pp. 123–124).

Professor Randelzhofer considers that there is no room for the concept of humanitarian intervention either in the Charter or in customary law.

And lastly, we have the views of Professor Bruno Simma, writing in the *European Journal of International Law* (Vol. 10 (1999) available on the Internet). He regards the use of force for humanitarian purposes as incompatible with the United Nations Charter in the absence of the authorization of the Security Council * * *.

Mr. President, these sources cover a period of 30 years and constitute the careful opinions of well-known authorities of various nationalities.

V. On the facts, this attack on Yugoslavia cannot qualify as humanitarian intervention

Mr. President, aside from the legal issues, there are very strong grounds for the disqualification of the so-called air strikes as a humanitarian intervention.

> *First*: There is no genuine humanitarian purpose. The action against Yugoslavia, as many diplomats know, forms part of an ongoing geopolitical agenda unrelated to human rights. When in 1995, 600,000 Serbs were forced out of the Krajina, the respondent States stayed silent.

> *Secondly*: The modalities selected disqualify the mission as a humanitarian one. Bombing the populated areas of Yugoslavia and using high performance ordnance and anti-personnel weapons involve policies completely inimical to humanitarian intervention. Moreover, bombing from a height of 15,000 feet inevitably endangers civilians, and this operational mode is intended exclusively to prevent risks to combat personnel.

The population of Yugoslavia as a whole is being subjected to inhumane treatment and punishment for political reasons. One thousand two hundred civilians—1,200 civilians—have been killed so far, and 4,500 seriously injured.

Some groups of civilians, including television personnel—including television personnel—have been deliberately targeted. Several attempts have been made to assassinate the Head of State of Yugoslavia. And so, in our view, these modalities clearly disqualify the claim to act on humanitarian grounds.

Thirdly: The selection of a bombing campaign is disproportionate to the declared aims of the action. Thus, in order to protect one minority in one region all the other communities in the whole of Yugoslavia are placed at risk of intensive bombing.

Fourthly: The pattern of targets and the geographical extent of the bombing indicates broad political purposes unrelated to humanitarian issues.

VI. Major considerations of international public order disqualifying the bombing as a humanitarian action

Mr. President, in addition to these factual elements, there are major considerations of international public order which, both individually and cumulatively, disqualify the bombing of Yugoslavia as a humanitarian action.

First: As the respondent States know very well, the so-called crisis originated in the deliberate fomenting of civil strife in Kosovo and the subsequent intervention by NATO States in the civil war. This interference is continuing. In such conditions those States responsible for the civil strife and the intervention are estopped from pleading humanitarian purposes.

In this context it is relevant to recall that the International Law Commission draft of 1980 on State Responsibility provides in Article 33 (in material part) that:

"2.   In any case, a state of necessity may not be invoked by a State as a ground for precluding wrongfulness: ...

(c) if the State in question has contributed to the occurrence of the state of necessity." (*YILC*, 1980, Vol. II (Part Two), pp. 34–52).

Secondly: The threats of massive use of force go back seven months and have throughout been intended to produce not a genuine peaceful settlement but a dictated result. The massive air campaign was planned some time ago for the purposes of general coercion in order to force Yugoslavia to accept NATO demands. NATO first threatened air strikes in October of last year, and this is a matter of public knowledge.

Thirdly: There has been no attempt to obtain Security Council authorization. Members of the Court if this was an obviously humanitarian intervention acceptable to the international community as a whole, why was it not possible to ask for the authorization of the Security Council.

Fourthly: There is no evidence that the *jus cogens* principle concerning the use of force has been replaced by any other principle of *jus cogens*.

VII.   The exponents of humanitarian intervention in the literature envisaged a radically different model

Mr. President, my next point is this. If the views of the few exponents of humanitarian intervention are studied, it becomes clear that they did not envisage anything like the NATO bombing of the populated areas of Yugoslavia, the damage to the system of health care, the destruction of the civilian infrastructure, the use of prohibited weapons, and the destruction of cultural property on a large scale.

Finally, the respondent States are jointly and severally responsible for the actions of the NATO military command structure, which in my submission constitutes an instrumentality of the respondent States.

* * *

Argument of the United Kingdom

* * *

12.   Mr. President, we must not let our careful and lawyerly analysis of these jurisdictional factors obscure our view of the real situation in Kosovo, of the human misery and suffering caused by the planned and deliberate actions and policies of the Government whom our opponents come here to represent, of the massive and shocking oppression of an entire ethnic population and the dire effects of this on neighbouring States. Let me simply give you a description containing some facts and figures—some of which you have had already—which I will do as dispassionately as I can despite the great indignation and outrage they have caused amongst ordinary people in my country. I do so, Mr. President, not in my words or the words of the British Government, but in those of the United Nations High Commissioner for Refugees, briefing in person the members of the Security Council on 5 May of this year—a week after these proceedings were started.

13.   "The situation of women, men and children fleeing the Province of Kosovo and Metohija, in the Federal Republic of Yugoslavia, is increasingly desperate. Kosovo is being emptied—brutally and methodically—of its ethnic Albanian popu-

lation. In the last three days alone [she said], about 37,000 new refugees and internally displaced people have arrived in Albania, the former Yugoslav Republic of Macedonia, and the Republic of Montenegro. More trains with thousands of refugees have arrived last night at the Yugoslav/Macedonian border. Ethnic cleansing and mass forced expulsions are yielding their tragic results faster than we can respond.... Fragile and unprepared countries are bearing the brunt of one of the largest refugee flows Europe has seen in the twentieth century. Seven hundred thousand people have already been forced to leave their homes."

14. Mrs. Ogata went on to say, in a passage which is very important to put the allegations you heard from counsel for the Federal Republic of Yugoslavia in their right perspective:

"This refugee crisis is not new. Last year, more than a quarter of all asylum requests in Europe were by people from Kosovo. Up to 23 March, when UNHCR had to reluctantly leave the province following a decision of the United Nations Security Coordinator, it was providing assistance to 400,000 people displaced or otherwise affected by fighting inside the province, and to 90,000 refugees and displaced people outside Kosovo."

15. So, Mr. President, the Applicant has brought before you claims that 1,200 of its civilians have been killed in a seven-week military campaign—all civilian deaths are a source of sadness—but expects you to ignore that over 700,000 Kosovars have been driven from their homes: 700,000, nearly three-quarters of a million, over one-third of the entire population of Kosovo. How could anyone remain unmoved by that description, by those figures? They are of course confirmed by reports we get from our own diplomatic missions in neighbouring countries. Isn't it strange that there is not one word about them in the Application and request filed with the Court? Mrs. Ogata is in no doubt that the root cause is (and I quote again) "the systematic and intolerable violence being waged against an entire population, and the failure to prevent it". Nor could anyone who simply watches the television screen and reads the newspapers. Doesn't that make one pause and think about the true motive and purpose behind the attempt of the Federal Republic of Yugoslavia to move this Court to action in its favour?

16. This Court is of course familiar, Mr. President, with cases in which one litigating party says that a dispute is about such and-such and the other party complains that so-and-so has also to be brought within it or taken into account. Those cases have to be judged each on its own merits. This case is however one that can *only* be understood against the background of why my country (together with others) is waging the military action complained of, and that is precisely (in Mrs. Ogata's words again) to prevent the systematic and intolerable violence being waged against an entire

population. Everyone knows that, as does the applicant State itself. I will allow myself one final quotation—this time from a British source—to show that what we are doing is not *against* any people or population, but *for* the rescue of the Kosovar Albanians from their desperate plight.

17. Speaking, Mr. President, in the Security Council on 24 March, the day the military action began, the United Kingdom's Permanent Representative described it as "an exceptional measure to prevent an overwhelming humanitarian catastrophe".

> "Under present circumstances in Kosovo [he went on] there is convincing evidence that such a catastrophe is imminent. Renewed acts of repression by the authorities of the Federal Republic of Yugoslavia would cause further loss of civilian life and would lead to displacement of the civilian population on a large scale and in hostile conditions. Every means short of force has been tried to avert this situation.... The force now proposed is directed exclusively to averting a humanitarian catastrophe, and is the minimum judged necessary for that purpose."

18. Contrary to what was suggested by counsel for the Applicant yesterday, those have always been the terms in which the British Government have presented their position in Parliament. My learned friend, Professor Brownlie, referred to a statement by the Prime Minister in the House of Commons on 23 March of this year. He suggested that this statement revealed an ambivalence on the part of my Government about the motives and legal basis for our action. Mr. President, it does nothing of the kind. What the Prime Minister said was that we would act "primarily to avert what would otherwise be a humanitarian disaster in Kosovo". Later in his statement he said:

> "We must act to save thousands of innocent men, women and children from humanitarian catastrophe—from death, barbarism and ethnic cleansing by a brutal dictatorship...."

The motives for our action could not have been more clearly stated. They give the lie to counsel's suggestion yesterday that, in acting to halt humanitarian catastrophe in one Province of the Federal Republic of Yugoslavia, the British Government should have been seeking to bring humanitarian catastrophe to the civilian population in any other part of their country, still less intending to destroy any population group as such.

19. Mr. President, I will not deal in detail with the jurisdiction element. Professor Greenwood will cover that. I only want respectfully to remind you that, even if the Applicant's optional clause declaration was a valid acceptance of the Court's jurisdiction, its application against the United Kingdom is plainly excluded by the 12–month clause in our acceptance. But to the Applicant that

crucial fact seems to be of no account. In fact, judging from what we have been hearing in Court over the last two days, the Applicant seems to have launched claims in pretty well identical terms against a whole series of different respondents without any regard to the terms on which each respondent may be within the jurisdiction of the Court—in fact without regard to whether some respondents are within the jurisdiction at all. That is hardly a sign of respect towards the judicial process of the Court.

20. Apart from the optional clause, which is clearly not applicable, the only other basis invoked is Article IX of the Genocide Convention. But, Mr. President, the same cavalier attitude permeates the Applicant's submissions on this point too. They give us virtually no indication of what conduct is actually alleged against the United Kingdom or of how that conduct might fall within the scope of the Genocide Convention. Nothing in the Applicant's written or oral submissions comes even near to a plausible allegation that the United Kingdom has breached its obligations under the Convention or threatens to do so. The factual allegations recited, even if all were proved true and even if we were responsible for them, are not genocide. Nor is there the slightest shred of evidence of genocidal intent. So where is there in any meaningful sense a dispute between us over the interpretation, application or fulfilment of the Genocide Convention?

21. I have explained, Mr. President, that what we are doing is designed to save one ethnic group, not—*not*—to destroy another. But what we do know with absolute certainty is that the authorities of the Federal Republic of Yugoslavia have been systematically engaged in what has acquired the eerie name of "ethnic cleansing". I gave you the shocking figures earlier. There is ample evidence that the ultimate aim is the forced removal of the entire ethnic Albanian population from the geographical area.

22. Mr. President, distinguished Members of the Court, the Applicant would have you believe that the situation in Kosovo is simple, a case of unwarranted external intervention. Counsel told you yesterday that if once the external intervention was stopped, the situation inside Kosovo would resolve itself into a model of ethnic harmony. You will know that such a depiction is wholly incredible. It is a travesty of the facts. It tries to banish from view the desperate humanitarian circumstances which led to our actions and the relief of which is our sole purpose. Not only that, but it tries to blind you to what happened since, as a result of the calculated policies of the Federal Republic of Yugoslavia. What the world requires—what in our submission international law requires—is that the inhabitants of Kosovo are able to return to their homes, are able to live there in peace and to rebuild their shattered lives. It is obvious that that requires far more than just the application of some simplistic nostrum: "stop the bombing". It

means that the people of Kosovo must be protected against new atrocities. That is the reason why the G–8 Foreign Ministers adopted on 6 May seven principles designed to ensure the safe and free return of all refugees and displaced persons and conditions for a peaceful and normal life for all inhabitants in Kosovo.

23.   So the Court, with respect, must ask itself what the effect would be of granting the provisional measures which the Federal Republic of Yugoslavia is urging upon it. The Court, with respect, is bound to consider that. But the Court may readily reach the conclusion that what the Federal Republic of Yugoslavia wants to achieve is to use the Court's processes to secure for itself a free hand to complete its planned campaign of "ethnic cleansing". At present the military action, directed specifically at the means of pursuing the oppression of the Kosovar Albanians, is the only thing holding the oppressors back. Imagine, imagine what the situation would be in the refugees' tented camps next winter if that restraint were lifted. Imagine the public reaction if a judicial proceeding in this Court were to lead to that result.

24.   I come therefore, Mr. President, to my final point. This is whether the Court ought to be entertaining this request from the Federal Republic of Yugoslavia at all. I have already described it, in its careless disregard of the legal requirements, as an abuse of the process of the Court. It deserves to be dismissed on that ground alone. There is, however, Mr. President, a deeper point. In my own legal system a remedy like "provisional measures" would lie at the discretion of the Court. In considering whether or not to exercise that discretion, the Court would weigh up all the equities. In weighing up all the equities, the Court would pay particular attention as to whether the party seeking its assistance came with clean hands. The Court would not, however, allow its process to be used as an engine to assist turpitude. I can see no reason why exactly the same principles should not be applied by this honourable Court. They are deeply rooted in the essential nature of the judicial function. They should be regarded as "general principles of law" within the meaning of Article 38 of the Statute.

25.   For this reason, as much as for any other, the Court should summarily dismiss the request.

* * *

C.   NOTES, QUESTIONS, AND PROBLEMS

1.   If NATO felt that Russia or China would veto a request for Security Council authorization to bomb Yugoslavia, why did NATO members not go to the General Assembly and request action there under the Uniting for Peace Resolution?

2. Do you see any legal restrictions in the Charter limiting the Security Council? Some have argued that it has full discretion when making a determination of what is a threat to the peace, breach of the peace, or act of aggression, and in how it responds. Judge Weeramantry however, expressed a different view the Lockerbie Case: "The history of the United Nations Charter corroborates the view that a clear limitation on the plenitude of the Security Council's powers is that those powers must be exercised in accordance with well-established principles of international law." Case Concerning Questions of Interpretation and Application of the 1971 Montreal Convention Arising from the Aerial Incident at Lockerbie (Libya v. U.S.), (Libya v. U.K.) ICJ Reports (1992) (Request for Provisional Measures)(dissenting opinion of Judge Weeramantry) 114, at 174–176. For more see ERIKA DE WET, THE CHAPTER VII POWERS OF THE UNITED NATIONS SECURITY COUNCIL (2004).

3. Compare and contrast peacekeeping and peace enforcement. Is there a danger for an entity like the United Nations in creating new structures such as peacekeeping without formal amendment of the Charter? Was the evolution of peacekeeping to peace enforcement a progressive development as either a matter of law or policy?

4. On February 29, 2004, the UN Security Council in Resolution 1529 (p. 344) once again authorized member states to send troops to Haiti pending the organization of a UN peacekeeping force. On June 1, 2004, the Security Council authorized the United Nations Stabilization Mission in Haiti (MINUSTAH) to take over for the non-UN forces, mainly US and French troops. The UN force that took over was to have 6700 troops, but, by July 1, it still had no more than 2081 troops and that despite a report released by Amnesty International on June 20 finding:

> Armed groups throughout the country are carrying out human rights abuses, such as attacks on judges, journalists and other civilians. These abuses have in part been fuelled by easy availability and widespread possession of guns.... If Haiti and the international community are to learn from the mistakes made following the 1994 multinational intervention in Haiti, every effort should be made to disarm all unofficial armed groups.... Unless Haiti can demonstrate that no one is above the law, and that law is applied impartially to both government supporters and opponents, impunity will continue to be rife and there will be no end to the violence and instability that has plagued Haiti for so long.

Haiti: Breaking the Cycle of Violence—A Last Chance? (June 20, 2004) http://www.amnestyusa.org.

How likely do you think it is that the lessons of 1994–5 from Haiti, Rwanda, and Srebrenica have been or will be learned? Or do you think the problem is not one of being able to learn lessons, but something else?

5. International humanitarian aid agencies have long operated under a principle of "do no harm." Such agencies have stopped work even in situations of tremendous suffering if they feel that on balance remaining will prolong that suffering such as by aiding fighters. Should the UN adopt such principles to guide the decision to send peacekeeping missions? What about other *in bello* rules such as necessity and proportionality? Should these principles bind the UN? Should it bear them in mind when authorizing peacekeeping or peace enforcement? On the obligations of humanitarian aid organizations, *see*, Thomas Weiss, *Principles, Politics and Humanitarian Action*, 13 ETHICS AND INTERNATIONAL AFFAIRS 1 (1999). On the *in bello* obligations of the United Nations, see Michael Reisman & Douglas Stevick, *The Applicability of International Law Standards to United Nations Economic Sanctions Programmes*, 9 EUR. J. INT'L L. 86, at 94–95 (1998).

6.   See also various internal reports of the United Nations on the organization's role in peace and security, e.g., the Security–General's establishment of a panel to review the functioning of the Security Council, discussed in the Annual Report of the Secretary–General on the Work of the Organization, U.N. Doc. A/58/1 (2003), available at www.un.org/documents/secretariat.htm; the Comprehensive Review of the Whole Question of Peacekeeping Operations in All Their Aspects, U.N. SCOR, 55 Sess., Item 87 of the Prov. Agenda, U.N. Doc. A/55/305–S/2000/809 (2000)(Brahimi Report), and the Supplement to an Agenda for Peace, UN Doc. A/50/60–S1995/1.

7.   A former US ambassador to the United Nations, Richard Holbrooke, has taken the position that NATO did not need Security Council authorization to take part in IFOR in Bosnia or KFOR in Kosovo. "No serious policy maker would advocate subordinating American national security interests to the United Nations; for this reason President Clinton twice used force in the Balkans (in Bosnia in 1995 and in Kosovo in 1999) without Security Council authority." Richard Holbrooke, *Last Best Hope*, N.Y. TIMES BOOK REV., Sept. 28, 2003, at 14–15. He has explained that the fact the Clinton Administration requested Security Council Resolution 1031 for IFOR was simply to satisfy the Europeans. Regardless of the reason the resolution was sought, does its existence undermine Ambassador Holbrooke's position? Or do his statements limit the legal impact of the resolution? It says in pertinent part that the Security Council "Acting under Chapter VII. . . 15. Authorizes the member States. . . to take all necessary measures to effect the implementation of and to ensure compliance with Annex 1–A of the Peace Agreement. . . ." Resolution 1244 has similar language respecting NATO peacekeeping in Kosovo. Besides these resolutions, what other arguments support or undermine Ambassador Holbrooke's position? *See* Jules Lobel & Michael Ratner, *Bypassing the Security Council: Ambiguous Authorizations to Use Force, Ceasefires and the Iraqi Inspection Regime*, 93 AM. J. INT'L L. 124 (1999).

8.   Problem: State A gives consent by treaty to the Organization of States A, B & C, to allow States B & C to intervene in State A in the case that serious human rights violations occur in State A. When States B & C decide to intervene, however, State A says it has withdrawn its consent and invokes Article 2(4) of the UN Charter. Do B & C have the right to intervene? Recall that the ICJ said in the Nicaragua Case that the prohibition on the use of force is a *jus cogens* principle. The Vienna Convention on the Law of Treaties says that treaties may not contravene *jus cogens* principles. Do such treaties contravene a *jus cogens* principle? Important human rights principles are also *jus cogens*, including the prohibitions on torture, slavery, and arbitrary killing. For discussions of the meaning of the intervention provisions of the African Charter, see *Panel: Peacemaking Practices "from the South": Africa's Influence*, 2002 PROC. AM. SOC'Y INT'L L. 135. See also the note on the Cyprus Treaty of Guarantee, pp. 319–320 above. *See also*, Jeremy I. Levitt, *The Peace and Security Council of the African Union: The Known Unknowns*, 13 TRANS. L. & CONT. PROBS. 109 (2003).

CHAPTER NINE

THE BASIC LAW AND INSTITUTIONS ON APPLICATION OF FORCE

We last looked at regulating the application of force in Chapter Five. There we discussed the origins of the contemporary law from Roman times until the Tokyo trials after the Second World War. Now we take-up the contemporary law. Recall that the Hague Conventions of 1907 (including, importantly, the Hague Regulations on Land Warfare annexed to Hague IV) remain in force and are part of current law. Indeed, the Hague Regulations are widely viewed as part of customary international law.[1] In addition, after the Second World War, four new conventions were drafted for the protection of victims of armed conflict. The first of the four Geneva Conventions, the Convention for the Amelioration of the Condition of the Wounded and Sick in Armed Forces in the Field grew from the similarly named Geneva Convention of 1864. The second Geneva Convention adapted the rules of the First Convention for the wounded, sick, and injured at sea and the shipwrecked. The Third Geneva Convention Relative to Prisoners of War drew on the 1929 Prisoners of War Convention, and the Fourth Geneva Convention of 1949 Relative to the Protection of Civilian Persons in Time of War took as its foundation the 1934 draft Tokyo Convention.[2]

In addition to the Hague Regulations and the 1949 Geneva Conventions, UNESCO, (the United Nations Educational, Scientific and Cultural Organization) sponsored the 1954 Hague Convention for the Protection of Cultural Property in the Event of Armed Conflict. And in 1977, the parties to the 1949 Geneva Conventions updated the four conventions with two additional protocols—one for international armed conflict and one for internal armed conflict. In 1993 the UN Security Council formed the first international criminal tribunal since Nuremberg to try war crimes, and crimes against humanity, the International Criminal Tribunal for the Former Yugoslavia (ICTY).[3] In 1994 it added the International Criminal Tribunal for Rwanda (ICTR) to prosecute crimes resulting from the Rwandan

---

1. George H. Aldrich & Christine Chinkin, *A Century of Achievement and Unfinished Work*, 94 Am. J. Int'l L. 90, 93, *citing* United States v. Von Leeb [High Command Case], 11 Trials of War Criminals Before the Nuernberg Military Tribunal Under Control Council Law No. 10, 462 (1950); *see also* 2 Lassa Oppenheim, International Law 234–36 (Hersch Lauterpacht ed., 7th ed. 1952).

2. Find the convention texts, current list of parties, reservations, declarations and other information at the website of the International Committee of the Red Cross, www.icrc.org.

3. 1993 Statute of the International Criminal Tribunal for the Former Yugoslavia, UN Doc. S/25704 (May 3, 1993).

genocide in 1994.[4] The ICTY in particular has produced important decisions relevant to the international law on the use of force as we have seen throughout this book. The contributions of both courts influenced the founding of a court with general jurisdiction over war crimes, crime against humanity and the crime of aggression. The Statute for the International Criminal Court was negotiated in Rome in the summer of 1998, and came into effect July 1, 2002.[5] The Rome Statute includes important provisions developed from the Hague and Geneva Conventions, making it the latest major convention relevant to the *jus in bello*.

While these are the core agreements on the law of armed conflict since the Second World War, they are part of a much larger network of treaties falling in two main categories: human rights and arms control. Both categories contain dozens of agreements and are the subject of whole courses in their own right. We will only refer to them briefly in conjunction with the *in bello* rules we consider in more detail below. It is important to be aware, however, that in considering any use of force question an arms control or human rights convention may hold the answer or part of the answer. It may also be important to consider whether provisions of any of the contemporary treaties have become part of customary international law.[6]

In addition to reviewing the substantive rules on the application of force, this Chapter also looks briefly at one of the most important institution for the *jus in bello*, the International Committee of the Red Cross. International courts and other organizations such as the United Nations are also very important, but we will focus on the organization specially devoted to the promotion and implementation of this law.

Despite the wealth of treaties and judicial decisions, the *jus in bello* does not have standard contemporary terms. Some writers still divide the *jus in bello* between "Hague law" and "Geneva law." (Some also equate Hague law with the phrase "laws of war" or "law of armed conflict" and Geneva law with "humanitarian law.") Hague law does tend more in the direction of regulating the "means and methods" of warfare, while the various Geneva conventions do tend more toward the protection of war victims. "Means" of warfare refers to the weapons that are used and "methods" to the military objectives sought and strategies employed in armed conflict.

---

4. Statute of the International Tribunal for Rwanda, UN Doc. SC/5974 (Jan. 12, 1995).

5. U.N. Doc. No. A/Conf. 183/9, art. 1, (1998), 37 I.L.M. 999 (1998). *See generally* THE INTERNATIONAL CRIMINAL COURT, THE MAKING OF THE ROME STATUTE (ROY S. LEE, ed. 1999); Mahnoush H. Arsanjani, *Developments in International Criminal Law; The Rome Statute of the International Criminal Court*, 93 AM. J. INT'L L. 22 (1999) (discussing the negotiations and the extensive debate over the scope of the Statute).

6. *See e.g.*, Theodor Meron, *The Geneva Conventions as Customary Law*, 81 AM. J. INT'L L. 348 (1987); Michael Matheson, *Session One: The United States Position on the Relation of Customary International Law to the 1977 Protocols Additional to the 1949 Geneva Conventions*, 2 AM. U. J. INT'L L. & POL'Y 419–31 (1987); *see also* UNITED STATES ARMY JUDGE ADVOCATE GENERAL CORPS, OPERATIONAL LAW HANDBOOK (2005).

Geneva focuses on civilians, prisoners, the sick and wounded. These two bodies of rules do, however, have considerable overlap. Some provisions have been brought together in both of the Additional Protocols to the 1949 Geneva Conventions and the Rome Statute,[7] and for these reasons we do not make a strict distinction between the two areas of rules here. For example, the rule against killing prisoners of war appears in both the Hague Regulations and the Third Geneva Convention. Parties to a conflict may not make the killing prisoners a military objective (Hague law); prisoners must be protected (Geneva law.) We will see other intersections as we review the important post-Second World War agreements below.[8] The International Court of Justice in the Nuclear Weapons Case (p. 278, above) referred to the requirement of respecting humanitarian law in any use of nuclear weapons. The Court was discussing both the legality of the use of a certain kind of weapon and the disproportionate impact it might have on victims. To refer to all the law relevant in the application of force the phrase "international humanitarian law" (IHL) will be used here from time to time as a substitute for *jus in bello.*

IHL is by now a very large body of law. Our focus will be toward the rules relating to civilians and combatants.

A.   POST-WAR DEVELOPMENTS

As you learned in Chapter Five, "Geneva law" has its origins on the battlefield of Solferino, Italy in 1859. From there, the Red Cross Movement was founded and a series of treaties for the protection of war victims began to be formed. In 1949, the four basic conventions were adopted. For fifty-five years since the adoption of the 1949 Conventions we have seen no similar move to replace them, as occurred after the Second World War when the 1949 Conventions replaced earlier treaties. Rather, the 1949 Conventions have been added to by protocols, supplemented by treaties on specific topics; and have been part of developing customary international law. After the September 11, 2001, attacks in the United States some

7. According to Greenwood, Hague Convention IV of 1907 and the Hague Regulations annexed thereto "remain of the utmost importance. Arts. 42–56 HagueReg still constitute the principal text on the government of occupied territory and the treatment of property in occupied territory. In addition the provisions on methods and means of warfare, on spies, on flags of truce and on armistices retain importance even though for parties to Additional Protocol I the sections on spies and methods and means of warfare have now been largely superseded. The International Military Tribunal at Nuremberg held that the provisions of the Regulations had become part of customary international law by 1939 and accordingly they are binding on all states." Christopher Greenwood, *Historical Development and Legal Basis, in* THE HANDBOOK OF HUMANITARIAN LAW IN ARMED CONFLICTS 1, 24–25 (Dieter Fleck ed., 1995).

8. Basic texts on the contemporary law *in bello* include, YORAM DINSTEIN, THE CONDUCT OF HOSTILITIES UNDER THE LAW OF INTERNATIONAL ARMED CONFLICT (2004); FRITS KALSHOVEN & LIESBETH ZEVGELD, CONTRAINTS ON THE WAGING OF WAR (3d ed. 2001). INGRID DETTER, THE LAW OF WAR (2d ed. 2000); L.C. GREEN THE CONTEMPORARY LAW OF ARMED CONFLICT (2d ed. 2000); HUMANITARIAN LAW (Judith Gardam ed., Library of Essays in International Law 1999); MARCO SASSÒLI & ANTOINE A. BOUVIER, HOW DOES LAW PROTECT IN WAR? (1999); THE HANDBOOK OF HUMANITARIAN LAW IN ARMED CONFLICTS (Dieter Fleck ed., 1995); HILAIRE MCCOUBREY INTERNATIONAL HUMANITARIAN LAW (1990).

Americans have called into question whether the Conventions are still viable in a time of terror. (President Bush's lawyer, the White House Counsel Judge Alberto Gonzalez, called them "obsolete" and "quaint."[9]) Yet, as with the United Nations Charter many decades after its adoption, the very longevity of the 1949 Conventions has given them stature in the law that few are willing to lose by replacing them wholesale. And, again, as with the Charter, while problems with the Conventions can easily be found, better solutions to those problems than the ones already agreed to are not so easily found. Consider as you read further what the problems might be in the Conventions that Judge Gonzalez might have been referring to and how you might solve the problems with politically acceptable solutions.

A key factor in making changes to international law has always been the mood of the times. You saw in both chapters on the development of international law how rapid development often followed particularly brutal wars. The same was true of the 1949 Conventions.

Frits Kalshoven, Geneva

Constraints on the Waging of War 10–11 (1987).

* * *

The tragic events, successively, of the Spanish Civil War and the Second World War provided the incentive for yet another major revision and further development of the law of Geneva. To this end a diplomatic conference met in 1949 in Geneva, once again at the instigation of the ICRC and by invitation of the Swiss Government. The three Conventions in force (one of 1907 and two of 1929) were substituted by new Conventions, giving improved versions of many existing rules and filling lacunae that practice had brought to light. To give just one example, the armed resistance in several European countries under German occupation during the Second World War led to the express recognition that members of organized resistance movements which fulfil a number of (severe) conditions would qualify as prisoners of war.

Then the law of Geneva was enriched by an entirely novel Convention on the protection of civilian persons in time of war. This Convention serves to protect two categories of civilians in particular: enemy civilians in the territory of a belligerent party, and the inhabitants of occupied territory; categories of civilians, that is, who as a consequence of the armed conflict find themselves in the power of the enemy. With this latest addition the law of Geneva had come to comprise four Conventions, dealing with the wounded and sick on land; the wounded, sick and shipwrecked at sea; prisoners of war; and protected civilians.

---

9. Alberto R. Gonzales, Decision re Application of the Geneva Convention on Prisoners of War to the Conflict with Al Qaeda and the Taliban, Jan. 25, 2002, available at http://www2.gwu.edu/~nsar-chiv/NSAEBB/NSAEBB/27/

The Diplomatic Conference of 1949 produced one further innovation of such major importance that it needs to be mentioned here. Thus far, the Conventions of Geneva had always been regarded as applicable primarily in wars between States. The Spanish Civil War had demonstrated the difficulty of making the parties to such an internal armed conflict respect even the most basic principles of the law of Geneva. In the light of this experience the Conference decided, on the one hand, that the Conventions would continue to apply in their entirety to international armed conflicts. On the other hand, it introduced into all four Conventions of 1949 a common Article 3, "applicable in the case of armed conflict not of an international character occurring in the territory of one of the High Contracting Parties", and providing for such an event a list of fundamental rules the parties are "bound to apply, as a minimum". The adoption of the Article signified a tremendous step forward in that it proved the possibility of laying down rules of international law expressly and exclusively addressing the situation of internal armed conflict.

In 1951, Josef Kunz called passionately for a revision of Hague law (that he refers to as the laws of war) comparable to the revision of Geneva law:

Josef Kunz, The Chaotic Status of the Law of War and the Urgent Necessity for Their Revision

45 AM. J. INT'L L. 37, 57–60 (1951)*

As war or use of force has not been abolished in law and is possible in fact, the laws of war, actually in a chaotic condition, urgently need revision. This revision certainly poses many problems. Writers have asked whether the revised rules of war should make a distinction between "small" and "major" wars. Clearly not every possible war must be a world war; and one is not justified in thinking only in terms of a new world war and not being interested in "little wars." After all, the law of contracts applies not only to contracts which involve hundreds of millions of dollars.

* * *

Already the four new Geneva Conventions of 1949 have been signed by 44 states. This great achievement is primarily due to the efforts of the International Red Cross, which took the initiative in 1945, and to the Swiss Government. The United States actively supported the initiative of the International Red Cross in 1945.

---

* Some footnotes omitted. For more details on the negotiations of the Geneva Conventions, see, Catherine Rey–Schyrr, *Les* *Conventions de Genève de 1949: une percée décisive*, 81 RICR/IRRC 209 (1999).

The International Red Cross[a] was inspired by the rich experience it gained in the second World War and in the experience gained by the National Red Cross Societies which were convoked in a preliminary conference held from June to August, 1946. In 1947 a Conference of Government Experts was held, in which the United States participated and at which a report[b] was elaborated. Then followed the XVIIth International Conference of the Red Cross at Stockholm in 1948, in which the United States also participated, at which Draft Conventions I–IV[c] were approved. Finally, the Swiss Government convoked a diplomatic conference which took place from April 21 to August 12, 1949, in Geneva, at which fifty-nine states, including the United States and the Soviet Union, took part. Although there was unanimous agreement to conclude these conventions, some doubted the wisdom of the action, because of the impression on public opinion. But the Swiss Foreign Minister stated that it is necessary and an imperative duty to establish such conventions in time of peace; that it is of the utmost urgency to do so to prevent the repetition of the terrible horrors perpetrated in the second World War. And at the time of signature, on December 8, 1949, he said that the conventions were signed "on the unhappy assumption that a new war is not impossible."

The new Geneva Conventions of August 12, 1949, deal only with the protection of the victims of war. Convention II is a revision of the Xth Hague Convention (Hospital Ship Convention). Conventions I and III are revisions of the two Geneva Conventions of 1929. Convention III (Prisoners of War) contains a new and somewhat controversial rule, which, it seems, was adopted under strong insistence by the Soviet Union; this new rule, corresponding to a pressing problem appearing in the second World War and hitherto unregulated, gives to members of underground resistance movements in occupied territory under certain conditions the status of prisoners of war. All three conventions constitute strong improvements. Convention IV deals with a new, hitherto unregulated problem, urgently in need of regulation, namely, the treatment of civilians in wartime. It is a great step forward in the development of international law. All the conventions are based, as it should be, on practical and realistic considerations, striking, in the words of the Swiss Foreign Minister, Max Petitpierre, an equilibrium between the cruel necessities of war and humanitarian ideals.

a. See Max Huber, Principles, Tasks and Problems of the Red Cross in International Law (Geneva, 1946).

b. *Commission d'Experts Gouvernementaux pour l'étude des Conventions protégeant les victims de la guerre. . . . Rapport sur les travaux* (Geneva, 1947).

c. Projets de Conventions . . . IVIIc Conférence Internaionale de la Croix Rouge (Geneva, May, 1948). See also volumes for 1948, 1949 of the Revue Internationale de la Croix Rouge (Geneva).

Rules of war, including rules of combat, are essential, as said earlier, even in time of peace. They are essential to protect soldiers and civilians in war; they are essential in these times to guarantee the survival of our whole civilization, if not of mankind itself. They are essential, representing, in the words of Jessup, not a matter of sentiment, but of military necessity. An army, as distinguished from a savage horde, must know what to expect, must know under what rules fighting is to be carried on. They are essential for the law of war crimes. A situation cannot be called legal, in which both belligerent groups will do what they like, and then the victors "will try the vanquished for having committed crimes determined unilaterally and with retroactive force by the victors."[d] That is why rules of war for the actual conduct of fighting are indispensable. If the United Nations is unwilling or unable to draft such rules, it must be done outside of the organization, just as were the four new Geneva Conventions. But just as the efforts at disarmament by the League of Nations dealt in effect to a great degree with the laws of war, so do the efforts of the United Nations Commission for Conventional Armaments and the Atomic Energy Commission. The envisaged prohibition of the use of the atomic bomb pertains to the rules of war and shows that even in the United Nations large-scale fighting, whether legal or illegal, is considered possible; otherwise why try to enact this prohibition? This Commission has, further, to deal with all other weapons of mass destruction. Secretary General Trygve Lie suggested even in 1948 that the United Nations forbid chemical and bacteriological warfare, and he suggested in 1950 that the United Nations begin the study of controlling germ warfare, and that the hydrogen bomb is a United Nations topic. The International Committee of the Red Cross has recently appealed to all signatories of the new Geneva Conventions to take appropriate steps to reach agreement on a prohibition of atomic weapons and of all weapons of non-directed mass-death-missiles.

We have already answered the arguments of those optimists who believe that war is "abolished" and, therefore, laws of war do not and cannot exist. Let us state once more that naturally all must be done to prevent wars diplomatically and to restrict, and ultimately eliminate, war legally. This is the higher goal. But this does not exclude the necessity of regulating large-scale fighting, legal or illegal, as long as the first goal is not reached. That the first goal has not yet been reached and is not likely to be reached within the near future is clear. To abandon the smaller progress achieved through the laws of war in favor of a higher goal not reached would be folly. It is indeed paradoxical that, in the words of Erich Hula, "though men despaired of being able to attain the compara-

---

d. H. Kelsen, "Will the Nuremberg Trial Constitute a Precedent", International Law Quarterly, Vol. II, No. 2 (1947), pp. 153–171, at p. 171.

tively modest goal of regulating war, they entertained strangely enough, the more excessive hope of being able to eliminate war altogether." Such an attitude "is unfortunately rather the symptom of grim prospects for the future conduct of wars than a guarantee of the elimination of war as such."

It must also be stressed that the laws of war pertain rather to the law of peace, that they are "a part of human rights."

B. The Conventions

1. The 1949 Geneva Conventions

Nearly every state in the world is a party to the Geneva Conventions. Indeed, they along with the UN Charter have more parties than most other treaties. "The law of Geneva serves to provide protection for all those who, as a consequence of an armed conflict, have fallen into the hands of the adversary. The protection envisaged here is, hence, not protection against the violence of war itself, but against the arbitrary power which one belligerent party acquires in the course of the war over persons belonging to the other party."[10] Thus, Geneva law focuses most essentially on combatants no longer fighting (*hors de combat*) and civilians. The excerpts below include some of the most important provisions in, first, the Prisoners Convention and then the Civilians Convention. All four conventions contain Common Article 3, also reproduced below. This article is sort of restatement of the core principles for the treatment of persons in any armed conflict.

The 1949 Geneva Conventions were intended to have broad application. The drafters designed them to apply in all armed conflicts, not just cases of traditional or declared war. According to the official commentary:

> Any difference arising between two States and leading to the intervention of members of the armed forces is an armed conflict within the meaning of * * * [the Conventions], even if one of the Parties denies the existence of a state of war. It makes no difference how long the conflict lasts, how much slaughter takes place or how numerous are the participating forces....[11]

The Civilians Convention also requires the existence of *de facto* hostilities,[12] but the Prisoners Convention may apply even without fighting as long as persons covered by the Convention are detained.[13]

---

10. Kalshoven, *supra*, note 8, at 40 (1987).

11. III Commentary to the 1949 Geneva Convention Relative to the Treatment of Prisoners of War 23 (Jean Pictet ed., 1960).

12. IV Commentary to the 1949 Geneva Convention Relative to the Protection of Civilian Persons in Time of War 20 (Jean Pictet ed., 1958).

13. III Commentary to the 1949 Geneva Convention Relative to the Treatment of Prisoners of War, *supra* note 11, at 23.

Should there be any doubt about the conditions necessary for the application of the Conventions, it is to be resolved in favor of extending protections: "It must not be forgotten that the Conventions have been drawn up first and foremost to protect individuals, and not to serve State interests. Even if the existence of a state of war is disputed, Article 3 can be applied."[14] The scope of application of Article 3, was, in turn intended to be "as wide as possible."[15] However, the official commentary's description of the conflicts covered by Article 3 indicates a triggering threshold above lawlessness and criminality: "Speaking generally, it must be recognized that the conflicts referred to in Article 3 are armed conflicts, with *armed forces* on either side engaged in *hostilities*—conflicts, in short, which are in many respects similar to an international war, but take place within the confines of a single country."[16]

Geneva Convention Relative to the Treatment of Prisoners of War of August 12, 1949

75 U.N.T.S. 135 (1950).

* * *

PART I—GENERAL PROVISIONS

Article 1

The High Contracting Parties undertake to respect and to ensure respect for the present Convention in all circumstances.

Article 2

In addition to the provisions which shall be implemented in peace time, the present Convention shall apply to all cases of declared war or of any other armed conflict which may arise between two or more of the High Contracting Parties, even if the state of war is not recognized by one of them.

The Convention shall also apply to all cases of partial or total occupation of the territory of a High Contracting Party, even if the said occupation meets with no armed resistance.

Although one of the Powers in conflict may not be a party to the present Convention, the Powers who are parties thereto shall remain bound by it in their mutual relations. They shall furthermore be bound by the Convention in relation to the said Power, if the latter accepts and applies the provisions thereof.

Article 3

In the case of armed conflict not of an international character occurring in the territory of one of the High Contracting Parties,

14. *Id.*

15. *Id.* at 36.

16. *Id.* at 37 (emphasis in original.)

each Party to the conflict shall be bound to apply, as a minimum, the following provisions:

(1) Persons taking no active part in the hostilities, including members of armed forces who have laid down their arms and those placed *hors de combat* by sickness, wounds, detention, or any other cause, shall in all circumstances be treated humanely, without any adverse distinction founded on race, colour, religion or faith, sex, birth or wealth, or any other similar criteria.

To this end, the following acts are and shall remain prohibited at any time and in any place whatsoever with respect to the above-mentioned persons:

(a) violence to life and person, in particular murder of all kinds, mutilation, cruel treatment and torture;

(b) taking of hostages;

(c) outrages upon personal dignity, in particular humiliating and degrading treatment;

(d) the passing of sentences and the carrying out of executions without previous judgment pronounced by a regularly constituted court affording all the judicial guarantees, which are recognized as indispensable by civilized peoples.

(2) The wounded and sick shall be collected and cared for. An impartial humanitarian body, such as the International Committee of the Red Cross, may offer its services to the Parties to the conflict.

The Parties to the conflict should further endeavour to bring into force, by means of special agreements, all or part of the other provisions of the present Convention.

The application of the preceding provisions shall not affect the legal status of the Parties to the conflict.

Article 4

A. Prisoners of war, in the sense of the present Convention, are persons belonging to one of the following categories, who have fallen into the power of the enemy:

(1) Members of the armed forces of a Party to the conflict as well as members of militias or volunteer corps forming part of such armed forces.

(2) Members of other militias and members of other volunteer corps, including those of organized resistance movements, belonging to a Party to the conflict and operating in or outside their own territory, even if this territory is occupied, provided that such militias or volunteer corps, including such organized resistance movements, fulfil the following condition:

(a) that of being commanded by a person responsible for his subordinates;

(b) that of having a fixed distinctive sign recognizable at a distance;

(c) that of carrying arms openly;

(d) that of conducting their operations in accordance with the laws and customs of war.

* * *

(6) Inhabitants of a non-occupied territory, who on the approach of the enemy spontaneously take up arms to resist the invading forces, without having had time to form themselves into regular armed units, provided they carry arms openly and respect the laws and customs of war.

* * *

Article 5

The present Convention shall apply to the persons referred to in Article 4 from the time they fall into the power of the enemy and until their final release and repatriation.

Should any doubt arise as to whether persons, having committed a belligerent act and having fallen into the hands of the enemy, belong to any of the categories enumerated in Article 4, such persons shall enjoy the protection of the present Convention until such time as their status has been determined by a competent tribunal.

* * *

PART II—GENERAL PROTECTION OF PRISONERS OF WAR

* * *

Article 13

Prisoners of war must at all times be humanely treated. Any unlawful act or omission by the Detaining Power causing death or seriously endangering the health of a prisoner of war in its custody is prohibited, and will be regarded as a serious breach of the present Convention. In particular, no prisoner of war may be subjected to physical mutilation or to medical or scientific experiments of any kind which are not justified by the medical, dental or hospital treatment of the prisoner concerned and carried out in his interest.

Likewise, prisoners of war must at all times be protected, particularly against acts of violence or intimidation and against insults and public curiosity.

Measures of reprisal against prisoners of war are prohibited.

Article 14

Prisoners of war are entitled in all circumstances to respect for their persons and their honour.

Women shall be treated with all the regard due to their sex and shall in all cases benefit by treatment as favourable as that granted to men.

* * *

PART III—CAPTIVITY

SECTION I—BEGINNING OF CAPTIVITY

Article 17

Every prisoner of war, when questioned on the subject, is bound to give only his surname, first names and rank, date of birth, and army, regimental, personal or serial number, or failing this, equivalent information.

If he willfully infringes this rule, he may render himself liable to a restriction of the privileges accorded to his rank or status.

Each Party to a conflict is required to furnish the persons under its jurisdiction who are liable to become prisoners of war, with an identity card showing the owner's surname, first names, rank, army, regimental, personal or serial number or equivalent information. * * *

No physical or mental torture, nor any other form of coercion, may be inflicted on prisoners of war to secure from them information of any kind whatever. Prisoners of war who refuse to answer may not be threatened, insulted, or exposed to unpleasant or disadvantageous treatment of any kind.

* * *

SECTION II—RELEASE AND REPATRIATION OF PRISONERS OF WAR AT THE CLOSE OF HOSTILITIES

Article 118

Prisoners of war shall be released and repatriated without delay after the cessation of active hostilities.

In the absence of stipulations to the above effect in any agreement concluded between the Parties to the conflict with a view to the cessation of hostilities, or failing any such agreement, each of the Detaining Powers shall itself establish and execute without delay a plan of repatriation in conformity with the principle laid down in the foregoing paragraph.

* * *

Part VI—Execution of the Convention

Section I—General Provisions

* * *

Article 127

The High Contracting Parties undertake, in time of peace as in time of war, to disseminate the text of the present Convention as widely as possible in their respective countries, and, in particular, to include the study thereof in their programmes of military and, if possible, civil instruction, so that the principles thereof may become know to all their armed forces and to the entire populations.

Any military or other authorities, who in time of war assume responsibilities in respect of prisoners of war, must possess the text of the Convention and be specially instructed as to its provisions.

* * *

Article 129

The High Contracting Parties undertake to enact any legislation necessary to provide effective penal sanctions for persons committing, or ordering to be committed, any of the grave breaches of the present Convention defined in the following Article.

Each High Contracting Party shall be under the obligation to search for persons alleged to have committed, or to have ordered to be committed, such grave breaches, and shall bring such persons, regardless of their nationality, before its own courts. It may also, if it prefers, and in accordance with the provisions of its own legislation, hand such persons over for trial to another High Contracting Party concerned, provided such High Contracting Party has made out of *prima facie* case.

Each High Contracting Party shall take measures necessary for the suppression of all acts contrary to the provisions of the present Convention other than grave breaches defined in the following Article.

* * *

Article 130

Grave breaches to which the preceding Article relates shall be those involving any of the following acts, if committed against persons or property protected by the Convention: wilful killing, torture or inhuman treatment, including biological experiments, willfully causing great suffering or serious injury to body or health, compelling a prisoner of war to serve in the forces of the hostile Power, or willfully depriving a prisoner of war of the rights of fair and regular trial prescribed in this Convention.

Geneva Convention Relative to the Protection of Civilian Persons in Time of War of August 12, 1949

5 U.N.T.S. 287 (1950).

Articles 1–3 [See PW arts. 1–3, pp. 390–391 above]

Article 4

Persons protected by the Convention are those who, at a given moment, and in any manner whatsoever, find themselves, in case of a conflict or occupation, in the hands of a Party to the conflict or Occupying Power of which they are not nationals.

* * *

PART II—GENERAL PROTECTION OF POPULATIONS AGAINST CERTAIN CONSEQUENCES OF WAR

Article 13

The provisions of Part II cover the whole of the populations of the countries in conflict, without any adverse distinction based, in particular, on race, nationality, religion or political opinion, and are intended to alleviate the sufferings caused by war.

Article 14

In time of peace, the High Contracting Parties and, after the outbreak of hostilities, the Parties thereto, may establish in their own territory and, if the need arises, in occupied areas, hospital and safety zones and localities so organized as to protect from the effects of war, wounded, sick and aged persons, children under fifteen, expectant mothers and mothers of children under seven.
* * *

Article 15

Any Party to the conflict may, either direct or through a neutral State or some humanitarian organization, propose to the adverse Party to establish, in the regions where fighting is taking place, neutralized zones intended to shelter from the effects of war the following persons, without distinction:

(*a*) wounded and sick combatants or non-combatants;

(*b*) civilian persons who take no part in hostilities, and who, while they reside in the zones, perform no work of a military character.

* * *

Article 23

Each High Contracting Party shall allow the free passage of all consignments of medical and hospital stores and objects necessary for religious worship intended only for civilians of another High

Contracting Party, even if the latter is its adversary. It shall likewise permit the free passage of all consignments of essential foodstuffs, clothing and tonics intended for children under fifteen, expectant mothers and maternity cases.

* * *

PART III—STATUS AND TREATMENT OF PROTECTED PERSONS

SECTION I—PROVISIONS COMMON TO THE TERRITORIES OF THE PARTIES TO THE CONFLICT AND TO OCCUPIED TERRITORIES

Article 27

Protected persons are entitled, in all circumstances, to respect for their persons, their honour, their family rights, their religious convictions and practices, and their manners and customs. They shall at all times be humanely treated, and shall be protected especially against all acts of violence or threats thereof and against insults and public curiosity.

Women shall be especially protected against any attack on their honour, in particular against rape, enforced prostitution, or any form of indecent assault.

Without prejudice to the provisions relating to their state of health, age and sex, all protected persons shall be treated with the same consideration by the Party to the conflict in whose power they are, without any adverse distinction based, in particular, on race, religion or political opinion.

However, the Parties to the conflict may take such measures of control and security in regard to protected persons as may be necessary as a result of the war.

Article 28

The presence of a protected person may not be used to render certain points or areas immune from military operations.

Article 29

The Party to the conflict in whose hands protected persons may be, is responsible for the treatment accorded to them by its agents, irrespective of any individual responsibility which may be incurred.

* * *

Article 31

No physical or moral coercion shall be exercised against protected persons, in particular to obtain information from them or from third parties.

Article 32

The High Contracting Parties specifically agree that each of them is prohibited from taking any measure of such character as to cause the physical suffering or extermination of protected persons in their hands. This prohibition applies not only to murder, torture, corporal punishment, mutilation and medical or scientific experiments not necessitated by the medical treatment of a protected person, but also to any other measures of brutality whether applied by civilian or military agents.

Article 33

No protected person may be punished for an offence he or she has not personally committed. Collective penalties and likewise all measures of intimidation or of terrorism are prohibited.

Pillage is prohibited.

* * *

SECTION III—OCCUPIED TERRITORIES

Article 49

Individual or mass forcible transfers, as well as deportations of protected persons from occupied territory to the territory of the Occupying Power or to that of any other country, occupied or not, are prohibited, regardless of their motive.

Nevertheless, the Occupying Power may undertake total or partial evacuation of a given area if the security of the population or imperative military reasons so demand. Such evacuations may not involve the displacement of protected persons outside the bounds of the occupied territory except when for material reasons it is impossible to avoid such displacement. Persons thus evacuated shall be transferred back to their homes as soon as hostilities in the area in question have ceased. * * *

The Occupying Power shall not detain protected persons in an area particularly exposed to the dangers of war unless the security of the population or imperative military reasons so demand.

The Occupying Power shall not deport or transfer parts of its own civilian population into the territory it occupies.

* * *

Article 53

Any destruction by the Occupying Power of real or personal property belonging individually or collectively to private persons, or to the State, or to other public authorities, or to social or cooperative organizations, is prohibited, except where such destruction is rendered absolutely necessary by military operations.

Article 54

The Occupying Power may not alter the status of public officials or judges in the occupied territories, or in any way apply sanctions to or take any measures of coercion or discrimination against them, should they abstain from fulfilling their functions for reasons of conscience.

This prohibition does not prejudice the application of the second paragraph of Article 51. It does not affect the right of the Occupying Power to remove public officials from their posts.

Article 55

To the fullest extent of the means available to it, the Occupying Power has the duty of ensuring the food and medical supplies of the population; it should, in particular, bring in the necessary foodstuffs, medical stores and other articles if the resources of the occupied territory are inadequate.

* * *

Part IV—Execution of the Convention
Section I—General Provisions

* * *

Article 144

[See PW Art. 127, p. 394 above.]

* * *

Article 146

[See PW Art. 129, p. 394 above.]

Article 147

Grave breaches to which the preceding Article relates shall be those involving any of the following acts, if committed against persons or property protected by the present Convention: willful killing, torture or inhuman treatment, including biological experiments, willfully causing great suffering or serious injury to body or health, unlawful deportation or transfer or unlawful confinement of a protected person, compelling a protected person to serve in the forces of a hostile Power, or willfully depriving a protected person of the rights of fair and regular trial prescribed in the present Convention, taking of hostages and extensive destruction and appropriation of property, not justified by military necessity and carried out unlawfully and wantonly.

Both the Prisoners Convention and the Civilians Convention apply to persons in the power of the adversary. The Conventions divide such persons among prisoners-of-war and civilians. "[R]esistance fighters, or, more generally, guerilla fighters, who do not meet all four conditions mentioned above [PW Art. 4] cannot claim a right to be treated as prisoners of war; they may, on the other hand, be entitled to the (lesser) protection of the Civilians Convention."[17] In cases of doubt, the practice has been to treat captured persons as prisoners of war, at least until a tribunal (PW Art. 5) can determine that the person does not qualify.[18]

(Additional Protocol I of 1977 creates a third category of persons who have taken up arms and are, therefore, no longer civilians, but who do not meet the criteria of prisoners of war.)

Binding the Conventions together is the basic principle of humanity. Persons in the power of the adverse party must be treated humanely. For prisoners of war, this means they may not be killed. This is true even if the Detaining Power has no secure place to hold prisoners or sufficient supplies to feed them and their own forces. "Self-preservation or military necessity on the part of the captor can never provide an excuse for the murder of prisoners."[19] Nor may prisoners be subjected to inhumane treatment of any kind to obtain information. They must be evacuated from a combat zone to a safe place. They must receive food, water, and medical attention. They may communicate with the outside world. Prisoners of war must be released at the end of hostilities. The Detaining Power may enforce the law against prisoners when the Detaining Power has evidence that the individual has committed an offense. The Detaining Power may bring proceedings against those who infringe applicable laws, regulations or orders. (PW Arts. 82 & 85) Prisoners of war may be disciplined for attempting to escape.

Humane treatment of civilians means the Occupying Power (or adverse party in control of civilians) may not murder or mutilate them. These protections imply the Occupying Power must respect the right to life of civilians.[20] An Occupying Power may not inhibit the free passage of medicine and food to certain vulnerable members of the population. Collective punishment is prohibited and, again, no coercion is permitted to obtain information. The Occupying Power may not take hostages, forcibly transfers civilians, or take reprisals. Civilian property must be protected from pillage and other unlawful destruction. Civilians must be protected from fighting under the terms of the Civilians Convention if they are in zones set aside for the purpose (CC Arts. 14 and 15). A person who takes up arms to resist an Occupying Power and who does not qualify for prisoner of war status need not receive all the privileges of a prisoner of war. Such a person need not be allowed, for example, to communicate with the outside world. And she may be subject to criminal proceedings. Nevertheless, she must be treated humanely at all times. The Occupying Party may take additional

---

17.   KALSHOVEN, *supra* note 8, at 41.

18.   *Id.* at 42.

19.   L.C. GREEN, *supra* note 8, at 206.

20.   *Id.* at 235.

measures to maintain security, including interning civilians, but all detention of civilians is subject to review. (CW Arts. 42–43, 68–71, and 75.)

2.   THE 1954 HAGUE CONVENTION

Some protection of cultural property was included in 1949 in the Civilians Convention. However, detailed protection of cultural property was provided for only in 1954:[21]

1954 Convention for the Protection of Cultural Property in the Event of an Armed Conflict

249 U.N.T.S. 240.

> Article 1. For the purposes of the present Convention, the term "cultural property" shall cover, irrespective of origin or ownership:
>
> > (a) movable or immovable property of great importance to the cultural heritage of every people, such as monuments of architecture, art or history, whether religious or secular; archaeological sites; groups of buildings which, as a whole, are of historical or artistic interest; works of art; manuscripts, books and other objects of artistic, historical or archaeological interest; as well as scientific collections and important collections of books or archives or of reproductions of the property defined above;
> >
> > (b) buildings whose main and effective purpose is to preserve or exhibit the movable cultural property defined in subparagraph (a) such as museums, large libraries and depositories of archives, and refuges intended to shelter, in the event of armed conflict, the movable cultural property defined in subparagraph (a);
> >
> > (c) centers containing a large amount of cultural property as defined in subparagraphs (a) and (b), to be known as "centers containing monuments."

* * *

> Article 4(3): "The High Contracting Parties further undertake to prohibit, prevent and, if necessary, put a stop to any form of theft,

---

21. 1954 Convention for the Protection of Cultural Property in the Event of an Armed Conflict, 249 U.N.T.S. 240, art. 4(3). (The US and UK are signatories only to this convention but its basic provisions, such as those in article 4 are considered part of customary international law.) *See* Jan Hladik, *The 1954 Hague Convention for the Protection of Cultural Property in the Event of Armed Conflict and the Notion of Military Necessity,* 81 RICR/IRRC 621 (1999).

pillage or misappropriation of, and any acts of vandalism directed against, cultural property.''

The United States and United Kingdom are signatories only to this convention. As signatories they have at least the obligation not to defeat the objects and purposes of the treaty pending its coming into force. Vienna Convention on the Law of Treaties, May 23, 1969, art. 8, 1155 UNTS 331. The United States has not ruled out ratifying the 1954 Convention, so the Convention is still "pending its coming into force." In 1994, the lawyers at the United States Departments of State and Defense reviewed the Convention and supported its submission to the Senate for ratification.

3. The 1977 Additional Protocols

The Biafran War in Nigeria (1967–70) and the Vietnam War (1958–1974) encouraged the ICRC to attempt to increase the protections of victims in armed conflict.[22] Biafra cost between 2 and 3 million civilian lives, mostly from hunger and disease. Biafra demonstrated that parties needed to respect Common Article 3, but, also, that Common Article 3 plainly had gaps that needed filling. In Vietnam, the problem of guerilla fighters and the torture and abuse of American prisoners by the North Vietnamese were prominent issues. The ICRC wanted to signal to all warring parties that Common Article 3 was customary law and binding on them, whether or not they were parties to the Conventions. The ICRC began undertaking studies and engaging in consultations on supplementing the 1949 Conventions as early as the 1960's. By 1974 two draft protocols were ready for presentation to a diplomatic conference.[23] What became Protocol I was designed to extend the protections of victims of international armed conflict. The other draft, eventually Protocol II, aimed at increasing the protections in non-international armed conflicts. During the four years of negotiations, the delegates decided to include wars against colonial domination and alien occupation in Protocol I. This decision was criticized by a number of delegations, including the United States. The result, "suffice it to say . . . certain countries' interest in Protocol II diminished."[24] And in the end, Protocol II emerged a simpler instrument than the ICRC originally planned—only 28 Articles. Nevertheless, those contained important additions as a supplement to Common Article 3.[25]

---

22. Commentary on the Additional Protocols of 8 June 1977 to the Geneva Conventions of 12 August 1949 (Yves Sandoz et al. eds., 1987); *see also* Christopher Greenwood, *A Critique of the Additional Protocols to the Geneva Conventions of 1949, in* The Changing Face of Conflict and the Efficacy of International Humanitarian Law 3, 7 (H. Durham & T.L.H. McCormack eds., 1999).

23. Sylvie Junod, *Additional Protocol II: History and Scope,* 33 Am. U. L. Rev. 29, 31 (1983).

24. *Id.* at 33.

25. Mary Ellen O'Connell, *Humanitarian Assistance in Non–International Armed Conflict, The Fourth Wave of Rights, Duties and Remedies,* 31 Israel Ybk. on Human Rights 183 (2000).

Protocol II applies in only a narrower range of non-international armed conflict—arguably narrower than Article 3. According to Article 1(1), it applies when an armed conflict takes place

> [i]n the territory of a High Contracting Party between its armed forces and dissident armed forces or other organized armed groups which, under responsible command, exercise such control over a part of its territory as to enable them to carry out sustained and concerted military operations and to implement this Protocol.

Protocol II does not apply to "situations of international disturbances and tensions, such as riots, isolated and sporadic acts of violence and other acts of a similar nature."[26] Despite Protocol II's narrow scope, states included Article 3(2) to provide further protection of domestic jurisdiction:

> Nothing in this Protocol shall be invoked as a justification for intervening, directly or indirectly, for any reason whatever, in the armed conflict or in the internal or external affairs of the High Contracting Party in the territory of which that conflict occurs.

Where Protocol II does apply, the provisions on humanitarian assistance enhance those of the Common Article 3, especially regarding: "modalities of care for the sick and wounded. Persons engaged in medical activities are awarded special protection and the Red Cross emblem is specifically protected ... Furthermore, the guarantees of humane treatment ... have been developed.... In addition, article 3 and Protocol II are binding not only on the established government, but also on the insurgent party."[27]

On December 12, 1977, the United States signed Additional Protocols I & II. During the Reagan Administration, the State Department did a thorough review of the Protocols and decided to submit APII to the Congress for advice and consent on the question of ratification. With respect to API, it decided that it would not submit it for advice and consent but rather declare certain provisions binding as customary international law.[28] As of July 2004, the United States had not become party to either Protocol, but over 150 other states, including the United Kingdom, are parties.

1977 Geneva Protocol I Additional to the Geneva Conventions of 12 August 1949, and Relating to the Protection of Victims of International Armed Conflicts

1125 U.N.T.S. 3 (1979).

PART I—GENERAL PROVISIONS

Article 1—General principles and scope of application

    1. The High Contracting Parties undertake to respect and to ensure respect for this Protocol in all circumstances.

---

26. Protocol II, art. 1(2).

27. Junod, *supra* note 23, at 33.

28. *See* Matheson, *supra* note 6, at 419–31.

2. In cases not covered by this Protocol or by other international agreements, civilians and combatants remain under the protection and authority of the principles of international law derived from established custom, from the principles of humanity and from the dictates of public conscience.

3. This Protocol, which supplements the Geneva Conventions of 12 August 1949 for the protection of war victims, shall apply in situations referred to in Article 2 common to those Conventions.

4. The situations referred to in the preceding paragraph include armed conflicts in which peoples are fighting against colonial domination and alien occupation and against racist régimes in the exercise of their right of self-determination, as enshrined in the Charter of the United Nations and the Declaration on Principles of International Law concerning Friendly Relations and Co-operation among States in accordance with the Charter of the United Nations.

* * *

Article 11—Protection of persons

1. The physical or mental health and integrity of persons who are in the power of the adverse Party or who are interned, detained or otherwise deprived of liberty as a result of a situation referred to in Article 1 shall not be endangered by any unjustified act or omission. Accordingly, it is prohibited to subject the persons described in this Article to any medical procedure which is not indicated by the state of health of the person concerned and which is not consistent with generally accepted medical standards which would be applied under similar medical circumstances to persons who are nationals of the Party conducting the procedure and who are in no way deprived of liberty.

* * *

PART III—METHODS AND MEANS OF WARFARE, COMBATANT AND PRISONER-OF-WAR STATUS

SECTION I—METHODS AND MEANS OF WARFARE

Article 35—Basic rules

1. In any armed conflict, the right of the Parties to the conflict to choose methods or means of warfare is not unlimited.

2. It is prohibited to employ weapons, projectiles and material and methods of warfare of a nature to cause superfluous injury or unnecessary suffering.

3. It is prohibited to employ methods or means of warfare which are intended, or may be expected, to cause widespread, long-term and severe damage to the natural environment.

Article 36—New weapons

In the study, development, acquisition or adoption of a new weapon, means or method of warfare, a High Contracting Party is under an obligation to determine whether its employment would, in some or all circumstances, be prohibited by this Protocol or by any other rule of international law applicable to the High Contracting Party.

Article 37—Prohibition of perfidy

1.   It is prohibited to kill, injure or capture an adversary by resort to perfidy. Acts inviting the confidence of an adversary to lead him to believe that he is entitled to, or is obliged to accord, protection under the rules of international law applicable in armed conflict, with intent to betray that confidence, shall constitute perfidy. The following acts are examples of perfidy:

(*a*) the feigning of an intent to negotiate under a flag of truce or of a surrender;

(*b*) the feigning of an incapacitation by wounds or sickness;

(*c*) the feigning of civilian, non-combatant status; and

(*d*) the feigning of protected status by the use of signs, emblems or uniforms of the United Nations or of neutral or other States not Parties to the conflict.

2.   Ruses of war are not prohibited. Such ruses are acts which are intended to mislead an adversary or to induce him to act recklessly but which infringe no rule of international law applicable in armed conflict and which are not perfidious because they do not invite the confidence of any adversary with respect to protection under the law. The following are examples of such ruses: the use of camouflage, decoys, mock operations and misinformation.

Article 38—Recognized emblems

1.   It is prohibited to make improper use of the distinctive emblem of the red cross, red crescent or red lion and sun or of other emblems, signs or signals provided for by the Conventions or by this Protocol. It is also prohibited to misuse deliberately in an armed conflict other internationally recognized protective emblems, signs or signals, including the flag of truce, and the protective emblem of cultural property.

* * *

Article 40—Quarter

It is prohibited to order that there shall be no survivors, to threaten an adversary therewith or to conduct hostilities on this basis.

Article 41—Safeguard of an enemy hors de combat

1.   A person who is recognized or who, in the circumstances, should be recognized to be *hors de combat* shall not be made the object of attack.

2.   A person is *hors de combat* if:

(*a*) he is in the power of an adverse Party;

(*b*) he clearly expresses an intention to surrender; or

(*c*) he has been rendered unconscious or is otherwise in incapacitated by wounds or sickness, and therefore is incapable of defending himself; provided, that in any of these cases he abstains from any hostile act and does not attempt to escape;

3.   When persons entitled to protection as prisoners of war have fallen into the power of an adverse Party under unusual conditions of combat which prevent their evacuation as provided for in Part III, Section I, of the Third Convention, they shall be released and all feasible precautions shall be taken to ensure their safety.

* * *

SECTION II—COMBATANT AND PRISONER-OF-WAR STATUS

Article 43—Armed forces

1.   The armed forces of a Party to a conflict consist of all organized armed forces, groups and units which are under a command responsible to that Party for the conduct of its subordinates, even if that Party is represented by a government or an authority not recognized by an adverse Party. Such armed forces shall be subject to an internal disciplinary system which, *inter alia*, shall enforce compliance with the rules of international law applicable in armed conflict. * * *

Article 44—Combatants and prisoners of war

1.   Any combatant, as defined in Article 43, who falls into the power of an adverse Party shall be a prisoner of war.

2.   While all combatants are obliged to comply with the rules of international law applicable in armed conflict, violations of these rules shall not deprive a combatant of his right to be a combatant or, if he falls into the power of an adverse Party, of his right to be a prisoner of war, except as provided in paragraphs 3 and 4.

3.   In order to promote the protection of the civilian population from the effects of hostilities, combatants are obliged to distinguish themselves from the civilian population while they are engaged in an attack or in a military operation preparatory to an attack. Recognizing, however, that there are situations in armed

conflicts where, owing to the nature of the hostilities an armed combatant cannot so distinguish himself, he shall retain his status as a combatant, provided that, in such situations, he carries his arms openly:

(*a*) during each military engagement, and

(*b*) during such time as he is visible to the adversary while he is engaged in a military deployment preceding the launching of an attack in which he is to participate.

Acts which comply with the requirements of this paragraph shall not be considered as perfidious within the meaning of Article 37, paragraph 1 (*c*).

4.   A combatant who falls into the power of an adverse Party while failing to meet the requirements set fourth in the second sentence of paragraph 3 shall forfeit his right to be a prisoner of war, but he shall, nevertheless, be given protections equivalent in all respects to those accorded to prisoners of war by the Third Convention and by this Protocol. This protection includes protections equivalent to those accorded to prisoners of war by the Third Convention in the case where such a person is tried and punished for any offences he has committed.

5.   Any combatant who falls into the power of an adverse Party while not engaged in an attack or in a military operation preparatory to an attack shall not forfeit his rights to be a combatant and a prisoner of war by virtue of his prior activities.

* * *

7.   This Article is not intended to change the generally accepted practice of States with respect to the wearing of the uniform by combatants assigned to the regular, uniformed armed units of a Party to the conflict.

* * *

Article 45—Protection of persons who have taken part in hostilities

1.   A person who takes part in hostilities and falls into the power of an adverse Party shall be presumed to be a prisoner of war, and therefore shall be protected by the Third Convention, if he claims the status of prisoner of war, or if he appears to be entitled to such status, or if the Party on which he depends claims such status on his behalf by notification to the detaining Power or the Protecting Power. Should any doubt arise as to whether any such person is entitled to the status of prisoner of war, he shall continue to have such status and, therefore, to be protected by the Third Convention and this Protocol until such time as his status has been determined by a competent tribunal.

* * *

Part IV—Civilian Population

Section I—General Protection Against Effects of Hostilities

Chapter I—*Basic Rule and Field of Application*

Article 48—Basic Rule

In order to ensure respect for and protection of the civilian population and civilian objects, the Parties to the conflict shall at all times distinguish between the civilian population and combatants and between civilian objects and military objectives and accordingly shall direct their operations only against military objectives.

Article 49—Definition of attacks and scope of application

1. (Attacks) means acts of violence against the adversary, whether in offence or in defence.

2. The provisions of this Protocol with respect to attacks apply to all attacks in whatever territory conducted, including the national territory belonging to a Party to the conflict but under the control of an adverse Party.

* * *

Chapter II—*Civilians and Civilian Population*

Article 50—Definition of civilians and civilian population

1. A civilian is any person who does not belong to one of the categories of persons referred to in Article 4 A (1), (2), (3) and (6) of the Third Convention and in Article 43 of this Protocol. In case of doubt whether a person is a civilian, that person shall be considered to be a civilian.

2. The civilian population comprises all persons who are civilians.

3. The presence within the civilian population of individuals who do not come within the definition of civilians does not deprive the population of its civilian character.

Article 51—Protection of the civilian population

1. The civilian population and individual civilians shall enjoy general protection against dangers arising from military operations. To give effect to this protection, the following rules, which are additional to other applicable rules of international law, shall be observed in all circumstances.

2. The civilian population as such, as well as individual civilians, shall not be the object of attack. Acts or threats of violence the primary purpose of which is to spread terror among the civilian population are prohibited.

3.   Civilians shall enjoy the protection afforded by this Section, unless and for such time as they take a direct part in hostilities.

4.   Indiscriminate attacks are prohibited.

* * *

Article 75—Fundamental guarantees

1.   In so far as they are affected by a situation referred to in Article 1 of this Protocol, persons who are in the power of a Party to the conflict and who do not benefit from more favourable treatment under the Conventions or under this Protocol shall be treated humanely in all circumstances and shall enjoy, as a minimum, the protection provided by this Article without any adverse distinction based upon race, colour, sex, language, religion or belief, political or other opinion, national or social origin, wealth, birth or other status, or on any other similar criteria. Each Party shall respect the person, honour, convictions and religious practices of all such persons.

2.   The following acts are and shall remain prohibited at any time and in any place whatsoever, whether committed by civilian or by military agents:

(*a*) violence to the life, health, or physical or mental well-being of persons, in particular:

(i) murder;

(ii) torture of all kinds, whether physical or mental;

(iii) corporal punishment; and

(iv) mutilation;

(*b*) outrages upon personal dignity, in particular humiliating and degrading treatment, enforced prostitution and any form of indecent assault;

(*c*) the taking of hostages;

(*d*) collective punishments; and

(*e*) threats to commit any of the foregoing acts.

3.   Any person arrested, detained or interned for actions related to the armed conflict shall be informed promptly, in a language he understands, of the reasons why these measures have been taken. Except in cases of arrest or detention for penal offences, such persons shall be released with the minimum delay possible and in any event as soon as the circumstances justifying the arrest, detention or internment have ceased to exist.

4.   No sentence may be passed and no penalty may be executed on a person found guilty of a penal offence related to the armed conflict except pursuant to a conviction pronounced by an impar-

tial and regularly constituted court respecting the generally recognized principles of regular judicial procedure * * *.

* * *

SECTION II—REPRESSION OF BREACHES OF THE
CONVENTIONS AND OF THIS PROTOCOL

Article 85—Repression of breaches of this Protocol

1.   The provisions of the Conventions relating to the repression of breaches and grave breaches, supplemented by this Section, shall apply to the repression of breaches and grave breaches of this Protocol.

2.   Acts described as grave breaches in the Conventions are grave breaches of this Protocol if committed against persons in the power of an adverse Party protected by Articles 44, 45 and 73 of this Protocol, or against the wounded, sick and shipwrecked of the adverse Party who are protected by this Protocol, or against those medical or religious personnel, medical units or medical transports which are under the control of the adverse Party and are protected by this Protocol.

3.   In addition to the grave breaches defined in Article 11, the following acts shall be regarded as grave breaches of this Protocol, when committed wilfully, in violation of the relevant provisions of this Protocol, and causing death or serious injury to body or health:

(*a*) making the civilian population or individual civilians the object of attack;

(*b*) launching an indiscriminate attack affecting the civilian population or civilian objects in the knowledge that such attack will cause excessive loss of life, injury to civilians or damage to civilian objects, as defined in Article 57, paragraph 2(*a*) (iii);

(*c*) launching an attack against works or installations containing dangerous forces in the knowledge that such attack will cause excessive loss of life, injury to civilians or damage to civilian objects, as defined in Article 57, paragraph 2(*a*) (iii);

(*d*) making non-defended localities and demilitarized zones the object of attack;

(*e*) making a person the object of attack in the knowledge that he is *hors de combat*;

(*f*) the perfidious use, in violation of Article 37, of the distinctive emblem of the red cross, red crescent or red lion and sun or of other protective signs recognized by the Conventions or this Protocol.

4. In addition to the grave breaches defined in the preceding paragraphs and in the Conventions, the following shall be regarded as grave breaches of this Protocol, when committed wilfully and in violation of the Conventions or the Protocol:

(*a*) the transfer by the Occupying Power of parts of its own civilian population into the territory it occupies, or the deportation or transfer of all or parts of the population of the occupied territory within or outside this territory, in violation of Article 49 of the Fourth Convention;

(*b*) unjustifiable delay in the repatriation of prisoners of war or civilians;

(*c*) practices of *apartheid* and other inhuman and degrading practices involving outrages upon personal dignity, based on racial discrimination;

(*d*) making the clearly-recognized historic monuments, works of art or places of worship which constitute the cultural or spiritual heritage of peoples and to which special protection has been given by special arrangement, for example, within the framework of a competent international organization, the object of attack, causing as a result extensive destruction thereof, where there is no evidence of the violation by the adverse Party of Article 53, sub-paragraph (*b*), and when such historic monuments, works of art and places of worship are not located in the immediate proximity of military objectives;

(*e*) depriving a person protected by the Conventions or referred to in paragraph 2 of this Article of the rights of fair and regular trial.

5. Without prejudice to the application of the Conventions and of this Protocol, grave breaches of these instruments shall be regarded as war crimes.

Article 86—Failure to act

1. The High Contracting Parties and the Parties to the conflict shall repress grave breaches, and take measures necessary to suppress all other breaches, of the Conventions or of this Protocol which result from a failure to act when under a duty to do so.

2. The fact that a breach of the Conventions or of this Protocol was committed by a subordinate does not absolve his superiors from penal or disciplinary responsibility, as the case may be, if they knew, or had information which should have enabled them to conclude in the circumstances at the time, that he was committing or was going to commit such a breach and if they did not take all feasible measures within their power to prevent or repress the breach.

Article 87—Duty of commanders

1. The High Contracting Parties and the Parties to the conflict shall require military commanders, with respect to members of the armed forces under their command and other persons under their control, to prevent and, where necessary, to suppress and to report to competent authorities breaches of the Conventions and of this Protocol.

2. In order to prevent and suppress breaches, High Contracting Parties and Parties to the conflict shall require that, commensurate with their level of responsibility, commanders ensure that members of the armed forces under their command are aware of their obligations under the Conventions and this Protocol.

3. The High Contracting Parties and Parties to the conflict shall require any commander who is aware that subordinates or other persons under his control are going to commit or have committed a breach of the Conventions or of this Protocol, to initiate such steps as are necessary to prevent such violations of the Conventions or this Protocol, and, where appropriate, to initiate disciplinary or penal action against violators thereof.

* * *

Protocol Additional to the Geneva Conventions of 12 August 1949, and Relating to the Protection of Victims of Non–International Armed Conflicts (Protocol II)

1125 U.N.T.S. 609 (1979).

Part I—Scope of this Protocol

Article 1—Material field of application

1. This Protocol, which develops and supplements Article 3 common to the Geneva Conventions of 12 August 1949 without modifying its existing conditions of application, shall apply to all armed conflicts which are not covered by Article 1 of the Protocol Additional to the Geneva Conventions of 12 August 1949, and relating to the Protection of Victims of International Armed Conflicts (Protocol I) and which take place in the territory of a High Contracting Party between its armed forces and dissident armed forces or other organized armed groups which, under responsible command, exercise such control over a part of its territory as to enable them to carry out sustained and concerted military operations and to implement this Protocol.

2. This Protocol shall not apply to situations of internal disturbances and tensions, such as riots, isolated and sporadic acts of violence, and other acts of a similar nature, as not being armed conflicts.

Article 2—Personal field of application

1.   This Protocol shall be applied without any adverse distinction founded on race, colour, sex, language, religion or belief, political or other opinion, national or social origin, wealth, birth or other status, or on any other similar criteria (hereinafter referred to as 'adverse distinction') to all persons affected by an armed conflict as defined in Article 1.

2.   At the end of the armed conflict, all the persons who have been, deprived of their liberty or whose liberty has been restricted, for reasons related to such conflict, as well as those deprived of their liberty or whose liberty is restricted after the conflict for the same reasons, shall enjoy the protection of Articles 5 and 6 until the end of such deprivation or restriction of liberty.

Article 3—Non-intervention

1.   Nothing in this Protocol shall be invoked for the purpose of affecting the sovereignty of a State or the responsibility of the government, by all legitimate means, to maintain or re-establish law and order in the State or to defend the national unity and territorial integrity of the State.

2.   Nothing in this Protocol shall be invoked as a justification for intervening, directly or indirectly, for any reason whatever, in the armed conflict or in the internal or external affairs of the High Contracting Party in the territory of which that conflict occurs.

PART II—HUMANE TREATMENT

Article 4—Fundamental guarantees

1.   All persons who do not take a direct part or who have ceased to take a part in hostilities, whether or not their liberty has been restricted, are entitled to respect for their person, honour and convictions and religious practices. They shall in all circumstances be treated humanely, without any adverse distinction. It is prohibited to order there shall be no survivors:

2.   * * * (*a*) violence to the life, health and physical or mental well-being of persons, in particular murder as well as cruel treatment such as torture, mutilation or any form of corporal punishment;

(*b*) collective punishments;

(*c*) taking of hostages;

(*d*) acts of terrorism;

(*e*) outrages upon personal dignity, in particular humiliating and degrading treatment, rape, enforced prostitution and any form of indecent assault;

(*f*) slavery and the slave trade in all their forms;

(*g*) pillage;

(*h*) threats to commit any of the foregoing acts.

3. Children shall be provided with the care and aid they require* * *.

* * *

Article 6—Penal prosecutions

1. This Article applies to the prosecution and punishment of criminal offences related to the armed conflict.

2. No sentence shall be passed and no penalty shall be executed on a person found guilty of an offence except pursuant to a conviction pronounced by a court offering the essential guarantees of independence and impartiality. In particular:

(*a*) the procedure shall provide for an accused to be informed without delay of the particulars of the offence alleged against him and shall afford the accused before and during his trial all necessary rights and means of defence;

(*b*) no one shall be convicted of an offence except on the basis of individual penal responsibility;

(*c*) no one shall be held guilty of any criminal offence on account of any act or omission which did not constitute a criminal offence, under the law, at the time when it was committed; nor shall a heavier penalty be imposed than that which was applicable at the time when the criminal offence was committed; if, after the commission of the offence, provision is made by law for the imposition of a lighter penalty, the offender shall benefit thereby;

(*d*) anyone charged with an offence is presumed innocent until proved guilty according to law;

(*e*) anyone charged with an offence shall have the right to be tried in his presence;

(*f*) no one shall be compelled to testify against himself or to confess guilt.

3. A convicted person shall be advised on conviction of his judicial and other remedies and of the time-limits within which they may be exercised.

4. The death penalty shall not be pronounced on persons who were under the age of eighteen years at the time of the offence and shall not be carried out on pregnant women or mothers of young children.

5. At the end of hostilities, the authorities in power shall endeavour to grant the broadest possible amnesty to persons who have participated in the armed conflict, or those deprived of their

liberty for reasons related to the armed conflict, whether they are interned or detained.

* * *

Letter of Transmittal from Ronald Reagan, President of the United States of America to the United States Senate

The White House, January 29, 1987.*

To the Senate of the United States:

I transmit herewith, for the advice and consent of the Senate to ratification, Protocol II Additional to the Geneva Conventions of 12 August 1949, concluded at Geneva on June 10, 1977. I also enclose for the information of the Senate the report of the Department of State on the Protocol.

The United States has traditionally been in the forefront of efforts to codify and improve the international rules of humanitarian law in armed conflict, with the objective of giving the greatest possible protection to victims of such conflicts, consistent with legitimate military requirements. The agreement that I am transmitting today is, with certain exceptions, a positive step toward this goal. Its ratification by the United States will assist us in continuing to exercise leadership in the international community in these matters.

The Protocol is described in detail in the attached report of the Department of State. Protocol II to the 1949 Geneva Conventions is essentially an expansion of the fundamental humanitarian provisions contained in the 1949 Geneva Conventions with respect to non-international armed conflicts, including humane treatment and basic due process for detained persons, protection of the wounded, sick and medical units, and protection of noncombatants from attack and deliberate starvation. If these fundamental rules were observed, many of the worst human tragedies of current internal armed conflicts could be avoided. In particular, among other things, the mass murder of civilians is made illegal, even if such killings would not amount to genocide because they lacked racial or religious motives. Several Senators asked me to keep this objective in mind when adopting the Genocide Convention. I remember my commitment to them. This Protocol makes clear that any deliberate killing of a noncombatant in the course of a non-international armed conflict is a violation of the laws of war and a crime against humanity, and is therefore also punishable as murder.

* *Reprinted in* 81 AM. J. INT'L L. 910 (1987) (footnotes omitted).

While I recommend that the Senate grant advice and consent to this agreement, I have at the same time concluded that the United States cannot ratify a second agreement on the law of armed conflict negotiated during the same period. I am referring to Protocol I additional to the 1949 Geneva Conventions, which would revise the rules applicable to international armed conflicts. Like all other efforts associated with the International Committee of the Red Cross, this agreement has certain meritorious elements. But Protocol I is fundamentally and irreconcilably flawed. It contains provisions that would undermine humanitarian law and endanger civilians in war. One of its provisions, for example, would automatically treat as an international conflict any so-called "war of national liberation." Whether such wars are international or non-international should turn exclusively on objective reality, not on one's view of the moral qualities of each conflict. To rest on such subjective distinctions based on a war's alleged purposes would politicize humanitarian law and eliminate the distinction between international and non-international conflicts. It would give special status to "wars of national liberation," an ill-defined concept expressed in vague, subjective, politicized terminology. Another provision would grant combatant status to irregular forces even if they do not satisfy the traditional requirements to distinguish themselves from the civilian population and otherwise comply with the laws of war. This would endanger civilians among whom terrorists and other irregulars attempt to conceal themselves. These problems are so fundamental in character that they cannot be remedied through reservations, and I therefore have decided not to submit the Protocol to the Senate in any form, and I would invite an expression of the sense of the Senate that it shares this view. Finally, the Joint Chiefs of Staff have also concluded that a number of the provisions of the Protocol are militarily unacceptable.

It is unfortunate that Protocol I must be rejected. We would have preferred to ratify such a convention, which as I said contains certain sound elements. But we cannot allow other nations of the world, however numerous, to impose upon us and our allies and friends an unacceptable and thoroughly distasteful price for joining a convention drawn to advance the laws of war. In fact, we must not, and need not, give recognition and protection to terrorist groups as a price for progress in humanitarian law.

The time has come for us to devise a solution for this problem, with which the United States is from time to time confronted. In this case, for example, we can reject Protocol I as a reference for humanitarian law, and at the same time devise an alternative reference for the positive provisions of Protocol I that could be of real humanitarian benefit if generally observed by parties to international armed conflicts. We are therefore in the process of consulting with our allies to develop appropriate methods for incorporating these positive provisions into the rules that govern our military operations, and as customary international law. I will advise the Senate of the results of this initiative as soon as it is possible to do so.

I believe that these actions are a significant step in defense of traditional humanitarian law and in opposition to the intense efforts of terrorist organizations and their supporters to promote the legitimacy of their aims and practices. The repudiation of Protocol I is one additional step, at the ideological level so important to terrorist organizations, to deny these groups legitimacy as international actors.

Therefore, I request that the Senate act promptly to give advice and consent to the ratification of the agreement I am transmitting today, subject to the understandings and reservations that are described more fully in the attached report. I would also invite an expression of the sense of the Senate that it shares the view that the United States should not ratify Protocol I, thereby reaffirming its support for traditional humanitarian law, and its opposition to the politicization of that law by groups that employ terrorist practices.

Ronald Reagan

Hans–Peter Gasser, An Appeal for Ratification by the United States

81 AM. J. INT'L L. 912, 912–22 (1987).*

The President of the United States sent a message to the Senate on January 29, 1987 asking for its consent to the ratification of Protocol II Additional to the Geneva Conventions of 12 August 1949, and relating to the Protection of Victims of Non–International Armed Conflicts, adopted on June 8, 1977 by a Diplomatic Conference in Geneva. The decision to recommend this treaty for ratification, subject to certain understandings and reservations, is a welcome contribution to the development of international humanitarian law applicable in noninternational armed conflicts. The proposed declaration of understanding to the effect that Protocol II will be applied whenever Article 3 common to the four Geneva Conventions is applicable is a positive step forward that should set an example for other states.

The message also explains why the United States should not ratify Protocol I Additional to the Geneva Conventions of 12 August 1949, and relating to the Protection of Victims of International Armed Conflicts, adopted by the same Diplomatic Conference on June 8, 1977. While recognizing that certain of its provisions reflect customary international law and that others appear to be

* (Footnotes omitted).

positive new developments, the President's letter of transmittal finds that Protocol I, applicable in international armed conflicts, is "fundamentally and irreconcilably flawed"; in the words of the Department of State, the rejection of Protocol I should be recognized as "a repudiation of the collectivist apology for attacks on non-combatants."

These are strong words about a treaty of humanitarian character that belongs to what is also called "Red Cross law." In this short presentation it will be shown that they are hardly an accurate evaluation of Protocol I, that Protocol I indeed resulted from the most serious effort ever undertaken to strengthen the protection of noncombatants from the effects of modern warfare and that, contrary to the claims in the President's letter, Protocol I neither recognizes terrorist groups nor legitimizes terrorist acts. Although Protocol I does not deal with terrorism as a distinct phenomenon, several of its rules make a decisive contribution to the outlawing of terrorist acts and thus to the fight against terrorism.

SUBSTANCE AND HISTORY OF PROTOCOL I

Protocol I codifies and develops rules on the protection of war victims during international armed conflicts. Without modifying the text of the four 1949 Geneva Conventions—the universally accepted treaties on humanitarian law applicable in armed conflict—Protocol I updates and strengthens the "law of Geneva," i.e., the rules on the protection of the wounded, sick and shipwrecked, prisoners of war (POWs), civilian detainees and the civilian population. * * *

Protocol I also reaffirms and considerably develops existing rules of customary law governing the conduct of hostilities and protecting the civilian population against their effects (the so-called law of The Hague). Protocol I thus codifies the basic principle of international humanitarian law, that *the right of parties to a conflict to choose the methods and means of warfare is not unlimited*, and it elaborates that principle. The treaty also reaffirms another, equally fundamental rule: *the principle of distinction*. That principle provides that in their military operations, combatants must always distinguish between the civilian population and enemy combatants. Civilians must be spared. A major part of Protocol I is devoted to transforming this principle into operational provisions.

Protocol I was neither a momentary inspiration nor the sudden product of political pressure by one or another political alliance. Indeed, its drafting history goes as far back as the 1950s, when the International Committee of the Red Cross (ICRC)—still feeling the impact of the Second World War and the immeasurable suffering of the civilian population—submitted to the attention of governments a set of rules designed to strengthen protection of the civilian population in wartime. However, no action was taken then.

It took the wars of the sixties (in Vietnam, Nigeria, the Middle East and elsewhere) and decolonization to make governments and armed forces aware of the need to update the law of armed conflict.

After extensive preparatory work by the ICRC, including numerous consultations with military and legal experts from governments throughout the world, the Swiss Government convened the Diplomatic Conference on the Reaffirmation and Development of International Humanitarian Law Applicable in Armed Conflicts. That conference was a truly global gathering: more than a hundred governments, representing every continent and every political persuasion, sent delegations to Geneva, which ensured that all views were taken into account. As this was the first time that nations from the Third World had the opportunity to participate in a conference on the codification of humanitarian law, it was quite natural and legitimate that they voiced their special concerns—as, indeed, did all participants. Several "liberation movements," together with other observers, were also invited to follow the work of the conference but had no voting rights.

The first session was confronted with the Third World's request that "wars of national liberation" be qualified under certain conditions as international armed conflicts and no longer as internal conflicts. After a lengthy and sometimes emotionally charged debate, this proposal was adopted in committee by a majority vote. Thereafter, the way was clear for the negotiation of new humanitarian law, a very delicate task accomplished by qualified legal and military experts with the assistance of diplomats. To the great regret of many, the Third World was not as well represented in that second (and much longer) part of the conference as it should have been, mainly because of a lack of experts in the field. A glance at the attendance lists would thus refute the argument that Protocol I as a whole is the product of any "automatic majority." The conference adopted the two Protocols without a vote (by consensus).

* * *

The delegation of the United States played an outstanding role throughout the Diplomatic Conference. The presence of that most respected legal authority, Richard R. Baxter, subsequently a judge of the International Court of Justice (to name but one member of the delegation), was proof of the seriousness with which the U.S. Government took up the task. The United States joined all other participating governments in adopting the two Protocols by consensus. On December 12, 1978, the United States *signed* both Protocols. As the U.S. Government is not known for taking hasty decisions on signature and ratification of important multilateral agreements, Washington's decision to sign the two Protocols, especially Protocol I, is of great significance. It reflected the U.S. delegation's positive assessment of the Diplomatic Conference.

THE NEW RULE ON STRUGGLES FOR SELF-DETERMINATION

The first of the two reasons given for rejecting Protocol I in the President's message is that the new rule on struggles for self-determination "elevates the international legal status of self-described 'national liberation' groups that make a practice of terrorism." This is not so. Article 1(4) of the Protocol lays down that international armed conflicts shall include

> armed conflicts in which peoples are fighting against colonial domination and alien occupation and against racist régimes in the exercise of their right of self-determination, as enshrined in the Charter of the United Nations and the Declaration on Principles of International Law concerning Friendly Relations and Co-operation among States in accordance with the Charter of the United Nations.

With this rule, Protocol I does not break major new ground; it has merely transferred into humanitarian law a concept that has been part of international law for some time. The principle of self-determination of peoples is of course enshrined in the Charter of the United Nations. The concept has been developed by the Declaration on the Granting of Independence to Colonial Countries and Peoples, the two 1966 Human Rights Covenants and the Declaration on Principles of International Law concerning Friendly Relations and Co-operation among States in accordance with the Charter of the United Nations. According to prevailing views, only peoples that have not yet exercised their right to self-determination may qualify. It is therefore difficult to understand why "any radical group" may now invoke the new rule of Protocol I. In any event, Protocol I deals only with specific types of armed conflict and not with the legal status of particular groups. The Friendly Relations Declaration furthermore makes clear that the territorial integrity of existing states shall not be impaired, which means that a secessionist movement cannot expect its struggle against the central government to be recognized as a war of national liberation. Neither minorities dissatisfied with the majority nor political opponents of the government may therefore rely on the right of self-determination to voice their grievances. This limited concept of self-determination is unlikely to be broadened to any significant degree, since no government has any interest in undermining the territorial integrity of the state or, implicitly, its own position. The scope of application of the new rule is consequently very limited and it will probably remain so.

GUERRILLAS AND TERRORISTS

The President's letter of transmittal states further that "[a]nother provision would grant combatant status to irregular forces even if they do not satisfy the traditional requirements to distinguish themselves from the civilian population and otherwise comply with the laws of war." In the same context, the Department of State report says: "As the essence of terrorist criminality is the obliteration of the distinction between combatants and non-combatants, it would be hard to square ratification of this Protocol with the United States' announced policy of combatting terrorism." A former Deputy Assistant Secretary of Defense observes in this regard that the Diplomatic Conference "lays waste the legal and moral achievements of ages."

What happened in Geneva to evoke such harsh judgments? Does the new law permit terrorist acts or even confer legitimacy on terrorists? Of course not. The implications of these accusations, however, are such that a thorough look at the new regime on the rights and duties of combatants is necessary.

The Diplomatic Conference had to negotiate a solution to an age-old challenge to the law of war: guerrilla warfare. The issue, in short, is the following: there are times in armed conflicts when one side, the weaker side, comes to the conclusion that unless it accepts defeat, it cannot abide by the classic requirements that combatants must fulfill under current law, in particular the requirement to wear a uniform. It was contended that such situations arise mainly during occupations by foreign armed forces or in wars of national liberation. History provides many examples in which guerrilla warfare was the only way for a people to survive and to save its honor. On the other hand, the ability to distinguish between combatants and noncombatants is crucial to the proper functioning of the law of war. The principle of distinction requires that those who may be attacked (because they themselves are exercising the right to attack) must distinguish themselves from those who may not be attacked. Only thus does it become possible, in practical terms, to spare the civilian population from the effects of hostilities.

* * *

"Armed forces" in the sense of Protocol I must belong to a party to an international armed conflict; that is, they have to be under the control of such a party. Groups that do not meet that requirement may not claim a privileged position under international law. All members of armed forces (other than medical personnel and chaplains) are combatants; "that is to say, they have the right to participate directly in hostilities." A person not belonging to such armed forces who commits an act of violence in the course of an armed conflict, e.g., an act of terrorism, never enjoys the privilege of combatant status. He must be prosecuted and punished according to national law, provided that certain judicial guarantees are respected. Under the new law, armed forces of a liberation movement would have to conform to the same criteria as any other forces. In particular, they "shall be subject to an internal disciplinary system which, *inter alia*, shall enforce compliance with the rules of international law applicable in armed conflict." An essential characteristic of armed forces is that they are required to comply with the laws of war. Therefore, if a liberation movement should reject, as a matter of policy, humanitarian law as a whole, those "armed forces" would lose their status under Article 43, and members of the group would no longer have the privilege of combatant status. That does not mean, however, that any violation of the law of war committed by individual combatants would have the effect of divesting armed forces of their status as such. Violations by individuals are to be dealt with according to the rules on individual penal responsibility of all members of armed forces.

* * *

[T]he new law recognizes that there are *exceptional* situations in which combatants may dispense with the necessity of identifying themselves: under certain conditions they may "go underground" or hide in the civilian population, as guerrilleros have done since time immemorial. But they may not *fight* in civilian disguise! Indeed, in these exceptional circumstances combatants must carry their arms openly and thus distinguish themselves from the civilian population *at the very least during the actual military engagement and in the preceding phase of deployment.*

* * *

A combatant who does not comply with the requirements of distinction forfeits his right to be considered a combatant and, consequently, a prisoner of war if captured. He must, however, be given treatment equivalent to that accorded to POWs and he shall enjoy the same procedural safeguards in case of criminal prosecution. That is hardly an unacceptable burden for a civilized nation. Having forfeited his (privileged) status of combatant, he may indeed be tried (and punished), not only for possible violations of the law of war, but also (in the case of a war of national liberation) for having taken up arms against his own government. The situation of those members of armed forces who do not respect the minimum requirement of bearing arms openly in combat is therefore hardly enviable, even under Protocol I.

The new law on the status of combatants bears all the signs of a compromise. And indeed it was: the final text was negotiated by the American and Vietnamese delegations, both of whom knew what they were talking about, the experience of the Vietnam War still being fresh in their minds. During the war in Vietnam, members of Vietcong guerrilla units who were captured while actually engaged in combat ("carrying arms openly") were *treated* by the U.S. Military Assistance Command as prisoners of war (but not granted formal POW status), whereas a Vietcong who had committed an act of terrorism did not receive that treatment. In a nutshell, that practice is identical with what is required by Protocol I, and the new rules thus go no further than American practice in Vietnam. Officers who served in Vietnam (from the United States and allied nations) have told the present writer that, according to their experience, the system adopted by Article 44(3) should work in practice.

Having shown that the new rules neither "produce" nor "recognize" terrorists, we now ask how the law deals with terrorist acts committed by a member of an armed force (whether of a state or of a liberation movement). If such a combatant kills, injures or captures anybody while in civilian disguise, he is guilty of perfidy, the "feigning of civilian, non-combatant status" being an example of a prohibited, perfidious act. In addition, any conceivable act of terrorism is specifically prohibited by the Geneva Conventions and Protocol I. In particular, Article 51(2) of Protocol I deserves to be quoted in full: "The civilian population as such, as well as individual civilians, shall not be the object of attack. Acts or threats of violence the primary purpose of which is to spread terror among the civilian population are prohibited."

If an attack on civilians is committed deliberately and causes death or serious injury, then it is a grave breach of the Protocol—in other words, a war crime. Persons suspected of war crimes *must* be prosecuted (or extradited to another jurisdiction) by a party to an armed conflict or by any other party to the Geneva Conventions. The value of such an *obligation* either *to prosecute or to extradite* to another jurisdiction that has expressed its readiness to prosecute cannot be overestimated.

---

4. THE 1998 ROME STATUTE OF THE INTERNATIONAL CRIMINAL COURT

The excerpts from the Geneva Conventions and Additional Protocols above all contain provisions on criminal enforcement of any grave breaches of the conventions. Yet, few trials have occurred to enforce this law since Nuremberg and Tokyo despite the many violations. We will look at a few of the trials that have taken place in national courts and at the International Criminal Tribunal for Yugoslavia in the next Chapters. The overall unimpressive record of enforcement compelled states and international organizations to finally agree to an international criminal court to enforce the law prohibiting serious human rights violations, war crimes and the crime of aggression. On July 17, 1998, 120 states voted in favor of the Rome Statute of the International Criminal Court and it opened for signature that day.

On July 1, 2002, the Statute came into force and the Court was subsequently established. At time of writing, it has 97 states party, but no cases, although the prosecutor is looking into charges stemming from the brutal fighting waged in the Congo beginning in 1994.[29]

The United States turned from being an early supporter of the ICC, to a vehement opponent. The US under the Clinton Administration voted against adoption of the Statute at Rome, one of only seven states to vote against (21 abstained.) The US opposition to the Court has engendered a huge literature that we cannot delve into here. The key issue was US concern that Americans might be prosecuted on political grounds. The US was given no ultimate control over the prosecutor's decisions to prevent such feared abuse. For our purposes, the Rome Statute's provisions on war crimes are where we wish to focus.[30]

Leila Nadya Sadat, The Evolution of the ICC: From The Hague to Rome and Back Again

THE UNITED STATES AND THE INTERNATIONAL CRIMINAL COURT,
NATIONAL SECURITY AND INTERNATIONAL LAW 31, 36–40
(Sara B. Sewal & Carl Kaysen eds., 2000).*

* * *

CONFLICT: U.N. STRUGGLES FOLLOWING WORLD WAR II

Nuremberg helped overcome objections to an international criminal court on the basis of sovereignty. * * * Thus it is not surprising that the United Nations considered the establishment of a permanent international criminal court immediately after the war, in connection with the formulation and adoption of the Genocide Convention. But although the Genocide Convention was adopted relatively quickly, efforts to create the international criminal tribunal envisaged in Article VI of the Convention failed. * * *

In a resolution accompanying the adoption of the Genocide Convention, the U.N. General Assembly invited the newly established International Law Commission (ILC) to "study the desirability and possibility of establishing an international judicial organ

---

29. *See* UNITED NATIONS DIPLOMATIC CONFERENCE OF PLENIPOTENTIARIES ON THE ESTABLISHMENT OF AN INTERNATIONAL CRIMINAL COURT, ROME, 15 JUNE–17 JUNE 1998: OFFICIAL RECORDS. The literature on the ICC is already vast, see, e.g., WILLIAM A. SCHABAS, AN INTRODUCTION TO THE INTERNATIONAL CRIMINAL COURT (2d ed. 2004); THE PERMANENT INTERNATIONAL CRIMINAL COURT: LEGAL AND POLICY ISSUES (Dominic McGoldrick et al. eds., 2004); YOUNG SOK KIM THE INTERNATIONAL CRIMINAL COURT: A COMMENTARY OF THE ROME STATUTE (2003); THE ROME STATUTE OF THE INTERNATIONAL CRIMINAL COURT (Antonio Cassese et al., eds. 2002); LEILA NAD-

YA SADAT, THE INTERNATIONAL CRIMINAL COURT AND THE TRANSFORMATION OF INTERNATIONAL LAW: JUSTICE FOR THE NEW MILLENIUM (2002); THE INTERANTIONAL CRIMINAL COURT: THE MAKING OF THE ROME STATUTE, ISSUES, NEGOTIATIONS, RESULTS (Roy S. Lee ed., 1999).

30. For a detailed analysis of the war crimes section of the Rome Statute, see Michael Bothe, *War Crimes, in* 1 THE ROME STATUTE OF THE INTERNATIONAL CRIMINAL COURT, chap. 11.3 (Antonio Cassese et al. eds., 2002).

* Footnotes omitted.

for the trial of persons charged with genocide or other crimes over which jurisdiction will be conferred upon that organ by international conventions." It also requested that the Commission consider the possibility that this might be accomplished through the creation of a Criminal Chamber of the International Court of Justice. Thus instructed, the International Law Commission embarked on what would prove to be a frustrating and long endeavor.

The ILC ultimately voted at its Second Session in 1950 to support the desirability and feasibility of creating an international criminal court. However, an examination of the summary records and reports on the topic shows that the Commission was deeply divided on this subject. Indeed, two separate reports were submitted to the Commission regarding the international criminal court, one supporting the court's establishment and a second rejecting it. After heated debate, the ILC voted eight to one, with two abstentions, that it was *desirable* to establish an international penal judicial organ, and seven to three, with one abstention, that the establishment of an international criminal judicial organ was *possible.*

Although the Commission ultimately adopted a Draft Code of Offenses Against the Peace and Security of Mankind in 1954, the General Assembly removed the question of the court that might enforce such a code from the ILC and vested it in a committee composed of the representatives of seventeen Member States. As was later pointed out, the General Assembly's action involved a reversal of roles that was curious, to say the least: it had asked a body of jurists a political question (whether the creation of the court was desirable) and had subsequently entrusted a political body with the technical task of elaborating a draft statute. The Committee on International Criminal Jurisdiction met in Geneva, Switzerland, during August 1951, by the end of which it had agreed to a draft statute (the Geneva draft) for an international criminal court. It comprised many features that reappeared in the * * * 1998 Rome Statute. First, the Committee believed it would be most satisfactory to establish the court as a United Nations organ. However, in light of the practical difficulties involved in amending the [U.N.] Charter and the legal difficulties of establishing the court by General Assembly Resolution, the Committee concluded that a multilateral convention would be the most appropriate mechanism for the court's creation. This was the solution ultimately adopted at Rome. Although a multilateral convention was perhaps the only means to ensure the court's establishment, it placed the court and its operations outside the U.N. system, suggesting that political support for the court is in many ways quite weak. The Committee envisaged the Court as a "semi-permanent" institution that would hold sessions only when matters before it required consideration, an idea that the ILC retained in subsequent incarnations of the court's statute, but that was ultimately discarded at Rome.

The court envisaged by the 1951 Committee would have heard cases against natural persons only, including heads of state or agents of government. The question of the criminality of states thus disappeared permanently from the agenda. The court's subject-matter jurisdiction was limited to international crimes "provided in conventions or special agreements among States parties" to the statute. This seemed to exclude from the proposal many of the most serious international crimes, including aggression, although the opacity of the formula leaves the scope of the proposed court's jurisdiction quite unclear. Finally, cases could proceed only if the state or states of the accused's nationality and the state or states in which the crime was alleged to have been committed expressly conferred jurisdiction upon the court.

Very few governments commented on the proposed statute. The United Kingdom expressed the view that "the whole project [was] fundamentally unsound." The French and the Dutch delegations were more optimistic, and the General Assembly requested the formation of another seventeen-member-state committee to reexamine several of the issues and to prepare another report. The second Committee met in New York during the summer of 1953 and issued its report with an amended version of the statute annexed thereto. The 1953 Committee modified the Geneva text in some respects, although not fundamentally.

The 1951 and 1953 Committee Reports were never implemented for lack of a political consensus on the desirability of creating an ICC. Instead, the idea stalled in the United Nations for the next thirty-five years. The General Assembly, which had postponed consideration of the Draft Code of Offenses until a definition of aggression could be adopted, took twenty years to complete its task, although the ILC produced several excellent reports on the topic.

The Cold War rendered action on the Draft Code of Offenses and the ICC virtually impossible, although the Draft Code remained on the General Assembly's agenda. But with the gradual reopening of East–West relations, work on an international criminal court could resume, and in 1989 the General Assembly specifically requested the ILC to address the question of establishing an international criminal court.

The ILC provisionally adopted a Draft Code of Crimes in 1991 and, in its forty-fourth session in 1992, created a working group on an international criminal court. The Working Group produced an extensive report outlining the general bases on which, in its opinion, the establishment of the ICC could proceed.

Not all the ILC's members were pleased with the relatively modest proposals made by the Working Group. But as the group's chair, Abdul Koroma, pointed out, the proposals represented a compromise between those who would have gone much further and those who felt that nothing should be done at all. With the exception of the Court's jurisdiction, which expanded in the 1994 Draft Statute, these proposals (which were themselves largely based on the work of the 1951 and 1953 committees) were substantially adopted in the 1994 Draft Statute issued by the ILC, and many of them found their way into the Rome Statute as well.

RESOLUTION: THE ROAD TO ROME

Following the ILC's report, the U.N. General Assembly granted the ILC a mandate to elaborate a draft statute "as a matter of priority," although many countries (including the United States) did not support the Draft Code of Crimes. The project gained momentum after the U.N. Security Council created the International Criminal Tribunal for the Former Yugoslavia (ICTY). The adoption of the ICTY's statute suggested not only that a permanent court was needed but also that governments, including the United States, would be willing to support its establishment, at least under some circumstances. The creation of the International Criminal Tribunal for Rwanda (ICTR) shortly thereafter underscored the need for the establishment of an international institution that could address serious violations of international humanitarian law. The problems that the two ad hoc tribunals faced in recruiting top-flight prosecutors and judges, financing their activities, and obtaining custody of suspects—not to mention the allegations of corruption that beset the Rwanda tribunal—did not dampen enthusiasm for the ICC. Rather, they underlined the urgent need for a stable, new, permanent institution that would be ready for any situation.

The ILC considered two draft statutes before finally adopting a sixty-article version in 1994. Deferential to the politics of states and perhaps wary of having its work shelved once again, the ILC took no position on some of the more difficult political questions involved in drafting the Statute (such as the definitions of crimes and the financing of the Court) or took positions deferential to state sovereignty on others (such as jurisdictional regimes and organizational structure).

The basic premise on which the ILC proceeded was that the Court should "complement" national prosecutions, rather than replace them, and that it should try only those accused of the most serious violations of international criminal law in cases in which national trials would not occur or would be ineffective. The ILC did not envisage the Court as an institution that would unify or construct international criminal law and, thus, did not grant the

Court any advisory jurisdiction, although there was some discussion among Commission members as to the desirability of doing so.

The ILC envisaged a Court with jurisdiction over both treaty crimes and violations of international humanitarian law. It would act only when cases were submitted to it by States Parties or the U.N. Security Council. It would be in all instances, except for U.N. Security Council referrals, completely dependent on State consent for its operation. Indeed, the proposed State consent regime and system of jurisdictional reservations probably would have completely crippled the proposed Court, except in cases involving affirmative action by the Security Council.

* * *

The ILC's draft statute then returned to the U.N. General Assembly for consideration. The General Assembly established an "Ad Hoc Committee," which met in four weeks of sessions from April to August 1995 and prepared a report that became the basis for the General Assembly to establish a Preparatory Committee to consider the ILC 1994 Draft Statute. The Preparatory Committee, open to all members of the United Nations as well as members of specialized agencies, was charged with "preparing a widely acceptable consolidated text of a convention for an international criminal court as a next step towards consideration by a conference of plenipotentiaries." In 1996 and 1997 the Preparatory Committee held six sessions, each lasting approximately two weeks, and issued a consolidated text of a Draft Statute in April 1998 for the consideration of a Diplomatic Conference later that summer.

The Diplomatic Conference was held in Rome from June 15 to July 17, 1998. The consolidated text that was the starting point of the negotiations was a complex document containing 116 articles, including some 1,300 phrases in brackets. It was extremely difficult to read, let alone understand, and virtually all of the difficult political issues that had been debated for more than two years during the Preparatory Committee meetings leading up to the Rome conference remained unresolved. The Conference was well attended, by both governments and NGOs; and the debates, while often intense, proved extremely fruitful. While a successful conclusion to the Conference was by no means a foregone conclusion, after five weeks of grueling negotiations, a statute was adopted on the last day of the Conference.

The Rome Statute is substantially longer and more complex than any of its predecessor instruments. The 128–article text not only outlines the Court's jurisdiction, but also goes into extensive detail as to the ICC's structure, operations, and functioning. Structurally, the Rome Conference largely adopted the ILC's proposal but added a Pretrial Division and an Assembly of States Parties (for oversight) to the overall structure. It also permits the

Prosecutor to bring cases to the Court on his or her own initiative (ex proprio motu), subject to judicial supervision, a provision that was highly controversial and to which the United States was adamantly opposed. Importantly, the Rome Conference rejected the conception of the Court as a "stand-by" institution in favor of a truly permanent structure.

The ILC's 1994 Draft had taken the position that its function was neither to define nor to codify crimes under general international law; rather it viewed the Court's Statute "primarily as an adjectival and procedural instrument." The drafters at Rome took the opposite view and defined the crimes within the Court's jurisdiction. This involved protracted and difficult negotiations between States that wanted broad definitions and States that wanted narrow definitions that would be difficult to apply. The result, as one might imagine, is a compromise text that is not always easy to interpret. The definitions of crimes will be further explicated in an annex to the Statute adopted by Parties to the Treaty (States Parties).

The Statute evidences a constant tension between supranationalism and deference to state sovereignty. It builds on the experience of Nuremberg, Tokyo, and the ICTY and the ICTR. The Court's jurisdiction, at least for the immediate future, is limited to crimes against humanity, genocide, war crimes, and possibly aggression. Until the Statute has been amended to define *aggression*, * * * and thus the Statute, in its current form, prohibits only war crimes, not war itself. The Statute represents a significant improvement over the ILC draft in many respects, particularly institutional structure and jurisdiction. In a significant victory for proponents of a strong and independent Court, it is the Court, not States Parties, that will decide whether cases are admissible, whether the Court has jurisdiction, whether a state's investigation or prosecution is "genuine" in determining complementarity, and whether evidence is admissible or not.

* * *

1998 Rome Statute of the International Court

UN Doc. A/CONF.183/9* (July 17, 1998)

Article 8—War crimes

1. The Court shall have jurisdiction in respect of war crimes in particular when committed as part of a plan or policy or as part of a large-scale commission of such crimes.

2. For the purpose of this Statute, "war crimes" means:

* Corrections issued Sept. 1998.

(*a*) Grave breaches of the Geneva Conventions of 12 August 1949, namely, any of the following acts against persons or property protected under the provisions of the relevant Geneva Convention:

(i) Wilful killing;

(ii) Torture or inhuman treatment, including biological experiments;

(iii) Wilfully causing great suffering, or serious injury to body or health;

(iv) Extensive destruction and appropriation of property, not justified by military necessity and carried out unlawfully and wantonly;

(v) Compelling a prisoner of war or other protected person to serve in the forces of a hostile Power;

(vi) Wilfully depriving a prisoner of war or other protected person of the rights of fair and regular trial;

(vii) Unlawful deportation or transfer or unlawful confinement;

(viii) Taking of hostages.

(*b*) Other serious violations of the laws and customs applicable in international armed conflict, within the established framework of international law, namely, any of the following acts:

(i) Intentionally directing attacks against the civilian population as such or against individual civilians not taking direct part in hostilities;

(ii) Intentionally directing attacks against civilian objects, that is, objects which are not military objectives;

(iii) Intentionally directing attacks against personnel, installations, material, units or vehicles involved in a humanitarian assistance or peacekeeping mission in accordance with the Charter of the United Nations, as long as they are entitled to the protection given to civilians or civilian objects under the international law of armed conflict;

(iv) Intentionally launching an attack in the knowledge that such attack will cause incidental loss of life or injury to civilians or damage to civilian objects or widespread, long-term and severe damage to the natural environment which would be clearly excessive in relation to the concrete and direct overall military advantage anticipated;

(v) Attacking or bombarding, by whatever means, towns, villages, dwellings or buildings which are undefended and which are not military objectives;

(vi) Killing or wounding a combatant who, having laid down his arms or having no longer means of defence, has surrendered at discretion;

(vii) Making improper use of a flag of truce, of the flag or of the military insignia and uniform of the enemy or of the United Nations, as well as of the distinctive emblems of the Geneva Conventions, resulting in death or serious personal injury;

(viii) The transfer, directly or indirectly, by the Occupying Power of parts of its own civilian population into the territory it occupies, or the deportation or transfer of all or parts of the population of the occupied territory within or outside this territory;

(ix) Intentionally directing attacks against buildings dedicated to religion, education, art, science or charitable purposes, historic monuments, hospitals and places where the sick and wounded are collected, provided they are not military objectives;

(x) Subjecting persons who are in the power of an adverse party to physical mutilation or to medical or scientific experiments of any kind which are neither justified by the medical, dental or hospital treatment of the person concerned nor carried out in his or her interest, and which cause death to or seriously endanger the health of such person or persons;

(xi) Killing or wounding treacherously individuals belonging to the hostile nation or army;

(xii) Declaring that no quarter will be given;

(xiii) Destroying or seizing the enemy's property unless such destruction or seizure be imperatively demanded by the necessities of war;

(xiv) Declaring abolished, suspended or inadmissible in a court of law the rights and actions of the nationals of the hostile party;

(xv) Compelling the nationals of the hostile party to take part in the operations of war directed against their own country, even if they were in the belligerent's service before the commencement of the war;

(xvi) Pillaging a town or place, even when taken by assault;

(xvii) Employing poison or poisoned weapons;

(xviii) Employing asphyxiating, poisonous or other gases, and all analogous liquids, materials or devices;

(xix) Employing bullets which expand or flatten easily in the human body, such as bullets with a hard envelope which does not entirely cover the core or is pierced with incisions;

(xx) Employing weapons, projectiles and material and methods of warfare which are of a nature to cause superfluous injury or unnecessary suffering or which are inherently indiscriminate in violation of the international law of armed conflict, provided that such weapons, projectiles and material and methods of warfare are the subject of a comprehensive prohibition and are included in an annex to this Statute, by an amendment in accordance with the relevant provisions set forth in articles 121 and 123;

(xxi) Committing outrages upon personal dignity, in particular humiliating and degrading treatment;

(xxii) Committing rape, sexual slavery, enforced prostitution, forced pregnancy, as defined in article 7, paragraph 2 (f), enforced sterilization, or any other form of sexual violence also constituting a grave breach of the Geneva Conventions;

(xxiii) Utilizing the presence of a civilian or other protected person to render certain points, areas or military forces immune from military operations;

(xxiv) Intentionally directing attacks against buildings, material, medical units and transport, and personnel using the distinctive emblems of the Geneva Conventions in conformity with international law;

(xxv) Intentionally using starvation of civilians as a method of warfare by depriving them of objects indispensable to their survival, including wilfully impeding relief supplies as provided for under the Geneva Conventions;

(xxvi) Conscripting or enlisting children under the age of fifteen years into the national armed forces or using them to participate actively in hostilities.

(c) In the case of an armed conflict not of an international character, serious violations of article 3 common to the four Geneva Conventions of 12 August 1949, namely, any of the following acts committed against persons taking no active part in the hostilities, including members of armed forces who have laid down their arms and those placed hors de combat by sickness, wounds, detention or any other cause:

(i) Violence to life and person, in particular murder of all kinds, mutilation, cruel treatment and torture;

(ii) Committing outrages upon personal dignity, in particular humiliating and degrading treatment;

(iii) Taking of hostages;

(iv) The passing of sentences and the carrying out of executions without previous judgement pronounced by a regularly constituted court, affording all judicial guarantees which are generally recognized as indispensable.

(*d*) Paragraph 2 (c) applies to armed conflicts not of an international character and thus does not apply to situations of internal disturbances and tensions, such as riots, isolated and sporadic acts of violence or other acts of a similar nature.

(*e*) Other serious violations of the laws and customs applicable in armed conflicts not of an international character, within the established framework of international law, namely, any of the following acts:

(i) Intentionally directing attacks against the civilian population as such or against individual civilians not taking direct part in hostilities;

(ii) Intentionally directing attacks against buildings, material, medical units and transport, and personnel using the distinctive emblems of the Geneva Conventions in conformity with international law;

(iii) Intentionally directing attacks against personnel, installations, material, units or vehicles involved in a humanitarian assistance or peacekeeping mission in accordance with the Charter of the United Nations, as long as they are entitled to the protection given to civilians or civilian objects under the international law of armed conflict;

(iv) Intentionally directing attacks against buildings dedicated to religion, education, art, science or charitable purposes, historic monuments, hospitals and places where the sick and wounded are collected, provided they are not military objectives;

(v) Pillaging a town or place, even when taken by assault;

(vi) Committing rape, sexual slavery, enforced prostitution, forced pregnancy, as defined in article 7, paragraph 2 (f), enforced sterilization, and any other form of sexual violence also constituting a serious violation of article 3 common to the four Geneva Conventions;

(vii) Conscripting or enlisting children under the age of fifteen years into armed forces or groups or using them to participate actively in hostilities;

(viii) Ordering the displacement of the civilian population for reasons related to the conflict, unless the security of the civilians involved or imperative military reasons so demand;

(ix) Killing or wounding treacherously a combatant adversary;

(x) Declaring that no quarter will be given;

(xi) Subjecting persons who are in the power of another party to the conflict to physical mutilation or to medical or scientific experiments of any kind which are neither justified by the medical, dental or hospital treatment of the person concerned nor carried out in his or her interest, and which cause death to or seriously endanger the health of such person or persons;

(xii) Destroying or seizing the property of an adversary unless such destruction or seizure be imperatively demanded by the necessities of the conflict;

(f) Paragraph 2 (e) applies to armed conflicts not of an international character and thus does not apply to situations of internal disturbances and tensions, such as riots, isolated and sporadic acts of violence or other acts of a similar nature. It applies to armed conflicts that take place in the territory of a State when there is protracted armed conflict between governmental authorities and organized armed groups or between such groups.

3. Nothing in paragraph 2 (c) and (e) shall affect the responsibility of a Government to maintain or re-establish law and order in the State or to defend the unity and territorial integrity of the State, by all legitimate means.

Knut Dörmann & Louis Maresca, International Criminal Court ("ICC")

The International Committee of the Red Cross and Its Contribution to the Development of International Humanitarian Law in Specialized Instruments, 5 CHI. J. INT'L L. 217, 224–28 (2004).*

The negotiations leading to the establishment of the ICC are another example of considerable ICRC involvement in the development of international humanitarian law. Why were these negotiations important to the ICRC? It believes that it is essential for international humanitarian law—as well as for any other body of law—to be properly respected and applied in practice. There are certainly various ways of ensuring this, but it is obvious that a law that is not supported by sanctions is generally difficult to enforce. Impunity for the most serious violations is therefore clearly unacceptable.

* Footnotes omitted.

Existing treaties of international humanitarian law prior to the Rome Statute establishing the ICC placed the responsibility to enact legislation and to provide for effective penal sanctions on the individual state parties. The Geneva Conventions and Additional Protocol I specifically require states parties to repress grave breaches of international humanitarian law, which are considered war crimes. In accordance with the respective provisions, state parties are obliged to search for persons alleged to have committed, or to have ordered to be committed, such breaches and to bring such persons, regardless of their nationality, before their own courts. They may also, if they prefer, hand such persons over for trial to another state party. For other breaches of the Conventions and of Protocol I, the state parties must take the measures needed to suppress them. In spite of these rules, however, states rarely fulfilled their duty to provide for or exercise their jurisdiction. Regardless of the appeals made by the ICRC and others asking states to comply with their obligations under the Geneva Conventions and Additional Protocol I, the situation remained static. Until the mid–1990s, the vast majority of war crimes trials were limited to crimes committed during the Second World War.

The creation of international tribunals was a solution to this rather unsatisfactory situation. With the establishment of two ad hoc tribunals, one for serious violations committed in the territory of the former Yugoslavia since 1991 ("ICTY"), and the other for serious violations committed in Rwanda or by Rwandan citizens between 1 January 1994 and 31 December 1994 ("ICTR"), the situation improved slightly.

* * *

A.   Preparatory Work and the Diplomatic Conference in Rome

The ICRC was active throughout the process of negotiating the Rome Statute. It had observer status at the various preparatory meetings and at the diplomatic conference that negotiated and adopted the Statute. The ICRC's main concerns were war crimes, which directly relate to international humanitarian law. Thus it paid particular attention to the definitions of these crimes. It took the view that the ICC's jurisdiction must cover all grave breaches of the Geneva Conventions as well as of Additional Protocol I. Moreover, it believed that other serious violations of international humanitarian law, in particular those committed in non-international armed conflicts, must also be included. In the ICRC's view, this was essential to giving the ICC the appropriate tools to end impunity for crimes committed in the majority of contemporary armed conflicts. Taking into account the legislative developments in many states since the early 1990s, the decisions made in the Statute for the Rwanda Tribunal and the case law of the ICTY, the exclusion of war crimes from the Rome Statute committed in non-international armed conflicts would have been a major setback.

In addition to these substantive matters, and with a view to making the ICC truly effective, the ICRC was particularly interested in making the exercise of the ICC's jurisdiction effective and in ensuring the independence of the prosecutor. With these aims in mind, it tried to convince states of its positions through official statements in formal and informal meetings, networking, and lobbying. Moreover, in 1997, the ICRC prepared a draft list of war crimes, together with a commentary for the February session of the Preparatory Committee, and submitted a paper entitled State Consent Regime vs. Universal Jurisdiction.

The diplomatic conference in Rome was strongly influenced by the extremely active and productive role played by some 230 non-governmental organizations. There is no doubt that their activities had an important influence on the group of like-minded states supporting the establishment of an effective court. Many of the ICRC's concerns and interests were shared by states and NGOs and thus its views fell on fertile ground.

In retrospect, it may be difficult to assess what concrete impact the specific work of ICRC had on the outcome. It may, however, be safe to say that the ICRC's expertise in international humanitarian law influenced in a significant way the final list of war crimes adopted. Regrettably, not all serious violations of international humanitarian law have been included in Article 8 of the Statute—namely, some grave breaches of Additional Protocol I were not retained. But most of the crimes in the 1997 ICRC proposal found their way into the Statute. The inclusion of crimes committed in non-international armed conflicts was a particular success. It clearly confirmed the acceptance of individual criminal responsibility for serious violations of international humanitarian law committed in non-international armed conflicts, a consensus that developed in the early 1990s.

C. THE INTERNATIONAL COMMITTEE OF THE RED CROSS

As we just read the ICRC was very active at the Rome Conference and of course was largely responsible for the Geneva Conventions and Additional Protocols. Supporting the development of humanitarian law is a vital part of the ICRC's mission, but it also plays an active role implementing the Geneva Conventions. Its structure is unique in the world of international organizations. It is neither a true non-governmental organization, like Amnesty International, nor a true inter-governmental organization like the United Nations:[31]

---

31. The ICRC has an excellent website with a wealth of further information on the organization: http://www.icrc.org.

The International Committee of the Red Cross (ICRC) is an impartial, neutral and independent organization whose exclusively humanitarian mission is to protect the lives and dignity of victims of war and internal violence and to provide them with assistance. It directs and coordinates the international relief activities conducted by the Movement in situations of conflict. It also endeavours to prevent suffering by promoting and strengthening humanitarian law and universal humanitarian principles.[32]

The International Committee of the Red Cross is organized as a private association under Swiss law, but it is mandated to carry out functions under the various humanitarian law conventions.[33] The headquarters of the association is in Geneva. The Committee proper is composed of fifteen to twenty-five members, all Swiss nationals. The restriction to Swiss nationals supports the ICRC's neutrality as Switzerland is a traditionally neutral country. From its founding in 1863, the ICRC has offered its services to protect and assist war victims. It is referred to in 15 articles of the Prisoners Convention, 22 articles of the Civilians Convention, eight articles in Additional Protocol I and two in Additional Protocol II. These references constitute the following tasks:

To visit and interview without witness prisoners of war and protected civilians, in particular when they are interned or detained;[a]

To provide relief to protected civilians, prisoners of war and to the population of occupied territories;[b]

To search for missing persons and trace * * * prisoners of war and civilians and forward their family messages;[c]

To offer its good offices to facilitate the creation of hospital and safety zones;[d]

To function as a substitute for Protecting Powers or as quasi-substitute;[e]

In the event of *non-international armed conflicts*, Article 3 common to the four Geneva Conventions of 1949 provides that the ICRC may "offer its services to the Parties to the conflict."[34]

---

32. The International Committee of the Red Cross (ICRC)–Its Ambitions and Its Will to Act, http://www.icrc.org.

33. In addition to the ICRC, the International Red Cross and Red Crescent Movement is made up of National Red Cross and Red Crescent Societies, and of the Federation of the Red Cross and Red Crescent Societies. (The Red Shield of David is used by Israel in lieu of a red cross or red crescent.)

a. *Cf.* Art. 126 of Convention III and Art. 143 of Convention IV.

b. *Cf.* Arts. 73 and 125 of Convention III, Arts 59, 61, and 142 of Convention IV.

c. *Cf.* Art. 123 of Convention III, Art. 140 of Convention IV, and Art. 33 of Protocol I.

d. *Cf.* Art 23 of Convention I and Art. 14 of Convention IV.

e. *Cf.* Arts. 9/9/9/10 respectively of the four conventions.

34. Marco Sassòli & Antoine A. Bociver, How Does Law Protect in War? 275 (1999).

Fritz Kalshoven, Constraints on the Waging of War,

8 (1987)

Around the middle of the 19th century the circumstances of wounded soldiers on the battlefield left nearly everything to be desired. Care for the wounded was primitive and insufficient in all respects: there was a dearth of military, medical and auxiliary personnel; surgery and other treatment usually had to be applied in very primitive conditions; insight into the need for sterile wound treatment was lacking; antibiotics and blood plasma did not yet exist; and so on and so forth. Nor was this all: perhaps the worst fact of all was that the Napoleonic wars of the beginning of the century had brought an end to the customary practice of sparing the enemy's field hospitals and leaving both the medical personnel and the wounded untouched.

Instead, field hospitals were shelled and doctors and stretcher-bearers on the battlefield subjected to fire; and whoever fell into enemy hands, whether wounded or not and regardless of whether he belonged to the fighting forces or to the medical or auxiliary personnel, was taken prisoner. The net result was that often, upon the approach of enemy forces, or even when their approach was merely rumoured, the doctors and nurses in the field hospitals fled with the primitive ambulances at their disposal, taking with them as many wounded as they could and leaving the others untended.

On top of all this, aid for the wounded could not always be expected from the inhabitants of nearby localities either: one could never be entirely sure which way the fortunes of battle would go, and he who tended a wounded soldier of one party ran the risk of being regarded as an active supporter of that party by the other side.

The disastrous consequences of this accumulation of adverse factors were widely known. Yet it would take the initiative of one man, the Genevese businessman J. Henry Dunant, for the world to do something effective about it. In 1859, in the aftermath of the battle of Solferino in Northern Italy, Dunant found himself, more or less by accident, amidst the thousands of French and Austrian wounded who had been brought to the nearby village of Castiglione. For days, he and a few other volunteers did what they could to treat the wounded and alleviate the sufferings of the dying.

Then, deeply affected by the misery he had witnessed, he retired for a while from active life and wrote his experiences down in a book which he gave the title *Un souvenir de Solferino* (A Memory of Solferino). Published in 1862, the book created an immediate stir throughout Europe, especially in elite circles where the realization was sharp that the existing situation could no longer be left unchanged. In effect, Dunant had indicated in his book the two steps that he regarded as indispensable: first, in each country, the establishment of a national private aid organization to assist the military medical services in a task the latter were not, by far, equipped to perform; and secondly, for States to conclude a treaty that would facilitate the work of these organizations and guarantee a better treatment of the wounded.

The realization of both ideas took surprisingly little time. As early as 1863 a few Genevese citizens, with Henry Dunant among them, established the "International Committee for Aid to the Wounded", with the self-appointed task of promoting the twin aim of the creation of national aid societies and the conclusion of a treaty facilitating their work. (The Committee was soon renamed International Committee of the Red Cross; it shall be referred to hereinafter as the ICRC). In the same year, the first national society was established in Wurtemberg; Oldenburg, Belgium and Prussia followed in 1864, The Netherlands in 1866. These early national societies were succeeded in the course of the years by similar societies in nearly every country, under the name of Red Cross or Red Crescent societies.

The desired treaty was hardly longer in coming. A group of enthusiastic propagandists—an action group, one is tempted to say—seized upon the first opportunity, an international congress on statistics held in Berlin in 1863, to start spreading the idea that such a treaty was urgently needed. As a result of this and similar efforts, a diplomatic conference convened in 1864 in Geneva, and on 22 August of that same year the Conference adopted the "Convention for the Amelioration of the Condition of the Wounded in Armies in the Field".

The most important features of the new Convention were the following: in war on land, ambulances and military hospitals would be "recognized as neutral, and as such, protected and respected by the belligerents as long as they accommodate wounded and sick"; the hospital and ambulance personnel, far from being taken prisoner or made the target of fire, would have "the benefit of the same neutrality when on duty, and while there remain any wounded to be brought in or assisted"; "wounded and sick combatants, to whatever nation they may belong, shall be collected and cared for"; last but not least, "hospitals, ambulances and evacuation parties" would be distinguished by a uniform flag bearing "a red cross on a white ground".

The ICRC carries out these tasks guided by the Fundamental Principles of the Red Cross and Red Crescent Movement:

Statutes of the International Red Cross and Red Crescent Movements

* * *

Humanity The International Red Cross and Red Crescent Movement, born of a desire to bring assistance without discrimination to the wounded on the battlefield, endeavours, in its international and national capacity, to prevent and alleviate human suffering wherever it may be found. Its purpose is to protect life and health and to ensure respect for the human being. It promotes mutual understanding, friendship, co-operation and lasting peace amongst all peoples.

Impartiality It makes no discrimination as to nationality, race, religious beliefs, class or political opinions. It endeavours to relieve the suffering of individuals, being guided solely by their needs, and to give priority to the most urgent cases of distress.

Neutrality In order to continue to enjoy the confidence of all, the Movement may not take sides in hostilities or engage at any time in controversies of a political, racial, religious or ideological nature.

Independence The Movement is independent. The National Societies, while auxiliaries in the humanitarian services of their governments and subject to the laws of their respective countries, must always maintain their autonomy so that they may be able at all times to act in accordance with the principles of the Movement.

Voluntary Service It is a voluntary relief movement not prompted in any manner by desire for gain.

Unity There can be only one Red Cross or one Red Crescent Society in any one country. It must be open to all. It must carry on its humanitarian work throughout its territory.

Universality The International Red Cross and Red Crescent Movement, in which all Societies have equal status and share equal responsibilities and duties in helping each other, is worldwide.

* * *

Declares that, by its humanitarian work and the dissemination of its ideals, the Movement promotes a lasting peace, which is not simply the absence of war, but is a dynamic process of co-operation among all States and peoples, co-operation founded on respect for freedom, independence, national sovereignty, equality, human rights, as well as on a fair and equitable distribution of resources to meet the needs of peoples.

D.   NOTES, QUESTIONS, AND PROBLEMS

1. Compare Article 8 of the Rome Statute (p. 428–434) with Articles 11 and 85 of Additional Protocol I (p. 403, 410) Dörmann and Maresca (p. 433) note that *not* all the grave breaches of Additional Protocol I were included in Article 8. What was left out? Do you agree that these were regrettable omissions? Or is "over-criminalization" potentially a problem, especially when it comes to military action? Is "over-criminalization" more of a problem when it occurs in international criminal law as opposed to domestic criminal law?

2. Compare Article 3 common to the Geneva Conventions (p. 390 above) with the excerpts from the Geneva Prisoners Convention and the Civilians Convention. Find some protections that apply in international armed conflicts that do not apply in non-international armed conflict. Now look at Additional Protocol II (pp. 411–414 above). Was Common Article 3 expanded upon in any meaningful way in APII? Note also the differences between international and non-international armed conflict in Article 8 of the Rome Statute. Should the rules be different for international versus internal armed conflict? (The facts in the problem below may help you decide.) *See* LINDSAY MOIR, THE LAW OF INTERNAL ARMED CONFLICT (2002).

3. The United States has signed the 1954 Hague Convention, Additional Protocol I and Additional Protocol II. So it has signatory obligations under all three. It has also declared certain provisions of these agreements binding as customary international law. Significantly, Article 75 of Additional Protocol I is cited as binding on the United States. (The United States has also claimed provisions of the United Nations Convention on the Law of the Sea are binding as customary law. UNCLOS is a treaty important to the US Navy.) For a detailed discussion of AP I articles officially identified as customary, see, Michael Matheson, *Session One: The United States Position on the Relation of Customary International Law to the 1977 Protocols Additional to the 1949 Geneva Conventions*, 2 AM. U. J. INT'L L. & POL' Y 419–31 (1987); *see also* UNITED STATES ARMY JUDGE ADVOCATE GENERAL CORPS. OPERATIONAL LAW HANDBOOK 2001 (2002).

4. "One of the major shortcomings of the law of armed conflict is the failure of that regime to provide for adequate means of enforcing those laws. Belligerent reprisals have been employed on the battlefield for centuries and are one of the few available sanctions of the laws of war. They are defined as 'intentional violations of a given rule of the law of armed conflict, committed by a Party to the conflict with the aim of inducing the authorities of the adverse party to discontinue a policy of violation of the same or another rule of that body of law.' " Shane Darcy, *The Evolution of the Law of Belligerent Reprisals*, 175 MIL. L. REV. 184, 184 (*quoting* FRITS KALSHOVEN, CONSTRAINTS ON THE WAGING OF WAR 65 (1987).)

The Geneva Conventions place some restrictions on the taking of reprisals during armed conflict (belligerent reprisals not to be confused with armed reprisals or countermeasures.) Additional Protocol I has prohibited all reprisals against the civilian population in Article 51. This is one of the articles the United States does *not* recognize as customary international law. When the United Kingdom became a party to Additional Protocol I, it made a reservation to this Article:

The obligations of Articles 51 and 55 are accepted on the basis that any adverse party against which the United Kingdom might be engaged will itself scrupulously observe those obligations. If an adverse party makes serious and deliberate attacks, in violation of Article 51 or Article 52 against the civilian population or civilians or against civilian objects, or, in violation of Articles 53, 54 and 55, on objects or items protected by those Articles, the United Kingdom will regard itself as entitled to take measures otherwise prohibited by the Articles in question to the extent that it considers such measures necessary for the sole purpose of compelling the adverse party to cease committing violations under those Articles, but only after formal warning to the adverse party requiring cessation of the violations has been disregarded and then only after a decision taken at the highest level of government. Any measures thus taken by the United Kingdom will not be disproportionate to the violations giving rise there to and will not involve any action prohibited by the Geneva Conventions of 1949 nor will such measures be continued after the violations have ceased. The United Kingdom will notify the Protecting Powers of any such formal warning given to an adverse party, and if that warning has been disregarded, of any measures taken as a result.

Reprinted in id., at 227.

How does Additional Protocol I provide for enforcement? Are AP I's provisions an adequate alternative to the use of reprisals? Consider why the British government is so keen to hold on to at least some right to take reprisals against civilians and their objects in armed conflict.

5. The International Committee of the Red Cross was heavily criticized following the Second World War for not making greater protests about the treatment of persons detained by Germany's Third Reich, especially regarding forced labor, abuse, and mass murder of Jews, gypsies, Slavs, gays, the handicapped and other groups. The ICRC has long maintained that it does not publicly criticize member states in order to preserve its neutral position among warring parties. It believes maintaining neutrality is the key to gaining access to prisoners and to governments where they can work quietly behind the scenes. The ICRC was again criticized for this policy in respect of the abuse of persons detained by the United States post September 11. What do you think of the policy? Can it go too far?

6. Problem: In the excerpt by Gasser (pp. 416–422, above) he refers to the "age-old challenge to the law of war: guerilla warfare." The Afghan conflict of the 1980s pitted irregular, guerrilla fighters against the Soviet Red Army. Guerillas are rarely are in a position to implement the 550 articles of the Geneva Conventions. Since guerillas are frequently on the move and often have little food or water to spare, prisoners can be a burden and are often executed. This was certainly true of the Afghan conflict. The ICRC proposed a solution described below while the armed conflict was going on:

In [a] 1982 agreement, Afghan rebels agreed to turn over to the ICRC Soviet prisoners in their custody. The Swiss government in turn agreed to detain these prisoners on behalf of the ICRC, which does not have the facilities to hold the prisoners itself. The Soviet Union will pay for the cost of internment, which is a departure from the Geneva Conventions; normally under Article 15 the detaining power pays all costs. In exchange for allowing Swiss detention, the Kabul authorities agreed to allow the ICRC to inspect prisons in Kabul where rebels are being held in order to certify that conditions and treatment are humane.

* * *

* * * [O]nly nine prisoners [went] to Switzerland. One prisoner escaped in July 1983 to the Federal Republic of Germany * * * seeking asylum. The Swiss government holds the remaining prisoners in a "special camp" designed for Swiss citizens who commit minor infractions while on their annual three week military training. Conditions appear to be excellent. The prisoners have regular mail and access to the media. They have outings and opportunities to earn money. Their only visitors, however, are officials of the ICRC and Soviet authorities who may visit once every two months.

Human rights organizations such as Amnesty International and International Commission of [Jurists] have been denied visits to the camp. These groups have become increasingly concerned about the prisoners, not because of prison conditions, but rather because of the issue of repatriation. A spokeswoman for Freedom House has suggested that the lives of the prisoners may be endangered by sending them back to the Soviet Union.

The Soviet Union has asked for a pledge from the ICRC that it will in fact repatriate the prisoners. The Soviets have a good legal argument that the soldiers in fact should be repatriated since the men agreed in writing to the arrangement, which includes repatriation at the end of two years. Moreover, the Soviet Union believes that international law requires forcible repatriation of prisoners of war. At the Geneva negotiating sessions, the Soviets pointed out that Article 118 of the prisoners convention requires forcible repatriation.[a]

The ICRC has made it clear that it rejects the Soviet Union's legal arguments and will not repatriate the prisoners against their wishes. It says that its position is based, among other things, on "prevailing legal opinion regarding the problem of repatriation and the interpretation of Article 118 of the Third Geneva Convention." It must be noted, however, that the ICRC has only said that *it* will not forcibly repatriate the prisoners. It says that at the end

---

a. The article states that "[p]risoners of war shall be released and repatriated without delay after the cessation of active hostilities." * * * The Soviet Union argued for this interpretation again during the Korean prisoner repatriation controversy. *See also* Gutteridge, *The Repatriation of Prisoners*, 22 INT'L & COMP. L. Q. 207–16 (1953) for an account of the Korean controversy. The Soviets believe that prisoners of war are in no position to make a truly independent decision and should therefore be repatriated automatically. *Id.*

of internment of any prisoner not wishing to return to the Soviet Union will come under Swiss jurisdiction; it will be for the Swiss government "to proceed in accordance with ... legislation in force." In May 1984, two prisoners did return to the Soviet Union from Switzerland. It is assumed that they wished to return.

The Swiss have * * * faced * * * such a decision before. After World War II, approximately 9,000 Soviet soldiers who had escaped from German prisoner-of-war camps were in Switzerland. The Swiss government sent them back to the Soviet Union where Stalin had them exiled to Siberia. * * * Granting asylum to Soviet prisoners would displease the Soviet Union, and thus would jeopardize the ICRC agreement and the lives of the prisoners held by the rebels in Afghanistan. This is the cost of allowing a few men to remain in Switzerland.

The * * * uncertainty may be why so few prisoners have agreed to go to Switzerland. (After negotiations were completed, it was thought that hundreds would go within a few months.) Further, the rebels have stopped allowing the soldiers to be transferred to the ICRC and have charged that the Soviets have failed to fulfill their end of the bargain.

Mary Ellen O'Connell, *Soviet Prisoners in the Afghan Conflict*, 23 COL. J. TRANS. L. 497, 499, 501–03 (1985). What should the Swiss authorities have done? Was the original idea of removing Soviet prisoners to Switzerland a good one? Can you think of ways that the agreement might have been made to work better than it did? Develop arguments opposed to forcible repatriation and arguments in support.

This case demonstrates the central dilemma of law aimed at mitigating the effects of war. The costs of the war in Afghanistan are clearly one of the reasons the Soviet Union fell. The costs were not just monetary. The Soviet intervention was unlawful and generated severe criticism and sanctions by other countries, in particular by the United States. The war was also hugely unpopular in the Soviet Union in part because it was so brutal. The killing of Soviet prisoners was a part of the brutality. If prisoners had been saved, the cost of the war to the Soviets would have been lessened. Would that necessarily have been a good thing in the long run? An argument we saw in Chapter Three is that mitigating the effects of war only creates longer wars. A variation on the argument is that those fighting a lawful war should not be restrained in how they do so. (This might have been part of the mindset behind why only the Axis leaders were tried for war crimes at the end of the Second World War.) What are the answers to these arguments?

Conversely, Ove Bring has suggested wars fought for humanitarian purposes should meet a higher standard of protection of the civilian population, since it is so hard to justify any collateral civilian deaths and injuries in the name of protecting human rights. *See* Ove Bring, *International Humanitarian Law after Kosovo: Is Lex Lata Sufficient?*, in *Legal and Ethical Lessons of NATO's Kosovo Campaign*, 78 INT'L L. STUDIES 257 (Andru Wall ed., Naval War College 2002). *See* Chapter Twelve pp. 606–611.

CHAPTER TEN

CIVILIANS

As we have seen in previous chapters, the *jus in bello* provides protections for civilians during hostilities and in the aftermath of hostilities when a party to a conflict controls its opponent's territory. Civilians are generally those persons who are neither members of the armed forces nor take direct part in hostilities.[1] Civilian objects are generally those objects not used for a military purpose. Most critically, during hostilities, the law prohibits directly targeting civilians and civilian objects.[2] Civilians and civilian objects must be protected from direct attack during hostilities, and, in the aftermath of hostilities, an occupying power must treat civilians humanely, providing for order and the basic needs of the civilian population. These are the two basic categories we will explore in this Chapter—civilian protections during hostilities and protections during occupation. Issues abound as to who really qualifies as a civilian—what does it mean to take no direct part in hostilities? How far does the obligation of protection extend? During occupation, does the definition of a civilian change? How does an occupying power both treat the civilian population humanely and provide for order?

Protecting civilians requires distinguishing them from combatants. Thus, civilian protection rests on the "principle of distinction:"

> The basic axiom underlying International Humanitarian Law (IHL), that even in an armed conflict only the weakening of the military potential of the enemy is acceptable, implies that IHL has to define who may be considered part of that potential and, therefore, may be attacked, participate directly in hostilities, but may not be punished for such participation under ordinary municipal law. Under the principle of distinction, all involved in armed conflict must distinguish between the persons thus defined, the combatants, on the one hand, and civilians, on the other hand. Combatants must, therefore, distinguish themselves (*i.e.*, allow their enemies to identify them, from all other persons, the civilians, who may not be attacked nor directly participate in hostilities.)[3]

In the next Chapter we take up the topic of combatants. We will consider how to determine who a combatant is beyond the general understanding

---

1. YORAM DINSTEIN, THE CONDUCT OF HOSTILITIES UNDER THE LAW OF INTERNATIONAL ARMED CONFLICT 113 (2004).

2. L.C. GREEN, THE CONTEMPORARY LAW OF ARMED CONFLICT 229 (2d ed., 2000).

3. MARCO SASSÒLI & ANTHOINE A. BOUVIER, HOW DOES LAW PROTECT IN WAR? 117 (1999).

that they are members of the armed forces and those taking an active part in hostilities. We will also look at the obligations combatants have both with respect to the limits on the means and methods of conducting hostilities, and the rights of a combatant detained by the adverse party. Some of these combatant protections indirectly protect civilians,[4] as some of the protections for civilians indirectly protect combatants. Our primary focus here, however, will be on further defining who civilians are and what their primary rights are in hostilities and in periods of occupation.

A.   CIVILIAN STATUS AND PROTECTIONS IN HOSTILITIES

The excerpts that follow are cases and materials discussing the protections owed to civilians in hostilities. Several excerpts define civilians and civilian objects and explain how civilians and their property can lose their protected status. The first excerpt is from the trial of General Stanislav Galic before the International Criminal Tribunal for Yugoslavia.

Prosecutor v. Stanislav Galić

ICTY, Case No. IT–98–29–T, Dec. 23, 2003.*

I.   INTRODUCTION

1.   Trial Chamber I of the International Tribunal (the "Trial Chamber") is seized of a case which concerns events surrounding the military encirclement of the city of Sarajevo in 1992 by Bosnian Serb forces.

2.   The Prosecution alleges that "The siege of Sarajevo, as it came to be popularly known, was an episode of such notoriety in the conflict in the former Yugoslavia that one must go back to World War II to find a parallel in European history. Not since then had a professional army conducted a campaign of unrelenting violence against the inhabitants of a European city so as to reduce them to a state of medieval deprivation in which they were in constant fear of death. In the period covered in this Indictment, there was nowhere safe for a Sarajevan, not at home, at school, in a hospital, from deliberate attack".

3.   In the course of the three and a half years of the armed conflict in and around Sarajevo, three officers commanded the unit of the Bosnian–Serb Army ("VRS") operating in the area of Sarajevo, the Sarajevo Romanija Corps ("SRK"). The second of those three officers, Major–General Stanislav Galić, is the accused in this case ("the Accused"). He was the commander for the longest period, almost two years, from around 10 September 1992

---

4. Hans–Peter Gasser, *Protection of the Civilian Population, in* THE HANDBOOK OF HUMANITARIAN LAW IN ARMED CONFLICTS 209, 211–12 (Dieter Fleck ed., 1995).

* www.un.org/icty/ (footnotes omitted).

to 10 August 1994. The Prosecution alleges that over this period he conducted a protracted campaign of sniping and shelling against civilians in Sarajevo. Two schedules to the Indictment "set forth a small representative number of individual incidents for specificity of pleading". At the end of the Prosecution case and pursuant to Rule 98 *bis* of the Rules of Procedure and Evidence of the International Tribunal, the Trial Chamber decided upon the Defence Motion for Acquittal that the Prosecution had failed to prove some of these scheduled sniping incidents.

4. The Prosecution alleges that General Galić incurs individual criminal responsibility under Articles 7(1) and 7(3) of the Statute for his acts and omissions in relation to the crime of terror (count 1), attacks on civilians (counts 4 and 7), murder (counts 2 and 5) and inhumane acts (counts 3 and 6) committed against civilians in the city of Sarajevo.

* * *

(ii) Discussion

41. Although the Indictment refers in general terms to Article 51 of Additional Protocol I, the Trial Chamber understands the first sentence of the second paragraph of that article to be the legal basis of the charges of attack on civilians in Counts 4 and 7. This sentence will hereinafter be referred to as "the first part" of the second paragraph of Article 51 of Additional Protocol I, or simply as the "first part of Article 51(2)".

42. The constitutive elements of the offence of attack on civilians have not yet been the subject of a definitive statement by the Appeals Chamber. In only two cases before the Tribunal have persons been charged and tried of attack on civilians under Article 3 of the Statute pursuant to Article 51(2) of Additional Protocol I. In each case a brief exposition was given of the offence, together with the offence of attacks on civilian property. In the *Blaškić* case the Trial Chamber observed in relation to the *actus reus* that "the attack must have caused deaths and/or serious bodily injury within the civilian population or damage to civilian property. [...] Targeting civilians or civilian property is an offence when not justified by military necessity." On the *mens rea* it found that "such an attack must have been conducted intentionally in the knowledge, or when it was impossible not to know, that civilians or civilian property were being targeted not through military necessity". The Trial Chamber in the *Kordić and Cerkez* case held that "prohibited attacks are those launched deliberately against civilians or civilian objects in the course of an armed conflict and are not justified by military necessity. They must have caused deaths and/or serious bodily injuries within the civilian population or extensive damage to civilian objects".

43. The Trial Chamber follows the above-mentioned jurisprudence to the extent that it states that an attack which causes death or serious bodily injury within the civilian population constitutes an offence. As noted above, such an attack when committed wilfully is punishable as a grave breach of Additional Protocol I. The question remains whether attacks resulting in non-serious civilian casualties, or in no casualties at all, may also entail the individual criminal responsibility of the perpetrator under the type of charge considered here, and thus fall within the jurisdiction of the Tribunal, even though they do not amount to grave breaches of Additional Protocol I. The present Indictment refers only to killing and wounding of civilians; therefore the Trial Chamber does not deem it necessary to express its opinion on that question.

44. The Trial Chamber does not however subscribe to the view that the prohibited conduct set out in the first part of Article 51(2) of Additional Protocol I is adequately described as "targeting civilians when not justified by military necessity". This provision states in clear language that civilians and the civilian population as such should not be the object of attack. It does not mention any exceptions. In particular, it does not contemplate derogating from this rule by invoking military necessity.

45. The Trial Chamber recalls that the provision in question explicitly confirms the customary rule that civilians must enjoy general protection against the danger arising from hostilities. The prohibition against attacking civilians stems from a fundamental principle of international humanitarian law, the principle of distinction, which obliges warring parties to distinguish *at all times* between the civilian population and combatants and between civilian objects and military objectives and accordingly to direct their operations only against military objectives. In its Advisory Opinion on the Legality of Nuclear Weapons, the International Court of Justice described the principle of distinction, along with the principle of protection of the civilian population, as "the cardinal principles contained in the texts constituting the fabric of humanitarian law" and stated that "States must never make civilians the object of attack [...]."

46. Part IV of Additional Protocol I, entitled "Civilian Population" (articles 48 to 58), develops and augments earlier legal protections afforded to civilians through specific rules aimed at guiding belligerents to respect and protect the civilian population and individual civilians during the conduct of hostilities. The general prohibition mentioned above forms [an] integral part of and is complemented and reinforced by this set of rules. In order to properly define the conduct outlawed in the first part of Article 51 (2) of Additional Protocol I, this rule must be interpreted in light of the ordinary meaning of the terms of Additional Protocol I, as well as of its spirit and purpose.

47. As already stated, the first part of Article 51(2) of Additional Protocol I proscribes making the civilian population as such, or individual civilians, the object of attack. According to Article 50 of Additional Protocol I, "a civilian is any person who does not belong to one of the categories of persons referred to in Article 4(A)(1), (2), (3) and (6) of the Third Geneva Convention and in Article 43 of Additional Protocol I." For the purpose of the protection of victims of armed conflict, the term "civilian" is defined negatively as anyone who is not a member of the armed forces or of an organized military group belonging to a party to the conflict. It is a matter of evidence in each particular case to determine whether an individual has the status of civilian.

48. The protection from attack afforded to individual civilians by Article 51 of Additional Protocol I is suspended when and for such time as they directly participate in hostilities. To take a "direct" part in the hostilities means acts of war which by their nature or purpose are likely to cause actual harm to the personnel or matériel of the enemy armed forces. As the *Kupreskić* Trial Chamber explained:

> the protection of civilian and civilian objects provided by modern international law may cease entirely or be reduced or suspended [. . .] if a group of civilians takes up arms [. . .] and engages in fighting against the enemy belligerent, they may be legitimately attacked by the enemy belligerent whether or not they meet the requirements laid down in Article 4(A)(2) of the Third Geneva Convention of 1949.

Combatants and other individuals directly engaged in hostilities are considered to be legitimate military targets.

49. The civilian population comprises all persons who are civilians, as defined above. The use of the expression "civilian population *as such*" in Article 51(2) of Additional Protocol I indicates that "the population must never be used as a target or as a tactical objective".

50. The presence of individual combatants within the population does not change its civilian character. In order to promote the protection of civilians, combatants are under the obligation to distinguish themselves at all times from the civilian population; the generally accepted practice is that they do so by wearing uniforms, or at least a distinctive sign, and by carrying their weapons openly. In certain situations it may be difficult to ascertain the status of particular persons in the population. The clothing, activity, age, or sex of a person are among the factors which may be considered in deciding whether he or she is a civilian. A person shall be considered to be a civilian for as long as there is a doubt as to his or her real status. The Commentary to Additional Protocol I explains that the presumption of civilian status concerns "persons who have not committed hostile acts, but whose status

seems doubtful because of the circumstances. They should be considered to be civilians until further information is available, and should therefore not be attacked". The Trial Chamber understands that a person shall not be made the object of attack when it is not reasonable to believe, in the circumstances of the person contemplating the attack, including the information available to the latter, that the potential target is a combatant.

51. As mentioned above, in accordance with the principles of distinction and protection of the civilian population, only military objectives may be lawfully attacked. A widely accepted definition of military objectives is given by Article 52 of Additional Protocol I as "those objects which by their nature, location, purpose or use make an effective contribution to military action and whose total or partial destruction, capture or neutralization, in the circumstances ruling at the time, offers a definite military advantage". In case of doubt as to whether an object which is normally dedicated to civilian purposes is being used to make an effective contribution to military action, it shall be presumed not to be so used. The Trial Chamber understands that such an object shall not be attacked when it is not reasonable to believe, in the circumstances of the person contemplating the attack, including the information available to the latter, that the object is being used to make an effective contribution to military action.

52. "Attack" is defined in Article 49 of Additional Protocol I as "acts of violence against the adversary, whether in offence or in defence." The Commentary makes the point that "attack" is a technical term relating to a specific military operation limited in time and place, and covers attacks carried out both in offence and in defence. The jurisprudence of the Tribunal has defined "attack" as a course of conduct involving the commission of acts of violence. In order to be punishable under Article 3 of the [ICTY] Statute, these acts have to be carried out during the course of an armed conflict.

53. In light of the discussion above, the Trial Chamber holds that the prohibited conduct set out in the first part of Article 51(2) is to direct an attack (as defined in Article 49 of Additional Protocol I) against the civilian population and against individual civilians not taking part in hostilities.

54. The Trial Chamber will now consider the mental element of the offence of attack on civilians, when it results in death or serious injury to body or health. Article 85 of Additional Protocol I explains the intent required for the application of the first part of Article 51(2). It expressly qualifies as a grave breach the act of *wilfully* "making the civilian population or individual civilians the object of attack". The Commentary to Article 85 of Additional Protocol I explains the term as follows:

wilfully: the accused must have acted consciously and with intent, i.e., with his mind on the act and its consequences, and willing them ('criminal intent' or 'malice aforethought'); this encompasses the concepts of 'wrongful intent' or 'reckless-ness', viz., the attitude of an agent who, without being certain of a particular result, accepts the possibility of it happening; on the other hand, ordinary negligence or lack of foresight is not covered, i.e., when a man acts without having his mind on the act or its consequences.

The Trial Chamber accepts this explanation, according to which the notion of "wilfully" incorporates the concept of recklessness, whilst excluding mere negligence. The perpetrator who recklessly attacks civilians acts "wilfully".

55.   For the *mens rea* recognized by Additional Protocol I to be proven, the Prosecution must show that the perpetrator was aware or should have been aware of the civilian status of the persons attacked. In case of doubt as to the status of a person, that person shall be considered to be a civilian. However, in such cases, the Prosecution must show that in the given circumstances a reason-able person could not have believed that the individual he or she attacked was a combatant.

56.   In sum, the Trial Chamber finds that the crime of attack on civilians is constituted of the elements common to offences falling under Article 3 of the Statute, as well as of the following specific elements:

1.   Acts of violence directed against the civilian population or individual civilians not taking direct part in hostilities causing death or serious injury to body or health within the civilian population.

2.   The offender wilfully made the civilian population or individual civilians not taking direct part in hostilities the object of those acts of violence.

57.   As regards the first element, the Trial Chamber agrees with previous Trial Chambers that indiscriminate attacks, that is to say, attacks which strike civilians or civilian objects and military objectives without distinction, may qualify as direct attacks against civilians. It notes that indiscriminate attacks are expressly prohib-ited by Additional Protocol I. This prohibition reflects a well-established rule of customary law applicable in all armed conflicts.

58.   One type of indiscriminate attack violated the principle of proportionality. The practical application of the principle of dis-tinction requires that those who plan or launch an attack take all feasible precautions to verify that the objectives attacked are neither civilians nor civilian objects, so as to spare civilians as much as possible. Once the military character of a target has been ascertained, commanders must consider whether striking this tar-

get is "expected to cause incidental loss of life, injury to civilians, damage to civilian objectives or a combination thereof, which would be excessive in relation to the concrete and direct military advantage anticipated." If such casualties are expected to result, the attack should not be pursued. The basic obligation to spare civilians and civilian objects as much as possible must guide the attacking party when considering the proportionality of an attack. In determining whether an attack was proportionate it is necessary to examine whether a reasonably well-informed person in the circumstances of the actual perpetrator, making reasonable use of the information available to him or her, could have expected excessive civilian casualties to result from the attack.

59. To establish the *mens rea* of a disproportionate attack the Prosecution must prove, instead of the above-mentioned *mens rea* requirement, that the attack was launched wilfully and in knowledge of circumstances giving rise to the expectation of excessive civilian casualties.

60. The Trial Chamber considers that certain apparently disproportionate attacks may give rise to the inference that civilians were actually the object of attack. This is to be determined on a case-by-case basis in light of the available evidence.

61. As suggested by the Defence, the parties to a conflict are under an obligation to remove civilians, to the maximum extent feasible from the vicinity of military objectives and to avoid locating military objectives within or near densely populated areas. However, the failure of a party to abide by this obligation does not relieve the attacking side of its duty to abide by the principles of distinction and proportionality when launching an attack.

(f) Conclusion

62. The Trial Chamber finds that an attack on civilian[s] can be brought under Article 3 by virtue of customary international law and, in the instant case, also by virtue of conventional law and is constituted of acts of violence willfully directed against the civilian population or individual civilians not taking direct part in hostilities causing death or serious injury to body or health within the civilian population.

* * *

The next excerpt is from the well-known case of Lt. William Calley. It considers the obligations owed to civilians in hostilities as well as the issue of obedience to superior orders as a defense for failure to respect those obligations.

The case is also an example of enforcement of IHL through national courts.

U.S. v. Calley

U.S. Court of Military Appeals, No. 26,875, Dec. 21, 1973.

On petition of the accused below. CM 426402, reported below at 46 CMR 1131. Affirmed

* * *

OPINION

QUINN, Judge:

* * *

First Lieutenant Calley stands convicted of the premeditated murder of 22 infants, children, women, and old men, and of assault with intent to murder a child of about 2 years of age. All the killings and the assault took place on March 16, 1968 in the area of the village of My Lai in the Republic of South Vietnam. The Army Court of Military Review affirmed the findings of guilty and the sentence, which, as reduced by the convening authority, includes dismissal and confinement at hard labor for 20 years. The accused petitioned this Court for further review, alleging 30 assignments of error. We granted three of these assignments.

* * *

In his second assignment of error the accused contends that the evidence is insufficient to establish his guilt beyond a reasonable doubt. Summarized, the pertinent evidence is as follows:

Lieutenant Calley was a platoon leader in C Company, a unit that was part of an organization known as Task Force Barker, whose mission was to subdue and drive out the enemy in an area in the Republic of Vietnam known popularly as Pinkville. Before March 16, 1968, this area, which included the village of My Lai 4, was a Viet Cong stronghold. C Company had operated in the area several times. Each time the unit had entered the area it suffered casualties by sniper fire, machine gun fire, mines, and other forms of attack. Lieutenant Calley had accompanied his platoon on some of the incursions.

On March 15, 1968, a memorial service for members of the company killed in the area during the preceding weeks was held. After the service Captain Ernest L. Medina, the commanding officer of C Company, briefed the company on a mission in the Pinkville area set for the next day. C Company was to serve as the main attack formation for Task Force Barker. In that role it would assault and neutralize My Lai 4, 5, and 6 and then mass for an assault on My Lai 1. Intelligence reports indicated that the unit would be opposed by a veteran enemy battalion, and that all civilians would be absent from the area. The objective was to destroy the enemy. Disagreement exists as to the instructions on the specifics of destruction.

Captain Medina testified that he instructed his troops that they were to destroy My Lai 4 by "burning the hootches, to kill the livestock, to close the wells and to destroy the food crops." Asked if women and children were to be killed, Medina said he replied in the negative, adding that, "You must use common sense. If they have a weapon and are trying to engage you, then you can shoot back, but you must use common sense." However, Lieutenant Calley testified that Captain Medina informed the troops they were to kill every living thing—men, women, children, and animals—and under no circumstances were they to leave any Vietnamese behind them as they passed through the villages en route to their final objective. Other witnesses gave more or less support to both versions of the briefing.

On March 16, 1968, the operation began with interdicting fire. C Company was then brought to the area by helicopters. Lieutenant Calley's platoon was on the first lift. This platoon formed a defense perimeter until the remainder of the force was landed. The unit received no hostile fire from the village.

Calley's platoon passed the approaches to the village with his men firing heavily. Entering the village, the platoon encountered only unarmed, unresisting men, women, and children. The villagers, including infants held in their mothers' arms, were assembled and moved in separate groups to collection points. Calley * * * testified that during this time he was radioed twice by Captain Medina, who demanded to know what was delaying the platoon. On being told that a large number of villagers had been detained, Calley said Medina ordered him to "waste them." Calley further testified that he obeyed the orders because he had been taught the doctrine of obedience throughout his military career. Medina denied that he gave any such order.

One of the collection points for the villagers was in the southern part of the village. There, Private First Class Paul D. Meadlo guarded a group of between 30 to 40 old men, women, and children. Lieutenant Calley approached Meadlo and told him, " 'You know what to do,' " and left. He returned shortly and asked Meadlo why the people were not yet dead. Meadlo replied he did not know that Calley had meant that they should be killed. Calley declared that he wanted them dead. He and Meadlo then opened fire on the group, until all but a few children fell. Calley then personally shot these children. He expended 4 or 5 magazines from his M–16 rifle in the incident.

Lieutenant Calley and Meadlo moved from this point to an irrigation ditch on the east side of My Lai 4. There, they encountered another group of civilians being held by several soldiers. Meadlo estimated that this group contained from 75 to 100 persons. Calley stated, " 'We got another job to do, Meadlo,' " and he ordered the group into the ditch. When all were in the ditch, Calley and Meadlo opened fire on them. Although ordered by Calley to shoot, Private First Class James J. Dursi refused to join in the killings, and Specialist Four Robert E. Maples refused to give his machine gun to Calley for use in the killings. Lieutenant Calley admitted that he fired into the ditch, with the muzzle of his weapon within 5 feet of people in it. He expended between 10 to 15 magazines of ammunition on this occasion.

With his radio operator, Private Charles Sledge, Calley moved to the north end of the ditch. There, he found an elderly Vietnamese monk, whom he interrogated. Calley struck the man with his rifle butt and then shot him in the head. Other testimony indicates that immediately afterwards a young child was observed running toward the village. Calley seized him by the arm, threw him into the ditch, and fired at him. Calley admitted interrogating and striking the monk, but denied shooting him. He also denied the incident involving the child.

Appellate defense counsel contend that the evidence is insufficient to establish the accused's guilt. They do not dispute Calley's participation in the homicides, but they argue that he did not act with the malice or mens rea essential to a conviction of murder; that the orders he received to kill everyone in the village were not palpably illegal; that he was acting in ignorance of the laws of war; that since he was told that only "the enemy" would be in the village, his honest belief that there were no innocent civilians in the village exonerates him of criminal responsibility for their deaths; and, finally, that his actions were in the heat of passion caused by reasonable provocation.

[3]   In assessing the sufficiency of the evidence to support findings of guilty, we cannot reevaluate the credibility of the witnesses or resolve conflicts in their testimony and thus decide anew whether the accused's guilt was established beyond a reasonable doubt. Our function is more limited; it is to determine whether the record contains enough evidence for the triers of the facts to find beyond a reasonable doubt each element of the offenses involved. United States v Papenheim, 19 USCMA 203, 41 CMR 203 (1970); United States v Wilson, 13 USCMA 670, 33 CMR 202 (1963).

[4]   The testimony of Meadlo and others provided the court members with ample evidence from which to find that Lieutenant Calley directed and personally participated in the intentional killing of men, women, and children, who were unarmed and in the custody of armed soldiers of C Company. If the prosecution's witnesses are believed, there is also ample evidence to support a finding that the accused deliberately shot the Vietnamese monk whom he interrogated, and that he seized, threw into a ditch, and fired on a child with the intent to kill.

[5] Enemy prisoners are not subject to summary execution by their captors. Military law has long held that the killing of an unresisting prisoner is murder. Winthrop's Military Law and Precedents, 2d ed., 1920 Reprint, at 788–91.

> While it is lawful to kill an enemy "in the heat and exercise of war," yet "to kill such an enemy after he has laid down his arms . . . is murder."

Digest of Opinions of the Judge Advocates General of the Army, 1912, at 1074–75 n. 3.

[6] Conceding for the purposes of this assignment of error that Calley believed the villagers were part of "the enemy," the uncontradicted evidence is that they were under the control of armed soldiers and were offering no resistance. In his testimony, Calley admitted he was aware of the requirement that prisoners be treated with respect. He also admitted he knew that the normal practice was to interrogate villagers, release those who could satisfactorily account for themselves, and evacuate the suspect among them for further examination. Instead of proceeding in the usual way, Calley executed all, without regard to age, condition, or possibility of suspicion. On the evidence, the court-martial could reasonably find Calley guilty of the offenses before us.

[7] At trial, Calley's principal defense was that he acted in execution of Captain Medina's order to kill everyone in My Lai 4. Appellate defense counsel urge this defense as the most important factor in assessment of the legal sufficiency of the evidence. The argument, however, is inapplicable to whether the evidence is legally sufficient. Captain Medina denied that he issued any such order, either during the previous day's briefing or on the date the killings were carried out. Resolution of the conflict between his testimony and that of the accused was for the triers of the facts. United States v Guerra, 13 USCMA 463, 32 CMR 463 (1963). The general findings of guilty, with exceptions as to the number of persons killed, does not indicate whether the court members found that Captain Medina did not issue the alleged order to kill, or whether, if he did, the court members believed that the accused knew the order was illegal. For the purpose of the legal sufficiency of the evidence, the record supports the findings of guilty.

In the third assignment of error, appellate defense counsel assert gross deficiencies in the military judge's instructions to the court members. Only two assertions merit discussion. One contention is that the judge should have, but did not, advise the court members of the necessity to find the existence of "malice aforethought" in connection with the murder charges; the second allegation is that the defense of compliance with superior orders was not properly submitted to the court members.

* * *

[9]   The trial judge delineated the elements of premeditated murder for the court members in accordance with the statutory language. He instructed them that to convict Lieutenant Calley, they must be convinced beyond a reasonable doubt that the victims were dead; that their respective deaths resulted from specified acts of the accused; that the killings were unlawful; and that Calley acted with a premeditated design to kill. The judge defined accurately the meaning of an unlawful killing and the meaning of a "premeditated design to kill." These instructions comported fully with requirements of existing law for the offense of premeditated murder, and neither statute nor judicial precedent requires that reference also be made to the pre-Code concept of malice.

We turn to the contention that the judge erred in his submission of the defense of superior orders to the court. After fairly summarizing the evidence, the judge gave the following instructions pertinent to the issue:

> The killing of resisting or fleeing enemy forces is generally recognized as a justifiable act of war, and you may consider any such killings justifiable in this case. The law attempts to protect those persons not actually engaged in warfare, however; and limits the circumstances under which their lives may be taken.

> Both combatants captured by and noncombatants detained by the opposing force, regardless of their loyalties, political views, or prior acts, have the right to be treated as prisoners until released, confined, or executed, in accordance with law and established procedures, by competent authority sitting in judgment of such detained or captured individuals. Summary execution of detainees or prisoners is forbidden by law. Further, it's clear under the evidence presented in this case, that hostile acts or support of the enemy North Vietnamese or Viet Cong forces by inhabitants of My Lai (4) at some time prior to 16 March 1968, would not justify the summary execution of all or a part of the occupants of My Lai (4) on 16 March, nor would hostile acts committed that day, if, following the hostility, the belligerents surrendered or were captured by our forces. I therefore instruct you, as a matter of law, that if unresisting human beings were killed at My Lai (4) while within the effective custody and control of our military forces, their deaths cannot be considered justified, and any order to kill such people would be, as a matter of law, an illegal order. Thus, if you find that Lieutenant Calley received an order directing him to kill unresisting Vietnamese within his control or within the control of his troops, that order would be an illegal order.

A determination that an order is illegal does not, of itself, assign criminal responsibility to the person following the order for acts done in compliance with it. Soldiers are taught to follow orders, and special attention is given to obedience of orders on the battlefield. Military effectiveness depends upon obedience to orders. On the other hand, the obedience of a soldier is not the obedience of an automaton. A soldier is a reasoning agent, obliged to respond, not as a machine, but as a person. The law takes these factors into account in assessing criminal responsibility for acts done in compliance with illegal orders.

The acts of a subordinate done in compliance with an unlawful order given him by his superior are excused and impose no criminal liability upon him unless the superior's order is one which a man of ordinary sense and understanding would, under the circumstances, know to be unlawful, or if the order in question is actually known to the accused to be unlawful.

* * *

... In determining what orders, if any, Lieutenant Calley acted under, if you find him to have acted, you should consider all of the matters which he has testified reached him and which you can infer from other evidence that he saw and heard. Then, unless you find beyond a reasonable doubt that he was not acting under orders directing him in substance and effect to kill unresisting occupants of My Lai (4), you must determine whether Lieutenant Calley actually knew those orders to be unlawful.

... In determining whether or not Lieutenant Calley had knowledge of the unlawfulness of any order found by you to have been given, you may consider all relevant facts and circumstances, including Lieutenant Calley's rank; educational background; OCS [officer candidate] schooling; other training while in the Army, including basic training, and his training in Hawaii and Vietnam; his experience on prior operations involving contact with hostile and friendly Vietnamese; his age; and any other evidence tending to prove or disprove that on 16 March 1968, Lieutenant Calley knew the order was unlawful. If you find beyond a reasonable doubt, on the basis of all the evidence, that Lieutenant Calley actually knew the order under which he asserts he operated was unlawful, the fact that the order was given operates as no defense.

Unless you find beyond reasonable doubt that the accused acted with actual knowledge that the order was unlawful, you must proceed to determine whether, under the circumstances, a man of ordinary sense and understanding would have known the order was unlawful. Your deliberations on this question do not focus on Lieutenant Calley and the manner in which he perceived the legality of the order found to have been given him. The standard is that of a man of ordinary sense and understanding under the circumstances.

Think back to the events of 15 and 16 March 1968.... Then determine, in light of all the surrounding circumstances, whether the order, which to reach this point you will have found him to be operating in accordance with, is one which a man of ordinary sense and understanding would know to be unlawful. Apply this to each charged act which you have found Lieutenant Calley to have committed. Unless you are satisfied from the evidence, beyond a reasonable doubt, that a man of ordinary sense and understanding would have known the order to be unlawful, you must acquit Lieutenant Calley for committing acts done in accordance with the order. * * *

Appellate defense counsel contend that these instructions are prejudicially erroneous in that they require the court members to determine that Lieutenant Calley knew that an order to kill human beings in the circumstances under which he killed was illegal by the standard of whether "a man of ordinary sense and understanding" would know the order was illegal. They urge us to adopt as the governing test whether the order is so palpably or manifestly illegal that a person of "the commonest understanding" would be aware of its illegality. They maintain the standard stated by the judge is too strict and unjust; that it confronts members of the armed forces who are not persons of ordinary sense and understanding with the dilemma of choosing between the penalty of death for disobedience of an order in time of war on the one hand and the equally serious punishment for obedience on the other. Some thoughtful commentators on military law have presented much the same argument.[a]

The "ordinary sense and understanding" standard is set forth in the present Manual for Courts–Martial, United States, 1969 (Rev) and was the standard accepted by this Court in United States v Schultz, 18 USCMA 133, 39 CMR 133 (1969) and United States v Keenan, 18 USCMA 108, 39 CMR 108 (1969). It appeared as early as 1917. Manual for Courts–Martial, U.S. Army, 1917, paragraph 442. Apparently, it originated in a quotation from F. Wharton, Homicide § 485 (3d ed. 1907). Wharton's authority is Riggs v

---

a. In the words of one author: "If the standard of reasonableness continues to be applied, we run the unacceptable risk of applying serious punishment to one whose only crime is the slowness of his wit or his stupidity. The soldier, who honestly believes that he must obey an order to kill and is punished for it, is convicted not of murder but of simple negligence." Finkelstein, Duty to Obey as a Defense, March 9, 1970 (unpublished essay, Army War College). *See also* L. Norene, Obedience to Orders as a Defense to a Criminal Act, March 1971 (unpublished thesis presented to The Judge Advocate General's School, U.S. Army).

State, 3 Coldwell 85, 91 American Decisions 272, 273 (Tenn 1866), in which the court approved a charge to the jury as follows:

> "[I]n its substance being clearly illegal, so that a man of ordinary sense and understanding would know as soon as he heard the order read or given that such order was illegal, would afford a private no protection for a crime committed under such order."

Other courts have used other language to define the substance of the defense. Typical is McCall v McDowell, 15 F Cas 1235, 1240 (CCD Cal 1867), in which the court said:

> But I am not satisfied that Douglas ought to be held liable to the plaintiff at all. He acted not as a volunteer, but as a subordinate in obedience to the order of his superior. Except in a plain case of excess of authority, where at first blush it is apparent and palpable to the commonest understanding that the order is illegal, I cannot but think that the law should excuse the military subordinate when acting in obedience to the orders of his commander. Otherwise he is placed in the dangerous dilemma of being liable in damages to third persons for obedience to an order, or to the loss of his commission and disgrace for disobedience thereto.... The first duty of a soldier is obedience, and without this there can be neither discipline nor efficiency in an army. If every subordinate officer and soldier were at liberty to question the legality of the orders of the commander, and obey them or not as they may consider them valid or invalid, the camp would be turned into a debating school, where the precious moment for action would be wasted in wordy conflicts between the advocates of conflicting opinions.

Colonel William Winthrop, the leading American commentator on military law, notes:

> But for the inferior to assume to determine the question of the lawfulness of an order given him by a superior would of itself, as a general rule, amount to insubordination, and such an assumption carried into practice would subvert military discipline. Where the order is apparently regular and lawful on its face, he is not to go behind it to satisfy himself that his superior has proceeded with authority, but is to obey it according to its terms, the only exceptions recognized to the rule of obedience being cases of orders so manifestly beyond the legal power or discretion of the commander as to admit of no rational doubt of their unlawfulness....

> Except in such instances of palpable illegality, which must be of rare occurrence, the inferior should presume that the order was lawful and authorized and obey it accordingly, and in

obeying it can scarcely fail to be held justified by a military court.

Winthrop's Military Law and Precedents, 2d ed., 1920 Reprint, at 296–297 (footnotes omitted) * * *.

In the stress of combat, a member of the armed forces cannot reasonably be expected to make a refined legal judgment and be held criminally responsible if he guesses wrong on a question as to which there may be considerable disagreement. But there is no disagreement as to the illegality of the order to kill in this case. For 100 years, it has been a settled rule of American law that even in war the summary killing of an enemy, who has submitted to, and is under, effective physical control, is murder. Appellate defense counsel acknowledge that rule of law and its continued viability, but they say that Lieutenant Calley should not be held accountable for the men, women and children he killed because the court-martial could have found that he was a person of "commonest understanding" and such a person might not know what our law provides; that his captain had ordered him to kill these unarmed and submissive people and he only carried out that order as a good disciplined soldier should.

[10]   Whether Lieutenant Calley was the most ignorant person in the United States Army in Vietnam, or the most intelligent, he must be presumed to know that he could not kill the people involved here. The United States Supreme Court has pointed out that "[t]he rule that 'ignorance of the law will not excuse' [a positive act that constitutes a crime] . . . is deep in our law." Lambert v California, 355 US 225, 228 (1957). An order to kill infants and unarmed civilians who were so demonstrably incapable of resistance to the armed might of a military force as were those killed by Lieutenant Calley is, in my opinion, so palpably illegal that whatever conceptional difference there may be between a person of "commonest understanding" and a person of "common understanding," that difference could not have had any "impact on a court of lay members receiving the respective wordings in instructions," as appellate defense counsel contend. In my judgment, there is no possibility of prejudice to Lieutenant Calley in the trial judge's reliance upon the established standard of excuse of criminal conduct, rather than the standard of "commonest understanding" presented by the defense, or by the new variable test postulated in the dissent, which, with the inclusion of such factors for consideration as grade and experience, would appear to exact a higher standard of understanding from Lieutenant Calley than that of the person of ordinary understanding.

In summary, as reflected in the record, the judge was capable and fair, and dedicated to assuring the accused a trial on the merits as provided by law; his instructions on all issues were comprehensive and correct. Lieutenant Calley was given every consideration to which he was entitled, and perhaps more. We are impressed with the absence of bias or prejudice on the part of the court members. They were instructed to determine the truth according to the law and this they did with due deliberation and full consideration of the evidence. Their findings of guilty represent the truth of the facts as they determined them to be * * *.

* * *

DUNCAN, Judge (concurring in the result):

My difference of opinion from Judge Quinn's view of the defense of obedience to orders is narrow. The issue of obedience to orders was raised in defense by the evidence. Contrary to Judge Quinn, I do not consider that a presumption arose that the appellant knew he could not kill the people involved. The Government, as I see it, is not entitled to a presumption of what the appellant knew of the illegality of an order. It is a matter for the factfinders under proper instructions.

* * *

DARDEN, Chief Judge (dissenting):

Although the charge the military judge gave on the defense of superior orders was not inconsistent with the Manual treatment of this subject, I believe the Manual provision is too strict in a combat environment.[b] Among other things, this standard permits serious punishment of persons whose training and attitude incline them either to be enthusiastic about compliance with orders or not to challenge the authority of their superiors. The standard also permits conviction of members who are not persons of ordinary sense and understanding.

The principal opinion has accurately traced the history of the current standard. Since this Manual provision is one of substantive law rather than one relating to procedure or modes of proof, the Manual rule is not binding on this Court, which has the responsibility for determining the principles that govern justification in the law of homicide. United States v Smith, 13 USCMA 105, 32 CMR 105 (1962). My impression is that the weight of authority, including the commentators whose articles are mentioned in the principal opinion, supports a more liberal approach to the defense of superior orders. Under this approach, superior orders should constitute a defense except "in a plain case of excess of authority, where at first blush it is apparent and palpable to the commonest understanding that the order is illegal." McCall v McDowell, 15 F Cas 1235, 1240 (No. 8,673) (CCD Cal 1867); In re

---

b. I agree with the majority opinion that the military judge was eminently fair and I do not blame him for this error.

Fair, 100 F 149, 155 (CCD Neb 1900); Winthrop's Military Law and Precedents, 2d ed, 1920 Reprint, at 296–97.

The next excerpts return to a conflict in the Balkans—this time the 1999 NATO bombing of Yugoslavia. Basic facts of the conflict are provided in the first excerpt, an application to the European Court of Human Rights, a court that hears complaints under the European Convention for the Protection of Human Rights and Fundamental Freedoms.[5] The Court found it did not have jurisdiction in the case, Yugoslavia not being a party to the European Convention.[6] Nevertheless, the Application sets out a complaint by civilians alleging a violation of the Convention and IHL when a television studio was bombed in the city of Belgrade. The Application argues that violations of IHL can come within the scope of the Convention. Following the Application is an excerpt from a Report for the ICTY prosecutor on the same incident—the bombing of the television studio, among other alleged violations of IHL. The ICTY prosecutor found she did have jurisdiction over IHL violations even by NATO against the former Yugoslavia. The Report found, however, that no allegations justified prosecution.

Banković and Others v The Contracting States also parties to the North Atlantic Treaty

European Court of Human Rights, (Application of Oct. 21, 1999).*

* * *

The Background to bombing of the RTS building on 23rd April 1999

7.   The historical background to the conflict between the Serbian government in Belgrade, including its military and police forces, and the Kosovar Albanian forces, is well documented. During 1998, open conflict between Serbian military and police forces and Kosovar Albanian forces resulted in the deaths of over 1,500 Kosovar Albanians and forced 400,000 people from their homes. The international community became gravely concerned about the escalating conflict, its humanitarian consequences, and the risk of it spreading to other countries.

* * *

12.   Notwithstanding [several multinational] initiatives, by January 1999 the situation had deteriorated further. Renewed international efforts were made to give new political impetus to finding a

---

5. Nov. 4, 1950, 213 U.N.T.S. 221.

6. *See*, Bankovic v. Belgium, Eur. Ct. H.R. (2001), *reprinted in* 123 I.L.R. 94 (2001).

* Some footnotes omitted.

peaceful solution to the conflict. A six-nation Contact Group, consisting of France, Germany, Russia, Italy, the United States and the United Kingdom, which had been established by the 1992 London Conference on the Former Yugoslavia, met on 29 January. It agreed to convene urgent negotiations between the parties to the conflict, under international mediation. The following day the use of air strikes "if required", was threatened by NATO. These concerted initiatives culminated in a further round of negotiations in Rambouillet near Paris, from 6 to 23 February, followed by a second round in Paris, from 15 to 18 March. At the end of the second round of talks, the Kosovar Albanian delegation signed the proposed peace agreement, but the talks broke up without a signature from the Serbian delegation.

13. On 23rd March 1999, the commencement of the NATO bombing campaign was announced by Dr. Javier Solana, the Secretary General [of NATO], with the following words:—

> "I have just directed SACEUR, General Clark, to initiate air operations in the Federal Republic of Yugoslavia.
>
> I have taken this decision after extensive consultations in recent days with all the Allies, and after it became clear that the final diplomatic effort of Ambassador Holbrooke in Belgrade has not met with success.
>
> All efforts to achieve a negotiated, political solution to the Kosovo crisis having failed, no alternative is open but to take military action.
>
> We are taking action following the Federal Republic of Yugoslavia Government's refusal of the International Community's demands:
>
> - Acceptance of the interim political settlement which has been negotiated at Rambouillet;
> - Full observance of limits on the Serb Army and Special Police Forces agreed on 25 October;
> - Ending of excessive and disproportionate use of force in Kosovo."[a]

He went on to say:—

> "Let me be clear: NATO is not waging war against Yugoslavia. We have no quarrel with the people of Yugoslavia who for too long have been isolated in Europe because of the policies of their government.
>
> Our objective is to prevent more human suffering and more repression and violence against the civilian population of

a. NATO Press Release 23rd March 040e.htm)
1999 (http:///www.nato.int/docu/pr/1999/p99–

Kosovo. We must also act to prevent instability spreading in the region. NATO is united behind this.''

* * *

17. By early April 1999, as the bombing campaign intensified, concern was being expressed over a possible widening of targets, and specific reassurances were being sought by the International Federation of Journalists (IFJ) concerning NATO's policy towards the media during Operation Allied Force. On 9th April 1999 Mr Aiden White, the General Secretary of IFJ wrote to [NATO spokesman] Mr. Shea seeking assurances that television and radio facilities in the Federal Republic of Yugoslavia, which were being used extensively by the world media, would not be targeted. In his reply dated 12th April 1999 * * * Mr Shea confirmed:—

''. . . There is no policy to strike television and radio transmitters as such . . .''.

> "Allied air missions are planned to avoid civilian casualties, including of course journalists, and have been frequently aborted when it has proven impossible to distinguish between military and civilian targets."

18. Notwithstanding this re-assurance, by the third week of April 1999 concerns with regard to a possible widening of NATO targets were increasing. The RTS building, which housed the central control room for the state television service, was also being used daily by television crews from many western countries to file reports, and the American company CNN was using the facilities to make live broadcasts. Much of the output from the building however, was state propaganda issued on behalf of the Milosevic government, directed against the NATO bombing campaign. One Journalist (Julian Manyon of the British Independent Television Network) has reported that this propaganda was angering the allied forces, and particularly the NATO supreme commander, General Wesley K. Clark:—

> ''. . . General Wesley K. Clark, was apparently infuriated by the station's mixture of defiant rhetoric and crude but effective visual jibes at NATO, one showing the NATO star turning into a flaming swastika, another featuring a pudgy Bill Clinton puppet playing his jazz saxophone in front of rows of tombstones.''[b]

* * *

20. To the best of the Applicant's knowledge and belief, there was and is no evidence that the RTS building in Belgrade was, at any point, part of the Milosevic ''war machine''. Whilst noted

b. http://www.itn.co.uk/World/
world19990429/ 032903.htm.

internationally for it slavish support for the regime, there was no evidence that it formed part of the command and control network for the military apparatus of the state, nor that any military personnel were stationed there. A series of surveys carried out in FRY have established that, although a substantial majority of the population of Belgrade watched RTS Channel 1 evening news, only a tiny proportion of these mostly believed what they saw and heard.[c]

21. Notwithstanding Mr Shea's comments at the end of his address on 18th April 1999, no further mention was made of the RTS prior to the attack which took place on the building on the 23rd April. Other targets, which were referred to by the NATO spokesmen as "high value targets", and described as part of President Milosevic's "propaganda machine" were hit.

* * *

22. General Marani's comments concerning NATO's efforts to "degrade the FRY propaganda machine" are believed to be within the first official articulation of a policy of attacking facilities with FRY which propagated information (however inaccurate) but which did not represent part of the command and control structure of the military apparatus of the regime.

23. One the same day the General Secretary of the IFJ again wrote to the Secretary General of NATO protesting at the targeting of media outlets. The IFJ was concerned that such a policy threatened the lives of all journalists in Serbia and Kosova:—

> "For almost ten years the IFJ has worked in Serbia and Kosova, alongside many other professional organisations, to build confidence in democracy and media freedom. We have tried to nurture a culture of transparency and professionalism in defence of democratic pluralism and human rights. We are, therefore, profoundly dismayed by NATO's action. It will reinforce cynicism amongst many governments that NATO's commitment to universal principles of freedom of expression and press freedom is subject to achieving primarily its military objectives."[d]

24. Within 48 hours of the letter having been written NATO bombers had destroyed the RTS building in central Belgrade, with

---

c. See survey results published by Mark Thompson, "Forging War: The Media in Serbia, Croatia, Bosnia and Hercegovina", Luton, University of Luton Press, 1999. P118 (also endorsed by Article 19). These suggest that by March 1997 only 4.1% of the popula-tion of Belgrade believed what they saw and heard on RTS news.

d. Extract from letter from Aiden White, General Secretary of IFJ, dates 21st April 1999, to Secretary General Solana. A copy of the letter is included in Appendix 4.

the attendant loss of civilian lives amongst the media personnel on duty there necessarily involved in such a raid.

* * *

41.   Official casualty figures published by FRY indicated there were 16 fatalities in the attack and another 16 civilians were injured sufficiently seriously to require hospital treatment. * * *

* * *

Statement of Violations of the [European] Convention

* * *

Article 2

111.   Article 2 of the Convention provides:—

"1. Everyone's right to life shall be protected by law. No one shall be deprived of his life intentionally save in the execution of a sentence of a court following his conviction of a crime for which this penalty is provided for by law.

2.   Deprivation of life shall not be regarded as inflicted in contravention of this article when it results from the use of force which is no more than absolutely necessary:

> a.   in defence of any person from unlawful violence;
>
> b.   in order to effect a lawful arrest or to prevent the escape of a person lawfully detained;
>
> c.   in action taken for the purpose of quelling a riot or insurrection."

* * *

118.   The use of such force is only compatible with Article 2 if it satisfies two cumulative conditions. First, it must be for one of the purposes listed in paragraph 2 and second the force used must be "absolutely necessary" in the attainment of that purpose. If the use of force did not satisfy that test, it was unlawful. The applicants submit that neither condition was satisfied in this case.

purpose of the use of force

119.   The respondent Governments claimed a variety of reasons for attacking targets in the former Republic of Yugoslavia, including "humanitarian intervention" to protect the Kosovar ethnic Albanians from attack by Serb military and paramilitary forces. The only conceivably relevant purpose for the use of force in this case was the defence of persons from unlawful violence.

120.   The fact that the use of force is sought to be justified on this ground does not, of itself, justify any and every attack. In order to be for this purpose, the particular attack must relate to the

protection of those threatened. In the McCann Case, the Court stated:—

> "In particular, the force used must be strictly proportionate *to the achievement of the aims* set out in sub-paragraphs 2 (a), (b) and (c) of Article 2." (ibid, para. 149, emphasis added)

121. A use of force cannot be strictly proportionate to the achievement of the aim if it is not related to it. In other words there is a necessary prior condition, before one considers the strict proportionality of the measure. One must first consider whether the particular attack was related to the protection of those being defended from unlawful violence.

122. Those allegedly at risk were in Kosovo. Their protection might require the use of force against those attacking them. If, and only if, it could be shown that those attacking them were receiving material support and reinforcements from the territory of Serbia, that might be argued to be sufficiently closely connected with the threat to justify attacks against the means by which such material support and reinforcements were provided. Material support must be related to the threatened unlawful violence (e.g. providing the means by which it is carried out, the personnel carrying it out or possibly essential food supplies for those carrying it out). Unless a very close connection can be established between the thing attacked and those threatening people with unlawful violence, the attack can not be justified under sub-paragraph (a). General political support for the regime does not constitute material support for those engaging in or threatening unlawful violence (see para. 130 below). It should also be noted that opinion poll evidence suggests that only a tiny proportion of the population of Belgrade believed what they saw and heard on RTS news (para. 20 above and footnote 9).

123. There is no doubt that RTS was a State controlled media and certain programmes output by RTS were used as propaganda tools. Such programmes were highly selective in their representation of the facts and broadcast as fact claims for which there was no evidence (see para. 19, p.8 above). It should be noted that the NATO spokesman complained that it was claimed that NATO was engaging in unlawful attacks (e.g. deliberately bombing the elderly and retarded) or that NATO casualties were much higher than they in fact were. He did not claim that the broadcasts were inciting acts of violence against the Kosovar Albanians.

124. Neither the television station itself nor those working in it nor the broadcasts posed any threat of unlawful violence to the Kosovar Albanians. It was not suggested at the time by any of the respondent Governments or the NATO spokesman that the broadcasts incited attacks against Kosovar Albanians on account of their national, ethnic or religious origin. (That was suggested later, when the Board of Signatories of EUTELSTAT ordered the sus-

pension of broadcasts on 26 May 1999. No evidence has been produced to support that claim. See para. 30 above.) The complaint has rather been that the broadcasts represented propaganda. They satirised NATO political leaders and represented a very one-sided view of the situation. The destruction of the television station did not have any effect at all on the threat of unlawful violence to the Kosovar Albanians. The attack was therefore not for the purpose of defending people from unlawful violence. It can, therefore, not be justified under sub-paragraph (a) of Article 2(2). The purposes listed in sub-paragraphs (b) and (c) are irrelevant on the facts. *The use of force was not for any purpose listed in Article 2 and was therefore unlawful.*

The use of force was more than "strictly necessary" in the circumstances

125.   If the attack against the television station is regarded as having been undertaken "in defence of any person from unlawful violence", it is submitted that the force used was not "absolutely necessary" to achieve that purpose. As already indicated, the Court applies a strict test of necessity and examines both the planning and control of the actions under examination.

* * *

130.   It is submitted that propaganda is not unlawful. It is a normal incident of war. The respondent Governments engaged in propaganda themselves. The propaganda broadcast by RTS was broadcast within the territory of the former Republic of Yugoslavia. It's content did not incite genocide or the commission of crimes against humanity. The International Military Tribunal at Nuremberg dealt with two "propagandists". Streicher was the publisher of *Der Sturmer*, a weekly anti-Semitic newspaper.

> "Streicher's incitement to murder and extermination at the time when Jews in the East were being killed under the most horrible conditions clearly constitutes persecution on political and racial grounds in connection with War Crimes as defined by the Charter, and constitutes a Crime against Humanity."[f]

131.   Streicher was convicted and sentenced to death. Fritsche, on the other hand, was ministerial head of the Radio Division of the Reich Ministry of Propaganda and Enlightenment. The aim of his use of the media:—

"... was rather to arouse popular sentiment in support of Hitler and the German war effort" (ibid at p. 328), rather than to incite Germans to commit atrocities. Fritsche was acquitted.

* * *

f. Judgment of the International Mili-   p. 172 at p. 296
tary Tribunal at Nuremberg, 41 AJIL (1947)

133. * * * [T]he only effect of the destruction of the television station which lasted more than five hours was the death and injuries to those inside the building. The transmissions were resumed within five hours (para. 41 above). Given modern technology, it was foreseeable that transmission would resume within a few hours. Since any attack could only disrupt transmissions for a very brief period of time, no attack could be justified which would forseeably result in loss of life in return for a brief break in transmission.

134. Since the attack was clearly disproportionate to any conceivably legitimate aim and since the transmissions could have been interrupted for longer by different means which would have resulted in fewer civilian casualties, it is submitted that the real purpose of the attack appears rather to have been to attack the morale of the civilian population and to spread fear amongst the population of Belgrade that they would be attacked. This may raise issues under Article 51.2 of Protocol I to the four Geneva Conventions, which provides:—

> "Acts or threats of violence the primary purpose of which is to spread terror among the civilian population are prohibited."

(see further below).

135. *It is submitted that the destruction of the television station by bombardment, which forseeably resulted in the deaths of and injury to innocent civilians, was not "absolutely necessary" for the attainment of any aim which might be legitimate under Article 2 of the Convention.*

* * *

Article 15

141. The scope of Article 2 may, in certain circumstances, be modified by Article 15 of the Convention, where that is applicable. * * *

[Article 15,1. In time of war or other public emergency threatening the life of the nation any High Contracting Party may take measures derogating from its obligations under this Convention to the extent strictly required by the exigencies of the situation, provided that such measures are not inconsistent with its other obligations under international law. 2. No derogation from Article 2, except in respect of deaths resulting from lawful acts of war, * * * shall be made under this provision. 3. Any High Contracting Party availing itself of this right of derogation shall keep the Secretary General of the Council of Europe fully informed of the measures which it has taken and the reasons therefore. * * *]

* * *

Article 15 of the Convention is not applicable as none of the Respondent Governments submitted a notice of derogation

* * *

Alternatively,

if Article 15 can be applicable even without notice of derogation and even if it is applicable in this situation and even if any derogation was not a nullity,

> **I there was a violation of the procedural obligation in Article 15(3) and**

> **II the attack in question was not a lawful act of war.**

* * *

160.   Any State seeking to derogate from its obligations under the Convention may only do so:—

> "... to the extent strictly required by the exigencies of the situation, *provided that such measures are not inconsistent with its other obligations under international law.*" (Article 15(1), emphasis added)

161.   The other obligations in question must, by definition, be applicable in time of war or other public emergency. They include the four Geneva Conventions of 1949 and Protocol I thereto, together with any other customary law rules of the law of armed conflicts and any other relevant treaty obligations. That "other obligations under international law" includes the laws of war is made clear by Article 15(2), which provides that there can be no derogation from Article 2, "except in respect of deaths resulting from lawful acts of war." (See also Cyprus v. Turkey, Report of 10 July 1996, paras. 509–10). The fact that, under Article 15(2), it is possible to modify but not to eliminate a State's obligations under Article 2 in time of war or other armed conflict, demonstrates conclusively that Article 2 remains applicable, although potentially in a modified form, during a war or other armed conflict.

162.   In determining what constitutes a lawful act of war, the Court should have regard to the conventional and customary law of war obligations of States, as *lex specialis*. In the Abella case (also known as La Tablada, case 11, 137, report 55/97), the Inter–American Commission of Human Rights had to analyse an intense but very localised and short-lived armed confrontation. The Inter–American Commission of Human Rights based itself on common Article 3 of the Geneva Conventions of 1949 and the customary international law applicable in non-international armed conflicts, as the *lex specialis*. Furthermore, the two dissenting members of the Commission in the case of Cyprus v. Turkey, who were prepared to treat the situation as an emergency, regarded it as

axiomatic that the Geneva Conventions of 1949 were applicable to the situation (Report of the Commission, 10 July 1976, pp.170–171, paras. 5–7).

* * *

167.   The provisions of the Protocol on which the applicants rely (Articles 48, 50, 51 paras.2–5, 51.3, 52.2, 57.2(c) and 79) represent customary law * * *.

168.   In an article published in 1991, an expert on the laws of war, Professor Christopher Greenwood, stated that the principle of distinction (Article 48), the clarification of some of its implications (e.g. the prohibition of terror attacks, Article 51.2), the definition of military objective (Article 52.2), the provisions as to precautions to be taken in attack (Article 57.2(c)) and the protection of journalists (Article 79) reflect principles of customary international law (Greenwood C., "Customary Law Status of the 1977 Geneva Protocols", in Delissen & Tanja (Eds.), <u>Humanitarian Law of Armed Conflict: Challenges Ahead</u>, Nijhoff, 1991, p. 93 at pp. 108–111 and pp. 102–103). It should be emphasised that Greenwood did *not* maintain that all the provisions of Protocol I had the status of customary international law, but all the provisions on which the applicants seek to rely do have that status.

169.   In order for an attack to be lawful, it must respect the principle of distinction. In the case of attacks against objects, an attack can only be launched against a military objective and must not be indiscriminate. In the case of the execution of an otherwise lawful attack, the attackers must take the precaution of giving an effective advance warning. The applicants maintain that the RTS building was not a military objective and that the attack was indiscriminate in view of the non-existent or minimal direct military advantage anticipated. Either element is sufficient to render the attack unlawful. If the Court disagrees as to the characterisation of the attack as unlawful, the applicants maintain that the conduct of the operation was unlawful, on account of the failure to give an effective advance warning. These elements will be discussed in turn.

170.   It should be noted that the elements relevant to the analysis of a lawful act of war are similar to those already used by the Court in examining a use of potentially lethal force under Article 2 of the Convention. Thus, the issue of whether RTS was a "military objective" is similar to the question of whether there was a sufficiently close relationship between the RTS building and the persons to be protected from unlawful violence. The analysis of whether the attack was indiscriminate is closely related to the arguments as to whether the bombardment of the RTS building was "absolutely necessary". Both of these elements relate to the planning of the attack. The precautions that need to be taken in

attack, notably the question of advance warning, concerns the conduct of the operation. In other words, in applying the laws of war to a military operation to determine whether there has been a breach of the Convention, the Court will be using a structure of analysis with which it is already familiar, even though the rules may be expressed in a different language.

Principle of Distinction

171.   The "principle of distinction" requires that the parties to a conflict:—

"... Shall at all times distinguish between the civilian population and combatants and between civilian objects and military objectives and accordingly shall direct their operations only against military objectives." (Protocol I, Art. 48)

172.   The respondent Governments stated that the attack was directed against the RTS building, rather than the people inside. In order to determine whether the attack was indiscriminate (see below), it is necessary to establish whether the media workers were civilians. Civilians are all those persons who do not come within the definition of combatant (ibid, Art. 50.1). Civilians enjoy the protection of this part of the Protocol:—

"unless and for such time as they take a direct part in hostilities." (ibid, Art.51.3) Journalists shall be considered as civilians within the meaning of Article 50.1 (ibid, Art.79).

173.   As civilians, the media workers were entitled to the following protection:—

"The civilian population as such, as well as individual civilians, shall not be the object of attack. Acts or threats of violence the primary purpose of which is to spread terror among the civilian population are prohibited." (ibid, Art.52.2)

"The civilian population and individual civilians shall enjoy general protection against dangers arising from military operations." (ibid, Art.51.1)

174.   It is submitted that it is clear that the media workers were civilians and that, as such, they were entitled to protection from the dangers arising from military operations.

Military Objectives

175.   In order for the attack against the RTS building to be lawful, the building must have constituted a "military objective". The term is defined in Article 52.2, which provides:—

"In so far as objects are concerned, military objectives are limited to those objects which by their nature location, purpose or use make an effective contribution to military action and whose total or partial destruction, capture or neutralization, in the circumstances ruling at the time, offers a definite military advantage.''

176.   Certain introductory comments need to be made about this definition. First, there is no substantive definition of civilian objects. They are, rather, defined negatively as ''all objects which are not military objectives as defined in paragraph 2.'' (ibid, Article 52.1) In other words, any object which falls outside the definition in Article 52.2 is, by definition, a civilian object. Second, there are no categories or classes of legitimate military targets. The decision has to be taken on the facts in each case. For example, in the case of a garrison, it is almost inevitable that any given garrison will satisfy the test. In the case of a bridge, however, it will depend on the use being made of it at the time and the advantage to be anticipated from its destruction. Even if some bridges are legitimate targets, others will not be. Third, there is no provision for dual-use targets. Where both military and civilian use is made of an object, the initial question is whether that use brings it within the definition. If so, it will *prima facie* be a legitimate target of attack. It will then be necessary to address the second issue, which is whether the attack will cause disproportionate casualties. Amongst other things, that will depend on the means available for attacking it and the timing of the attack (e.g. if the civilians only use it during the day, it should be attacked at night).

177.   There are two separate reasons why the RTS building was not a military objective.

178.   First, it has never been claimed by the respondent Governments that it was used to relay military communications. Previously transmitters which relayed military communications had been attacked on that basis (e.g. ''The other attack was on a radio relay and TV transmitting station near Novi Sad. This facility was an important link in the air defence command and control communications net, and also a local area TV repeater.'' General Marani, see para. 21 above). Until such time as the RTS building and the facilities housed inside it were used as part of the military war effort, it was not an object the purpose or use of which made an effective contribution to *military* action. This is confirmed by an examination of the Commentaries on the Protocol. The ICRC Commentary (Sandoz, Swinarski & Zimmermann (Eds.), <u>Commentary on the Additional Protocols</u>, ICRC, 1987) clarifies the distinction between ''purpose'' and ''use'':—

> ''The criterion of *purpose* is concerned with the intended future use of an object, while that of *use* is concerned with its present function. Most civilian objects can become useful objects to the armed forces. Thus, for example, a school or a hotel is a civilian object, but if they are used to accommodate troops or headquarters staff, they become military objectives.'' (p.636 para.2022)

179.   In other words, the status of the object depends on the use being made of it at the time. The use to which the object is being put must make an "effective contribution to military action". That does not require a direct connection with combat operations but does require that the object:-

> "... provides an effective contribution to the *military* phase of a Party's overall war effort." (Bothe, Partsch & Solf, <u>New Rules for Victims of Armed Conflicts</u>, Nijhoff, 1982, p.324, para.2.4.3)

180.   The promotion of general political support for the war effort by means of propaganda does not represent an effective contribution to *military* action. The political leaders of the respondent Governments and the NATO spokeman did not claim that the RTS broadcasts contributed to military action. Their complaint was that the broadcasts were part of Milosevic's propaganda machine (see the facts above). As has already been established in the context of Article 2, the use of propaganda is not unlawful.

181.   The second reason why the RTS building did not come within the definition of a military objective is that its destruction or neutralization did not offer a "definite military advantage". This is a second, cumulative, element in the definition (Bothe, Partsch & Solf, supra, p.324, para.2.4.4). The only potential military advantage in attacking the television station was to put an end to the broadcasts. As seen above, an attack on the RTS building was forseeably not capable of doing that. It could only interrupt transmission for a very brief period of time. Furthermore, putting an end to the broadcasts would not offer a *military* advantage, far less a "definite military advantage".

* * *

183.   The applicants submit that the RTS building was not a military objective because:—

> 183.1.   neither its purpose nor use made an effective contribution to *military action;* and

> 183.2.   neither its destruction nor neutralization offered a definite *military advantage.*

184.   The attack was therefore unlawful *ab initio,* irrespective of whether it was also indiscriminate and whether any effective advance warning was given.

* * *

[The Application goes on to argue the attack violated AP1 Article 51(4), prohibition on indiscriminate attacks; Article 57(2)(c) warning, and Article 91 on compensation to victims of violations of the Protocol.]

Final Report To The Prosecutor By The Committee Established To Review The Nato Bombing Campaign Against The Federal Republic Of Yugoslavia

June 13, 2000*

I. Background and Mandate

1.   The North Atlantic Treaty Organization (NATO) conducted a bombing campaign against the Federal Republic of Yugoslavia (FRY) from 24 March 1999 to 9 June 1999. During and since that period, the Prosecutor has received numerous requests that she investigate allegations that senior political and military figures from NATO countries committed serious violations of international humanitarian law during the campaign, and that she prepares indictments pursuant to Article 18(1) & (4) of the Statute.

2.   Criticism of the NATO bombing campaign has included allegations of varying weight: a) that, as the resort to force was illegal, all NATO actions were illegal, and b) that the NATO forces deliberately attacked civilian infrastructure targets (and that such attacks were unlawful), deliberately or recklessly attacked the civilian population, and deliberately or recklessly caused excessive civilian casualties in disregard of the rule of proportionality by trying to fight a "zero casualty" war for their own side. Allegations concerning the "zero casualty" war involve suggestions that, for example, NATO aircraft operated at heights which enabled them to avoid attack by Yugoslav defences and, consequently, made it impossible for them to properly distinguish between military or civilian objects on the ground. Certain allegations went so far as to accuse NATO of crimes against humanity and genocide.

3.   Article 18 of the Tribunal's Statute provides:

> "The Prosecutor shall initiate investigations ex officio or on the basis of information obtained from any source, particularly from Governments, United Nations organs, intergovernmental and non-governmental organizations. The Prosecutor shall assess the information received or obtained and decide whether there is sufficient basis to proceed".

On 14 May 99 the then Prosecutor established a committee to assess the allegations and material accompanying them, and advise the Prosecutor and Deputy Prosecutor whether or not there is a sufficient basis to proceed with an investigation into some or all

---

* Available at www.un.org/icty/pressre-al/nato061300.htm

the allegations or into other incidents related to the NATO bombing.

4.   In the course of its work, the committee has not addressed in detail the issue of the fundamental legality of the use of force by NATO members against the FRY as, if such activity was unlawful, it could constitute a crime against peace and the ICTY has no jurisdiction over this offence. (See, however, paras 30–34 below). It is noted that the legitimacy of the recourse to force by NATO is a subject before the International Court of Justice in a case brought by the FRY against various NATO countries.

* * *

iv.   Legal Issues Related to Target Selection

a.   Overview of Applicable Law

28.   In brief, in combat military commanders are required: a) to direct their operations against military objectives, and b) when directing their operations against military objectives, to ensure that the losses to the civilian population and the damage to civilian property are not disproportionate to the concrete and direct military advantage anticipated. Attacks which are not directed against military objectives (particularly attacks directed against the civilian population) and attacks which cause disproportionate civilian casualties or civilian property damage may constitute the *actus reus* for the offence of unlawful attack under Article 3 of the ICTY Statute. The *mens rea* for the offence is intention or recklessness, not simple negligence. In determining whether or not the *mens rea* requirement has been met, it should be borne in mind that commanders deciding on an attack have duties:

> a) to do everything practicable to verify that the objectives to be attacked are military objectives,
>
> b) to take all practicable precautions in the choice of methods and means of warfare with a view to avoiding or, in any event to minimizing incidental civilian casualties or civilian property damage, and
>
> c) to refrain from launching attacks which may be expected to cause disproportionate civilian casualties or civilian property damage.

29.   One of the principles underlying international humanitarian law is the principle of distinction, which obligates military commanders to distinguish between military objectives and civilian persons or objects. The practical application of this principle is effectively encapsulated in Article 57 of Additional Protocol I which, in part, obligates those who plan or decide upon an attack to "do everything feasible to verify that the objectives to be attacked are neither civilians nor civilian objects". The obligation to do everything feasible is high but not absolute. A military

commander must set up an effective intelligence gathering system to collect and evaluate information concerning potential targets. The commander must also direct his forces to use available technical means to properly identify targets during operations. Both the commander and the aircrew actually engaged in operations must have some range of discretion to determine which available resources shall be used and how they shall be used. Further, a determination that inadequate efforts have been made to distinguish between military objectives and civilians or civilian objects should not necessarily focus exclusively on a specific incident. If precautionary measures have worked adequately in a very high percentage of cases then the fact they have not worked well in a small number of cases does not necessarily mean they are generally inadequate.

* * *

c.   The military objective

35.   The most widely accepted definition of "military objective" is that in Article 52 of Additional Protocol I which states in part:

> In so far as objects are concerned, military objectives are limited to those objects which by their nature, location, purpose or use make an effective contribution to military action and whose total or partial destruction, capture or neutralization, in the circumstances ruling at the time, offers a definite military advantage.

36.   Where objects are concerned, the definition has two elements: (a) their nature, location, purpose or use must make an effective contribution to military action, and (b) their total or partial destruction, capture or neutralization must offer a definite military advantage in the circumstances ruling at the time. Although this definition does not refer to persons, in general, members of the armed forces are considered combatants, who have the right to participate directly in hostilities, and as a corollary, may also be attacked.

37.   The definition is supposed to provide a means whereby informed objective observers (and decision makers in a conflict) can determine whether or not a particular object constitutes a military objective. It accomplishes this purpose in simple cases. Everyone will agree that a munitions factory is a military objective and an unoccupied church is a civilian object. When the definition is applied to dual-use objects which have some civilian uses and some actual or potential military use (communications systems, transportation systems, petrochemical complexes, manufacturing plants of some types), opinions *may* differ. The application of the definition to particular objects *may* also differ depending on the scope and objectives of the conflict. Further, the scope and objectives of the conflict *may* change during the conflict.

38. Using the Protocol I definition and his own review of state practice, Major General A.P.V. Rogers, a former Director of British Army Legal Services has advanced a tentative list of military objectives:

> military personnel and persons who take part in the fighting without being members of the armed forces, military facilities, military equipment, including military vehicles, weapons, munitions and stores of fuel, military works, including defensive works and fortifications, military depots and establishments, including War and Supply Ministries, works producing or developing military supplies and other supplies of military value, including metallurgical, engineering and chemical industries supporting the war effort; areas of land of military significance such as hills, defiles and bridgeheads; railways, ports, airfields, bridges, main roads as well as tunnels and canals; oil and other power installations; communications installations, including broadcasting and television stations and telephone and telegraph stations used for military communications. (Rogers, *Law on the Battlefield* (1996) 37)

The list was not intended to be exhaustive. It remains a requirement that both elements of the definition must be met before a target can be properly considered an appropriate military objective.

39. In 1956, the International Committee of the Red Cross (ICRC) drew up [a] proposed list of categories of military objectives: * * *

The following however, are excepted from the foregoing list:

> (1) Persons, constructions, installations or transports which are protected under the Geneva Conventions I, II, III, of August 12, 1949;

> (2) Non-combatants in the armed forces who obviously take no active or direct part in hostilities.

40. The Protocol I definition of military objective has been criticized by W. Hays Parks, the Special Assistant for Law of War Matters to the U.S. Army Judge Advocate General as being focused too narrowly on definite military advantage and paying too little heed to war sustaining capability, including economic targets such as export industries. (W. Hays Parks, "Air War and the Law of War," 32 *A.F.L. Rev.* 1, 135–45 (1990)). On the other hand, some critics of Coalition conduct in the Gulf War have suggested that the Coalition air campaign, directed admittedly against legitimate military objectives within the scope of the Protocol I definition, caused excessive long-term damage to the Iraqi economic infrastructure with a consequential adverse effect on the civilian population. (Middle East Watch, *Needless Deaths in the Gulf War: Civilian Casualties during the Air Campaign and Violations of the*

Laws of War (1991); Judith G. Gardam, "Proportionality and Force in International Law," 87 *Am. J. Int'l L.* 391, 404–10 (1993)).

* * *

d) The Principle of Proportionality

48.   The main problem with the principle of proportionality is not whether or not it exists but what it means and how it is to be applied. It is relatively simple to state that there must be an acceptable relation between the legitimate destructive effect and undesirable collateral effects. For example, bombing a refugee camp is obviously prohibited if its only military significance is that people in the camp are knitting socks for soldiers. Conversely, an air strike on an ammunition dump should not be prohibited merely because a farmer is plowing a field in the area. Unfortunately, most applications of the principle of proportionality are not quite so clear cut. It is much easier to formulate the principle of proportionality in general terms than it is to apply it to a particular set of circumstances because the comparison is often between unlike quantities and values. One cannot easily assess the value of innocent human lives as opposed to capturing a particular military objective.

49.   The questions which remain unresolved once one decides to apply the principle of proportionality include the following:

a) What are the relative values to be assigned to the military advantage gained and the injury to noncombatants and or the damage to civilian objects?

b) What do you include or exclude in totaling your sums?

c) What is the standard of measurement in time or space? and

d) To what extent is a military commander obligated to expose his own forces to danger in order to limit civilian casualties or damage to civilian objects?

50.   The answers to these questions are not simple. It may be necessary to resolve them on a case by case basis, and the answers may differ depending on the background and values of the decision maker. It is unlikely that a human rights lawyer and an experienced combat commander would assign the same relative values to military advantage and to injury to noncombatants. Further, it is unlikely that military commanders with different doctrinal backgrounds and differing degrees of combat experience or national military histories would always agree in close cases. It is suggested that the determination of relative values must be that of the "reasonable military commander". Although there will be room for argument in close cases, there will be many cases where reasonable military commanders will agree that the injury to noncombat-

ants or the damage to civilian objects was clearly disproportionate to the military advantage gained.

51.   Much of the material submitted to the OTP consisted of reports that civilians had been killed, often inviting the conclusion to be drawn that crimes had therefore been committed. Collateral casualties to civilians and collateral damage to civilian objects can occur for a variety of reasons. Despite an obligation to avoid locating military objectives within or near densely populated areas, to remove civilians from the vicinity of military objectives, and to protect their civilians from the dangers of military operations, very little prevention may be feasible in many cases. Today's technological society has given rise to many dual use facilities and resources. City planners rarely pay heed to the possibility of future warfare. Military objectives are often located in densely populated areas and fighting occasionally occurs in such areas. Civilians present within or near military objectives must, however, be taken into account in the proportionality equation even if a party to the conflict has failed to exercise its obligation to remove them.

52.   In the *Kupreskic* Judgment (Case No: IT–95–16–T 14 Jan 2000) the Trial Chamber addressed the issue of proportionality as follows:

> "526.   As an example of the way in which the Martens clause may be utilised, regard might be had to considerations such as the cumulative effect of attacks on military objectives causing incidental damage to civilians. In other words, it may happen that single attacks on military objectives causing incidental damage to civilians, although they may raise doubts as to their lawfulness, nevertheless do not appear on their face to fall foul *per se* of the loose prescriptions of Articles 57 and 58 (or of the corresponding customary rules). However, in case of repeated attacks, all or most of them falling within the grey area between indisputable legality and unlawfulness, it might be warranted to conclude that the cumulative effect of such acts entails that they may not be in keeping with international law. Indeed, this pattern of military conduct may turn out to jeopardise excessively the lives and assets of civilians, contrary to the demands of humanity."

This formulation in *Kupreskic* can be regarded as a progressive statement of the applicable law with regard to the obligation to protect civilians. Its practical import, however, is somewhat ambiguous and its application far from clear. It is the committee's view that where individual (and legitimate) attacks on military objectives are concerned, the mere *cumulation* of such instances, all of which are deemed to have been lawful, cannot *ipso facto* be said to amount to a crime. The committee understands the above formulation, instead, to refer to an *overall* assessment of the totality of civilian victims as against the goals of the military campaign.

V Casualty Figures

53. In its report, *Civilian Deaths in the NATO Air Campaign,* Human Rights Watch documented some 500 civilian deaths in 90 separate incidents. It concluded: "on the basis available on these ninety incidents that as few as 488 and as many as 527 Yugoslav civilians were killed as a result of NATO bombing. Between 62 and 66 percent of the total registered civilian deaths occurred in just twelve incidents. These twelve incidents accounted for 303 to 352 civilian deaths. These were the only incidents among the ninety documented in which ten or more civilian deaths were confirmed." Ten of these twelve incidents were included among the incidents which were reviewed with considerable care by the committee * * * and our estimate was that between 273 and 317 civilians were killed in these ten incidents. Human Rights Watch also found the FRY Ministry of Foreign Affairs publication NATO Crimes in Yugoslavia to be largely credible on the basis of its own filed research and correlation with other sources. A review of this publication indicates it provides an estimated total of approximately 495 civilians killed and 820 civilians wounded in specific documented instances. For the purposes of this report, the committee operates on the basis of the number of persons allegedly killed as found in both publications. It appears that a figure similar to both publications would be in the range of 500 civilians killed.

VI General Asses[s]ment of the Bombing Campaign

54. During the bombing campaign, NATO aircraft flew 38,400 sorties, including 10,484 strike sorties. During these sorties, 23,-614 air munitions were released (figures from NATO). As indicated in the preceding paragraph, it appears that approximately 500 civilians were killed during the campaign. These figures do not indicate that NATO may have conducted a campaign aimed at causing substantial civilian casualties either directly or incidentally.

55. The choice of targets by NATO * * * includes some loosely defined categories such as military-industrial infrastructure and government ministries and some potential problem categories such as media and refineries. All targets must meet the criteria for military objectives * * *. If they do not do so, they are unlawful. A general label is insufficient. The targeted components of the military-industrial infrastructure and of government ministries must make an effective contribution to military action and their total or partial destruction must offer a definite military advantage in the circumstances ruling at the time. Refineries are certainly traditional military objectives but tradition is not enough and due regard must be paid to environmental damage if they are attacked * * *. The media as such is not a traditional target category. To the extent particular media components are part of the C3 (command, control and communications) network they are military

objectives. If media components are not part of the C3 network then they may become military objectives depending upon their use. As a bottom line, civilians, civilian objects and civilian morale as such are not legitimate military objectives. The media does have an effect on civilian morale. If that effect is merely to foster support for the war effort, the media is not a legitimate military objective. If the media is used to incite crimes, as in Rwanda, it can become a legitimate military objective. If the media is the nerve system that keeps a war-monger in power and thus perpetuates the war effort, it may fall within the definition of a legitimate military objective. As a general statement, in the particular incidents reviewed by the committee, it is the view of the committee that NATO was attempting to attack objects it perceived to be legitimate military objectives.

56.   The committee agrees there is nothing inherently unlawful about flying above the height which can be reached by enemy air defences. However, NATO air commanders have a duty to take practicable measures to distinguish military objectives from civilians or civilian objectives. The 15,000 feet minimum altitude adopted for part of the campaign may have meant the target could not be verified with the naked eye. However, it appears that with the use of modern technology, the obligation to distinguish was effectively carried out in that they may not be in the vast majority of cases during the bombing campaign.

B.   Specific Incidents

* * *

iii) The Bombing of the RTS (Serbian TV and Radio Station) in Belgrade on 23/4/99

71.   On 23 April 1999, at 0220, NATO intentionally bombed the central studio of the RTS (state-owned) broadcasting corporation at 1 Aberdareva Street in the centre of Belgrade. The missiles hit the entrance area, which caved in at the place where the Aberdareva Street building was connected to the Takovska Street building. While there is some doubt over exact casualty figures, between 10 and 17 people are estimated to have been killed.

72.   The bombing of the TV studio was part of a planned attack aimed at disrupting and degrading the C3 (Command, Control and Communications) network. In co-ordinated attacks, on the same night, radio relay buildings and towers were hit along with electrical power transformer stations. At a press conference on 27 April 1999, NATO officials justified this attack in terms of the dual military and civilian use to which the FRY communication system was routinely put, describing this as a

> "very hardened and redundant command and control communications system [which ...] uses commercial telephone, [...] military cable, [...] fibre optic cable, [...] high frequency

radio communication, [...] microwave communication and everything can be interconnected. There are literally dozens, more than 100 radio relay sites around the country, and [...] everything is wired in through dual use. Most of the commercial system serves the military and the military system can be put to use for the commercial system [...]."

Accordingly, NATO stressed the dual-use to which such communications systems were put, describing civilian television as "heavily dependent on the military command and control system and military traffic is also routed through the civilian system" (press conference of 27 April, *ibid*).

73. At an earlier press conference on 23 April 1999, NATO officials reported that the TV building also housed a large multipurpose communications satellite antenna dish, and that "radio relay control buildings and towers were targeted in the ongoing campaign to degrade the FRY's command, control and communications network". In a communication of 17 April 1999 to Amnesty International, NATO claimed that the RTS facilities were being used "as radio relay stations and transmitters to support the activities of the FRY military and special police forces, and therefore they represent legitimate military targets" (Amnesty International Report, *NATO/Federal Republic of Yugoslavia: Violations of the Laws of War by NATO during Operation Allied Force,* June 2000, p. 42).

74. Of the electrical power transformer stations targeted, one transformer station supplied power to the air defence co-ordination network while the other supplied power to the northern-sector operations centre. Both these facilities were key control elements in the FRY integrated air-defence system. In this regard, NATO indicated that

> "we are not targeting the Serb people as we repeatedly have stated nor do we target President Milosevic personally, we are attacking the control system that is used to manipulate the military and security forces."

More controversially, however, the bombing was also justified on the basis of the propaganda purpose to which it was employed:

> "[We need to] directly strike at the very central nerve system of Milosovic's regime. This of course are those assets which are used to plan and direct and to create the political environment of tolerance in Yugoslavia in which these brutalities can not only be accepted but even condoned. [...] Strikes against TV transmitters and broadcast facilities are part of our campaign to dismantle the FRY propaganda machinery which is a vital part of President Milosevic's control mechanism."

In a similar statement, British Prime Minister Tony Blair was reported as saying in *The Times* that the media "is the apparatus that keeps him [Milosevic] in power and we are entirely justified as NATO allies in damaging and taking on those targets" (24 April, 1999). In a statement of 8 April 1999, NATO also indicated that the TV studios would be targeted unless they broadcast 6 hours per day of Western media reports: "If President Milosevic would provide equal time for Western news broadcasts in its programmes without censorship 3 hours a day between noon and 1800 and 3 hours a day between 1800 and midnight, then his TV could be an acceptable instrument of public information."

75.   NATO intentionally bombed the Radio and TV station and the persons killed or injured were civilians. The questions are: was the station a legitimate military objective and; if it was, were the civilian casualties disproportionate to the military advantage gained by the attack? For the station to be a military objective within the definition in Article 52 of Protocol I: a) its nature, purpose or use must make an effective contribution to military action and b) its total or partial destruction must offer a definite military advantage in the circumstances ruling at the time. The 1956 ICRC list of military objectives, drafted before the Additional Protocols, included the installations of broadcasting and television stations of fundamental military importance as military objectives (para. 39 above). The list prepared by Major General Rogers included broadcasting and television stations if they meet the military objective criteria (para. 38 above). As indicated in paras. 72 and 73 above, the attack appears to have been justified by NATO as part of a more general attack aimed at disrupting the FRY Command, Control and Communications network, the nerve centre and apparatus that keeps Milosevic in power, and also as an attempt to dismantle the FRY propaganda machinery. Insofar as the attack actually was aimed at disrupting the communications network, it was legally acceptable.

76.   If, however, the attack was made because equal time was not provided for Western news broadcasts, that is, because the station was part of the propaganda machinery, the legal basis was more debatable. Disrupting government propaganda may help to undermine the morale of the population and the armed forces, but justifying an attack on a civilian facility on such grounds alone may not meet the "effective contribution to military action" and "definite military advantage" criteria required by the Additional Protocols (see paras. 35–36, above). The ICRC Commentary on the Additional Protocols interprets the expression "definite military advantage anticipated" to exclude "an attack which only offers potential or indeterminate advantages" and interprets the expression "concrete and direct" as intended to show that the advantage concerned should be substantial and relatively close rather than hardly perceptible and likely to appear only in the long term (ICRC Commentary on the Additional Protocols of 8 June 1977, para. 2209). While stopping such propaganda may serve to demo-

ralize the Yugoslav population and undermine the government's political support, it is unlikely that either of these purposes would offer the "concrete and direct" military advantage necessary to make them a legitimate military objective. NATO believed that Yugoslav broadcast facilities were "used entirely to incite hatred and propaganda" and alleged that the Yugoslav government had put all private TV and radio stations in Serbia under military control (NATO press conferences of 28 and 30 April 1999). However, it was not claimed that they were being used to incite violence akin to *Radio Milles Collines* during the Rwandan genocide, which might have justified their destruction * * *. At worst, the Yugoslav government was using the broadcasting networks to issue propaganda supportive of its war effort: a circumstance which does not, in and of itself, amount to a war crime (see in this regard the judgment of the International Military Tribunal in Nuremberg in 1946 in the case of Hans Fritzsche, who served as a senior official in the Propaganda ministry alleged to have incited and encouraged the commission of crimes. The IMT held that although Fritzsche clearly made strong statements of a propagandistic nature, it was nevertheless not prepared to find that they were intended to incite the commission of atrocities, but rather, were aimed at arousing popular sentiment in support of Hitler and the German war effort *(American Journal* of *International Law,* vol. 41 (1947) 32)). The committee finds that if the attack on the RTS was justified by reference to its propaganda purpose alone, its legality might well be questioned by some experts in the field of international humanitarian law. It appears, however, that NATO's targeting of the RTS building for propaganda purposes was an incidental (albeit complementary) aim of its primary goal of disabling the Serbian military command and control system and to destroy the nerve system and apparatus that keeps Milosevic in power. In a press conference of 9 April 1999, NATO declared that TV transmitters were not targeted directly but that "in Yugoslavia military radio relay stations are often combined with TV transmitters [so] we attack the military target. If there is damage to the TV transmitters, it is a secondary effect but it is not [our] primary intention to do that." A NATO spokesperson, Jamie Shea, also wrote to the Brussels-based International Federation of Journalists on 12 April claiming that Operation Allied Force "target[ed] military targets only and television and radio towers are only struck if they [were] integrated into military facilities ... There is no policy to strike television and radio transmitters as such" (cited in Amnesty International Report, *ibid,* June 2000).

77. Assuming the station was a legitimate objective, the civilian casualties were unfortunately high but do not appear to be clearly disproportionate.

Although NATO alleged that it made "every possible effort to avoid civilian casualties and collateral damage" (Amnesty International Report, *ibid,* June 2000, p. 42), some doubts have been expressed as to the specificity of the warning given to civilians by NATO of its intended strike, and whether the notice would have constituted "effective warning . . . of attacks which may affect the civililan [sic] population, unless circumstances do not permit" as required by Article 57(2) of Additional Protocol I.

Evidence on this point is somewhat contradictory. On the one hand, NATO officials in Brussels are alleged to have told Amnesty International that they did not give a specific warning as it would have endangered the pilots (Amnesty International Report, *ibid,* June 2000, at p. 47; see also para. 49 above re: proportionality and the extent to which a military commander is obligated to expose his own forces to danger in order to limit civilian casualties or damage). On this view, it is possible that casualties among civilians working at the RTS may have been heightened because of NATO's apparent failure to provide clear advance warning of the attack, as required by Article 57(2).

On the other hand, foreign media representatives were apparently forewarned of the attack (Amnesty International Report, *ibid).* As Western journalists were reportedly warned by their employers to stay away from the television station before the attack, it would also appear that some Yugoslav officials may have expected that the building was about to be struck. Consequently, UK Prime Minister Tony Blair blamed Yugoslav officials for not evacuating the building, claiming that "[t]hey could have moved those people out of the building. They knew it was a target and they didn't . . . [I]t was probably for . . . very clear propaganda reasons." *(ibid,* citing *Moral combat—NATO at war,* broadcast on BBC2 on 12 March 2000). Although knowledge on the part of Yugoslav officials of the impending attack would not divest NATO of its obligation to forewarn civilians under Article 57(2), it may nevertheless imply that the Yugoslav authorities may be partially responsible for the civilian casualties resulting from the attack and may suggest that the advance notice given by NATO may have in fact been sufficient under the circumstances.

78.   Assuming the RTS building to be a legitimate military target, it appeared that NATO realised that attacking the RTS building would only interrupt broadcasting for a brief period. Indeed, broadcasting allegedly recommenced within hours of the strike, thus raising the issue of the importance of the military advantage gained by the attack *vis-à-vis* the civilian casualties incurred. The FRY command and control network was alleged by NATO to comprise a complex web and that could thus not be disabled in one strike. As noted by General Wesley Clark, NATO "knew when we struck that there would be alternate means of getting the Serb Television. There's no single switch to turn off everything but we thought it was a good move to strike it and the political leadership

agreed with us" *(ibid,* citing "Moral combat, NATO at War," broadcast on BBC2 on 12 March 2000). At a press conference on 27 April 1999, another NATO spokesperson similarly described the dual-use Yugoslav command and control network as "incapable of being dealt with in 'a single knock-out blow *(ibid)'* ". The proportionality or otherwise of an attack should not necessarily focus exclusively on a specific incident. (See in this regard para. 52, above, referring to the need for an overall assessment of the totality of civilian victims as against the goals of the military campaign). With regard to these goals, the strategic target of these attacks was the Yugoslav command and control network. The attack on the RTS building must therefore be seen as forming part of an integrated attack against numerous objects, including transmission towers and control buildings of the Yugoslav radio relay network which were "essential to Milosevic's ability to direct and control the repressive activities of his army and special police forces in Kosovo" (NATO press release, 1 May 1999) and which comprised "a key element in the Yugoslav air-defence network" *(ibid,* 1 May1999). Attacks were also aimed at electricity grids that fed the command and control structures of the Yugoslav Army *(ibid,* 3 May 1999). Other strategic targets included additional command and control assets such as the radio and TV relay sites at Novi Pazar, Kosovaka and Krusevac *(ibid)* and command posts *(ibid,* 30 April). Of the electrical power transformer stations targeted, one transformer station supplied power to the air-defence coordination network while the other supplied power to the northern sector operations centre. Both these facilities were key control elements in the FRY integrated air-defence system *(ibid,* 23 April 1999). The radio relay and TV transmitting station near Novi Sad was also an important link in the air defence command and control communications network. Not only were these targets central to the Federal Republic of Yugoslavia's governing apparatus, but formed, from a military point of view, an integral part of the strategic communications network which enabled both the military and national command authorities to direct the repression and atrocities taking place in Kosovo *(ibid,* 21 April 1999).

79. On the basis of the above analysis and on the information currently available to it, the committee recommends that the OTP not commence an investigation related to the bombing of the Serbian TV and Radio Station.

* * *

91. On the basis of information available, the committee recommends that no investigation be commenced by the OTP in relation to the NATO bombing campaign or incidents occurring during the campaign.

B.   Protections During Occupation

When territory comes under the control of armed forces of an adversary that territory is occupied. The adversary becomes an occupying power with the obligation to restore and maintain public order. Civilians and civilian objects under the control of an occupying power may not be attacked. The occupying power must provide for the basic needs of the population. "None of these rights prevents a party from taking measures necessary for its security, including restrictions on the freedom of movement of protected persons."[7] Occupation is meant to be a temporary situation in which the occupying power makes only necessary changes to the *status quo.*

Beit Sourik Village Council v.
1. The Government of Israel
2.   Commander of the IDF Forces in the West Bank

The Supreme Court Sitting as the High Court of Justice, June 30, 2004.

JUDGEMENT

President A. Barak

The Commander of the IDF Forces in Judea and Samaria issued orders to take possession of plots of land in the area of Judea and Samaria. The purpose of the seizure was to erect a Separation Fence on the land. The question before us is whether the orders and the Fence are legal.

Background

1.   Since 1967, Israel has been holding the areas of Judea and Samaria [hereinafter—the area] in belligerent occupation. In 1993 Israel began a political process with the PLO, and signed a number of agreements transferring control over parts of the area to the Palestinian Authority. Israel and the PLO continued political negotiations in an attempt to solve the remaining problems. The negotiations, whose final stages took place at Camp David in Maryland, USA, failed in July 2000.

From respondents' affidavit in answer to an *order nisi* we learned that, a short time after the failure of the Camp David talks, the Israeli–Palestinian conflict reached new heights of violence. In September 2000, the Palestinian side began a campaign of terror against Israel and Israelis. Terror attacks take place both in the area and in Israel. They are directed against citizens and soldiers, men and women, elderly people and infants, regular citizens and public figures. Terror attacks are carried out everywhere: in public transportation, in shopping centers and markets, in coffee houses and in restaurants. Terror organizations use

---

7.   Green, *supra* note 2, at 235.

gunfire attacks, suicide attacks, mortar fire, Katyusha rocket fire, and car bombs. From September 2000 until the beginning of April 2004, more than 780 attacks were carried out within Israel. During the same period, more than 8200 attacks were carried out in the area.

The armed conflict claimed (as of April 2004) the lives of 900 Israeli citizens and residents. More than 6000 were injured, some with serious wounds that have left them severely handicapped. The armed conflict has left many dead and wounded on the Palestinian side as well. Bereavement and pain wash over us.

In HCJ 7015/02 *Ajuri v. IDF Commander*, at 358, I described the security situation:

> Israel's fight is complex. Together with other means, the Palestinians use guided human bombs. These suicide bombers reach every place that Israelis can be found (within the boundaries of the State of Israel and in the Jewish communities in Judea and Samaria and the Gaza Strip). They sew destruction and spill blood in the cities and towns. The forces fighting against Israel are terrorists: they are not members of a regular army; they do not wear uniforms; they hide among the civilian Palestinian population in the territories, including inside holy sites; they are supported by part of the civilian population, and by their families and relatives.

2. These terror acts have caused Israel to take security precautions on several levels. The government, for example, decided to carry out various military operations, such as operation "Defensive Wall" (March 2002) and operation "Determined Path" (June 2002). The objective of these military actions was to defeat the Palestinian terrorist infrastructure and to prevent terror attacks. *See* HCJ 3239/02 *Marab v. IDF Commander in the West Bank,* at 355; HCJ 3278/02 *Center for Defense of the Individual v. IDF Commander*, at 389. These combat operations—which are not regular police operations, but embody all the characteristics of armed conflict—did not provide a sufficient answer to the immediate need to stop the terror. The Ministers' Committee on National Security considered a list of steps intended to prevent additional terror acts and to deter potential terrorists from participating in such acts. *See Ajuri*, at 359. Despite all these measures, the terror did not come to an end. The attacks did not cease. Innocent people paid with both life and limb. This is the background behind the decision to construct the Separation Fence.

The Decision to Construct the Separation Fence

3. The Ministers' Committee for National Security reached a decision (on April 14, 2002) regarding deployment in the "Seam Area" between Israel and the area. [Note to English translation: the "Seam Area" is roughly the interface between Judea and

Samaria on the one hand, and Israel as per the 1949 armistice agreement on the other.] *See* HCJ 8532/02 *Ibraheem v. Commander of the IDF Forces in the West Bank.* The purpose behind the decision was "to improve and strengthen operational capability in the framework of fighting terror, and to prevent the penetration of terrorists from the area of Judea and Samaria into Israel." The IDF and the police were given the task of preventing the passage of Palestinians into the State of Israel. As a temporary solution, it was decided to erect an obstacle in the three regions found to be most vulnerable to the passage of terrorists into Israel: the Umm El–Fahm region and the villages split between Israel and the area (Baka and Barta'a); the Qalqilya–Tulkarm region; and the Greater Jerusalem region. It was further decided to create a team of Ministers, headed by the Prime Minister, which would examine long-term solutions to prevent the infiltration of Palestinians, including terrorists, into Israel.

4.   The Government of Israel held deliberations on the "Seam Area" program (June 23, 2002). The armed services presented their proposal to erect an obstacle on the "Seam." The government approved stage 1 of the project, which provides a solution to the operational problem of terrorist infiltration into the north of the country, the center of the country and the Jerusalem area. The obstacle that was approved begins in the area of the Salam village, adjacent to the Meggido junction, and continues until the trans-Samaria road. An additional obstacle in the Jerusalem area was also approved. The entire obstacle, as approved, is 116 km long.

* * *

The Normative Framework

23.   The general point of departure of all parties—which is also our point of departure—is that Israel holds the area in belligerent occupation (*occupatio bellica*). *See* HCJ 619/78 *"El Tal'ia" Weekly v. Minister of Defense*; HCJ 69/81 *Abu Ita v. Commander of the Area of Judea and Samaria*; HCJ 606/78 *Ayoob v. Minister of Defense*; HCJ 393/82 *Jam'iat Ascan Elma'almoon Eltha'aooniah Elmahduda Elmaoolieh v. Commander of the IDF Forces in the Area of Judea and Samaria.* In the areas relevant to this petition, military administration, headed by the military commander, continues to apply. *Compare* HCJ 2717/96 *Wafa v. Minister of Defense* (application of the military administration in "Area C"). The authority of the military commander flows from the provisions of public international law regarding belligerent occupation. These rules are established principally in the Regulations Concerning the Laws and Customs of War on Land, The Hague, 18 October 1907 [hereinafter—the Hague Regulations]. These regulations reflect customary international law. The military commander's authority is also anchored in IV Geneva Convention Relative

to the Protection of Civilian Persons in Time of War 1949. [herein-
after—the Fourth Geneva Convention]. The question of the application of the Fourth Geneva Convention has come up more than
once in this Court. *See* HCJ 390/79 *Duikat v. Government of Israel*;
HCJ 61/80 *Haetzni v. State of Israel*, at 597. The question is not
before us now, since the parties agree that the humanitarian rules
of the Fourth Geneva Convention apply to the issue under review.
See HCJ 698/80 *Kawasme v. Minister of Defense*; *Jam'iyat Ascan*,
at 794; *Ajuri*, at 364; HCJ 3278/02 *Center for the Defense of the
Individual v. Commander of the IDF Forces in the West Bank Area*,
at 396. *See also* Meir Shamgar, *The Observance of International
Law in the Administered Territories*, 1 Israel Yearbook on Human
Rights 262 (1971).

24.   Together with the provisions of international law, "the
principles of the Israeli administrative law regarding the use of
governing authority" apply to the military commander. *See
Jam'iyat Ascan*, at 793. Thus, the norms of substantive and
procedural fairness (such as the right to have arguments heard
before expropriation, seizure, or other governing actions), the
obligation to act reasonably, and the norm of proportionality apply
to the military commander. *See Abu Ita*, at 231; HCJ 591/88 *Taha
v. Minister of Defense*, at 52; *Ajuri*, at 382; HJC 10356/02 *Hess v.
Commander of the IDF Forces in the West Bank*. Indeed, "[e]very
Israeli soldier carries, in his pack, the provisions of public international law regarding the laws of war and the basic provisions of
Israeli administrative law." *Jam'iyat Ascan*, at 810.

25.   This petition raises two separate questions. The first
question: is the military commander in Judea and Samaria authorized, by the law applying to him, to construct the Separation Fence
in Judea and Samaria? An affirmative answer to this question
raises a second question concerning the location of the Separation
Fence. Both questions were raised before us in the petition, in the
response, and in the parties' arguments. The parties, however,
concentrated on the second question; only a small part of the
arguments before us dealt with the first question. The question of
the authority to erect the Fence in the area is complex and
multifaceted, and it did not receive full expression in the arguments before us. Without exhausting it, we too shall occupy
ourselves briefly with the first question, dealing only with the
arguments raised by the parties, and will then move to focus our
discussion on the second question.

Authority to Erect the Separation Fence

26.   Petitioners rest their assertion that the military commander does not have authority to construct the Fence on two
claims. The first is that the military commander does not have the
authority to order construction of the Fence since his decision is
founded upon political—and not military—considerations.

27. We accept that the military commander cannot order the construction of the Separation Fence if his reasons are political. The Separation Fence cannot be motivated by a desire to "annex" territories to the state of Israel. The purpose of the Separation Fence cannot be to draw a political border. In *Duikat*, at 17, this Court discussed whether it is possible to seize land in order to build a Jewish civilian town, when the purpose of the building of the town is not the security needs and defense of the area (as it was in *Ayoob*), but rather based upon a Zionist perspective of settling the entire land of Israel. This question was answered by this Court in the negative. The Vice–President of this Court, Justice Landau, quoted the Prime Minister (the late Mr. Menachem Begin), regarding the right of the Jewish people to settle in Judea and Samaria. In his judgment, Justice Landau stated:

The view regarding the right of the Jewish people, expressed in these words, is built upon Zionist ideology. However, the question before this Court is whether this ideology justifies the taking of the property of the individual in an area under control of the military administration. The answer to that depends upon the interpretation of article 52 of the Hague Regulations. It is my opinion that the needs of the army mentioned in that article cannot include, by way of any reasonable interpretation, national security needs in broad meaning of the term.

* * *

Indeed, the military commander of territory held in belligerent occupation must balance between the needs of the army on one hand, and the needs of the local inhabitants on the other. In the framework of this delicate balance, there is no room for an additional system of considerations, whether they be political considerations, the annexation of territory, or the establishment of the permanent borders of the state. This Court has emphasized time and time again that the authority of the military commander is inherently temporary, as belligerent occupation is inherently temporary. Permanent arrangements are not the affair of the military commander. True, the belligerent occupation of the area has gone on for many years. This fact affects the scope of the military commander's authority. *See Jam'iyat Ascan*, at 800. The passage of time, however, cannot extend the authority of the military commander and allow him to take into account considerations beyond the proper administration of the area under belligerent occupation.

28. We examined petitioners' arguments, and have come to the conclusion, based upon the facts before us, that the Fence is motivated by security concerns. As we have seen in the government decisions concerning the construction of the Fence, the government has emphasized, numerous times, that "the Fence,

like the additional obstacles, is a security measure. Its construction does not express a political border, or any other border." (decision of June 23, 2002). "The obstacle that will be erected pursuant to this decision, like other segments of the obstacle in the 'Seam Area,' is a security measure for the prevention of terror attacks and does not mark a national border or any other border." (decision of October 1, 2003).

29. The Commander of the IDF Forces in the area of Judea and Samaria (respondent no. 2), Major General M. Kaplinsky, submitted an affidavit to the Court. In his affidavit he stated that "the objective of the security Fence is to help contend with the threat of Palestinian terror. Specifically, the Fence is intended to prevent the unchecked passage of inhabitants of the area into Israel and their infiltration into Israeli towns located in the area. Based on this security consideration we determined the topographic route of the Fence." (affidavit of April 15, sections 22–23). The commander of the area detailed his considerations for the choice of the route. He noted the necessity that the Fence pass through territory that topographically controls its surroundings, that, in order to allow surveillance of it, its route be as flat as possible, and that a "security zone" be established which will delay infiltration into Israel. These are security considerations *par excellence*. In an additional affidavit, Major General Kaplinsky testified that "it is not a permanent Fence, but rather a temporary Fence erected for security needs." (affidavit of April 19, 2004, section 4). We have no reason not to give this testimony less than full weight, and we have no reason not to believe the sincerity of the military commander.

30. Petitioners, by pointing to the route of the Fence, attempt to prove that the construction of the Fence is not motivated by security considerations, but by political ones. They argue that if the Fence was primarily motivated by security considerations, it would be constructed on the "Green Line," that is to say, on the armistice line between Israel and Jordan after the War of Independence. We cannot accept this argument. The opposite is the case: it is the security perspective—and not the political one—which must examine a route based on its security merits alone, without regard for the location of the Green Line. The members of the Council for Peace and Security, whose affidavits were brought before us by agreement of the parties, do not recommend following the Green Line. They do not even argue that the considerations of the military commander are political. Rather, they dispute the proper route of the Separation Fence based on security considerations themselves.

* * *

Regarding the central question raised before us, our opinion is that the military commander is authorized—by the international law applicable to an area under belligerent occupation—to take possession of land, if this is necessary for the needs of the army. *See* articles 23(g) and 52 of the Hague Convention; article 53 of the Fourth Geneva Convention. He must, of course, provide compensation for his use of the land. *See* HCJ 606/78 *Ayoob v. Minster of Defense*; HCJ 401/88 *Abu Rian v. Commander of the IDF Forces in the Area of Judea and Samaria; Timraz*. Indeed, on the basis of the provisions of the Hague Convention and the Geneva Convention, this Court has recognized the legality of land and house seizure for various military needs, including the construction of military facilities (HCJ 834/78 *Salama v. Minister of Defense*), the paving of detour roads (HCJ 202/81 *Tabib v. Minister of Defense; Wafa*), the building of fences around outposts (*Timraz*), the temporary housing of soldiers (HCJ 290/89 *Jora v. Commander of IDF Forces in Judea and Samaria*), the ensuring of unimpaired traffic on the roads of the area (*Abu Rian*), the construction of civilian administration offices (HCJ 1987/90 *Shadid v. Commander of IDF Forces in the Area of Judea and Samaria*), the seizing of buildings for the deployment of a military force, (HCJ 8286/00 *Association for Civil Rights in Israel v. Commander of the IDF Forces in the Area of Judea and Samaria*). Of course, regarding all of these acts, the military commander must consider the needs of the local population. Assuming that this condition is met, there is no doubt that the military commander is authorized to take possession of land in areas under his control. The construction of the Separation Fence falls within this framework. The infringement of property rights is insufficient, in and of itself, to take away the authority to build it. It is permitted, by the international law applicable to an area under belligerent occupation, to take possession of an individual's land in order to erect a separation fence upon it, on the condition that this is necessitated by military needs. To the extent that construction of the Fence is a military necessity, it is permitted, therefore, by international law. Indeed, the obstacle is intended to take the place of combat military operations, by physically blocking terrorist infiltration into Israeli population centers. The building of the obstacle, to the extent it is done out of military necessity, is within the authority of the military commander. Of course, the route of the Separation Fence must take the needs of the local population into account. That issue, however, concerns the route of the Fence and not the authority to erect it. After reaching this conclusion, we must now contend with the second question before us: the question that constitutes the bulk of the arguments before us. This question is the legality of the location and route of the Separation Fence. We will now turn to this question.

The Route of the Separation Fence

33. The focus of this petition is the legality of the route chosen for the construction of the Separation Fence. This question stands on its own, and it requires a straightforward, real answer. It is not sufficient that the Fence be motivated by security considerations, as opposed to political considerations. The military commander is not at liberty to pursue, in the area he holds in belligerent occupation, every activity primarily motivated by security considerations. The discretion of the military commander is restricted by the normative system in which he acts, which is the source of his authority. Indeed, the military commander is not the sovereign in the occupied territory. *See* Oppenheim, *The Legal Relations Between an Occupying Power and the Inhabitants*, 33 Law Q. Rev., 363, 364 (1917); Y. Dinstein, The Law of War 210 (1983). He must act within the law that establishes his authority in a situation of belligerent occupation. What is the content of this law?

34. The law of belligerent occupation recognizes the authority of the military commander to maintain security in the area and to protect the security of his country and her citizens. However, it imposes conditions on the use of this authority. This authority must be properly balanced against the rights, needs, and interests of the local population:

> The law of war usually creates a delicate balance between two poles: military necessity on one hand and humanitarian considerations on the other.

Dinstein, *Legislative Authority in the Administered Territories*, 2 Iyunei Mishpat 505, 509 (1973)

This Court has emphasized, in its case law since the Six Day War, that "together with the right to administer comes the obligation to provide for the well being of the population." HCJ 337/71 *Al-jamaya Al-masihiye L'alararchi Elmakdasa v. Minister of Defense*, at 581 (Sussman, D.P.).

> The obligations and rights of a military administration are defined, on one hand, by its own military needs and, on the other, by the need to ensure, to the extent possible, the normal daily life of the local population.

HCJ 256/72 *Jerusalem District Electric Company v. Defense Minister*, at 138 (Landau, J.).

* * *

35. The approach of this Court is well anchored in the humanitarian law of public international law. This is set forth in Regulation 46 of the Hague Regulations and Article 27 of the Fourth Geneva Convention. Regulation 46 of the Hague Regulations provides:

Family honour and rights, the lives of persons, and private property, as well as religious convictions and practice, must be respected. Private property cannot be confiscated.

Article 27 of the Fourth Geneva Convention provides:

Protected persons are entitled, in all circumstances, to respect for their persons, their honour, their family rights, their religious convictions and practices, and their manners and customs. They shall at all times be humanely treated, and shall be protected especially against all acts of violence or threats thereof.... However, the Parties to the conflict may take such measures of control and security in regard to protected persons as may be necessary as a result of the war.

These rules are founded upon a recognition of the value of man and the sanctity of his life. *See Physicians for Human Rights*, at para. 11. Interpreting Article 27 of the Fourth Geneva Convention, Pictet writes:

Article 27 ... occupies a key position among the articles of the Convention. It is the basis of the Convention, proclaiming as it does the principles on which the whole "Geneva Law" is founded. It proclaims the principle of respect for the human person and the inviolable character of the basic rights of individual men and women ... the right of respect for the person must be understood in its widest sense: it covers all the rights of the individual, that is, the rights and qualities which are inseparable from the human being by the very fact of his existence and his mental and physical powers, it includes, in particular, the right to physical, moral and intellectual integrity—one essential attribute of the human person.

The rules in Regulation 46 of the Hague Regulations and in Article 27 of the Fourth Geneva Convention cast a double obligation upon the military commander: he must refrain from actions that injure the local inhabitants. This is his "negative" obligation. He must take the legally required actions in order to ensure that the local inhabitants shall not be injured. This is his "positive" obligation. *See Physicians for Human Rights*. In addition to these fundamental provisions, there are additional provisions that deal with specifics, such as the seizure of land. *See* Regulation 23(g) and 52 of the Hague Regulations; Article 53 of the Fourth Geneva Convention. These provisions create a single tapestry of norms that recognize both human rights and the needs of the local population as well security needs from the perspective of the military commander. Among these conflicting norms, a proper balance must be found. What is that balance?

Proportionality

36. The problem of balancing security and liberty is not specific to the discretion of a military commander of an area under

belligerent occupation. It is a general problem in the law, both domestic and international. Its solution is universal. It is found deep in the general principles of law, which include reasonableness and good faith. *See* B. Cheng, General Principles of Law as Applied By International Courts and Tribunals (1987); T. Meron, Human Rights and Humanitarian Norms as Customary Law (1989); S. Rosenne, The Perplexities of Modern International Law 63 (2002). One of these foundational principles, which balances the legitimate objective with the means for achieving it, is the principle of proportionality. According to this principle, the liberty of the individual can be limited (in this case, the liberty of the local inhabitants under belligerent occupation), on the condition that the restriction is proportionate. This approach applies to all types of law. In the framework of the petition before us, its importance is twofold: first, it is a basic principle in international law in general and specifically in the law of belligerent occupation; second, it is a central standard in Israeli administrative law, which applies to the area under belligerent occupation. We shall now briefly discuss each of these.

37.   Proportionality is recognized today as a general principle of international law. *See* Meron, at 65; R. Higgins, Problems and Process: International Law and How We Use It 219 (1994); Delbruck, *Proportionality*, 3 Encyclopedia of Public International Law 1140, 1144 (1997). Proportionality plays a central role in the law regarding armed conflict. During such conflicts, there is frequently a need to balance military needs with humanitarian considerations. *See* Gardam, *Proportionality and Force in International Law*, 87 Am. J. Int'l L. 391 (1993); [Gardam], *Legal Restraints on Security Council Military Enforcement Action*, 17 Mich. J. Int'l L. 285 (1996); Dinstein, *Military Necessity*, 3 Encyclopedia of Public International Law 395 (1997); Medenica, *Protocol I and Operation Allied Force: Did NATO Abide by Principles of Proportionality?*, 23 Loy. L. A. Int'l & Comp. L. Rev. 329 (2001); Roberts, *The Laws of War in the War on Terror*, 32 Isr. Yearbook of Hum. Rights. 1999 (2002). Proportionality is a standard for balancing. Pictet writes:

> In modern terms, the conduct of hostilities, and, at all times the maintenance of public order, must not treat with disrespect the irreducible demands of humanitarian law.

> From the foregoing principle springs the Principle of Humanitarian Law (or that of the law of war):

> Belligerents shall not inflict harm on their adversaries out of proportion with the object of warfare, which is to destroy or weaken the strength of the enemy.

J. S. Pictet, Developments and Principles of International Humanitarian Law 62 (1985). Similarly, Fenrick has stated:

[T]here is a requirement for a subordinate rule to perform the balancing function between military and humanitarian requirements. This rule is the rule of proportionality.

Fenrick, *The Rule of Proportionality and Protocol I in Conventional Warfare*, 98 Military L. Rev. 91, 94 (1982). Gasser repeats the same idea:

International humanitarian law takes into account losses and damage as incidental consequences of (lawful) military operations.... The criterion is the principle of proportionality.

Gasser, *Protection of the Civilian Population*, The Handbook of Humanitarian Law in Armed Conflicts 220 (D. Fleck ed., 1995).

* * *

Overview of the Proportionality of the Injury Caused by the Orders

82.   Having completed the examination of the proportionality of each order separately, it is appropriate that we lift our gaze and look out over the proportionality of the entire route of the part of the Separation Fence which is the subject of this petition. The length of the part of the Separation Fence to which these orders apply is approximately forty kilometers. It causes injury to the lives of 35,000 local inhabitants. 4000 dunams of their lands are taken up by the route of the Fence itself, and thousands of olive trees growing along the route itself are uprooted. The Fence separates the eight villages in which the local inhabitants live from more than 30,000 dunams of their lands. The great majority of these lands are cultivated, and they include tens of thousands of olive trees, fruit trees and other agricultural crops. The licensing regime which the military commander wishes to establish cannot prevent or substantially decrease the extent of the severe injury to the local farmers. Access to the lands depends upon the possibility of crossing the gates, which are very distant from each other and not always open. Security checks, which are likely to prevent the passage of vehicles and which will naturally cause long lines and many hours of waiting, will be performed at the gates. These do not go hand in hand with the farmer's ability to work his land. There will inevitably be areas where the Security Fence will have to separate the local inhabitants from their lands. In these areas, the commander should allow passage which will reduce, to the extent possible, the injury to the farmers.

83.   During the hearings, we asked respondent whether it would be possible to compensate petitioners by offering them other lands in exchange for the lands that were taken to build the Fence and the lands that they will be separated from. We did not receive a satisfactory answer. This petition concerns farmers that make their living from the land. Taking petitioners' lands obligates the

respondent, under the circumstances, to attempt to find other lands in exchange for the lands taken from the petitioners. Monetary compensation may only be offered if there are no substitute lands.

84. The injury caused by the Separation Fence is not restricted to the lands of the inhabitants or to their access to these lands. The injury is of far wider scope. It is the fabric of life of the entire population. In many locations, the Separation Fence passes right by their homes. In certain places (like Beit Sourik), the Separation Fence surrounds the village from the west, the south and the east. The Fence directly impedes the access of the local inhabitants to the urban centers (Bir Nabbala and Ramallah). This access is impeded even without the Separation Fence. This difficulty is increased sevenfold by the construction of the Fence.

85. The task of the military commander is not easy. He must delicately balance security needs with the needs of the local inhabitants. We were impressed by the sincere desire of the military commander to find this balance, and his willingness to change the original plan in order to reach a more proportionate solution. We found no stubbornness on his part. Despite all this, we are of the opinion that the balance determined by the military commander is not proportionate. There is no escaping, therefore, a renewed examination of the route of the Fence, according to the standards of proportionality that we have set out.

Epilogue

86. Our task is difficult. We are members of Israeli society. Although we are sometimes in an ivory tower, that tower is in the heart of Jerusalem, which is not infrequently struck by ruthless terror. We are aware of the killing and destruction wrought by terror against the state and its citizens. As any other Israelis, we too recognize the need to defend the country and its citizens against the wounds inflicted by terror. We are aware that in the short term, this judgment will not make the state's struggle against those rising up against it easier. But we are judges. When we sit in judgment, we are subject to judgment. We act according to our best conscience and understanding. Regarding the state's struggle against the terror that rises up against it, we are convinced that at the end of the day, a struggle according to the law will strengthen her power and her spirit. There is no security without law. Satisfying the provisions of the law is an aspect of national security. I discussed this point in HCJ 5100/94 *The Public Committee against Torture in Israel v. The Government of Israel,* at 845:

> We are aware that this decision does make it easier to deal with that reality. This is the destiny of a democracy—she does not see all means as acceptable, and the ways of her enemies are not always open before her. A democracy must sometimes

fight with one arm tied behind her back. Even so, a democracy has the upper hand. The rule of law and individual liberties constitute an important aspect of her security stance. At the end of the day, they strengthen her spirit and this strength allows her to overcome her difficulties.

That goes for this case as well. Only a Separation Fence built on a base of law will grant security to the state and its citizens. Only a separation route based on the path of law will lead the state to the security so yearned for.

* * *

Legal Consequences of the Construction of a Wall in the Occupied Palestinian Territory

2004 I.C.J. (Advisory Opinion (July 9)).

* * *

70.   Palestine was part of the Ottoman Empire. At the end of the First World War, a class "A" Mandate for Palestine was entrusted to Great Britain by the League of Nations, pursuant to paragraph 4 of Article 22 of the Covenant * * *.

* * *

73.   In the 1967 armed conflict, Israeli forces occupied all the territories which had constituted Palestine under British Mandate (including those known as the West Bank, lying to the east of the Green Line).

74.   On 22 November 1967, the Security Council unanimously adopted resolution 242 (1967), which emphasized the inadmissibility of acquisition of territory by war and called for the "Withdrawal of Israel armed forces from territories occupied in the recent conflict", and "Termination of all claims or states of belligerency".

75.   From 1967 onwards, Israel took a number of measures in these territories aimed at changing the status of the City of Jerusalem. The Security Council, after recalling on a number of occasions "the principle that acquisition of territory by military conquest is inadmissible", condemned those measures and, by resolution 298 (1971) of 25 September 1971, confirmed in the clearest possible terms that:

> "all legislative and administrative actions taken by Israel to change the status of the City of Jerusalem, including expropriation of land and properties, transfer of populations and legislation aimed at the incorporation of the occupied section, are totally invalid and cannot change that status".

Later, following the adoption by Israel on 30 July 1980 of the Basic Law making Jerusalem the "complete and united" capital of Israel, the Security Council, by resolution 478 (1980) of 20 August 1980, stated that the enactment of that Law constituted a violation of international law and that "all legislative and administrative measures and actions taken by Israel, the occupying Power, which have altered or purport to alter the character and status of the Holy City of Jerusalem ... are null and void". It further decided "not to recognize the 'basic law' and such other actions by Israel that, as a result of this law, seek to alter the character and status of Jerusalem".

76. Subsequently, a peace treaty was signed on 26 October 1994 between Israel and Jordan. That treaty fixed the boundary between the two States "with reference to the boundary definition under the Mandate as is shown in Annex I (a) ... without prejudice to the status of any territories that came under Israeli military government control in 1967" (Article 3, paragraphs 1 and 2). Annex I provided the corresponding maps and added that, with regard to the "territory that came under Israeli military government control in 1967", the line indicated "is the administrative boundary" with Jordan.

77. Lastly, a number of agreements have been signed since 1993 between Israel and the Palestine Liberation Organization imposing various obligations on each party. Those agreements *inter alia* required Israel to transfer to Palestinian authorities certain powers and responsibilities exercised in the Occupied Palestinian Territory by its military authorities and civil administration. Such transfers have taken place, but, as a result of subsequent events, they remained partial and limited.

78. The Court would observe that, under customary international law as reflected (see paragraph 89 below) in Article 42 of the Regulations Respecting the Laws and Customs of War on Land annexed to the Fourth Hague Convention of 18 October 1907 (hereinafter "the Hague Regulations of 1907"), territory is considered occupied when it is actually placed under the authority of the hostile army, and the occupation extends only to the territory where such authority has been established and can be exercised.

The territories situated between the Green Line * * * and the former eastern boundary of Palestine under the Mandate were occupied by Israel in 1967 during the armed conflict between Israel and Jordan. Under customary international law, these were therefore occupied territories in which Israel had the status of occupying Power. Subsequent events in these territories, as described in paragraphs 75 to 77 above, have done nothing to alter this situation. All these territories (including East Jerusalem) remain occupied territories and Israel has continued to have the status of occupying Power.

* * *

79. It is essentially in these territories that Israel has constructed or plans to construct the works described in the report of the Secretary–General. The Court will now describe those works, basing itself on that report. For developments subsequent to the publication of that report, the Court will refer to complementary information contained in the Written Statement of the United Nations, which was intended by the Secretary–General to supplement his report (hereinafter "Written Statement of the Secretary–General").

80. The report of the Secretary–General states that "The Government of Israel has since 1996 considered plans to halt infiltration into Israel from the central and northern West Bank ..." (Para. 4.) According to that report, a plan of this type was approved for the first time by the Israeli Cabinet in July 2001. Then, on 14 April 2002, the Cabinet adopted a decision for the construction of works, forming what Israel describes as a "security fence", 80 kilometres in length, in three areas of the West Bank.

* * *

81. According to the Written Statement of the Secretary–General, the first part of these works (Phase A), which ultimately extends for a distance of 150 kilometres, was declared completed on 31 July 2003. It is reported that approximately 56,000 Palestinians would be encompassed in enclaves. During this phase, two sections totalling 19.5 kilometres were built around Jerusalem. In November 2003 construction of a new section was begun along the Green Line to the west of the Nazlat Issa–Baqa al-Sharqiya enclave, which in January 2004 was close to completion at the time when the Secretary–General submitted his Written Statement.

* * *

82. According to the description in the report and the Written Statement of the Secretary General, the works planned or completed have resulted or will result in a complex consisting essentially of:

(1) a fence with electronic sensors;

(2) a ditch (up to 4 metres deep);

(3) a two lane asphalt patrol road;

(4) a trace road (a strip of sand smoothed to detect footprints) running parallel to the fence;

(5) a stack of six coils of barbed wire marking the perimeter of the complex.

The complex has a width of 50 to 70 metres, increasing to as much as 100 metres in some places. "Depth barriers" may be added to these works.

The approximately 180 kilometres of the complex completed or under construction as of the time when the Secretary–General submitted his report included some 8.5 kilometres of concrete wall. These are generally found where Palestinian population centres are close to or abut Israel (such as near Qalqiliya and Tulkarm or in parts of Jerusalem).

83. According to the report of the Secretary–General, in its northernmost part, the wall as completed or under construction barely deviates from the Green Line. It nevertheless lies within occupied territories for most of its course. The works deviate more than 7.5 kilometres from the Green Line in certain places to encompass settlements, while encircling Palestinian population areas. A stretch of 1 to 2 kilometres west of Tulkarm appears to run on the Israeli side of the Green Line. Elsewhere, on the other hand, the planned route would deviate eastward by up to 22 kilometres. In the case of Jerusalem, the existing works and the planned route lie well beyond the Green Line and even in some cases beyond the eastern municipal boundary of Jerusalem as fixed by Israel.

84. On the basis of that route, approximately 975 square kilometres (or 16.6 per cent of the West Bank) would, according to the report of the Secretary–General, lie between the Green Line and the wall. This area is stated to be home to 237,000 Palestinians. If the full wall were completed as planned, another 160,000 Palestinians would live in almost completely encircled communities, described as enclaves in the report. As a result of the planned route, nearly 320,000 Israeli settlers (of whom 178,000 in East Jerusalem) would be living in the area between the Green Line and the wall.

* * *

86. The Court will now determine the rules and principles of international law which are relevant in assessing the legality of the measures taken by Israel. Such rules and principles can be found in the United Nations Charter and certain other treaties, in customary international law and in the relevant resolutions adopted pursuant to the Charter by the General Assembly and the Security Council. However, doubts have been expressed by Israel as to the applicability in the Occupied Palestinian Territory of certain rules of international humanitarian law and human rights instruments. The Court will now consider these various questions.

87.   The Court first recalls that, pursuant to Article 2, paragraph 4, of the United Nations Charter:

> "All Members shall refrain in their international relations from the threat or use of force against the territorial integrity or political independence of any State, or in any other manner inconsistent with the Purposes of the United Nations."

On 24 October 1970, the General Assembly adopted resolution 2625 (XXV), entitled "Declaration on Principles of International Law concerning Friendly Relations and Co-operation among States" (hereinafter "resolution 2625 (XXV)"), in which it emphasized that "No territorial acquisition resulting from the threat or use of force shall be recognized as legal." As the Court stated in its Judgment in the case concerning *Military and Paramilitary Activities in and against Nicaragua (Nicaragua v. United States of America)*, the principles as to the use of force incorporated in the Charter reflect customary international law (see *I.C.J. Reports 1986*, pp. 98–101, paras. 187–190); the same is true of its corollary entailing the illegality of territorial acquisition resulting from the threat or use of force.

[The Court then discussed the application of General Assembly Resolution 2625 and its provisions on the right of self-determination as well as various decisions of the Court on the same subject. It next turned to international humanitarian law concluding that the customary international law provisions of the Hague Regulations and the Geneva Civilians Convention apply in the occupied territories.]

89.   As regards international humanitarian law, the Court would first note that Israel is not a party to the Fourth Hague Convention of 1907, to which the Hague Regulations are annexed. The Court observes that, in the words of the Convention, those Regulations were prepared "to revise the general laws and customs of war" existing at that time. Since then, however, the International Military Tribunal of Nuremberg has found that the "rules laid down in the Convention were recognised by all civilised nations, and were regarded as being declaratory of the laws and customs of war" (Judgment of the International Military Tribunal of Nuremberg, 30 September and 1 October 1946, p. 65). The Court itself reached the same conclusion when examining the rights and duties of belligerents in their conduct of military operations (*Legality of the Threat or Use of Nuclear Weapons, Advisory Opinion, I.C.J. Reports 1996 (I)*, p. 256, para. 75). The Court considers that the provisions of the Hague Regulations have become part of customary law, as is in fact recognized by all the participants in the proceedings before the Court.

The Court also observes that, pursuant to Article 154 of the Fourth Geneva Convention, that Convention is supplementary to Sections II and III of the Hague Regulations. Section III of those

Regulations, which concerns "Military authority over the territory of the hostile State", is particularly pertinent in the present case.

90. Secondly, with regard to the Fourth Geneva Convention, differing views have been expressed by the participants in these proceedings. Israel, contrary to the great majority of the other participants, disputes the applicability *de jure* of the Convention to the Occupied Palestinian Territory. In particular, in paragraph 3 of Annex I to the report of the Secretary–General, entitled "Summary Legal Position of the Government of Israel", it is stated that Israel does not agree that the Fourth Geneva Convention "is applicable to the occupied Palestinian Territory", citing "the lack of recognition of the territory as sovereign prior to its annexation by Jordan and Egypt" and inferring that it is "not a territory of a High Contracting Party as required by the Convention".

91. The Court would recall that the Fourth Geneva Convention was ratified by Israel on 6 July 1951 and that Israel is a party to that Convention. Jordan has also been a party thereto since 29 May 1951. Neither of the two States has made any reservation that would be pertinent to the present proceedings.

Furthermore, Palestine gave a unilateral undertaking, by declaration of 7 June 1982, to apply the Fourth Geneva Convention. Switzerland, as depositary State, considered that unilateral undertaking valid. It concluded, however, that it "[was] not—as a depositary—in a position to decide whether" "the request [dated 14 June 1989] from the Palestine Liberation Movement in the name of the 'State of Palestine' to accede" *inter alia* to the Fourth Geneva Convention "can be considered as an instrument of accession".

92. Moreover, for the purpose of determining the scope of application of the Fourth Geneva Convention, it should be recalled that under common Article 2 of the four Conventions of 12 August 1949:

> "In addition to the provisions which shall be implemented in peacetime, the present Convention shall apply to all cases of declared war or of any other armed conflict which may arise between two or more of the High Contracting Parties, even if the state of war is not recognized by one of them.
>
> The Convention shall also apply to all cases of partial or total occupation of the territory of a High Contracting Party, even if the said occupation meets with no armed resistance.
>
> Although one of the Powers in conflict may not be a party to the present Convention, the Powers who are parties thereto shall remain bound by it in their mutual relations. They shall furthermore be bound by the Convention in relation to the said Power, if the latter accepts and applies the provisions thereof."

93.   After the occupation of the West Bank in 1967, the Israeli authorities issued an order No. 3 stating in its Article 35 that:

> "the Military Court ... must apply the provisions of the Geneva Convention dated 12 August 1949 relative to the Protection of Civilian Persons in Time of War with respect to judicial procedures. In case of conflict between this Order and the said Convention, the Convention shall prevail."

Subsequently, the Israeli authorities have indicated on a number of occasions that in fact they generally apply the humanitarian provisions of the Fourth Geneva Convention within the occupied territories. However, according to Israel's position as briefly recalled in paragraph 90 above, that Convention is not applicable *de jure* within those territories because, under Article 2, paragraph 2, it applies only in the case of occupation of territories falling under the sovereignty of a High Contracting Party involved in an armed conflict. Israel explains that Jordan was admittedly a party to the Fourth Geneva Convention in 1967, and that an armed conflict broke out at that time between Israel and Jordan, but it goes on to observe that the territories occupied by Israel subsequent to that conflict had not previously fallen under Jordanian sovereignty. It infers from this that that Convention is not applicable *de jure* in those territories. According however to the great majority of other participants in the proceedings, the Fourth Geneva Convention is applicable to those territories pursuant to Article 2, paragraph 1, whether or not Jordan had any rights in respect thereof prior to 1967.

94.   The Court would recall that, according to customary international law as expressed in Article 31 of the Vienna Convention on the Law of Treaties of 23 May 1969, a treaty must be interpreted in good faith in accordance with the ordinary meaning to be given to its terms in their context and in the light of its object and purpose. Article 32 provides that:

> "Recourse may be had to supplementary means of interpretation, including the preparatory work of the treaty and the circumstances of its conclusion, in order to confirm the meaning resulting from the application of article 31, or to determine the meaning when the interpretation according to article 31 ... leaves the meaning ambiguous or obscure; or ... leads to a result which is manifestly obscure or unreasonable." (See *Oil Platforms (Islamic Republic of Iran v. United States of America), Preliminary Objections, I.C.J. Reports 1996 (II)*, p. 812, para. 23; see, similarly, *Kasikili/Sedudu Island (Botswana/Namibia), I.C.J. Reports 1999 (II)*, p. 1059, para. 18, and *Sovereignty over Pulau Ligitan and Pulau Sipadan (Indonesia/Malaysia), Judgment, I.C.J. Reports 2002*, p. 645, para. 37.)

95. The Court notes that, according to the first paragraph of Article 2 of the Fourth Geneva Convention, that Convention is applicable when two conditions are fulfilled: that there exists an armed conflict (whether or not a state of war has been recognized); and that the conflict has arisen between two contracting parties. If those two conditions are satisfied, the Convention applies, in particular, in any territory occupied in the course of the conflict by one of the contracting parties.

The object of the second paragraph of Article 2 is not to restrict the scope of application of the Convention, as defined by the first paragraph, by excluding therefrom territories not falling under the sovereignty of one of the contracting parties. It is directed simply to making it clear that, even if occupation effected during the conflict met no armed resistance, the Convention is still applicable.

This interpretation reflects the intention of the drafters of the Fourth Geneva Convention to protect civilians who find themselves, in whatever way, in the hands of the occupying Power. Whilst the drafters of the Hague Regulations of 1907 were as much concerned with protecting the rights of a State whose territory is occupied, as with protecting the inhabitants of that territory, the drafters of the Fourth Geneva Convention sought to guarantee the protection of civilians in time of war, regardless of the status of the occupied territories, as is shown by Article 47 of the Convention.

That interpretation is confirmed by the Convention's *travaux préparatoires*. The Conference of Government Experts convened by the International Committee of the Red Cross (hereinafter, "ICRC") in the aftermath of the Second World War for the purpose of preparing the new Geneva Conventions recommended that these conventions be applicable to any armed conflict "whether [it] is or is not recognized as a state of war by the parties" and "in cases of occupation of territories in the absence of any state of war" (*Report on the Work of the Conference of Government Experts for the Study of the Conventions for the Protection of War Victims, Geneva, 14–26 April 1947*, p. 8). The drafters of the second paragraph of Article 2 thus had no intention, when they inserted that paragraph into the Convention, of restricting the latter's scope of application. They were merely seeking to provide for cases of occupation without combat, such as the occupation of Bohemia and Moravia by Germany in 1939.

96. The Court would moreover note that the States parties to the Fourth Geneva Convention approved that interpretation at their Conference on 15 July 1999. They issued a statement in which they "reaffirmed the applicability of the Fourth Geneva Convention to the Occupied Palestinian Territory, including East Jerusalem". Subsequently, on 5 December 2001, the High Contracting Parties, referring in particular to Article 1 of the Fourth Geneva

Convention of 1949, once again reaffirmed the "applicability of the Fourth Geneva Convention to the Occupied Palestinian Territory, including East Jerusalem". They further reminded the Contracting Parties participating in the Conference, the parties to the conflict, and the State of Israel as occupying Power, of their respective obligations.

97. Moreover, the Court would observe that the ICRC, whose special position with respect to execution of the Fourth Geneva Convention must be "recognized and respected at all times" by the parties pursuant to Article 142 of the Convention, has also expressed its opinion on the interpretation to be given to the Convention. In a declaration of 5 December 2001, it recalled that "the ICRC has always affirmed the *de jure* applicability of the Fourth Geneva Convention to the territories occupied since 1967 by the State of Israel, including East Jerusalem".

98. The Court notes that the General Assembly has, in many of its resolutions, taken a position to the same effect. Thus on 10 December 2001 and 9 December 2003, in resolutions 56/60 and 58/97, it reaffirmed "that the Geneva Convention relative to the Protection of Civilian Persons in Time of War, of 12 August 1949, is applicable to the Occupied Palestinian Territory, including East Jerusalem, and other Arab territories occupied by Israel since 1967".

99. The Security Council, for its part, had already on 14 June 1967 taken the view in resolution 237 (1967) that "all the obligations of the Geneva Convention relative to the Treatment of Prisoners of War ... should be complied with by the parties involved in the conflict".

Subsequently, on 15 September 1969, the Security Council, in resolution 271 (1969), called upon "Israel scrupulously to observe the provisions of the Geneva Conventions and international law governing military occupation".

Ten years later, the Security Council examined "the policy and practices of Israel in establishing settlements in the Palestinian and other Arab territories occupied since 1967". In resolution 446 (1979) of 22 March 1979, the Security Council considered that those settlements had "no legal validity" and affirmed "*once more* that the Geneva Convention relative to the Protection of Civilian Persons in Time of War, of 12 August 1949, is applicable to the Arab territories occupied by Israel since 1967, including Jerusalem". It called "*once more upon* Israel, as the occupying Power, to abide scrupulously" by that Convention.

On 20 December 1990, the Security Council, in resolution 681 (1990), urged "the Government of Israel to accept the *de jure* applicability of the Fourth Geneva Convention ... to all the territories occupied by Israel since 1967 and to abide scrupulously by the provisions of the Convention". It further called upon "the high contracting parties to the said Fourth Geneva Convention to ensure respect by Israel, the occupying Power, for its obligations under the Convention in accordance with article 1 thereof".

Lastly, in resolutions 799 (1992) of 18 December 1992 and 904 (1994) of 18 March 1994, the Security Council reaffirmed its position concerning the applicability of the Fourth Geneva Convention in the occupied territories.

100. The Court would note finally that the Supreme Court of Israel, in a judgment dated 30 May 2004, also found that:

> "The military operations of the [Israeli Defence Forces] in Rafah, to the extent they affect civilians, are governed by Hague Convention IV Respecting the Laws and Customs of War on Land 1907 ... and the Geneva Convention Relative to the Protection of Civilian Persons in Time of War 1949."

101. In view of the foregoing, the Court considers that the Fourth Geneva Convention is applicable in any occupied territory in the event of an armed conflict arising between two or more High Contracting Parties. Israel and Jordan were parties to that Convention when the 1967 armed conflict broke out. The Court accordingly finds that that Convention is applicable in the Palestinian territories which before the conflict lay to the east of the Green Line and which, during that conflict, were occupied by Israel, there being no need for any enquiry into the precise prior status of those territories.

* * *

102. The participants in the proceedings before the Court also disagree whether the international human rights conventions to which Israel is party apply within the Occupied Palestinian Territory. Annex I to the report of the Secretary–General states:

> "4. Israel denies that the International Covenant on Civil and Political Rights and the International Covenant on Economic, Social and Cultural Rights, both of which it has signed, are applicable to the occupied Palestinian territory. It asserts that humanitarian law is the protection granted in a conflict situation such as the one in the West Bank and Gaza Strip, whereas human rights treaties were intended for the protection of citizens from their own Government in times of peace."

Of the other participants in the proceedings, those who addressed this issue contend that, on the contrary, both Covenants are applicable within the Occupied Palestinian Territory.

103. On 3 October 1991 Israel ratified both the International Covenant on Economic, Social and Cultural Rights of 19 December 1966 and the International Covenant on Civil and Political Rights

of the same date, as well as the United Nations Convention on the Rights of the Child of 20 November 1989. It is a party to these three instruments.

104.   In order to determine whether these texts are applicable in the Occupied Palestinian Territory, the Court will first address the issue of the relationship between international humanitarian law and human rights law and then that of the applicability of human rights instruments outside national territory.

105.   In its Advisory Opinion of 8 July 1996 on the *Legality of the Threat or Use of Nuclear Weapons*, the Court had occasion to address the first of these issues in relation to the International Covenant on Civil and Political Rights. In those proceedings certain States had argued that "the Covenant was directed to the protection of human rights in peacetime, but that questions relating to unlawful loss of life in hostilities were governed by the law applicable in armed conflict" (*I.C.J. Reports 1996 (I)*, p. 239, para. 24).

The Court rejected this argument, stating that:

> "the protection of the International Covenant of Civil and Political Rights does not cease in times of war, except by operation of Article 4 of the Covenant whereby certain provisions may be derogated from in a time of national emergency. Respect for the right to life is not, however, such a provision. In principle, the right not arbitrarily to be deprived of one's life applies also in hostilities. The test of what is an arbitrary deprivation of life, however, then falls to be determined by the applicable *lex specialis*, namely, the law applicable in armed conflict which is designed to regulate the conduct of hostilities." *(Ibid.*, p. 240, para. 25.)

106.   More generally, the Court considers that the protection offered by human rights conventions does not cease in case of armed conflict, save through the effect of provisions for derogation of the kind to be found in Article 4 of the International Covenant on Civil and Political Rights. As regards the relationship between international humanitarian law and human rights law, there are thus three possible situations: some rights may be exclusively matters of international humanitarian law; others may be exclusively matters of human rights law; yet others may be matters of both these branches of international law. In order to answer the question put to it, the Court will have to take into consideration both these branches of international law, namely human rights law and, as *lex specialis*, international humanitarian law.

107.   It remains to be determined whether the two international Covenants and the Convention on the Rights of the Child are applicable only on the territories of the States parties thereto or

whether they are also applicable outside those territories and, if so, in what circumstances.

108. The scope of application of the International Covenant on Civil and Political Rights is defined by Article 2, paragraph 1, thereof, which provides:

"Each State Party to the present Covenant undertakes to respect and to ensure to all individuals within its territory and subject to its jurisdiction the rights recognized in the present Covenant, without distinction of any kind, such as race, colour, sex, language, religion, political or other opinion, national or social origin, property, birth or other status."

This provision can be interpreted as covering only individuals who are both present within a State's territory and subject to that State's jurisdiction. It can also be construed as covering both individuals present within a State's territory and those outside that territory but subject to that State's jurisdiction. The Court will thus seek to determine the meaning to be given to this text.

109. The Court would observe that, while the jurisdiction of States is primarily territorial, it may sometimes be exercised outside the national territory. Considering the object and purpose of the International Covenant on Civil and Political Rights, it would seem natural that, even when such is the case, States parties to the Covenant should be bound to comply with its provisions.

The constant practice of the Human Rights Committee is consistent with this. Thus, the Committee has found the Covenant applicable where the State exercises its jurisdiction on foreign territory. It has ruled on the legality of acts by Uruguay in cases of arrests carried out by Uruguayan agents in Brazil or Argentina (case No. 52/79, *López Burgos v. Uruguay*; case No. 56/79, *Lilian Celiberti de Casariego v. Uruguay*). It decided to the same effect in the case of the confiscation of a passport by a Uruguayan consulate in Germany (case No. 106/81, *Montero v. Uruguay*).

The *travaux préparatoires* of the Covenant confirm the Committee's interpretation of Article 2 of that instrument. These show that, in adopting the wording chosen, the drafters of the Covenant did not intend to allow States to escape from their obligations when they exercise jurisdiction outside their national territory. They only intended to prevent persons residing abroad from asserting, *vis-à-vis* their State of origin, rights that do not fall within the competence of that State, but of that of the State of residence (see the discussion of the preliminary draft in the Commission on Human Rights, E/CN.4/SR.194, para. 46; and United Nations, *Official Records of the General Assembly, Tenth Session, Annexes*, A/2929, Part II, Chap. V, para. 4 (1955)).

110. The Court takes note in this connection of the position taken by Israel, in relation to the applicability of the Covenant, in its communications to the Human Rights Committee, and of the view of the Committee.

In 1998, Israel stated that, when preparing its report to the Committee, it had had to face the question "whether individuals resident in the occupied territories were indeed subject to Israel's jurisdiction" for purposes of the application of the Covenant (CCPR/C/SR.1675, para. 21). Israel took the position that "the Covenant and similar instruments did not apply directly to the current situation in the occupied territories" (*ibid.*, para. 27).

The Committee, in its concluding observations after examination of the report, expressed concern at Israel's attitude and pointed "to the long-standing presence of Israel in [the occupied] territories, Israel's ambiguous attitude towards their future status, as well as the exercise of effective jurisdiction by Israeli security forces therein" (CCPR/C/79/Add.93, para. 10). In 2003 in face of Israel's consistent position, to the effect that "the Covenant does not apply beyond its own territory, notably in the West Bank and Gaza . . .", the Committee reached the following conclusion:

> "in the current circumstances, the provisions of the Covenant apply to the benefit of the population of the Occupied Territories, for all conduct by the State party's authorities or agents in those territories that affect the enjoyment of rights enshrined in the Covenant and fall within the ambit of State responsibility of Israel under the principles of public international law" (CCPR/CO/78/ISR, para. 11).

111. In conclusion, the Court considers that the International Covenant on Civil and Political Rights is applicable in respect of acts done by a State in the exercise of its jurisdiction outside its own territory.

* * *

113. As regards the Convention on the Rights of the Child of 20 November 1989, that instrument contains an Article 2 according to which "States Parties shall respect and ensure the rights set forth in the . . . Convention to each child within their jurisdiction . . .". That Convention is therefore applicable within the Occupied Palestinian Territory.

* * *

114. Having determined the rules and principles of international law relevant to reply to the question posed by the General Assembly, and having ruled in particular on the applicability within the Occupied Palestinian Territory of international humanitarian law and human rights law, the Court will now seek to ascertain

whether the construction of the wall has violated those rules and principles.

* * *

116.   For its part, Israel has argued that the wall's sole purpose is to enable it effectively to combat terrorist attacks launched from the West Bank. Furthermore, Israel has repeatedly stated that the Barrier is a temporary measure (see report of the Secretary–General, para. 29). It did so *inter alia* through its Permanent Representative to the United Nations at the Security Council meeting of 14 October 2003, emphasizing that "[the fence] does not annex territories to the State of Israel", and that Israel is "ready and able, at tremendous cost, to adjust or dismantle a fence if so required as part of a political settlement" (S/PV.4841, p. 10). Israel's Permanent Representative restated this view before the General Assembly on 20 October and 8 December 2003. On this latter occasion, he added: "As soon as the terror ends, the fence will no longer be necessary. The fence is not a border and has no political significance. It does not change the legal status of the territory in any way." (A/ES–10/PV.23, p. 6.)

* * *

119.   The Court notes that the route of the wall as fixed by the Israeli Government includes within the "Closed Area" (see paragraph 85 above) some 80 per cent of the settlers living in the Occupied Palestinian Territory. Moreover, it is apparent from an examination of the map mentioned in paragraph 80 above that the wall's sinuous route has been traced in such a way as to include within that area the great majority of the Israeli settlements in the occupied Palestinian Territory (including East Jerusalem).

120.   As regards these settlements, the Court notes that Article 49, paragraph 6, of the Fourth Geneva Convention provides: "The Occupying Power shall not deport or transfer parts of its own civilian population into the territory it occupies." That provision prohibits not only deportations or forced transfers of population such as those carried out during the Second World War, but also any measures taken by an occupying Power in order to organize or encourage transfers of parts of its own population into the occupied territory.

In this respect, the information provided to the Court shows that, since 1977, Israel has conducted a policy and developed practices involving the establishment of settlements in the Occupied Palestinian Territory, contrary to the terms of Article 49, paragraph 6, just cited.

The Security Council has thus taken the view that such policy and practices "have no legal validity". It has also called upon "Israel, as the occupying Power, to abide scrupulously" by the Fourth Geneva Convention and:

> "to rescind its previous measures and to desist from taking any action which would result in changing the legal status and geographical nature and materially affecting the demographic composition of the Arab territories occupied since 1967, including Jerusalem and, in particular, not to transfer parts of its own civilian population into the occupied Arab territories" (resolution 446 (1979) of 22 March 1979).

The Council reaffirmed its position in resolutions 452 (1979) of 20 July 1979 and 465 (1980) of 1 March 1980. Indeed, in the latter case it described "Israel's policy and practices of settling parts of its population and new immigrants in [the occupied] territories" as a "flagrant violation" of the Fourth Geneva Convention.

The Court concludes that the Israeli settlements in the Occupied Palestinian Territory (including East Jerusalem) have been established in breach of international law.

121.   Whilst the Court notes the assurance given by Israel that the construction of the wall does not amount to annexation and that the wall is of a temporary nature (see paragraph 116 above), it nevertheless cannot remain indifferent to certain fears expressed to it that the route of the wall will prejudge the future frontier between Israel and Palestine, and the fear that Israel may integrate the settlements and their means of access. The Court considers that the construction of the wall and its associated régime create a "fait accompli" on the ground that could well become permanent, in which case, and notwithstanding the formal characterization of the wall by Israel, it would be tantamount to de facto annexation.

122.   The Court recalls moreover that, according to the report of the Secretary–General, the planned route would incorporate in the area between the Green Line and the wall more than 16 per cent of the territory of the West Bank. Around 80 per cent of the settlers living in the Occupied Palestinian Territory, that is 320,-000 individuals, would reside in that area, as well as 237,000 Palestinians. Moreover, as a result of the construction of the wall, around 160,000 other Palestinians would reside in almost completely encircled communities * * *.

* * *

Section III of the Hague Regulations includes Articles 43, 46 and 52, which are applicable in the Occupied Palestinian Territory. Article 43 imposes a duty on the occupant to "take all measures within his power to restore, and, as far as possible, to insure public order and life, respecting the laws in force in the country". Article 46 adds that private property must be "respected" and that it cannot "be confiscated". Lastly, Article 52 authorizes, within certain limits, requisitions in kind and services for the needs of the army of occupation.

125.   A distinction is also made in the Fourth Geneva Convention between provisions applying during military operations leading to occupation and those that remain applicable throughout the entire period of occupation. It thus states in Article 6:

"The present Convention shall apply from the outset of any conflict or occupation mentioned in Article 2.

In the territory of Parties to the conflict, the application of the present Convention shall cease on the general close of military operations.

In the case of occupied territory, the application of the present Convention shall cease one year after the general close of military operations; however, the Occupying Power shall be bound, for the duration of the occupation, to the extent that such Power exercises the functions of government in such territory, by the provisions of the following Articles of the present Convention: 1 to 12, 27, 29 to 34, 47, 49, 51, 52, 53, 59, 61 to 77, 143.

Protected persons whose release, repatriation or re-establishment may take place after such dates shall meanwhile continue to benefit by the present Convention."

Since the military operations leading to the occupation of the West Bank in 1967 ended a long time ago, only those Articles of the Fourth Geneva Convention referred to in Article 6, paragraph 3, remain applicable in that occupied territory.

126.   These provisions include Articles 47, 49, 52, 53 and 59 of the Fourth Geneva Convention.

* * *

132.   From the information submitted to the Court, particularly the report of the Secretary–General, it appears that the construction of the wall has led to the destruction or requisition of properties under conditions which contravene the requirements of Articles 46 and 52 of the Hague Regulations of 1907 and of Article 53 of the Fourth Geneva Convention.

* * *

151.   Israel accordingly has the obligation to cease forthwith the works of construction of the wall being built by it in the Occupied Palestinian Territory, including in and around East Jerusalem. Moreover, in view of the Court's finding (see paragraph 143 above) that Israel's violations of its international obligations stem from the construction of the wall and from its associated régime, cessa-

tion of those violations entails the dismantling forthwith of those parts of that structure situated within the Occupied Palestinian Territory, including in and around East Jerusalem. All legislative and regulatory acts adopted with a view to its construction, and to the establishment of its associated régime, must forthwith be repealed or rendered ineffective, except in so far as such acts, by providing for compensation or other forms of reparation for the Palestinian population, may continue to be relevant for compliance by Israel with the obligations referred to in paragraph 153 below.

152.   Moreover, given that the construction of the wall in the Occupied Palestinian Territory has, *inter alia*, entailed the requisition and destruction of homes, businesses and agricultural holdings, the Court finds further that Israel has the obligation to make reparation for the damage caused to all the natural or legal persons concerned. The Court would recall that the essential forms of reparation in customary law were laid down by the Permanent Court of International Justice in the following terms:

> "The essential principle contained in the actual notion of an illegal act—a principle which seems to be established by international practice and in particular by the decisions of arbitral tribunals—is that reparation must, as far as possible, wipe out all the consequences of the illegal act and reestablish the situation which would, in all probability, have existed if that act had not been committed. Restitution in kind, or, if this is not possible, payment of a sum corresponding to the value which a restitution in kind would bear; the award, if need be, of damages for loss sustained which would not be covered by restitution in kind or payment in place of it—such are the principles which should serve to determine the amount of compensation due for an act contrary to international law." (*Factory at Chorzów, Merits, Judgment No. 13, 1928, P.C.I.J., Series A, No. 17*, p. 47.)

153.   Israel is accordingly under an obligation to return the land, orchards, olive groves and other immovable property seized from any natural or legal person for purposes of construction of the wall in the Occupied Palestinian Territory. In the event that such restitution should prove to be materially impossible, Israel has an obligation to compensate the persons in question for the damage suffered. The Court considers that Israel also has an obligation to compensate, in accordance with the applicable rules of international law, all natural or legal persons having suffered any form of material damage as a result of the wall's construction.

* * *

154.   The Court will now consider the legal consequences of the internationally wrongful acts flowing from Israel's construction of the wall as regards other States.

155. The Court would observe that the obligations violated by Israel include certain obligations *erga omnes*. As the Court indicated in the *Barcelona Traction* case, such obligations are by their very nature "the concern of all States" and, "In view of the importance of the rights involved, all States can be held to have a legal interest in their protection." (*Barcelona Traction, Light and Power Company, Limited, Second Phase, Judgment, I.C.J. Reports 1970*, p. 32, para. 33.) The obligations *erga omnes* violated by Israel are the obligation to respect the right of the Palestinian people to self-determination, and certain of its obligations under international humanitarian law.

156. As regards the first of these, the Court has already observed * * * that in the *East Timor* case, it described as "irreproachable" the assertion that "the right of peoples to self-determination, as it evolved from the Charter and from United Nations practice, has an *erga omnes* character" (*I.C.J. Reports 1995*, p. 102, para. 29). The Court would also recall that under the terms of General Assembly resolution 2625 (XXV), already mentioned above * * *,

> "Every State has the duty to promote, through joint and separate action, realization of the principle of equal rights and self-determination of peoples, in accordance with the provisions of the Charter, and to render assistance to the United Nations in carrying out the responsibilities entrusted to it by the Charter regarding the implementation of the principle...."

157. With regard to international humanitarian law, the Court recalls that in its Advisory Opinion on the *Legality of the Threat or Use of Nuclear Weapons*, it stated that "a great many rules of humanitarian law applicable in armed conflict are so fundamental to the respect of the human person and 'elementary considerations of humanity' ...", that they are "to be observed by all States whether or not they have ratified the conventions that contain them, because they constitute intransgressible principles of international customary law" (*I.C.J. Reports 1996 (I)*, p. 257, para. 79). In the Court's view, these rules incorporate obligations which are essentially of an *erga omnes* character.

158. The Court would also emphasize that Article 1 of the Fourth Geneva Convention, a provision common to the four Geneva Conventions, provides that "The High Contracting Parties undertake to respect and to ensure respect for the present Convention in all circumstances." It follows from that provision that every State party to that Convention, whether or not it is a party to a specific conflict, is under an obligation to ensure that the requirements of the instruments in question are complied with.

159. Given the character and the importance of the rights and obligations involved, the Court is of the view that all States are under an obligation not to recognize the illegal situation resulting

from the construction of the wall in the Occupied Palestinian Territory, including in and around East Jerusalem. They are also under an obligation not to render aid or assistance in maintaining the situation created by such construction. It is also for all States, while respecting the United Nations Charter and international law, to see to it that any impediment, resulting from the construction of the wall, to the exercise by the Palestinian people of its right to self-determination is brought to an end. In addition, all the States parties to the Geneva Convention relative to the Protection of Civilian Persons in Time of War of 12 August 1949 are under an obligation, while respecting the United Nations Charter and international law, to ensure compliance by Israel with international humanitarian law as embodied in that Convention.

160.   Finally, the Court is of the view that the United Nations, and especially the General Assembly and the Security Council, should consider what further action is required to bring to an end the illegal situation resulting from the construction of the wall and the associated régime, taking due account of the present Advisory Opinion.

C. NOTES, QUESTIONS, AND PROBLEMS

1.   Civilians may defend themselves from the effects of military operations. Such "civil defense" is not considered participation in hostilities and civilians do not lose their protected status for taking part in civil defense. *See*, AP I, art. 61.

2.   Compare the cases of Gen. Galić and Lt. Calley. What is the source of the law the two courts look to? What *mens rea* is required in the two cases? What *mens rea* should be required to convict a soldier of intentionally targeting civilians or persons *hors de combat* during hostilities? Compare the two trials—one international, one national. What are the pros and cons of each type of procedure? Consider the fact that Gen. Galić was sentenced to twenty years in prison. Lt. Calley was originally sentenced to life in prison, but President Richard Nixon reduced that to approximately three years of house arrest.

3.   The trial of Lt. William Calley is most famous as a discussion of superior orders. When should a member of the military disobey a direct superior? When should a superior be held responsible for the acts of those to whom she gives orders? *See* Prosecutor v. Zejnil Delalić (Čelebići Case) Judgment of Nov. 16, 1998, Case No. IT–96–21; Matthew Lippman, *Humanitarian Law: The Uncertain Contours of Command Responsibility*, 9 TULSA J. COMP. & INT'L L. 1 (2001).

4.   Compare the two excerpts on NATO's bombing of the RTS television station in 1999. Do the two differ in any significant ways regarding the substantive law applicable to the incident? Is it on the basis of the applicable law that the authors reach such different conclusions or the application of the law? Which conclusion is more persuasive to you?

5. The Report to the ICTY prosecutor on NATO bombing in Yugoslavia is highly controversial. NATO countries were incensed that the prosecutor would look into the legality of their actions. On the other hand, independent academics have pointed out that the investigating commission lacked neutrality. All members of the commission but one came from NATO countries. The chair and deputy chair were retired members of the Canadian and US armed forces, respectively. *See* Anthony J. Colangelo, *Manipulating International Criminal Procedure: The Decision of the ICTY Office of the Independent Prosecutor Not to Investigate NATO Bombing in the Former Yugoslavia*, 97 Nw. U. L. Rev. 1393 (2003). What do you think? Is it at least noteworthy that some attempt was made to hold the purported victors in Yugoslavia to account? Recall the aftermath of the First and Second World War where only the vanquished were tried.

In addition to international judicial proceedings and national criminal trials, like Lt. Calley's (pp. 452–462) and national public law cases like Beit Sourik Village Council (pp. 488–500) some national civil trials have occurred in which victims of IHL violations have sought money damages. One of the best known such cases is *Kadic v. Karadžić*, 70 F.3d 232 (2d Cir. 1995), *cert. denied*, 518 U.S. 1005 (1996), in which Bosnian victims sued the leader of the Bosnian Serbs. They won a very sizable judgment but are unable to collect it.

6. NATO countries are among the wealthiest in the world. Yugoslavia, as a result of the years of armed conflict and break-up into mini-states became one of the poorest. Should a state's wealth affect its obligations under the *jus in bello*? Should wealthier states with more advanced technology be held to a higher standard than poorer ones? Does wealth not became part of the calculus of necessity and proportionality? Is it not part of the calculus of assessing good faith efforts to comply with these and other principles of the *jus in bello*?

7. Compare Israel's High Court of Justice decision respecting the security structure (or wall) and the ICJ advisory opinion. Do the two opinions analyze the applicable law consistently? Can you explain the different outcome based on findings of law or the application of law to fact? Which opinion is more persuasive? Both cases discuss the occupying power's responsibility to the civilian population. What are the obligations of the civilian population toward the occupying power, if any? If persons in occupied territory take up arms to oppose the occupying power, can they qualify for POW status? If they do not, what rules do apply to their detention? *See* Note 11 below on p. 521.

8. The ICJ's Wall Case is an advisory opinion, meaning it is not binding on Israel in the same way that an order of the Court would be in a contentious case between two states. On the other hand, can Israel ignore the Advisory Opinion? Israel filed a lengthy document in the case urging the ICJ not to take jurisdiction. It decided not to participate in the hearings. Why might a party, especially one disputing jurisdiction, decide to participate in only a limited way in a case? What are the risks of such a strategy? See the decision of the ICJ as to jurisdiction at the Court's website: www.icj-cij.org.

9. Occupation is meant to be a temporary situation, and, yet, Israel has been in occupation of certain Palestinian territory since 1967. Do the rules applicable to occupation make sense to you for long-term situations like this one? Should a different set of rules be developed for these cases? Suggest some new rules for long-term occupation not found in the existing law. What are the dangers of developing new rules for long-term occupation or any aspects of hostilities and occupation? *See* Adam Roberts, *Prolonged Military Occupation: The Israeli–Occupied Territories Since* 1967, 84 Am. J. Int'l L. 44 (1990).

10. For a discussion of the rules applicable to controlling violence during an occupation, see, Kenneth Watkin, *Controlling the Use of Force: A Role for Human Rights Norms in Contemporary Armed Conflict*, 98 Am. J. Int'l L. 1, 26–28 (2004). For a discussion of other issues regarding administration of occupation, see David J. Scheffer, *Beyond Occupation Law*, 97 Am. J. Int'l L. 872 (2003).

11. An Occupying Power may detain civilians as an exercise of its authority. The first and most basic requirement of lawful confinement is that no one be detained except for the reasons set out in the Convention in particular in Articles 42–43, 68–71 and 75. These provisions have been summarized by Sassòli. Under the Fourth Geneva Convention:

> Protected civilians may be detained only for two reasons: first, under domestic legislation for the prosecution and punishment of criminal offenses (including for direct participation in hostilities); second, civilians may be interned for imperative security reasons, upon individual decision made in a regular procedure, which has to be prescribed by the belligerent concerned, and must include a right of appeal. Such civilians are civil internees whose treatment is governed by extremely detailed provisions of Convention IV and whose cases must be reviewed every six months.

Marco Sassòli, *Use and Abuse of the Laws of War in the "War on Terrorism,"* 22 Law & Ineq. 195, 206 (2004). In other words, everyone except a prisoner of war under the Third Geneva Convention is owed some form of legal review of confinement, whether the limited review of internee status or the rights of full and fair trial for those accused of crimes.

12. Arguably the targeting rules discussed in this Chapter apply to international and non-international armed conflicts alike. Or do you see a basis for applying different rules for the two types of conflicts? By contrast, the occupation rules do not apply in non-international armed conflict. Or, again, do you see a basis for applying at least some of them? *See* Lindsay Moir, The Law of Internal Armed Conflict 2002.

13. Problem: During the Gulf War, coalition forces decided to bomb electricity production facilities in Iraq. Their reasons for doing so were multiple: electricity played a key role in military operations. It was essential to the operation of radar sites used to warn Iraq of incoming Coalition air attacks; it was used to operate Iraq's air defense system; it powered computers essential to military command, control and communication; it powered refrigeration of biological weapons, and it powered nuclear weapon production facilities. Electricity was also key to Iraq's industry. Coalition planners also feared Iraq would pump oil into fire trenches in southern Iraq as a defense to a Coalition ground attack. Electricity was needed to operate oil pumps. *See* Michael W. Lewis, *The Law of Aerial Bombardment in the 1991 Gulf War*, 97 AM. J. INT'L L. 481, 495–506 (2003).

Coalition planners determined that to prevent these military uses, all of Iraq's electricity production would need to be targeted. As a result of the targeting, Iraq was left at the end of the war with 15% of its pre-war electricity. Water purification and sewage treatment plants were shut down leading to deaths among the civilian population ranging between 40,000 and 110,000 persons. *Id.* at 504. Planners had determined that facilities should only be bombed in a way that shut them down but allowed fairly easy repair. This determination, however, did not reach wing commanders until several weeks after the campaign began. Commanders chose targets easy to hit, like generator halls, but hard to repair. The damage was greater than intended by planners and the resulting deaths and suffering by civilians was greater, too. CONDUCT OF THE PERSIAN GULF WAR, FINAL REPORT TO CONGRESS 180 (April 1992).

Did the planners violate any *in bello* rules? Did the wing commanders?

CHAPTER ELEVEN

Combatants

While civilians and civilian objects may not be attacked, combatants and military objects may be targeted. This Chapter may appear like the mirror image of the previous one. Combatants and military objects are defined in distinction to civilians and civilian objects. Combatants are generally members of the armed forces of a party to a conflict or persons taking active part in hostilities. They are not civilians. Military objects are "those objects which by their nature, location, purpose or use make an effective contribution to military action and whose total or partial destruction, capture or neutralization, in the circumstances ruling at the time, offers a definite military advantage."[1] Even as to lawful targets, however, restraints apply.

Two large categories of restraints are found in first, the limits on means and methods of warfare, and, second in the requirements respecting the treatment of combatants no longer taking an active part in hostilities. "Means and methods of warfare" refers to the types of weapons and tactics employed to defeat the enemy. A core principle of IHL is that the means and methods of warfare are not unlimited. There are a variety of specific rules that limit means and methods, some of which we will see below. In addition to specific rules, general principles apply to the conduct of hostilities, such as the prohibition on causing unnecessary suffering and the principles of discrimination, necessity and proportionality. Another major category of combatant protection is the prohibition on targeting combatants who are no longer taking an active part in hostilities. Combatants may be targeted "but only so long as they are capable of fighting, willing to fight or resist capture. Once incapable in this sense, so *hors de combat*, they are immune from attack, but may be taken prisoner."[2] Once taken prisoner, combatants have other rights.

In this Chapter we consider in more detail the definition of combatant and the various categories of combatants. We also consider procedures that should be employed when a detaining power is uncertain as to whether an individual is a combatant or civilian, and if a combatant, whether a combatant deserving prisoner-of-war status or not. We also take up the rules and principles as to the lawful conditions of detention for prisoners-of-war and other detained persons. The final section of the Chapter returns to the topic of command responsibility.

---

1. AP I, art. 52(2).

2. L.C. Green, The Contemporary Law of Armed Conflict 124–125 (2d ed., 2000).

A. Combatant Status and Detention

Only a combatant may be targeted and detained without any further grounds than his status. Thus, the determination of this status is a key aspect of the *jus in bello*. Review the Calley and Galić cases in Chapter Ten for examples of the need to distinguish on the battlefield between combatants and civilians. The excerpts that follow concern determining the combatant status of individuals in custody. The excerpts provide both indications of the substantive definition of a combatant as well as procedures for determining combatant status in unclear cases.

Hamdi v. Rumsfeld

Supreme Court of the United States, 2004.
542 U.S. ___ (2004).

> Justice O'Connor announced the judgment of the Court and delivered an opinion, in which The Chief Justice, Justice Kennedy, and Justice Breyer join.
>
> At this difficult time in our Nation's history, we are called upon to consider the legality of the Government's detention of a United States citizen on United States soil as an "enemy combatant" and to address the process that is constitutionally owed to one who seeks to challenge his classification as such. The United States Court of Appeals for the Fourth Circuit held that petitioner's detention was legally authorized and that he was entitled to no further opportunity to challenge his enemy-combatant label. We now vacate and remand. We hold that although Congress authorized the detention of combatants in the narrow circumstances alleged here, due process demands that a citizen held in the United States as an enemy combatant be given a meaningful opportunity to contest the factual basis for that detention before a neutral decisionmaker.
>
> On September 11, 2001, the I al Qaeda terrorist network used hijacked commercial airliners to attack prominent targets in the United States. Approximately 3,000 people were killed in those attacks. One week later, in response to these "acts of treacherous violence," Congress passed a resolution authorizing the President to "use all necessary and appropriate force against those nations, organizations, or persons he determines planned, authorized, committed, or aided the terrorist attacks" or "harbored such organizations or persons, in order to prevent any future acts of international terrorism against the United States by such nations, organizations or persons." Authorization for Use of Military Force ("the AUMF"), 115 Stat. 224. Soon thereafter, the President ordered United States Armed Forces to Afghanistan, with a mission to subdue al Qaeda and quell the Taliban regime that was known to support it.

This case arises out of the detention of a man whom the Government alleges took up arms with the Taliban during this conflict. His name is Yaser Esam Hamdi. Born an American citizen in Louisiana in 1980, Hamdi moved with his family to Saudi Arabia as a child. By 2001, the parties agree, he resided in Afghanistan. At some point that year, he was seized by members of the Northern Alliance, a coalition of military groups opposed to the Taliban government, and eventually was turned over to the United States military. The Government asserts that it initially detained and interrogated Hamdi in Afghanistan before transferring him to the United States Naval Base in Guantanamo Bay in January 2002. In April 2002, upon learning that Hamdi is an American citizen, authorities transferred him to a naval brig in Norfolk, Virginia, where he remained until a recent transfer to a brig in Charleston, South Carolina. The Government contends that Hamdi is an "enemy combatant," and that this status justifies holding him in the United States indefinitely—without formal charges or proceedings—unless and until it makes the determination that access to counsel or further process is warranted.

In June 2002, Hamdi's father, Esam Fouad Hamdi, filed the present petition for a writ of habeas corpus under 28 U.S.C. § 2241 in the Eastern District of Virginia, naming as petitioners his son and himself as next friend. * * * Although his habeas petition provides no details with regard to the factual circumstances surrounding his son's capture and detention, Hamdi's father has asserted in documents found elsewhere in the record that his son went to Afghanistan to do "relief work," and that he had been in that country less than two months before September 11, 2001, and could not have received military training. *Id.*, at 188–189. The 20–year-old was traveling on his own for the first time, his father says, and "[b]ecause of his lack of experience, he was trapped in Afghanistan once that military campaign began." *Id.*, at 188–189.

The District Court found that Hamdi's father was a proper next friend, appointed the federal public defender as counsel for the petitioners, and ordered that counsel be given access to Hamdi. *Id.*, at 113–116. The United States Court of Appeals for the Fourth Circuit reversed that order, holding that the District Court had failed to extend appropriate deference to the Government's security and intelligence interests. 296 F.3d 278, 279, 283 (2002). It directed the District Court to consider "the most cautious procedures first," *Id.*, at 284, and to conduct a deferential inquiry into Hamdi's status, *Id.*, at 283. It opined that "if Hamdi is indeed an 'enemy combatant' who was captured during hostilities in Afghanistan, the government's present detention of him is a lawful one." *Ibid.*

On remand, the Government filed a response and a motion to dismiss the petition. It attached to its response a declaration from one Michael Mobbs (hereinafter "Mobbs Declaration"), who identified himself as Special Advisor to the Under Secretary of Defense for Policy. Mobbs indicated that in this position, he has been "substantially involved with matters related to the detention of enemy combatants in the current war against the al Qaeda terrorists and those who support and harbor them (including the Taliban)." App. 148. He expressed his "familiar[ity]" with Department of Defense and United States military policies and procedures applicable to the detention, control, and transfer of al Qaeda and Taliban personnel, and declared that "[b]ased upon my review of relevant records and reports, I am also familiar with the facts and circumstances related to the capture of . . . Hamdi and his detention by U.S. military forces." *Ibid.*

Mobbs then set forth what remains the sole evidentiary support that the Government has provided to the courts for Hamdi's detention. The declaration states that Hamdi "traveled to Afghanistan" in July or August 2001, and that he thereafter "affiliated with a Taliban military unit and received weapons training." *Ibid.* It asserts that Hamdi "remained with his Taliban unit following the attacks of September 11" and that, during the time when Northern Alliance forces were "engaged in battle with the Taliban," "Hamdi's Taliban unit surrendered" to those forces, after which he "surrender[ed] his Kalishnikov assault rifle" to them. *Id.*, at 148–149. The Mobbs Declaration also states that, because al Qaeda and the Taliban "were and are hostile forces engaged in armed conflict with the armed forces of the United States," "individuals associated with" those groups "were and continue to be enemy combatants." *Id.*, at 149. Mobbs states that Hamdi was labeled an enemy combatant "[b]ased upon his interviews and in light of his association with the Taliban." *Ibid.* According to the declaration, a series of "U.S. military screening team[s]" determined that Hamdi met "the criteria for enemy combatants," and "a subsequent interview of Hamdi has confirmed that he surrendered and gave his firearm to Northern Alliance forces, which supports his classification as an enemy combatant." *Id.*, at 149–150.

After the Government submitted this declaration, the Fourth Circuit directed the District Court to proceed in accordance with its earlier ruling and, specifically, to " 'consider the sufficiency of the Mobbs Declaration as an independent matter before proceeding further.' " 316 F.3d at 450, 462 (C.A.4 2003). The District Court found that the Mobbs Declaration fell "far short" of supporting Hamdi's detention. App. 292. It criticized the generic and hearsay nature of the affidavit, calling it "little more than the government's 'say-so.'" *Id.*, at 298. It ordered the Government to turn over numerous materials for *in camera* review.

* * *

II

The threshold question before us is whether the Executive has the authority to detain citizens who qualify as "enemy combatants." There is some debate as to the proper scope of this term, and the Government has never provided any court with the full criteria that it uses in classifying individuals as such. It has made clear, however, that, for purposes of this case, the "enemy combatant" that it is seeking to detain is an individual who, it alleges, was "'part of or supporting forces hostile to the United States or coalition partners'" in Afghanistan and who "'engaged in an armed conflict against the United States'" there. Brief for Respondents 3. We therefore answer only the narrow question before us: whether the detention of citizens falling within that definition is authorized. * * *

The capture and detention of lawful combatants and the capture, detention, and trial of unlawful combatants, by "universal agreement and practice," are "important incident[s] of war." *Ex parte Quirin*, 317 U.S., at 28, 63 S.Ct. 2. The purpose of detention is to prevent captured individuals from returning to the field of battle and taking up arms once again. Naqvi, Doubtful Prisoner-of-War Status, 84 Int'l Rev. Red Cross 571, 572 (2002) ("[C]aptivity in war is 'neither revenge, nor punishment, but solely protective custody, the only purpose of which is to prevent the prisoners of war from further participation in the war'") (quoting decision of Nuremberg Military Tribunal, reprinted in 41 Am. J. Int'l L. 172, 229 (1947)); W. Winthrop, Military Law and Precedents 788 (rev. 2d ed. 1920) ("The time has long passed when 'no quarter' was the rule on the battlefield.... It is now recognized that 'Captivity is neither a punishment nor an act of vengeance,' but 'merely a temporary detention which is devoid of all penal character.' ... 'A prisoner of war is no convict; his imprisonment is a simple war measure.'" (citations omitted)); cf. *In re Territo*, 156 F.2d 142, 145 (C.A.9 1946) ("The object of capture is to prevent the captured individual from serving the enemy. He is disarmed and from then on must be removed as completely as practicable from the front, treated humanely, and in time exchanged, repatriated, or otherwise released" (footnotes omitted)).

There is no bar to this Nation's holding one of its own citizens as an enemy combatant. In *Quirin*, one of the detainees, Haupt, alleged that he was a naturalized United States citizen. 317 U.S., at 20, 63 S.Ct. 2. We held that "[c]itizens who associate themselves with the military arm of the enemy government, and with its aid, guidance and direction enter this country bent on hostile acts, are enemy belligerents within the meaning of . . . the law of war." *Id.*, at 37–38, 63 S.Ct. 2. While Haupt was tried for violations of the law of war, nothing in Quirin suggests that his citizenship would have precluded his mere detention for the duration of the relevant hostilities. See *Id.*, at 30–31, 63 S.Ct. 2. See also Lieber Code, ¶ 153, Instructions for the Government of Armies of the United States in the Field, Gen. Order No. 100 (1863), reprinted in 2 Lieber, Miscellaneous Writings, p. 273 (contemplating, in code binding the Union Army during the Civil War, that "captured rebels" would be treated "as prisoners of war"). Nor can we see any reason for drawing such a line here. A citizen, no less than an alien, can be "part of or supporting forces hostile to the United States or coalition partners" and "engaged in an armed conflict against the United States," Brief for Respondents 3; such a citizen, if released, would pose the same threat of returning to the front during the ongoing conflict.

* * *

[The Court's discussion of when detention must end is included in Part C below.]

* * *

III

Even in cases in which the detention of enemy combatants is legally authorized, there remains the question of what process is constitutionally due to a citizen who disputes his enemy-combatant status. Hamdi argues that he is owed a meaningful and timely hearing and that "extra-judicial detention [that] begins and ends with the submission of an affidavit based on third-hand hearsay" does not comport with the Fifth and Fourteenth Amendments. Brief for Petitioners 16. The Government counters that any more process than was provided below would be both unworkable and "constitutionally intolerable." Brief for Respondents 46. Our resolution of this dispute requires a careful examination both of the writ of habeas corpus, which Hamdi now seeks to employ as a mechanism of judicial review, and of the Due Process Clause, which informs the procedural contours of that mechanism in this instance.

* * *

First, the Government urges the adoption of the Fourth Circuit's holding below—that because it is "undisputed" that Hamdi's seizure took place in a combat zone, the habeas determination can be made purely as a matter of law, with no further hearing or factfinding necessary. This argument is easily rejected. * * * Under the definition of enemy combatant that we accept today as falling within the scope of Congress' authorization, Hamdi would need to be "part of or supporting forces hostile to the United States or coalition partners" and "engaged in an armed conflict against the United States" to justify his detention in the United States for the duration of the relevant conflict. Brief for Respondents 3. The habeas petition states only that "[w]hen seized by the United States Government, Mr. Hamdi resided in Afghanistan." App. 104. An assertion that one resided in a country in which combat operations are taking place is not a concession that one was "*captured* in a zone of active combat operations in a foreign theater of war," 316 F.3d, at 459 (emphasis added), and certainly is not a concession that one was "part of or supporting forces hostile to the United States or coalition partners" and "engaged in an armed conflict against the United States." Accordingly, we reject any argument that Hamdi has made concessions that eliminate any right to further process.

* * *

We * * * hold that a citizen-detainee seeking to challenge his classification as an enemy combatant must receive notice of the factual basis for his classification, and a fair opportunity to rebut the Government's factual assertions before a neutral decisionmaker. See *Cleveland Bd. of Ed. v. Loudermill*, 470 U.S. 532, 542, 105 S.Ct. 1487, 84 L.Ed.2d 494 (1985) ("An essential principle of due process is that a deprivation of life, liberty, or property 'be preceded by notice and opportunity for hearing appropriate to the nature of the case' ") (quoting *Mullane v. Central Hanover Bank & Trust Co.*, 339 U.S. 306, 313, 70 S.Ct. 652, 94 L.Ed. 865 (1950)); *Concrete Pipe & Products of Cal., Inc. v. Construction Laborers Pension Trust for Southern Cal.*, 508 U.S. 602, 617, 113 S.Ct. 2264, 124 L.Ed.2d 539 (1993) ("due process requires a 'neutral and detached judge in the first instance' ") (quoting *Ward v. Monroeville*, 409 U.S. 57, 61–62, 93 S.Ct. 80, 34 L.Ed.2d 267 (1972)). "For more than a century the central meaning of procedural due process has been clear: 'Parties whose rights are to be affected are entitled to be heard; and in order that they may enjoy that right they must first be notified.' It is equally fundamental that the right to notice and an opportunity to be heard 'must be granted at a meaningful time and in a meaningful manner.' " *Fuentes v. Shevin*, 407 U.S. 67, 80, 92 S.Ct. 1983, 32 L.Ed.2d 556 (1972) (quoting *Baldwin v. Hale*, 1 Wall. 223, 233, 17 L.Ed. 531 (1864); *Armstrong v. Manzo*, 380 U.S. 545, 552, 85 S.Ct. 1187, 14 L.Ed.2d 62 (1965) (other citations omitted)). These essential constitutional promises may not be eroded.

At the same time, the exigencies of the circumstances may demand that, aside from these core elements, enemy combatant proceedings may be tailored to alleviate their uncommon potential to burden the Executive at a time of ongoing military conflict. Hearsay, for example, may need to be accepted as the most reliable available evidence from the Government in such a proceeding. Likewise, the Constitution would not be offended by a presumption in favor of the Government's evidence, so long as that presumption remained a rebuttable one and fair opportunity for rebuttal were provided. Thus, once the Government puts forth credible evidence that the habeas petitioner meets the enemy-combatant criteria, the onus could shift to the petitioner to rebut that evidence with more persuasive evidence that he falls outside the criteria. A burden-shifting scheme of this sort would meet the goal of ensuring that the errant tourist, embedded journalist, or local aid worker has a chance to prove military error while giving due regard to the Executive once it has put forth meaningful support for its conclusion that the detainee is in fact an enemy combatant. In the words of *Mathews*, process of this sort would sufficiently address the "risk of erroneous deprivation" of a detainee's liberty interest while eliminating certain procedures that have questionable additional value in light of the burden on the Government. 424 U.S., at 335, 96 S.Ct. 893.[a]

We think it unlikely that this basic process will have the dire impact on the central functions of warmaking that the Government forecasts. The parties agree that initial captures on the battlefield need not receive the process we have discussed here; that process is due only when the determination is made to *continue* to hold those who have been seized. The Government has made clear in its briefing that documentation regarding battlefield detainees already is kept in the ordinary course of military affairs. Brief for Respondents 3–4. Any factfinding imposition created by requiring a knowledgeable affiant to summarize these records to an independent tribunal is a minimal one. Likewise, arguments that military officers ought not have to wage war under the threat of litigation lose much of their steam when factual disputes at enemy-combatant hearings are limited to the alleged combatant's acts. This focus meddles little, if at all, in the strategy or conduct of war, inquiring only into the appropriateness of continuing to detain an individual claimed to have taken up arms against the United States. While we accord the greatest respect and consideration to the judgments of military authorities in matters relating to the actual prosecution of a war, and recognize that the scope of that discretion necessarily is wide, it does not infringe on the core role of the military for the courts to exercise their own time-honored and constitutionally mandated roles of reviewing and resolving claims like those presented here. Cf. *Korematsu v. United States*, 323 U.S. 214, 233–234, 65 S.Ct. 193, 89 L.Ed. 194 (1944) (Murphy, J., dissenting) ("[L]ike other claims conflicting with the

a. Because we hold that Hamdi is constitutionally entitled to the process described above, we need not address at this time whether any treaty guarantees him similar access to a tribunal for a determination of his status.

asserted constitutional rights of the individual, the military claim must subject itself to the judicial process of having its reasonableness determined and its conflicts with other interests reconciled"); *Sterling v. Constantin*, 287 U.S. 378, 401, 53 S.Ct. 190, 77 L.Ed. 375 (1932) ("What are the allowable limits of military discretion, and whether or not they have been overstepped in a particular case, are judicial questions").

In sum, while the full protections that accompany challenges to detentions in other settings may prove unworkable and inappropriate in the enemy-combatant setting, the threats to military operations posed by a basic system of independent review are not so weighty as to trump a citizen's core rights to challenge meaningfully the Government's case and to be heard by an impartial adjudicator.

* * *

There remains the possibility that the standards we have articulated could be met by an appropriately authorized and properly constituted military tribunal. Indeed, it is notable that military regulations already provide for such process in related instances, dictating that tribunals be made available to determine the status of enemy detainees who assert prisoner-of-war status under the Geneva Convention. See Enemy Prisoners of War, Retained Personnel, Civilian Internees and Other Detainees, Army Regulation 190–8, § 1–6 (1997). In the absence of such process, however, a court that receives a petition for a writ of habeas corpus from an alleged enemy combatant must itself ensure that the minimum requirements of due process are achieved.

* * *

The judgment of the United States Court of Appeals for the Fourth Circuit is vacated, and the case is remanded for further proceedings.

It is so ordered.

Memorandum
To: Members of the ASIL–CFR Roundtable
From: William J. Haynes II, General Counsel of the Department of Defense
Subject: Enemy Combatants*

There is no doubt that the attacks of September 11, 2001 constituted acts of war. They possessed the intensity and scale of war.

---

* http://cfr.org/publication_print.php?id=5312 (Dec. 12, 2002).

They involved at least one military target, the Pentagon, and they came on the heels of a decade of attacks by al Qaida on U.S. military and civilian targets. Congress on September 18, 2001 authorized the President to use force in response to the attacks. And both the United Nations and NATO recognized that the attacks were "armed attacks" within the meaning of the UN Charter and NATO treaty. Since September 11th (and perhaps before then), we have been at war—both legally and in fact.

War implies legal powers and rules that are not available during peacetime. Among other things, the war context gives the President the authority to detain enemy combatants at least until hostilities cease.

Enemy Combatant

An "enemy combatant" is an individual who, under the laws and customs of war, may be detained for the duration of an armed conflict. In the current conflict with al Qaida and the Taliban, the term includes a member, agent, or associate of al Qaida or the Taliban. In applying this definition, the United States government has acted consistently with the observation of the Supreme Court of the United States in Ex parte Quirin, 317 U.S. 1, 37–38 (1942): "Citizens who associate themselves with the military arm of the enemy government, and with its aid, guidance and direction enter this country bent on hostile acts are enemy belligerents within the meaning of the Hague Convention and the law of war."

"Enemy combatant" is a general category that subsumes two sub-categories: lawful and unlawful combatants. See Quirin, 317 U.S. at 37–38. Lawful combatants receive prisoner of war (POW) status and the protections of the Third Geneva Convention. Unlawful combatants do not receive POW status and do not receive the full protections of the Third Geneva Convention. (The treatment accorded to unlawful combatants is discussed below).

The President has determined that al Qaida members are unlawful combatants because (among other reasons) they are members of a non-state actor terrorist group that does not receive the protections of the Third Geneva Convention. He additionally determined that the Taliban detainees are unlawful combatants because they do not satisfy the criteria for POW status set out in Article 4 of the Third Geneva Convention. Although the President's determination on this issue is final, courts have concurred with his determination.

Authority to Detain

The President has unquestioned authority to detain enemy combatants, including those who are U.S. citizens, during wartime. See, e.g., Quirin, 317 U.S. at 31, 37 (1942); Colepaugh v. Looney, 235 F.2d 429, 432 (10th Cir. 1956); In re Territo, 156 F.2d 142,

145 (9th Cir. 1946). The Fourth Circuit recently reaffirmed this proposition. See Hamdi v. Rumsfeld, 296 F.3d 278, 281, 283 (4th Cir. 2002). The authority to detain enemy combatants flows primarily from Article II of the Constitution. In the current conflict, the President's authority is bolstered by Congress's Joint Resolution of September 18, 2001, which authorized "the President ... to use all necessary and appropriate force" against al Qaida and against those nations, organizations, or persons he determines "committed or aided in the September 11 attacks." Pub. L. No. 107–40, § 2(a), 115 Stat. 224 (2001) * * *. This congressional action clearly triggers (if any trigger were necessary) the President's traditional authority to detain enemy combatants as Commander in Chief.

Presidents (and their delegates) have detained enemy combatants in every major conflict in the Nation's history, including recent conflicts such as the Gulf, Vietnam, and Korean wars. During World War II, the United States detained hundreds of thousands of POWs in the United States (some of whom were U.S. citizens) without trial or counsel. Then as now, the purposes of detaining enemy combatants during wartime are, among other things, to gather intelligence and to ensure that detainees do not return to assist the enemy.

Who Decides

The determination of enemy combatant status has traditionally resided with the military commander who is authorized to engage the enemy with deadly force. In this regard, the task ultimately falls within the President's constitutional responsibility as Commander in Chief to identify which forces and persons to engage or capture and detain during an armed conflict. Of course, there is no requirement that the President make such determinations personally, and in the vast majority of cases he does not do so. Rather, consistent with longstanding historical practice and applicable rules of engagement, the task is normally a function of the military command structure.

In the current conflict, military personnel ordinarily make enemy combatant determinations during combat operations, under the combatant commander's direction. With respect to individuals captured in the United States, to date DoD has detained only Abdullah al Muhajir, also known as Jose Padilla. The President, as Commander in Chief, determined that Mr. Padilla is an enemy combatant.

Detainee Rights

All of the detainees are unlawful combatants and thus do not as a matter of law receive the protections of the Third Geneva Convention. However, the United States armed forces are treating, and will continue to treat, all enemy combatants humanely and, to the extent appropriate and consistent with military necessity, in a manner consistent with the principles of the Third Geneva Convention of 1949. Among many other things, this means that they receive: three meals a day that meet Muslim dietary laws; medical care; clothing and shoes; shelter; showers; soap and toilet articles; the opportunity to worship; the means to send mail and receive mail, subject to security screening; and the ability to receive packages of food and clothing, also subject to security screening. In addition, the International Committee of the Red Cross has visited and will continue to visit the detainees privately. The detainees will be permitted to raise concerns about their conditions, and we will attempt to address those concerns consistent with security.

The non-citizen detainees in Guantanamo have no right to habeas corpus relief in U.S. courts. See, e.g., Coalition of Clergy v. Bush, 189 F. Supp.2d 1036 (C.D. Cal. 2002), affirmed on other grounds, 310 F.3d 1153 (9th Cir. 2002). As noted above, however, we have permitted the ICRC access to the detainees, and we have notified each detainee's country of origin that the detainee is in DoD control.

U.S. citizen enemy combatants who are detained in the United States may challenge their detention by a petition for habeas corpus. In the view of the U.S. government, enemy combatants have no right to counsel to challenge their detention. Providing enemy combatants a right of access to counsel could thwart our ability to collect critical information and could imperil efforts to prevent further terrorist attacks. It might also enable detained enemy combatants to pass concealed messages to the enemy.

In Padilla v. Bush, 233 F. Supp.2d 564 (S.D.N.Y. 2002), the U.S. District Court for the Southern District of New York recently upheld the government's ability to detain U.S. citizen enemy combatants in the United States but required the government to provide access to Padilla by his attorneys for limited purposes. We are currently reviewing the court's decision.

Length of Detention

Many have claimed that enemy combatants are being detained "indefinitely." The suggestion appears to be that they are being detained lawlessly and without limit. That is not true. As explained above, the constitutional power to detain during wartime is well settled. In addition, international law—including the Third Geneva Convention—unambiguously permits a government to detain enemy combatants at least until hostilities cease. There may be uncertainty about when hostilities cease in the novel conflict with al Qaida. But disquiet about indefinite detention is misplaced for two reasons.

First, the concern is premature. In prior wars combatants (including U.S. POWs) have been legally detained for years. We have not yet approached that point in the current conflict. Second, the government has no interest in detaining enemy combatants any longer than necessary, and the Department of Defense reviews the status of all enemy combatants on a case-by-case basis to determine whether they should continue to be detained. Since we first captured or came to control detainees in Afghanistan, we have released many thousands, and we recently released additional detainees from the United States Naval Base in Guantanamo Bay, Cuba. But as long as hostilities continue and the detainees present a threat or retain intelligence or law enforcement value, no law requires that the detainees be released, and it would be imprudent to do so.

* * *

George H. Aldrich, The Taliban, Al Qaeda, and the Determination of Illegal Combatants*

96 AM. J. INT'L L.. 891 (2002)

On September 11, 2001, a small number of men who belonged to a fanatical group known as "Al Qaeda" carried out a suicidal armed attack upon the United States that resulted in very substantial material damage and loss of life by some three thousand persons, the great majority of whom were civilians. In response, the United States and a number of allies have taken action to find, capture, or kill as many members of the Qaeda organization as possible and deprive it of funds, support, and sanctuary.

As the leaders of Al Qaeda and a large part of its membership and facilities were located within the territory of Afghanistan, the Taliban, who controlled all but a small part of that country and were consequently its effective government, were requested to assist in this effort. The Taliban refused to do so and made clear that they would continue to give sanctuary to Al Qaeda. As a result, the United States and its allies attacked the armed forces of the Taliban, as well as those of Al Qaeda, in the process killing and capturing a considerable number of soldiers belonging to both entities. Since these persons were captured in the course of an international armed conflict, questions immediately arose as to their legal status and the protections to which they might be entitled pursuant to international humanitarian law, particularly as at least some of them were clearly bound to face criminal proceedings for terrorist acts and other crimes.

In February [2002], President Bush determined the position of the United States on at least some of these questions. In essence, as announced by the White House press secretary on February 7, 2002, he decided that:

---

* Some footnotes omitted.

(1) the 1949 Geneva Convention on the treatment of prisoners of war, to which both Afghanistan and the United States are parties, applies to the armed conflict in Afghanistan between the Taliban and the United States;

(2) that Convention does not apply to the armed conflict in Afghanistan and elsewhere between Al Qaeda and the United States;

(3) neither captured Taliban personnel nor captured Qaeda personnel are entitled to be prisoners of war (POWs) under that Convention; and

(4) nevertheless, all captured Taliban and Qaeda personnel are to be treated humanely, consistently with the general principles of the Convention, and delegates of the International Committee of the Red Cross may privately visit each detainee.[a]

* * *

Turning to the applicable law and the choices the president faced, I suggest that the decision to consider that two separate armed conflicts are being waged is correct. The first, the conflict with Al Qaeda, is not limited to the territory of Afghanistan. Al Qaeda is evidently a clandestine organization consisting of elements in many countries and apparently composed of people of various nationalities; it is dedicated to advancing certain political and religious objectives by means of terrorist acts directed against the United States and other, largely Western, nations. As such, Al Qaeda does not in any respect resemble a state, is not a subject of international law, and lacks international legal personality. It is not a party to the Geneva Conventions, and it could not be a party to them or to any international agreement.[b] Its methods brand it as a criminal organization under national laws and as an international outlaw. Its members are properly subject to trial and punishment under national criminal laws for any crimes that they commit.

Analytically, the armed attack against the Taliban in Afghanistan is a separate armed attack that was rendered necessary because the Taliban, as the effective government of Afghanistan, refused all requests to expel Al Qaeda and instead gave it sanctuary. While the United States, like almost all other countries, refused to

a. Ari Fleischer, Special White House Announcement Re: Application of Geneva Conventions in Afghanistan (Feb. 7, 2002), available in LEXIS, Legis Library, Fednew File; see also White House Fact Sheet: Status of Detainees at Guantanamo (Feb. 7, 2002), at <http://www.whitehouse.gov/news/releases/2002/02/>.

b. *Accord* Joan Fitzpatrick, *Jurisdiction of Military Commissions and the Ambiguous War on Terrorism*, 96 AJIL 345, 348 (2002). *But see id.* at 353 (stating that some Qaeda combatants "may also be entitled to presumptive POW status").

extend diplomatic recognition to the Taliban, both Afghanistan and the United States are parties to the Geneva Conventions of 1949, and the armed attacks by the United States and other nations against the armed forces of the Taliban in Afghanistan clearly constitute an international armed conflict to which those Conventions, as well as customary international humanitarian law, apply.

Despite the analytical clarity of this distinction, one must recognize that practical problems are likely to arise in some circumstances, for example, when Qaeda personnel are captured while accompanying Taliban armed forces, to whom the Geneva Conventions are applicable; but, once the Qaeda personnel are identified, they would clearly not be entitled to POW status.[c] As persons who were combatants in hostilities and are not entitled to POW status, they are entitled, under customary international law, to humane treatment of the same nature as that prescribed by Article 3 common to the four Geneva Conventions of 1949 and, in more detail, by Article 75 of Additional Protocol I to those Conventions of 1977; but they may be lawfully prosecuted and punished under national laws for taking part in the hostilities and for any other crimes, such as murder and assault, that they may have committed. They were illegal combatants, or, as the late Professor and Judge Richard Baxter once described such persons, they were "unprivileged belligerents," that is, belligerent persons who lack the privilege enjoyed by the armed forces of a state to engage in warfare with immunity from any liability under national or international law, except as prescribed by the international laws of war. This vulnerability to prosecution for simply taking part in an armed conflict and for injuries that may have been caused in that connection is the sanction prescribed by the law to deter illegal combatants.

Turning to the Taliban, I find it quite difficult to understand the reasons for President Bush's decision that all Taliban soldiers lack entitlement to POW status. The White House press secretary gave the following cryptic explanation of that decision:

> Under Article 4 of the Geneva Convention, . . . Taliban detainees are not entitled to POW status. To qualify as POWs under Article 4, al Qaeda and Taliban detainees would have to have satisfied four conditions: They would have to be part of a military hierarchy; they would have to have worn uniforms or other distinctive signs visible at a distance; they would have to have carried arms openly; and they would have to have conducted their military operations in accordance with the laws and customs of war.

---

c. I know of no evidence suggesting that Qaeda personnel were incorporated in Taliban military units as part of the Taliban armed forces.

The Taliban have not effectively distinguished themselves from the civilian population of Afghanistan. Moreover, they have not conducted their operations in accordance with the laws and customs of war. Instead, they have knowingly adopted and provided support to the unlawful terrorist objectives of the al Qaeda.

Clearly, the press secretary was summarizing the provisions of paragraph A(2) of that article, a paragraph that deals only with members of militias or other volunteer corps that are not part of the armed forces of a party to the armed conflict.

Members of the press attending a press conference probably do not carry with them copies of the Geneva Convention. If they did, they might well have asked the press secretary what happened to the first provision of Article 4, which provides as follows:

> A. Prisoners of war, in the sense of the present Convention, are persons belonging to one of the following categories, who have fallen into the power of the enemy:

> (1) Members of the armed forces of a Party to the conflict as well as members of militias or volunteer corps forming part of such armed forces.

It is only with respect to the second category of POWs that we come to the four conditions referred to by the press secretary as justifying the president's decision, and that category relates solely to militias and volunteer corps that do not form part of the armed forces of a party to the conflict. Are the Taliban soldiers not members of the armed forces of a party to the conflict? Or, at least, are they not members of militias or volunteer corps forming part of those armed forces? On the basis of the public record to date, we cannot know the answer of the United States to those questions. We are forced to speculate. Perhaps the United States might argue that Afghanistan has no armed forces within the meaning of that sub-paragraph 1 but, rather, only armies of competing warlords; but that, I suggest, would not be fully convincing given the general perception that, when the attacks began, the Taliban government was in effective control of most of Afghanistan.

* * *

In view of the reasons given by the press secretary, it seems most likely that the United States is relying upon a different argument, i.e., that the conditions specified for POW status by Article 4A(2) for militias and volunteer corps that are not part of the armed forces somehow apply to all armed forces of a state, and that two of those four categories—wearing uniforms or other distinctive signs visible at a distance and conducting their operations in accordance with the laws and customs of war—are not complied with by the armed forces of the Taliban. Apparently, the United

States does not question the Taliban's compliance with the other two conditions—being commanded by a person responsible for his subordinates and carrying their arms openly.

Whether the four conditions applicable under Article 4A(2) to members of militias and other volunteer corps that are not part of the armed forces of a state are also inherent requirements of any of a state's armed forces is a debatable question. While contrary to textual logic, that assertion has occasionally been made.[d] Certainly, I would not deny that, to qualify for POW status under the Convention, all armed forces must belong to the state in the sense of being subject to a command responsible to that state for that group's conduct and for its compliance with the rules of international law applicable in international armed conflict. On the other hand, each state is normally free to determine the nature of the clothing to be worn by its armed forces. While I certainly do not know whether or not some or all of the members of the Taliban's armed forces were distinguishable from civilians, either by wearing black turbans or by some other visible sign, it seems insufficient for the United States merely to assert an absence of distinction without adducing evidence, and it appears most unlikely in any event that all units of the Taliban's armed forces were indistinguishable from civilians.

With respect to the requirement that armed forces conduct their operations in compliance with the applicable laws of war, I note that the only allegation by the press secretary is that the Taliban "have knowingly adopted and provided support to the unlawful terrorist objectives of the al Qaeda." Providing sanctuary to Al Qaeda and sympathizing with it are wrongs, but they are not the same as failing to conduct their own military operations in accordance with the laws of war.[e] A nation that assists an aggressor thereby commits a wrong, but its armed forces should not, as a consequence, lose their entitlement, if captured, to POW status. Moreover, asserted noncompliance with this fourth requirement is a dangerous argument to make in defense of denial of POW status, because it can so easily be abused, as it was by North Korea and North Vietnam, to deny POW treatment to all members of a state's armed forces on the ground that their state was an aggressor or that some of the members of its armed forces allegedly committed war crimes.[f] Even in a conflict where substantial war

d. *See, e.g.,* ALLAN ROSAS, THE LEGAL STATUS OF PRISONERS OF WAR 328 (1976); W. Thomas Mallison & Sally V. Mallison, The Juridical Status of Irregular Combatants Under the International Humanitarian Law of Armed Conflict, 9 CASE W. RES. J. INT'L L. 39, 44, 48 (1977). * * * *see* Ruth Wedgwood, Al Qaeda, Terrorism, and Military Commissions, 96 AJIL 328, 335 (2002), but Michael J. Matheson * * * implies that the four conditions do not apply to the armed forces of a state, see Michael J. Matheson, U.S. Military Commissions: One of Several Options, 96 AJIL 354, 355 (2002).

e. *Contra* Wedgwood, supra note d, at 335.

f. All of the then-Communist states made a reservation to Article 85 of Geneva Convention No. III to the effect that they

crimes were committed by a state's armed forces, this argument would be a bad idea. Those who commit war crimes should be punished, but their crimes should not be used as an excuse to deprive others of the protections due POWs.

I believe that it would be much easier and more convincing for the United States to conclude that the members of the armed forces of the effective government of most of Afghanistan should, upon capture, be treated as POWs. This is what we did in Vietnam, where we found it desirable to give virtually all enemy prisoners POW status. The different treatment of the Taliban causes me to suspect that some unexplained reason may lie behind the decision. I am forced to ask why the United States would wish to deprive all Taliban soldiers of POW status when they have been defending the government whose armed forces they are. Does it intend to prosecute them simply for participating in the conflict? I must doubt that. Does it intend to prosecute them for crimes under United States law? For crimes under some Afghan law? If a few of them are guilty of war crimes or crimes against humanity, they could be prosecuted while remaining POWs. Probably, POW status might be thought to inhibit interrogation, as it would prohibit confinement except for penal or disciplinary sanctions.[g] Such confinement may well facilitate successful interrogation. The detainees in Cuba are evidently confined in separate pens.[h]

* * *

Without a doubt, the most difficult element to defend of the decisions made by President Bush in February with respect to the status of prisoners taken in Afghanistan is the blanket nature of the decision to deny POW status to the Taliban prisoners. By one sweeping determination, the president ruled that not a single Taliban soldier, presumably not even the army commander, could qualify for POW status under the Geneva Convention. While armed forces in the past doubtless made some decisions related to army units or other groups as a whole, one cannot help but question the all-encompassing nature of this one. Can it possibly exclude any doubt? Moreover, can it legitimately preclude any contest by an individual prisoner?

refused to accept continued POW status for prisoners of war who were tried and convicted of war crimes or crimes against humanity. North Korea and North Vietnam, however, denied POW status to all American prisoners solely on the basis of the allegation that they were all war criminals. George H. Aldrich, *The Laws of War on Land*, 94 AJIL 42, 62 n.100 (2000).

g. Geneva Convention No. III, supra note 3, Arts. 21, 95, 97, 98.

h. Note that Article 17 of Convention No. III provides, inter alia:

No physical or mental torture, nor any other form of coercion, may be inflicted on prisoners of war to secure from them information of any kind whatever. Prisoners of war who refuse to answer may not be threatened, insulted, or exposed to unpleasant or disadvantageous treatment of any kind.

Article 5 of the Convention states the following cautionary rule:

> Should any doubt arise as to whether persons, having committed a belligerent act and having fallen into the hands of the enemy, belong to any of the categories enumerated in Article 4, such persons shall enjoy the protection of the present Convention until such time as their status has been determined by a competent tribunal.

Given that provision and the fact that the president is not a tribunal and cannot substitute for a tribunal under Article 5, either the United States must maintain that no doubt could arise with respect to any Taliban prisoner, or it must preserve the option of a determination by a tribunal in the event that any doubt does arise concerning a group or an individual prisoner. The spokesman of the Department of State indicated in his press briefing on February 8 of this year that the United States would be prepared to review its determination about the applicability of Article 4 of the Convention should any genuine doubt about status arise in individual cases.[i] I do not know whether such a "review" would be made by a tribunal, as required by the Convention, or by the president. Review by a competent tribunal in individual cases would certainly be helpful if it could be meaningful. Only if reviews occur in practice can that be determined. The broad and definitive nature of the president's determination would appear to entail the risk that any review by a tribunal might well have to be limited to resolving doubts as to whether a prisoner was, in fact, a member of the Taliban armed forces, not whether the unit in which he served, or those armed forces in general, met the standards of Article 4. If so limited, a right to individual review would fall far short of a right to determination of POW entitlement by an Article 5 tribunal.

The United States probably believes that its screening of Taliban captives prior to their transfer to the camp in Cuba is thorough and as fully adequate as scrutiny by a tribunal to ensure that they are legitimately detained for purposes of further criminal investigation. That may well be true, but, in view of the president's determination, such screening could have no effect on their entitlement to POW status.

In my view, international humanitarian law provides all too few opportunities for individuals to challenge state action,[j] but one of those few is the right of access to a tribunal granted by Article 5. It would be regrettable if in practice this right proves to have been

---

i. Richard Boucher, Spokesman, Daily Press Briefing (Feb. 8, 2002), at <http://www.state.gov/r/pa/prs/dpb/>.

j. George H. Aldrich, Individuals as Subjects of International Humanitarian Law, *in* THEORY OF INTERNATIONAL LAW AT THE THRESHOLD OF THE 21ST CENTURY: ESSAYS IN HONOUR OF KRZYSZT OF SKUBISZEWSKI 851, 855–56 (Jerzy Makarczyk ed., 1996).

effectively negated for Taliban prisoners. In this connection, I note that, since 1956, the United States Army Field Manual *The Law of Land Warfare* has made the following interpretation of Article 5 of the Convention:

> b. *Interpretation.* The foregoing provision applies to any person not appearing to be entitled to prisoner-of-war status who has committed a belligerent act or has engaged in hostile activities in aid of the armed forces and who asserts that he is entitled to treatment as a prisoner of war or concerning whom any other doubt of a like nature exists.

This interpretation clearly indicates that doubt arises and a tribunal is required whenever a captive who has participated in hostilities asserts the right to be a POW. That is a point we were careful to state in Article 45, paragraph 1 of Protocol I when we negotiated it in the seventies, and, in my view, it is now part of customary international law. In that connection, I should point out that, when the armed forces of countries that are parties to the Geneva Protocol capture Taliban soldiers, they will obviously be required by Article 45, paragraph 1 to give them POW status until a tribunal decides otherwise. Given the president's decisions of February 7, 2002, this obligation might also prevent the transfer of such prisoners to the United States.

Also relevant to prisoners facing criminal prosecution is paragraph 2 of Article 45 of Protocol I, which establishes a separate right of any person who has fallen into the power of an adverse party that intends to try him for an offense arising out of the hostilities to have his entitlement to POW status determined by a judicial tribunal. When that text was negotiated, the United States government was painfully aware of the experiences in Korea and Vietnam, where many American military personnel were mistreated by their captors and denied POW status by mere allegations that they were all criminals. Time evidently dulls memory.

Detainees at Guantanamo Bay, Cuba, Request for Precautionary Measures

Decision on Inter–American Commission on Human Rights (IACHR) March 12, 2002, 41 I.L.M. 532 (2002).

* * *

[W]hile its specific mandate is to secure the observance of international human rights protections in the Hemisphere, this Commission has in the past looked to and applied definitional standards and relevant rules of international humanitarian law in interpreting the American Declaration and other Inter–American human rights instruments in situations of armed conflict.[a]

In taking this approach, the Commission has drawn upon certain basic principles that inform the interrelationship between international human rights and humanitarian law. It is well-recognized that international human rights law applies at all times, in peacetime and in situations of armed conflict.[b] In contrast, international humanitarian law generally does not apply in peacetime and its principal purpose is to place restraints on the conduct of warfare in order to limit or contain the damaging effects of hostilities and to protect the victims of armed conflict, including civilians and combatants who have laid down their arms or have been placed hors de combat.[c] Further, in situations of armed conflict, the protections under international human rights and humanitarian law may complement and reinforce one another, sharing as they do a common nucleus of non-derogable rights and a common purpose of promoting human life and dignity.[d] In certain circumstances, however, the test for evaluating the observance of a particular right, such as the right to liberty, in a situation of armed conflict may be distinct from that applicable in time of peace. In such situations, international law, including the jurisprudence of this Commission, dictates that it may be necessary to deduce the applicable standard by reference to international humanitarian law as the applicable *lex specialis*.[e]

Accordingly, where persons find themselves within the authority and control of a state and where a circumstance of armed conflict may be involved, their fundamental rights may be determined in part by reference to international humanitarian law as well as international human rights law. Where it may be considered that the protections of international humanitarian law do not apply, however, such persons remain the beneficiaries at least of the non-derogable protections under international human rights law. In short, no person under the authority and control of a state, regardless of his or her circumstances, is devoid of legal protection for his or her fundamental and non-derogable human rights.

This basic precept is reflected in the Martens clause common to numerous long-standing humanitarian law treaties, including the Hague Conventions of 1899 and 1907 respecting the laws and customs of war on land, according to which human persons who do

---

a. *See generally* Abella v. Argentina, Case No. 11.137, Report No. 5/97, Annual Report of the IACHR 1997; Coard et al. v. United States, supra; IACHR, Third Report on the Situation of Human Rights in Colombia, OEA/Ser.L/V/II.102 doc. 9 rev. 1, 26 February 1999.

b. Abella Case, *supra*, para. 158.

c. *Id.*, para. 159.

d. *Id.*, para. 160–1.

e. ICJ, *Advisory Opinion on the Legality of the Threat or Use of Nuclear Weapons,* ICJ Reports 1996, para. 25. *See also* Abella Case, *supra*, para. 161; Coard et al. Case, *supra*, para. 42.

not fall within the protection of those treaties or other international agreements remain under the protection of the principles of the law of nations, as they result from the usages established among civilized peoples, from the laws of humanity, and the dictates of the public conscience. And according to international norms applicable in peacetime and wartime, such as those reflected in Article 5 of the Third Geneva Convention and Article XVIII of the American Declaration of the Rights and Duties of Man, a competent court or tribunal, as opposed to a political authority, must be charged with ensuring respect for the legal status and rights of persons falling under the authority and control of a state.

Specifically with regard to the request for precautionary measures presently before it, the Commission observes that certain pertinent facts concerning the detainees at Guantanamo Bay are well-known and do not appear to be the subject of controversy. These include the fact that the government of the United States considers itself to be at war with an international network of terrorists,[f] that the United States undertook a military operation in Afghanistan beginning in October 2001 in defending this war,[g] and that most of the detainees in Guantanamo Bay were apprehended in connection with this military operation and remain wholly within the authority and control of the United States government.[h]

It is also well-known that doubts exists as to the legal status of the detainees. This includes the question of whether and to what extent the Third Geneva Convention and/or other provisions of international humanitarian law apply to some or all of the detainees and what implications this may have for their international human rights protections. According to official statements from the United States government, its Executive Branch has most recently declined to extend prisoner of war status under the Third Geneva Convention to the detainees, without submitting the issue for determination by a competent tribunal or otherwise ascertaining the rights and protections to which the detainees are entitled under US domestic or international law.[i] To the contrary, the information available suggests that the detainees remain entirely at the unfettered discretion of the United States government. Absent clarification of the legal status of the detainees, the Com-

---

f. *See e.g.* Remarks by the President in Photo Opportunity with the National Security Team, Office of the Press Secretary, September 12, 2001, http://whitehouse.gov/news/releases/2001/09/20010912-4.html.

g. *See e.g.* Radio Address of the President to the Nation, Office of the Press Secretary, October 13, 2001, http://www.whitehouse.gov/news/releases/2001/10/20011013.html.

h. *See e.g.* Jim Garamone, 50 Detainees now at Gitmo; All Treated Humanely, American Forces Press Service, January 15, 2002, http://www.defenselink.mil/news/Jan2002/n01152002_200201151.html.

i. *See* White House Fact Sheet, Status of Detainees at Guantanamo, Office of the Press Secretary, February 7, 2002, http://www.whitehouse.gov/news/releases/2002/02/ 20020207-13.html.

mission considers that the rights and protections to which they may be entitled under international or domestic law cannot be said to be the subject of effective legal protection by the State.

In light of the foregoing considerations, and without prejudging the possible application of international humanitarian law to the detainees at Guantanamo Bay, the Commission considers that precautionary measures are both appropriate and necessary in the present circumstances, in order to ensure that the legal status of each of the detainees is clarified and that they are afforded the legal protections commensurate with the status that they are found to possess, which may in no case fall below the minimum standards of non-derogable rights. On this basis, the Commission hereby requests that the United States take the urgent measures necessary to have the legal status of the detainees at Guantanamo Bay determined by a competent tribunal.

In the case of Rasul v. Bush, 542 U.S. ___ (2004), the US Supreme Court ruled that detainees held at Guantànamo Bay had a right to challenge the legality of their detention in Federal Court. The decision was based on principles of United States law and thus is not excerpted here. The next excerpts concern not who may be detained but how, including how long may detention last and may detainees be interrogated during detention.

Combatants may be targeted until they are in the control of the adverse party. Then they must be treated with humanity in all cases, at a minimum. Those who qualify for prisoner of war status receive the rights set out in the Geneva Prisoner's Convention and Additional Protocol I. Perhaps the greatest right is that they must be released at the end of the hostilities in which they were captured.

Hamdi v. Rumsfeld, Cont'd

Supreme Court of the United States, 2004.
542 U.S. ___ (2004).

Hamdi objects, nevertheless, that Congress has not authorized the *indefinite* detention to which he is now subject. The Government responds that "the detention of enemy combatants during World War II was just as 'indefinite' while that war was being fought." *Id.*, at 16. We take Hamdi's objection to be not to the lack of certainty regarding the date on which the conflict will end, but to the substantial prospect of perpetual detention. We recognize that the national security underpinnings of the "war on terror," although crucially important, are broad and malleable. As the Government concedes, "given its unconventional nature, the current conflict is unlikely to end with a formal cease-fire agreement." *Ibid*. The prospect Hamdi raises is therefore not far-fetched. If the

Government does not consider this unconventional war won for two generations, and if it maintains during that time that Hamdi might, if released, rejoin forces fighting against the United States, then the position it has taken throughout the litigation of this case suggests that Hamdi's detention could last for the rest of his life.

It is a clearly established principle of the law of war that detention may last no longer than active hostilities. See Article 118 of the Geneva Convention (III) Relative to the Treatment of Prisoners of War, Aug. 12, 1949, [1955] 6 U.S.T. 3316, 3406, T.I.A.S. No. 3364 ("Prisoners of war shall be released and repatriated without delay after the cessation of active hostilities"). See also Article 20 of the Hague Convention (II) on Laws and Customs of War on Land, July 29, 1899, 32 Stat. 1817 (as soon as possible after "conclusion of peace"); Hague Convention (IV), *supra*, Oct. 18, 1907, 36 Stat. 2301("conclusion of peace" (Art. 20)); Geneva Convention, *supra*, July 27, 1929, 47 Stat.2055 (repatriation should be accomplished with the least possible delay after conclusion of peace (Art. 75)); P[]aust, Judicial Power to Determine the Status and Rights of Persons Detained without Trial, 44 Harv. Int'l L.J. 503, 510–511 (2003) (prisoners of war "can be detained during an armed conflict, but the detaining country must release and repatriate them 'without delay after the cessation of active hostilities,' unless they are being lawfully prosecuted or have been lawfully convicted of crimes and are serving sentences" (citing Arts. 118, 85, 99, 119, 129, Geneva Convention (III), 6 T.I.A.S., at 3384, 3392, 3406, 3418)).

Hamdi contends that the AUMF [Congress's Authorization for the Use of Military Force] does not authorize indefinite or perpetual detention. Certainly, we agree that indefinite detention for the purpose of interrogation is not authorized. Further, we understand Congress' grant of authority for the use of "necessary and appropriate force" to include the authority to detain for the duration of the relevant conflict, and our understanding is based on longstanding law-of-war principles. If the practical circumstances of a given conflict are entirely unlike those of the conflicts that informed the development of the law of war, that understanding may unravel. But that is not the situation we face as of this date. Active combat operations against Taliban fighters apparently are ongoing in Afghanistan. See, *e.g.,* Constable, U.S. Launches New Operation in Afghanistan, Washington Post, Mar. 14, 2004, p. A22 (reporting that 13,500 United States troops remain in Afghanistan, including several thousand new arrivals); J. Abizaid, Dept. of Defense, Gen. Abizaid Central Command Operations Update Briefing, Apr. 30, 2004, http://www.defenselink.mil/transcripts/2004/tr20040430–1402.html (as visited June 8, 2004, and available in the Clerk of Court's case file) (media briefing describing ongoing operations in Afghanistan involving 20,000 United States troops). The United States may detain, for the duration of these hostilities, individuals legitimately determined to be Taliban combatants who "engaged in an armed conflict against the United States." If the record establishes that United States troops are still involved in active combat in Afghanistan, those detentions are part of the exercise of "necessary and appropriate force," and therefore are authorized by the AUMF.

———————

The next two excerpts concern the lawful conditions of detention. The first focuses on consequences for the detaining power when conditions do not meet the international legal standard. The second excerpt concerns consequences for an individual found guilty of abusing combatant detainees.

Between May 1998 and June 2000, Eritrea and Ethiopia fought a bitter and costly war over their mutual boundary that left tens of thousands dead. As part of the peace agreement, in addition to agreeing to settle the boundary dispute, the two states agreed to establish a commission to settle claims growing out of the conduct of the war.

Prisoners of War Ethiopia's Claim 4 (Part 3), (Partial Award)

ERITREA ETHIOPIA CLAIMS COMMISSION* (July 1, 2003).

I.   INTRODUCTION

   A.   Summary of the Positions of the Parties

1.   This Claim ("Ethiopia's Claim 4;" "ETO4") has been brought to the Commission by the Claimant, the Federal Democratic Republic of Ethiopia ("Ethiopia"), pursuant to Article 5 of the Agreement between the Government of the Federal Democratic Republic of Ethiopia and the Government of the State of Eritrea of December 12, 2000 ("the Agreement"). The Claim seeks a finding of the liability of the Respondent, the State of Eritrea ("Eritrea"), for loss, damage and injury suffered by the Claimant as a result of the Respondent's alleged unlawful treatment of its Prisoners of War ("POWs") who were nationals of the Claimant. In its Statement of Claim, the Claimant requested monetary compensation, and in its Memorial, it proposed that compensation be determined by a mass claims process based upon the five permanent camps in which those POWs were held.

   2.   The Respondent asserts that it fully complied with international law in its treatment of POWs.

* * *

   C.   General Comment

* www.pca-cpa.org

12.   As the findings in this Award and in the related Award in Eritrea's Claim 17 describe, there were significant difficulties in both Parties' performance of important legal obligations for the protection of prisoners of war. Nevertheless, the Commission must record an important preliminary point that provides essential context for what follows. Based on the extensive evidence adduced during these proceedings, the Commission believes that both Parties had a commitment to the most fundamental principles bearing on prisoners of war. Both parties conducted organized, official training programs to instruct their troops on procedures to be followed when POWs are taken. In contrast to many other contemporary armed conflicts, both Eritrea and Ethiopia regularly and consistently took POWs. Enemy personnel who were *hors de combat* were moved away from the battlefield to conditions of greater safety. Further, although these case involve two of the poorest countries in the world, both made significant efforts to provide for the sustenance and care of the POWs in their custody.

13.   There were deficiencies of performance on both sides, sometimes significant, occasionally grave. Nevertheless, the evidence in these cases shows that both Eritrea and Ethiopia endeavored to observe their fundamental humanitarian obligations to collect and protect enemy soldiers unable to resist on the battlefield. The Awards in these cases, and the difficulties that they identify, must be read against this background.

* * *

2.   Eritrea's Refusal to Permit the ICRC to Visit POWs

55.   From the outset of the armed conflict in 1998, the ICRC was permitted by Ethiopia to visit the Eritrean POWs and the camps in which they were held. It was also permitted to provide relief to them and to assist them in corresponding with their families in Eritrea, although there is evidence that Eritrea refused to permit communications from those POWs to be passed on to their families.[a] In Eritrea, the ICRC had a limited role in the 1998 repatriation of seventy sick or wounded POWs, but all efforts by the ICRC to visit the Ethiopian POWs held by Eritrea were refused by Eritrea until August 2000, just after Eritrea acceded to the 1949 Geneva Conventions. The Commission must decide whether, as alleged by Ethiopia, such refusal by Eritrea constituted a violation of its legal obligations under the applicable law.

56.   Eritrea argues that the right of access by the ICRC to POWs is a treaty-based right and that the provisions of Geneva Convention III granting such access to the ICRC should not be considered provisions that express customary international law. While recog-

a.   *See* Ethiopia's Claims 4, Prisoners of War, Counter-Memorial to ET 04, filed by   Eritrea on November 1, 2002, p. 140 and note 856.

nizing that most of the provisions of the Convention have become customary law, Eritrea asserts that the provisions dealing with the access of the ICRC are among the detailed or procedural provisions that have not attained such status.

57.   That the ICRC did not agree with Eritrea is demonstrated by a press statement it issued on May 7, 1999, in which it recounted its visits to POWs and interned civilians held by Ethiopia and said: "In Eritrea, meanwhile, the ICRC is pursuing its efforts to gain access, as required by the Third Geneva Convention, to Ethiopian POWs captured since the conflict erupted last year."[b]

58.   The ICRC is assigned significant responsibilities in a number of articles of the Convention.[c] These provisions make clear that the ICRC may function in at least two different capacities—as a humanitarian organization providing relief and as an organization providing necessary and vital external scrutiny of the treatment of POWs, either supplementary to a Protecting Power or as a substitute when there is no Protecting Power. There is no evidence before the Commission that Protecting Powers were proposed by either Ethiopia or Eritrea, and it seems evident that none was appointed. Nevertheless, the Convention clearly requires external scrutiny of the treatment of POWs[d] and, in Article 10, where there is no Protecting Power or other functioning oversight body, it requires Detaining Powers to "accept ... the offer of the services of a humanitarian organization, such as the International Committee of the Red Cross, to assume the humanitarian functions performed by Protecting Powers under the present Convention." In that event, Article 10 also provides that all mention of Protecting Powers in the Convention applies to such substitute organizations.

59.   The right of the ICRC to have access to POWs is not limited to a situation covered by Article 10 in which it serves as a substitute for a Protecting Power. Article 126 specifies clear and critical rights of Protecting Powers with respect to access to camps and to POWs, including the right to interview POWs without witnesses, and it states that the delegates of the ICRC "shall enjoy the same prerogatives." Ethiopia relies primarily on Article 126 in its allegation that Eritrea violated its legal obligations by refusing the ICRC access to its POWs.

60.   Professor Levie points out in his monumental study of the treatment of POWs in international armed conflicts that the ICRC "has played an indispensable humanitarian role in every armed conflict for more than a century."[e] He also notes that, in addition

---

b.   ICRC, *Ethiopia/Eritrea: ICRC Visits Newly Captured Prisoners,* ICRC NEWS, May 7, 1999, *in* ET04 MEM, Annex XV, Tab 94.

c.   *See* Articles 9, 10, 73, 81 and 126.

d.   *See* Articles 8 and 10.

e.   Howard S. Levie, *Prisoners of War in International Armed Conflict, in* INTERNATION-

to the work by the many Protecting Powers, the ICRC played a vital role in protecting POWs during the Second World War, when it made a total of 11,175 visits to installations where POWs and civilian internees were confined.[f] Levie also lists the places where the ICRC and protecting powers have been excluded in recent times—the Soviet Union (1940–45), North Korea and the Peoples Republic of China (1950–53), and North Vietnam (1965–73).[g] It is common knowledge that the treatment of POWs by the named Parties in those four places where the ICRC was unlawfully excluded was far worse than that required by the standards of applicable law. The long term result of these exclusions has been a reinforcement of the general understanding of the crucial role played by outside observers in the effective functioning of the legal regime for the protection of POWs.

61. The Commission cannot agree with Eritrea's argument that provisions of the Convention requiring external scrutiny of the treatment of POWs and access to POWs by the ICRC are mere details or simply implementing procedural provisions that have not, in half a century, become part of customary international law. These provisions are an essential part of the regime for protecting POWs that has developed in international practice, as reflected in Geneva Convention III. These requirements are, indeed, "treaty-based" in the sense that they are articulated in the Convention; but, as such, they incorporate past practices that had standing of their own in customary law, and they are of such importance for the prospects of compliance with the law that it would be irresponsible for the Commission to consider them inapplicable as customary international law. As the International Court of Justice said in its Advisory Opinion on the Legality of the Threat or Use of Nuclear Weapons:

> 79. It is undoubtedly because a great many rules of humanitarian law applicable in armed conflict are so fundamental to the respect of the human person and "elementary considerations of humanity" as the Court put it in its Judgment of 9 April 1949 in the *Corfu Channel Case* (*I.C.J. Reports* 1949, p. 22), that the Hague and Geneva Conventions have enjoyed a broad accession. Further these fundamental rules are to be observed by all States whether or not they have ratified the conventions that contain them, because they constitute intransgressible principles of international customary law.[h]

62. For the above reasons, the Commission holds that Eritrea violated customary international law from May 1998 until August 2000 by refusing to permit the ICRC to send its delegates to visit

AL LAW STUDIES, Volume 59, p. 312 (United States Naval War College Press 1978).

f. *Id.* at p. 310.

g. *Id.* at p. 312.

h. Legality of the Threat or Use Nuclear Weapons, * * *

all places where Ethiopian POWs were detained, to register those POWs, to interview them without witnesses, and to provide them with the customary relief and services. Consequently, Eritrea is liable for the suffering caused by that refusal.

    3.   Mistreatment of POWs at Capture and its Immediate Aftermath

63.   Of the thirty Ethiopian POW declarants, at least twenty were already wounded at capture and nearly all testified to treatment of the sick or wounded by Eritrean forces upon capture at the front and during evacuation. Consequently, in addition to the customary international law standards reflected in Geneva Convention III, the Commission also applies the standards reflected in the Geneva Convention for the Amelioration of the Condition of the Wounded and Sick in Armed Forces in the Field on August 12, 1949 ("Geneva Convention I").[i] For a wounded or sick POW, the provisions of Geneva Convention I apply along with Geneva Convention III. Among other provisions, Article 12 of Geneva Convention I demands respect and protection of wounded or sick members of the armed forces in "all circumstances."

64.   A State's obligation to ensure humane treatment of enemy soldiers can be severely tested in the heated and confused moments immediately following capture or surrender and during evacuation from the battlefront to the rear. Nevertheless, customary international law as reflected in Geneva Conventions I and III absolutely prohibits the killing of POWs, requires the wounded and sick to be collected and cared for, the dead to be collected, and demands prompt and humane evacuation of POWs.[j]

    a. Abusive Treatment

65.   Ethiopia alleged that Eritrean troops regularly beat and frequently killed Ethiopians upon capture and its immediate aftermath. Ethiopia presented a *prima facie* case, through clear and convincing evidence, to support this allegation.

66.   One-third of the Ethiopian POW declarations contain accounts of Eritrean soldiers deliberately killing Ethiopian POWs, most wounded, at capture or evacuation. Particularly troubling are accounts in three declarations of Eritrean officers ordering troops to kill Ethiopian POWs or beating them for not doing so. More than half of the Ethiopian POW declarants described repeated and brutal beatings, both at the front and during evacuation, including blows purposefully inflicted on wounds. Fortunately, these accounts were countered to a degree by several other accounts from Ethiopian declarants of Eritrean officers and soldiers intervening to curtail physical abuse and prevent killings.

---

i. 75 U.N.T.S. p. 31; 6 U.S.T. p. 3114.

j. Common Article 3(1)(a), (2); Geneva Convention I, Articles 12, 15; Geneva Convention III, Articles 13, 20, 130.

67. In rebuttal, Eritrea offered detailed and persuasive evidence that Eritrean troops and officers had received extensive instruction during their basic training, both on the basic requirements of the Geneva Conventions on the taking of POWs and on the policies and practices of the Eritrean People's Liberation Front ("EPLF") in the war against the prior Ethiopian government, the Derg, for independence, which had emphasized the importance of humane treatment of prisoners. What is lacking in the record, however, is evidence of what steps Eritrea took, if any, to ensure that its forces actually put this extensive training to use in the field. There is no evidence that Eritrea conducted inquiries into incidents of physical abuse or pursued disciplinary measures under Article 121 of Geneva Convention III.

68. The Commission concludes that Eritrea has not rebutted the *prima facie* case presented by Ethiopia and, consequently, holds that Eritrea failed to comply with the fundamental obligation of customary international law that POWs, even when wounded, must be protected and may not, under any circumstances, be killed. Consequently, Eritrea is liable for failing to protect Ethiopian POWs from being killed at capture or its immediate aftermath, and for permitting beatings and other physical abuse of Ethiopian POWs at capture or its immediate aftermath.

b. Medical Care Immediately Following Capture

69. Ethiopia alleges that Eritrea failed to provide necessary medical attention to Ethiopian POWs after capture and during evacuation, as required under customary international law reflected in Geneva Conventions I (Article 12) and III (Articles 20 and 15). Many Ethiopian declarants testified that their wounds were not cleaned and bandaged at or shortly after capture, leading to infection and other complications. Eritrea presented rebuttal evidence that its troops provided rudimentary first aid as soon as possible, including in transit camps.

70. The Commission believes that the requirement to provide POWs with medical care during the initial period after capture must be assessed in light of the harsh conditions on the battlefield and the limited extent of medical training and equipment available to front line troops. On balance, and recognizing the logistical and resource limitations faced by both Parties to the conflict, the Commission finds that Eritrea is not liable for failing to provide medical care to Ethiopian POWs at the front and during evacuation.

c. Evacuation Conditions

71. Ethiopia also alleges that, in addition to poor medical care, Eritrea failed to ensure humane evacuation conditions. As reflected in Articles 19 and 20 of Geneva Convention III, the Detaining Power is obliged to evacuate prisoners humanely, safely

and as soon as possible from combat zones; only if there is a greater risk in evacuation may the wounded or sick be temporarily kept in the combat zone, and they must not be unnecessarily exposed to danger. The measure of a humane evacuation is that, as set out in Article 20, POWs should be evacuated "in conditions similar to those for the forces of the Detaining Power."

72.   Turning first to the timing of evacuation, Eritrea submitted clear and convincing evidence that, given the reality of battle, the great majority of Ethiopians POWs were evacuated from the various fronts in a timely manner. Despite one disquieting incident in which a wounded Ethiopian POW allegedly was forced to spend a night on top of a trench while artillery exchanges occurred and his Eritrean captors took refuge in the trench, the Commission concludes that Eritrea generally took the necessary measures to evacuate its prisoners promptly.

73.   Timing aside, the Ethiopian POW declarants described extremely onerous conditions of evacuation. The POWs were forced to walk from the front for hours or days over rough terrain, often in pain from their own wounds, often carrying wounded comrades and Eritrean supplies, often in harsh weather, and often with little or no food and water. Eritrea offered rebuttal evidence that its soldiers faced nearly the same unavoidably difficult conditions, particularly given the lack of paved roads in Eritrea.

74.   Subject to the holding above concerning unlawful physical abuse during evacuation and with one exception, the Commission finds that Eritrean troops satisfied the legal requirements for evacuations from the battlefield under the harsh geographic, military and logistical circumstances. The exception is the Eritrean practice of seizing the footwear of all Ethiopian POWs, testified to by many declarants. Although the harshness of the terrain and weather on the marches to the camps may have been out of Eritrea's control, to force the POWs to walk barefoot in such conditions unnecessarily compounded their misery. The Commission finds Eritrea liable for inhumane treatment during evacuations from the battlefield as a result of its forcing Ethiopian POWs to go without footwear during evacuation marches.

d.   Coercive Interrogation

75.   Ethiopia alleges frequent abuse in Eritrea's interrogation of POWs, commencing at capture and evacuation. International law does not prohibit the interrogation of POWs, but it does restrict the information they are obliged to reveal and prohibits torture or other measures of coercion, including threats and "unpleasant or disadvantageous treatment of any kind."[k]

---

k.   Geneva Convention III, Article 17.

76.   Ethiopia presented clear and convincing evidence, unrebutted by Eritrea, that Eritrean interrogators frequently threatened or beat POWs during interrogation, particularly when they were dissatisfied with the prisoner's answers. The Commission must conclude that Eritrea either failed to train its interrogators in the relevant legal restraints or to make it clear that they are imperative. Consequently, Eritrea is liable for permitting such coercive interrogation.

* * *

4.   Physical and Mental Abuse in POW Camps

81.   Ethiopia's evidence of physical and mental abuse of Ethiopian POWs in Eritrean POW camps takes several forms. First, there was the testimony before the Commission of a former POW; second, Ethiopia filed with its Memorial forty signed declarations, including thirty by former POWs in which they described their treatment while captive; third, Ethiopia filed many unsigned statements and claims forms of former POWs; and fourth, Ethiopia filed data it had drawn from the claims forms of other former POWs. The Commission has relied heavily on the first two of these forms of evidence, as it considers the others of uncertain probative value for the proof of liability.

82.   The testimony at the hearing of a former POW and the declarations of the other POWs are consistent and persuasive that the Eritrean guards at the various POW camps relied often upon brutal force for the enforcement of rules and as means of punishment. All thirty POW declarations described frequent beatings of POWs by camp guards. Several guards accused of regularly abusing POWs were identified by name in numerous declarations. The evidence indicates that many of the same guards remained in charge as the numbers of POWs increased and as they were moved from one camp to another, and the conclusion is unavoidable that guards who regularly beat POWs were not replaced as a result. Beatings with wooden sticks were common and, on occasion, resulted in broken bones and lack of consciousness. There were multiple, consistent accounts that, at Digdigta, several POWs who had attempted to escape were beaten senseless, with one losing an eye, prior to their disappearance. Being forced to hold heavy objects over one's head for long periods of time, being punched or kicked, being required to roll on stony or thorny ground, to look at the sun, and to undergo periods of confinement in hot metal containers were notable among the other abuses, all of which violated customary international law, as exemplified by Articles 13, 42, 87 and 89 of Geneva Convention III. Regrettably, the evidence also indicates that the camp commanders did little to restrain these abuses and, in some cases, even threatened POWs by telling them that, as there was (prior to the first ICRC visits in August

2000) no list of prisoners, they could do anything they wanted to the POWs and could not be held accountable.

83.   In addition to the fear and mental anguish that accompanied these physical abuses, there is clear evidence that some POWs, particularly Tigrayans, were treated worse than others and that several POWs were treated as deserters and given favored treatment. (Those given favored treatment were not among those who signed the thirty declarations relied on by Ethiopia on this issue.) Such discrimination is, of course, prohibited by Article 16 of Geneva Convention III.

84.   The evidence is persuasive that beatings were common at all camps: Barentu, Embakala, Digdigta, Afabet and Nakfa. Solitary confinement of three months or more occurred at least at Digdigta and Afabet. At Nakfa, much of the evidence of beatings and other brutal punishments relates to POWs away from camp working on labor projects and occurred when fatigue slowed their work. After ICRC visits began, there is some evidence that POWs were threatened with physical punishment if they reported abuses to the ICRC.

85.   Eritrea introduced little, if any, evidence to counter Ethiopia's evidence of physical and mental abuse of POWs. Eritrea sought to undermine the credibility of Ethiopia's witnesses by pointing to some discrepancies in their declarations or testimony on medical and food issues. Eritrea also asserted that the allegations of physical abuse were not sufficiently specific to make it possible to investigate or rebut them. However, Eritrea chose not to introduce any witnesses from among its camp commanders, and it did not unequivocally deny that specific abuses, such as the beating of the attempted escapees at Digdigta, had occurred.

86.   In conclusion, the Commission holds that Eritrea violated international law from May 1998 until the last Ethiopian POWs were released and repatriated in August 2002 by permitting the pervasive and continuous physical and mental abuse of Ethiopian POWs in Eritrean POW camps. Consequently, Eritrea is liable for such abuse.

* * *

6.   Inadequate Medical Care in Camps

104.   A Detaining Power has the obligation to provide in its POW camps the medical assistance on which the POWs depend to heal their battle wounds and to prevent further damage to their health. This duty is particularly crucial in camps with a large population and a greater risk of transmission of contagious diseases.

105.   The protections provided by Articles 15, 20, 29, 30, 31, 109 and 110 of Geneva Convention III are unconditional. These rules, which are based on similar rules in Articles 4, 13, 14, 15 and 68 of

the Geneva Convention Relative to the Treatment of Prisoners of War of July 27, 1929,[1] are part of customary international law.

106.   Many of these rules are broadly phrased and do not characterize precisely the quality or extent of medical care necessary for POWs. Article 15 speaks of the "medical attention *required* by their state of health;" Article 30 requires infirmaries to provide prisoners "the attention they *require*" (emphasis added). The lack of definition regarding the quality or extent of care "required" led to difficulties in assessing this claim. Indeed, standards of medical practice vary around the world, and there may be room for varying assessments of what is required in a specific situation. Moreover, the Commission is mindful that it is dealing here with two countries with very limited resources.

107.   Nevertheless, the Commission believes certain principles can be applied in assessing the medical care provided to POWs. The Commission began by considering Article 15's concept of the maintenance of POWs, which it understands to mean that a Detaining Power must do those things required to prevent significant deterioration of a prisoner's health. Next, the Commission paid particular attention to measures that are specifically required by Geneva Convention III, such as the requirements for segregation of prisoners with infectious diseases and for regular physical examinations.

* * *

c.   The Commission's Conclusions

116.   Overall, while the Commission is satisfied from the evidence that Eritrea made efforts to provide medical care and that some care was available at each permanent camp, Eritrea's evidence is inadequate to allow the Commission to form judgements regarding the extent or quality of health care sufficient to overcome Ethiopia's *prima facie* case.

117.   The camp clinic logs (where readable) do show that numerous POWs went to the clinics, but they cannot establish that care was appropriate or that all POWs in need of medical attention were treated in a timely manner over the full course of their captivity. For example, from the records it appears that the clinics did not register patients on a daily basis. Under international humanitarian law, a POW has the right to seek medical attention on his or her own initiative and to receive the continuous medical attention required by his or her state of health—which requires daily access to a clinic.

118.   International humanitarian law also requires that POWs be treated at a specialized hospital or facility when required medical care cannot be given in a camp clinic. The hospital records

---

1.   118 L.N.T.S. pp. 343–411.

submitted by Eritrea, however, are not sufficient to establish that all POWs in need of specialized treatment were referred to hospitals. Moreover, a quantitative analysis of those records shows that, while a few relate to treatment in the first half of 1999 at Digdigta, nearly one half relate to the period from August to December 2000 and one quarter to 2001 and 2002, *i.e.*, the time period after Eritrea acceded to the Geneva Conventions and ICRC camp visits started. Only a few records relate to treatment between July 1999 and May 2000, when the POWs were detained at Afabet, and none relates to the time when Barentu and Embakala were open.

119.   Likewise, the medicine supply reports submitted by Eritrea indicate that Eritrea distributed some drugs and vitamins to the POWs, but they do not prove that Eritrea provided adequate drugs to all POWs in the camps. It is striking that, according to the evidence submitted, Eritrea apparently distributed substantially more Vitamin A, B and C and multi-vitamins to POWs after August 2000 than before.

120.   Preventive care is a matter of particular concern to the Commission. As evidenced by their prominence in Geneva Convention III, regular medical examinations of all POWs are vital to maintaining good health in a closed environment where diseases are easily spread. The Commission considers monthly examinations of the camp population to be a preventive measure forming part of the Detaining Power's obligations under international customary law.

121.   The Commission must conclude that Eritrea failed to take several important preventative care measures specifically mandated by international law. In assessing this issue, the Commission looked not just to Ethiopia but also to Eritrea, which administered the camps and had the best knowledge of its own practices.

122.   As noted, Ethiopia submitted several declarations indicating that no regular medical examinations took place. Eritrea failed to submit records in rebuttal demonstrating that personal POW medical data, including weight records, were maintained on a regular basis. It appears that health inspections were performed only in the last months of captivity.

123.   The evidence also reflects that Eritrea failed to segregate certain infected prisoners. POWs are particularly susceptible to contagious diseases such as tuberculosis, and customary international law (reflecting proper basic health care) requires that infected POWs be isolated from the general POW population. Several Ethiopian POW declarants describe how tuberculosis patients were lodged with the other POWs, evidence which was not effectively rebutted by Eritrea. The camp authorities should have detected contagious diseases as early as possible and organized special wards.

124. Accordingly, the Commission holds that Eritrea violated international law from May 1998 until the last Ethiopian POWs were released and repatriated in August 2002, by failing to provide Ethiopian POWs with the required minimum standard of medical care. Consequently, Eritrea is liable for this violation of customary international law.

125. In closing, the Commission notes its recognition that Eritrea and Ethiopia cannot, at least at present, be required to have the same standards for medical treatment as developed countries. However, scarcity of finances and infrastructure cannot excuse a failure to grant the minimum standard of medical care required by international humanitarian law. The cost of such care is not, in any event, substantial in comparison with the other costs imposed by the armed conflict.

* * *

The Director of Public Prosecutions vs T

Sentence passed by the Eastern High Court (3rd Division) on 22 November 1994 (Denmark)*

In this case, tried by jury, the Chief Prosecutor for Zealand has changed T upon an indictment of 19 October 1994 and a supplementary indictment of 4 November 1994, as these were amended during the trial of the case, under para. 5 of Section 8 of the Danish Penal Code, cf. articles 129 and 130, respectively articles 146 and 147 of the 3rd and 4th Geneva Conventions of 1949 relative to the protection of victims of armed conflicts, for conviction

1.

of assault of a particularly cruel, brutal or dangerous nature and of such a malicious character and with such grave consequences as to constitute particularly aggravating circumstances as set out in section 246, cf. section 245, of the Penal Code, as on 5 August 1993 in the Croation POW camp of Dretelj in Bosnia, in association with some Croatian military police officers and another warder A ("Trebinjac" alias "Bunda") for about 45 minutes he beat up and maltreated B with fist blows, kicks, bludgeoning with wooden clubs and by stamping on B while he was lying down, which maltreatment caused B to die,

of assault of a particularly cruel, brutal or dangerous nature and of such a malicious character and with such grave consequences as to constitute particularly aggravating circumstances as set out in

* Danish Ministry of Foreign Affairs, unofficial translation.

section 246, cf. section 245, of the Penal Code, as in early August 1993 in the Croatian POW Camp of Dretelj in Bosnia, in association with Croatian military police officers among others, he maltreated C several times with fist blows, and kicks, last by having again dealt kicks to the head and body of C for a period of about 20–30 minutes, all of which maltreatment had the result that C died the same evening or night, * * *

> [Twenty-two more descriptions follow of a similar nature to 1. & 2., although no other victims apparently died of their injuries.]

The Prosecution has claimed in pursuance of section 73 of the Penal Code, that the accused shall be admitted to a psychiatric hospital until it may be possible to carry out the sentence imposed.

Moreover, the Prosecution has claimed an increase of the sentence according to section 88(1)(2) of the Penal Code.

Finally, the Prosecution has claimed expulsion of the accused from the Kingdom, with a ban on re-entry applicable forever.

The accused has pleaded not guilty of all counts.

The accused has been subjected to a mental examination at the Clinic of Forensic Psychiatry of the Ministry of Justice, from which a report of 17 May 1994 has been submitted.

Based on the mental report as well as other information available in the case, the Medico–Legal Council reported on 29 June 1944 that "prior to his arrival in Denmark, T had not with certainty offered signs of mental disturbance or disease.["]

He is currently described as insane, harbouring delusions with megalomaniac content as well as hallucinations and magic thinking. His appearance is exalted, with a speech pressure and with an inclination to get lost in details. Emotional contact takes place on his premises. In diagnostic terms, he is most likely to suffer from an acute, polymorphous psychosis (previously denoted reactive psychosis), triggered by emotional strain.

It is thus improbable that he was insane at the time of the committing the acts charged, whereas he has later developed a state of insanity that is not just of short duration. His intelligence level is deemed to be in the normal range. There are no signs that at the time of the acts charged he was in a pathological state of ecstasy.

As a consequence of his present state and the language and cultural conditions related to the mental observation, the Medico–Legal Council do not find it possible, with a reasonable degree of certainty, to report on his habitual personality features. Thus, it cannot be determined with certainty whether he is subject to section 69(1) of the Penal Code. However, he is now, with great probability, in a state corresponding to that referred to in section

16 of the same Act. In accordance with section 73 (1) of the Penal Code, the Medico–Legal Council recommend, as the most expedient measure, in case he is found guilty, that he should be admitted to a hospital for the mentally ill, until it may become possible to carry out any sentence".

* * *

The accused has appealed against the sentence, claiming acquittal on counts 3, 6, 7, 8, 10, 11, 14, 18, 19, 22, 23 and 25 of the case, referring to an allegation that these offences are not subject to Danish criminal jurisdiction. * * *

In support of his claim for acquittal, the accused has specifically pleaded that the offences referred to in this claim—which should be assessed separately—are not subject to Danish criminal jurisdiction because they cannot be characterized as "grave breaches" such as this concept is defined in article 130 of the 3rd Geneva Convention relative to the treatment of prisoners of war and in article 147 of the 4th Geneva Convention relative to the protection of civilians in times of war.

* * *

Article 129 of the 3rd Geneva Convention of August 12, 1949 relative to the treatment of prisoners of war is commenced as follows: "The High Contracting Parties undertake to enact any legislation necessary to provide effective penal sanctions for persons committing, or ordering to be committed, any of the grave breaches of the present Convention defined in the following Article".

Article 130 reads as follows:

"Grave breaches to which the preceding Article relates shall be those involving any of the following acts, if committed against persons or property protected by the Convention: wilful killing, torture or inhuman treatment, including biological experiments, wilfully causing great suffering or serious injury to body or health, compelling a prisoner of war to serve in the forces of the hostile Power, or wilfully depriving a prisoner of war of the rights of fair and regular trial prescribed in this Convention".

The provisions of Articles 146 and 147 of the 4th Geneva Convention of August 12, 1049 relative to the protection of civilians in times of war have the same wordings as to the issues relevant to this trial.

It appears from the evidence that the accused who is a Bosnian muslim, and who was himself a prisoner of war, was a "watchman", and that the violence was committed against fellow prisoners.

During the trial before the High Court, the Defence applied for an adjournment in order to procure detailed information about whether and when eight witnesses requested by the Defence could be heard by the High Court, referring to section 880(2), cf. section 881 of the Administration of Justice Act. Alternatively, the Defence requested leave to produce a written statement as well as a number of police reports in evidence.

In this connection, the High Court issued an Order of 18 November 1994, reading as follows:

"The Order is based on the circumstance that prior to and during the trial such steps as are possible have been taken by the Prosecution in order to find the witnesses in question.["]

Since it is considered only slightly probable, in view of the situation in Bosnia, that an adjournment of the trial will make it possible to conduct the requested examination of witnesses within a foreseeable time, the application for an adjournment shall not be granted.

Because this trial has involved quite exceptional difficulties for the production of evidence by the Defence, the mentioned documents shall, as an exception, be admitted in evidence as requested by the Defence.

* * *

Comments of the Supreme Court

Taking account of the fact that the large number of offences—of which several are very grave—were committed in quite uniform circumstances, the Supreme Court find that all counts related to the Conventions shall be considered as whole. This approach, which is considered to conform most appropriately to the objectives of the Conventions, implies that the requirements set out in the Conventions as to "grave breaches" have been met in the case of all counts of the indictment. Consequently, the Court cannot find for the claim for acquittal of the accused on the grounds of non-applicability of Danish criminal jurisdiction.

Since the Supreme Court accede to the reasons given in the Order issued by the High Court on November 18, 1994, the Supreme Court find that the High Court have not failed to observe any procedural rule by trying the case on the basis of the available witness evidence, cf. section 943 of the Administration of Justice Act.

The High Court have not either committed any procedural error in relation to the requirement as to the evidence cited in the sentence of the Court of Impeachment, which may be considered a reflection of the principle generally applicable in the administration of criminal justice that any reasonable doubt shall benefit the accused.

Consequently, the Supreme Court cannot find in favour of the claim of the accused for reversal and remission.

The offences charged on count 14 and on counts 3, 19, 22 and 25 have been committed at the Dretelj Camp against exhausted, defenceless prisoners who were without any possibility of protection by authorities or others from outrage which the victims might fear could continue for a long time and at mounting severity. These counts are thus found to have been lawfully tried with reference to section 246, cf. 245, as well as section 245 of the Penal Code.

Consequently, the Supreme Court shall not consider the claims of the accused in relation to the increase of the sentence imposed under section 88 of the Penal Code.

The Supreme Court have found no grounds for reducing the sentence.

[The High Court imposed a sentence of 8 years.]

In conformity with the claim of the Prosecution, the sentence is thus upheld by the Supreme Court.

The accused has continuously been detained during the hearing of the appeal.

The findings of the Supreme Court are as follows:

> *The sentence passed by the High Court shall be upheld.*

> [The High Court imposed a sentence of 8 years.]

> *The accused shall pay the costs of the trial of the case by the Supreme Court.*

The excerpt from the Eritrea Ethiopia Claims Commission above at pp. 546–557 discusses interrogation of POWs at paragraphs 75 and 76 of the award. The excerpt that follows is from the United States Army Field Manual 34–52 stating the US Army's view as to the law and policy regarding the use of coercion in interrogation.

FM 34–52

HEADQUARTERS

DEPARTMENTS OF THE ARMY

Washington, DC, 8 May 1987

FM 34-52

INTELLIGENCE INTERROGATION

---

* * *

Chapter 1

Interrogation and the Interrogator

Interrogation is the art of questioning and examining a source to obtain the maximum amount of usable information. The goal of any interrogation is to obtain usable and reliable information, in a lawful manner and in the least amount of time, which meets intelligence requirements of any echelon of command. Sources may be civilian internees, insurgents, EPWs [enemy prisoners of war], defectors, refugees, displaced persons, and agents or suspected agents. A successful interrogation produces needed information which is timely, complete, clear, and accurate. An interrogation involves the interaction of two personalities: the source and the interrogator. Each contact between these two differs to some degree because of their individual characteristics and capabilities, and because the circumstances of each contact and the physical environment vary.

* * *

PROHIBITION AGAINST USE OF FORCE

The use of force, mental torture, threats, insults, or exposure to unpleasant and inhumane treatment of any kind is prohibited by law and is neither authorized nor condoned by the US Government. Experience indicates that the use of force is not necessary to gain the cooperation of sources for interrogation. Therefore, the use of force is a poor technique, as it yields unreliable results, may damage subsequent collection efforts, and can induce the source to say whatever he thinks the interrogator wants to hear. However, the use of force is not to be confused with psychological ploys, verbal trickery, or other nonviolent and noncoercive ruses used by the interrogator in questioning hesitant or uncooperative sources.

Can you think of anything that might have changed to lead the US government to rethink this policy after September 11? What might have turned coercion from a "poor technique" to a useable one? The Ethiopia Eritrea Claims commissioners made their partial award in 2003. Do they indicate the law prohibiting coercion had changed after 2001?

B.   Restrictions in Hostilities

The previous Chapter focused on the protections that must be afforded civilians during hostilities. These protections are also restrictions on combatants. We include below another excerpt from the report for the ICTY prosecutor regarding the NATO bombing of Yugoslavia in 1999. While the report in general is concerned with unlawful killing of civilians and focuses on the rules for civilian protection, this excerpt focuses on the combatant, a US Air Force jet pilot and the decisions he had to make in the course of bombing a railroad bridge.

Following the excerpt from the ICTY report, we look at other decisions on the battlefield and restrictions on combatants with respect to other combatants.

> Final Report to the Prosecutor by the Committee Established to Review the NATO Bombing Campaign Against the Federal Republic of Yugoslavia, cont'd*
>
> i.   The Attack on a Civilian Passenger Train at the Grdelica Gorge on 12/4/99
>
> 58.   On 12 April 1999, a NATO aircraft launched two laser guided bombs at the Leskovac railway bridge over the Grdelica gorge and Juzna Morava river, in eastern Serbia. A 5–carriage passenger train, travelling from Belgrade to Ristovac on the Macedonian border, was crossing the bridge at the time, and was struck by both missiles. The various reports made of this incident concur that the incident occurred at about 11.40 a.m. At least ten people were killed in this incident and at least 15 individuals were injured. The designated target was the railway bridge, which was claimed to be part of a re-supply route being used for Serb forces in Kosovo. After launching the first bomb, the person controlling the weapon, at the last instant before impact, sighted movement on the bridge. The controller was unable to dump the bomb at that stage and it hit the train, the impact of the bomb cutting the second of the passenger coaches in half. Realising the bridge was still intact, the controller picked a second aim point on the bridge at the opposite end from where the train had come and launched the second bomb. In the meantime the train had slid forward as a result of the original impact and parts of the train were also hit by the second bomb.
>
> 59.   It does not appear that the train was targeted deliberately. US Deputy Defense Secretary John Hamre stated that "one of our electro-optically guided bombs homed in on a railroad bridge just

* Available at www.un.org/icty/pressre-al/nato061300.htm

when a passenger train raced to the aim point. We never wanted to destroy that train or kill its occupants. We did want to destroy the bridge and we regret this accident.'' The substantive part of the explanation, both for the failure to detect the approach of the passenger train and for firing a second missile once it had been hit by the first, was given by General Wesley Clark, NATO's Supreme Allied Commander for Europe and is here reprinted in full:

> "[T]his was a case where a pilot was assigned to strike a railroad bridge that is part of the integrated communications supply network in Serbia. He launched his missile from his aircraft that was many miles away, he was not able to put his eyes on the bridge, it was a remotely directed attack. And as he stared intently at the desired target point on the bridge, and I talked to the team at Aviano who was directly engaged in this operation, as the pilot stared intently at the desired aim point on the bridge and worked it, and worked it and worked it, and all of a sudden at the very last instant with less than a second to go he caught a flash of movement that came into the screen and it was the train coming in.

> Unfortunately he couldn't dump the bomb at that point, it was locked, it was going into the target and it was an unfortunate incident which he, and the crew, and all of us very much regret. We certainly don't want to do collateral damage.

> The mission was to take out the bridge. He realised when it had happened that he had not hit the bridge, but what he had hit was the train. He had another aim point on the bridge, it was a relatively long bridge and he believed he still had to accomplish his mission, the pilot circled back around. He put his aim point on the other end of the bridge from where the train had come, by the time the bomb got close to the bridge it was covered with smoke and clouds and at the last minute again in an uncanny accident, the train had slid forward from the original impact and parts of the train had moved across the bridge, and so that by striking the other end of the bridge he actually caused additional damage to the train." (Press Conference, NATO HQ, Brussels, 13 April).

General Clark then showed the cockpit video of the plane which fired on the bridge:

> "The pilot in the aircraft is looking at about a 5–inch screen, he is seeing about this much and in here you can see this is the railroad bridge which is a much better view than he actually had, you can see the tracks running this way.

> Look very intently at the aim point, concentrate right there and you can see how, if you were focused right on your job as a pilot, suddenly that train appeared. It was really unfortunate.

Here, he came back around to try to strike a different point on the bridge because he was trying to do a job to take the bridge down. Look at this aim point—you can see smoke and other obscuration there—he couldn't tell what this was exactly.

Focus intently right at the centre of the cross. He is bringing these two crosses together and suddenly he recognises at the very last instant that the train that was struck here has moved on across the bridge and so the engine apparently was struck by the second bomb." (Press Conference, NATO HQ, Brussels, 13 April).

* * *

62. It is the opinion of the committee that the bridge was a legitimate military objective. The passenger train was not deliberately targeted. The person controlling the bombs, pilot or WSO, targeted the bridge and, over a very short period of time, failed to recognize the arrival of the train while the first bomb was in flight. The train was on the bridge when the bridge was targeted a second time and the bridge length has been estimated at 50 meters (Wenz study para. 6 g above at p.25). It is the opinion of the committee that the information in relation to the attack with the first bomb does not provide a sufficient basis to initiate an investigation. The committee has divided views concerning the attack with the second bomb in relation to whether there was an element of recklessness in the conduct of the pilot or WSO. Despite this, the committee is in agreement that, based on the criteria for initiating an investigation (see para. 5 above), this incident should not be investigated. In relation to whether there is information warranting consideration of command responsibility, the committee is of the view that there is no information from which to conclude that an investigation is necessary into the criminal responsibility of persons higher in the chain of command. Based on the information available to it, it is the opinion of the committee that the attack on the train at Grdelica Gorge should not be investigated by the OTP.

The Concept of "Surrender" in the Conduct of Combat Operations

United States Defense Department Report to Congress
on the Conduct of the Persian Gulf War*

The law of war obligates a party to a conflict to accept the surrender of enemy personnel and thereafter treat them in accordance with the provisions of the 1949 Geneva Conventions for the

* Appendix O, The Role of the Law of
War, 629–632 (April 10, 1992).

Protection of War Victims. Article 23 (d) of Hague IV prohibits the denial of quarter, that is the refusal to accept an enemy's surrender, while other provisions in that treaty address the use of flags of truce and capitulation.

However, there is a gap in the law of war in defining precisely when surrender takes effect or how it may be accomplished in practical terms. Surrender involves an offer by the surrendering party (a unit or an individual soldier) and an ability to accept on the part of his opponent. The latter may not refuse an offer of surrender when communicated, but that communication must be made at a time when it can be received and properly acted upon an attempt at surrender in the midst of a hard-fought battle is neither easily communicated nor received. The issue is one of reasonableness.

A combatant force involved in an armed conflict is not obligated to offer its opponent an opportunity to surrender before carrying out an attack. To minimize Iraqi and Coalition casualties, however, the Coalition engaged in a major psychological operations campaign to encourage Iraqi soldiers to surrender before the Coalition ground offensive. Once that offensive began, the Coalition effort was to defeat Iraqi forces as quickly as possible to minimize the loss of Coalition lives. In the process, Coalition forces continued to accept legitimate Iraqi offers of surrender in a manner consistent with the law of war. The large number of Iraqi prisoners of war is evidence of Coalition compliance with its law of war obligations with regard to surrendering forces.

Situations arose in the course of Operation Desert Storm that have been questioned by some in the post-conflict environment. Two specific cases involve the Coalition's breach of the Iraqi defensive line and attack of Iraqi military forces leaving Kuwait City. Neither situation involved an offer of surrender by Iraqi forces, but it is necessary to discuss each in the context of the law of war concept of surrender.

[R]apid breach of the Iraqi defense in depth was crucial to the success of the Coalition ground campaign. When the ground campaign began, Iraq had not yet used its air force or extensive helicopter fleet in combat operations, the Iraqi Scud capability had not been eliminated, and most importantly, chemical warfare by Iraq remained a distinct possibility. It was uncertain whether the Coalition deception plan had worked or whether the Coalition effort had lost the element of surprise and there was also no definitive information about the strength and morale of the defending Iraqi soldiers. Because of these uncertainties, and the need to minimize loss of US and other Coalition lives, military necessity required that the assault through the forward Iraqi defensive line be conducted with maximum speed and violence.

The VII Corps main effort was the initial breaching operation through Iraqi defensive fortifications. This crucial mission was assigned to the 1st Infantry Division (Mechanized). The Division's mission was to conduct a deliberate breach of the Iraqi defensive positions as quickly as possible to expand and secure the breach site, and to pass the 1st UK Armored Division through the lines to continue the attack against the Iraqi forces.

To accomplish the deliberate breaching operations, the 1st Infantry Division (Mechanized) moved forward and plowed through the berms and mine fields erected by the Iraqis. Many Iraqis surrendered during this phase of the attack and were taken prisoner. The division then assaulted the trenches containing other Iraqi, soldiers. Once astride the trench lines, the division turned the plow blades of its tanks and combat earthmovers along the Iraqi defense line and, covered by fire from its M–2/–3 armored infantry fighting vehicles, began to fill in the trench line and its heavily bunkered, mutually supporting fighting positions.

In the process, many more Iraqi soldiers surrendered to division personnel; others died in the course of the attack and destruction or bulldozing of their defensive positions.

By nightfall, the division had breached the Iraqi defenses, consolidated its position, and prepared to pass the 1st UK Armoured Division through the lines. Hundreds of Iraqi soldiers had been taken prisoner; US casualties were extremely light.

The tactic used by the 1st Infantry Division (Mechanized) resulted in a number of Iraqi soldiers dying in their defensive positions as those positions were bulldozed. Marine Corps breaching operations along its axis of attack into Kuwait used different, but also legally acceptable, techniques of assault by fire, bayonet, and the blasting of enemy defensive positions. Both tactics were entirely consistent with the law of war.

Tactics involving the use of armored vehicles against dug-in infantry forces have been common since the first use of armored vehicles in combat. The tactic of using armored vehicles to crush or bury enemy soldiers was briefly discussed in the course of the UN Conference on Certain Conventional Weapons, conducted in Geneva from 1978 to 1980 and attended by the United States and more than 100 other nations. It was left unregulated, however, as it was recognized by the participants to be a common long-standing tactic entirely consistent with the law of war.

In the case in point, military necessity required violent, rapid attack. Had the breaching operation stalled, the VII Corps main effort would have been delayed or, at worst, blunted. This would have had an adverse effect on the entire ground campaign, lengthening the time required to liberate Kuwait, and increasing overall Coalition casualties.

As first stated in US Army General Orders No. 100 (1863), otherwise known as the Lieber Code, military necessity "consists in the necessity of those measures which are indispensable for securing the ends of war, and which are lawful according to the modern law and usages of war. . . . [It] admits of all direct destruction of life or limb of armed enemies." As developed by the practice of nations since that time, the law of war has placed restrictions on the application of force against enemy combatants in very few circumstances (e.g., the first use of chemical or biological weapons). None of these restrictions were at issue during the breaching operations during Operation Desert Storm.

The law of war principle complementary to military necessity is that of unnecessary suffering (or superfluous injury). That principle does not preclude combat actions that otherwise are lawful, such as that used by the 1st Infantry Division (Mechanized).

In the course of the breaching operations, the Iraqi defenders were given the opportunity to surrender, as indicated by the large number of EPWs taken by the division. However, soldiers must make their intent to surrender clear and equivocal, and do so rapidly. Fighting from fortified emplacements is not a manifestation of an intent to surrender, and a soldier who fights until the very last possible moment assumes certain risks. His opponent either may not see his surrender, may not recognize his actions as an attempt to surrender in the heat and confusion of battle, or may find it difficult (if not impossible) to halt an onrushing assault to accept a soldier's last-minute effort surrender.

It was in this context that the breach of the Iraqi defense line occurred. The scenario Coalition forces faced and described herein illustrates the difficulty of defining or effecting "surrender." Nonetheless, the breaching tactics used by US Army and Marine Corps forces assigned this assault mission were entirely consistent with US law of war obligations.

In the early hours of 27 February, CENTCOM received a report that a concentration of vehicles was forming in Kuwait City. It was surmised that Iraqi forces were preparing to depart under the cover of darkness. CINCCENT was concerned about the redeployment of Iraqi forces in Kuwait City, fearing they could join with and provide reinforcements for Republican Guard units west of Kuwait City in an effort to stop the Coalition advance or otherwise endanger Coalition forces.

The concentration of Iraqi military personnel and vehicles, including tanks, invited attack. CINCCENT decides against attack of the Iraqi forces in Kuwait City, since it could lead to substantial collateral damage to Kuwait civilian property and could cause surviving Iraqi units to decide to mount a defense from Kuwait City rather than depart. Iraqi units remaining in Kuwait City would cause the Coalition to engage in military operations in urban terrain, a form of fighting that is costly to attacker, defender, innocent civilians, and civilian objects.

The decision was made to permit Iraqi forces to leave Kuwait City and engage them in the unpopulated area to the north. Once departed, the Iraqi force was stopped by barricades of mines deployed across the highway in front of and behind the column. Air attacks on the trapped vehicles began about 0200. The following morning, CENTCOM leadership viewed the resulting damage. More than two hundred Iraqi tanks had been trapped and destroyed in the ambush, along with hundreds of other military vehicles and various forms of civilian transportation confiscated or seized by Iraqi forces for the redeployment. The vehicles in turn were full of property pillaged from Kuwaiti civilians: appliances, clothing, jewelry, compact disc players, tape recorders, and money, the last step in the Iraqi looting of Kuwait.

Throughout the ground campaign Coalition leaflets had warned Iraqi soldiers that their tanks and other vehicles were subject to attack, but that Iraqi soldiers would not be attacked if they abandoned their vehicles—yet another way in which the Coalition endeavored to minimize Iraqi casualties while encouraging their defection and/or surrender. When the convoy was stopped by the mining operations that blocked the Iraqi axis of advance, most Iraqi soldiers in the vehicles immediately abandoned their vehicles and fled into the desert to avoid attack.

In the aftermath of Operation Desert Storm, some questions were raised regarding this attack, apparently on the supposition that the Iraqi force was retreating. The attack was entirely consistent with military doctrine and the law of war. The law of war permits the attack of enemy combatants and enemy equipment at any time, wherever located, whether advancing, retreating, or standing still. Retreat does not prevent further attack. At the small-unit level, for example, once an objective has been seized and the position consolidated, an attacking force is trained to fire upon the retreating enemy to discourage or prevent a counterattack.

Attacks on retreating enemy forces have been common throughout history. Napoleon suffered some of his worst losses in his retreat from Russia, as did the German We[h]rmacht more than a century later. It is recognized by military professionals that a retreating force remains dangerous. The 1st Marine Division and its 4,000 attached US Army forces and British Royal Marines, in the famous 1950 march out of the Chosin Reservoir in North Korea, fighting outnumbered by a 4:1 margin, turned its "retreat" into a battle in which it defeated the 20th and 26th Chinese Armies trying to annihilate it, much as Xenophon and his "immortal 10,000" did as they fought their way through hostile Persian forces to the Black Sea in 401 BC.

In the case at hand, neither the composition, degree of unit cohesiveness, nor intent of the Iraqi military forces engaged was known at the time of the attack. At no time did any element within the formation offer to surrender. CENTCOM was under no law of war obligation to offer the Iraqi forces an opportunity to surrender before the attack.

C. COMMAND RESPONSIBILITY

Violation of IHL typically occurs at a distance from the headquarters of generals and the offices of civilian leaders. These high-ranking individuals rarely commit violations personally but are may be held accountable depending on the test of command responsibility for what occurs in hostilities and occupation. The ICTY has dealt with several cases concerning the appropriate test or standard of command responsibility.[3]

Prosecutor v. Tihomir Blaškić

IT–95–14–A, 29 July 2004*

JUDGEMENT

* * *

2. The events giving rise to this appeal took place during the conflict between the Croatian Defense Council ("HVO") and the Bosnian Muslim Army in the Lašva Valley region of Central Bosnia in the period from May 1992 until January 1994. The Appellant Tihomir Blaškić was the Commander of the HVO Armed Forces in Central Bosnia at the time the crimes at issue were committed.

3. The Trial Chamber convicted the Appellant on the basis of nineteen counts set forth in the Indictment, in relation to crimes occurring in the Vitez, Busovača, and Kiseljak municipalities. These counts encompassed violations of Articles 2, 3, and 5 of the Statute of the International Tribunal ("Statute"). The Appellant was convicted on the basis of Article 7(1) of the Statute for ordering the crimes at issue in this appeal.[a] The Trial Chamber also stated in the disposition of the judgement that "[i]n any event, as a commander, he failed to take the necessary and reasonable measures which would have allowed these crimes to be prevented or the perpetrators thereof to be punished..." There-

---

3. *See* ILIAS BANTEKAS, PRINCIPLES OF DIRECT AND SUPERIOR RESPONSIBILITY (2002).

* International Tribunal for the Prosecution of Persons Responsible for Serious Violations of International Humanitarian Law Committed in the Territory of the Former Yugoslavia since 1991 (footnotes omitted).

a. Art. 7(1) A person who planned, instigated, ordered, committed or otherwise aided and abetted in the planning, preparation or execution of a crime referred to in articles 2 to 5 of the present Statute, shall be individually responsible for the crime.

fore, the Trial Chamber also convicted the Appellant under Article 7(3) of the Statute.[b] The Trial Chamber imposed a single sentence of 45 years' imprisonment.

* * *

A. Individual Criminal Responsibility under Article 7(1) of the Statute

1. Planning, Instigating, and Ordering

27. According to the Appellant, the standards set forth in the Trial Judgement concerning the forms of criminal participation consisting of planning, instigating, and ordering under Article 7(1) of the Statute deviate from those established by the jurisprudence of the International Tribunal and the ICTR, customary international law, and national legislation. The Appellant submits that the correct standard of *mens rea* for these three forms of criminal participation is "direct or specific intent," rather than the "indirect" or recklessness standard adopted by the Trial Chamber in this case. In addition, he alleges that the Trial Chamber failed to differentiate between the recklessness standard and that of *dolus eventualis*, and improperly applied these concepts.

* * *

32. At the outset, the Appeals Chamber notes that the Appellant was not convicted for planning or instigating crimes. As a result, it declines to consider the issues raised in this ground of appeal in relation to these two modes of participation. The issue which the Appeals Chamber will address is whether a standard of *mens rea* that is lower than direct intent may apply in relation to ordering under Article 7(1) of the Statute, and if so, how it should be defined.

33. The Appeals Chamber has not had the occasion to pronounce on this issue in previous decisions. In the *Vasiljević* Appeal Judgement, the Appeals Chamber considered the issue of *mens rea*, but in relation to the extended form of joint criminal enterprise. * * *

34. In further examining the issue of whether a standard of *mens rea* that is lower than direct intent may apply in relation to ordering under Article 7(1) of the Statute, the Appeals Chamber deems it useful to consider the approaches of national jurisdictions. In common law systems, the *mens rea* of recklessness is sufficient to ground liability for serious crimes such as murder or manslaughter. In the United States, for example, the concept of

b. Art. 7(3) The fact that any of the acts referred to in articles 2 to 5 of the present Statute was committed by a subordinate does not relieve his superior of criminal responsibility if he knew or had reason to know that the subordinate was about to commit such acts or had done so and the superior failed to take the necessary and reasonable measures to prevent such acts or to punish the perpetrators thereof.

recklessness in criminal cases has been defined in the Model Penal Code as follows:

> a conscious disregard of a substantial and unjustifiable risk that the material element exists or will result from [the actor's] conduct. The risk must be of such a nature and degree that, considering the nature and purpose of the actor's conduct and the circumstances known to him, its disregard involves a gross deviation from the standard of conduct that a law-abiding person would observe in the actor's situation.

According to the Model Penal Code, therefore, the degree of risk involved must be substantial and unjustifiable; a mere possibility of risk is not enough.

35.   In the United Kingdom, the House of Lords in the case of *R v. G and another* considered the ambit of recklessness within the meaning of section 1 of the Criminal Damage Act of 1971. Lord Bingham's opinion, with which his colleagues agreed, was that

> [A] person acts recklessly within the meaning of section 1 of the Criminal Damage Act 1971 with respect to—(i) a circumstance when he is aware of a risk that it exists or will exist; (ii) a result when he is aware of a risk that it will occur; and it is, in the circumstances known to him, unreasonable to take the risk...

According to this opinion, the risk involved must be unreasonable; furthermore, with respect to a particular result, the actor in question must be aware of a risk that such a result will occur, not merely that it may occur.

36.   In the Australian High Court decision of *R v. Crabbe*, the Court considered "whether the knowledge which an accused person must possess in order to render him guilty of murder when he lacks an actual intent to kill or to do grievous bodily harm must be knowledge of the probability that his acts will cause death or grievous bodily harm (. . .) or whether knowledge of a possibility is enough." The High Court determined that:

> The conclusion that a person is guilty of murder if he commits a fatal act knowing that it will probably cause death or grievous bodily harm but (absent an intention to kill or do grievous bodily harm) is not guilty of murder if he knew only that his act might possibly cause death or grievous bodily harm is not only supported by a preponderance of authority but is sound in principle. The conduct of a person who does an act, knowing that death or grievous bodily harm is a *probable consequence*, can naturally be regarded for the purposes of the criminal law as just as blameworthy as the conduct of one who does an act intended to kill or to do grievous bodily harm.

37. The High Court in *R v. Crabbe* also considered the situation where a person's knowledge of the probable consequence of his act is accompanied by indifference, finding that:

> A person who does an act causing death knowing that it is probable that the act will cause death or grievous bodily harm is...guilty of murder, although such knowledge is accompanied by indifference whether death or grievous bodily harm might not be caused or not, or even by a wish that death or grievous bodily harm might not be caused. That does not mean that reckless indifference is an element of the mental state necessary to constitute the crime of murder. It is not the offender's indifference to the consequences of his act but his knowledge that those consequences will probably occur that is the relevant element.

38. In the common law jurisdictions examined above, the *mens rea* of recklessness incorporates the awareness of a risk that the result or consequence will occur or will probably occur, and the risk must be unjustifiable or unreasonable. The mere possibility of a risk that a crime or crimes will occur as a result of the actor's conduct generally does not suffice to ground criminal responsibility.

39. In civil law systems, the concept of *dolus eventualis* may constitute the requisite *mens rea* for crimes. In French law, for example, this has been characterized as the taking of a risk and the acceptance of the eventuality that harm may result. Although the harm in question was not desired by the actor, it was caused by his dangerous behaviour, which was carried out deliberately and with the knowledge that harm may occur. In Italian law, the principle is expressed as follows: the occurrence of the fact constituting a crime, even though it is not desired by the perpetrator, is foreseen and accepted as a possible consequence of his own conduct. The German Federal Supreme Court (Bundesgerichtshof, BGH) has found that acting with *dolus eventualis* requires that the perpetrator perceive the occurrence of the criminal result as possible and not completely remote, and that he endorse it or at least come to terms with it for the sake of the desired goal. It has further stated that in the case of extremely dangerous, violent acts, it is obvious that the perpetrator takes into account the possibility of the victim's death and, since he continues to carry out the act, accepts such a result. The volitional element denotes the borderline between *dolus eventualis* and advertent or conscious negligence.

40. In the present case, the Trial Chamber in paragraph 474 of the Trial Judgement articulated the following standard:

> Even if doubt were still cast in spite of everything on whether the accused ordered the attack with the clear

intention that the massacre would be committed, he would still be liable under Article 7(1) of the Statute for ordering the crimes. As has been explained above, any person who, in ordering an act, knows that there is a risk of crimes being committed and accepts that risk, shows the degree of intention necessary (recklessness) [*le dol éventuel* in the original French text] so as to incur responsibility for having ordered, planned or incited the commitment of the crimes.

Although the Trial Chamber, citing in a footnote its "above, discussion on Article 7 of the Statute," indicated that the standard it was articulating in paragraph 474 had already been explained earlier in the Trial Judgement, an examination of previous paragraphs pertaining to the legal elements of Article 7 demonstrates that the Trial Chamber did not actually do so. Other paragraphs in the Trial Judgement articulated the standard set out in paragraph 474 using different expressions. These paragraphs are quoted below:

562.   The Trial Chamber concludes that General Blaškić is responsible for the crimes committed in the three villages on the basis of his negligence [*dol éventuel* in the French text], in other words for having ordered acts which he could only reasonably have anticipated would lead to crimes.

592.   The Trial Chamber is also convinced beyond any reasonable doubt that by giving orders to the Military Police in April 1993, when he knew full well that there were criminals in its ranks[], the accused intentionally took the risk that very violent crimes would result from their participation in the offensives. . . .

653.   The Trial Chamber maintains that even though General Blaškić did not explicitly order the expulsion and killing of the civilian Muslim populations, he deliberately ran the risk of making them and their property the primary targets of the "sealing off" and offensives launched on 18 April 1993. . . .

661.   The Trial Chamber is of the view that the content of the military orders sent to the Ban Jelačić Brigade commander, the systematic and widespread aspect of the crimes perpetrated and the general context in which these acts fit permit the assertion that the accused ordered the attacks effected in April and June 1993 against the Muslim villages in the Kiseljak region. It also appears ["Il appert également" in the French text] that General Blaškić clearly had to have known that by ordering the Ban Jelačić Brigade to launch such wide-ranging attacks against essentially civilian targets extremely violent

crimes would necessarily result. Lastly, it emerges from those same facts that the accused did not pursue a purely military objective but that by using military assets he also sought to implement the policy of persecution of the Muslim civilian populations set by the highest HVO authorities and that, through these offensives, he intended to make the populations in the Kiseljak municipality take flight.

738. With particular regard for the degree of organisation required, the Trial Chamber concludes that General Blaškić ordered the use of detainees to dig trenches, including under dangerous conditions at the front. The Trial Chamber also adjudges that by ordering the forced labour Blaškić knowingly took the risk that his soldiers might commit violent acts against vulnerable detainees, especially in a context of extreme tensions.

741. The Trial Chamber concludes that although General Blaškić did not order that hostages be taken, it is inconceivable that as commander he did not order the defence of the town where his headquarters were located. In so doing, Blaškić deliberately ran the risk that many detainees might be taken hostage for this purpose.

41. Having examined the approaches of national systems as well as International Tribunal precedents, the Appeals Chamber considers that none of the Trial Chamber's above articulations of the *mens rea* for ordering under Article 7(1) of the Statute, in relation to a culpable mental state that is lower than direct intent, is correct. The knowledge of any kind of risk, however low, does not suffice for the imposition of criminal responsibility for serious violations of international humanitarian law. The Trial Chamber does not specify what degree of risk must be proven. Indeed, it appears that under the Trial Chamber's standard, any military commander who issues an order would be criminally responsible, because there is always a possibility that violations could occur. The Appeals Chamber considers that an awareness of a higher likelihood of risk and a volitional element must be incorporated in the legal standard.

42. The Appeals Chamber therefore holds that a person who orders an act or omission with the awareness of the substantial likelihood that a crime will be committed in the execution of that order, has the requisite *mens rea* for establishing liability under Article 7(1) pursuant to ordering. Ordering with such awareness has to be regarded as accepting that crime.

* * *

D. NOTES, QUESTIONS, AND PROBLEMS

1. In the Hamdi case, Justice O'Connor refers to the US government's basis for considering Hamdi an "enemy combatant." "The Mobbs Declaration also states that, because al Qaeda and the Taliban 'were and are hostile forces engaged in armed conflict with the armed forces of the United States,' 'individuals associated with' those groups 'were and continue to be enemy combatants.'" See also the memorandum by Haynes, pp. 531–535, above. Is mere "association" with a group sufficient under IHL to be a "combatant?" What more must be shown? What definition does Justice O'Connor herself apply for purposes of the case?

2. In the Ethiopia–Eritrea Prisoner of War Claims, the Commission notes that Eritrea and Ethiopia cannot be held to the same standard as developed countries for medical treatment. They can be held to provide a minimum standard. What does this mean for IHL? Are the United States, Britain and other developed states expected to provide a higher level of medical treatment to POWs or is it also only required to provide the same minimum as Ethiopia and Eritrea? Should they be held to a higher standard? In the area of international environmental law, differential responsibility between developed and developing countries does feature in the law. (See, e.g., the Rio Declaration on Environment and Development.) Should "differential responsibility" be part of IHL, too? Reconsider the problem at the end of Chapter 9 on Soviet prisoners in the Afghan conflict and the difficulty rebel fighters in Afghanistan had in meeting their obligations regarding POWs. What is the argument against differential responsibility? What are the alternatives for poor states or rebel or insurgent fighters if they do not have the resources or the practical ability to meet IHL standards respecting POWs and other detainees? See also Note 6, Chapter 10, p. 519.

3. Torture, coercion and abuse of persons in detention are prohibited by, among other principles, the Third Geneva Convention, art. 17, Additional Protocol I, art. 75 and Additional Protocol II, art. 4(2). In 1999, Israel's Supreme Court generally prohibited the use of torture by Israel's General Security Service in Judgment Concerning the Legality of the General Security Service's Interrogation Methods, Sept. 6, 1999, http://www.israel-mfa.gov.il/mfa/home.asp. The Court did, however, make one exception to the general ban: "Our decision does not negate the possibility that the 'necessity' defence be available to GSS investigators, be within the discretion of the Attorney General, if he decides to prosecute, or if criminal charges are brought against them, as per the Court's discretion." *Id.* at 1489. The Committee Against Torture which monitors respect for the Convention Against Torture raised this aspect of the decision as a point of concern: "While acknowledging the importance of the September 1999 Supreme Court decision, the Committee regrets certain consequences of it: ... The Court indicated that ISA interrogators who use physical pressure in extreme circumstances (ticking bomb cases) might not be criminally liable as they may be able to rely on the 'defence of necessity.'" Conclusions and Recommendations of the Committee against Torture: Israel, UN

Doc.   CAT/C/XXVII/Concl.5.(ConcludingObservations/Comments),   http://www.ohchr.org

Does the *jus in bello* have any necessity exception with regard to methods used in interrogating person in military detention?

4.   Compare the tests of command responsibility in the Yamashita Case, pp. 192–205 and the Blaškić Case, pp. 570–575. Consider the various violations of IHL found in the Ethiopia's Claim 4. Can you argue that an Eritrean civilian defense minister might be responsible for any of those violations? What further facts would you need to make a case for responsibility under the Yamashita Case or under the Blaškić Case?

5.   When does war end for purposes of IHL? When must prisoners of war be released? In the Ethiopia–Eritrea War an effective cease-fire was established in June 2002. Is that what it takes to end a war? Or must there be a peace agreement? Ethiopia and Eritrea set up the peace settlement system by agreement only in December 2002. In the conflict in Afghanistan that began October 2001, fighting was still on going according to Justice O'Connor in June 2004, when the Hamdi Case was decided. On the other hand, the government had changed in Afghanistan from the Taliban to the regime of Hamid Karzai. Can you argue that as of the time of the Hamdi decision, no international armed conflict was occurring in Afghanistan and so only the rules of non-international armed conflict applied?

6.   During the Iran–Iraq War, Iraq used chemical weapons against Iranian soldiers and civilians. "A U.N. report last week accused Iraq of widespread use of chemical weapons against Iranian civilians and soldiers in the first proven use of the outlawed arms since World War I." *Gulf War Cease-fire to Begin Aug. 20*, Seattle Times, Aug. 8, 1988, at A1. Even if chemical weapons were not outlawed specifically by treaty for use against enemy soldiers, can you find other principles that would forbid their use?

Controversy has arisen over the use of depleted uranium weapons by the United States. Studies by the US military have not found unintended health affects from the weapons as of 2004. Other studies have shown at least a relationship between exposure to the spent casings of uranium weapons and elevated radiation in people's blood. Should there be a precautionary principle regarding new weapons? Until they can be proven to have only the harmful affects intended, should they be produced? Would such a standard not hold weapons—already inherently dangerous—to a higher standard than most consumer products? *See* Dan Beaulieu, *New Fear in Iraq Over US Use of Depleted Uranium in War*, Agence France-Presse, May 8, 2003, 2003 WL 2797719.

7.   Sophisticated militaries provide their members with instructions on how to conduct themselves during particular hostilities. These instructions are called "rules of engagement." ROE are directives issued by a commander that clearly define when and how force can be used. At the tactical level, ROE typically address under what circumstances a soldier can fire his/her weapon. At the strategic level, ROE discuss the circumstances and restrictions under which a force will initiate and/or continue engagement with the enemy. ROE can be mission-specific or standardized for a theater of operations. ROE play a critical role in ensuring that combatants respect IHL restraints. *See Rules of Engagement, in* UNITED STATES ARMY JUDGE ADVOCATE GENERAL CORPS, OPERATIONAL LAW HANDBOOK 2005, 89–90 (2004); Mark Martins, *Rules of Engagement for Land Forces: A Matter of Training, Not Lawyering*, 143 MIL L. REV. 1, 30–33 (1994).

8. In addition to the various references throughout the chapter, see also, A.P.V. ROGERS, LAW ON THE BATTLEFIELD (2d ed. 2004); REFLECTIONS ON LAW AND ARMED CONFLICTS: THE SELECTED WORKS ON THE LAWS OF WAR BY THE LATE PROFESSOR COLONEL G.I.A.D. DRAPER, OBE (Michael A. Meyer & Hilaire McCoubrey eds., 1998).

9. Problem: "On November 3, 2002, agents of the CIA, using an unmanned Predator drone, fired a Hellfire missile against a vehicle in remote Yemen killing six men. One of those men was suspected of being a high-ranking Al Qaeda lieutenant. According to the media, Yemen had knowledge of the operation. Following the strike, National Security Adviser Condoleezza Rice stated, 'We are in a new kind of war. And we've made very clear that it is important that this new kind of war be fought on different battlefields.' * * * Yemen was involved in a civil war for years, but Yemen's authorities recognize that war ended in 1994. Following the attack on the USS *Cole* in 2000, the United States sent agents of the Federal Bureau of Investigation to work with Yemeni authorities to solve the case. Police techniques were used. Conditions in Yemen at the time of the Predator strike had not changed markedly from the time of the *Cole* attack." Mary Ellen O'Connell, *Ad Hoc War, in* KRISENSICHERUNG UND HUMANITÄRER SCHUTZ–CRISIS MANAGEMENT AND HUMANITARIAN PROTECTION 405, 415–16 (Horst Fischer et al., eds., 2004). *See also*, Michael Schmitt, *"Direct Participation in Hostilities" and 21st Century Armed Conflict*, in *id*., at 505. The CIA suspected that the alleged high-ranking Al Qaeda lieutenant had participated in some way in the attack on the *Cole* in which 17 US sailors lost their lives. Little is know of the others riding in the vehicle with him other than that one was a US citizen.

Was the alleged Al Qaeda lieutenant a combatant when he was targeted? If he was, was the use of an unmanned drone to fire a missile at him an acceptable means of attack? Did it conform with the principles of necessity, proportionality, and distinction? There is currently no treaty prohibiting the use of unmanned aerial vehicles. Based on the treaty provisions and customary principles you have studied in this and other Chapters, make an argument both for and against the legality of using unmanned vehicles.

CHAPTER TWELVE

PROPOSING THE FUTURE

Law is never static. It must continue to adapt to the ever-changing realities of human existence. We have seen throughout this book how the international law on the use of force has changed over time. It is clear that it will continue to change and the law of the future will look different from the law contained in the preceding pages. Those pages do contain some indications of how the law is likely to develop. We have seen that gaps in the law exist, and can predict that those are likely to be filled. We have seen controversies over the correct interpretation current law and know that those could be settled. We have seen arguments for new interpretations of the law that courts and other bodies may one day adopt. These are all areas to watch for the law of the future. This Chapter adds another area of consideration to all the indications of future developments you have already seen. It gathers together several proposals for outright, fundamental change in the law. These proposals require dramatic departures from the current rules and institutions of the international law on the use of force. If these proposals are adopted, the law will definitely change. Consider, in reading them, what the strengths and weaknesses are in the proposals. Think about the underlying policies and principles of existing law when deciding whether these proposals constitute changes for the better. Bear in mind the impact of any radical change on the authority of law in general. Most legal change occurs incrementally, but from time-to-time radical change is needed and does occur.[1] Consider, also, what proposals you would make for improving the international law on the use of force.

A. AD BELLUM PROPOSALS

Karl M. Meessen, Unilateral Recourse to Military Force Against Terrorist Attacks

28 YALE INT'L L. J. 341, 341–50 (2003)*

I. A New Response to a Not So New Challenge

If a state that has been victimized by a large-scale terrorist attack seeks recourse to military force against another state, it can be expected to do so at a scale well above the threshold set by Article 2(4) of the Charter of the United Nations. Such threat or exercise

---

1. For an article proposing incremental change, *see* W. Michael Reisman, ASSESSING CLAIMS TO REVISE THE LAWS OF WAR, 97 AM. J. INT'L L. 82 (2003).

* Footnotes omitted.

of military force is prohibited by that rule unless it is authorized under the provisions on collective security laid down in Chapter VII of the U.N. Charter or unless it occurs in legitimate self-defense. Under Chapter VII, it is for the multilateral decision-making of the Security Council to qualify a terrorist attack as a "threat to the peace" and then to decide what remedy is appropriate. The question to be discussed in this paper, however, refers to the legality of "unilateral" acts of military force in response to terrorist attacks. The discussion will therefore have to address the self-defense exception to the general prohibition on the use of force. Unilateral acts, it should be added, are here understood to include "plurilateral" acts, that is, acts undertaken by two or more states.

Under Article 51, "nothing in the present Charter," which includes the prohibition on the use of force in Article 2(4), "shall impair the inherent right of individual or collective self-defense if an armed attack occurs against a member of the United Nations, until the Security Council has taken measures necessary to maintain international peace and security." A terrorist attack masterminded by, or otherwise attributable to, a particular foreign state may constitute an "armed attack" in the sense of Article 51 and then be answered by the unilateral or plurilateral exercise of the right of self-defense. However, September 11, 2001, and its aftermath, has shown that terrorist attacks need not be state-sponsored at all, and that sometimes no evidence for any state-sponsorship may be available. Terrorist attacks out of the clear blue sky, like those of 9/11, lack the government connotation of the term "armed attack." Such terrorist attacks are society-induced. Is responding to them covered by Article 51 all the same?

Shortly after the Iraqi invasion of Kuwait in 1990, Francois Mitterand, the then president of France, spoke of the "logic of war" (logique de guerre) as the principle driving events at the time. The fight against society-induced terrorism, too, follows its own logic. That logic is equally inescapable but also quite different from the logic of war President Mitterand had in mind. While the potential of society-induced crossborder terrorism may only have become manifest on September 11, trying to fight it on a world-wide scale certainly is an entirely new phenomenon. The precise properties of the logic of that fight, one is glad to note, are unknown so far. Conjectural considerations cannot altogether be avoided.

Legal rules, even of written law, rarely precede factual developments. Understandably, therefore, every conceivable effort is undertaken to apply the existing rules to the new phenomenon of a worldwide fight against society-induced terrorism so as either to render an early verdict of illegality on unilateral action, or to pave the ground for a more favorable assessment by extending, or overextending, the meaning of the existing law. In the post–9/11 literature, only a few authors advocate a new approach. To leave the well-trodden paths means incurring a high risk, but such an approach at least offers the chance of viewing the structure of the rules in accordance with the pattern of the practice they are designed both to reflect and orient.

* * *

The fight against terrorism is taking place in an asymmetrical setting. On September 11, 2001, the most powerful state the world has ever known, both in absolute and relative terms, was hit in the heart of both its military and commercial prowess by just a few men of daunting courage. In addition to the terrorists' resolve to sacrifice their lives, it is their invisibility that gives them the capacity to launch attacks of such horrible effectiveness. * * *

* * *

[I]t may from time to time be necessary to send the terrorists and their sympathizers a message of one's own determination, one's courage, and one's preparedness for sacrifice. The foregoing observations do not exactly propound a call to arms. All that can be said at this point is that the fight against terrorism has to be envisaged—as it actually is—at many different levels at a time. If there is a decisive battle to be fought against terrorism, it must be fought and won on the psychological level, which may involve signaling the resolve of Western society to take risks for its conception of world peace. The widely held view of the incapacitating effects of the "post-heroic age" may need to be refuted. If military action is to be taken, neither the unilateral option, because of the probable unavailability of effective multilateral action, nor the option of preemptive strikes, because of the greater damage they might help to avoid, can be generally left aside. But those very options also present a particular challenge to legal analysis.

III.   The Right to Survival in the Bounds of Legal Rationality

The procedural posture of the Nicaragua case prevented the International Court of Justice from applying multilateral treaty law, including the legal rules contained in the U.N. Charter. The Court therefore had to base its decision on the merits on other sources of international law, such as bilateral treaties and customary international law. Referring to the language of the Charter—"inherent right" in the English text and "droit naturel" in the French text—the Court held that the right of self-defense is granted under both treaty law and customary international law.

Relying on the "Definition of Aggression" annexed to General Assembly Resolution 3314 (XXIX) of December 14, 1974, the Court went on to define the terms "armed attack" and "agression armée" as suggesting some link to one or more particular states backing the action. In the Nicaragua case, the mere "assistance to rebels in the form of provision of weapons or logistical or other support" was explicitly denied the effect of attributing the responsibility for private operations to a particular state.

Under that standard, the attack on the World Trade Center and the Pentagon can hardly be qualified as an armed attack on the part of Afghanistan against the United States. To be sure, arguing for a lower standard than the one set by the Court is possible, albeit unrelated to the logic of fighting society-induced terrorist attacks. Yet there is, as will be elaborated below, an emerging rule of customary law that directly addresses society-induced terrorist attacks. That rule focuses on fighting terrorism rather than fending off ongoing attacks launched by one or more foreign states under the standard developed by the Court.

* * *

* * * [D]evelopment of new customary law, [] may allow for a unilateral recourse to military action against society-induced terrorist attacks. Neither that fact, nor the actual interventions in Afghanistan and Iraq, suffice to establish a new rule of customary law. On the conceptual side, however, the grounds for an emerging rule of customary law seem well prepared. The pertinent concepts can be derived from the traditional law of self-defense as it has been developed by the International Court of Justice.

The principle found to underlie the right of self-defense is the right of a state to fight for its survival. In the Nuclear Weapons advisory opinion, the Court stated that right in the context of a state taking resort to self-defense in a desperate situation, "when its survival is at stake." With regard to resorting to nuclear weapons, the judges proved unable to agree on the legal consequences to draw from that principle. With regard to fending off terrorism, however, survival seems a principle clearly in point: terrorists, if equipped with weapons of mass destruction, may threaten the physical survival of the victim state. It is not, as in the case of employing nuclear weapons, the other way around. Moreover, the situation of a people living under the constant threat of a recurrence of 9/11–type events falls short of survival in human dignity.

The exercise of the right to survival, as of any other right, is bounded by rationality. Rationality in law may generally be expressed by the principles of necessity and proportionality. The International Court of Justice was right to find that those principles constitute corollaries of the right of self-defense. That finding applies to the right of self-defense against society-induced terrorist attacks as well. By limiting a state's exercise of its right to survival, the principles of necessity and proportionality give guidance to the evolution of operative rules on self-defense against society-induced terrorist attacks.

IV.   Necessity and Proportionality of Military Responses

In the face of less intrusive alternatives, a military response is bound to prove unnecessary and thus illegal. Similarly, measures that cannot possibly reach their objectives would not constitute a necessary response. In addition, proportionality requires the intrusiveness of the measures applied to be commensurate with the goals pursued.

* * *

A.   Subsidiarity of Unilateral Action

Had a terrorist attack of the September 11 variety occurred before the end of the Cold War, collective security would almost certainly have been unavailable to the state victim of the attack. Since the end of the Cold War the prospects for the Council to use its powers under Chapter VII, and to assume effective control of a crisis situation, may have improved. But satisfactory results cannot be taken for granted. The victim state's choice of unilateral response might, for a variety of reasons, fail to draw the support of the majority of the member states represented in the Council and, of course, the casting of a "nyet" in the terms of good old Stalinist times by one or more of the permanent members of the Council still constitutes more than a faint possibility.

To be sure, there may be sound reasons for a permanent member to cast a veto and, even more so, for a majority of members to block the mounting of an effective response to a society-induced terrorist attack. Such lack of support is likely to reflect policy concerns that correspond to shortcomings under the legal principles of necessity or proportionality. But there may also be cases where the grounds for refusing support are not so sound and quite unrelated to the issue under review. In that case, should an exercise of the right of self-defense be barred merely on account of a refusal of support by the Security Council? If so, possible target states that wish to obtain legal protection against military action responding to terrorist attacks would merely have to secure the veto of a single permanent member of the Security Council or to obstruct the taking of a majority vote. The exercise of a state's right to survival can hardly be considered dependent on the opportunism of members of the Security Council. To safeguard the right to survival, unilateral action may eventually prove necessary.

Multilateral action, however, remains the preferable course of action also as a matter of law. The necessity of multilateral action can be more easily established. Sympathizers may be led to realize that world public opinion as expressed by a unanimous or majority vote of the Security Council is turning against them. Furthermore, the appraisal of the facts and of the law in a particular case is less prone to misjudgment if it can be based on the opinion of the many rather than the few.

From a normative viewpoint, the two statements made above—on the residual necessity of unilateral action and the preferability of multilateral action—can be reconciled by a rule of subsidiarity: unilateral recourse to military force is permitted if effective multilateral action proves unavailable. Multilateral action must be sufficiently effective before it can be considered "available" in the sense of that rule. Of course, this approach requires an amount of fine-tuning of the subsidiarity rule that only further discussion of various scenarios can provide.

Lee Feinstein and Anne–Marie Slaughter, A Duty to Prevent

83 Foreign Affairs 136–138, 139–140, 142–149 (2004)

* * *

In the name of protecting state sovereignty, international law traditionally prohibited states from intervening in one another's affairs, with military force or otherwise. But members of the human rights and humanitarian protection communities came to realize that, in light of the humanitarian catastrophes of the 1990s, from famine to genocide to ethnic cleansing, those principles will not do. The world could no longer sit and wait, reacting only when a crisis caused massive human suffering or spilled across borders, posing more conventional threats to international peace and security. As a result, in late 2001, an international commission of legal practitioners and scholars, responding to a challenge from the UN secretary-general, proposed a new doctrine, which they called "The Responsibility to Protect." This far-reaching principle holds that today UN member states have a responsibility to protect the lives, liberty, and basic human rights of their citizens, and that if they fail or are unable to carry it out, the international community has a responsibility to step in.

We propose a corollary principle in the field of global security: a collective "duty to prevent" nations run by rulers without internal checks on their power from acquiring or using [weapons of mass destruction]. For many years, a small but determined group of regimes has pursued proliferation in spite of—and, to a certain extent, without breaking—the international rules barring such activity. Some of these nations cooperate with one another, trading missile technology for uranium-enrichment know-how, for example. Their cooperation, dangerous in itself, also creates incentives for others to develop a nuclear capacity in response. These regimes can also provide a ready source of weapons and technology to individuals and terrorists. The threat is gravest when the states pursuing WMD are closed societies headed by rulers who menace their own citizens as much as they do their neighbors and potential adversaries.

Such threats demand a global response. Like the responsibility to protect, the duty to prevent begins from the premise that the rules now governing the use of force, devised in 1945 and embedded in the UN Charter, are inadequate. Both new principles respond to a growing recognition, born of logic and experience, that in the twenty-first century maintaining global peace and security requires states to be proactive rather than reactive. And both recognize that UN members have responsibilities as well as rights.

The duty to prevent has three critical features. First, it seeks to control not only the proliferation of WMD but also people who possess them. Second, it emphasizes prevention, calling on the international community to act early in order to be effective and develop a menu of potential measures aimed at particular governments—especially measures that can be taken well short of any use of force. Third, the duty to prevent should be exercised collectively, through a global or regional organization.

OLD RULES, NEW THREATS

We live in a world of old rules and new threats. This period did not begin on September 11, 2001. Before then, politicians and public figures were already lacing their millennium speeches with calls for a new global financial architecture, new definitions of national self-interest and humanitarian intervention, and new ways of organizing international institutions. They recognized that the existing rules and institutions created to address the economic, political, and security problems of the last century were inadequate for solving a new generation of threats to world order: failed states; regional economic crises; sovereign bankruptcies; the spread of HIV/AIDS and other new viruses; global warming; the rise of global criminal networks; and trafficking in arms, money, women, workers, and drugs.

Although the worst threats to the international order in the 1990s arose from internal conflicts—civil wars, ethnic bloodletting, and resurgent nationalism—the cardinal doctrines of the post–1945 order apply to wars between nations, not within them. The UN Charter binds states only to refrain from the use or threat of force in "their international relations" and explicitly protects their "domestic jurisdiction" from outside interference. And a broad doctrine prohibiting intervention in a state's internal affairs is well established in customary law.

Granted, under the charter, the UN Security Council may take action when it determines the existence of a threat to international peace and security. And nothing prevents it from identifying a government with no internal checks on its power that possesses or seeks to acquire WMD as a threat to the peace and taking measures against it. But articulating and acknowledging a specific duty to prevent such governments from even acquiring WMD will shift the burden of proof from suspicious nations to suspected nations and create the presumption of a need for early and, therefore, more effective action.

* * *

The inability to prevent WMD proliferation by dangerous regimes is a concern that has confounded at least the last three U.S. administrations. President George H.W. Bush defined the issue in terms of "outlaw" states, to distinguish regimes that followed international rules from those that defied them. President Bill Clinton used the term "rogue states" until 2000, when his administration began referring to "states of concern" to signal that the goal of U.S. policy was eventually to reintegrate states, if not their dictatorial rulers, into the international system. The present administration's use of the term "axis of evil" suggests a sterner version of the first Bush administration's approach. It leaves little room for diplomacy, forcing the United States to either advocate regime change or do nothing.

All these approaches, moreover, miss a key point. It is not states that are the danger, but their rulers—a relatively small group of identifiable individuals who seek absolute power at home or sponsor terrorism abroad. These rulers and their regimes can be identified by evaluating their behavior according to criteria already documented in the UN system: the rule of law and human rights; rights of association and organization; freedom of expression and belief; and personal autonomy and economic rights. The international system remains uncomfortable distinguishing one country from another, but such distinctions are already embedded in the UN system and they should be emphasized as the basis for effective international action to deal with the dangers we now face.

* * *

The duty to prevent is the responsibility of states to work in concert to prevent governments that lack internal checks on their power from acquiring WMD or the means to deliver them. In cases where such regimes already possess such weapons, the first responsibility is to halt these programs and prevent the regimes from transferring WMD capabilities or actual weapons. The duty to prevent would also apply to states that sponsor terrorism and are seeking to obtain WMD.

This responsibility would apply to cases where the underlying set of agreements restricting WMD programs—the Nonproliferation Treaty (NPT), the Biological Weapons Convention, and the Chemical Weapons Convention—has not prevented a regime without internal checks from pursuing dangerous weapons, or when such a state withdraws from its obligations or cheats on them, or when a gap in existing rules needs to be filled to prevent such a regime from acquiring WMD or the means to deliver them.

Why emphasize the absence of internal checks on a government's power? We are not trying to distinguish "good" governments from "bad" governments, much less democracies from nondemocracies. Nor are we arguing that governments that have internal checks on their behavior always obey international law; they are bound by the same international norms restricting the development and use of weapons of WMD as are other states, and their compliance must be monitored too. But the behavior of open societies is subject to scrutiny, criticism, and countermeasures by opponents, at home and abroad. Also, existing nonproliferation agreements can circumscribe these states' behavior or, if political circumstances change dramatically, as they did, say, in South Africa in 1989 and in Argentina and Brazil in the 1990s, they can provide a path for states to give up their nuclear ambitions or, in the case of Pretoria, even their weapons.

On the other hand, the international community may only discover the danger posed by a closed society with no opposition when it is too late. In such cases, standard diplomatic tools are simply not up to the job. The greatest potential danger to the international community is posed by rulers whose power over their own people and territory is so absolute that no matter how brutal, aggressive, or irrational they become, no force within their own society can stop them. Their rule is absolute precisely because they have terrified, brainwashed, and isolated their populations and have either destroyed internal opposition or subdued it by "closing" their societies, restricting information as much as possible. Such leaders may simply seek to consolidate their power and to be left alone. But if they choose to menace other countries or support terrorist groups, it is far more difficult to find out what they are doing and take effective measures to stop them.

Just as the responsibility to protect cannot apply to all regimes that abuse their citizens' human rights, the duty to prevent cannot apply to all closed societies with WMD programs. To be practical, the duty has to be limited and applied to cases when it can produce beneficial results. It applies to Kim Jong Il's North Korea, but not to Hu Jintao's (or even Mao's) China. Existing nonproliferation tools, updated to close loopholes, would continue to apply to most countries, and the effectiveness of these rules would be reinforced by the perception of greater determination to deal firmly with the most serious cases.

THE USUAL SUSPECTS

The main international nonproliferation agreements stigmatize weapons or certain categories of weapons rather than regimes or leaders. Aiming at the weapons themselves rather than the states or regimes that develop or acquire them has been judged to be a more objective basis for international action. The problem with this approach is that its opening proposition is to treat North Korea as if it were Norway. This flaw has exposed the nonproliferation regime to abuse by determined and defiant regimes, especially those headed by dictatorial rulers. It is also the weakness that makes the NPT and, more broadly, the nonproliferation system vulnerable to charges that the only ones restrained by nonproliferation agreements are those nations that do not need restraining.

In truth, the NPT—the cornerstone of international efforts to prevent the spread of WMD—has helped stanch nuclear proliferation in the overwhelming majority of cases. It has also provided a pathway for states seeking to terminate their nuclear programs. But the NPT has not prevented a small group of determined states, including Iran, Iraq, and North Korea, from traveling down the nuclear path. These states, sometimes operating within the scope of the treaty, managed to develop advanced nuclear programs and, in the case of North Korea, the material for actually producing nuclear weapons.

* * *

EARLY ACTION

Like intervention for humanitarian purposes, international action to counter WMD proliferation can take the form of diplomatic pressure or incentives, economic measures, or coercive action, often in combination. It can also incorporate new strategies, such as indicting individual leaders before the International Criminal Court or a special court for crimes against humanity, grave war crimes, or genocide when such charges apply, as they certainly would have with Saddam Hussein and possibly with Kim Jong Il. Still another alternative could be support for nonviolent resistance movements that are dedicated to democratizing their governments.

To be effective, incentives must be tailored to a state's particular needs. Where a state seeks WMD for their perceived deterrent value, security assurances by a nation or group of nations, formally organized or not, may make adequate alternatives. Where a state trades in sensitive technologies in exchange for hard currency, economic incentives—including assistance from international financial institutions, direct bilateral aid, and trade incentives—may be more appropriate.

Coercive action may take the form of economic penalties, including measures targeted at the state's rulers, their close associates, and their families. Curbs on financial flows or on sensitive trade that provides financial support for a state's weapons programs, including a crackdown on black-market trade, can be a very effective brake. (Counterfeiting and the illegal drug trade are believed to support North Korea's WMD programs.) Coercive action can also include embargoes, informal or otherwise, to block the transfer of weapons or relevant technologies and material. The Bush administration's Proliferation Security Initiative, an 11–nation effort to stop the shipment of WMD, their delivery systems, and related materials at sea, by air, or on land, is a step in the right direction. The initiative is intended to prevent the transfer of nuclear weapons, weapons materials, and missiles, as well as trade in contraband that supports these weapons programs. France and Germany are participating, despite their opposition to the Iraq war, but not China and Russia, whose cooperation is critical to making it an effective system.

A jugular issue is how to monitor compliance with any pledges to freeze or reverse nuclear programs. The Iraq experience suggests that UN inspections stopped being effective when Baghdad succeeded in dividing the Security Council and international support for them broke down. When UN Security Council Resolution 1441 revived the inspections, with the unanimous backing of the Security Council, Baghdad grudgingly cooperated with inspectors. Intrusive inspections endorsed by a united Security Council, backed up by the threat of force, may have worked better than they have been given credit for. Although it is easy to dismiss the effectiveness of inspections in closed societies, we need to review systematically the experience of international inspections for lessons learned. It may be that intense international pressure can make a system of rigorous inspections effective enough.

The Bush administration's announcement of a preemption doctrine set off alarm bells in the United States and abroad, chiefly because of the precedent it would set in terms of a unilateral determination that another state poses a sufficient threat to justify a preemptive strike. In truth, the use of force to preempt an imminent threat has always been part of international law, and it has been an option that the United States has held in quiet reserve and occasionally used. In cases in which terrorists appear poised to strike, preemption is clearly the preferred course of action.

Unfortunately, the preemptive use of force is often difficult to justify because clear evidence that a threat is imminent is rare. The U.S. strike on a pharmaceutical plant in Sudan in 1998 was intended as a preemptive strike against a facility suspected of producing chemical weapons, but evidence that activities there were illicit remains thin. Furthermore, preemption is usually impractical because suspected facilities are often difficult to spot or hit. States have taken precautions in recent years in response to the Israeli bombing of Iraq's Osiraq reactor in 1981 and to the NATO and U.S. bombing campaigns in the Balkans and the Middle East. Many facilities are buried in bunkers deep underground and dispersed over wide areas. They are especially difficult to locate in closed societies. This is not to suggest that the use of force should be discounted as ineffective but to highlight that the most effective action is preventive, because undoing a nuclear program is orders of magnitude more difficult than preventing one in the first place.

Nevertheless, as in the Iraq case, keeping force on the table is often a critical ingredient in making diplomacy work. It may be especially necessary for effective inspections and monitoring of WMD programs in closed societies. Force may be considered as part of an interdiction effort, may be targeted at specific dangerous facilities, or may be part of broader military action as a last resort.

The utility of force in dealing with the most serious proliferation dangers is not a controversial proposition. In a little-noticed statement last June [2003], the EU announced a "strategy against proliferation," identifying "coercive measures, including as a last resort the use of force in accordance with the UN Charter" as one of its "key elements." Later that month, the G–8 group of leading industrialized countries, which includes Russia, approached the subject more gingerly but nonetheless agreed that WMD and the spread of international terrorism were "the preeminent threat to international security," and that force ("other measures in accordance with international law") may be needed to deal with them. And, as noted earlier, Kofi Annan himself called on the Security Council to develop criteria for the early authorization of coercive measures.

IN IT TOGETHER

The contentious issue is who decides when and how to use force. No one nation can or should shoulder alone the obligation to prevent a repressive regime from acquiring WMD. Although the Security Council, still reeling from the Iraq crisis * * * now seems more interested in papering over its differences than in tackling these questions, it remains the preferred enforcer of collective measures. The unmatched legitimacy that the UN lends to Security Council actions makes it easier for member states to carry them out and harder for targeted governments to evade them by playing political games. On the other hand, rifts within the council allow states to pursue WMD to advance their programs, leaving individual nations to take matters into their own hands, which further erodes the stature and credibility of the United Nations.

Given the Security Council's propensity for paralysis, alternative means of enforcement must be considered. The second most legitimate enforcer is the regional organization that is most likely to be affected by the emerging threat. After that, the next best option would be another regional organization, such as NATO, with a less direct connection to the targeted state but with a sufficiently broad membership to permit serious deliberation over the exercise of a collective duty. It is only after these options are tried in good faith that unilateral action or coalitions of the willing should be considered.

In any event, the resort to force is subject to certain "precautionary principles." All nonmilitary alternatives that could achieve the same ends must be tried before force may be used, unless they can reasonably be said to be futile. Force must be exerted on the smallest scale, for the shortest time, and at the lowest intensity necessary to achieve its objective; the objective itself must be reasonably attainable when measured against the likelihood of making matters worse. Finally, force should be governed by fundamental principles of the laws of war: it must be a measure of last resort, used in proportion to the harm or the threat of the harm it targets, and with due care to spare civilians.

B.   In Bello Proposals

Francisco Forrest Martin, Using International Human Rights Law for Establishing a Unified Use of Force Rule in the Law of Armed Conflict

64 Sask. L. Rev. 347–348, 360–381*

* * *

The topic of this article is *Using International Human Rights Law for Establishing a Unified Use of Force Rule in the Law of Armed Conflict*. I will argue that international human rights law can be used to interpret some aspects of the law of armed conflict and, thereby, create greater restraints on the use of force. The result of this effort will be a Unified Use of Force Rule that not only makes the conduct of war and "operations other than war" (OOTW) more humane, but also enables military personnel to adhere more effectively to the law of armed conflict.

* * *

III.   THE APPLICATION OF INTERNATIONAL HUMAN RIGHTS LAW TO THE LAW OF ARMED CONFLICT

The law of armed conflict has incorporated numerous human rights guarantees. These are located primarily in the common Article 3 provisions of the *Geneva Conventions* that are universally guaranteed regardless of how the armed conflict is characterized. These guarantees include prohibitions of violence to life and person, hostage-taking, outrages upon personal dignity, extrajudicial executions, discriminatory treatment, and a duty to care for the wounded and sick. Reflected in common Article 3 provisions are two human rights guarantees: the right to life and the right to

---

* Footnotes omitted.

humane treatment. Let us first address the right to life. Article 6 of the International Covenant on Civil and Political Rights [ICCPR] states:

> Every human being has the inherent right to life. This right shall be protected by law. No one shall be arbitrarily deprived of his life.

Article 2 of the *European Convention for the Protection of Human Rights and Fundamental Freedoms* [ECHR] is even more precise. It states in relevant part:

> 1. Everyone's right to life shall be protected by law....
>
> 2. Deprivation of life shall not be regarded as inflicted in contravention of this article when it results from the use of force which is no more than *absolutely necessary*:
>
>> (a) in defence of any person from unlawful violence;
>>
>> (b) in order to effect a lawful arrest ...;
>>
>> (c) in action lawfully taken for the purpose of quelling a[n] ... insurrection.

The right to humane treatment is guaranteed by Article 7 of the ICCPR, which states in relevant part:

> No one shall be subjected to torture, or to cruel, inhuman or degrading treatment or punishment.

Article 3 of the ECHR is nearly identical to the ICCPR. Article 3 states:

> No one shall be subjected to torture or to inhuman or degrading treatment or punishment.

Relevant to the application of these rights to war and OOTW are the non-derogability provisions in the ICCPR and ECHR. Both the ICCPR and ECHR allow no derogation from the right to humane treatment. However, the ECHR differs from the ICCPR in regard to the right to life. Unlike the ICCPR, the ECHR does allow derogation from the right to life during war. Article 4 of the ICCPR states in relevant part:

> 1. In time of public emergency which threatens the life of the nation and the existence of which is officially proclaimed, the States parties to the present Covenant may take measures derogating from their obligations under the present Covenant to the extent strictly required by the exigencies of the situation, provided that such measures are not inconsistent with their other obligations under international law and do not involve discrimination solely on the ground of race, colour, sex, language, religion or social origin.
>
> 2. No derogation from articles 6 [right to life], 7 [right against inhuman treatment] ... may be made under this provision.

Article 15 of the ECHR states in relevant part:

> 1. In time of war or other public emergency threatening the life of the nation any High Contracting Party may take measures derogating from its obligations under this Convention to the extent strictly required by the exigencies of the situation, provided that such measures are not inconsistent with its other obligations under international law.
>
> 2. No derogation from Article 2 [right to life], except in respect of deaths resulting from lawful acts of war, or from Article[] 3 [right to humane treatment] ... shall be made under this provision.

Other major human rights treaties also allow no derogation from the rights to life and humane treatment during war or other national emergencies. What is important to recognize about the nonderogability of these rights during war (except the right to life guaranteed by the ECHR) and other national emergencies is that they reflect *jus cogens* norms. *Jus cogens* is non-derogable, peremptory law that binds all nations at all times. Multilateral treaties guaranteeing non-derogable rights are a source for *jus cogens* norms.

A.   THE RIGHT TO LIFE AND THE *McCANN* RULE

The European Court of Human Rights has repeatedly interpreted the right to life guaranteed by the ECHR in the context of military use of lethal force. In *McCann and Others v. United Kingdom*, the Grand Chamber of the European Court of Human Rights considered a case involving the shootings of three suspected Irish Republican Army terrorists by members of the Special Air Service (SAS) and the police in Gibralter in March 1988. The UK, Spanish, and Gibralter authorities had reason to believe that a terrorist attack was planned in Gibralter, and that the target was probably the Band and Guard of the Royal Anglican Regiment during a ceremony in 1988. The authorities knew that the suspects were active IRA members and were attempting to enter Gibralter. However, the authorities did not prevent the suspects from entering because the authorities had insufficient evidence to successfully prosecute them.

Fearing that the suspects would detonate a remote-controlled bomb, the authorities shot and killed them. Although the suspects, indeed, had planned an attack and planted a bomb, the method of detonation was not a remote device that could be set off instantaneously. Moreover, the evidence claiming that it was such a device was dubious, having been provided by a non-expert.

Family members of the deceased suspects claimed a violation of the suspects' rights to life under the ECHR. It was alleged that, on the evidence, the level of force used was more than absolutely necessary because shooting the three suspects was not necessary to prevent the bombing. The European Court found a violation of the right to life because the authorities had used lethal force that was not "absolutely necessary in defence of persons from unlawful violence." The Court's decision was based on the facts that the authorities (i) had not prevented the IRA suspects from travelling to Gibraltar; (ii) had "failed to make sufficient allowances for the possibility that their intelligence assessments might, in some respects at least, be erroneous"; and (iii) had failed to stop their soldiers from automatically using lethal force. The Court noted that the right to life allows no derogation in times of national emergency, and as such it must be strictly construed. Thus, the deprivation of life must be subjected to the most careful scrutiny, taking into consideration both the actions of the authorities and the surrounding circumstances, including the planning and control of the operation.

The Court accepted that the soldiers honestly believed that it was necessary to shoot the suspects in order to prevent remote detonation of the device. Their beliefs were based on erroneous information with which they had been supplied. However, the Court found that their commanders had failed to organize the operation as a whole in conformity with the right to life, including the information and instructions given to the soldiers. Consequently, the organization of the operation inevitably required the use of lethal force and failed to adequately respect the suspects' right to life.

For convenience, let's call the Court's application of the right to life to military operations the "*McCann* Rule." It is important to note that the *McCann* Rule allows military authorities to use lethal measures only if there are no other alternatives to taking life. Accordingly, they must consider and use non-lethal measures if they can achieve their lawful objectives by such means.

The use of the *McCann* Rule is not limited to tactical operations. It also extends to strategic operations. The U.S. Department of Defense has noted that non-lethal weapon employment is not limited to operations in the lower spectrum of conflict (i.e., peace-keeping, peace-enforcement, and humanitarian missions that generally are associated with discrete, independent, relatively small operations). Rather, the employment of non-lethal means and methods of warfare can apply across the range of military operations where, to quote the U.S. Department of Defense, they can "enhance the ... effectiveness and efficiency [of] ... military operations". To comply with the *McCann* Rule, military forces would need to be further trained in tactics and strategy using non-lethal measures, and several senior military authorities already have argued for such training. Of course, military forces must be given access to these non-lethal means and methods.

What is the relevance of the *McCann* Rule to the law of armed conflict, and how does it place greater restraints on the use of force? First, the *McCann* Rule is a clearer and better defined rule to implement than the * * * Proportionality Rules. The *McCann* Rule only allows the taking of life *if there is no other alternative.* Second, the right to life applies to both civilians and combatants, the latter application as illustrated by the *McCann* Rule. The ECHR (as well as most other human rights treaties, including the ICCPR) makes no distinction between civilians and combatants. The Proportionality Rule does not extend such protection to combatants when they are the only targets. Third, although the *McCann* Rule was formulated in the context of a non-international conflict, the Rule also is applicable to international conflicts, because several international tribunals have repeatedly held that international liability for human rights violations—including violations of the right to life—extends outside a nation's territory. Moreover, the enemy forces (whether state or non-state) need not be a party to the ECHR because the right to life guaranteed by the ECHR reflects not only regional international law norms but also global international law norms. Furthermore, there is no *si omnes* or general participation clause in the ECHR that allows state-parties to exempt themselves from their ECHR obligations when such enemy forces are not parties to the ECHR. Even if the ECHR had such a general participation clause (such as Article 2 of the *Hague Convention (IV)* for states or Article 96(2) of the *Geneva Convention—Protocol I* for non-states), the general participation clause has fallen into disuse.

Although the ECHR allows a state-party to take measures derogating from the right to life "in respect of deaths resulting from lawful acts of war" (Art. 15(2)), such measures are allowed only "to the extent *strictly required* by the exigencies of the situation" (Art. 15(1)) [emphasis added]. This strict necessity requirement is identical to the absolute necessity test articulated by the *McCann* Rule because both operate identically. Furthermore, Article 15(1) creates an additional requirement that such measures taken by a state-party in derogation of the right to life during war must "not be inconsistent with its other obligations under international law." As we shall see below, the right to *humane treatment* under international human rights law requires that states may use force only if there is no other alternative to inflicting suffering and that such use of force—if absolutely necessary—must employ a means or method of warfare of a nature to cause the *least possible* amount of suffering. The right to humane treatment is non-derogable during war. Therefore, a state-party's "other obligations under international law"—*i.e.*, under the right to humane treatment—would require that a state-party may only use force if absolutely necessary. This fortifies the *McCann* Rule because the taking of life by use of force also must meet an identical absolute necessity threshold under the right to humane treatment. Unless the taking of life occurs without any suffering, the taking of life must be absolutely necessary under the right to humane treatment.

Clearly, the *McCann* Rule is an emerging rule that will increasingly acquire greater recognition. But what about the use of non-lethal force that still causes unnecessary suffering or superfluous injury? To address this issue, let us now turn to the right to humane treatment under international human rights law.

B. THE RIGHT TO HUMANE TREATMENT AND THE *SATIK* RULE

The right to humane treatment under international human rights law can be used to interpret and clarify the * * * Proportionality Rules. Although international human rights law absolutely prohibits inhumane treatment, *exactly what* constitutes such inhumane treatment depends on the context—in terms of both the conditions requiring use of force and the foreseeable level of suffering imposed. In other words, it may be lawful to use force that causes suffering, but the level of suffering caused by that use of force may violate the right to humane treatment.

In *Satik and Others v. Turkey*, a case concerning a detainee, the European Court of Human Rights held that "recourse to physical force which had not been made *strictly necessary* by [the victim's] own conduct diminishes human dignity and is in principle an infringement" of the right to humane treatment. In cases involving unlawful behaviour by the victim, the Court recognizes that some acts causing suffering may indeed be lawful if strictly necessary to achieve a lawful objective. In *Satik*, the European Court noted the absence of governmental justification for the commission of certain harmful acts and then held that such acts were unlawfully inhumane. The *Satik* case is important because its strict necessity rule can interpret and supplement the * * * [proportionality], which does not say what level of necessity is required for allowing the use of particular means and methods of warfare that cause suffering or injury. We can call this strict necessity rule the "*Satik* Rule".

However, in other cases only involving innocent victims, the Court is less clear. For example, in *Selçuk and Asker v. Turkey*, the European Court of Human Rights examined the burning of civilian Kurdish homes by Turkish military authorities and noted:

> [E]ven if it were the case that the acts in question were carried out without any intention of punishing the applicants,

but instead to prevent their homes being used by terrorists or as a discouragement to others, this would not provide a justification for the ill-treatment.

The Court does not explain whether it was the Turkish authorities' decision to use force, or the level of suffering caused by the burning of the applicants' homes, that violated the right to humane treatment.

This brings us to the level of suffering imposed. Under the right to humane treatment guaranteed by the ICCPR, the means or method of warfare must—at least—cause the least suffering. In *Ng v. Canada*, the UN Human Rights Committee held that the lawful execution of a convicted prisoner "must be carried out in such a way as to cause the *least possible physical and mental suffering*" in order to comply with the right to humane punishment under the ICCPR. However, it is important to note that *Ng v. Canada* did not deal with innocent persons—as is the case with mixed civilian-combatant targets during armed conflict. This suggests that innocent persons may receive greater protection than convicted persons; namely, that innocent persons may not be subjected to *any* physical or mental suffering. This suggestion casts doubt on the legal validity of the Proportionality Rule, which still allows innocent civilians to be targeted. Until a court determines whether the right to humane treatment prohibits the subjection of innocent persons to any suffering during armed conflict, it is at least safe to say that the subjection of innocent civilians to any use of force because they constitute part of a mixed civilian-combatant target must be carried out in a way so as to cause the least possible physical and mental suffering. Nevertheless, for combatants, the least possible suffering requirement under *Ng v. Canada* still provides greater protection and serves to interpret and augment the SIrUS Rule.

The *Satik* Rule—like the *McCann* Rule—requires strict or absolute necessity. Although the *Satik* Rule was articulated outside the context of war, the non-derogable provision of the ECHR does not allow derogation of the right to humane treatment guaranteed by Article 3. Therefore, it probably is not relevant that the *Satik* Case did not address warfare.

In the context of armed conflict, the right to life is closely associated with the right to humane treatment. Both address the use of force, and both rights are applicable to the contexts of war and OOTW. Using identical necessity thresholds for uses of force that can entail death and suffering would bring the right to humane treatment in line with the right to life. Consistency and uniformity are not just important for creating elegant legal systems, but also for practical operational reasons. First, not using the absolute or strict necessity threshold * * * can foreseeably lead to a violation of both the *McCann* Rule and the *Geneva Convention–Protocol I*.

Article 57 of the *Geneva Convention—Protocol I* also suggests a strict necessity requirement for attacking mixed combatant-civilian targets:

> When a choice is possible between several military objectives for obtaining a similar military advantage, the objective to be selected shall be that the attack on which may be expected to cause the least danger to civilian lives and to civilian objects.

For example, instead of the less potentially lethal water cannon, one chooses to use rubber bullets (given that both means can achieve the objective) and death does in fact result, the *Geneva Convention–Protocol I* would have been violated with respect to civilians, and the *McCann* Rule would have been violated with respect to combatants. If the *Geneva Convention–Protocol I* and the *McCann* Rule are to be effective, the law governing the use of force—lethal and non-lethal—must be consistent. If combatants are going to be held accountable to a law of armed conflict, then that law of armed conflict must be clear, precise, and operationally practical, and violations of the law of armed conflict must be foreseeable.

Second, applying international human rights law to the law of armed conflict today helps render irrelevant the observance of the combatant-civilian Distinction Rule. This collapse of the combatant-civilian distinction reflects a practical reality because the use of force against military targets often entail collateral civilian suffering or injury. A recent twist on this development is the voluntary protection of military targets by civilians. After the Gulf War, Iraqi civilians surrounded potential targets on several occasions to protect the targets from air attacks by Gulf Coalition forces. Although these civilians removed themselves from international legal protection afforded to persons placed *hors de combat* because they took part in the hostilities, they still were unarmed. Furthermore, some civilians may have been children who were forced to participate by relatives. If Coalition forces had used lethal force, the world community probably would have been outraged. Nonetheless, such use of lethal force would have probably been lawful under the old law of armed conflict, because it did not violate the Proportionality * * * Rules.

Third, applying international human rights law to the law of armed conflict furthers the collapse between the law governing international conflicts and the law governing non-international conflicts, because international human rights law addressing the rights to life and humane treatment recognizes no distinction between international and non-international conflicts. This collapse is imperative today because armed conflicts increasingly have become non-international. Moreover, international human rights law applies even to those grey situations (*e.g.*, "riots, isolated and sporadic acts of violence") in which a party to the conflict claims that neither the law governing international conflicts nor the law governing non-international conflicts applies.

In summary, contemporary armed conflicts have made the combatant-civilian distinction requirement increasingly unworkable, and international human rights law has made the distinction requirement increasingly irrelevant. This is not to say that compliance with the Distinction Rule is no longer legally required. Rather, the greater intermingling of military and civilian objects and personnel that has been brought about by, *inter alia*, the internet, placement of military-related computer and programming development in commercial non-defense sectors, and civilian-military shared telephone networks and electrical power grids makes it increasingly difficult to comply with the Distinction Rule (and by implication the Proportionality Rule).

By applying an absolute necessity threshold borrowed from international human rights law to the law of armed conflict, we can articulate a new use of force rule that unifies not only international human rights law and the law of armed conflict but also the rules governing the uses of lethal and non-lethal force against combatants and civilians. It also makes warfare more humane. Let's call this new rule the "Unified Use of Force Rule".

IV. THE UNIFIED USE OF FORCE RULE

The Unified Use of Force Rule is a three-part rule with the following requirements.

> First, military authorities may use force against combatants or mixed combatant-civilian targets only if there is no other alternative to inflicting injury and suffering for achieving lawful objectives, both tactical and strategic. Second, if the means or method per se of such use of force is not illegal, the employed means or method must inflict only the least possible amount of suffering and injury. Third, suffering and injury may be escalated incrementally through the additional use of force by the original or another means or method of warfare only if at each incremental use, the use of such means or method is absolutely necessary for achieving the lawful objectives.

The consequence of this new Rule is that the use of force has to be re-conceptualized. Military authorities must not approach their use of force decisions by way of "ratcheting down" from use of lethal force. The proper approach is to "ratchet up" when absolutely necessary—recognizing and using a range of means or methods of force with escalating degrees of suffering and injury. No longer can the decision be an "either-or"—between the use of no force and the use of lethal force. No longer can the decision alone be whether to use or not use a means or method of warfare that already has been held legal *per se*.

Let us examine this new Rule more closely.

A. MILITARY AUTHORITIES MAY USE FORCE AGAINST COMBATANTS OR MIXED COMBATANT–CIVILIAN TARGETS ONLY IF THERE IS NO OTHER ALTERNATIVE TO INFLICTING INJURY AND SUFFERING FOR ACHIEVING LAWFUL OBJECTIVES, BOTH TACTICAL *AND* STRATEGIC

The first part of the Unified Use of Force Rule constitutes the primary guiding principle for use of force and concerns the initial decision to use it. Reaching that decision requires that strategic and tactical objectives themselves be lawful and that a legal assessment of both means and ends be carried out, according to the absolute necessity threshold from international human rights law. We already have addressed the absolute necessity threshold in international human rights law. The remaining issue to be examined is the subject of lawful objectives.

Force can lawfully be used against military targets (*i.e.*, combatants) under the rights to life and humane treatment if absolutely necessary. However, as previously discussed, it is less clear whether any force causing suffering can be used against non-combatants under the right to humane treatment if they constitute part of a mixed combatant-civilian target. Because of this ambiguity and because the Proportionality Rule does allow use of force against civilians, it is at least safe to say that the use of force executed must cause the least possible suffering. This may be a troubling humanitarian conclusion given that innocents still can be targeted, but disallowing such targeting would absolutely immunize military targets from attack. As a result, enemy military authorities would be encouraged to place such targets among civilian populations, and the inability to attack some military targets—such as nuclear missile sites—can have devastating consequences on friendly and other civilian populations. Implementation of the Unified Use of Force Rule at least ensures that such attacks inflict the least possible degree of injury and suffering on the civilians surrounding the target.

Strategically speaking, force may be used lawfully against enemy forces only for protecting a state's sovereignty, territorial integrity, or political independence; maintaining peace or international security; and arguably for preventing international crimes (*e.g.*, genocide, war crimes, crimes against humanity, terrorism) and humanitarian catastrophes (*e.g.*, as seen in Somalia), because such crimes and catastrophes are inconsistent with the *UN Charter* and represent a threat to international security. Therefore, only these six strategic objectives are lawful: (i) defense of sovereignty, (ii) defense of territorial integrity, (iii) defense of political independence,

(iv) maintenance of peace, (v) maintenance of international security, and, arguably, (vi) prevention of international crimes and humanitarian catastrophes.

However, it is illegal to use *lethal* force to obtain any of these six strategic objectives in cases *not* involving (i) the defense of persons from unlawful violence, (ii) lawful arrest or prevention of escape of persons lawfully detained, or (iii) the quelling of a riot or insurrection. The right to life guaranteed by the ECHR allows the use of lethal force only in these three cases. For example, it is unlawful to use lethal force in response to enemy infection of one's computer with a virus to destroy intelligence information if such infection cannot foreseeably cause unlawful violence to persons. It is less clear whether *non-lethal* force could be used because the right to humane treatment does not address which objectives could be lawfully pursued through the infliction of suffering.

Tactically speaking, the lawfulness of targeting military objects or personnel must be made on the basis of each individual attack, not on a cumulative basis, under the Proportionality Rule. Targeting a military objective in order to reduce the enemy's general war-making capability is unlawful because this merely addresses means, not ends. International law has rejected the doctrine of *Kriegsraison* because the doctrine provides no standard as to the lawfulness of means. After all, even lawful ends never justify unlawful means. The only lawful tactical objective for using force is the neutralization or deterrence of enemy force, which can take place by surrender, withdrawal, and/or isolation of enemy combatants or military assets. Neutralization or deterrence does not necessarily mean the destruction of military objects or the infliction of injury or suffering upon combatants. Indeed, temporary neutralization or deterrence would be especially preferable because permanent damage can have the collateral effects of discouraging resolution of conflict and creating long-term harmful conditions for civilians. As Colonel Siniscalchi has observed in the case of non-lethal weapons:

> Non-lethal weapons enable effective conflict termination. The reversibility of most non-lethal effects limits the duration of the "damage." Assuming that the political objective is to re-establish stability, it becomes necessary to assist the failed state to restore economic and political processes. A non-lethal strategy provides one option.

Therefore, the first part of the Unified Use of Force Rule, "military authorities may use force against combatants or mixed combatant-civilian targets only if there is no other alternative to inflicting injury and suffering for achieving lawful objectives, both strategic and tactical," ensures that both the means *and* ends are part of the calculus for using force.

B. IF THE MEANS OR METHOD PER SE OF SUCH USE OF FORCE IS NOT ILLEGAL, THE EMPLOYED MEANS OR METHOD MUST INFLICT ONLY THE *LEAST POSSIBLE* AMOUNT OF SUFFERING AND INJURY

The second part of the Unified Use of Force Rule addresses the execution of the decision to use force by assessing the means and methods of warfare according to the absolute necessity threshold standard. The second part requires that "if the means or method *per se* of such use of force is not illegal, the employed means or method must inflict only the *least possible* amount of suffering and injury." Suffering or injury that is not absolutely necessary does not constitute the least possible amount of suffering or injury.

Certain means and methods of warfare are already *per se* illegal under international law. Under the Unified Use of Force Rule, the use of these means and methods remain prohibited. However, as already discussed, there are other means and methods of warfare that are not illegal *per se*. Therefore, one needs to grade different means and methods of warfare according to their foreseeable consequences in terms of suffering and injury, as well as in terms of their efficacy in achieving a lawful objective. As for grading efficacy, military authorities and arms manufacturers already employ different models for such measurement. For example, each branch of the U.S. military issues publications called "Joint Munitions Effectiveness Manuals" that use a four-tier approach in measuring the effectiveness of different munitions.

However, these manuals do not grade these weapons according to relative injury or suffering, and the *Geneva Convention–Protocol I* requires such grading:

> In the study, development, acquisition or adoption of a new weapon, means or method of warfare, a High Contracting Party is under an obligation to determine whether its employment would, *in some or all circumstances*, be prohibited by this Protocol or by any other rule of international law applicable to the High Contracting Party.

Therefore, in order to comply with the *Geneva Convention–Protocol I*, states must provide such grading. Unfortunately, military authorities have adopted only the weapons design approach that does not limit particular applications of weapons in different contexts if the weapon already has been determined to be lawful per se. Therefore, governments must grade those different means and methods of warfare that inflict foreseeable suffering and injury along a continuum.

Furthermore, states must make non-lethal weapons available to their military forces. The European Court of Human Rights has already held that military authorities must have access to non-lethal weapons and use such weapons for achieving lawful objectives. For example, in *Güleç v. Turkey*, the European Court of Human Rights examined a case in which the applicant's son, Ahmet Güleç, was shot by the Turkish security forces on his way home from school during an unauthorised demonstration in 1991. The Turkish Government alleged that he was a terrorist belonging to the Kurdish Worker's Party (PKK) and that there were armed terrorists among the demonstrators, requiring police to open fire on the protestors in order to disperse the demonstration. Subsequently, it was shown that the protestors were not armed. The applicant claimed that the police could have used less force, but the government stated that no other weapons were available at the scene of the incident. The Court held that the lack of equipment such as tear gas, rubber bullets, water cannons, and truncheons was "incomprehensible", given that the province of Sirnak where the protest took place was "in a region in which a state of emergency had been declared" and where disorder could therefore be expected. In these circumstances, the Court unanimously declared that the force used was not absolutely necessary and, therefore, constituted a violation of the right to life. This case is important because the Court addressed particular non-lethal measures that should have been made accessible to and used by the Turkish military forces.

Although commanders probably will be inclined to use force that does not cause the least possible suffering or injury in order to successfully achieve their lawful objective, the use of the Unified Use of Force Rule is operationally better than ratcheting down because it ensures that less suffering or injury would occur, given the availability of a spectrum of means and methods of warfare that produce different levels of suffering or injury. For example, in the case of neutralizing an enemy military radar, the use of force that would produce the least suffering and injury would be viral infection (including the advance deposit of probes or benign viruses for determining the extent of future damage) of the enemy's computer radar system. However, the enemy may be able to immunize against such infections. Therefore, one may be inclined to ratchet up the use of force by precision-guided munitions (PGMs or "smart bombs"). Nevertheless, this use of PGMs still would cause less suffering or injury than carpet bombardment.

This operational advantage afforded by the Unified Use of Force Rule is also applicable to cases of less technologically advanced militaries. For example, in order to compel the surrender or withdrawal of enemy troops from a fixed fortified position, the playing of loud, obnoxious music over public address systems for a long period of time (as the U.S. did during the Panamanian invasion), is an effective method of warfare that causes the least suffering or injury, but this may not have immediate effects. Therefore, one may be inclined to ratchet up the use of force by storming the enemy fortification and employing stun-grenades and rubber bullets or tasers. Nevertheless, this still would cause less suffering or injury than the use of rifle-propelled grenades or artillery.

This Rule also solves some problematic scenarios in contemporary armed conflicts. For example, where there is a mixed combatant-civilian target whose destruction will probably result in collateral harm to civilians, and where it is anticipated that the destruction of such target is barely proportional for achieving a military advantage, the Unified Use of Force Rule ensures that proportionality is, in fact, maintained. The Rule requires that military authorities start with using a means or method of warfare that causes the least suffering and injury to not only combatants but also civilians. Use of such a means or method—such as the deployment of carbon fiber chaff over an electrical power plant to disrupt electricity production also warns civilians who are not aware of their proximity to a military target, which is in compliance with the *Geneva Convention—Protocol I*. In cases of voluntary protection of military targets by unarmed civilians (as seen in the post-Gulf War example) or involuntary protection by POWs (as seen during the Vietnam War), the application of the Unified Use of Force Rule would have been more acceptable to the international community because the Rule requires the use of a means or method that causes the least suffering or injury, and such would probably also effectively disperse the crowd of civilians surrounding the targets.

C. SUFFERING AND INJURY MAY BE ESCALATED INCREMENTALLY THROUGH THE ADDITIONAL USE OF FORCE BY THE ORIGINAL OR ANOTHER MEANS OR METHOD OF WARFARE ONLY IF AT EACH INCREMENTAL USE, THE USE OF SUCH MEANS OR METHOD IS ABSOLUTELY NECESSARY FOR ACHIEVING THE LAWFUL OBJECTIVES

The third part of the Unified Use of Force Rule also addresses the execution of use of force decisions. Specifically, the third part deals with cases in which the initially chosen means or method of warfare fails to achieve its lawful objective. The third part of the Rule allows "suffering and injury to be escalated incrementally through the additional use of force by the original or another means or method of warfare only if at each incremental use, the use of such means or method is absolutely necessary for achieving the lawful objectives." Again, the absolute necessity threshold standard is used because another discrete attack, and possibly additional attacks, may be executed. This development now requires not only a re-visitation to the first part of the Rule, but also a modification to allow for incremental escalation of suffering and

injury. The assessment of the absolute necessity for each incremental escalation of suffering and injury ensures that once military authorities use force and such use of force does not achieve its
objective, they do not overreact and use disproportionate force.

Of course, incremental escalation of force can be advantageous to
enemy forces by providing them with an opportunity to, for
example, refortify or reinforce their position, or move their military assets. Therefore, it is necessary that one is able to disrupt
the enemy's OODA (observe, orient, decide, act) loop in the first
attack in order to shape the battlespace to one's advantage before
the enemy can, as well as to quickly ratchet-up the use of force if
absolutely necessary after the first attack. In this regard, the
importance of information warfare (IW) cannot be overstated. The
use of IW means and methods that produce no foreseeable suffering or injury could be used in combination with use of force under
the Unified Use of Force Rule. Indeed, this would be a preferable
method because the disruption of the enemy's OODA loop in a
first strike probably would weaken the enemy, thereby allowing a
ratcheting-down of force on a subsequent attack(s) or even the
surrender, withdrawal, leapfrogging, or isolation of enemy forces.

Ove Bring, International Humanitarian Law After Kosovo: Is Lex Lata Sufficient?

in Legal and Ethical Lessons of NATO's Kosovo Campaign, 78 INT'L
L. STUDIES 257 (Andru Wall ed., Naval War College 2002).*

* * *

Did Protocol I Mean Anything in Kosovo?

International humanitarian law as it related to the Kosovo crisis
was discussed in the March 2000 issue of the International Review
of the Red Cross. A perspective *de lege ferenda* was put forward in
an article by Peter Rowe, Professor of Law at the University of
Lancaster. Rowe first put the question of whether in fact the
constraints of modern IHL influenced NATO behavior during the
conflict. The subtitle of his article is: "Have the provisions of
Additional Protocol I withstood the test?"[a] Rowe's position is that
Protocol I did not add anything to the protection of the civilian
population beyond the customary law protection that was already
applicable before 1977. He concludes that the Protocol had little
impact or influence upon the decisions of the air campaign—that
"all the detailed rules so carefully drafted in 1977 were of little
consequence." In his view, the objects that military commanders

---

* Some footnotes omitted.

a. Peter Rowe, *Kosovo 1999: The air
campaign*, 82 INTERNATIONAL REVIEW OF THE RED
CROSS 147 (2000).

for military reasons wished to attack were attacked. There was nothing more to it.

If this argumentation is intended to imply that modern international law played no part in the crisis, it should be refuted. International humanitarian law clearly influenced decision-makers in Kosovo. Moreover, Additional Protocol I contributed to the role that law played in decision-making. During the conflict, as during the Gulf War, legal advice was sought and considered. In both cases it was extremely important, for political and public image reasons, to be seen as acting in conformity with international law. The opposite would imply a political cost and setback that had to be avoided at a time when political support was essential. During the Gulf War General Schwarzkopf was adamant that "we didn't want any war crimes on our hands." The same feeling obviously dominated NATO thinking in the spring of 1999. Protocol I, although it has not been ratified by all NATO States (not by the United States, France and Turkey at the time; France is now a party), has contributed much to the awareness of IHL standards in military and political circles. The United States position is that many of the rules of Protocol I are applicable as customary law. Moreover, the non-governmental organizations and informed public opinion are very much aware of the IHL standards. They continuously monitor relevant situations—and the politicians know it. Thus, it was in the self-interest of NATO to involve its legal advisers in the planning and targeting process.

The US military lawyer James Burger has written in the same March issue of the International Review of the Red Cross the following: "While there may be disagreement over the application of the rules by commentators who write about it after the event, there can be no doubt that full consideration was given, as required by the laws of armed conflict, to the advice of legal counsel and the application of the rules." We can probably safely conclude that in Kosovo there was a greater respect for humanitarian normative restraints than would have been the case had the adoption of Protocol I never taken place.

The Weakness of Protocol I and the Need for Reform

The Protocol only offers weak protection for civilians. Here one could easily agree with Peter Rowe, when he argues that the Protocol, when it comes to the test, is very weak in determining what may and what may not be attacked. "It is when civilians are most likely to be placed in danger that Protocol I, designed to protect them, shows its faults." One reason for this is that the Protocol sets the dividing line between legal and illegal attacks on the basis of military expectations before the attack is commenced. As Rowe states: "At this stage of military operations those planning the attack are at their most optimistic and civilians are at most risk." This criticism mainly relates to the principle of proportionality and the acceptance of collateral damage. An even more important flaw with the Protocol, in this writer's view, is the wide interpretations of legitimate military objectives that the Protocol harbors. This interpretation flows only indirectly from the text of Article 52, but rather through a perception that the Protocol has codified a liberal customary law regime. The effect is an increased risk of extensive collateral damage.

With regard to Kosovo it has already been indicated that collateral damage was a serious problem, but that the problem was not so much related to violations of IHL standards as it was to the flexible interpretation of the definition of military objectives. Should a reform of IHL be considered to address these matters, one point of departure would be that Additional Protocol I should stand as it is. A revision of the Protocol is neither realistic nor necessary. There is another way to approach the problem.

Suggestions De Lege Ferenda

Rowe suggests a new additional protocol to the 1980 Conventional Weapons Convention. Such an additional protocol would be adapted to the use of air-delivered "smart" weapons and it would introduce the same restrictions on such weapons as now exist with regard to air-delivered incendiary weapons. The relevant formulation would then read as follows:

> It is prohibited to make any military objective located within a concentration of civilians the object of attack, except when such military objective is clearly separated from the concentration of civilians, and all feasible precautions are taken with a view to limiting the effects of the attack to the military objective and to avoiding, and in any event to minimizing, incidental loss of civilian life, injury to civilians and damage to civilian objects.

The suggested text almost copies the 1980 restrictions on incendiaries. It would be a *lex specialis* for mainly air warfare, overriding the balancing act of the principle of proportionality, a principle that has its main application in air warfare. According to such a *lex specialis*—and rethinking air warfare in history—no buildings in Berlin, Baghdad or Belgrade could be attacked. It is difficult to believe that States would be willing to accept an erosion of the principle of proportionality and give up their military freedom of assessing military advantage against civilian damage. Protocol I has established a sort of balance between military necessity and proportionality and also between proportionality and feasible precautions. It does not seem realistic to expect that States would be willing to renounce the advantages of that approach.

Another problem with the text suggested by Rowe is that it is envisaged as a protocol additional to the 1980 Weapons Convention, although the text only covers *methods* and not *means* of warfare. It does not (like the other Protocols attached to the Weapons Convention) refer to a specific weapon category, although it may indirectly focus on air-delivered "smart" weapons.

On the other hand, one could imagine another solution. The Independent International Commission on Kosovo has suggested the drafting of an additional protocol III to the Geneva Conventions. Such a protocol would not detract from or compete with Protocol I, because the new protocol would have another scope of application. It would be limited to conflicts of an interventionist nature where the intervening side is a coalition enforcing a mandate against a militarily inferior party to the conflict. The coalition would not be fighting for its national security, vital interests or political survival, but for the purpose of limited crisis management. The new protocol would be limited to peace-enforcement operations conducted on behalf of the international community, or other interventions within the framework of regional crisis management, whether they are labeled humanitarian or not. It is important to state that such a new protocol would not address the *jus ad bellum* legality of humanitarian or other interventions (it would not introduce a "Just War" doctrine); it would stick to the traditional IHL method of describing a scope of application based on factual circumstances. In this case the scope of application would be linked to the limited nature of the international armed conflict. Should the State under attack plead self-defense and respond with counter-attacks, thus escalating the level of armed conflict, the limited scope of application of the new protocol would no longer describe the situation accurately and Protocol I would become applicable. In line with this thinking Michael Hoffman, the American Red Cross Officer for International Humanitarian Law, has suggested that we may witness emerging rules for "interventional armed conflict," for example in peace enforcement operations, whether authorized by the UN Security Council or conducted otherwise by regional organizations.

The UK Secretary of State for Defence said about the Kosovo air campaign on March 25, 1999 that "This is not a war, it is an operation designed to prevent what everybody recognizes is about to be a humanitarian catastrophe: ethnic cleansing, savagery.... That is what we are in there to prevent, that is not war, it is a humanitarian objective very clearly defined as such." Nevertheless, NATO relied on the traditional law of war developed for inter-State armed conflict during the air campaign, including the definition of military objectives and the rules on targeting, proportionality and collateral damage linked to that definition. The liberal definition of military objectives and the generous acceptance of collateral damage are part of a legal regime that envisages a full-scale war. The Geneva Conventions and Additional Protocol I were drafted against the background of World War II and partly with a possible clash between NATO and the Warsaw Pact in mind.

International humanitarian law is built upon a balance between acceptance of military interests on the one hand and humanitarian concerns on the other. NATO's "no-body-bag policy" showed that this balance was upset in the Kosovo conflict's limited type of war. NATO could use the liberal definition of military objectives—thus benefiting from the rules favorable to the military interest—while at the same time attacking from such altitudes that humanitarian concerns could not be met. This problem could be addressed in a new protocol for interventional types of conflict, through a sharpening of the definition of military objectives. One could require that only those objectives be attacked which *are* making an effective contribution to military action, or which imminently are about to make such a contribution. A requirement of imminence should be added, somewhat along the lines of the famous *Caroline* case. This would protect a number of dual-use objects and increase the protection of the civilian population.

Such a sharpening of the definition of legitimate military objectives would have its consequences with regard to the implementation of the principles of proportionality and feasible precautions. A stricter application of these two principles will follow from a more strict definition of military objectives. A stricter application of the principle of proportionality would somewhat reduce the problem of collateral damage flowing from that principle. The concepts of proportionality and feasible precautions would not themselves need to be sharpened. They would stand as they are today—in all types of international armed conflict. However, in interventionist conflicts a better balance with regard to precautionary measures would result from the suggested change; i.e., precautionary measures would, as intended by the drafters of Protocol I, genuinely protect civilians on the ground, and not only the attackers flying high.

Although the above suggestion is the main *de lege ferenda* thrust of this paper, it should be mentioned that a further additional protocol could be imagined—a protocol attached to the 1980 Weapons Convention that would explicitly prohibit the use of cluster bombs. This type of multiple sub-munitions affected the civilian population in Kosovo and Serbia on several occasions, often more so than the intended military targets. A protocol on multiple weapons was in fact debated, in the years 1977–1980, as a follow-up to Additional Protocols I and II for inclusion in the 1980 Conventional Weapons Convention. But time was not ripe for it then, during the Cold War, and the situation does not seem to have changed that much today. Or has it? During the Kosovo air campaign, after alarming media reports about civilian casualties caused by cluster bombs, some decision-makers reconsidered things. The NATO attack targeted on the Nis airfield on May 7 went wrong. The cluster bomb container opened right away after release from the aircraft, instead of opening over the airfield. As a consequence it projected the sub-munitions into the city of Nis. Following the media coverage of this incident there was a decision by the White House to prohibit the further use of cluster bombs during the conflict. However, this was a unilateral US decision. The British command in London did not follow suit and more cluster bombs were dropped on targets in Serbia and Kosovo in the spring of 1999.

Whether States in the future may in fact be willing to forgo weapons of the cluster bomb type in interventionist types of conflicts is not clear. Further thinking on this issue of means of warfare could perhaps usefully be channeled into the kind of discussion I have tried to promote in this paper, a discussion on the possibilities of increased protections for civilians in conflicts of a limited nature.

Are you surprised to find that the two proposals regarding the *jus ad bellum* want to expand the right of states to use armed force, while the two *in bello* proposals seek to restrict the rights of states? Steven Ratner has found an indication that after September 11, 2001, "global elites" were prepared to allow the United States more leeway regarding resort to force than with regard to the treatment of detainees.[2] Perhaps it makes sense that so long as the *in bello* rules are strictly observed, the world can tolerate more use of force? On the other hand, if the *jus in bello* were strictly observed or even enhanced,[3] would that not mean less resort to armed force in the first place? If force were used only when necessary and only to the extent necessary to accomplish a military objective, using proportionate force, how many wars occurring in the world today could have been resorted to in the first place? How many initial uses of unlawful force have seen a lawful response under this paradigm? The future of international law on the use of force may well see an increasing convergence of the law *in bello* and *ad bellum* around the concepts of necessity and proportionality—resulting in greater restrictions on both the resort to force and the conduct of hostilities.

C. NOTES AND QUESTIONS

1. As for proposals respecting collective action, see the report of the United Nations Secretary General's High Level Panel of Eminent Persons, due for release at the end of 2004. Advance information indicates the Panel

---

2. *See* Steven R. Ratner, Jus Ad Bellum and Jus In Bello *after September* 11, 96 AM. J. INT'L L. 905, 913 (2002).

3. *See* Roger Normand & Chris af Jochnick, *The Legitimation of Violence: A Critical Analysis of the Gulf War*, 35 HARV. INT'L L. J. 387, 413–16 (1994).

will call for expanding membership of the Security Council and of adopting the view the Council has a "responsibility to protect." *See A Winning Recipe for Reform? The United Nations, Reforming the UN After Iraq, Some Ideas for Rescuing the UN*, ECONOMIST, July 24, 2004, 2004 WL 62018788.

2. For alternative views to Meessen's proposal for the *jus ad bellum* rules in an era of terrorism, see, Jutta Brunneé & Stephen J. Toope, *The Use of Force: International Law After Iraq*, 53 INT'L & COMP. L. Q. 785 (2004); see also, Written evidence submitted by Jutta Brunneé, Professor of Law, University of Toronto, Canada, and Stephen J. Toope, Professor of Law, McGill University, Canada, U.K. House of Commons Foreign Affairs Committee, June 29, 2004, http://www.publications.parliament.uk/pa/cm 200304/cmselect/441/441we43.htm

3. For an alternative view to Feinstein and Slaughter's proposal for a right of preventive war, see United Kingdom House of Commons Minutes of Evidence Taken Before Foreign Affairs Committee (Professor Philippe Sands, Q.C., Mr. Daniel Bethlehem, Q.C.) http://www.publications.parliament.uk/pa/cm200304/cmselect/cmfaff/uc631–vi/uc63102.htm. *See also* Mary Ellen O'Connell, The Myth of Preemptive Self–Defense, Report of the American Society of International Law Taskforce on Terrorism, Aug. 2002, http://www.asil.org/taskforce/oconnell.pdf; Louis Henkin, *Use of Force: Law and U.S. Policy, in* MIGHT V. RIGHT, INTERNATIONAL LAW AND THE USE OF FORCE 45 (Louis Henkin et al. eds., 2d ed. 1989).

4. For responses to Forrest Martin's proposal regarding a unified theory of law on the use of force, see, Jordan J. Paust, *The Right to Life in Human Rights and the Laws of War*, 65 SASK. L. REV. 463 (2002); L.C. Green, *The "Unified Use of Force Rule" and the Law of Armed Conflict: A Reply to Professor Martin, id.* at 427.

5. For responses to Bring's proposal regarding the *jus in bello* during humanitarian intervention, see Yves Sandoz, *Commentary*, LEGAL AND ETHICAL LESSONS OF NATO'S KOSOVO CAMPAIGN, 78 INT'L L. STUD. 273 (Andru Wall ed., 2002); W. Hays Parks, Commentary, *id.* at 281. *See also*, ICRC, Report on International Humanitarian Law and the Challenges of Contemporary Armed Conflicts, ICRC, 28th Sess. (2003).

INDEX

†